Occupational
Information

Guidance, Counseling, and Student Personnel in Education

WALTER F. JOHNSON, *Consulting Editor*

Arbuckle, *Counseling and Psychotherapy: An Overview*
Bailard and Strang, *Parent-Teacher Conferences*
Bennett, *Guidance and Counseling in Groups*
Berdie, *Testing in Guidance and Counseling*
Bernhardt, *Discipline and Child Guidance*
Detjen and Detjen, *Elementary School Guidance*
Downing, *Guidance and Counseling Services: An Introduction*
Hoppock, *Occupational Information*
Johnson, Stefflre, and Edelfelt, *Pupil Personnel and Guidance Services*
Jones, *Principles of Guidance*
Stefflre, *Theories of Counseling*
Warters, *Techniques of Counseling*
Williamson, *Vocational Counseling*

McGraw-Hill Series in Education

HAROLD BENJAMIN   *Consulting Editor-in-Chief*

ARNO A. BELLACK   *Teachers College, Columbia University*
CONSULTING EDITOR, CURRICULUM AND METHODS IN EDUCATION

HAROLD BENJAMIN   *Emeritus Professor of Education*
George Peabody College for Teachers
CONSULTING EDITOR, FOUNDATIONS IN EDUCATION

HARLAN HAGMAN   *Wayne State University*
CONSULTING EDITOR, ADMINISTRATION IN EDUCATION

WALTER F. JOHNSON   *Michigan State University*
CONSULTING EDITOR, GUIDANCE, COUNSELING,
AND STUDENT PERSONNEL IN EDUCATION

Occupational Information

WHERE TO GET IT AND HOW TO USE IT
IN COUNSELING AND IN TEACHING

Robert Hoppock

PROFESSOR OF EDUCATION, NEW YORK UNIVERSITY

Third Edition

McGraw-Hill Book Company

NEW YORK   ST. LOUIS
SAN FRANCISCO   TORONTO   LONDON   SYDNEY

To
Shawn, Shannon,
and Michael

Occupational Information

Library of Congress Catalog Card Number: 67–14672
ISBN 07-030325-8

8 9 0 M P 7 4 3 2

No two persons are born exactly alike, but each differs from each in natural endowments, one being suited for one occupation and another for another . . . all things will be produced in superior quantity and quality and with greater ease, when each man works at a single occupation in accordance with his natural gifts.

PLATO

. . . we must decide what manner of men we wish to be and what calling in life we would follow; and this is the most difficult problem in the world.

CICERO

Preface

This is a textbook for use in the education of counselors, teachers, psychologists, rehabilitation officers, school and college administrators, social workers, employment interviewers, personnel directors, librarians, parents, clergymen, psychiatrists, and others to whom people turn when they want facts about jobs to help them to decide what they will do to earn a living. Parts of the book may interest economists and sociologists who are concerned with problems of occupational choice, distribution, mobility, and adjustment.

Many of the illustrations in this book are taken from educational institutions. The basic principles, however, remain the same, whether the counselor meets his client in school, in the employment service, in industry, in a social agency, or in a veterans' hospital. The social worker may not organize a course in occupations, but he will find most of the teaching techniques useful in his group work program. The counseling psychologist and the employment counselor may approach the client from quite different orientations, but both must turn to the same sources for the same facts.

The word "counselor" appears frequently in this book. It is used here to designate anyone who is trying to help another person to choose an occupation or to get occupational information. This counselor may be a professional or an amateur; he may devote all or part of his time to vocational guidance; he may help many persons or only one; he may be employed as a teacher of occupations or be just a friend of someone who has come to him for help. He is, in short, the reader, who may never have thought of himself as a counselor but who becomes one the moment he undertakes to help another person think through a problem—in this case the problem of choosing an occupation.

The general plan of the book is as follows: Chapters 1 to 6 identify the kinds of occupational information that counselors and clients need and suggest where to get it and how to appraise, classify, and file it. Chapters 7 to 11 discuss basic theories of vocational choice and development and the use of occupational information in counseling. Chapters 12 to 25 consider the principles and methods of teaching occupations and describe a variety of ways in which occupational information may be presented to groups of all kinds. Several of the recommended procedures involve active audience participation in compiling from primary sources the information which members of the group need and want. Appendixes A to H are referred to in various chapters. Appendixes I to O are supplemental to the text. Appendixes Y and Z offer suggested lesson plans and assignments for the convenience of the instructor who is teaching occupational information for the first time; most of the suggestions have been tested in the author's classes. Although the lesson plans and assignments were designed for university courses, some of them could be used in elementary and secondary schools and in other settings with other groups.

To the author, the most exciting new developments reported in this edition are:

The research of Youngberg [532] and Weitz [507] both of whom reduced turnover among newly hired life insurance salesmen by thirty percent when they provided job applicants with more accurate job descriptions. See pages 382–390.

The demonstration by Ziegler [334, 537] of the impressive effect of a three-hour course in how to find a job. See pages 383 and 390.

Toporowski's [480] experiment in which three *interested* social studies teachers taught an occupational information unit to high school seniors. Six months after graduation the experimental group was significantly superior to the control group in job satisfaction, in earnings, and in numbers employed. Previous researches have indicated similar results from courses in occupations taught by counselors. Toporowski is the first to report such results from units taught by social studies teachers. See pages 381–382.

I am still skeptical of the *typical* units taught by teachers who are neither interested nor competent to teach them, but I am now more hopeful of units taught by counselors and teachers who *want* to teach them and will take the time and trouble to make themselves competent to teach them. We still need more research to learn whether *good* semester courses produce even better results than *good* units, and whether *motivated* counselors produce better results than *motivated* social studies teachers.

Other new materials included in this edition are:

New appendixes on automation, on the handicapped, and on counseling interviews.

The results of new research showing the impact of occupational information on career plans. See Chapter 25.

Descriptions of many new ways in which counselors, teachers, and others have presented occupational information to groups. See Chapters 12 to 21.

In addition:

The summarized theories of vocational choice and development by Holland, Roe, Super, and Tiedeman now include excerpts from the most recent publications suggested by their authors.

All references to the *Dictionary of Occupational Titles* have been revised to conform to the latest edition of it.

All descriptions of filing plans now reflect the revisions which their authors have made since the new *D.O.T.* was published.

From the Bibliography, 32 obsolete references have been deleted and replaced by 131 new ones. Some older references have been retained for their historical value or because nothing equally good has been published more recently.

The reader who is already familiar with the second edition of this book and who wishes now to read only the new material, will find it all on the following pages: 1–2, 9, 14, 18, 20, 22, 29–33, 35–36, 38–40, 50, 58, 60–62, 64–65, 67–70, 72–73, 76–80, 88–90, 94–96, 99, 106–108, 135–136, 149, 151–154, 157, 160, 166–167, 169–170, 174, 179–183, 194, 203, 208, 213–214, 216, 221, 224, 232, 236, 241–243, 245–246, 249–250, 252, 255, 257–258, 261–262, 264–265, 268, 273, 283, 287, 291–292, 294–295, 298, 307, 309, 315, 319–320, 326, 329–331, 333–334, 336–337, 342, 344, 346, 349–351, 358–361, 363–364, 367–368, 371–372, 379–383, 386, 388–391, 393–394, 398–399, 401, 410–412, 480, 485, 488, 496, 501–502, 507–508, 515, 518–520, 523–524, 526, 531, 535, 537, 539–547, 551–553, 556–559.

Robert Hoppock

Acknowledgments

To Theodore J. Cote, George E. Leonard, Morton Margules, T. N. Stephens, and to my daughter Joan, each of whom has read parts of the manuscript,

To Amelia Ashe, Catherine Avent, Margaret Blair, Henry Borow, James W. Costar, Eleanor Fried, Harold Goldstein, John L. Holland, Charles I. Jones, Bernard Kaplan, John T. Klepper, James W. Moore, Evelyn Murray, Clyde L. Reed, Anne Roe, Donald E. Super, David V. Tiedeman, T. T. Toporowski, Joseph Weitz, Seymour Wolfbein, Charles F. Youngberg and Ray A. Ziegler, all of whom contributed or helped me to find information which I needed,

To Daniel Sinick for permission to reprint his article, which appears in Appendix O,

To Sam N. Wolk for permission to reprint "The Facts of Life,"

To the other authors who have generously granted permission to use the new quotations from their works, and to their publishers: the American Psychological Association, Appleton-Century-Crofts, Blaisdell Publishing Company, the Kiplinger Washington Editors, the College Entrance Examination Board, Harper and Row, the *High School Journal*, the *Journal of Counseling Psychology*, the *Vocational Guidance Quarterly*, and the Cleveland Vocational Guidance and Rehabilitation Services,

To Ruth F. Cowell, Irma B. Fontana, Marie R. Klein, Sylvia Levin, and the staff of the Manhasset Public Library for their professional help in finding materials and for making a harried author feel welcome,

To the many other friends, acquaintances, and students whose information and ideas I have appropriated without recognition or recall,

To my wife and her mother who patiently endured repeated interruptions in their own work whenever I needed help,

To all these I am greatly indebted and deeply grateful.

Will You Help?

If you use any of the information or ideas in this book, will you share your experience with the author? Many of the reports of current practice in this revision have come from the readers of earlier editions. Your experience may help some future reader. It will also help the author to decide what should be retained in the next revision. A brief note on what you did and how you feel about the results will be much appreciated.

Contents

1
Why
Study
Occupations?

Both the reader and the author of this book have made decisions which we hoped would facilitate our progress in the direction of careers which appeared attractive to us. We shall make more such decisions in the future. Each decision has been or will be based in part upon our own occupational information, however inadequate that information may be.

These decisions, in sequence, help to determine our careers. Together they constitute our choice of an occupation for the near or distant future. As time passes and conditions change, we may or may not change both our jobs and our occupations. We may thus make one or many occupational choices. The more choices we make, the more occupational information we need. There are at least five reasons why the wise choice of an occupation is important and why facts about jobs are essential to this choice.

The choice of an occupation may determine whether one will be employed or unemployed. In some occupations employment is notoriously irregular; in others it is much more stable and secure. By choosing an occupation in which employment is known to be relatively stable, one may increase the probability that he will have a job even when millions of other persons are out of work.

In severe economic depressions as many as 75 percent of the workers in some occupations and industries have been unemployed. At the same time less than 10 percent of the workers in other fields were out of work, and in some occupations employment actually increased.

Even in very mild recessions there are striking differences in the rates of unemployment among different groups of workers. In April, 1961, for example, 18 percent of the workers in construction were unemployed, but only 6 percent of those in transportation and public utilities and only 2 percent of those in government were out of work.

The choice of an occupation may determine success or failure. Many things affect success. They include effort, luck, and knowing the right people. They include also the ability of the worker to perform satisfactorily the tasks assigned to him. People differ in both the nature and the level of their abilities, and occupations differ in the abilities required for their acceptable performance. By choosing an occupation which will utilize his strengths and make only minimum demands upon his weaknesses, one may increase the probability of his own success.

The choice of an occupation may determine whether one will enjoy or detest his work. There are probably few, if any, occupations in which a person never has to do anything that he dislikes, but there is no need for most of us to work at jobs in which we dislike most of the things we have to do. Despite popular impressions to the contrary, modern mass production does not condemn all factory workers to misery. Robinson [396][1] and others have summarized twenty-eight years of research and 450 attempts to measure the percentage of workers who are dissatisfied with their jobs. The reported percentages range from 1 to 92 with a median of 13 percent dissatisfied. Many of the studies were made on factory populations, several different criteria of job satisfaction were used, and in the vast majority of the studies a minority of the workers was reported to be dissatisfied.

By the wise choice of an occupation one may find a large share of life's pleasures and satisfactions in his work. Although we have had much research on vocational aptitudes and vocational interests, we have had comparatively little on what might be called the emotional fitness of a man for a job or of a job for a man. How important this aspect of vocational choice can be was well expressed years ago by the distinguished psychiatrist, who was then the medical director of the National Committee for Mental Hygiene, Frankwood E. Williams [516].

> One's job must furnish an outlet suitable to one's particular, personal emotional needs. The greatest part of one's emotional life is lived in one's job, not elsewhere, as is commonly supposed. Different professions and vocations . . . offer quite different emotional outlets; even specialties within a profession offer different outlets. One may be more than adequately equipped intellectually, and with special ability for a given profession, but if that profession does not offer the emotional outlet peculiar to one's own needs, unhappiness and discontent follow. Even though material and professional success may come, it is likely to be as dust in the mouth. After considerable trial and error, other partial outlets are found that make the situation

[1] Numbers in brackets refer to the bibliography at the back of this book.

bearable, but there is likely to be an element of frustration through-out that makes for unhappiness.

The choice of an occupation influences almost every other aspect of life. It affects a woman's chances of marriage. It determines where the family will live, where the children will go to school, and how often they will move. It determines the persons with whom the worker will associate during much of the day and thus affects his choice of friends. In subtle ways it changes the values, the ideals, the standards, and the daily conduct of the worker and helps to determine the kind of person he will become. It helps to determine both the economic and the social status of the entire family. It may affect the worker's health, both mental and physical; the frequency with which he sees his family; and the amount of time that he spends with them.

Whether family income will increase or decrease with advancing age, whether it will be stable or erratic, whether it will provide for health and comfort or actually threaten survival in case of illness may depend on the occupational choice of the breadwinner.

Occupational choices determine how a democratic society will utilize its manpower. The modest young person who is choosing his own field of work may not think much about the impact of his choice upon human welfare, but the aggregate of thousands of such choices may determine where seri-ous shortages and surpluses of manpower will occur. Economic rewards, public policy, and military conscription all affect the distribution of manpower, but in a democratic society the final determinant of what any one person will do is that person himself. When too few persons choose to be teachers, the education of a whole generation may suffer. When too many persons prepare for a few popular professions and fail to find employment, precious human assets are wasted, and powerful future leaders begin to wonder about the political and economic systems under which they live.

Many investigators have observed the discrepancies between the occu-pational preferences of students and the occupational distribution of our employed population. One of the most vivid reports was based upon the announced choices of 1,658 boys and girls in the eighth grades of thirty-five public schools in Cincinnati, Ohio, described by Dale [114]:

> What would Cincinnati be like if these eighth grade students be-came the sole inhabitants of the city, in the jobs of their choice, ten years from now? . . . Health services would be very high, with every eighteen people supporting one doctor. . . . It may be, however, that

they would all be needed in a city that had no garbage disposal workers, no laundry workers, and no water supply, since no one chose to
do that kind of work. . . . The two bus drivers . . . will find that
their customers get tired of waiting, and use the services of the sixty-
seven airline pilots. It may be difficult getting to Crosley Field to see
the forty baseball players.

One need not be a genius to see that some of these students are going
to have to revise their choices and that they will need information about
many occupations which they are not seriously considering today.

Occupational information is indispensable. One cannot choose what one does not
know, and many occupations are unknown to most of us. One may
stumble into an appropriate occupation by sheer luck, but the wise
choice of an occupation requires accurate information about what occupations are available, what they require, and what they offer.

Occupational information alone is not enough. Knowledge and acceptance of one's own aptitudes, abilities, needs, limitations, interests,
values, feelings, fears, likes, and dislikes are essential also, as is clear
thinking about the relative significance of all the facts. Nothing in this
book is intended to imply that any of these other considerations is any
less important than occupational information.

It is obvious that knowledge of occupations can be effectively applied
only when one knows something about oneself. It is equally obvious that
knowledge of oneself can be effectively applied to the choice of an occupation only when one knows something about occupations. Either without the other is incomplete.

REVIEW QUESTIONS

1. How may a person increase the probability that he will have a
job even when millions of other persons are unemployed?

2. How may a person increase the probability of his own success?

3. Is vocational guidance for factory workers a waste of time? Has
modern mass production destroyed their opportunity to find job satisfaction?

4. Where is the greatest part of one's emotional life lived?

5. A person may be adequately equipped intellectually, he may
achieve success and yet be unhappy in his job if it does not offer
what?

6. What are some of the ways in which a person's occupation affects his family and his life off the job?

7. What kind of world would we have if occupational choices were
based only on the abilities, interests, and needs of the individual?

8. Has anything in this chapter surprised, provoked, or challenged you? Will any of this affect your future thoughts and actions? How?

9. What do you think of vocational counseling services which devote 90 percent of their resources to discovering the needs, abilities, and interests of the client and 10 percent to studying the changing employment market?

2
What the Counselor Should Know about Occupations

Definitions. In this book the term "occupational information" is used to mean any and all kinds of information regarding any position, job, or occupation, provided only that the information is potentially useful to a person who is choosing an occupation. More briefly stated, occupational information means facts about jobs for use in vocational guidance.

In this and subsequent chapters the word "client" is used to designate any person who seeks the help of any counselor. Obviously, the client may or may not also be a student and often will be if the counselor is employed in a school or college. The word "student" is used to designate any person enrolled in a school or college, whether or not he seeks the help of the counselor. Thus a student may or may not also be a client. Any counselor anywhere will, of course, have direct personal contact with his clients. The counselor who works in a school or college may also have direct or indirect contact with students who do not seek his help but who are served through teachers, group activities, or a course in occupations which the counselor may teach; he therefore has responsibilities to "students" as well as to "clients."

The beginning counselor is liable to be overwhelmed by the number of things he should know and by the infinite variety of the questions his clients bring to him. Obviously he cannot be a walking encyclopedia. He cannot answer every question on the spot. Like every teacher, he must, if he is honest, frequently admit his own ignorance.

The impossibility of knowing everything may lead the frightened beginner to take refuge in the idea that he need not know anything except where the library is and how to use it. He may, in desperation and ignorance, fall back upon the rationalization of the lazy and incompetent by deciding that it is better for his clients to search for the answers to their questions without his help. Clients should become familiar with the sources of occupational information. What better way is there to become familiar with any tool than by using it? Why not simply send the client to the library for his facts about jobs?

There are two important reasons for not taking this easy way out: many of the answers are not to be found in the library or in any publication, and much of the information in print is inaccurate, obsolete, or intentionally misleading. To turn the unsuspecting client loose in even the best library of occupational information is a little like turning him loose in a drugstore to write and fill his own prescription. The same may be said of sending him, unaided, to most of the other sources of occupational information.

Brayfield and Mickelson [39] tabulated the contents of 5,958 occupational publications and found that many occupations were inadequately represented.

The impossibility of knowing everything is no excuse for knowing nothing. No teacher of mathematics can know everything about mathematics, but he does not send his students to the library to learn algebra without his help. No teacher of French can know everything about the French language, literature, and life, but he does not send his students to the library to learn French without his help. The counselor must do what every teacher does. He must separate the essential from the nonessential, the important from the less important, and then master the essential information.

What then is essential?

First jobs. The counselor should know where his dropouts and graduates got their first jobs. The occupational interests and plans of school and college students often bear little relation to the employment opportunities of the area in which the students will look for work. Consequently, many of them never do find a job in the occupation of their choice. Disappointed and frustrated in their search for employment, too many of them drift into some substitute job in which they are neither effective nor satisfied.

This unhappy situation will be corrected only when students can base their occupational choices upon a realistic view of the kinds of jobs that will be open to them. This realistic view is best obtained by learning what jobs previous dropouts and graduates were able to get. This information is readily available in schools which make annual follow-up studies. The new counselor should inquire of his associates and supervisors whether or not such studies have been made. If they have not been, he should proceed promptly to make one himself, preferably with the aid of his students.

Any project of this kind, which involves public relations, should first be discussed with, and approved by, the counselor's immediate superior. If no recent studies have been made, the first one should cover the dropouts and graduates of the past five years unless a sample of several hundred can be obtained from more recent classes. A large sample is necessary in order to reveal clearly which occupations and employers have absorbed the largest numbers of former students.

Once made, the follow-up study should be repeated annually in order to discover changes when they appear. Each study should include, at least, all the dropouts and graduates of the past twelve months. Some schools follow up all former students at intervals of 1, 3, and 5 years after separation from school. Others prefer intervals of 1, 4, and 7 years, and still others like 1, 5, and 10.

High schools need to follow up their alumni after they have completed college and military or alternate service in order to find out where these former students got their first jobs. Without this information the vocational and educational guidance of prospective college students can be sadly unrealistic.

The follow-up study has two advantages over the community occupational survey as a means of learning what beginning jobs are likely to be available. First, it has no geographical limits; it goes wherever the former students have gone and thus reveals the true extent of the employment market with which the counselor must be concerned. Second, it reveals the kinds of jobs which dropouts and graduates are able to get in the open competition of the labor market. Employers may state, quite truthfully, that they frequently do have vacancies which could be filled by inexperienced young workers. With no intent to deceive, the employers may nevertheless not hire beginners when the vacancies occur if experienced workers are available at that time. Only the follow-up study reveals what kinds of jobs the beginners actually get.

Suggestions for conducting a follow-up study as a class or club project will be found in Chapter 13. If student participation is not feasible, the counselor may conduct the study himself. If no way can be found to communicate with former students, the counselor can get limited information about them by asking the teachers and students who are still in school to report the nature and place of employment of any former students whom they know.

All that has been said above about students, dropouts, and graduates applies also to the clients of counselors who do not work in schools or colleges. Every counselor should know what has happened to his former clients. Every agency which has clients should make periodic follow-up studies of the persons it has served.

Thus vocational rehabilitation counselors, counselors in community vocational guidance and placement services, counseling psychologists in veterans' hospitals and in private practice all need to know what has become of their former clients. Only in this way can the counselor find out whether he has helped or hindered his client in the client's attempt to evaluate the probability that he will be able to find employment in the occupation of his choice.

Principal employment opportunities. The counselor should know the other opportunities for his dropouts and graduates in his community. No technique is perfect. Desirable and indispensable as the follow-up study is, it will not do the whole job of revealing all employment opportunities to the counselor and his clients. Dropouts and graduates may have missed some excellent opportunities of which they were unaware. New opportunities may have arisen since the last class entered the employment market. To discover these, a survey of the employment market is desirable.

The extent of the employment market, already revealed by the follow-up studies, will vary greatly from one institution and from one community to another. High school dropouts and graduates usually find their first jobs in or near their hometowns, even in suburban areas, but this tendency is not universal. College alumni usually cover a much wider territory, but not always. Amateur counselors in rural areas sometimes assume that employment opportunities near home are too limited to permit much choice, but Handville [204] found 220 different occupations within a 25-mile radius of a rural school.

Any follow-up is likely to reveal a considerable concentration of alumni employed near the institution. A follow-up of alumni from the high school at Jamestown, N.Y., revealed that 74 percent of the respondents still gave Jamestown as their address five years after graduation [368]. Local employment opportunities, therefore, should never be slighted by the counselor.

The occupational survey may be as simple or as elaborate as the counselor's resources permit. The beginning counselor, coming into a new college or a new community, should begin his survey by browsing through the classified section of the local telephone directory, observing the kinds of organizations listed therein. Anyone who has not done this before will be surprised at the variety of industries and occupations that he might otherwise have overlooked.

The counselor should next call on the school or college placement officer, if there is one, and on any teachers who have helped their own students to get jobs. He should then go to the nearest office of his state employment service and to any private employment agencies in his community. The addresses of employment agencies are usually found in the classified telephone directory. If no office of the state employment service is listed in the local directory, a letter to the state employment service at the state capital will reveal the location of the nearest office.

To each placement officer the counselor should introduce himself, explain that he is trying to learn something about the local occupations that are likely to be open to his dropouts and graduates, and ask the placement officer if he can give the counselor any information or suggest where he might get any. Because the employment agency business is sometimes fiercely competitive, some placement officers are understandably reluctant to reveal trade secrets, including the names of the employers they serve. But most placement officers will be willing to indicate the kinds of jobs they find easy and hard to fill and the kinds of applicants they can and cannot place. Because the interest of any informant may sometimes be served by revealing only part of the truth, the counselor should accept all information gratefully but tentatively and check it against other sources at every opportunity. No information is perfect. No source is infallible. But excellent leads for further investigation may be obtained in a short time with little effort and almost no expense by calling on placement officers and employment agencies.

The beginning counselor should call next on the secretary of the local chamber of commerce, from whom he can usually obtain some information regarding the largest local employers, approximately how many persons they employ, and the nature of their business. If this information is not available locally, it may sometimes be obtained by writing to the state chamber of commerce at the state capital. In a very small community, a call at the local bank or a walk around town may be all that is needed.

After identifying the larger employers, the counselor's next calls should be on the personnel directors or employment managers of these companies and on the officers of the local labor unions with which these companies have contracts. If the counselor also teaches a course in occupations or another course in which industrial tours are appropriate, he may save time and improve his service to students by taking his class with him on these trips. How to conduct such tours and what questions to ask are described in Chapters 14 and 15. The same questions may be used in a private interview if the counselor goes alone.

The survey activities so far described can be and should be undertaken by the counselor himself. No appropriation is necessary if the counselor is willing to spend a little of his own money for postage stamps, telephone calls, and local transportation. Of course, if he can get expense money for these items, he can conserve his own funds for other things.

When these activities have been completed, the counselor may wish to undertake a more complete survey of the employment market for his graduates. This may be done at little or no expense as a student project in a course in occupations, or it may be undertaken by the counselor himself. Suggestions will be found in Chapter 16.

All that has been said above about counselors who work in schools and colleges is equally true of counselors who work in community agencies or elsewhere. Every counselor who attempts to help his clients make occupational choices should know the principal employment opportunities of the community in which he works.

Student interests. The counselor should know which occupations are being seriously considered by his students. Although the occupational preferences of students are often unrealistic, they are nevertheless important, if only because the students will show little real interest in exploring other occupations until they have explored their first choices. The counselor needs to know which are the currently popular occupations so that he can begin to make himself more familiar with them.

A tabulation of students' occupational preferences can be compiled quickly with the use of a simple mimeographed questionnaire. If mimeographing or other duplicating facilities are not available, plain paper may be used and the questions numbered and read to the students.

If the counselor does not wish to be misled, he will not ask only "What would you *like* to do when you finish school?" This question has been known to draw answers far removed from what the student expects or plans to do. A better approach is probably a series of questions such as "Considering what you now know of your own abilities, interests, and opportunities, what occupations do you think you are most likely to enter when you finish school? What other occupations are you seriously considering? What others would you like to enter if you could? Would you like to have more information about any of these occupations? If so, which ones?"

The results of this inquiry will interest not only the counselor, but other teachers and the school administrators may like to see a summary of the replies. Local newspapers will usually publish a story on them if given the chance. Again, because publication involves public relations, the counselor should get the approval of his supervisor before approaching the newspapers. Students' names should, of course, not be publicly identified with their choices.

The percentage of truthful responses may be increased by assuring the students that only the counselor and his clerical helpers will see the replies. If student clerks are to help in the tabulation, this fact should be stated frankly; the helpers should be chosen for their discretion as well as for their accuracy and then should be strongly indoctrinated in the confidential nature of their work. Truthfulness may be further encouraged by assuring the students that they need not put their names on the papers if they prefer not to. The counselor may, however, wish to risk a little candor in order to preserve identification. If the names are on the papers, these papers can help the counselor to get facts about specific occupations to the students who will be most interested in them.

The big three. The counselor should know almost everything about three occupations. As noted above, the counselor cannot know everything about every occupation, but he should be his community's best expert on at least three. These are, first, the occupation or industry or company which has employed the largest number of dropouts and graduates from his school or of clients from his agency; second, the occupation or industry or company which employs the largest number of persons in his community; and, third, the occupation or industry or company which is currently being seriously considered by the largest number of his students or clients. No counselor is too busy to make himself an authority on these three occupations; if he is, he is too busy doing the wrong things.

Obviously the counselor should know more than this. Having learned everything he can about these three occupations, by visits, by reading, by talking with his own alumni and with other employers and employees, the conscientious counselor will need no further urging to extend his knowledge of occupations as far as his time and resources permit, for he will have blushed more than once as he discovered how little he knew about these three occupations, how much of what he did "know" was not true, and how pitiably inadequate are the sources to which he previously referred the clients who came to him for occupational information. The counselor will also have learned how important it is to repeat his visits and his interviews at least once a year in order to learn what changes have occurred.

The counselor who postpones his own study of occupations until he finds the time for it will never find the time. The most effective way for a counselor to do occupational research is to set aside a fixed amount of time at regular intervals and then stick to the schedule as conscientiously as if he had a class to meet at this time. The counselors in one large city once set aside one full day a week for research on local occupations. The counselor who finds this schedule impossible may reserve one morning a week or one morning every two weeks. Mornings are suggested rather than afternoons because once the counselor appears in his office, he is liable to find it hard to get away.

A great deal can be accomplished in small units of time if one can just stick to a regular schedule. With as little as one morning every two weeks, the counselor can visit twenty places of employment in a school year. In five years he can visit a hundred. Any counselor who gives less time than this to occupational research should begin to suspect himself of malpractice.

The counselor who also teaches a course in occupations will find his time for occupational research automatically provided as he takes his students to visit local industries, brings alumni back to school for group conferences, and helps his students to get the facts they want about the occupations which interest them.

Sources of information. The counselor should know where to get information about occupations and how to appraise its accuracy. The average counselor is a college graduate who has spent at least sixteen years of his life as a student, looking in books and in libraries for the answers to most of his questions. It is not surprising that he thinks first of the library when he needs occupational information. A good library can be a useful source, but it is not the only one, and it is frequently not the best. For some kinds of information on some occupations, it can easily be the worst.

For fifteen years the author of this book planned and edited abstracts of the available literature on more than a hundred occupations. Over and over again, reviewers found the literature to be obsolete, inaccurate, inadequate, intentionally or unintentionally biased. One abstracter examined all the available literature published on one occupation over a period of twenty years and then reported that, twenty years earlier, three original investigations of this occupation had been made in three major cities, and nearly everything written on the occupation since that time had been copied from one of these old studies or from someone else who had copied from the originals.

There is good occupational literature in print, and some of it will be mentioned later in this book. What the beginning counselor needs to learn and to remember is that there is also bad occupational literature and that the average student, teacher, parent, librarian, psychologist, and social worker does not know how to tell the good from the bad.

No one source of occupational information is wholly good or wholly bad. Each source is good for some kinds of information and poor for others. The discriminating counselor must learn, and then he must teach his clients, where to look for the facts they want and how to appraise what they find. These topics are discussed at length in Chapters 4 and 5.

Labor legislation. One of the first tasks assigned to a school counselor is likely to be the issuance of employment certificates, which are frequently called "working papers." These are documents required by the state laws which regulate the employment of minors. Before an employer may legally hire children of certain ages for certain jobs, an employment certificate must be issued by the school, even though the student is already a high school graduate. State regulations vary, so the counselor should write to his own state departments of education and labor for full information regarding the regulations and his responsibilities in connection therewith.

Other legislation affecting workers, including beginners, has now reached such proportions that the effective counselor needs to know a good deal about it. License requirements will be discussed in Chapter 4. Other aspects of labor legislation are discussed in the *Handbook for Young Workers* [203]. A liberal education awaits the counselor who will visit his own state department of labor, confess his ignorance, and ask to be informed about things he should know and publications he should read.

REVIEW QUESTIONS

1. You have just been employed as a counselor in a community that is new to you. What are the quickest ways for you to learn something about its principal occupations and industries?

2. How can you best obtain a realistic view of the kinds of jobs most likely to be available to your clients?

3. What are the advantages of the follow-up study over the community occupational survey, and vice versa?

4. Since the counselor cannot be a walking encyclopedia of occupational information, what should he do?

5. Why is the occupational information library an inadequate source of occupational information?

6. Where do the graduates of suburban high schools usually find their first jobs?

7. How many different occupations did Handville find within a 25-mile radius of a rural school?

8. How can a busy counselor find time for occupational research?

9. Where can a counselor get information about "working papers"?

10. Is there anything in this chapter that you can use to improve your work? What? How?

3
What the
Client
Should Know
about Occupations

At some time, in some way, with or without the help of a counselor, every person who chooses an occupation looks at the various opportunities which he thinks are open to him, compares them, and selects the one which most appeals to him. He may do this thoroughly, systematically, and realistically; he may do it casually, impulsively, or fancifully.

Students and clients differ in their need for occupational information, just as they differ in abilities and interests. Some need a great deal of information, some need little or none, and some are already in a position to supply it.

Client needs differ. The beginning counselor will soon observe a few students whose need for occupational information appears to be negligible: the boy who expects to take over his father's business, who already works at it on Saturdays and on vacations, and who shows every indication of being successful and satisfied; the prospective nurse who visits hospitals at every opportunity and has been caring for the sick among her family and friends ever since she was big enough to carry a breakfast tray; and the electronics wizard who repairs all the neighborhood radios and television sets and has been accepted by the engineering college of his choice. Conceivably, any one of these persons might be more successful and better satisfied in some other occupation, but the average school or college counselor will find little time to explore such a remote possibility unless he sees some indication that the choice is not appropriate or that the student needs help on other problems. The competent counselor who knows something about occupations will be much too busy helping clients who obviously need and want his help.

Some clients have tentative choices which appear appropriate but which they want the counselor to help them review just to make sure they have not overlooked some consideration of importance. A checklist of questions for use in such cases appears later in this chapter.

Some clients are moving toward appropriate occupational choices on their own initiative. They neither need nor want extensive counseling, but they do need, want, and ask for specific information to use in arriving at their own decisions. One of the counselor's major responsibilities in occupational information is helping these clients to get the information they want, check its accuracy, and see its implications in terms of their own choices. Sources of information are discussed in Chapter 4. The ways in which the facts may affect the job satisfaction of the prospective worker are discussed in Chapter 11.

Other clients are positive about their plans but with less apparent justification. One of the problems which worries counselors most is what to do with the client who is certain of what he wants to do but whose choice seems unwise, because he lacks some essential qualification or because employment opportunities are negligible or because he anticipates some satisfaction that the counselor believes the occupation will not yield. There is no easy solution to this problem. If the client seems unable to face reality, psychotherapy may be tried. Even then, the counselor may find himself wholly ineffective until the client has followed his choice and failed. If and when this happens, the counselor faces one of his most challenging responsibilities, which is to help such clients find acceptable substitutes for the things they want to do and can't. At this point, occupational information in large doses may be indicated. Before this time, occupational information may or may not be helpful. For further discussion of this problem see Chapter 10.

Somewhat different is the problem of the client who has no idea of what he wants to do. Individual counselors differ in their approaches to this problem, but all of them come eventually to the place where they must acquaint the client with the occupations which are open to him. It is at this point that the counselor begins to use the information he has compiled from his follow-up studies, community occupational surveys, and other sources. For further discussion of this problem see Chapter 10.

Because the adequate presentation of information about a variety of occupations is a long and time-consuming process and because much of the information to be presented is needed by more than one client, a good course in occupations is sometimes a help to both the counselor and the client. Individual interviews will still be necessary, but more interview time can be used to discuss the individual aspects of the problem if the background information has already been presented by the same counselor to the same client in the more economical group situation. For more on this topic see Chapters 12 to 22.

Range of opportunities. The client should know what jobs are open to him. There has been much research on the range of occupations in which young persons express an interest. In general, the results indicate a disturbingly limited range, which can be quickly and easily extended by presenting information about additional occupations. For more on this research, see Chapter 25. For ways in which to present additional occupational information, see Chapters 13 to 16.

Sources of information. The client should know where to get information about occupations and how to appraise its accuracy. Contrary to a popular impression among many counselors, the best sources of occupational information are not to be found in libraries, not even in the average counselor's own special library of occupational information. The client cannot be taught what he should know about sources by the sink-or-swim method of sending him to the library, unaided, to find what often is not there. For more on sources of occupational information and how to make students familiar with them see Chapters 4, 5, and 13 to 16.

How to choose. The client should know how to choose an occupation. The bases on which some young persons choose their occupations have made more than one counselor shudder. From some vague source they have heard that a specific occupation pays well, is expanding, offers attractive opportunities for advancement. They have seen one glamorous aspect of the occupation and are attracted by it. They wish to be like someone they admire who is engaged in this field. They have taken an interest test, and it points in this direction. They liked this subject in school or did well on an aptitude test in this area. Any one of these reasons could be a good reason for considering the occupation. No one of them alone nor all of them in combination is sufficient basis for an intelligent choice. There are dozens of other considerations which may have more effect upon the success and satisfaction of the client than any of the items mentioned in this paragraph. How to choose an occupation is readably discussed in a short pamphlet by Byrn [51] published by the National Vocational Guidance Association. For more on this topic see Chapters 17 to 19.

How to find a job. Vocational counseling which does not stay with the client until he has been employed is frequently futile, because the counselor is not present when the client discovers that he cannot find anyone who will pay him to do just what his counselor and he have decided he should do. At this point the counselor may need to help his client to improve his job-hunting techniques or to reconsider his objective. Few clients know the most effective channels for finding vacancies. There is much which they can and should be taught, in the counseling interviews or in a good course in occupations. For more on this subject see the sections on "Practice Job Interviews," "Job Clinics," and "Practice on Employment Application Blanks" in Chapter 20.

Significant specifics. Krumboltz [282] has noted that some clients "not only do . . . not know the answers to some vital questions; they do not even know what questions to ask." The client should know many specific things about an occupation before he enters it. Most of these specifics are included in the checklist below. How significant some of these items are in determining the success and satisfaction of the client is discussed more fully in Chapter 11.

Eventually every person who is to be self-supporting comes to the point where he must commit himself to preparing for an occupation or seeking a job in it or accepting or refusing a job that he can have. If he has not previously examined the occupation or the job in terms of what he has to offer it and what it offers him, he may wish to do so at this time. The following checklist of questions which may be applied to any occupation is presented to help the counselor and the client to review a job or an occupation systematically. Not all these questions apply to all jobs, but the counselor will find here most of the important topics to consider. The reader is urged not to skip over this checklist unless he is already familiar with several other lists of this kind. The beginning counselor may find here a number of important considerations which will be new to him and which he should be thinking about from this point on.

A CHECKLIST OF FACTS ABOUT JOBS
FOR USE IN VOCATIONAL GUIDANCE

Employment prospects

Are workers in demand today? Is employment in this occupation expected to increase or decrease?

Nature of the work

What is the work of a typical day, week, month, year? What are all the things a worker may have to do in this occupation, the pleasant things, the unpleasant things, the big and little tasks, the important responsibilities, and the less glamorous details? Does he deal mainly with data, people, or things? With what kinds of tools, machines, and materials does he work? Must he walk, jump, run, balance, climb, crawl, kneel, stand, turn, stoop, crouch, sit, reach, lift, carry, throw, push, pull, handle, finger, feel, talk, hear, or see? Must he travel? Where and when?

Work environment

In what kind of surroundings is the work done? Hot, cold, humid, dry, wet, dusty, dirty, noisy? Indoor or outdoor? Is the worker exposed to sudden changes of temperature, offensive odors, vibration, mechanical hazards, moving objects, burns, electric shock, explosives, radiant energy, toxic conditions, or other hazards? Does he work in cramped quarters, in high places, or in any other unusual location? Are lighting, ventilation, and sanitation adequate? Does he work with others, near others, or alone? If with others, what is his relationship to them, and does it place him in a position of superiority, inferiority, equality, conflict, or stress?

Qualifications

Age. What are the upper and lower age limits for entrance and retirement?

Sex. Is this predominantly a male or female occupation? Are there reasonable opportunities for both? Is there any more active demand for one than for the other?

Height and weight. Are there any minimum or maximum requirements? What are they?

Other physical requirements. Are there any other measurable physical requirements, e.g., 20/20 vision, freedom from color blindness, average or superior hearing, physical strength, etc.?

Aptitudes. Has there been any research on aptitudes required, e.g., minimum or maximum intelligence quotient, percentile rank on specific tests of mechanical aptitude, clerical aptitude, finger dexterity, pitch discrimination, reaction time, etc.?

Interests. Have any vocational interest inventories been validated against workers in this occupation?

Tools and equipment. Must these be supplied by the worker at his own expense? What is the average cost? Can they be rented or bought on credit?

Legal requirements. Is a license or certificate required? What are the requirements for getting it?

Citizenship. Is it required?

Residence. Must the worker be a resident of the city or state in which he is employed?

In what other ways do workers in this occupation differ from other people?

Unions

Is the closed shop common or predominant? If so, what are the requirements for entrance to the union? Initiation fees? Dues? Does the union limit the number admitted?

Discrimination

Do employers, unions, or training institutions discriminate against minority groups?

Preparation

Distinguish clearly between what is desirable and what is indispensable.

How much and what kind of preparation is required to meet legal requirements and employers' standards?

How long does it take? What does it cost? What does it include?

Where can one get a list of approved schools?

What kind of high school or college program should precede entrance into the professional school? What subjects must or should be chosen?

What provisions, if any, are made for apprenticeship or other training on the job?

Is experience of some kind prerequisite to entrance?

Entrance

How does one get his first job? By taking an examination? By applying to employers? By joining a union? By registering with employment agencies? By saving to acquire capital and opening his own business? How much capital is required?

Advancement

What proportion of workers advance? To what? After how long and after what additional preparation or experience?

What are the related occupations to which this may lead, if any?

Earnings

What are the most dependable average figures on earnings by week, month, or year?

What is the range of the middle 50 percent?

Are earnings higher or lower in certain parts of the United States or in certain branches of the occupation?

Number and distribution of workers

Are the workers evenly distributed in proportion to population or concentrated in certain areas? Where? Why?

Can a person practice this occupation anywhere that he may wish to live?

Do conditions in small towns and rural areas differ materially from those in urban centers? How?

Are most of the workers employed by private industry, by government, by some other kind of organization, or are they self-employed? Are most of the employing organizations large or small?

Advantages and disadvantages

What do workers say they like best and dislike most about their jobs?

Are hours regular or irregular, long or short? Is there frequent overtime or night work? Sunday and holiday work?

What about vacations? Maternity leave?

Is employment steady, seasonal, or irregular? Does one earn more or less with advancing age?

Is the working lifetime shorter than average, e.g., as for professional athletes?

Are the skills acquired transferable to other occupations?

Is the work hazardous? What about accidents, occupational diseases?

How will the work affect the family of the worker?

In comparison with other occupations requiring about the same level of ability and training, in what ways is this one more or less attractive?

For college seniors who are comparing potential employers, Sherrill [427] prepared a helpful booklet which includes the following list:

QUESTIONS AND SUBJECTS
FREQUENTLY DISCUSSED IN INTERVIEWS

1 The Industry (or type of service).

Do the general characteristics of the industry have a definite interest for you?

Is it, or does it promise to be, sound in the national economy?

Has the industry a history of broad usefulness? Are expansions or diversifications contemplated? Are new developments challenging the industry?

2 The Company (or institution).

Has the company shown substantial growth as reflected by increased production, new products and services, sales over a period of years?

Has there been, or is there promise of considerable growth of products, technological changes and facilities which permit upgrading of qualified people? Has the company taken on new acquisitions? Are there prospects of a merger?

How does the company rate with Dun & Bradstreet, Standard & Poor, the local banker, and customers? What reputation does it have with the placement service, the faculty, and alumni?

Have the company's labor and public relations appeared normal over a period of time?

Does the company have today's usual fringe benefits such as group life insurance, hospitalization, sick benefits, retirement, and provisions for continuing education? What are the approximate contributory costs?

3   Stability.

Does the whole picture of the industry . . . the company, research and development, diversification of products and services, sales . . . appear progressive in this age of technological progress and obsolescence?

What is the company's financial condition? (Refer to annual statements of assets and liabilities; ratio of research expenditures to sales; the trend of earnings per share of stock. Extremely high or low positions may be important for your inquiry.)

Does the company appear well established and aggressively managed? What is its competitive position?

Does the company have many contracts subject to cancellation? What is the history of professional layoffs? What were the basic causes? (Turnover percentages can be misleading; definitions and interpretations are seldom identical.)

Could this hiring be for temporary work?

4   Assignments.

Is the work in line with your interests, and can your education and experience be well applied? What indoctrination, training, and work is offered during the first few years? What challenges are promised for you?

Do you want a job clearly defined with established responsibilities and hours of work?

Are schedules and days of work satisfactory?

Will you receive a permanent assignment or will you be expected to move from one location to another? Will extensive travel or time on business away from home impose restrictions on family or other obligations?

Would it be possible to obtain a transfer to another location should personal reasons demand?

5   Freedom for Ideas and Methods.

Does it appear that you will have reasonable freedom in assignments to use initiative in developing ideas and new methods?

What associations or foreman's clubs exist on a self-operating basis?

Are there meetings with the new people to discuss problems, ideas, new developments?

6   Professional Status.

Does it appear that you will have professional status or managerial responsibilities?

What are some of the privileges accorded a professional employee?

Will you be free to make decisions as you become qualified?

Are professional organizations nearby?

Does the company promote activities aiding professional growth such as participation in technical societies and seminars?

Are there aspects of publication of technical papers, patents, that would add to your professional stature and worth to the company?

7   Advancement.

While advancement depends much upon your efforts and abilities, you will want to consider all aspects of the business and your probable place in the organizational structure. What are the factors which seem unfavorable for your future advancement?

Is there evidence of real flexibility in management?

Will additional work become available to permit promotion as you develop new abilities?

Are there many cases of promotions through reassignments and transfers?

Do promotions come primarily from within the company or are outsiders brought in for key jobs to a large extent?

8   Salary.

What is the present average salary for those in your classification and state of preparation?

Consider reasons for unusually low or high salary offers.

Is the beginning salary apt to be static?

What is your salary potential? Are there many cases of salaries increasing as responsibilities increase?

Are there periodic reviews? On a merit basis? When and by whom?

Are salaries adjusted on an overall basis . . . as for a change in the cost of living?

9   Continuing Education.

Are there colleges within commuting distance offering courses useful to you?

Does the company encourage continuing education and does it subsidize tuition?

Does the company provide technical programs designed to strengthen the employee and the company?

10   Location (or possible future locations).

Is the area you are considering suitable for your progress and happiness? A number of factors deserve special attention if you have a family. Do you desire residence in a metropolitan or suburban area? Would living a considerable distance from home town and family obligations impose problems? Consider the effects of nearby institutions, community safety, health, welfare, available utilities, organized protection, the school system, and city management.

Are you seriously concerned about climate, excessive humidity, noise, odors?

11 Off-the-job Conditions.

Does the community appear progressive for your interests in recreational, social, professional, or other areas of activity?

What community activities now engage the interests of employees and their families?

How will family members adjust to the new environment? Do the town people seem friendly and willing to aid newcomers?

Are churches and service organizations adequate?

12 Housing.

Is housing available within a reasonable distance?

Are suitable rentals within your means?

Does the company assist in relocations? To what extent?

Does property appear a sound investment if you later want to sell?

13 Transportation.

Are transportation and communication services satisfactory? Consider main highways, rail, and air facilities.

Consider time and cost of daily travel to and from work.

14 Cost of Living.

Cost of living varies with location and depends primarily on what people are accustomed to and how they want to live.

Consider any special costs required by the job . . . expense of living in a specified area, social expectations, frequent assignments away from home.

Are there nearby business institutions (service, commerce, manufacturing) to help keep local taxation levies at a reasonable level?

15 Temporary Employment (undergraduate and postgraduate).

Is work available during periods before military service or intermittent periods while you are continuing your education?

What are the requirements for leaves-of-absence?

16 Military Commitments.

Will the company consider your employment in the event of probable military call after graduation?

Does the company cooperate with requirements for summer camp

(ROTC), National Guard, or reserve meetings? Is a salary adjustment made?

What is the policy regarding work and salary upon return from service?

17   Corporate Attitudes and Characteristics.

A company or other organization, like an individual, has certain predominant characteristics—the traits, interests, abilities which underlie its strengths and weaknesses. Some indicators of such character are participations in civic, government, and educational affairs; its attentions to individual improvements, high ethical standards, dealer and stockholder relationships. If you believe certain outstanding characteristics of a company will affect your progress and success, now is the time to investigate thoroughly.

In what ways does the company or its representatives serve in community affairs, service organizations, government? How extensively is safety promoted on the job and off, and how does the company's annual frequency rate compare with the industry's average? How many serve in youth organizations or lead in other public services? What meetings at colleges and technical groups are usually attended by company representatives? Will you be in line for any of these meetings?

REVIEW QUESTIONS

1. How do clients differ in their need for occupational information?

2. How can the range of occupations in which young persons express an interest be quickly and easily extended?

3. Where can you get for your clients a readable pamphlet on how to choose an occupation?

4. Vocational counseling which stops short of placement is frequently futile. Why?

5. What are some of the characteristics of the work environment that should be considered by a person choosing an occupation?

6. What are some of the physical requirements that a candidate for employment may have to meet?

7. What should a person who is choosing an occupation know about unions in any field he thinks of entering?

8. In considering preparation for an occupation what should the client and counselor "distinguish clearly between"?

9. What are some of the different ways in which a person may get his first job?

10. List some of the important considerations in the choice of an occupation that you think might be overlooked by a person who did not use a checklist similar to the one in this chapter.

11. How can you use what you have learned from this chapter?

4
Sources
of
Occupational
Information

One part of a counselor's work is to answer questions about occupations brought to him by clients, teachers, parents, and others. Often he will not know the answers, but he will know more than his questioner about where and how to find them. The purpose of this chapter and the next one is to help the counselor to find the information he wants on any occupation and to appraise the accuracy of what he finds.

Not every question can be answered. No one can predict with certainty the average earnings of journeyman plumbers four years ahead. No one can say precisely what combination of aptitudes and interests contributes most to successful teaching. But a great many questions can be answered, and reasonably good guesses can be made about many others if the counselor knows where and how to look for the necessary information.

ORIGINAL SOURCES

The original sources of all occupational information are very simple, very easy to remember. They are the worker who does the job, the person who pays him to do it, and the government bureau which issues licenses and regulates employment.

All other sources of occupational information are intermediate sources which, in some way at some time, obtained their information from these original sources or from someone else who went to the original sources.

The ultimate recourse for the counselor or client who wants occupational information and has trouble finding it is to turn to these original sources. The difficulties in doing so are obvious. Except in the government bureaus, the persons may be hard to find or reluctant to answer.

Those who can be reached may provide an atypical or a biased sample. They may have reasons for revealing only part of the truth or for stretching it a little. Despite the difficulties, the original source is often the best source and sometimes the only source from which to seek the desired information.

Workers and employers can be found in several ways: by examining the classified telephone directory; by consulting local offices of the state employment service and other placement services; by consulting the local chamber of commerce, labor unions, professional and trade associations, and banks; by asking one's students or clients to list the occupations of their relatives and friends; by making follow-up studies of former students and clients; and by making occupational surveys of the employment market.

When the original sources have already been consulted by a competent inquirer who has compiled and published the results, the counselor may, of course, turn first to such reports. Part of this chapter is devoted to explaining where and how such reports may be found. The succeeding chapter suggests how they may be appraised so that the client may be protected from information that is obsolete, incomplete, intentionally or unintentionally biased.

The total volume of information available in publications is impressive—dangerously so. Its sheer quantity may lead the counselor to the erroneous conclusion that a good library is a sufficient source of occupational information. It is not. The counselor who depends upon his library for all his occupational information will be unable to answer many of the questions that come to him, and his clients will be unable to find the answers without his help.

The author and his students once undertook to find the answers to questions which counselors had been asked but which they could not answer, such as "How do you get to be a tombstone cutter? Are there any opportunities for Negro girls in modeling? What do Good Humor salesmen do in the winter?" We found the answers, and we kept a record of where we found them. Most of the answers came from workers and their employers.

This chapter is intended to serve as a convenient reference to which the counselor may turn as questions arise. While there is no need to memorize every detail, the counselor is urged to read the chapter carefully in order to see what surprises it may contain for him; the beginner will be likely to find several, and even the experienced counselor may find one or two, as the author did when he prepared this material.

PUBLICATIONS

Publications usually available in schools and colleges. Perhaps the most widely used of all sources of occupational information is the *Occupational Outlook Handbook* [365] published biennially by the U.S. Bureau of Labor Statistics. It describes several hundred occupations. The descriptions include the nature of the work, where workers are employed, training, other qualifications, advancement, employment outlook, earnings, working conditions, and where to go for more information. While no publication of this kind can ever be perfect, the handbook is generally conceded to be the best document of its kind currently available. Most counselors who are looking for occupational information turn to it first. Some schools place a copy in every homeroom. Old editions should be discarded and replaced as new editions are published.

To supplement the handbook most schools maintain a collection of occupational pamphlets. Some publishers now offer collections of this kind, complete with filing cabinet, filing system, file folders, occupational pamphlets, and a service for supplying new materials as they are published. Some of these kits are described in Chapters 5 and 6.

Most college placement offices maintain a file of recruiting brochures, supplied by the companies which hope to hire some of the students about to graduate. Some of these brochures provide excellent descriptions of the jobs available. Regrettably, most of the brochures deal in glittering generalities and exemplify all the dangers of recruiting literature discussed in Chapter 5.

Other major reference works for the counselor's library. Less widely used but valuable for reference are the following, which belong in every counselor's library:

The *Dictionary of Occupational Titles* [123] is usually referred to as the *D.O.T.* In volume I of this book 21,741 separate occupations and 13,809 alternate job titles are listed alphabetically. Each title is defined in a short paragraph which describes what gets done, how, and why; and the functions performed by the worker in relation to data, people, and things. In volume II the job titles are arranged by categories and code numbers, by worker trait requirements, and by industry. How the *D.O.T.* may be used in counseling is discussed in Chapter 10.

The *Job Guide for Young Workers* [258] published by the U.S. Employment Service. Companion publications bearing similar titles are published by some state employment services. These present realistic information on the jobs most frequently available to beginning workers. Topics included for each occupation are usual duties, characteristics of the job, qualifications, employment prospects, advancement, and where jobs are found.

The *Counselor's Guide to Occupational and Other Manpower Information* [104], an annotated bibliography of federal and state government publications, including sections on job descriptions, careers in government, summer jobs, apprentices, minority groups, handicapped, older workers, labor standards, and part-time employment.

The local classified telephone directory. This provides a quick and easy way of revealing to the student or client the wide range of occupations locally available, and the names of possible employers. It can also reveal how limited are the opportunities for employment in some of the glamour fields.

How to build a library of occupational information is described in Chapter 5.

Where and how to find other publications. To locate books, pamphlets, and magazine articles describing different occupations, consult current and back issues of the *Career Index* [61], the *Career Guidance Index* [59], the *Counselors' Information Service* [105], the *Guidance Exchange* [197], the *Occupational Index* [364], and the lists of "Current Occupational Literature" recommended by the Career Information Review Service of the National Vocational Guidance Association and published in the *Vocational Guidance Quarterly* [494]. Earlier publications recommended by the Career Information Review Service may be found in the *NVGA Bibliography of Current Occupational Literature* [350].

The beginning counselor should write to the publishers of these indexes, ask for descriptive literature and sample copies, compare them, select and subscribe to the one he likes best, and be sure to save all issues for future reference.

One of these indexes should be among the first purchases made for any library of occupational information, for several reasons. As a file of back issues accumulates, the index will become the counselor's best guide to the most recently published information on any and all occupations. By calling the counselor's attention to several publications on the same subject, the index will facilitate more discriminating purchase; sometimes an inexpensive pamphlet will be better than an expensive book. Much free material is listed, and some of it is good. The index will more than pay for itself in what it will save on the purchase of new materials.

Another excellent bibliography is Forrester's *Occupational Literature* [163]. Being a single volume which covers the publications of several years, this is more convenient to use than the periodical indexes. Its one disadvantage is that it is published less frequently and thus includes none of the new publications which have come out since the last edition went to press.

After consulting these bibliographies, ask your students if any of them have relatives in the occupation from whom they can borrow occupational books or magazines for you to consult. Consult the card index and the pamphlet files of local libraries. Ask your librarian for back issues of professional journals and trade papers related to the occupation you are investigating.

To locate technical journals in any field consult *Ulrich's International Periodicals Directory*, now edited by Graves [190]. For articles in general magazines consult the *Readers' Guide to Periodical Literature* [386]; for recent news about any occupation watch the local newspapers and *The New York Times Index* [355]. All these are available in most large libraries and in many smaller ones. For guides to audio-visual materials containing occupational information see Chapter 20.

When you do not find the information you want among the publications or when you suspect the publications are out of date, biased, or otherwise inaccurate, consult the other sources listed below for information on specific topics.

KINDS OF INFORMATION AND WHERE TO FIND THEM

Employment opportunities. To determine the kinds of jobs most likely open to dropouts, graduates, or members of any other group, examine the results of follow-up studies to see what jobs were obtained by former members of the same group. Consult employment offices, and make a survey of employers. Review the discussion of these sources in Chapter 2.

Summer jobs.

Write to:

U.S. Bureau of Employment Security, Washington, D.C., for latest edition of *What To Do This Summer*.

Your own state employment service at the state capital. Ask if they publish a summer job bulletin.

U.S. Civil Service Commission, Washington, D.C., for pamphlet on *Summer Vacation Jobs in Federal Agencies*.

Commission on Youth Service Projects, 475 Riverside Drive, New

York, N.Y., for information about summer service jobs in the United States and abroad.

Alumnae Advisory Center, 541 Madison Ave., New York, N.Y., for titles and prices of their publications on summer jobs.

Read the following:

Babbott, Edward: "What Shall I Do This Summer?" *School Counselor*, March, 1964, pp. 154–156.

"Outlook for Summer Jobs—a Reappraisal," *Occupational Outlook Quarterly*, February, 1964, pp. 29–31.

Poppel, Norman: "Summer Activities for Students," *Vocational Guidance Quarterly*, Winter, 1963–1964, pp. 99–103.

Ask any college placement office to let you see the latest *College Placement Annual*. Look in the table of contents for the index to companies which hire college students for summer jobs. Then see the descriptions of the companies, arranged alphabetically in the front of the book.

Supply and demand for workers. Ask school and college placement offices and public employment services; they are in the best position to observe the supply and demand for workers in the occupations which they handle. Information from these sources is seldom more than twenty-four hours old. It is comparatively free from bias. In periods of depression, when many occupations are overcrowded, the employment office is favorably situated to observe where the crowding is least severe.

The information obtained from local agencies usually reflects local conditions, which may or may not follow national trends. For a broader picture, consult the *Occupational Outlook Handbook* [365] and write to the Occupational Outlook Service, U.S. Bureau of Labor Statistics, Washington, for any reports released since the last handbook went to press. See also the *Career Guide for Demand Occupations* [60].

Read slowly and carefully all statements about the occupational outlook. The hasty reader can easily draw the wrong inference from such statements as the following, if he fails to notice and to emphasize the words which I have put in capital letters.

Opportunities for TALENTED commercial artists are expected to be good.

WELL–QUALIFIED beginners with writing TALENT will have good employment opportunities.

Editors were actively seeking young reporters with EXCEPTIONAL TALENT.

Employment opportunities are favorable for TALENTED and WELL–TRAINED photographers. People with less ability and training are likely to encounter KEEN COMPETITION.

The correct inference from each of these statements may well be "You had better have a second-choice occupation to fall back on if you want to eat." In contrast, observe the following quotations from the same publication.

Home economists are expected to have very good employment opportunities. . . . NOT ENOUGH GRADUATES to satisfy the demand.
A nationwide SHORTAGE of trained librarians.

Be cautious about accepting statements of employers, employees, professional and trade associations, labor unions, and training institutions; frequently they have a selfish interest in increasing or restricting the supply of workers.

Employers seldom find the ideal applicant for work. Even in periods of unemployment, employers can and often will say quite truthfully, "There is still plenty of room for good people." Because the counselor deals most of the time with average persons, he must remember to emphasize the word "good" in the employer's statement. What the counselor considers good will sometimes be far removed from what the employer had in mind. Trade associations and other associations of employers are subject to similar bias.

Employees are subject to the same bias in reverse. Few of them are as successful as they would like to be. It is easy for them to believe that they would have been more successful if they had had less competition. It is not surprising that they notice, remember, and repeat anything which supports the opinion that their field is overcrowded. Labor unions and associations of professional workers are subject to similar bias. During economic depressions, it is common to find a professional association reporting that its field is overcrowded, rare to find one that encourages the recruitment of new workers. Labor unions quite frankly restrict the number of apprentices and the admission of new members to the union; some professional associations do the same thing less openly.

Not to be confused with the professional association is the association of professional schools, which reverses the bias again. When enrollments decline, educational administrators become apprehensive. College professors and vocational school teachers share their concern. Budgets are threatened. Salary increments and promotions are delayed. When enrollments go up, faculty meetings are concerned with excluding the incompetent applicant for admission in order to maintain standards, but when enrollments go down, all attention is focused on recruitment. Even the reputable, accredited, and endowed colleges have not been above stretching the truth a bit in some of their recruiting literature. Associations of schools and colleges reflect the biases of their members.

Future prospects. Consult the *Occupational Outlook Handbook* [365]. Write to the Occupational Outlook Service, U.S. Bureau of Labor Statistics, Washington. For local conditions, interview local employers and the officers of local unions, and compare what they say. Beware of biases noted above.

The forecast of prospects should extend into the future at least as far as the prospective worker's full-time education. Failure to consider this fact can result in some sad disappointments. When there is a widely advertised shortage of engineers, nurses, or elementary school teachers, there is a tendency to assume that the shortage will still exist when the present high school seniors are ready to look for jobs. Actually, by that time, so many other persons may have responded to the shortage and the demand may have so changed that there will be a surplus instead of a shortage of applicants for work. Conversely, a widely advertised surplus of workers can so discourage new entrants as to create a shortage in a few years. One cannot assume that surpluses and shortages will reverse themselves, but neither can one assume that they will not. Always one must look for the best available predictions and never forget that prediction is a hazardous business at best.

Dickinson [122] has noted that when one is comparing the number of new entrants who can be absorbed in an occupation with the number of persons in training for the occupation, it is important to remember that "very sizable percentages of those gaining degrees in such fields of study do not choose to enter these professions."

Nature of the work. Consult the *Dictionary of Occupational Titles,* volume I [123]. For more detailed descriptions of manufacturing occupations see the *Encyclopedia of Job Descriptions in Manufacturing* [146]. Visit and observe workers at their work. Ask several persons engaged in the occupation to tell you all the things they do and to indicate which things occupy most of their time. One of the best ways to do this is to ask the worker to describe in sequence everything that he has done since he came to work this morning and how much time he spent on each task, then ask what he did the day before that was different, then what else he has done as a part of his job during the past week, month, year. Without a detailed review of this kind, workers often forget to mention some of their activities.

Work environment. Go to see it if you can. Ask several workers and employers. Because working conditions in the same occupation may vary from one place of employment to another, be careful not to generalize from too few observations. Examine *Abstracts of Sociological Literature on Occupations* [1], *Sociological Studies of Occupations* [449], and back issues of the *Sociological Abstracts* [448].

Qualifications for employment. Ask employers not only what qualifications they seek but also what they have accepted. Distinguish between the qualifications which are indispensable and those which are desirable. Remember that few workers have all the desirable qualities.

For civil service jobs, consult the announcements of the most recent examinations. To get civil service announcements, write to the civil service commissions at the city hall, state capital, and Washington.

Physical demands. Do not overlook the physical demands of the occupation, which are often at least as important as the mental qualifications and which are sometimes much easier to discover. The first aptitude test applied to prospective soda dispensers by one vocational school is a tape measure around the hips; too much bulk at this point makes the worker a traffic hazard behind the counter. Some large cities have minimum and maximum height and weight requirements for policemen and firemen. One city will hire no teacher who weighs more than 300 pounds. Color blindness may handicap a chemist, a commercial artist, or a house painter. High blood pressure will exclude a truck driver from employment with some companies. A person who cannot stand on his feet all day will have to find an unusually favorable environment if he is to earn a living as a dentist or retail salesman. For facts on physical demands, ask local employers and employees, consult the *Dictionary of Occupational Titles*, volume I [123], the U.S. Employment Service, and the civil service commissions at the city hall, state capital, and Washington.

Aptitudes. Read Super and Crites [470]. See also the sections on worker trait groups in the *Dictionary of Occupational Titles* [123], volume II, pages 214–529 and 649–656. For more recent research, consult the back issues of the *Psychological Abstracts* [383]. In conversations with employers, beware of vague statements about such general characteristics as "initiative, dependability, honesty, punctuality, industry," etc., which are needed in nearly all occupations. The statements may be true enough, but they are of little help to the person who is trying to choose an occupation.

Interests. Consult the manual of instructions which accompanies available interest blanks to see if any research has been done on the relationship between scores on these blanks and success or satisfaction in the occupation. Beware of scores on blanks that have not been adequately validated. See also Super and Crites [470]. For more recent research, consult the back issues of the *Psychological Abstracts* [383].

Tools and equipment. Ask local employers, employees, and unions. Write to business, professional, and trade associations listed in the *Encyclopedia of Associations* [145], and in the *Directory of National Trade and Professional Associations of the United States* [131].

Legal requirements. Write to the appropriate city, state, and Federal licensing boards. If you do not know the name and address of the correct board, send your question to the mayor, governor, or President, and ask him to route it to the proper department.

Do not assume that a license is not required until you have made inquiries of city, state, and Federal authorities. The number of licensed occupations increases continually. Some occupations are licensed by some states or cities and not by others. Among the workers who must have licenses, in some or all places in the United States, are airplane mechanics, apprentice seamen, architects, auctioneers, awning contractors, barbers, beekeepers, boxers, cement-block manufacturers, chauffeurs, commission merchants, cosmetologists, dealers in firearms, dental hygienists, food handlers, fur dealers, gasoline-service-station attendants, ice-cream manufacturers, insurance agents, journeyman electricians, junk dealers, landscape gardeners, kennel owners, manicurists, minnow dealers, morticians, motor-vehicle dealers, nursery dealers, optometrists, parking-lot attendants, plumbers, public librarians, real estate salesmen, registered and practical nurses, residential builders, stationary engineers, structural welders, syrup manufacturers, teachers, veterinarians, and many others.

Among the government agencies which issue these licenses are the municipal departments of health, fire, police, buildings, and safety engineering; the state departments of aeronautics, agriculture, banking, conservation, health, education, insurance, labor, police, state, social welfare; the athletic board of control; the state board of libraries; the liquor-control commission; the U.S. Department of Agriculture; Coast Guard; Federal Aviation Agency; Federal Communications Commission; Interstate Commerce Commission; and U.S. Treasury Department. See also the section on "Labor Legislation" in Chapter 2.

Unions. Consult officers of local unions regarding requirements and costs of admission to the union. Ask both the union and the employers about closed-shop contracts and about what percentage of employees are union members.

Consult the *Directory of National and International Labor Unions in the United States* [130] and subsequent supplements. Select the appropriate unions, and write to them. The constitution and bylaws of a national union may say nothing about racial discrimination in the admission of new members, national policy may even forbid such discrimination, but a union local may nevertheless find ways to discriminate, just as an individual employer may evade the laws which prohibit him from discriminating. Because it may be impolitic for a union to tell the whole story, the counselor should always ask his former students and clients about their experiences in applying for union membership.

Discrimination. Ask employers, employees, and former students. Do not ask employers and unions, "Do you discriminate?" Ask employers, "How many Negroes do you employ now? In what jobs?" Ask unions, "How many of your members are Negroes?" Ask similar questions about all other groups with which you are concerned. Groups subject to discrimination include Negroes; Jews; Catholics; Protestants; Communists; alleged Communists; Chinese, Japanese, Mexicans, Puerto Ricans, other persons with distinctly foreign names, speech, or appearance; women; married women; pacifists; nonveterans; former prisoners; and persons over forty years of age.

Discriminatory practices include refusal to admit to union membership, refusal to refer qualified workers for employment, refusal to hire, unequal working conditions, refusal to upgrade, and dismissal without cause. Discrimination is practiced by government agencies as well as by private employers and labor unions and by individuals within these organizations even in opposition to organization policy.

For further information on discrimination against Negroes and Jews write to the National Urban League, 14 E. 48 St., and to the Jewish Occupational Council, 150 Fifth Ave., both in New York.[1]

Preparation. See sections on qualifications, legal requirements, and union requirements above; see approved schools and apprenticeship below; see the discussion of "Preparation" in Chapter 11.

---

[1] The addresses here and on subsequent pages were correct at date of publication but should be checked by any reader using this list.

Approved schools. Consult directories such as:

    Accredited Higher Institutions [3]
    Accredited Institutions of Higher Education [4]
    American Junior Colleges [183]
    American Universities and Colleges [69]
    Canadian Universities and Colleges [56]
    College Guide for Jewish Youth [152]
    Colleges Classified [353]
    Directory, National Association of Trade and Technical Schools [128]
    Directory of Vocational Training Sources [348]
    Guide to College Majors [198]
    A Guide to Graduate Study. Programs Leading to the Ph.D. Degree [189]
    Guide to Organized Occupational Curriculums in Higher Education [47]
    Lovejoy's College Guide [310]
    National Directory of Schools and Vocations [331]
    New American Guide to Colleges [208]
    S.O.S. Guidance Research Information Booklets [245]
    Technician Education Yearbook [474]

Write to business, trade, and professional associations listed in the *Encyclopedia of Associations* [145] and in the *Directory of National Trade and Professional Associations of the United States* [131]. Schools approved by some of the professional associations are so identified in some of the other directories.

Write to the U.S. Office of Education, Washington, D.C., and to your own state department of education for their most recent directories of approved and accredited vocational and professional schools and colleges and for a list of other directories of schools and colleges.

Write to the Accrediting Commission of the National Home Study Council, 1601–18 St., N.W., Washington, D.C., for its most recent list of approved correspondence schools [129]. Although correspondence study is even less likely than residence study to assure the student of subsequent employment, it can be of considerable value to the person who has a job and wants to become more proficient at it.

Shoemaker [428] asked university department heads to recommend ". . . some schools that are considered 'good' in your area of specialization." He got 133 responses from 91 areas of specialization.

The applicant who is not admitted to the college of his choice can sometimes find a school that will accept him if he seeks help from the following:

American College Admissions Center
12th and Walnut Streets
Philadelphia, Pa.
Catholic College Admissions and Information Center
3805 McKinley Street, N.W.
Washington, D.C.
College Admissions Assistance Center
41 E. 65 Street
New York, N.Y.
College Admissions Center
610 Church Street
Evanston, Ill.

Apprenticeship. Ask the person in charge of apprenticeship or of vocational education in your school. Ask employers. Ask union locals. Ask the nearest office of your state employment service. Write to the Bureau of Apprenticeship and Training, U.S. Department of Labor, Washington, for the addresses of the nearest regional and state apprenticeship agencies; then write to them. Ask the state agency if there are any apprenticeship councils near you, and consult them.

Apprentices are now trained in more than three hundred occupations. Among these are aircraft-engine mechanic, automobile mechanic, boat-builder, bookbinder, bricklayer, business-machine mechanic, cabinetmaker, carpenter, commercial photographer, cook, dental mechanic, draftsman, electrician, engraver, jeweler, landscape nurseryman, machinist, meatcutter, painter, patternmaker, photoengraver, plasterer, plumber, printer, radio and television repairman, refrigeration and air-conditioning mechanic, sewing-machine mechanic, sheet-metal worker, stonemason, tailor, tool and die maker, upholsterer, and watchmaker.

Methods of entrance. Ask employers, employees, and former students how a beginner gets his first job.

Capital. Ask proprietors and bankers how much capital a beginner needs to start in business. Read Metcalf [328]. Write to the United States Small Business Administration, Washington.

Advancement. Ask both employers and employees. Inquire what percentage of beginning workers subsequently advances to each level.

Related occupations. Consult the *Dictionary of Occupational Titles*, volume II

[123]. Ask employers, employees, and the local office of the state employment service.

Earnings. Write to the U.S. Bureau of Labor Statistics, Washington. It publishes reports on earnings in the whole range of occupations from the unskilled to professional and administrative. Write to the professional, trade, and business associations in the *Encyclopedia of Associations* [145] and in the *Directory of National Trade and Professional Associations of the United States* [131]. Write to the unions listed in the *Directory of National and International Labor Unions in the United States* [130]. For prevailing wages in local industry, try the local office of the state employment service. Try also the state department of labor. In large cities consult the local office of the U.S. Department of Labor. Ask local employers and unions, and compare their answers. Be sure to specify whether you are inquiring about wages for beginners or for experienced workers.

Starting salaries currently offered to college seniors in different curricula, by companies in different industries, are reported periodically in the College Placement Council's *Salary Survey* [413] which is distributed to all subscribers to the *Journal of College Placement* [262].

Beware of figures which may be accurate but misleading. Perhaps the most misleading of all are the top earnings of the most successful persons in an occupation. These are frequently reported in newspapers and in popular magazines. The optimistic young person may readily assume that if someone else can earn that much, perhaps he can, too. Perhaps he can, but the probabilities may be a thousand to one against him.

We know so little about how to predict the earning power of any individual that the best guess we can make usually is that he will earn about what the average worker earns in the occupation that he enters. Consequently the best figures to use in comparing occupations are the median, or the range of the middle 50 percent. Means may have to be used when medians are not available; means are less desirable because they may be unduly affected by the extremely high earnings of extremely few persons.

Even median earnings can be misleading if one does not consider the working lifetime. Show girls are old at twenty-three. Professional boxers are finished in their thirties. Heavy laborers may be unable to stand the physical strain in their forties and fifties. The choice of an occupation should be made only after a realistic look at probable life earnings. These are admittedly difficult to predict, but we can at least warn the young hopeful that in certain occupations his earnings will be likely to decline with his advancing age.

Hourly, daily, and weekly rates of pay can also be misleading. Coal miners, furriers, and hod carriers are employed in seasonal industries; they must expect several weeks or months of unemployment each year. Hourly, daily, and weekly earnings must be converted into annual earnings before they can be used properly in vocational guidance. In the conversion, allowance should be made for unemployment compensation.

The person who wants a steady job in a seasonal occupation may find it if he will look long enough. Some large companies, for example, hire carpenters for maintenance work and keep them busy all the time; such carpenters are usually paid less per hour than carpenters whose work is intermittent.

Other persons who budget their expenditures carefully enjoy the vacations provided by seasonal unemployment, during which they may collect unemployment compensation. It is, of course, not the counselor's responsibility to decide whether continuous or intermittent employment is preferable; it is the counselor's responsibility to see that his client knows which kind of employment he is choosing.

Number and distribution of workers. Write to the Bureau of the Census, U.S. Department of Commerce, Washington. Ask which census publication will give you the information you want.

If the facts you want have not been published, ask the Bureau of the Census if and how the data may be obtained. Some data are tabulated but not published, and transcripts of these data may be obtained at cost. Additional tabulations also may be contracted for under a cost arrangement.

It is possible to obtain data on the number employed in different occupations by age, race, and sex in any locality in the United States.

Hours. Ask local employers and employees. For national figures write to the U.S. Bureau of Labor Statistics, Washington; to the professional, trade, and business associations in the *Encyclopedia of Associations* [145]; and to the unions in the *Directory of National and International Labor Unions in the United States* [130].

Vacations. Ask employers and employees.

Stability of employment. Ask employers and employees how the number of persons employed was affected by the last economic depression, the last big war, and the end of the war. Ask also about seasonal changes, effects of weather, strikes, and anything else which may interfere with steady employment for a normal working lifetime. Consult the *Occupational Outlook Handbook* [365].

Some occupations are particularly responsive to increases or decreases in public appropriations. Employers and employees can usually report with some accuracy, and often with some feeling, the effects of public spending in the past and the extent to which employment in their field is or is not affected by it.

If one wishes to work in a seasonal occupation, he will, of course, find employment prospects best at the time of the year when employment is rising. Employers can usually predict when this time will be. In retail selling, for example, employment rises sharply before Christmas and declines sharply after, and this happens year after year through periods of prosperity and depression.

Hazards. Ask employers and employees, professional associations, and labor unions about accidents and occupational diseases. See the *Accident Prevention Manual for Industrial Operations* [2]. Write to the National Safety Council, Industrial Department, 425 N. Michigan Ave., Chicago.

Advantages and disadvantages. Ask several workers in the occupation, "What do you like best about your job? What do you dislike most about it?"

FINALLY

As the need for facts about jobs arises, the counselor who hopes to be effective will not rely solely upon the facts in his files or upon the occupational information that can be compiled by a client who has had no training in occupational research. The counselor who wants to do his job well will put his hat on his head and go out and talk with the employers and the employees of his community. He will turn to his telephone more often than to his files. How one community agency used a volunteer worker to get facts about jobs by means of field visits and telephone inquiries has been described by Miller [333].

REVIEW QUESTIONS

1. What are the original sources of all occupational information?
2. What sources provided most of the answers to questions that counselors could not answer?

3. What indexes periodically list new books, pamphlets, and magazine articles containing occupational information?

4. Which are the best sources of information on the relative supply and demand for workers in different occupations? Which are the biased sources, and why are they biased?

5. Which is the best source of information on future prospects for employment in many occupations?

6. Which is the best source of information on legal requirements for entrance to an occupation?

7. What are some of the groups that are subject to discrimination in employment other than Jews and Negroes?

8. Where can you write for general information about apprenticeship?

9. What organization publishes reports on earnings in the whole range of occupations?

10. What questions should be asked about stability of employment?

11. One of your clients wants to know all about an occupation that you have never even heard of. To what sources will you turn for information and in what sequence?

12. Your colleagues on your job know that you are taking this course. They ask you to talk to them for ten minutes about sources of occupational information. What will you tell them?

13. Is there anything in this chapter that you can use to improve your work? What? How?

5
Appraising
Occupational
Literature

The dubious quality of many books, pamphlets, and magazine articles which purport to describe occupations has been mentioned in preceding chapters. One very important responsibility of the counselor or teacher is to examine and appraise the accuracy of every piece of occupational literature to which his clients or students will be referred.

If the beginning counselor gets his first job in an organization which already has a substantial library of occupational information and if responsibility for the quality of this library has been assigned to some other member of the organization, the beginner should, of course, not make himself obnoxious by openly questioning or criticizing the quality of a colleague's work. But neither should he assume that he can refer his clients to this library without himself examining and appraising the materials that his clients will use.

Under these circumstances, the beginner may ask the librarian to show him the materials available and to explain the preferred procedures for using them; then he should examine them as thoroughly as his time permits. Usually, the counselor will not have time to do a very thorough job at this point.

Thereafter, every time the counselor refers a client to published occupational information, he should do one of two things: first, refer the client only to specific publications which the counselor has already examined and appraised, or, second, go with the client to the library and appraise each publication in the client's presence, at the same time teaching the client a little about how to appraise such materials himself. The counselor can avoid implied criticism of the librarian by explaining to the client that this library must serve the needs of many persons and that publications useful to other persons for their purposes may not be useful to this client for his purposes.

If the counselor also teaches a course in occupations to the students he counsels, he can and should include in this course both instruction and practice in the appraisal of occupational literature, but he can never escape ethical and professional responsibility for himself knowing the quality of the publications to which he refers his students any more than he can escape responsibility for knowing the validity of the aptitude tests he uses.

If the counselor is to be the only or the principal guidance officer in the organization which he serves, if he is himself to be responsible for the purchase of new materials, he should then order publications only on approval and reserve sufficient time to appraise each accession before it goes onto the shelves or into the files. He should also make a thorough examination of the occupational literature on hand when he arrives and ask the librarian if some way can be devised to separate the best materials from the others. In this connection, he must, of course, remember that he and his clients are not the only users of the library and that the librarian may not be able to do everything that would be desirable from the counselor's point of view.

FIVE CRITICAL QUESTIONS

In appraising occupational literature, the counselor will do well to memorize and always to ask himself at least these five questions: When? Where? Who? Why? How?

When? If the reader will go to any school or college library, ask to see the occupational shelves, and examine the copyright dates of the books thereon, he will find, almost invariably, at least one book that is twenty-five years old resting on the same shelf with books published in the current year, and there will be nothing to warn the unsuspecting reader that the statements in the older volume may be a quarter century behind the times.

Most counselors maintain a file of occupational pamphlets, to which new materials are added periodically, and from which no one ever throws anything away. Examination of one such file revealed 900 pamphlets that were more than five years old. Of these 300 were over ten years old, 20 were over twenty years old, and a few had been published thirty years before [236]. Occupational books and pamphlets that are obsolete should be burned or sold as scrap paper or at least transferred to the historical section of the library.

The date by which to judge a book is not the date which appears on the title page. This date is usually the year in which the volume was printed. The book may have been written years earlier and reprinted without revision. The important date is the first copyright date, which usually appears in small print on the back of the title page. Later copyright dates for revised editions may or may not be significant. A book can be technically considered "revised" if the author changes one comma to a semicolon, and some revised versions seem to have enjoyed just about this much change.

Certain kinds of occupational information become obsolete more quickly than others. The duties of a high school counselor have not changed greatly in the past ten years, but salaries have increased considerably. The ratio of supply to demand for beginners in engineering has changed radically within one year. Appropriate aptitudes and interests change only as the nature of the work changes. Hours and conditions of employment may change with each union contract negotiation. Hazards may change as rapidly as industrial processes. Industrial occupations may be wiped out completely by technological improvement, but it may take a thousand years to get an obsolete subject out of a school or college curriculum.

In appraising any publication the counselor should consider how rapid is the rate of change in the kind of information he seeks. He may then decide how old a publication may be and still serve his purposes. The beginner may not be very confident of his judgment on the rate of obsolescence, but if he will only pause long enough to consider it, he will avoid the inexcusable malpractice of referring clients to sources that are obviously out of date.

Where? All original occupational research has some kind of geographical limitation. It may cover conditions in one company, one city, one state, or one nation. In time it may cover one world. At present, much occupational literature purports to be national in its application but is based upon only scattered research covering a much smaller area or on the author's experience and reading. Careful appraisal therefore requires careful scrutiny of the research evidence upon which the author has based his statements. Is there any? If so, was the evidence compiled in the area in which the reader expects to seek employment? If not, are conditions likely to be similar or different in the two areas? Teacher salaries and training requirements, for example, tend to be much higher in wealthy urban or suburban areas than in poorer rural areas. Inability to gain entrance to an exclusive union may exclude an urban boy from his preferred occupation but be a matter of no concern to his cousin in a small town where the workers are not organized.

Who? Experienced workers in occupational research soon learn that certain of their colleagues invariably do careful, scholarly research and make only conservative statements which can be adequately documented. Other writers and some publishers become known for the superficial, inadequate, or biased nature of their material.

The beginning counselor will be somewhat at a loss to appraise the quality of authorship, but he can begin by noting anything that may be said about the author's qualifications and by asking for such information when the publishers do not supply it.

In general, the best material is that written by persons whose full-time job is occupational research, such as the staff of the Occupational Outlook Service, the occupational research workers in the U.S. Employment Service, the state employment services, and the Women's Bureau of the U.S. Department of Labor. But these are not the only sources of good material. One of the best descriptions of an occupation ever to appear in print was "A Day with a Social Worker" [117] prepared by Margaret O'Rourke Montgomery for *Glamour*'s job department. In complete detail this article reported everything that one social worker did from 9 A.M. to 6:15 P.M. on a typical day.

Why? Some occupational literature is written solely for purposes of professional vocational guidance by persons who have no desire to do other than present the pertinent facts as accurately as possible.

Some is written for purposes of entertainment; most articles in popular magazines are in this category. Material for these articles is selected because it makes interesting reading. Important facts may be omitted if they are dull. Peak salaries may be stated, and average salaries omitted. Glamorous activities may be described at length; the more time-consuming routine aspects of the job may be barely mentioned. As entertainment, for the general reader who is not choosing an occupation, such literature has its place. As occupational information, it often leaves the reader with a false impression.

Some occupational literature is written for the purpose of recruiting students or workers. This is particularly dangerous because so much of it is free; consequently, it finds its way into school and college libraries in disproportionately large quantities. It is often biased, emphasizing the attractions of the occupation, omitting or slighting its disadvantages, and sometimes intentionally conveying a false impression regarding opportunities, requirements, or rewards. The actual statements made are often true, as are the statements in patent-medicine advertising, but the total impression is often just as misleading and just as intentionally so. It is a sad commentary on our professions and our professional schools, but it is indisputably true, that some of the most respected of them have not been above creating false impressions in order to recruit high school and college students. The deliberate misrepresentation employed by recruiting officers for military services has been notorious for centuries. Gullible school counselors have been unwitting partners to the deception.

James Jones in *From Here to Eternity* [261] had his own comment on recruiting literature:

> Fatigue, in the Army, occupies fifty percent of the duty time; in the morning there is drill, in the afternoon Fatigue; but it is a fifty percent unmentioned in the enlistment campaigns and the pretty posters outside every Post Office in the nation that are constantly extolling the romance of a soldier's life, the chance for adventurous foreign travel (take the wife), the exceedingly high pay all unattached (if you get the rating), the chance to be a leader (if you get a commission), and the golden merits of learning a trade that will support you all your life. A recruit never finds out about Fatigue until some time after he has held up his right hand and then it is too late.

Southern and Colver [451] recommended that recruiting literature be used in counseling because of the useful information it contains but cautioned the counselor about his responsibilities when he uses it:

> Many counselors tend to feel that the use of free material, especially recruitment material, is not an acceptable practice. We question the wisdom of such an attitude. . . .
> Every company realizes that only a small percentage of those people who read the literature will apply for jobs, but that most readers are prospective customers, now or at some time in the future. In using this material for occupational information, the counselor has a responsibility for making the client fully aware of the fact that this is advertising and public relations material, as well as occupational information.

A few occupational articles are written for the express purpose of discouraging competition. In periods of general unemployment, nearly all occupations are temporarily "overcrowded." It is not unusual, at such times, for professional associations and labor unions to encourage the publication of news stories and magazine articles which describe the low earnings and the extensive unemployment among their own members. All that they say may be true, but if the same situation exists in most other occupations, the impression created may be misleading.

Biography and fiction are sometimes recommended for student reading because of their occupational content. A few such publications are good, but many biographies describe occupational conditions faced by the subject twenty or thirty years ago and do not warn the reader that conditions have changed. Many books of fiction convey mistakenly glamorous impressions of occupations. Both biography and fiction are usually written for purposes of entertainment rather than education. Necessarily they give most of their space to the entertaining aspects of whatever they present.

How? This question applies both to how the facts were collected and to how they are presented.

Questionnaire research has been described as a method of summarizing ignorance. Much occupational information has been collected by questionnaire. If the data sought concern matters on which the respondent is well informed such as his own hours and earnings, if the sample is adequate, and if there is no incentive for giving false replies, the questionnaire may be the best possible method of compilation. If the data concern matters of opinion, on which the respondent is ignorant or biased, the results may do more harm than good. Most workers really know very little about the aptitudes which determine success or failure in their work, although many of them think they know a great deal. The same may be said of supply and demand for workers.

Some occupational literature is based solely on library research. It is as good or as bad as the original studies which the author consulted. Usually these studies are not identified, and the reader can only guess how good or how recent they were. This kind of "research" is often found in textbooks on occupations prepared by school teachers or college professors. An exception to the rule is the *Occupational Abstracts* [363] which are clearly identified as based upon library research and which include an appraisal of the literature abstracted.

By inquiring about, and by carefully noting, how the information for any publication was collected, the counselor can sometimes get a much clearer idea of its probable accuracy. Guidelines for preparing and evaluating occupational materials [199] have been prepared and published by the National Vocational Guidance Association and revised from time to time. These standards are used by the association to appraise new occupational pamphlets as they appear. Recommended publications are listed periodically in the *Vocational Guidance Quarterly* [494].

Using the same criteria, Hill [216] developed *The Ohio University Check List and Rating Device for Evaluating Occupational Literature* which he has used "in helping counselor trainees to develop skill in evaluating . . . occupational literature."

How the facts are presented may determine whether or not the publication will be read and understood by the persons whom the counselor seeks to help. The difficult reading level of many occupational publications has been explored by Brayfield and Reed [40], by Diener and Kaczkowski [124], by Ruth [411], and by Watson, Rundquist, and Cottle [504]. *The Rochester Occupational Reading Series* [185] provides occupational information for "the slow and reluctant learner" in grades 6 to 10. Splaver [453, 454] and Oxhandler [370] have studied what makes occupational books and pamphlets popular. Unfortunately, the counselor often will have little opportunity to select publications on the basis of readability, popularity, or suitability. By the time he has eliminated those which are obsolete, biased, or otherwise unacceptable, he will frequently have little left from which to choose. The most readable material is of little value if the content is false. Accurate material is of little value to readers who will not read it; it can, however, be read by counselors, who probably ought to read much more occupational literature than they usually do.

TO SAVE TIME

The order of the five questions "When? Where? Who? Why? and How?" is intended to save the counselor's time. If he begins by asking "When?" he will find sometimes that he can reject a reference on this basis alone, without bothering to ask the other questions. "Where?" may reveal that the source of the data was too remote or too different from the area in which his client hopes to work. If the publication passes these two tests, "Who?" may indicate that the publication is so good or so bad that the remaining questions are needed only to confirm the counselor's judgment of the author. "Why?" will often spot a piece of recruiting literature to be avoided. Each of these first four questions can be asked and answered quickly for many publications, and a large number can be rejected or identified as questionable without further examination. Some of the questionable publications may be kept in the counselor's personal library for such use as he cares to make of them (perhaps as horrible examples in his course in occupations), but they should not be placed on open shelves or in open files for indiscriminate use by all students.

REVIEWS BY EXPERTS

If examination by the counselor indicates that a publication is probably acceptable, the counselor may then try to find someone engaged in the occupation who will read it as a check on the counselor's judgment. Often the parent of some student can be found to do this. Many parents are pleased at being asked to help, and good public relations may thus be incidentally established. Excerpts from the reader's report may, with his permission, be copied and pasted in the front of the publication for permanent record and as an aid to others who consult the publication. If this is done, the reviewer's name and position should be appended to the excerpts, along with the date of the review.

ANNUAL BOOK BURNING

Every library of occupational information should be thoroughly weeded once a year, at which time all obsolete publications should be removed. This need not be an onerous task. A student clerk can remove from the shelves and the files all publications which are more than five years old. The counselor who knows his literature can quickly decide which of these items to discard and which to keep for another year.

If you decide to keep anything that is more than five years old, put on the front cover some warning that the material may be out of date, for example, a red label reading:

OUT OF DATE

This document is more than five years old. Some of the information in it may now be out of date. Ask your counselor where to get more recent information.

For more on this subject see "Renovating an Occupational Information File" [236].

HOW TO BUILD A LIBRARY OF
OCCUPATIONAL INFORMATION

Occupational information kits, collections, and pamphlet series. The quickest and easiest way to acquire a library of occupational information is to buy it ready-made. Several publishers have produced sets of occupational pamphlets which cover many of the popular occupations. Some schools and libraries have bought complete sets of these pamphlets and then discovered that much of what they bought was already obsolete and should be discarded.

Caution. Before ordering any complete set of occupational pamphlets, ask the publisher for the copyright date of each pamphlet in the series, or order the set on approval and do not pay the bill until you have examined the copyright dates yourself.

The principal publishers of occupational pamphlets are listed in Appendix A of this book.

Science Research Associates, Inc., sells a Career Information Kit [62] which contains a collection of pamphlets from several publishers. Chronicle Guidance Publications offers a similar kit [84] containing its own pamphlets plus reprints of articles from various magazines. Careers (Largo, Fla.) publishes its own desk-top career file.

The ready-made pamphlet collection certainly saves the counselor considerable time that he would otherwise spend in reviewing, appraising, selecting, and purchasing individual pamphlets. This saving is an obvious advantage. There are less obvious disadvantages.

The pamphlets included may not all be appropriate for the persons who are to read them. If they are not, some money will be wasted.

The pamphlets included may not be the best on the subject if the best title was produced by another publisher.

Nearly every publisher who produces a set of pamphlets continues to produce new ones and to revise his old ones. But the revisions are not always made as frequently as they should be, nor are they always adequate. In the meantime, every publisher is tempted to sell his surplus publications even after they are obsolete; not all publishers resist the temptation.

Occasions are almost sure to arise when the counselor will want more information than the best pamphlet file can provide. He will need and want to supplement his pamphlet file with books which describe one or more occupations. And he will want to buy new pamphlets from many publishers as they appear.

For these reasons, the counselor will need to supplement and extend any collection of occupational pamphlets which he may buy ready-made. He may even prefer to build his own collection from the start. How to do this is described below.

To supplement the pamphlet collection. If you are in a school or college, ask all your students to answer the following questions on a mimeographed form:

When you think about what you will do after you finish school, which occupations are of most interest to you?

Would you like to read books and pamphlets which describe the opportunities and requirements in any of these occupations?

Which ones?

Tabulate the replies to the last question. Note the occupations in which the largest numbers of your students are interested.

If you are in a counseling organization where you meet your clients only one at a time, keep a record of the occupations in which they indicate an interest until you feel that you have a good sample.

Examine your present library to see if you have enough recent material on each of these occupations. If you have not, make a note to order more.

Subscribe to one or more of the indexes listed in Chapter 4 under "Publications," after comparing them as suggested there. Order all back issues of the current year and bound volumes for the five years preceding the current year.

From the back issues of the index select the publications needed to fill the gaps in your present library. Read carefully the annotations of all publications before you order them. Take one occupation at a time, and compare the available publications on it as to content, recency of publication, cost, and probable value to your students.

Order all publications on approval, and appraise them as suggested in this chapter.

Before placing any publication in the files or on the shelves, write the copyright date on the front cover. If the document is not dated, write the date received, thus: "Rec'd 1967." This date will help to remind you and your students to consider the possible obsolescence of the materials when you consult them. It will save hours of time when you weed your files.

If you keep and file any recruiting literature from employers, schools, or military services, put on the front cover some warning about recruiting literature, for example, a red label reading:

WARNING

This document comes from an author or publisher who could conceivably wish to recruit students or workers. Recruiting literature often says more about the attractions of an occupation than about the disadvantages. Ask your counselor about the disadvantages.

If possible, do not spend your entire first year's book budget at one time. Save from one-third to two-thirds of it to purchase future publications as they appear. Ask your supervisor if present regulations regarding book requisitions will permit you to order publications as you need them. If the answer is no, ask if the regulations can be changed. If the answer is still no, keep a record of the things you want and order them at the prescribed times.

Examine each new issue of the index when it arrives. Order immediately all the free and inexpensive pamphlets that you think will be of value to your students. The free publications that you can collect in this way will more than justify the cost of your subscription to the index.

Order books that cost more than a dollar only when you are sure you will have use for them. If you are not sure, order when a need for the books arises. Occasionally, you will regret having done this. You will need the books sooner than you can get them, or you will find them out of print when you want them. These annoyances are preferable to dissipating your book budget on publications you will never use.

Keep in close touch with your librarian to find out which publications on which occupations appear to be in greatest demand. Occasionally examine the library books yourself, and note which have been taken out most frequently.

An annual budget of $250 is adequate to keep a library of occupational information reasonably up to date. If your budget is less than this, you may find the Kiwanis or Rotary Club willing to contribute to it. Or you may get the school and the public librarian to divide between them the purchase of the materials you want so that unnecessary duplication is reduced or eliminated.

If your budget is very small, limit most of your purchases to inexpensive pamphlets and to books which describe more than one occupation. Watch especially for the new publications of the publishers listed in Appendix A. Do not buy complete sets of pamphlets from any of these publishers or from anyone else without first getting the copyright dates on all titles. The smaller your budget, the more you need a good current bibliography to bring you information about all the new publications that you can get free of charge.

When funds are inadequate. The author's students have asked, "When we can't buy all that we ought to buy, what should we buy first?" The author suggests that the first money available be used to provide the following, in this order:

The *Dictionary of Occupational Titles*, Volumes I and II [123] and the latest supplements to it.

One copy of the latest edition of the *Occupational Outlook Handbook* [365].

One copy of the *Job Guide for Young Workers* [258].

One copy of the local classified telephone directory, which can usually be obtained free from the business office of the local telephone company.

A simple, inexpensive filing system. See Chapter 6 for suggestions.

An annual subscription to one of the indexes listed in Chapter 4 under "Publications."

A list or a card file of companies which have hired former students or clients, cross-indexed by occupation. See Chapter 13 for suggestions on inexpensive follow-up studies.

A list or card file of other local employers who have said they will hire students, alumni, or clients, similarly cross-indexed by occupation. See Chapter 16 for suggestions on inexpensive surveys of beginning jobs.

Your own notes on jobs in local plants to which you have taken students or clients for plant tours. See Chapter 14.

Your own notes which you have taken during group conferences which you have arranged for your students and clients. See Chapter 15.

Clippings from newspapers and magazines which your students will bring to you at your request. Be sure to caution them not to deface publications which do not belong to them.

Free and inexpensive publications selected from the index you have chosen, appraised as suggested in this chapter.

REVIEW QUESTIONS

1. What should the counselor do whenever he refers a client to published occupational information?

2. What five questions should the counselor memorize and always ask about any piece of occupational literature?

3. What should be done with occupational books and pamphlets that are obsolete?

4. By what date should one judge a book for obsolescence?

5. What are some of the kinds of occupational information that change rapidly?

6. Why is it important to know where occupational information was collected?

7. Why do articles in popular magazines sometimes give false impressions of occupations?

8. Why is recruiting literature particularly dangerous?

9. What are the weaknesses of biography and fiction as sources of occupational information?

10. Who should check the counselor's judgment of occupational literature?

11. How often should a library of occupational information be thoroughly weeded?

12. How large an annual budget is needed to keep a library of occupational information reasonably up to date?

13. When funds are inadequate, what are the first things to buy?

14. You are a counselor in a school, college, or agency which has a collection of occupational information in its library. The librarian asks you to review the collection and recommend which publications should be kept and which removed. How will you proceed?

15. Will anything in this chapter affect your future thoughts and actions? What? How?

6
Classifying and Filing Occupational Information

The industrious counselor soon collects occupational pamphlets, books, and clippings by the hundreds. To these he adds his own notes on the information that he obtains from tours of local industries, from conversations with workers in different occupations, from follow-up studies of his own dropouts and alumni, and from other sources. Soon the volume of such material becomes so large that it must be classified and filed, so that he can find what he has on any one occupation when and as he needs it.

Depending on where he works, the counselor may or may not have the help of a librarian. If he has, the librarian may already have established a file of occupational information. The counselor may find that the existing file serves all essential purposes, that the librarian will be pleased to receive and to file any new material that the counselor may acquire, and that the counselor can turn his attention to other matters.

On the other hand there may be no librarian and no filing system, or the librarian may want the help of the counselor in setting up an occupational file, or the librarian and the counselor and their common administrator may agree that the counselor should maintain a separate file of occupational information in his office. In this case the sooner the counselor starts the better. Odgers [366] suggested that "Once he has accumulated a hundred or more pieces of occupational information . . . he may find the job of getting everything classified and filed is overwhelming. His best bet is to . . . classify and file materials as they arrive. Otherwise he may find himself with a week's work and no week in which to do it."

NOW WHERE DID I PUT THAT?

Many problems in filing arise from the fact that an occupation is a hard thing to define. Actually an occupation is just a classification of jobs which have something in common. Since jobs may have many things in common, they may be classified in many ways.

Jobs may be classified according to the activities involved, such as selling, teaching, typing.

Jobs may be classified according to their function, such as research, finance, manufacturing, distribution, education.

Jobs may be classified according to the product which they produce, such as automobiles, chemicals, steel.

Jobs may be classified according to the employer, for example American Cyanamid, General Electric, F. W. Woolworth.

Jobs may be classified according to the expressed interests of students or clients.

Jobs may be classified according to measured interest patterns, such as artistic, computational, persuasive.

Jobs may be classified according to the school subjects which help to prepare workers for them, such as mathematical, musical, scientific.

Jobs may be classified in other ways that may occur to the reader and in still other ways that have not yet been conceived.

Depending upon which classification is adopted as the basis for a filing system, information about the job of a salesman for the Ford Motor Co. might be filed under any one of the following headings: selling, distribution, automobiles, Ford, persuasive occupations, business education. If the person who files occupational materials is not to be hopelessly confused, if the person who wants to find information in the files is not to be continually frustrated, someone must do some pretty clear thinking about how to classify jobs and occupations and the publications which describe them.

In their search for the ideal, counselors have tried several different ways of classifying and filing occupational information. Some of these ways are described and compared below.

CLASSIFICATION AND
FILING SYSTEMS

Alphabetic files. Many counselors and librarians begin by classifying and filing their occupational information alphabetically by the name of the occupation. This appears at first to be simple, easy, and logical. Anyone who knows the alphabet can go to such a file and use it with a minimum of instruction. Materials on any one occupation are filed and found together.

When the assembled collection of occupational information is small, the alphabetic file may be reasonably satisfactory, but it does have disadvantages. Materials on related occupations are not grouped together unless they can all be filed under the same occupational title. Some occupations have more than one title. The counselor or librarian must decide whether materials on accounting and on bookkeeping will be filed together or separately. Similar decisions must be made for electrical engineering and mechanical engineering, for electrical engineering and electrical contracting, for electrical contracting and general contracting. Each time such a decision is made, it must be recorded, so that similar material may be similarly filed in the future. Numerous cross-reference cards must be placed in the file or in a separate cross index.

If the counselor finds that some of his original decisions on classification were unwise or inconsistent, materials must be refiled. As the number of occupational titles in the file rises into the hundreds, the number of decisions that must be made and remembered or recorded can become a bit of a burden. There is always the risk that valuable materials will be lost in the file because the counselor failed to think of one important title for cross indexing.

The counselor who prefers the alphabetic file can escape some of the difficulties by purchasing and following an alphabetic filing plan such as the Bennett plan which is described below. In this plan 828 decisions have already been made and recorded.

United States census classification. In the hope of avoiding some of the disadvantages of the alphabetic file, counselors have sought and tried other classification systems. In the early days of vocational guidance many filing systems were based upon the occupational and industrial classifications of the United States census, because these were then the most complete classifications that were readily available. The census provided an alphabetic and a classified index covering several thousand titles, which were classified in occupational and industry categories. It thus relieved the counselor of many decisions regarding classification and of the necessity for devising and labeling many cross references, since he could use the census index as a substitute for cross references.

The census has been largely abandoned as a basis for occupational filing systems since the publication of the *Dictionary of Occupational Titles* [123].

The Dictionary of Occupational Titles classification. As a basis for occupational filing systems the *D.O.T.* has all the advantages of the census, plus some new ones.

In volume I of the dictionary 21,741 job titles are listed alphabetically and are defined in short paragraphs. An additional 13,809 alternate titles are listed and cross-indexed. Each title is assigned a code number. For example:

PLACEMENT COUNSELOR (education) *see* PLACEMENT OFFICER.

PLACEMENT INTERVIEWER (education) *see* PLACEMENT OFFICER.

PLACEMENT OFFICER (education) **166.268.**
manager, student employment; placement counselor; placement interviewer; student-employment officer. Provides job placement service for students and graduates: Interviews applicants for full- or part-time employment to determine their qualifications on basis of education, ability, interest, and other employment factors, and eligibility for employment in accordance with school and municipal policies. Matches qualifications to job requirements as indicated by employer and refers applicant to job opening. Gives information to students regarding job opportunities, vocational choice, and desirable qualifications. Maintains file of applicants and record of placement and counseling activities. Develops job openings through employer contact. May arrange for administration and scoring of selected psychological tests. Assembles and maintains current labor market information and assists in developing library of occupational information. May specialize in placing specific groups, such as law students or undergraduates seeking part-time employment.

In volume II of the dictionary, all the titles have been arranged by code number to show the complete classification system. For example:

314.   Chefs and Cooks, Small Hotels and Restaurants
                This group includes occupations concerned with planning menus, estimating consumption, ordering supplies, and cooking food in small hotels and restaurants.

314.381   COOK, SHORT ORDER (hotel & rest.)
                    griddle man
                Cook, Griddle (hotel & rest.)
                Hamburger-Fry Cook (hotel & rest.)

314.781   COOK, SPECIALTY (hotel & rest.)
                Cook, Fish and Chips (hotel & rest.)
                Cook, Pizza (hotel & rest.)

314.878   COMBINATION MAN (hotel & rest.)
                Combination Girl (hotel & rest.)

Thus the code number for any occupational title can be found in volume I, and the occupational title for any code number can be found in volume II.

The beginning counselor will sometimes hear his colleagues refer to the "three-digit classification" or the "six-digit classification" of the D.O.T. At first this may sound bewildering. It is, however, very simple when once explained.

In each code number, the first digit indicates the major occupational category to which the occupation has been assigned, the next two digits indicate subgroups, the next three digits indicate specific occupations within the subgroups.

The six-digit classification therefore refers simply to individual occupations, while the three-digit classification refers to groups of occupations. The group to which any individual occupation belongs is indicated by the first three digits in its code number.

For example, in the code number 633.281 for **OFFICE-MACHINE-SERVICEMAN APPRENTICE** the first digit "6" indicates the major category of MACHINE TRADES OCCUPATIONS; the next two digits "33" indicate the subgroup **Business and Commercial Machine Repairmen;** the last three digits "281" indicate the job title OFFICE-MACHINE-SERVICEMAN APPRENTICE.

In filing systems which are based on the D.O.T., the appropriate D.O.T. code number is written on each publication. The publication is placed in a folder which bears the same code number. Folders are placed in the file in numerical order, rather than alphabetic. Occupational titles are written on the folders beside the code numbers. The code numbers have been so devised that consecutive numbers are assigned to closely related occupations; hence consecutive folders contain materials on related occupations.

The counselor can now avoid many of the difficulties of classification and cross-indexing by following the D.O.T. classification; 35,550 decisions have already been made for him and recorded in volume I of the D.O.T. The counselor will find that he still has some decisions to make himself, but not so many as with any other system.

The disadvantage of systems based on the D.O.T. is that a reader, a student, or a client must have the system explained to him before he can use the files, and he must refer frequently to the D.O.T. in order to find the code numbers of the occupations on which he is seeking information.

There have been some revisions of the D.O.T. in the past. There will be more, but probably not for a few years. The first three editions were published in 1939, 1949, and 1965. The counselor, of course, can decide whether or not he wishes to incorporate future revisions in his filing system. The necessary changes will take some time, but they can be made readily with the help of the *Conversion Table of Code and Title Changes* [100].

Filing plans which are based on the *D.O.T.* are described in more detail later in this chapter.

Classification by industry. Clients and students sometimes want to know what kinds of occupations may be found in specific industries, particularly if such industries are important sources of employment in the areas in which the clients expect to look for work, for example, the machine-tool industry in Cincinnati, the meat-packing industry in Chicago, the insurance business in Hartford. Clients whose occupational preferences may lead them into any of several industries—for example, machinists and comptometer operators—may wish to compare different industries. An industry itself, for purposes of recruitment or goodwill, may publish a pamphlet describing employment opportunities in the industry. A good deal of useful occupational information is published on an industry basis and is much more readily classified and filed by the industry than by the occupations within the industry.

Some means of filing such information by industry should be provided in any occupational filing system. The most complete and convenient basis for a filing system by industries is to be found in the *Standard Industrial Classification Manual* [456].

This manual resembles the *D.O.T.* in that it uses code numbers which designate major groups and subgroups. For example, the code number for **Meat packing plants** is **2011**. The first two digits of this number indicate **Major Group 20—FOOD AND KINDRED PRODUCTS**. The next digit indicates the subgroup **MEAT PRODUCTS**, and the last digit indicates the industry **Meat packing plants**. The Standard Industrial Classification thus has a two-digit classification for major groups, a three-digit classification for subgroups, and a four-digit classification for specific industries.

Industries are arranged alphabetically in one part of the manual and numerically in another, thus resembling the arrangements in the *D.O.T.* For filing by industry this manual may be used in the same way that the *D.O.T.* is used for filing by occupation.

The following excerpts from the manual illustrate the arrangement. The first excerpt is from the "Alphabetic Index"; the second is from the "Titles and Descriptions of Industries."

5634 Apparel accessory stores—retail
0122 Apple farms
7399 Appraisers, except real estate appraisers
6531 Appraisers, real estate
0122 Apricot orchards and farms
7213 Apron supply service
8421 Aquariums

Major Group 59—RETAIL TRADE—MISCELLANEOUS RETAIL STORES

Group No. Industry No.

594   **BOOK AND STATIONERY STORES**
     5942   Book stores
     5943   Stationery stores
595   **SPORTING GOODS AND BICYCLE SHOPS**
     5952   Sporting goods stores
     5953   Bicycle shops
596   **FARM AND GARDEN SUPPLY STORES**
     5962   Hay, grain, and feed stores

How to use the *Standard Industrial Classification Manual* in filing is described further in the section below on homemade filing plans.

Classification by employer. Colleges which are visited by recruiting officers from large companies often receive recruiting booklets and other publications about the companies. Public schools in industrial cities collect information about local employers as a result of tours, conferences, and follow-up studies. Such material may be filed by industry according to the *Standard Industrial Classification Manual* and arranged alphabetically by company within the industry.

If the collection of industrial materials consists almost exclusively of company publications, some institutions may find that a simple alphabetic file by company name is preferable to the industrial classification. Such a file will not help the counselor or his clients to find all the material on all the companies in one industry unless they can recall the names of the companies or can find them in a reference volume such as *Thomas Register of American Manufacturers* [476]. Since Thomas covers only manufacturers, additional directories would be needed to locate banks, utilities, and other kinds of employers.

Publications of some diversified companies may cover several different industries. General Motors and Chrysler, for example, manufacture refrigeration equipment as well as automobiles. Omnibus publications which cover several industries as well as several occupations require special indexing, which is described in detail later in this chapter under "Homemade Plans."

Geographical files. Some placement officers file some of their occupational information geographically by state and city. This is a convenient means of handling material which applicants may wish to consult when they are looking for work in certain localities. For example, the college student who wants to return to his hometown may wish to compile a list of potential employers from business directories, classified telephone directories, company brochures, and annual reports. The student who has been offered a teaching position in a public school system may want to see everything the placement office has on the local schools.

Geographical filing is not a convenient way of handling information on companies with numerous locations, such as Bethlehem Steel. Nor is it a serviceable plan for filing information on occupations which can be practiced almost universally, such as painting.

Academic-subject classifications. Students sometimes become interested and proficient in a school or college subject and want to know what occupations it may lead to. Teachers sometimes wish to tell their students about occupations related to their subjects. Consequently some attempts have been made to group occupations by related academic subjects, particularly in occupational pamphlets published by colleges for their own students or for recruiting purposes.

Occupational filing systems are seldom based upon academic-subject classifications, because so many occupations cannot be clearly identified with any one subject and because so many other occupations could be equally well assigned to any of several different subjects.

Measured interest classifications. Some counselors have tried to file occupational information in the categories which are found on vocational interest inventories, such as the Kuder Preference Record. This kind of classification has certain obvious advantages of convenience when discussing Kuder scores. It has equally obvious disadvantages. Some occupations do not fit neatly into any one of the categories. Others overlap two or more categories. This system requires the counselor to make many difficult and arbitrary decisions, necessitates many cross references, and may have to be completely revised if the institution ever decides to drop one interest inventory in favor of another with a different set of categories.

Expressed interest classifications. Cooley [101] analyzed "student perceptions to determine clusters of occupations which are viewed similarly by the people who have to make distinctions among them as they move into the world of work." In a five-year, overlapping longitudinal study, he found the occupational plans of 150 fifth-grade boys with above average general intelligence "to be based primarily on interest. At first, the only stable distinction among plans was the dichotomy" of science technology versus all other occupations.

> Of course, most of the boys gave more specific plans, but the boy who talked civil engineering one time in an interview perhaps was talking physics or even biochemistry in a subsequent interview. Also, those who said lawyer one time may have been talking business the next time. There was a great tendency of stability within this very broad dichotomy, science technology or not. . . .
>
> During and following junior high school it was possible to detect ability discriminations. For example, some of the science-technology group began to talk about professional careers in this broad area and others began to talk about being electricians or mechanics. Here again the ability discriminations were very gross, so that up through high school only four occupational categories were needed; namely, (a) college in science technology, (b) college in something other than science technology, (c) technology without college, and (d) neither college nor technology. The students did not seem to make consistent finer discriminations. . . . It was not possible to find attributes which could significantly distinguish between those planning to be lawyers and businessmen or between future chemists and engineers. During college it was possible to make finer distinctions with respect to college science majors. These distinctions were based primarily on what might be called values. . . .

Cooley did not propose a filing plan, but his classifications may be helpful to teachers and counselors who wish to discuss broad areas of occupations with students, or who wish to arrange exhibits, meetings, tours, printed materials, etc., in similarly broad categories.

Bennett Occupations Filing Plan and Bibliography, Sterling Powers Publishing Co., 18½ Palmer St., Athens, Ohio,[1] 1958. This is an alphabetic filing plan in which the subject headings are adapted from the *D.O.T.*, but the *D.O.T.* code numbers are not used. There are 270 subject headings for folders in which material may be filed; 501 printed labels for cross references are provided to be pasted on cards the same size as the folders. The subject headings are printed in capital letters and in red ink. The cross references are printed in capitals and small letters and in blue ink.

All the subject headings and cross references are combined in a single

---

[1] The addresses given in this chapter were correct at date of publication but should be checked by any reader who wishes to write to these sources.

alphabetic list and numbered consecutively to 771. These are followed by 58 headings that are supplements for related materials, making a total of 829 labels.

The printed labels may be pasted on folders as the need for them arises, but it is more efficient to paste them all on empty folders and cross-reference cards when the file is started; or the counselor may make his own labels by copying the subject headings and cross references from the list which comes with the plan.

To file materials by this plan, the counselor first examines the material to determine the content, then searches in the printed list of headings for the one which seems most appropriate. This heading and its corresponding number are written on the material to facilitate later refiling, and the material is then placed in the appropriate folder.

The subject headings in this plan include industries as well as occupations and other supplementary headings, as noted above. The following are excerpts from the list of headings:

26   AIR CONDITIONING AND REFRIGERATING INDUSTRIES. See also ENGINEERING: MECHANIC AND REPAIR WORK.
27   Air conditioning engineering. See AIR CONDITIONING AND REFRIGERATING INDUSTRIES; ENGINEERING.
46   ARCHITECTURE.
47   ARCHITECTURE, LANDSCAPE.
48   Architecture, Marine. See SHIP AND BOAT BUILDING AND REPAIRING.
196 DESIGNING, FASHION. See also GARMENT INDUSTRY.
197 DESIGNING, INDUSTRIAL.
198 Detective work. See CRIMINOLOGY.
199 Diamond cutting. See JEWELRY AND WATCHMAKING.
200 Die designing. See DRAFTING.
201 Die making. See TOOL AND DIE MAKING.
202 DIESEL ENGINE WORK. See also ENGINEERING; MECHANIC AND REPAIR WORK; MOTOR TRANSPORTATION; POWER PLANT WORK; RAILROAD WORK.

Nothing is said about what to do if no appropriate subject heading can be found in the printed list. Presumably the counselor can invent new headings and insert new folders for them, either in alphabetic order or as additional supplements at the back of the file.

Omnibus materials which cover several unrelated occupations are provided with a folder labeled "Sup. 13. COLLECTIONS (Several jobs described in one publication)." No suggestions are offered for indexing the contents of such publications by occupation. Cross-reference notations could, of course, be placed in all other appropriate folders. This plan is designed for filing unbound occupational information, but the subject headings can also be used for books, films, and tape recordings.

Career information kit, Science Research Associates, Inc., Chicago, 1965, available in a corrugated case, or in a portable metal file. This is a collection of over 600 publications on occupations, already filed in 212 coded and labeled folders. The materials were selected and the kit was prepared under the direction of A. H. Edgerton of the University of Wisconsin, who is a past president of the National Vocational Guidance Association.

The filing plan uses a numerical system based upon job-family relationships but not upon the *D.O.T.* Six major occupational fields are divided into 66 occupational areas and 132 job titles. A separate folder is provided for each major field and each subdivision. The subdivisions are arranged alphabetically and numbered accordingly. The code number and title appear on each folder.

A separate section of the kit consists of eight folders which contain publications of a more general nature classified as

> Educational Guidance
>> High School
>> Junior College and Technical School
>> College
>> Apprenticeship
> Personal-Social Guidance
> Vocational Guidance
> Employment Guidance

The complete kit includes the 212 labeled folders and their contents and a manual of directions. The manual contains a complete list of the code numbers and titles arranged as they appear on the folders and an alphabetic index which shows the code numbers for more than nine hundred occupations. Included in the index is a column of Dewey decimal classification numbers to facilitate the location of related materials in general libraries.

No provision is made for filing materials on unskilled occupations, but one or more folders for these could be added by the purchaser. Nothing is said in the manual about how to file omnibus materials which cover several unrelated occupations. The plan does not include directions for shelving books, films, and tape recordings. It does not include directions for filing materials which describe industries rather than specific occupations, except to a limited extent in the subdivisions of major fields.

Chronicle plan for filing unbound occupational information, Chronicle Guidance Publications, Moravia, N.Y., 1966, available with or without approximately 700 occupational briefs, reprints and posters, and a variety of filing cabinets.

The plan consists of reinforced manila folders for 9 major occupational categories, 80 main occupational divisions, and approximately 200 specific occupational subgroups, following the three-digit code of the *D.O.T.* Seven extra folders are provided for categories not in the *D.O.T.* code; these categories are "agricultural workers, apprentices, atomic energy workers, banking industry workers, department store workers, government workers, insurance industry workers."

Printed direction cards show the complete classification scheme and provide an alphabetic cross reference.

To file occupational materials by this plan, the counselor first examines the material in order to identify the occupation which it covers. He then refers to the alphabetic cross-reference list to find the code number for this occupation. He writes this code number on the material to facilitate later refiling, and then he places the material in the appropriate folder which bears this code number. If the occupational title is not found in the alphabetic cross-reference list, the counselor refers to the *D.O.T.* to get the code number.

Nothing is said in the directions about how to file omnibus materials which cover several unrelated occupations. Presumably they would be filed under one of the occupations, and cross-reference notations would be placed in all other appropriate folders. The plan is designed for unbound occupational information. It does not include directions for shelving books, films, and tape recordings. It does not include directions for filing materials which describe industries rather than specific occupations, except to a limited extent in the seven broad occupational fields for which the seven extra folders are provided.

Missouri filing plan for unbound materials on occupations, College of Education, University of Missouri, Columbia, Mo., 1950, 26 pp. Mimeographed copies are distributed free on request within Missouri. A limited number of copies are available to counselors, counselor educators, and administrators in other states. Reproduction is permitted without charge.

This plan uses 325 subject headings, which are grouped under eleven school subjects: agriculture, art and drawing, commercial, home economics, industrial arts, language arts, mathematics, music, physical education, science, and social science. Within these eleven groups, occupations are arranged alphabetically. "Cross-references are essential . . . because some occupations are closely related to more than one school subject."

To file occupational materials by this plan, the counselor refers to an ". . . alphabetical cross-reference list." Folders may be prepared in advance or as material is acquired. New folders with new titles can be inserted as desired. "Usually one or more school subjects are related to training for each occupation."

The plan is designed for unbound occupational information. Nothing is said about shelving books, films, and tape recordings.

New York State Plan for filing unbound occupational information, State Education Department, Bureau of Guidance, Albany, N.Y., 1961, 15 pp. Mimeographed copies are distributed free on request within New York State. A limited number of copies are available to counselors, counselor educators, and administrators in other states. Reproduction is permitted without charge.

This plan is based on the 1949 edition of the *D.O.T.* As this book went to press, revision of this plan was contemplated but not yet completed. The plan uses code numbers and occupational titles which are similar to, but not always identical with, those in the *D.O.T.* Twelve major occupational groups, from "Professional" to "Semiskilled Occupations," are divided into 111 occupational divisions. Within these divisions are 200 occupational titles. The 12 major occupational groups and the 111 occupational divisions use the three-digit code of the *D.O.T.* The 200 occupational titles use the five-digit and six-digit codes.

The plan includes an alphabetic arrangement of 367 occupational titles with their code numbers and a similar list of 37 industries with suggestions for filing materials on these industries under code numbers. For omnibus publications the plan suggests cross-indexing on 5- by 8-inch cards.

To file occupational materials by this plan, the counselor first examines the material in order to identify the occupation which it covers. He then refers to the alphabetic lists to find the code number for this occupation. He writes this code number on the material, and then he places the material in a folder which bears this code number. Folders may be prepared in advance or as material is acquired.

The plan is designed for unbound occupational information. Nothing is said about shelving books, films, and tape recordings. Nothing is said about what to do if the occupational title cannot be found among those included in the plan.

Occupational information reference file by A. M. Wellington, Counselor Education Press, State College, Pa. No date. A numerical code adapted from but not identical with the *D.O.T.* The plan consists of a mimeographed list of 14 occupational groups, about 150 occupational families, a flexible number of individual occupations, and an alphabetic index. Some of the groups include industrial titles. The purchaser supplies his own filing cabinet, file folders, and labels.

Homemade plans. After examining the filing plans which others have devised, the counselor may decide that no one of them exactly meets his needs. For the counselor who wishes to devise his own filing system the following suggestions are offered:

> Base your plan on the *D.O.T.* This will not solve all your problems, but it will save you the decisions that have already been made about how to classify and file material on 35,550 job titles.
>
> Use the *Standard Industrial Classification Manual* as a guide to filing industrial materials which cannot be filed under *D.O.T.* code numbers.
>
> Use a steel filing cabinet of letter size or larger to hold light, fragile materials such as your own notes, clippings, pictures, reprints, posters which can be folded, and small pamphlets. Place these materials in manila file folders. When the contents of a single folder become too bulky or heavy, remove them from the manila folder and put them in a heavier folder, such as the Vertical File Pocket No. 1514C made by the Oxford Filing Supply Co., Clinton Road, Garden City, N.Y.
>
> Use bookshelves to hold books, tape recordings, films, and other materials that are too bulky or too heavy for the file folders. These may all be kept on the same shelves, or books may be kept in one place, tape recordings in another, and films in another. Either way the arrangement should be by *D.O.T.* or *S.I.C.M.* code number.

How to use the D.O.T. Begin with nothing in the file and nothing on the shelves. For your first attempt at filing, select some small pamphlet which deals with a single, well-known occupation. Proceed as follows:

> 1. Review the section above on "The *Dictionary of Occupational Titles* Classification."
> 2. Consult volume I of the *D.O.T.*
> 3. In this find the title of the occupation which your pamphlet describes; beside it will be the code number.
> 4. Copy this code number on the pamphlet.
> 5. Copy the code number and the occupational title on a file folder.
> 6. Put the pamphlet in the folder.
> 7. Put the folder in the filing cabinet.

Repeat this process with additional materials on other occupations. As each new folder is added to the file, place it in numerical order in relation to the other folders. For protection against damage, place fragile clippings in transparent covers or in envelopes before putting them in folders with other materials; copy the D.O.T. number on the envelope, as well as on the clipping and the folder.

When you have trouble deciding where to file something, put it aside until you have filed everything that you can file easily. By then you will be more familiar with the D.O.T., and you may have less trouble with the difficult pieces.

To illustrate this procedure, if the title of the pamphlet you choose is "Architect," when you look in volume I of the D.O.T., on page 18 you will find **ARCHITECT** (profess. & kin.) **001.081.** You will write "001.081" on the pamphlet. On a file folder you will write "001.081 Architect." You will put the pamphlet in the folder and put the folder in the filing cabinet.

If the next pamphlet you file is entitled "Carpenter," when you turn to volume I of the D.O.T., you will find many titles and descriptions of different kinds of carpenters. If you are a beginner in vocational counseling, you will now learn something about the variety of occupations within occupations. A quick scanning of the job titles in the D.O.T. and a review of the pamphlet you wish to file may reveal that the pamphlet deals exclusively with carpenters who help to construct houses. If so, you will have no trouble identifying this occupation in the D.O.T. as **CARPENTER** (const.) **860.381.** You will write "860.381" on the pamphlet. On a file folder you will write "860.381 Carpenter (const.)." You will put the pamphlet in the folder and put the folder in the filing cabinet.

If, however, the pamphlet you wish to file describes several different kinds of carpenters, you may at first be puzzled. Then you will notice that most of the code numbers for the different kinds of carpenters begin with 860. Now look at volume II of the D.O.T. where all the titles are arranged by code number. Here on page 193 you will find a three-digit code number **"860. CARPENTERS AND RELATED OCCUPATIONS."** Under this you will find six-digit code numbers for many different kinds of carpenters. Because your pamphlet covers several of these different kinds of carpenters, you decide to file it under the three-digit code. So you write "860" on the pamphlet. On a file folder you write "860. Carpenters and Related Occupations." You put the pamphlet in the folder and put the folder in the filing cabinet.

You can put folders bearing three-digit code numbers in the same file with folders bearing six-digit code numbers simply by arranging the code numbers in the same way in which they are arranged in volume II of the *D.O.T.* After a little practice you will find this easy to do.

Difficulties in finding D.O.T. code numbers. Although the *D.O.T.* in volume I defines and cross-indexes 35,550 occupational titles, you will sometimes find that you have information on an occupation which you cannot readily locate in the dictionary.

The authors of the *D.O.T.* suggest that "When users of this publication need additional job definitions, new code numbers, or clarification of the classifications, they should write to the U.S. Employment Service, Bureau of Employment Security, Department of Labor, Washington."

How to use the Standard Industrial Classification Manual. When you wish to file something which describes an industry rather than an occupation, if you cannot logically file it in any *D.O.T.* category, the time has come to set up an industrial file, separate from your occupational file. Be sure to keep the two files separate and clearly labeled, because they will have separate systems of code numbers.

For your first attempt at filing industrial materials, select some simple pamphlet or document which describes a single, well-known industry. Proceed as follows:

1. Review the section above on "Classification by Industry."
2. Consult the *Standard Industrial Classification Manual.*
3. Look in the alphabetic index for the title of the industry which your document describes; beside it will be the code number.
4. Copy this code number on the document you wish to file.
5. Copy the code number and the industrial title on a file folder.
6. Put the document in the folder.
7. Put the folder in the industrial section of your files.

Repeat this process with additional materials on other industries. As each new folder is added to the file, place it in numerical order, in relation to the other folders, in the industrial section of your files.

To illustrate this procedure, if you wish to file a document that describes the past and probable future growth of commercial airlines and you try to file it under a *D.O.T.* code number, you will find yourself in trouble. The future growth of airlines affects the future prospects for employment and advancement of all kinds of workers in airline companies. Your document might therefore be filed under any of the following code numbers:

005.081   Airport engineer
196.283   Airplane pilot

352.878   Airplane stewardess
621.281   Airplane inspector
824.781   Airport electrician
912.368   Airplane-dispatch clerk

So you decide that this document should go in your industrial file.

You observe that commercial airlines seem to belong with nonmanufacturing industries, so you look in the *Standard Industrial Classification Manual*, part II, *Alphabetic Index, Nonmanufacturing Industries*. On page 237 of this volume you find several industry titles that begin with "Commercial," but "Commercial airlines" is not among them. You then look for "Airlines, commercial." On page 227 you will find several industry titles that begin with "Air," but "Airlines, commercial" is not among them. On the same page, however, you do find:

4511   Air cargo carriers, certificated
4511   Air passenger carriers, certificated
4511   Air transportation, by certificated carriers

This looks like what you want.

To verify your judgment you look for 4511 in part I of the same volume. On page 137 you find:

Major Group 45—TRANSPORTATION BY AIR
The Major Group as a Whole

This major group includes companies engaged in furnishing domestic and foreign transportation by air and also those operating airports and flying fields and furnishing terminal services. Companies primarily engaged in performing services which may incidentally use airplanes (crop dusting, aerial photography, etc.) are classified according to the service performed.

Group No.   Industry No.

451

4511

AIR TRANSPORTATION, CERTIFICATED CARRIERS

Air transportation, certificated carriers
Companies holding certificates of public convenience and necessity under the Civil Aeronautics Act, operating over fixed routes on fixed schedules, or in the case of certificated Alaskan carriers over fixed or irregular routes.

Now you know you have what you want. So you copy "4511" on your document. On a file folder you copy "4511" and the industry title "Air transportation, certificated carriers." You put your document in the folder. You put the folder in the industrial section of your files.

Difficulties in finding Standard Industrial Classification Manual code numbers. If you are doubtful about which of two classification code numbers to use, or if you cannot find the industry in the alphabetic indexes, refer to part I. Here you will find the complete classification structure with descriptions of the industries to be included in each classification. If you still cannot find the industry listed, choose the code which comes closest to it. For a manufacturing industry you may finally choose "3999 Manufacturing industries, not elsewhere classified." For a nonmanufacturing industry your final choice may be "99 Nonclassifiable establishments." In either case, whenever you have this much difficulty in choosing a code number, add a card to your cross-index file, and place on this card the title of the industry and the code number that you have chosen, so that you can readily find the material when you want it. If the industry may be known by two or more names, such as oil and petroleum, put in separate cards for each name.

If a publication deals primarily with industrial rather than occupational information but contains useful information on some occupations, it may be placed in the proper industrial classification and cross-indexed in the occupational card file.

You will not need 20,000 folders. Although the *D.O.T.* and the *Standard Industrial Classification Manual* provide code numbers for several thousand occupations and industries, you will not need an equal number of folders. You will probably never have materials to file on more than a few hundred occupations. Even if you should have, both code systems are so devised that you can easily file the materials on related occupations in a single folder by simply shortening the code number that you write on the folder.

Shelving books, films, and recordings. Occupational books are handled in the same way as notes, clippings, and pamphlets, except that the classification number is recorded on the spine of the book and on the title page and the books are arranged numerically on the shelves. Films and tape recordings may be placed on the shelves with the books after the proper code numbers have been written on the containers.

Omnibus books, pamphlets, films, and recordings. Books and other publications which describe several unrelated occupations cannot be properly classified under any one code number. They can readily be overlooked when you are seeking information on a specific occupation if you do not recall which omnibus book contains information on which occupation.

If such books are worth buying, they are worth using, and they can be fully utilized only if they are adequately cross-indexed. The clerical labor of cross-indexing a book that describes fifty or a hundred occupations is forbidding to busy counselors who have no clerical help, but the job must be done if the books are to be used. There are too many such books for the counselor or the client to examine all of them each time information on one occupation is needed. If you have one or more bright students as volunteer or paid clerical assistants, they can be taught to classify and cross-index the information in such books, with some help from you when they encounter difficulty.

Whoever does the indexing must first determine, for each occupation covered, whether or not the information in the book is of sufficient potential value to merit indexing. Casual mention of an occupation, in one or two sentences, is scarcely worth indexing if you have better material on the same subject. Each occupation to be indexed is then found in volume I of the D.O.T., the code number and title of the occupation are written on an index card, the book containing the information is identified on the same card, and the card is placed in the file. These index cards may be the same size as the file folders and may be placed in their proper numerical position in the filing cabinet, or they may be smaller cards kept in a separate file and arranged numerically therein. The books may then be arranged on the shelves by author or title, in a separate section for omnibus books. Films, tape recordings, and large pamphlets may be handled in the same way as books. Fragile materials may be filed in folders in a separate omnibus section of the filing cabinet, in which these materials are arranged by author or title.

All that has been said about occupations in this section on omnibus books applies equally to industries and industrial classification, except that the *Standard Industrial Classification Manual* should be used in place of the *D.O.T.*

Alternative procedures. The counselor who prefers to may use pamphlet boxes instead of file folders and shelves instead of a filing cabinet. D.O.T. code numbers and occupational titles will then appear on the pamphlet boxes instead of on file folders. Large, sturdy pamphlet boxes can be purchased from stationery stores and from library supply houses such as Gaylord Bros. of Syracuse, N.Y., and Stockton, Calif.

Some schools prefer filing cabinets consisting of many drawers in which the pamphlets lie flat. *D.O.T.* code numbers are combined so that the number of categories is reduced to the number of drawers in the file. Purcell [384] described such a file, which was introduced because in the former vertical file ". . . pamphlets were frequently misfiled, folders were continually flopping over, and not infrequently, entire folders were found out of sequence." To make the change to the new system four temporary employees worked one week. They discarded obsolete materials, marked the publication date and code number on all materials retained. "Students seem to enjoy using the file and can locate material quickly. Being able to remove an entire drawer of materials and carry it over to the work table for use is a real boon; and we find that under this system very few materials are misfiled." George DuBato has devised and used a similar plan in the high school at Roslyn, N.Y. An alphabetic index to the file is mounted on the wall above the cabinets.

Other plans. Burianek and Tennyson [50] have described a display rack for filing which ". . . has proved effective in motivating students to peruse occupational pamphlets. In a reception room where the study chairs face the display rack, a waiting youngster . . . tends to reach up and pull out a folder. . . ."

Diamond [120] has described a similar rack which was used by fifteen times as many students as had ever used the materials before.

Chervenik [77] described a similar plan for use in a university counseling office.

Corre [103] described a system based on the U.S. census in which the occupations are arranged alphabetically within the major groups.

Frank and Patten [167] described a homemade filing plan similar to the one suggested above. It uses both the *D.O.T.* and the *S.I.C.M.*

Gachet [171] described a plan designed for women college students, based on the *D.O.T.* and cross-indexed under fifty-three occupational classifications that were arranged alphabetically.

Huey [247] described a plan based on the U.S. census, which provided for cross-indexing of omnibus materials.

Kirk and Michels [277] described the filing plan used in the Counseling Center of the University of California at Berkeley. The plan includes subdivisions on occupations, trends and outlook, legislation, special groups, training, employment, scholarships, planning, and adjustment.

LeMay [290] described a loose-leaf notebook in which each page contains one job title, the corresponding *D.O.T.* number, and a list of all the sources from which the school has obtained useful information on the occupation, in pamphlet or other form. Counselors find the book helpful when they wish to re-order lost publications or seek additional information. ˜

Munson [344] described a filing plan for scholarship information and offered some suggestions for filing information on colleges.

Neal [352] described an alphabetic filing plan with cross-indexing and a plan for shelving books.

Schubert [420] described a plan based on the interest categories of the Kuder Preference Record.

Wyatt [530] described a display rack for company literature used in a college placement office.

TIME REQUIRED

The task of filing occupational information is not so formidable as it may appear to one who has just read this lengthy explanation. If no unusual difficulties are encountered, an experienced counselor should be able to find the correct code number, write the number on a pamphlet and a folder, and place both of them in the files in less than five minutes. A counselor who devotes ten minutes a day to filing, who works five days a week, forty weeks a year, could file 400 new pieces of occupational information each year. Few counselors will add even half that number of new publications to their libraries in an average year.

COST

A good occupational library with a homemade filing plan can be started and maintained at modest cost. The essential items and their estimated costs are:

Initial expenses

1	Steel filing cabinet	$75.00
500	Manila file folders	16.00
50	Heavy file folders	23.00
1	Bookcase	75.00
1	*Dictionary of Occupational Titles*, vols. I and II	9.25
1	*Standard Industrial Classification Manual*	2.50
1	*Occupational Literature* by Gertrude Forester	8.50
		$209.25

Recurring annual expenditures

1	Annual subscription to one of the indexes to new occupational books and pamphlets described in Chapter 4	10.00
	New file folders as needed	10.00
200	New books and pamphlets	230.00
		$250.00

CHARACTERISTICS OF A GOOD FILING SYSTEM

Before deciding upon a classification system, before choosing or devising a filing plan, the reader may wish to compare each possibility with the following suggested characteristics of a good filing system:

1. It should provide a safe place for housing written and printed documents, clippings from newspapers and magazines, posters, pictures, films, tape recordings, pamphlets, books, and anything else that may contain useful occupational information.

2. It should provide one and only one designated location for each item to be filed, so that there may be no confusion about where to file an item or where to find it.

3. It should be easy to use, so that all who use it can find what they want with a minimum of time and effort.

4. It should bring together as many as possible of the materials on any one occupation or industry or employer.

5. It should bring together related occupations or industries or employers.

6. It should provide some means of quickly finding material in omnibus books and other publications which describe several different occupations.

7. It should be expandable, so that it can grow as the collection grows.

8. It should provide for filing and finding related materials, such as the results of follow-up studies and community occupational surveys.

COMPARATIVE APPRAISAL OF FILING PLANS

The reader of this book will probably do better to choose his own filing plan than to follow anyone else's judgment. However, the author's students have asked for the author's judgment, so here it is.

For high schools, colleges, libraries, and other community agencies. For most counselors in these institutions, I would choose one of the following in this order of preference:

1. *A homemade plan,* because it is the only one that provides for adequate indexing of industrial as well as occupational materials, using both the D.O.T. and the *Standard Industrial Classification Manual,* and because it is the only one that provides directions for shelving books, films, and recordings.

2. *The Chronicle plan,* because it is based on the D.O.T. and it can be purchased with or without a collection of pamphlets.

3. *The Bennett plan* for those who want an alphabetic file rather than one which uses D.O.T. code numbers.

4. *The Science Research Associates kit* if the purchaser is just starting to collect occupational information and has no substantial investment in publications which might be duplicated.

All these plans have the disadvantage of requiring a little time to learn how to file material and to find it. This may even be an advantage if it prevents the counselor from sending his client to the files alone when the counselor ought to go with him.

Although the last three plans do not provide directions for shelving books, films, and recordings or for indexing omnibus books, the directions under homemade plans may be adapted for use in combination with any of these plans.

For employment offices which use the D.O.T. code. For these I would choose for the reasons stated above:

1. *A homemade plan*
2. *The Chronicle plan*

For teachers colleges. For placement officers in teachers colleges, whose only interest is jobs in education, I would choose:

1. *The Missouri plan* supplemented by
2. *A geographical file* by state and city for information on potential employers, particularly public schools and colleges.

For teachers. For teachers of academic subjects whose only interest in occupational information is in connection with their own subjects, I would choose:

An academic subject file. While the total amount of material is small, some simple alphabetic arrangement within the subject field may serve all essential purposes. When and if the collection becomes large, I would switch to one of the four plans listed above for counselors.

For students. For the student or client who is collecting information on a small number of occupations to help him in his own choice of an occupation, I would choose:

An alphabetic file, because it is the simplest to use when the number of occupations and the amount of material are small. If he loses anything in the files he can search the entire collection in a short time. If he is in doubt about where to file something, he can put it in a "Miscellaneous" category and examine this category every time he seeks material on any subject.

SUGGESTIONS FOR BEGINNERS

Because occupational information may be classified in so many different ways, no filing system will ever be perfect. Because information may be sought for so many different purposes, no filing system will yield all its useful contents with uniform speed and precision. Don't expect too much. Don't try to do too much. And don't blame yourself or your files when they do not work perfectly for all purposes.

Spend an evening with all the volumes of the *Dictionary of Occupational Titles* and the *Standard Industrial Classification Manual*. Read the introductory and explanatory parts of each volume. Examine the remaining contents. Take time to understand what the classification structure is and to see how you can use it for your own purposes. Take several of your own occupational materials and decide how you would classify and file them if you were to develop your own filing system.

If you have the time and the inclination, write for and examine the filing plans listed above. Get them on approval, and try filing and finding the same materials in these systems.

Select the system which seems best to meet your needs, which you find easy to understand and comfortable to work with. Install it, use it, change and adapt it to suit your own purposes, and use plenty of cross references.

Once a year go through your file, weeding out and throwing away every document that is more than five years old unless you have some good reason for keeping it. Your student clerk can remove these obsolete materials for you. Then it will not take much of your time to look at them and tell him which to put back.

To facilitate weeding, put the copyright date or the accession date on the front of each pamphlet before you file it.

FILING RELATED MATERIALS

The counselor needs some place to file information on child labor laws, work certificates, unemployment insurance, and other materials that are related to occupational information but that do not describe occupations or industries.

Baer and Roeber [14] prepared a filing plan for "supplementary occupational and educational information" on sixty-six topics including apprenticeships, automation, child labor, community agencies, dropouts, employment agencies, handicapped individuals, job finding, job satisfaction, labor laws, labor organizations, and scholarships.

A *Counselor's Professional File* [106] provides 171 printed folders in sixteen broad areas of guidance which include articulation, orientation, associations, counseling, educational information, evaluation, group guidance, mental hygiene, placement, publishers, and testing.

ON COOPERATION WITH THE LIBRARIAN

The counselor who starts on a new job may find that the librarian in his institution already has an occupational file but that the filing system does not serve the counselor's purposes. The librarian will usually be a staff colleague of equal rank to whom the counselor cannot issue orders and with whom he will wish to establish and maintain cordial working relationships.

Librarians have their problems, too. They must try to meet the needs and the demands of the entire staff and clientele. These demands sometimes conflict; they sometimes cannot be met with the staff at the librarian's disposal. Administrative policy or good library practice may discourage the development of separate departmental libraries, and this may bring the librarian into conflict with counselors and others who would like to have their own separate bookshelves and pamphlet files in their own offices. Librarians have learned from sad experience that complex filing systems discourage readers from using the files. The librarian who has a file that seems to serve and satisfy his readers may be understandably reluctant to change it.

Before the counselor concludes that an existing system is inadequate, he should recall that no filing system is perfect. Each system has some advantages and some disadvantages. Each will serve one purpose best, at the expense of other purposes. The counselor who wants to maintain good human relations will respect the needs of his colleagues who use the same files. If careful examination reveals that the existing files will not meet the counselor's reasonable needs, there are several things he may do.

If the librarian is cooperative, the whole problem may be discussed freely and some solution reached. In rare cases the librarian may welcome the help of the counselor in revising his files, he may offer to change his filing system, or he may invite the counselor to assume responsibility for this part of the library. More frequently, perhaps, the librarian will suggest that the counselor set up a separate file of occupational information in his own office. The counselor, in turn, will recognize that the librarian must serve other staff members whose needs may conflict with those of the counselor; he will recognize that the librarian may know some things the counselor does not know about the ways in which students and others use the files; and he will respect the librarian's professional training and experience in selecting, acquiring, housing, and distributing all kinds of library materials. The cooperative counselor will be willing to give a little in the interest of his colleagues and of cordial human relations.

If the librarian is unapproachable, the counselor may get along as well as he can with the files as they exist, or he may set up his own file in his own office. If a separate file is contemplated, the counselor may be wise to discuss this possibility with his immediate superior before he mentions it to anyone else. If the librarian disapproves and resents the separate file, personnel problems may be created that will be worse than the filing problems.

If the librarian is approachable but insecure or reluctant to make immediate changes, the counselor may become the most frequent user of the files and ask the librarian for help whenever he has difficulty. After the librarian has had time to acquire some confidence in the counselor's integrity and competence, the counselor may offer his help in acquiring new materials. Later he may offer to help weed out the obsolete. Eventually the librarian may be willing to consider the counselor's offer to revise the filing system.

Important as a good filing system can be, it may in the long run be less important than good working relationships. A librarian can be of great help to young people who seek occupational information and to the counselor who is trying to help them. Everyone in the school, from the principal to the janitor, is going to be asked by some student at some time for information about some occupation. If the counselor has alienated his colleagues, the students will get poorer service than if the staff is working together in friendly cooperation with mutual consideration for one another's needs and problems and limitations.

REVIEW QUESTIONS

1. What are some of the different ways in which jobs can be classified?

2. You are a member of a committee appointed to recommend a filing system for the occupational information that is to be collected in the library of a new high school. Your colleagues favor an alphabetic system because of its simplicity. They ask you what are its disadvantages. What will you tell them?

3. After you have answered the preceding question, one person asks if the *D.O.T.* provides an adequate guide for filing all the materials that your collection will be likely to include. How will you answer him?

4. You are dean of students in a college. The college placement office is under your supervision. It has a collection of recruiting pamphlets filed by companies. You have just hired a new placement officer. He wants to change to an alphabetic filing system by occupation. Will you approve the change? Why? Why not?

5. You are a dormitory counselor in a small college. Your dean has asked you to start a collection of occupational information for the use of students and faculty advisers. Some faculty members want the materials filed by academic subjects. Will you follow their wishes or suggest another method? If so, what? Why?

6. You are a counselor in a psychological testing center, and you are assigned to reorganize the collection of occupational information. Some of your colleagues want the material filed by interest classifications on one of the vocational interest tests which they use. What will you do? Why?

7. You are employed as a counselor in the high school or the undergraduate college that you attended. You are free to file occupational information in any way you choose. How will you file it? Why? How many filing cabinets will you need? How will you file omnibus books? Tape recordings?

8. How much of your time as a counselor will you need to spend in filing occupational information in order to keep your collection up to date?

9. What is the probable cost of setting up and maintaining a good homemade filing system?

7
Theories of Vocational Choice and Development

Any attempt to help any person make vocational plans or choices implies some theory of vocational choice or development. Such a theory expresses our expectation, or belief, or hypothesis about the way in which vocational plans or choices are made.

Thus counseling implies a belief that decisions are influenced by what the counselor says or does, or by what happens to the client in the counseling relationship. The use of vocational aptitude tests and interest inventories implies a belief that decisions are influenced by the information which these instruments may contribute to the client's knowledge of himself. The provision of occupational information implies a belief that decisions are influenced by what the client knows about occupations.

There are many theories of vocational choice and development—too many for all of them to be reviewed in a book devoted to another subject. But explanation and discussion of a selected sample of theories may help the counselor to see more clearly the beliefs implied in his own behavior, and perhaps to reconsider some of the things that he does.

Several excerpts from other writers are presented and discussed in this chapter. The quotations are necessarily brief. From much longer documents, I have chosen the parts which seem to me most likely to interest counselors; these are not always the quotations most likely to interest other research workers. Nor do these brief passages really do justice to the writers. The reader who is interested in theory is urged to read each writer's full statement in the original.

The quotations include theories which have been carefully drafted and documented, research evidence which supports or challenges the theories, hypotheses proposed for further investigation, conclusions from research completed, and some casual but provocative expressions of opinion. Some of the writers explain occupational choice in terms of external economic, sociologic, and educational influences; others find their explanations in the conscious and unconscious internal motivations of the individual. There is sharp conflict on some points, considerable agreement on others.

In this chapter each writer's statement is first presented with a minimum of comment. The arrangement is alphabetic. Comparison and discussion follow in the latter part of the chapter. The student who is approaching this subject for the first time may find the conflicting statements somewhat confusing, especially if he tries to remember them all. This chapter may be more useful to the beginner if he will read it as he might examine a display of merchandise in a store, looking at each excerpt critically, rejecting those ideas which contribute nothing to his own thinking, and marking for review those which provoke his interest.

THE THEORIES

Brill [43] in his *Basic Principles of Psychoanalysis* suggested that

. . . the normal individual needs no advice or suggestion in the selection of a vocation, he usually senses best what activity to follow. . . .

The surgeon and the butcher have both conquered their sadistic impulses and sublimate the same for useful purposes. . . .

The professions of prize fighters, wrestlers, bullfighters, warriors, and mighty hunters are direct descendants of pure sadism, and the need for the sadistic outlet is well shown by the popularity of these vocations. . . .

Unconscious and sometimes conscious feelings of guilt and remorse as a reaction to real or imaginary sins are often the basis of theological callings. . . . The actor and the professional soldier are sublimated exhibitionists par excellence; the latter is also unconsciously dominated by a strong aggressive component. . . .

There is always some psychic determinant which laid the foundation for the later vocation, and if not interfered with the individual is unconsciously guided to express his sublimation in that particular form. . . .

As in the selection of a mate, a sensible person needs no advice and wants none in choosing his vocation; and fools will fail in spite of the best guidance. . . .

Caplow [58] reviewed the evidence from sociologic research on occupational choice and concluded that

> . . . error and accident often play a larger part than the subject himself is willing to concede.
> . . . almost all farmers are recruited from farmers' sons.
> . . . occupational choices are made at a time when the student is still remote from the world of work. They are made in terms of school requirements, which may call for quite different abilities and tastes from those which will be related to the eventual job.
> . . . occupational choices are made in the schoolroom, under the impersonal pressure of the curriculum, and remote from many of the realities of the working situation. . . .
> Realistic choices typically involve the abandonment of old aspirations in favor of more limited objectives. . . . Not until late in his career will the average man be able to sum up his total expectations with some degree of finality and measure them against his remaining aspirations so as to arrive at a permanent sense of frustration, a permanent glow of complacency, or an irregular oscillation from one to the other.

Clark. The effect of earnings on job choice has been discussed by economists ever since the division of labor was invented. Difference of opinion exists as to the relative importance of income and other influences, and individual differences in responsiveness to income are conceded, but few would deny that a substantial change in rates of pay is a potent force in moving workers from one occupation to another. This aspect of occupational choice was discussed at length by Clark [86] in his *Economic Theory and Correct Occupation Distribution,* in which he expressed the conviction that "Proper information regarding wages, if sufficiently impressed upon people, will lead to correct choice of occupation and correct number, provided barriers to occupations have been removed."

Forer [161] found the explanation of occupational choices largely in the personality and the emotional needs of the individual, often operating unconsciously:

> 1. Choice of a vocation is not primarily rational or logical, but is a somewhat blind, impulsive, emotional, and automatic process and is not always subject to practical and reasonable considerations.
> 2. Primary reasons for selecting a particular vocation are unconscious in the sense that when the individual is pressed to elaborate beyond the superficial rationalization of economic advantage and opportunity, he is forced to admit that he does not know why; he simply has to build bridges or can't stand paper work. These activities have

immediate appeal or distaste for him. We are saying that interests and references have unconscious roots. . . .

3. Both of these factors point ultimately to the purposive nature of occupational choice. Obviously it is necessary for most persons to find gainful employment. But the economic motive is secondary. Occupational choice, the specific occupation chosen or the fact of lack of preference, is an expression of basic personality organization and can and should satisfy basic needs.

4. Selection of a vocation, like the expression of other interests, is a personal process, a culmination of the individual's unique psychological development. . . .

Ginzberg, Ginsburg, Axelrad, and Herma [180] reviewed earlier theories of occupational choice and then interviewed sixty-four students at Horace Mann–Lincoln School and Columbia University, both in New York City. The educational level of the students at the time of the interviews ranged from sixth grade to graduate school. All the students were male, Protestant or Catholic, of Anglo-Saxon background, reared in an urban environment, with parents in the upper middle income group. As a check on this research, the investigators also interviewed seventeen sons of dock workers, truck drivers, and semiskilled factory workers and ten girls from Barnard College. The following excerpts are from their report:

> Our analysis points to the fact that the foundation for an effective occupational choice must lie in the values and goals of an individual, for it is these which enable him to order his current activities with reference to the future. The essential element in occupational decision-making is the effective link of present action to future objectives. Certainly, capacities and interests must be considered, but the individual will not make an effective occupational choice unless he has support from his value scheme. . . .
>
> We found that the process of occupational decision-making could be analyzed in terms of three periods—fantasy, tentative, and realistic choices. These can be differentiated by the way in which the individual "translates" his impulses and needs into an occupational choice. In the fantasy period the youngster thinks about an occupation in terms of his wish to be an adult. He cannot assess his capacities or the opportunities and limitations of reality. He believes that he can be whatever he wants to be. His translations are arbitrary.
>
> The tentative period is characterized by the individual's recognition of the problem of deciding on a future occupation. The solution must be sought in terms of probable future satisfactions rather than in terms of current satisfactions. During this period, however, the translation is still almost exclusively in terms of subjective factors: interests, capacities, and values. In fact, as most individuals reach the end of this period, they recognize that their approach has been too subjective. They, therefore, consider their choices tentative, for they real-

ize that an effective resolution requires the incorporation of reality considerations and this will be possible only on the basis of additional experience.

During the realistic period, the translation is so heavily weighted by reality considerations that a synthesis is difficult. The individual recognizes that he must work out a compromise between what he wants and the opportunities which are available to him. . . .

At the age of about seventeen, reality considerations which were on the periphery of consciousness, move into a more central position. In large part this shift reflects the fact that the values which an individual hopes to realize through work are deeply embedded in the social and economic structure to which he must adjust himself. . . .

The decision concerning an occupational choice is, in the last analysis, a compromise whereby an individual hopes to gain the maximum degree of satisfaction out of his working life by pursuing a career in which he can make as much use as possible of his interests and capacities, in a situation which will satisfy as many of his values and goals as possible. In seeking an appropriate choice, he must weigh the actual opportunities and limitations and the extent to which they will contribute to or detract from maximum work satisfaction. . . .

This, then, is our general theory. First, occupational choice is a process which takes place over a minimum of six or seven years, and more typically, over ten years or more. Secondly, since each decision during adolescence is related to one's experience up to that point, and in turn has an influence on the future, the process of decision-making is basically irreversible. Finally, since occupational choice involves the balancing of a series of subjective elements with the opportunities and limitations of reality, the crystallization of occupational choice inevitably has the quality of a compromise.

Holland [219] summarized his theory in these words:

> These working assumptions constitute the heart of the theory. . . .
>
> *In our culture, most persons can be categorized as one of six types —Realistic, Intellectual, Social, Conventional, Enterprising, and Artistic.* . . .
>
> *There are six kinds of environments: Realistic, Intellectual, Social, Conventional, Enterprising, and Artistic.* . . .
>
> *People search for environments and vocations that will permit them to exercise their skills and abilities, to express their attitudes and values, to take on agreeable problems and roles, and to avoid disagreeable ones.* Consequently, Realistic types seek Realistic environments, Intellectual types seek Intellectual environments, and so forth. To a lesser degree, environments also search for people through recruiting practices. The person's search for environments is carried on in many ways, at several levels of consciousness, and over a long period of time. . . .
>
> As a child grows up, he learns through his parents, social class, schools, and community what he does well, what he does poorly, and

what he likes to do. He also acquires some useful though not always accurate vocational images. . . . When he graduates from school and takes his first job, his choice is a resolution of a complex set of forces that include his hierarchy of choices . . . the range of job opportunities available to him, the influence of parents and friends, and various chance factors. In the present theory, a person's first and subsequent decisions are explained in terms of personality pattern and environmental model only. A more complete theory would incorporate economic and sociological influence.

A person's behavior can be explained by the interaction of his personality pattern and his environment.

Hollingshead [220] from his research on *Elmtown's Youth* reported that

The pattern of vocational choices corresponds roughly with the job patterns associated with each class in the adult work world. Therefore, we believe that the adolescents' ideas of desirable jobs are a reflection of their experiences in the class and family culture complexes. . . .

The surprising thing to us is not the high percentage of youngsters in class II who want to go into business and the professions, but the low percentages in classes IV and V. Apparently these lower class youngsters, on the average, have adjusted their job desires to what they may hope to achieve. By so doing, they have limited their horizons to the class horizon, and in the process they have unconsciously placed themselves in such a position that they will occupy in the class system the same levels as their parents.

Kline and Schneck [279], in reporting "An Hypnotic Experimental Approach to the Genesis of Occupational Interests and Choice," expressed their belief that

What has not been stressed in vocational guidance is the origin of vocational interests, their relationship to personality organisation and their relationship to individual aptitudes. There is evidence that changes in personality organisation greatly influence not only occupational interests but the level of job adjustment, and that in fact the prescribed approach to vocational maladjustment in a great number of cases appears to be psychotherapy rather than vocational guidance. A manipulation of the expressed occupational interests of an individual does not in fact prove to effect adjustment in cases of vocational maladjustment. Psychotherapy involving distinct changes in personality organisation has on the other hand been capable of altering occupational factors to the extent of effecting adjustment out of maladjustment.

In their experiment Kline and Schneck placed three persons under hypnosis and then said to them, "I'm going to count from one to five and when I reach five you will be able to visualize a scene involving an occupation for which you have a real interest, even though this interest may be unknown to you now."

One subject was a married woman, age twenty-four, about to be fired from her job as a clerical office worker because of frequent clashes with her supervisor. Under hypnosis she said, "I am a singer and I am singing before a large audience. They like me very much and ask me to sing again. They give me a lot of attention and applause." The examiner asked, "Why do you really enjoy it?" The woman replied, "Because I am showing my mother that I can be successful and that people really do like me."

Another subject was a twenty-three-year-old actress who repeatedly failed just as she seemed to be on the verge of success. Under hypnosis she first saw herself drawing fashion copy, next as an executive in an office. Then she said, "I'm resisting myself. I won't let myself think of other jobs. I can't. Please—no more scenes. I'm afraid I will find out that I really don't want to be an actress and will want to go into some other type of work, and I'm afraid that people will laugh at me if I should."

Miller and Form [332] in their book on *Industrial Sociology* expressed the view that

> The network of interrelated social factors that have been demonstrated to be associated with occupational levels might become the basis of a *social* causation theory of career patterns. Such a theory would impute the origin and development of a career to those social factors that have been identified. Relationships can be demonstrated between occupational level of a worker and (1) the father's occupation, (2) the historical circumstances, (3) the father's income and education, (4) financial aid and influential contacts, (5) social and economic conditions. An accurate weighing of the facts will demonstrate that the social background of the worker is a base of opportunities and limitations. As opportunities are enlarged the *possibilities* of occupational mobility are increased. Personal motivation and native ability are necessary to an enlarging career pattern. However, there is good evidence that the social backgrounds of workers are the crucial determiners in the *number* who are able to come into various occupational levels. . . .
>
> *Social background, native ability, historical circumstance, and acquired personality traits* are the influences determining a given career pattern. These forces may be considered as intertwined and pulling upon each worker with different intensities at various times in his career. By the time a man or woman reaches 35 or 40 years of age the forces often become equilibrated, and what the occupational history is from 35 years to 60 years is a fair index of whatever stability the worker will experience.

Roe [397] sees

> . . . the job as a source of satisfaction of many needs. . . . When I speak of the job . . . I mean not only what he does but the total setting within which he does it. A major part of most jobs, in terms of the satisfactions to be derived from them, is the social interaction, and the social status which is linked to the job. . . . The intrinsic interest of the task varies pretty constantly with the level of the job . . . and as the relative importance of intrinsic interest declines, the importance of the job setting increases. . . . To understand how a man functions in a job one must know what his needs are and where and how they are satisfied. . . .

All persons have physiological needs which

> . . . can vary only within a very limited range, but . . . need for understanding, need for beauty, etc., will have extremely wide variation among individuals. . . . For example, aesthetic needs are very strong in some individuals, and may then be extremely important in vocational choice, but of no importance at all for other persons. . . .
>
> The modes and degrees of need satisfaction determine which needs will become the strongest motivators. The nature of the motivation may be quite unconscious. . . .

Roe accepts Maslow's [320] concept of a hierarchy of needs, which Roe lists in the following order:

1. The physiological needs.
2. The safety needs.
3. The need for belongingness and love.
4. The need for importance, respect, self-esteem, independence.
5. The need for information.
6. The need for understanding.
7. The need for beauty.
8. The need for self-actualization.

In this list the lower-numbered needs are frequently referred to as the basic or "lower order" needs. The higher-numbered are called the "higher order" needs.

Roe suggests that

> Needs, for which even minimum satisfaction is rarely achieved, will, if higher order, become in effect expunged, or will, if lower order, prevent the appearance of higher order needs, and will become dominant and restricting motivators. . . .
>
> A child whose expressions of natural curiosity are thoroughly blocked may cease to be curious. . . .
>
> Needs, the satisfaction of which is delayed but eventually accomplished, will become (unconscious) motivators, depending largely upon the degree of satisfaction felt. . . .

This is the key to the development of interests.

Interests . . . are . . . the focus of effortless, active attention, which becomes progressively differentiated. . . .

The first and greatest differentiation is between person-directed attention and non-person-directed attention. Person-directed attention may refer to other persons or to the self, and it may be a resultant of excessive thwarting from persons, or of major satisfactions connected with persons. And I think that this differentiation is probably fixed, for all practical purposes . . . by kindergarten age. . . .

What the counselor needs to know is the major orientation of the child, his patterns of interpersonal relations, and especially the situations which the child finds satisfying and those which he dislikes. The counselor should be able to extract from these experiences some estimate of the need hierarchy of the child, and of need strengths. . . . The counselor must also know what the socio-economic background of the family is, and what their attitudes and value systems are, and their expectations for the child. . . .

If high school is to be the last of formal educational training . . . specific vocational counseling is necessary, and I would strongly urge that it not be primarily task oriented, but be oriented first to the general situation and then to the specific task. And that it include some discussion of what satisfactions the job can and cannot be expected to supply. . . .

At the college level ". . . the importance of the task is very much greater. This is largely because of the shift from extrinsic to intrinsic interests occurring with difference in job level."

Schaffer [416] studied job satisfaction as related to need satisfaction among seventy-two employed men, most of whom were in professional and semiprofessional occupations. His theory formally stated is this:

Over-all satisfaction will vary directly with the extent to which those needs of an individual which can be satisfied in a job are actually satisfied; the stronger the need, the more closely will job satisfaction depend on its fulfillment. . . .

The most accurate prediction of over-all job satisfaction can be made from the measure of the extent to which each person's strongest two or three needs are satisfied. . . .

Twelve needs . . . were chosen. . . .

A. *Recognition and Approbation.* The need to have one's self, one's works, and other things associated with one's self known and approved by others.

B. *Affection and Interpersonal Relationships.* The need to have a feeling of acceptance by and belongingness with other people. The need to have people with whom to form these affective relationships.

C. *Mastery and Achievement.* The need to perform satisfactorily according to one's own standards. The need to perform well in accordance with the self-perception of one's abilities.

D. *Dominance.* The need to have power and control of others.

E. *Social Welfare.* The need to help others, and to have one's efforts result in benefits to others.

F. *Self-expression.* The need to have one's behavior consistent with one's self-concept.

G. *Socioeconomic Status.* The need to maintain one's self and one's family in accordance with certain group standards with respect to material matters.

H. *Moral Value Scheme.* The need to have one's behavior consistent with some moral code or structure.

I. *Dependence.* The need to be controlled by others. Dislike of responsibility for one's own behavior.

J. *Creativity and Challenge.* The need for meeting new problems requiring initiative and inventiveness, and for producing new and original works.

K. *Economic Security.* The need to feel assured of a continuing income. Unwillingness to "take a chance" in any financial matters.

L. *Independence.* The need to direct one's own behavior rather than to be subject to the direction of others.

Super in 1953 proposed "A Theory of Vocational Development" [469] which he has since revised and expanded in *The Psychology of Careers* [468], in *The Vocational Maturity of Ninth Grade Boys* [471], and in *Career Development: Self-Concept Theory* [472].

From *The Psychology of Careers* [468]:

The term *vocational choice,* widely used in discussions and studies of vocational development and adjustment, conveys a misleading notion of neatness and precision in time. . . .

Choice is, in fact, a process rather than an event. . . . The term should denote a whole series of choices, generally resulting in the elimination of some alternatives and the retention of others, until in due course the narrowing down process results in what might perhaps be called an occupational choice. . . .

Vocational development is conceived of as one aspect of individual development. . . .

Vocational maturity is used to denote the degree of development, the place reached on the continuum of vocational development from exploration to decline. . . .

The choice of an occupation is one of the points in life at which a young person is called upon to state rather explicitly his concept of himself, to say definitely "I am this or that kind of person."

Similarly, holding and adjusting to a job is for the typical beginning worker a process of finding out, first, whether that job permits him to play the kind of role he wants to play; secondly, whether the role the job makes him play is compatible with his self-concept—

whether the unforeseen elements in it can be assimilated into the self or modified to suit the self; and, finally, it is a process of testing his self-concept against reality, of finding out whether he can actually live up to his picture of himself.

From *Career Development: Self-Concept Theory* [472]:

> *Elements of a self-concept theory of vocational development* . . . may be identified as the processes of formation, translation, and implementation of the self concept.
> *Self-concept formation.* In infancy the individual begins the process of forming a concept of himself, developing a sense of identity as a person distinct from but at the same time resembling other persons. This is essentially an exploratory process which goes on throughout the entire course of life until selfhood ceases and identity is lost to the sight of man as we know him. How does this concept of self evolve?
> *Exploration* appears to be the first phase. . . . The self is an object of exploration as it develops and changes; so, too, is the environment.
> *Self differentiation* is a second phase . . . the baby notes "This is I, that is someone else." He goes on to ask, "What am I like?" . . .
> *Identification* is another process which goes on more or less simultaneously with differentiation. . . . The boy, whose father was at first his only male object of identification, finds that he can resemble a number of other males and assume a variety of masculine roles, can choose his identification on the basis of what appeals to him most. . . .
> *Role playing* is a type of behavior which accompanies or follows identification. . . . Whether the role playing is largely imaginative or overtly participatory it gives some opportunity to try the role on for size, to see how valid the concept of oneself as a left-handed baseball player, or as a student of biology preparing to be a physician. actually is.
> *Reality testing* stems as readily from role playing as role playing does from identification. Life offers many opportunities for reality testing, in the form of children's play, . . . in school courses, . . . in extracurricular activities, . . . and in part-time or temporary employment. . . . These reality testing experiences strengthen or modify self concepts, and confirm or contradict the way in which they have been tentatively translated into an occupational role.
> *Translation of self concepts into occupational terms.* The translation proceeds in several ways. . . . Identification with an adult. . . . Experience. . . . Awareness of the fact that one has attributes which are said to be important in a certain field of work. . . .
> *Implementation of the self concepts.* The implementation or actualizing of self concepts is the result of these processes as professional training is entered or as education is completed and the young man or woman moves from school or college into the world of work. . . .

These appear to be the elements of a self-concept theory of vocational development.

Tiedeman [478] says:

The conception of choos*ing* is now the primary conception in my evolving theory of the personally-determined career. . . .

Career development is not all thought; career development is the exercise of thought in work activities in ways such that action is somewhat guided by thought. However, action influences thought as well as the reverse. . . .

The adequate exercise of choice requires full use of thought, a conscious mechanism. . . .

Behavioral science does not honor the possibility of thought in any form except that of the investigator. . . .

Personal determination in career development originates from purposeful action provided that such action becomes related to the career realm of the person's experience. The cultivation of a union of purposeful action with career requires careful consideration of the mechanisms of time and sequence by subject and counselor. When the subject and counselor focus upon the previously explicated mechanisms of time and sequence in relation to the processes involved in vocational choosing, unconscious, pre-conscious, and conscious mechanisms provide means of analyzing the objects and bases of choice in the development of the personally-determined career. The expansion of career development through the incorporation into personal and career continuities of the discontinuities of new career opportunities gives rise to the processes of differentiation and integration associated with such incorporation. The attainment of integration during the incorporation of discontinuity into continuity requires commitment to such incorporation as well as the assumption of tentativeness towards that incorporation so that the person is master, not slave, of the possibility.

Obviously the development of maturity which incorporates the personally-determined career is a matter of considerable duration in the life of man. In fact, I am of the view that maturity is an always evolving condition, never an attained condition. Nevertheless, I do believe that patterns are discernible at different ages in relation to different problems in the evolution of career. . . .

A curriculum will have to be constructed which will teach students how to use . . . educational and vocational information . . . in the framing of vocational decisions. The assumption of responsibility during choice in vocational decisions will be the primary goal of this instruction. . . .

The *procedure* of making decisions will then become the explicit context within which the counselor's discourse in this task will find focus. Finally, the *process* of making informed decisions will become the professional context within which the counselor must operate. In other words, case by case, year after year, the counselor must focus upon the developed awareness of the student concerning *his* process of decision making in educational and vocational realms.

In response to a request for help in selecting the quotations which best summarize her theory, **Tyler** [487] replied, "What has happened over the years in my thinking is that I have become more and more interested in the general process of choice and less inclined to elaborate theories about vocational choice." Tyler suggested the following:

From "The Future of Vocational Guidance" [486], pages 61 and 62:

Another change we may expect as an outgrowth of this developmental view of vocational choice is that other aspects of life planning will inevitably come in for a great deal of consideration. It has always been true that vocational guidance for girls took a different shape from vocational guidance for boys, because girls are less able or perhaps less willing than boys are to think about the choosing of a career without reference to other considerations. A girl may see it as more important that she be acceptable to the kinds of people who matter to her, so that the kind of man she wants to marry will be likely to propose to her, than that she find just the occupation that best fits her talents and aptitudes. She regards choices of certain kinds of social groups and behavior patterns, certain kinds of leisure and recreational activities, certain kinds of values and standards, as more important than choices with regard to occupation alone. These are valid considerations, and with the progress of automation reducing the demand for many kinds of human effort, it may well be that non-work activities will require as much thoughtful planning and organization as work itself. One way of expressing what this trend means is to say that *vocational* guidance will be less and less likely to take place alone.

It is unfortunate that there seems to have developed in the minds of counselors and of the public at large a conception of counseling as *either* vocational *or* personal. Vocational counseling is viewed as a somewhat superficial, rather routine matter. Personal counseling, on the other hand, is thought of as a complex, challenging process calling for a high degree of psychological sophistication and skill. Seeing the task this way, a counselor provides some information about his own aptitudes and the world of work to a client whom he classifies in the first category, and launches into an involved analysis of symptoms, emotional reactions, and early experiences with a client whom he classifies in the second category. Neither of these ways of counseling can be very helpful to the client who needs most of all to think through what he wants from life in general. Which of the many kinds of rewards it holds out have most meaning for him? What philosophical questions is he seeking answers to? What kinds of human relationships does he want most to cultivate and maintain? What kind of contribution to the common good does he expect to make? . . . At this point it is sufficient to say that counselors of the future must attempt to apply what they have learned about the facilitation of a wise vocational choice that can serve as an organizing focus for the identity of an individual to the facilitation of the many other kinds of choices upon which individual identity rests in our modern world.

Warner and Abegglen [498] analyzed the social origins and careers of 8,000 major business executives in the United States. On the basis of incidence in the population, they computed how many persons from various kinds of families might be expected to become business leaders if family background had no effect upon occupational success. They then observed how many persons from each group did become business leaders. They found that

> For every 10 men who might have been expected to be business leaders on the basis of their occupational backgrounds and the proportion of such men in the general occupational population, there were approximately 80 sons of business leaders, 40 sons of small business men, about 40 sons of professional men, and slightly over 10 sons of foremen. . . . Fewer than 2 out of the expected 10 turn up for the semiskilled or unskilled and almost none for farm laborers. . . .
>
> A comparison of the findings of 1928 . . . indicate . . . an increase in the proportion of the men who come from the lower ranks. . . .
>
> Geographical regions . . . contributed disproportionately. . . . Corrected for the size of the population . . . the . . . Middle Atlantic states rank first. . . .
>
> Most of the men of the business elite were born in the big cities. . . .
>
> Seventy-six per cent of the men studied had gone to college, 57 per cent had graduated. . . .
>
> The laborer who "marries the boss's daughter" takes almost exactly the same amount of time for achievement as the one who marries someone from his own level of origin (25.9 years for the first, 26.1 for the latter).

COMMENTS ON THEORIES

The theories described above are pioneer attempts to find some rational explanation and some basis for understanding of what happens when a person chooses an occupation. They are theories in the broadest sense. Some have been called assumptions or postulates or hypotheses. All of them are based upon some evidence; all of them will require much more evidence before any one of them can be regarded as established. In the meantime, the counselor must rely upon his own experience and his own judgment in comparing conflicting theories, in accepting ideas which make sense to him, in rejecting those which do not, and in formulating his own theory to guide his own actions.

The comments which follow may be of some help to the reader in identifying the areas of agreement and the points of conflict among the theories described above, and in considering the implications of these theories for the use of occupational information in counseling and in teaching. The opinions expressed are the author's own, subject to all the errors of judgment based on inadequate data and subject to revision as these errors become apparent.

Vocational choice or vocational development? Super [468] has noted that "The term *vocational choice* . . . conveys a misleading notion of neatness and precision in time" whereas "Choice is, in fact, a process rather than an event." Super's introduction of the term "vocational development" has been widely accepted. It has served to emphasize what professional vocational counselors have always recognized, that vocational decisions are frequently influenced by earlier experiences and earlier decisions, as well as by the general growth and development of the individual.

The concept of vocational development does not, of course, deny the fact that every individual must someday decide that he will or will not accept a job that has been offered to him. He may, indeed, have to make several such decisions. Each decision may be affected by his vocational development up to that point, but his development will seldom make the decision for him. When the chips are down, he and he alone must make a vocational choice—to accept or to decline. Whether this decision is good or bad will always depend in part upon the accuracy and adequacy of the information which he has about the occupation under consideration.

All good things may be overdone. Current discussion of vocational development seems sometimes to suggest that vocational choices automatically become better as one grows older. There is no denying the obvious fact that they *sometimes* do. But that they *always* do is questionable.

Super and Overstreet [471] concluded that ". . . the typical ninth-grade boy has not yet reached a stage at which wisdom of vocational preference can be expected." They also noted that "The . . . information which these boys had about . . . duties, conditions of work, and other important characteristics" of their preferred occupations was found to be limited.

We do not yet know how wise ninth-grade boys might be about their vocational preferences if they did have accurate and adequate information about occupations. We do know that many college seniors are as naïve and as bewildered as ninth-grade boys, so apparently something more than maturity is needed to achieve wisdom. And we do know that a few individuals still do make stable choices even before the ninth grade. For example, in a twelve-year longitudinal study, Tyler [485] found the science interests in boys had crystallized by the time they were in the eighth grade. And in a study of seventy-five Science Talent Search winners, MacCurdy [314] found that thirty-seven of them had decided to become scientists ". . . *when they were in elementary school.*" MacCurdy also reported an unpublished study by Margaret Patterson and Watson Davis, who found that ". . . 94 per cent of the winners of the Science Talent Search followed their occupational choice. . . ." MacCurdy noted five other studies which revealed that "Career choices for science are made while the student scientist is young."

We do not know why the vocational choices of some persons improve with age, while others seem never to get any better, and still others seem to need no improvement. On theoretical grounds it seems quite possible that occupational information may have something to do with this phenomenon. Perhaps the person who makes the good early choice has had the good fortune to *discover* an appropriate occupation early in life. Perhaps the person whose choice never improves never does find a job that is right for him. Perhaps for other persons vocational choice improves as the individual discovers more ways of making a living and learns more about them. To the extent that this hypothesis proves to be true, we might hope to help young people to reach wiser decisions earlier in life if we could increase the accuracy and the adequacy of the occupational information at their disposal during what Ginzberg has called the "fantasy" and the "tentative" stages.

Something of this sort was doubtless hoped for when courses in occupations were first introduced into the public schools. Something of this sort may explain why the choices of some students who have had courses in occupations have proved to be better than the choices of comparable students who did not have such courses. For a review of the research evidence on the effectiveness of courses in occupations, see Chapter 25.

Unconscious motivations. Much of the vocational counseling of the past appears to have been based upon the assumption that occupational choices are made intellectually in terms of what the client knows about occupations and about himself. Currently there appears to be increasing recognition of the extent to which the client's emotional needs may affect his choices, with or without his awareness of these needs, as may be noted in the excerpts above from Brill, Forer, Kline and Schneck, and Roe. As with every new idea there are, and will continue to be, extremists who explain everything in terms of their one pet idea. Thus Brill sees no need for counseling or for testing or for occupational information; the client's emotions will lead him to a wise choice if the rest of us will only let him alone. In response to this blithe assumption, one may observe that the client's emotions can affect his choices among only those occupations of which the client is aware and that the emotional response to any contemplated choice is a response to what the client believes the occupation to be. Emotional responses sometimes change with alacrity when clients learn how mistaken were their concepts of what specific occupations involve.

Competent counselors will not discard all their previous knowledge and experience when they discover unconscious motivations; they will, perhaps, find it a little easier to understand why their clients sometimes appear to act irrationally. As we learn more about emotions and their effect upon choices, we may learn how to help clients to become more aware of their emotional needs and to act effectively to meet them. As we learn to do this, vocational counseling will make increasingly important contributions to the emotional health and welfare of the client as well as to his economic and social adjustment. So long as people choose occupations, there will be need for someone to help them to learn what occupations are accessible to them, what these occupations offer that may meet their needs, and what each occupation requires in exchange.

Is vocational adjustment basically emotional? There are probably some persons who are so maladjusted emotionally, who find it so difficult to live comfortably with themselves and with others, that they would be ineffective and dissatisfied in almost any occupation. Others may be so concerned with their own emotional anxieties that they find it impossible to face reality or to think rationally about the choice of an occupation. Such persons may well need psychotherapy more than they need vocational guidance, as Kline and Schneck suggest. Recognition of this fact has led some observers to assume that all vocational indecision and dissatisfaction is merely a symptom of emotional maladjustment, that the "real" problem is always within the individual, and that if the counselor can deal effectively with this "real" problem, the client will then be able to solve his own vocational problems without the help of occupational information or aptitude tests or "vocational" counseling.

In conflict with this assumption is the evidence of conspicuous change in vocational adjustment which has followed change in external conditions. Many an unhappy worker has become a contented worker overnight by a fortunate change of employment; basic emotional maladjustments are not cured so quickly.

Gaudet and Kulick [178] studied the emotional adjustment of ". . . individuals who seek vocational and educational guidance." They could find no noticeable difference between the ". . . emotional, social, and familial adjustment" of these clients and the emotional, social, and familial adjustment of "a normative sample" of the total population.

Instead of assuming that all vocational maladjustment is caused by emotional maladjustment, we might get nearer the truth if we explored the hypothesis that *in some cases* emotional maladjustment causes vocational maladjustment while *in some cases* vocational maladjustment causes emotional maladjustment. The frustration of daily competition in work at which one is obviously inept, with food for one's family dependent upon satisfactory performance, is hardly conducive to mental health.

It is probably true that a normally versatile person can succeed well enough to make a living in any one of several occupations. It is also true that most of us can think of several occupations in which our own limitations would put us at a serious disadvantage. Success and satisfaction and mental health may well depend upon finding one of the former and avoiding all of the latter.

The experience of psychiatrists with this problem of choosing an occupation is reflected in Menninger's [326] comment:

> Perhaps three-fourths of the patients who come to psychiatrists are suffering from an incapacitating impairment of their satisfaction in work or their ability to work. In many it is their chief complaint. . . .
> Another index of our lack of scientific thinking in regard to the function of labor is our colossal ignorance and neglect of the problem of vocational choice. Here is one of the momentous decisions that cast the lives of human beings in fixed though diverse channels. Perhaps next to the choice of a marital partner, it is the most important and far-reaching decision made by the individual. . . .
> If one has occasion to observe in a young adolescent about to be graduated from high school his struggles over a choice of college and, particularly, over his course of study in that college, one cannot but be grateful to those who have made some effort to put at his disposal a survey of the complicated activities of life in which he will soon be forced to participate in some capacity or other.

There is no essential conflict between psychotherapy and vocational counseling. Some persons need one; some need the other; some need both. In the case of those who need both, each may reinforce the other.

Recent literature on counseling has frequently mentioned that a client who needs and wants psychotherapy may present a vocational problem as an excuse for an initial interview, during which he may observe the counselor and decide whether or not to discuss his other problems. It is certainly desirable that counselors be aware of this possibility and alert to detect what the client does need and want. It is equally desirable that the counselor remember Gaudet and Kulick's evidence that most of the persons who seek vocational and educational guidance are normal people, that not every client is psychopathic or emotionally maladjusted or even unduly anxious about his problems. For more on this see Hoppock [233].

Psychotherapists are exposed daily to an atypical sample of the population. It is not surprising that they, like the rest of us, sometimes generalize from their own experience, without adequate allowance for the limitations which their specialization has imposed upon their experience. No reasonable person would deny the great unmet need for psychotherapy among multitudes of unhappy people. But the research on happiness in marriage, in work, in life as a whole has seldom shown a majority of the population to be unhappy. As a species of the animal kingdom, man has made a fairly tolerable adjustment.

There are a great many people in the world who are doing a pretty good job of handling their own emotional problems without professional assistance, who neither need nor want psychotherapy, but who do sometimes want and need information on which to base important decisions. Providing such information, tailored to their needs, and helping them to explore its significance in relation to their problems are essential parts of a counselor's professional responsibility. When the client's problem is the choice of an occupation, the counselor has an inescapable responsibility to use all his professional knowledge and skill to help the client to get the essential information about the occupations under consideration and to see to it that the information is accurate. Facts about jobs are quite as important as feelings about them.

To answer the question posed at the beginning of this section, vocational adjustment is basically emotional in some cases, but the evidence to date suggests that these cases constitute a minority of those who seek vocational and educational guidance. For the majority of clients, emotional needs are a part of the problem of choice, but they are not the whole problem. Clients do have economic needs and physical needs as well as emotional needs, and the client whose emotional needs are not met in his job can often correct this situation more readily by changing his job than by changing himself.

In a twenty-seven-year follow-up on job satisfaction of employed adults, Hoppock [230] found that ". . . changes in jobs did change job satisfaction promptly and in both directions" and that ". . . the greatest increases in job satisfaction were achieved by those who changed jobs."

Sociologic and economic influences. However potent may be the emotional and intellectual factors in determining occupational choice, there can be no escaping the fact that all effective choices *must* be made from the employment opportunities to which the client has access and *will* be made from those of which he is aware. Caplow, Clark, Hollingshead, Miller and Form, and Warner and Abegglen have given us convincing evidence that economic and sociologic factors do limit the range of occupations to which a person has access, do direct his attention to some occupations and away from others, and do affect the occupational distribution of the population.

Most counselors come from middle-class homes with middle-class values and middle-class awareness of middle-class opportunities. Only through disillusioning experience do some counselors learn that not all their clients share their values or respond as the counselors do to what they regard as attractive opportunities. The counselor who would work effectively with clients whose backgrounds differ from his own will study the economics of the labor market and the sociology of work as industriously as he studies psychology. He will listen to his clients and their parents as much as he talks to them. Slowly he will learn some of the economic and family and cultural influences which lead his clients to do things that sometimes appear incomprehensible to members of other cultures. The reader who wishes to explore this area of human knowledge will do well to start with Caplow's [58] fascinating and scholarly review of *The Sociology of Work* and follow this with Nosow and Form's *Man, Work, and Society* [362].

The teacher who feels underpaid, who toys with the idea that he might quit his job, go into business for himself, and make a lot of money, may be no more attuned to reality than the six-year-old child who plans to be an airline pilot or the retarded student who plans to be a physician. The desire for wealth, status, glamour, or anything else may lead a person to choose an occupation that he thinks will bring him these things. If he shows no interest in considering the demand for workers and his own qualifications for the work, he may reasonably be suspected of fantasy at any age.

One of the less pleasant tasks of the counselor is that of helping such persons to discover and to face reality before they burn their bridges behind them. One of the really professional tasks of the counselor is the highly technical job of determining what the demand for workers really is and what qualifications really are essential to success.

Ginzberg and Caplow on irreversibility. Not everyone has accepted Ginzberg's conclusion that ". . . the process of decision-making is basically irreversible." Some occupations require a long period of professional training before admission to practice; a person who has completed a substantial part of such training usually cannot change his objective to a wholly different field without considerable loss. Some occupations and some employers offer substantial rewards for long experience; a person who is reaping such a harvest usually cannot change his occupation without a sacrifice. In such cases, the unavoidable sacrifices may well make the original decisions irreversible for all practical purposes.

But not all occupations require or reward training or experience. Although automation may reduce the number of unskilled and semiskilled workers, particularly in large organizations, we still have thousands of deliverymen, taxi drivers, stock boys, salesclerks, waiters, busboys, doormen, ushers, helpers, and porters, whose occupations require little formal education, no experience, and only a short period of training on the job.

The persons who choose any of these occupations may change their choices as frequently as they can find employers to hire them. In prosperous times they can often increase their earnings by changing. Caplow has noted that they often do. Presumably Ginzberg intended his theory of irreversibility to apply only to those occupations in which training or experience is required or rewarded. His concept of irreversibility does serve to remind us of the great importance of educational choices which restrict future occupational choices and of the importance of first jobs in which a young person may acquire experience that will be too valuable to throw away.

Economists, sociologists, psychologists, and educators. There is no major conflict among the carefully formulated theories and the observations of economists, sociologists, psychologists, and educators unless one wishes to assert that the influence which he sees is the dominant influence.

Most reasonable people will agree that most of us need to earn a living, that we would like it to be a good living, and that few of us will accept a job without knowing what it pays. Most of us will also agree that the high average earnings of physicians and the low average earnings of workers in ancillary medical services help to explain why the medical profession is simultaneously turning away applicants for admission to medical schools and desperately recruiting candidates for other health occupations. The need to earn a living is one of the basic needs which most of us seek to meet when we choose an occupation.

Most reasonable people will agree that the family and the social class in which we were reared helped to determine the occupations with which we were familiar, the occupations in which employment opportunities were presented to us, the occupations which we considered respectable and questionable, and some of the social needs that we sought to meet in our occupational choices. Even the person who rebels against his family is influenced by it, and one can hardly deny the evidence that social origins have affected the occupational distribution of our population.

Most reasonable people will agree that there are observable differences in vocational interest and aptitude, that the same occupation may appear attractive to one person and repulsive to another, and that emotional needs do influence occupational choices consciously or unconsciously.

Most reasonable people will agree that there are some occupations which are extremely difficult to enter without the prescribed preparation and that education or the lack of it may permit or prevent a person from entering such an occupation.

Economists, sociologists, psychologists, and educators all are presumably correct when they assert that the forces with which they deal do affect occupational choice. Each of them may also correctly assert that in some cases the dominant influence is to be found in his field. Each of them is probably wrong if he thinks that all occupational choices, or even a majority of them, are dominated by the considerations which dominate his own interest. Vocational choice is not the exclusive province of the economist or the sociologist or the psychologist or the educator. It is the province of the person who is doing the choosing and who should be able to command the help of all the related disciplines in learning how best to make his choice.

IMPLICATIONS FOR COUNSELORS
Despite the differences which have been noted above, all the theories appear to have much more in common than in contrast.

Areas of agreement. There appears to be either explicit or tacit agreement
that both occupations and people differ; that the choice of an occupation may help or hinder success and satisfaction; that choices are
affected by needs and should be affected also by abilities and by employment opportunities; that some choices are realistic, some fantastic,
and some in between; that many persons make several different choices
before committing themselves to any one choice; that choices may continue to change throughout the working lifetime of the individual; and
that a counselor may sometimes help a person to make better choices
than he would make without help.

Reality testing. There is explicit agreement on the necessity for reality testing as a part of occupational choice.

Ginzberg suggested that in the fantasy period the child ". . . believes
that he can be whatever he wants to be." Well-intentioned but uninformed commencement orators, inspirational teachers, and amateur
counselors contribute to the preservation of this fantasy as they elo-
quently assure the younger generation that perseverance and. determination can overcome all obstacles to a cherished goal. Perhaps school
counselors should suggest to their colleagues on the faculty that inspiration of this kind be tempered by reality.

Today there is much concern with disadvantaged youth and with
efforts to raise their level of aspiration. It is difficult to express any
reservations about these efforts without appearing to oppose equal opportunity for all. But good intentions do not guarantee good results.

Rich or poor, privileged or persecuted, we each have our own abilities
and limitations, to which our own aspirations must be reasonably related. An indiscriminate effort to raise the aspirations of *all* disadvantaged youth may succeed only in aggravating the frustrations of those
individuals who lack the qualifications to achieve their newly acquired
aspirations.

Let us by all means remove racial barriers, but let us also remember
that in any group of students anywhere there are very likely to exist
some who could wisely raise their level of aspiration and some who
could wisely lower it.

Counselors should see their clients through placement. Ultimately every client tests
his occupational choice against the realities of occupational life when
he tries to make a living. Too often the client cannot get a job in the
occupation of his choice. He needs a job. He takes what he can get. It
is at this point of placement that much vocational counseling breaks

down because neither the client nor his counselor did enough reality testing in anticipation, during the process of vocational counseling. Because the client who fails to get a job seldom returns at this point, the counselor seldom learns of these failures.

We could make tremendous improvements in the quality of vocational guidance if we could require all counselors to do what good rehabilitation counselors do—follow the client through the process of placement and stay with him until his record indicates that the placement and the counseling have been successful. There would be some pretty red faces among counselors when they experienced this kind of reality testing for the first time, and the embarrassment of the counselors might in turn, provide the motivation needed to make future counseling more realistic.

Far too many counselors now are able to dispose of their clients before the success or failure of the counseling can be tested against reality. School and college counselors can dispose of their problems by graduating them. Client-centered counselors are relieved of their failures when the client no longer returns for counseling. Testing centers can get rid of their clients when the testing results have been interpreted. Counseling psychologists in veterans' hospitals can dispose of their patients by turning them over to the state employment service when they are ready to look for a job. Thus the counselors themselves can escape reality testing of their own work.

The American Board on Counseling Services, which was created by the American Personnel and Guidance Association, approves and certifies agencies and individuals as "professionally competent to perform . . . counseling about occupations and careers." Regrettably the Board's criteria for approval, printed in the 1965–1966 *Directory of Approved Counseling Agencies* [358] do not require the approved agency to know anything about what happens to its clients when they go to look for a job which the counselor has helped them to choose.

Fantasy in counseling. Too much of our vocational counseling today is in a stage which resembles the tentative period of Ginzberg's theory. This counseling operates almost ". . . exclusively in terms of subjective factors: interests, capacities, and values." The situation is bad enough in some of our public schools which give little attention to the realities of the employment market. The situation is even worse in some of the clinics and the testing centers which developed so rapidly in colleges and social agencies while the Veterans Administration was financing the service, in some of the counseling psychology programs in the Veterans Administration itself, and in some of the counseling agencies operated by psychologists in private practice.

Most of the professional employees of these agencies are psychometrists, clinical psychologists, and counseling psychologists, who are well trained to deal with the subjective factors. In the same agencies there are comparatively few counselors who are equally well trained to deal with the "reality considerations," who have the technical knowledge of occupations and the professional skill to help the client to ". . . work out a compromise between what he wants and the opportunities which are available to him." The imbalance of professional competence which prevails in such agencies today may permit a service which is better than none, as some evaluations already indicate, but it hardly seems calculated to produce the best results in terms of realistic choices.

There is fantasy in the belief that good vocational counseling can be provided by psychologists who know all about values and emotions and interests and capacities and who are not equally competent in the area of occupational information. What we now have in vocational counseling is far too many psychologists who regard placement as a dirty word and any direct contact with the employment market as degrading. If we are not someday to be charged with quackery, we should have in all vocational counseling services as many persons who are skilled in occupational information as we have persons who are skilled in psychology, or we should have a new breed of counselor whose training, experience, and competence in economics, in occupational information, and in placement equals his training, experience, and competence in psychology, in psychometrics, and in psychotherapy.

One of the most important uses of occupational information in counseling is in helping the client to test the reality of his choice against all the pertinent, known facts about the demand for workers, the qualifications for employment, and the ways in which the occupation may or may not meet the needs of the client if he is able to get and hold a job. How occupational information may be used to do this is discussed later in this book.

Self-appraisal. There is one aspect of occupational choice that has been mentioned infrequently in the theories and in the other literature of vocational guidance. We have impressive evidence of the inability of many persons to estimate their own aptitude for activities in which they have had little opportunity to experiment. From this evidence we may easily but mistakenly infer that the average person has little ability to estimate his aptitude for anything.

On the contrary, most persons, by the time they are ready for full-time employment, have had thousands of opportunities to try to do thousands of different things and to observe whether they do them better or less well than other people. The duties of most occupations include many activities in which the average person has had many opportunities to participate. When a person knows enough about an occupation to be thoroughly familiar with all the duties and activities that the occupation involves, he will often avoid choosing that occupation if it is one of those for which he is least fitted, and he will often lean toward it if it is one of those occupations for which he has more appropriate aptitudes. When people appear not to do this, their choices may be based upon inadequate knowledge of the occupation as well as upon ignorance of themselves. To the extent that we can help individuals to become thoroughly familiar with the activities of the principal occupations that are open to them, we may hope to contribute significantly to their adjustment even in some of the occupations for which no aptitude tests are yet available.

REVIEW QUESTIONS

    1. Which of all these theories most nearly approximates your own?
    2. With which do you disagree most vigorously? Why?
    3. To what extent do you think your past vocational choices have been affected by anything mentioned in any of these theories?

8
A
Composite
Theory
for
Counselors

Theories serve two purposes: for the research worker they provide hypotheses to be investigated; for the counselor they provide a way to make some sense out of the otherwise bewildering behavior of other people. In this chapter we are concerned with the counselor, and with how theories of vocational choice and development can help him to do his job.

When a person acts the way we expect him to act, he confirms and supports the theories on which we operate. We feel reassured, successful, and confident. And we keep on doing what we are doing.

When a person does not act the way we expect him to act, when he acts in a way directly contrary to our expectations, he contradicts the theories on which we operate. We feel insecure, uncertain of our success, and doubtful of our methods. We may even feel impatient with the person who obstinately refuses to act in the way our theories have led us to expect that he will act. But when we recover from our impatience, we begin to reexamine our theories, to look for others which offer better explanations of the way people behave and better bases for anticipating how our students and clients will respond to our efforts as counselors.

Not for many years, if ever, will we have enough research evidence to confirm or contradict each of the many theories of vocational choice and development already proposed, not to mention the new theories not yet devised. In the meantime, counselors must do the best they can.

What can a counselor extract from the conflicting theories now available? Must these theories only add to his confusion? Or can they help him to understand the behavior of the persons he tries to serve? Admittedly, what the counselor can infer from theories yet unconfirmed will still be speculative. But examination and comparison of several theories may provide the counselor with a broader base for his own speculations and thus bring him a little nearer to truth, whatever that truth may be.

The existence of several conflicting theories suggests the possibility that there may be some truth in all of them. The basic principle of individual differences, so familiar to counselors, suggests the same possibility. One theory may explain the behavior of some persons, but we may need another theory to explain the behavior of others.

The remainder of this chapter is the result of one counselor's attempts to understand the behavior of the persons who have sought his help in making their vocational plans and choices at various stages in their vocational development. This is presented not as a neat hypothesis for research, but as a series of speculations as to why people behave as they do when they are trying to reach vocational decisions. It will be apparent that these speculations draw freely on several of the theories reviewed in the preceding chapter.

A COMPOSITE THEORY

1. Occupations are chosen to meet needs.

2. The occupation that we choose is the one that we believe will best meet the needs that most concern us.

3. Needs may be intellectually perceived, or they may be only vaguely felt as attractions which draw us in certain directions. In either case, they may influence choices.

4. Vocational development begins when we first become aware that an occupation can help to meet our needs.

5. Vocational development progresses and occupational choice improves as we become better able to anticipate how well a prospective occupation will meet our needs. Our capacity thus to anticipate depends upon our knowledge of ourselves, our knowledge of occupations, and our ability to think clearly.

6. Information about ourselves affects occupational choice by helping us to recognize what we want and by helping us to anticipate whether or not we will be successful in collecting what the contemplated occupation offers to us.

7. Information about occupations affects occupational choice by helping us to discover the occupations that may meet our needs and by helping us to anticipate how well satisfied we may hope to be in one occupation as compared with another.

8. Job satisfaction depends upon the extent to which the job that we hold meets the needs that we feel it should meet. The degree of satisfaction is determined by the ratio between what we have and what we want.

9. Satisfaction can result from a job which meets our needs today or from a job which promises to meet them in the future.

10. Occupational choice is always subject to change when we believe that a change will better meet our needs.

EXPLANATIONS

Most human action is caused by feelings, by our desire to be more comfortable or less uncomfortable, more satisfied or less frustrated, in short, by our desire to feel better than we do. Human action is affected by intellect only after feelings have indicated that some kind of action is desirable and only to the extent that our intellect can convince us that a particular course of action will improve or relieve our feeling tone. Intellect gives direction to our actions when factual information or logical reasoning indicates that one course of action is more likely than another to bring us the satisfactions that we seek.

It may appear that human action sometimes is caused, not by a desire to feel better than we do, but by a desire to maintain the comfortable state that we have already attained. Certainly the latter desire can provide motivation for action, but only when we feel some concern that our comfortable state may deteriorate if we do not act. We then act to relieve our concern. In relieving our concern, we feel better. Thus we act in order to feel better.

It may appear that some persons enjoy unhappiness, persecute themselves, or sacrifice themselves for others. Such actions may not make the individual either happy or satisfied. They are, nevertheless, undertaken in the hope that they will make the individual less unhappy than he would be if he followed any other course of action. To the martyr, death is preferable to capitulation. He may be an atheist who expects no reward in heaven and yet prefer death to life on terms that would be intolerable to him. The person who persecutes himself does so in order to relieve a feeling of guilt or because for some other reason he finds relief or satisfaction in his own unhappiness. Paradoxical as it appears, perverted as it may be, he seeks unhappiness in order to enjoy it.

The client who is unable to face reality may distort information about occupations just as he may distort information about himself. He may accept those facts which support a course of action that appeals to him, while he rejects those facts which he finds disturbing. Wishful thinking is a fairly common characteristic of the human race. When people appear not to act rationally in choosing an occupation, their failure to do so may be traced to one of three causes: inadequate information about themselves, inadequate information about occupations, or inability to think clearly. Inability to face reality is one kind of inability to think clearly.

As noted previously, an occupation is only a name for a group of jobs which have something in common. The specific jobs within one occupation may differ in many ways. They may involve different supervisors, different employers, different locations, different physical surroundings, different associates. Because of these differences a person may be satisfied in one job and dissatisfied in another job in the same occupation if one of the jobs meets more of his needs than the other.

Needs and values sometimes change. A young person's eagerness for adventure may be replaced in later years by a preference for stability. An occupation which meets the needs of a client at age twenty may no longer meet his needs at age fifty. Participation in an occupation, daily association with the kinds of people who are attracted to it, acceptance of, and conformity to, the mores of the occupational group can in time have a subtle but substantial effect on a person's values. The result may be to make the occupation appear either more or less desirable than it seemed at first. If changes in needs and values are anticipated, they may affect the original choice of an occupation; if they are not anticipated, they may lead a person to change his occupation in later life.

Economic factors affect occupational choice by helping to determine the age at which a person terminates his formal education and enters the labor market on a full-time basis. The economic cycle, moving from periods of prosperity to depression and back again, helps to determine the number and nature of the employment opportunities available at the time a person is looking for a job. Immediate and potential future earnings affect the extent to which a contemplated occupation may be expected to meet one's economic needs.

Education influences occupational choice by opening the doors to some occupations that would otherwise be closed, by making a person aware of occupations of which he had no previous knowledge, by arousing or discouraging his interest in them, by providing tryout experiences which lead the student to anticipate success or failure in specific activities. For some students, school or college provides a new social group with which they identify and which profoundly influences the social and economic needs which they feel their occupations must meet.

Psychological factors influence occupational choice by helping to determine the extent to which one perceives his own needs, accepts or suppresses them, faces the realities of employment opportunities and of his own abilities and limitations, and thinks clearly about all these facts. The extent to which aptitudes and interests are general or specific will probably be argued as long as there are psychologists to speculate and statisticians to calculate probabilities, but there is little doubt that interests help to determine the occupations a person will consider and that aptitudes help to determine whether or not he will achieve enough success to get and to hold the job that he has chosen.

Sociologic factors affect occupational choice by helping to determine the occupations with which a person is familiar, by virtue of his contacts with family and friends. The cultural pattern of the social group in which a person has been reared and of the social group with which he currently identifies himself helps to determine the occupations which he will consider to be socially acceptable and socially preferred. Social patterns of exclusion or acceptance help to determine the occupations which are available to the individual; thus a union may admit relatives of members in preference to others, an employer may discriminate on racial or religious grounds, the qualifications for a job may include social contacts and social skills which are seldom acquired except through family associations. All these factors affect occupational choice by helping to determine the employment opportunities that will be available to an individual and those which he will consider, by influencing the social needs which he will feel that his occupation must meet and the extent to which he will expect any contemplated occupation to meet these needs.

THE THEORY IN OPERATION

How this theory may help us to understand the phenomena of occupational choice may be suggested by the following examples.

Perhaps the simplest illustration is one that has appeared in times of economic depression. A man is unemployed and destitute and hungry. He takes the first job he can get, despite the fact that the work is offensive to him and does not meet many of his obvious needs. At the moment the need of which he is most aware is the need for food. He will be miserable until that need is met. Other needs can wait. This job offers the most acceptable, available way to meet the need that he feels most acutely. He takes the job. Later, on a full stomach, with this job for temporary security, he will look for another job that will provide food and also meet more of his other needs.

At the other end of the scale is the complex case of the individual who is only vaguely aware, if at all, of the emotional needs which drive him toward a particular occupation. Thus, a brilliant student who has little skill in teaching, even less patience with slower learners, and no genuine desire to help others to learn may nevertheless choose teaching as his occupation because the only real success he has ever achieved has been in the classroom and he fears to leave the environment in which he has enjoyed success or because something in his past experience has left him with a desire to dominate other people and teaching is the only occupation in which he sees an opportunity to do so. He may not be conscious of either of these motives and yet may be driven by them more compulsively than if he were aware of them. He may even become a teacher and remain a teacher all his life, despite the fact that neither he nor his students really enjoy his teaching, because he never finds any other occupation that offers him the security of the familiar classroom or the opportunity to play the dominant role.

Abnormal as well as normal needs may find expression in the choice of an occupation, sometimes with unfortunate results. Comfort [97], in his book on *Authority and Delinquency in the Modern State: A Criminological Approach to the Problem of Power,* has observed that

There are many occupations in modern society, almost all of them concerned with the executive side of power, which confer a limited license for the infliction of pain or of arbitrary authority, and these occupations are of a type indispensable to the present pattern of life. . . . Tolerated delinquents appear in centralized cultures at two distinct levels. They may enter and control the machinery of legislative and political power, as policy-makers and rulers. They may also be found, and tend in general to be more numerous, in the machinery of enforcement which intervenes between the policy-maker and the citizen. We owe our present recognition of the presence and the role of these tolerated delinquents, and of their capacity for mischief, to the rise of totalitarian states, but the reappearance of delinquency and military tyranny as socially accepted policies in civilized states has led, and must lead, to a scrutiny of similar mechanisms within the social democracies. . . . By comparison with other employments, the enforcement services offer poor remuneration and a severer discipline. . . . There is, therefore, in centralized societies, a tendency for the personnel of these occupations to be drawn increasingly from those whose main preoccupation is a desire for authority, for power of control and of direction over others.

How the theory may help us to understand others. The needs and the demands of individuals are probably as varied and as complex as the individuals themselves, but if the individual sees or even subconsciously feels any way in which the choice of an occupation may help to meet his needs, then his needs will affect his choice. It is desirable that we as counselors understand this, not because the understanding will enable us to solve all the complex problems that will be brought to us, but because we may then better understand the less complex cases and be of more help to them. Without this understanding we may be baffled by the choices of individuals whose emotional needs or value patterns differ from ours. A choice that seems illogical to us, and would indeed be illogical if we made it for ourselves, becomes logical when we understand the needs and the values of the person who makes it.

Thus we smile and dismiss as fantasy the occupational choice of the little child who announces his serious intention to be a fireman when he grows up. It may not occur to us that the child, dominated by adults from morning until night and protected from every danger that can be anticipated, may feel a real need to be important and to embark upon some adventure more thrilling than the exploration of his own backyard. In terms of the needs that he feels and of the occupations with which he is familiar, his choice may be as logical as ours. In his place we might well make the same choice, and some of us did.

We consider immature the choice of the adolescent who is determined to enter the occupation of his current adult hero, for which work our student obviously lacks essential aptitudes. We overlook, perhaps, the fact that the adolescent is here showing the first sign of maturity. He is breaking away from home ties and has a real need to identify with some adult outside the family and to try to be like him, as in the past he tried to be like his parents. Knowing as little as he does about vocational aptitudes and about the requirements of occupations and being not yet ready to stand alone, we too might find security in such an occupational choice, and some of us did.

If we can even suspect the emotional needs behind what look to us like irrational choices, we may be more tolerant of them. If we can occasionally understand the connection between these needs and choices, we may then be of more help to our clients, sometimes by simply waiting for them to mature a little more, sometimes by helping them to understand and accept themselves, sometimes by helping them to discover more effective and attractive ways to satisfy their needs.

Aptitudes and interests are not enough. Perhaps this theory may explain in part the skepticism of some observers regarding the kind of vocational guidance that is given by counselors whose major interest is in aptitude and interest tests. Aptitude and interest are important, but they are only a part of the total picture of the client. A person may have a perfect pattern of measured abilities and interests for a specific occupation and firmly reject it if it fails to meet the needs which are most important to him. He may be happier and, conceivably, more effective in an occupation for which he has only average qualifications if the occupation meets more of the needs which are high in his scale of values.

Thus a man who values his role as a husband and father higher than his occupational success may reject a job for which he has perfect aptitudes, because it would require him to leave his family or to move them to a location that would aggravate one child's allergies.

Another person may value leisure more than money, prestige, or achievement and be happier in a job that is "beneath him" than in one which would utilize more of his talents but consume more of his time.

Another may prefer steady work and an assured weekly income in a job that he does moderately well rather than higher but irregular earnings in a field for which he may have superior aptitude and interest.

A child may feel a need to conform to or to resist his parents' wishes, to remain near them or to get away from them. His choice may be influenced more by such considerations than by others which may appear more rational to the counselor.

Self-concepts are needs, too. Most of us think enough about ourselves to develop some kind of self-concept. This concept may be realistic or fanciful. Either way it tends to affect our actions, including our occupational choices.

The healthy, well-adjusted client, who has a realistic concept of his own abilities and limitations, may seek an occupation appropriate to them. The person with a grandiose concept of himself may choose an objective far beyond his ability to attain. The person whose self-concept is one of inferiority may choose a job that is far beneath his capacities, or he may, in desperation, choose a job that is far above them, in the hope that the job will develop him into the kind of person he would like to be.

The person who likes to think of himself as a superior being whom others respect and admire may be strongly attracted to any occupation which permits him to be the center of attention. Given the requisite abilities, he may fulfill his self-concept by becoming a successful and considerate supervisor or employer, an expert tax consultant, a lawyer, physician, nurse, policeman, receptionist, or information clerk.

The person who feels secure only when he has someone else to tell him what to do may like to think of himself as the loyal, obedient, trusted assistant to someone whose strength and courage and competence he admires and in whose care he feels safe. Depending on his abilities he may meet his needs and fulfill his self-concept as a confidential assistant to the president of a corporation, as a private secretary, as a member of the clergy in a church with a strong hierarchy, or as a statistical clerk, a soldier, or a domestic servant.

The compassionate idealist may be able to think of himself comfortably only as a person whose life is devoted to the service of others. He may be so selfish in some respects that his friends are skeptical of his ideals yet be unable to respect himself unless he can do something that he feels will leave the world a better place because he was here. Depending on his abilities he may find satisfaction as a social worker, a political reformer, an inventor, an entrepreneur, a union organizer, or a Salvation Army musician.

Self-concepts and needs are closely related. The client who is choosing an occupation will often be influenced by a need to implement or to deny his own concept of himself.

How the theory explains illogical choices. A person chooses and prepares for an occupation, he accepts or rejects a job that is offered to him, he remains in or leaves a job he has held because he expects or hopes that this course of action will make him feel better. Most of us have seen ourselves, in some situation, act contrary to our intellectual convictions about what was the proper course of action. We could not explain to others or even to ourselves why we behaved so illogically. We only knew that we "just had to do it" or that we "just couldn't bring ourselves to do it." In these words we were saying that all our neat, logical processes had not really convinced us that the "logical" course of action would make us feel better.

When a young person chooses an occupation for which he is obviously not fitted, tenaciously resists all logical arguments against it, and stubbornly ignores the evidences of his inability to meet even the minimum qualifications, he is saying to us that something in this job promises to fulfill some emotional need which means a great deal to him. He will not give up this path to its fulfillment until he can find some more promising way in which to achieve the same satisfaction or relief that he thinks this occupation would bring him. If we and he can learn about other occupations, in which he can earn a living and in which he can also achieve some of the emotional satisfactions that he craves—then we may be able to help him to a more realistic choice.

One may, of course, try to change a client's emotional cravings or to find ways of meeting them outside his occupation. This is sometimes desirable and sometimes successful. In most cases there is nothing wrong with the emotional needs that the client feels, there is nothing wrong about his desire to satisfy these needs through his work, but he does require help in finding an occupation which will fulfill his needs and in which he can get and hold a job.

Needs may lead us to satisfactions. Fortunately, emotional needs do not always lead us to irrational occupational choices. They are, perhaps, more likely to lead us to occupations in which we may find reasonable satisfaction and success if we can be patient and industrious enough to examine the occupations that are open to us, to compare them in terms of what they can offer us and what we can offer them, and if we can be realistic enough to face facts, including the fact that we are unlikely ever to achieve complete satisfaction and that life would be pretty dull if we did.

If our knowledge of ourselves or of occupations is insufficient, we are less likely to make a wise choice and more liable to cling stubbornly to an unrealistic choice because it offers the only route we can see to what we want. We may then find ourselves unemployed because we chose an occupation in which jobs are scarce or unsuccessful because we chose a job for which we lack the requisite abilities or unhappy because we were misinformed about what the work was really like.

Conscious choice may not be necessary. Vocational development begins and occupational choice may take place at any time after a person first becomes aware that an occupation might be a means of meeting the needs that he feels. Choices may change as frequently as a person's awareness of his needs changes or as frequently as he discovers that another occupation might better meet his needs. Some persons choose early and never change—like Mozart, who was playing the piano at the age of four and composing at seven. Some persons never do find an occupation which meets enough of their needs to give them any real feeling of satisfaction. Some persons achieve satisfaction without ever having made an occupational choice in the sense in which counselors usually think of choice.

Much of our vocational guidance to date appears to have been based upon the assumption that our objective is to help someone reach a vocational choice which both he and we will consider appropriate. Until this choice has been consciously identified and announced, we feel that the client still needs counseling and that our job as vocational counselors or teachers of occupations is incomplete. Once the choice is announced, if we consider it a good choice, we enjoy a sense of successful achievement and are disposed to direct our attention elsewhere.

All this may be quite appropriate in some cases; it is not necessarily appropriate or logical in all cases. The wise and conscious choice of an occupation is not an end in itself; it is a means to an end. It is an intermediate objective. The ultimate objective is an individual who is reasonably useful and reasonably contented in his work. It is conceivable that this objective may sometimes be attained without the individual ever having consciously chosen a career.

We do not yet have sufficient evidence to prove that conscious vocational choice is either essential or not essential to good vocational adjustment. Perhaps one of the readers of this book will someday do the research to provide us with such evidence. Meanwhile, it seems at least conceivable that some persons may learn a good deal about themselves and a good deal about occupations and yet never make a vocational choice until they are offered a specific job which they must either accept or reject. It seems conceivable, also, that at this point their knowledge of occupations and of themselves may enable them to make wiser decisions than they would have made without such knowledge. The teacher of occupations may thus contribute to improved vocational adjustment, even if his students do not reach final vocational choices before they finish his course. Vocational development may proceed even though the results are not immediately apparent.

Needs are not always complex. Many persons do not ask or expect from their jobs much more than a fairly steady income that will enable them to maintain the modest standard of living to which they are accustomed. Not everyone is ambitious. Not everyone wants to be promoted and to assume added responsibilities. Christensen and Burns [83] quote one of their students: "I suppose that I am one of those people that . . . never uses all his abilities. But I'm satisfied if I get by. All I want out of life is a steady job, money enough to buy a home, raise a family and enjoy life without killing myself doing it."

Such persons do not talk much about "choosing an occupation"; they just "get a job," and when it terminates, they get another. Simple as this process may appear, it does involve an occupational choice every time the individual decides that he will look for a job in one place rather than another and every time that he decides to accept or reject a job that has been offered to him. Thus an unemployed person who has always worked in a retail store and liked it may refuse even to apply for a factory job until he has exhausted every possibility of finding another job in retailing. Though he may say he is only looking for a job, he is at the same time making an occupational choice just as truly as is the high school senior who makes the same decision about where he will look for work and whose decision has been preceded by aptitude and interest testing, counseling, and the examination of a wide range of occupational possibilities.

Much of our most successful vocational guidance is done on this simple level, with persons whose demands are modest enough to be met without great difficulty and who can be helped to find the kinds of jobs they want by counselors, placement officers, and teachers of occupations who know the local employment market. It is, perhaps, regrettable that so little of our discussion of occupational choice has dealt with these simple cases, for our preoccupation with the complex problems has led too many beginning counselors to measure their own success by their ability to satisfy the client whose demands preclude any reasonable possibility of satisfaction.

How occupational information helps. All the facts about jobs with which this book is concerned are important and essential because they help us to discover what jobs are available, what these jobs offer that may satisfy our needs, and what these jobs demand of us in return.

Courses in occupations may be useful in helping students to discover and to compare occupations which promise to meet their needs. While no one wants to dispense with individual counseling, it is conceivable that in some cases the course may be more effective than counseling, because the student does not understand himself and his needs well enough to reveal them to his counselor. But he does feel them, and when he sees an occupation that promises to meet his needs, he may feel strongly attracted to it. Without the opportunity to see it, as part of a general survey of occupations, neither he nor his counselor might ever have thought of it—he because he was unaware of its existence or its nature, his counselor because he was unaware of the need.

Needs are met in many ways, not all of them occupational. But when occupations are being chosen to meet needs, as they will be, the more occupations we counselors know and the more we know about them, the better is the chance that we will be able to help our clients to find occupations that will meet their needs and in which they can also get and hold jobs.

The ability to get and hold a job cannot be overlooked, even in a discussion of needs. The best occupation in the world will not meet our client's needs if he cannot get a job in it or hold it after he gets it or if he will not move to where the work must be done. Ultimately the compelling need for most of us is to eat; the occupational choice which overlooks this need is hardly realistic, however well it might serve as an emotional outlet. This is one more reason why we as counselors need a realistic knowledge of the occupations available to those we try to help.

One of the most cogent illustrations of this need for realistic occupational information occurs many times each year. A man recovers from tuberculosis. He is warned that if he returns to his former occupation, he may have a relapse. He looks for other work but finds none. His family suffers because of his inability to support them. He feels that he has failed them, that his life is futile. He wants to live, but he also wants to feel useful. He wants his own self-respect and the respect of others. He loves his family and wants to provide for them. Eventually, his desire to support his family becomes greater than his desire to protect his health. He is offered a job in his old occupation. He takes it. He has a relapse. The job failed to meet the need which may be most apparent to others—the need to protect his health. It did meet the need which at the moment he felt most strongly—the need to support himself and his family and to regain his self-respect. Adequate occupational information, provided perhaps by a rehabilitation counselor, might have helped him to find a way to be self-supporting without jeopardizing his health.

Implications for counselors. The use of occupational information is discussed later in this book. At this point, however, the author's students have asked, "What are the implications of this theory for counselors?" The following are suggested in response to this question:

> The counselor should always remember that the needs of his client may differ from the needs of the counselor.
> The counselor should operate within the framework of the client's needs.
> The counselor should provide every possible opportunity for the client to identify and to express his own needs.
> The counselor should be alert to notice and to remember the needs which the client reveals.
> The counselor should help the client to get whatever information the client wants about himself and about occupations.
> The counselor should help the client to discover the occupations which may meet his needs.
> The counselor should help the client to anticipate how well any contemplated occupation will meet the client's needs.
> The counselor should get the occupational information which the counselor needs in order to help the client to meet his needs.
> The counselor should stay with his client through the process of placement in order to provide the further counseling that will be needed if the desired job is not available.

The counselor should follow up his client some months after placement in order to see how well the job is meeting the needs which the client thought it would meet.

REVIEW QUESTIONS

1. Of all the statements in this chapter, which one could you endorse most heartily? About which one are you most skeptical? Why?

2. Will anything in this chapter affect your future thoughts and actions? What? How?

3. How do economic factors affect occupational choice?

4. How does education influence occupational choice?

5. How do psychological factors affect occupational choice?

6. How do sociologic factors affect occupational choice?

7. Some psychologists believe that only psychologists should be pemitted to do vocational counseling. What do you think? Why?

8. Why do some persons reject occupations for which they are well equipped in aptitude and interest?

9. Why do some clients stubbornly cling to occupational choices in the face of overwhelming evidence that the choices are not realistic?

10. What are some of the implications of this chapter for counselors?

9
Contributions of Client-centered Counseling to Vocational Counseling

The development and success of "nondirective," or "client-centered," counseling as a contribution to psychotherapy have led counselors in other fields properly to consider the possible uses of the client-centered approach in their own work. It is the purpose of this chapter to discuss the contributions and limitations of client-centered procedures in vocational counseling before discussing the use of occupational information in counseling. The reader who is not already familiar with client-centered counseling will find it described in Rogers [398, 399]. In the first of these two books, what is now called "client-centered" counseling was described as "nondirective" counseling. The terms "nondirective" and "client-centered" are now used interchangeably. An excellent summary of client-centered philosophy may be found in Rogers [400].

The nondirective approach. The completely nondirective approach to counseling may be summarized as follows: the nondirective counselor seeks to understand, accept, reflect, and clarify the feelings of the client; the counselor scrupulously refrains from directing the conversation, conveys little or no information, makes no suggestions, expresses no approval or disapproval, and generally seeks to focus his own and his client's attention upon the feelings being expressed by the client rather than upon the intellectual content of what he says.

In contrast to this, the directive counselor assumes responsibility for directing the interview, he asks questions, he answers questions, he supplies information and suggestions. He may or may not tell the client what he thinks the client should do.

Originally the proponents of nondirective counseling insisted that any digression from nondirective procedures tended to disturb the essential relationship between counselor and client and thus to impair the effectiveness of counseling. Recently there has been less insistence on this point. Many counselors who regard themselves as client-centered are no longer wholly nondirective in their counseling procedures. Many counselors who do not regard themselves as nondirective do sometimes use nondirective techniques.

Patterson [373] has well expressed the current view of many counselors:

> The client-centered approach is essentially an *attitude* rather than a series of techniques. The attitude may be implemented in different ways in different situations. In counseling on problems of personal adjustment the techniques of simple acceptance and reflection of feeling are sufficient. In counseling dealing with problems of vocational choice, tests may be used and occupational information provided. It is, or should be, done in ways which are consistent with the basic attitudes or assumptions of client-centered counseling. . . .

Terminology is now a bit confusing, since the reader often is not sure whether the writer is using the terms "nondirective" and "client-centered" to designate an attitude or a technique. In the remainder of this chapter these terms are used to designate the techniques of acceptance and reflection of feeling as described in Rogers's *Counseling and Psychotherapy* [399].

There is little if any controversy about the desirability of the client-centered *attitude*. Most well-informed counselors at least profess to accept it. There is, however, still considerable difference in the use of *techniques* other than acceptance and reflection of feeling, when the problem under discussion deals with vocational planning.

The potential value. The potential value of client-centered counseling in vocational guidance is considerable. Through client-centered counseling, both counselor and client may achieve a clearer understanding of the nature of the client's problems; of his feelings about them, his values, his conflicts, his perception and acceptance of reality; and of the bearing of accepted facts upon his own problems and plans. Client-centered counseling may relieve some of the client's emotional conflicts, so that he may function at a higher level of efficiency in trying to solve his own problems. The client may then be better able to perceive and accept and deal with facts which are readily obtainable but which he has previously overlooked or refused to face.

If, on the other hand, the counselor spends too little time listening to his client, accepting and reflecting his client's feelings, trying to understand his client's internal conflicts and values, the counselor may easily mistake the nature of the problem on which the client wants help. Or the counselor may identify the problem but overlook values, anxieties, or other feelings of the client that will be among the major determinants of the client's success and satisfaction. Disturbing and disconcerting facts presented to the client may be silently rejected or discounted, so that they will not function in the client's perception of reality. Dependence upon the counselor may be welcomed by the client as an escape from the discomfort of facing and dealing with his problem.

The inescapable limitation. The inescapable limitation of the *exclusively* nondirective approach to vocational counseling is that it functions solely within the client's perception of reality. If the client's perception is false, if he is dealing intellectually and emotionally with misconceptions of his own abilities and limitations or with mistaken concepts of occupational opportunities and requirements, he may make decisions and plans that are wholly unrealistic. If pertinent facts to correct the client's misconceptions are not readily accessible to him, if nothing in his experience or in his counseling suggests to him that his perception is false, he may take actions that would be wholly logical in terms of his perception but that are almost certain to lead to failure, frustration, and further maladjustment.

For example, if a person whose qualifications are minimal chooses an occupation that is chronically overcrowded, he may very well find that he cannot get a job. This would hardly be the best way for him to become self-supporting—economically or psychologically. If a person whose qualifications are adequate chooses an occupation without learning the exact nature of the work, he may well find that it is distressingly different from his expectations; this would hardly be the best way for him to achieve emotional equanimity or job satisfaction.

Client-centered counseling was developed by social workers and clinical psychologists whose major interest was in the internal emotional conflicts of anxious, unhappy persons. Client-centered counseling was designed to help such persons to resolve their internal conflicts, recognize and accept their own emotions, clarify their own value patterns, enhance their own feelings of worth and competence, and lead their own lives according to their own standards with less concern for the approval or disapproval of others. Client-centered counseling was not designed to help a person to find out where he could get a job or what kind of activity any specific occupation involves. Client-centered counseling was intended to help remove emotional obstacles to the perception and acceptance of reality, which obstacles may prevent a person from thinking clearly even when all pertinent facts are available to him. Client-centered procedures can be very helpful in vocational counseling; they were never intended to do the whole job of vocational counseling.

In an article on "Non-directive Techniques and Vocational Counseling," Combs [96] offered the following suggestions:

> Non-directive counseling might be defined as *an attempt to aid the individual by assisting him to a reorganization of attitudes, feelings, and emotions, such that he can make optimal use of his abilities and physical endowments.* . . .
>
> Non-directive and directive techniques are not antagonistic but complementary devices, each having a unique usefulness and efficiency, depending upon the type of problem the client presents. . . .
>
> Directive techniques seem most useful where the client's primary need is for information, education, or an opportunity for clarification of thinking through discussion. . . .
>
> Non-directive techniques have most to offer where the primary need of the client is for social or emotional adjustment, clarification of feelings and attitudes, or where a shift in personality integration or self concept is necessary. . . .
>
> From our own experience with both directive and non-directive methods, non-directive techniques appear to have particular applicability to vocational counseling in the following situations:
>
> 1. *As a preliminary interview technique.* . . .
> 2. *When the level of aspiration shows marked variation from demonstrated ability or when there is a wide discrepancy between expressed and measured interests.* . . .
> 3. *When the pre-counseling information from testing, observation, or reports from others indicates a pressing social, emotional, or personal problem.* . . .
> 4. *Whenever it is necessary for the client to make decisions.* . . .
> 5. *Whenever it is necessary to deal with parents.*

Current practice. It is now fairly common practice for a counselor to begin all interviews nondirectively and continue in this manner until the nature of the problem is identified. If it then appears that the problem is primarily one of emotional conflict, the counselor may continue nondirectively. If it appears that the problem is primarily caused by lack of information, the counselor may help the client to get the needed information. If the problem involves both emotional conflict and a lack of information, the counselor may try to help the client with both aspects of his problem. Sometimes a counselor will begin nondirectively, discover that his client needs information, supply the information, then resume his nondirective role while the client considers his own reaction to the information provided. The skillful interviewer tries to be ever alert to any expression of the client's feelings or opinions, to encourage and to facilitate such expression. If the counselor supplies information, he tries to do so when the client is ready for it and at a rate which permits the client to accept it and to use it effectively. For more on this see Kilby [275] and Patterson [373].

We are still a long way from knowing what are the most effective techniques of vocational counseling. On the basis of present knowledge it appears that neither directive nor nondirective procedures are wholly satisfactory and that we must seek some way to extract the benefits of both without destroying the effectiveness of either. Some nondirective counselors have sought to do this by referring their clients to other counselors for the study of capacities and of occupations. Whether or not this is the best approach remains to be seen. For the moment, referral is of little help to the counselor who has no referral resources available. Nor does it help the client who is sent to a source of occupational information from which he returns with a sadly distorted perception of the realities of employment opportunities and requirements, which can easily happen if he is referred to the usual occupational library.

The desire of some counselors to work in the area of their own interests rather than to follow the needs of the client wherever they may lead will doubtless result in many referrals, even if the results are not good. The counselor who is not critical of his own motives can always blame the failure on the lack of good referral resources. This may solve his own problem if not the client's.

It is sad but true that much of the vocational counseling done today is done by persons whose major interest and training are not in vocational guidance. Teachers, psychologists, social workers, and placement officers all dabble in vocational guidance and refer their clients elsewhere for essential parts of the process or depend upon their own superficial knowledge of the areas in which they are not expert. Teachers and social workers refer students to psychometrists for testing. Psychologists refer clients to libraries for occupational information. It is a rare counselor indeed who feels that he should be competent himself to see his client through the whole process of vocational guidance, who has acquired the training to do so, and who is interested enough in vocational guidance to let the needs of the client rather than the counselor's interests determine the counselor's activities.

Although at the present time most counselors profess to be client-centered in attitude, Murphy's [347] revealing study of "Counselor Dominance" suggests that counselors are often more dominant than they think they are, and also more dominant than they think they should be.

The unattainable ideal. There are very few ideal counselors or ideal clients or ideal interviews, but goals are worth having, even if not immediately attainable, for we progress more when we have something to progress toward. The ideal counselor would possess consummate skill in nondirective, or client-centered, counseling, with which to help his client to explore his feelings about what he wants most from his occupation and about how he anticipates that he would feel if he were engaged in any proposed occupation. The ideal counselor would know all there is to know about physiological, psychological, and sociologic techniques for discovering and measuring what the client has or can get to offer to an employer or a customer. With this knowledge he would help his client to know himself better and so to anticipate his success and satisfaction in any contemplated occupation. The ideal counselor would know everything about every occupation. With this knowledge he would help his client to discover occupations in which he could find the things he seeks, including self-support and job satisfaction. The ideal counselor would be able to combine nondirective counseling with directive, without impairing the effectiveness of either.

Since these ideals are, to the best of our present knowledge, as unattainable as is perfection in any other field of human endeavor, the counselor who values his own mental health will not expect to achieve perfection. He will rather seek to do as well as he can and hope that his efforts will at least help his client to do better than he would do with no help. The counselor will also, if he is truly professional, evaluate his work in order to learn how well he is doing and try to find how to do his job better than any of us knows how to do it now.

REVIEW QUESTIONS

1. What are the potential values of client-centered counseling in vocational counseling?

2. What is the inescapable limitation of a completely nondirective approach to vocational counseling?

3. How do the purposes of client-centered counseling differ from the purposes of vocational counseling?

4. In what kinds of situations would *you* begin a vocational counseling interview nondirectively? In what kind would you not? Why?

5. Will anything in this chapter affect your future thoughts and actions? What? How?

10
The Use
of
Occupational
Information
in
Counseling—General
Aspects

Occupational information is used in counseling for the same basic purpose for which the counselor uses any other kind of information. The purpose is to help the client to clarify the goal that he wants to reach and to move in the direction in which he wants to go, so long as the goal and the means of attaining it are not injurious to others.

WHAT COUNSELING IS NOT

It is not the purpose of counseling to recruit clients for occupations in which they are needed or which the counselor considers desirable.

It is not the purpose of counseling to divert clients from occupations for which the counselor believes them to be unqualified or of which the counselor disapproves.

It is not the purpose of counseling to encourage the bright student to go to college and the slow student to go to work.

It is not the purpose of counseling to substitute the values, the ideals, the ambitions, or the judgment of the counselor for those of the client, no matter how strongly the counselor may feel that he knows best.

It is not the purpose of counseling to make decisions for the client or even to bring him to the point of decision himself.

THE PURPOSE OF COUNSELING

The purpose of counseling is to help the client to recognize his own needs and values, to see how these affect the goals that he seeks to reach, to identify these goals and to arrange them as well as he can in order of priority, to discover the possible courses of action which may bring him closer to the goals he seeks, and to anticipate as accurately as possible the results of each course of action in terms of his own goals.

What the client decides and when he decides it are his business. The only exception to this limitation on the counselor's functions occurs when a client clearly intends to do something that will seriously injure another person. In such a case, the counselor may step out of his role as counselor and assume the role of policeman. He should recognize that when he does this, he ceases to be a counselor, and he may find it difficult to resume the counselor's role.

Not everyone who seeks the counselor's help wants or needs to go through the full process of counseling as described above. Many want only a small amount of help on one small part of the total process. They may prefer to handle the remainder of the process alone or with the help of other persons. In such cases the counselor does what he can, within the limits of what he is asked to do. If he thinks he might be helpful in additional ways, he may offer his services, but he does not intrude where he is not wanted.

Odgers [366] has observed that

> . . . a sizeable chunk of our population really have no preference —and should not be frightened or made perplexed or anxious by having a counselor stress the importance of choice. If Shartle's analysis is true—and there are many jobs which require no particular aptitude patterns, competencies, or training—then we may be doing a disservice by pushing *some* folks through a choice process which implies that they must really know themselves inside out—and know many details about many jobs. . . . Many people are relatively easily satisfied—and can do an acceptable job and get satisfaction from any of various jobs—(machine operator, routeman, carpenters' helper, mailman, truck driver or what have you). I have in mind a young man (about 30) who in the last ten years has been reasonably well adjusted as an ad clipper in a newspaper clipping service, a bread route man, a drill press operator, and a traveling salesman of housetrailer equipment. He left the first job because of salary, the second because lack of seniority got him bumped to a rural route with long hours, the third because of a prolonged strike. He never worried about self-concept, aptitudes, fantasies or the fact that he quit school just before graduating. He was concerned about a living wage, decent working conditions and hours, employment security, etc. . . . His best counselor was the want-ad section of the paper. I'm not saying we shouldn't

help fellows like this—but we shouldn't get them to thinking they are (or have) problems. Maybe it's fortunate that most of this type never get to a counselor.

To avoid misunderstanding, the reader is urged to keep in mind that this chapter deals only with *the use of occupational information* in counseling. The omission of other aspects of the counseling process from this discussion is not intended to imply that they are any less important.

THE USE OF OCCUPATIONAL INFORMATION

Individual goals differ, counseling techniques differ with them, and so does the use of occupational information in counseling. The goal may be as simple as finding a temporary job for the Christmas holidays or as complex as trying to discover whether or not a change of employment will help to relieve a serious case of emotional disturbance.

Occupational information is useful in counseling when and to the extent that it can help the client to solve his problem. If the client is fully capable of solving his own problem as soon as he has the necessary information, counseling may consist only of providing the information or of telling the client where he can find it; some counselors would not even call this counseling. But when the client needs help to get the essential information, to appraise its accuracy, or to see how it relates to his problems, or when he needs help in considering his own reaction to the information, then there may be need for all the competence and skill and patience that the counselor may possess.

The first step in counseling is to discover, and if necessary to help the client to discover, what it is that he wants. Is he seeking release from a feeling of anxiety or fear or insecurity? Is he a reasonably happy and contented individual who wants help in finding a job? Is he lacking any conscious vocational preference but facing a decision which will tend to restrict his future range of vocational choice? Has he a tentative choice that he wishes to review to see if it makes sense? Is he using questions about occupations as a means of getting acquainted with the counselor before bringing up some other problem?

The counselor will probably begin nondirectively, encourage his client to talk as long and as freely as the client will or as the counselor's time permits, until both client and counselor believe that the nature of the problem has been pretty well identified and agreed upon. Thereafter, counseling procedure may vary with the nature of the problem. If the problem does not involve occupational choice, the remainder of this chapter will not apply.

The client with no preferences. One of the most common and most difficult problems is that of the client who has no vocational choice and who comes to the counselor with the attitude "You are the expert; you tell me what to do." The counselor, of course, cannot accept this responsibility for leading another person's life; he may even believe that this attitude of dependence requires some exploration in the counseling situation. If the counselor decides, immediately or later, that he should try to help the client to reach an occupational choice, the counselor may begin by helping the client to review all that his past experiences may reveal about his needs, values, ambitions, and anxieties; his abilities, limitations, likes, and dislikes. The counselor or the client may wish to use physical examinations or psychological tests or sociologic inquiries or other means to add to their information about the individual. Whether they decide that much or little time needs to be spent in studying the individual, sooner or later they reach the point at which possible occupations must be examined to see which appear to be the most reasonable choices.

It is at this point that counseling breaks down if the counselor is not well informed about occupations. Here the weak counselor pools his own ignorance of occupations with the ignorance of the client and from this shallow pool tries to help the client to select an appropriate occupation. Here the well-informed counselor may achieve some of his most brilliant and effortless successes by the simple process of suggesting acceptable occupations or jobs unknown to the client. How readily the counselor can do this will depend in part upon how modest or excessive are the demands of the client. If all that the client wants is a job that he can do, for which he needs no further preparation, and that offers average or better earnings, the counselor who has the results of follow-up studies and community surveys may be well equipped to make suggestions. If the client's goals are more complex, he and the counselor together may need to go beyond their present knowledge and to explore the possibilities in a wider variety of occupations. At this point, they may turn to more extensive lists of occupations such as those in the *Dictionary of Occupational Titles* [123].

Although the *D.O.T.* was prepared for the use of employment service interviewers in classifying applicants for work, it can be effectively used in counseling if the counselor will take the time to examine it in leisurely fashion, to read the introductory and explanatory sections, and to practice using it on the kinds of problems that he and his clients are trying to solve.

In using the D.O.T., the counselor and client may proceed together as follows:

1. Start with volume II.

2. Examine the list of three-digit occupational groups on pages 3 to 24. Copy the code numbers of all occupational groups in which the client thinks he might find an appropriate occupation.

3. Look up each selected code number in the more detailed list of occupations on pages 33 to 213. Note all the occupations listed under the three-digit code numbers selected. Copy the code number and title of each occupation which the client thinks might offer a possibility for him.

4. Examine the worker trait groups on pages 215 and 216. Copy the names and page references for all worker trait groups in which the client thinks he might find an appropriate occupation.

5. Look up each selected worker trait group on the designated page.

6. Under each worker trait group read the brief descriptions of work performed, worker requirements, clues for relating applicants and requirements, training and methods of entry, and related classifications. Examine the qualifications profile, in which the usual qualifications are indicated by letter and number symbols. Refer to pages 651 to 656 to find what the symbols mean.

7. Under each worker trait group, look on the next page for a list of occupations. Copy the code number and title of each occupation which the client thinks might offer a possibility for him.

8. Look up each selected occupational title in volume I of the D.O.T. Read the description of the occupation. Look up each related occupation to which the description refers. This will take time; the selection of anything as important as an occupation ought to take time.

9. Eliminate those occupations which the client is certain he should not enter.

10. Arrange the remaining occupations in order of the client's present interest.

11. Investigate each occupation on the list until the client finds one that suits him or exhausts the list. Follow the suggestions below in the section on "The Tentative Choice."

12. If the client can find nothing appropriate on the list, suggest that he compile a new list by browsing through the complete classified list of occupations on pages 33 to 213 of volume II. If the client is attracted to any major industry, he can find on pages 531 to 635 a list of occupational titles arranged by industry, followed by an industry index on pages 637 to 639. For example, here are listed more than 75 occupations in air transportation, more than 100 occupations in radio and television broadcasting, more than 100 occupations in banking, and more than 350 occupations in printing and publishing. Here also are seven pages of occupations likely to be found in any industry.

13. When the new list has been compiled, repeat steps 8 to 11 above.

The client with no discernible preferences faces a problem that can be both perplexing and frightening to him. It is perhaps because of the prevalence of this problem that vocational aptitude and interest tests have been so frequently used by counselors and have been so eagerly sought by a credulous public. Such tests are sometimes helpful in directing the attention of the client to occupations that he might otherwise overlook, among which he may find an occupation appropriate for him. They are among many tools that the skillful counselor uses in helping his client to discover possible occupations and to anticipate his probable success and satisfaction in them. Other personal characteristics, leisure-time activities, previous education, and work experience all should be used as possible clues to occupations that may be considered.

To be sure, all this may lead to no immediate occupational choice that will be definite and satisfying. The client may find something unsatisfactory about every occupation that the counselor can suggest; he may even reject the entire *Dictionary of Occupational Titles* and in effect say to the counselor, "See! You're not so hot. You can't find anything that I like, either." This can, does, and will happen.

The counselor can, of course, escape this experience of rejection by refusing to make any suggestions, and there may be counselors who believe that this procedure would be best for the client. Certainly it bears some resemblance to the client-centered counseling which has proved so effective in helping people with their emotional problems. Until we have more evidence to indicate what kind of occupational counseling is most effective, the author of this book inclines to the belief that there may still be some value in making available to the student the occupational information that he wants, even if he does not always use it to our satisfaction. Certainly every successful placement officer and vocational rehabilitation counselor can recall instances in which satisfying occupational choices and improved occupational adjustment have followed the presentation of appropriate occupational information.

If the counselor is convinced that the client is unable to face reality or to make a decision, the counselor may work on this obstacle as a counseling problem; if the counselor lacks the time or the competence to deal with it, he may attempt referral or simply accept the fact and direct his attention to persons he can help.

Meanwhile the counselor's efforts may not have been wasted. To the extent that he has helped his client to know more about himself and more about occupations, to that extent he may have prepared his client to make a wiser decision when he finally goes looking for a job and must accept or reject a job that is offered to him. As noted in Chapter 8, some persons never will make an occupational choice until this time. Others may just not be ready to make a decision now but will be later.

Because counselors seldom have time to explore all the potential occupations with each client, the course in occupations may serve to supplement counseling by making the client more aware of occupations that might meet his needs. When the client has discovered something that appeals to him, he may return for further counseling.

The tentative choice. Less baffling is the problem of the client who has one or more tentative occupational choices and who seeks help in reviewing or comparing them. In this case again, the counselor may begin by encouraging the client to talk until both counselor and client are agreed on what the problem is and on what the client wants to find in and through his occupation. Then, together, they may review the checklist in Chapter 3 and consider each item in turn to see what it may reveal about the wisdom of a contemplated choice.

Time may be saved by considering first those items most likely to lead to a quick rejection if the client is misinformed. Time may be saved, also, by going all the way through the checklist on the basis of the client's and counselor's present knowledge of the occupation and simply marking those items on which more information is needed before compiling the additional information. Somewhere along the way, the checklist may call attention to a consideration which will convince the client that this occupation is not for him. If so, the time that might have been spent in compiling additional information on this occupation can be saved for the study of some more promising possibility. Should this happen, it may be wise to verify the facts which led to the rejection before the decision is made final.

Should this first review of the checklist leave the occupation still open to consideration, the counselor and client may then proceed to look for the additional facts they need, following the suggestions in Chapter 4. When the facts have been assembled, the checklist may be reexamined in the light of the new information. This time the client may find it helpful to list, on one side of a sheet of paper, all the reasons why this occupation appears attractive and on the other side all the reasons against choosing it, then to select the five strongest reasons on each side of the sheet, weigh them, and see if they point to any clear conclusion. If they do not, decision may be delayed pending similar study of other occupations which may be similarly summarized and with which the first occupation may be compared. In this kind of intensive study of an occupation the counselor or client may find it convenient to use the "Outline for the Study of an Occupation" in Appendix G. Tryout experiences in summer vacations, in part-time jobs, or in a program of cooperative work-experience education may be especially helpful at this point.

Should this further study and comparison still not lead to a decision with which the student is content, additional occupations may be similarly reviewed and compared until a satisfactory occupation is discovered or the client becomes exhausted and gives up or the counselor has exhausted his time and resources or the time arrives at which the client must find immediate employment. In some cases no decision will be reached until the client is ready to go to work, at which time he must accept or reject any jobs which may be offered to him. When he finally finds and accepts one, his decision for the present has been made. It may not be a permanent decision. Like many successful persons, the worker may change jobs several times in the first few years. He may even become a "job hopper" who never settles down. The counselor cannot assume responsibility for preventing this; he can only offer all the help that his knowledge and skill enable him to give. Decisions are made or not made by the client. But to the extent that the counselor has helped his client to become better acquainted with himself and with occupations, there is hope that his client may make better choices than he would have made otherwise.

Occasionally the client's choice will be between two occupations, or two facets of an occupation, neither of which requires further preparation. For example, should a prospective teacher of science, who has met all certification requirements, look for a job in a high school or a junior college, in a small town or a large city? Should a high school senior, with stenographic skills, take a civil service examination or look for a job in private industry? In such cases, it may be desirable to look for jobs in both areas, see what jobs are available, and make the final choice between specific job offers. Such a choice is sometimes much easier to make and more satisfying when made.

Occasionally, tentative choices can be confirmed or canceled by a preliminary exploration of the job market. One widow had no marketable skills other than those of homemaker and hostess. She was attracted by an advertisement of a school which offered training for hotel hostesses. Her counselor suggested that she call on several hotel managers, ask them about the job market for persons like herself, and inquire about the manager's opinion of the school. One manager hired her on the spot.

Similar exploration of the employment market is often advisable *before* the client begins his professional preparation. The tendency of too many students, parents, teachers, and counselors is to assume that jobs will be available for students who complete their professional or vocational programs with satisfactory records. Too often the young graduate finds too late that he has prepared for an occupation in which he has little chance of finding a job.

The impossible choice. In some ways the most difficult of counseling problems is that of the client who comes for help on how to achieve the impossible—how to enter and succeed in an occupation in which he is almost certain not to find a job. Some clients are realistic enough to accept the facts when they have them and to revise their plans. The more pertinent and convincing the facts that the counselor has to present, the better is the probability of a realistic decision. But some persons, like those described in Chapter 8, will cling desperately to an unrealistic choice because they can see no other course of action that holds out any more hope of achieving certain satisfactions which they feel they must have.

In some cases of this kind there is nothing to do but to let the person try and fail and then to help him to make a better second choice when he is ready to do so. In other cases, a well-informed, ingenious, and persistent counselor can find out what are the basic satisfactions the individual is seeking in his occupation and can find substitute occupations which will offer his client even more attractive prospects of getting what he wants.

It is in such cases that the counselor's knowledge of occupations within occupations may be invaluable. The average client knows so little about occupations that his announced choice may be much less specific than it appears to be. As the counselor helps the client to learn more about the broad area of his preference, the client may discover an occupation which he can enter and which will please him as much as the choice he first announced. Volume II of the *Dictionary of Occupational Titles* may be helpful in the search for such a related occupation.

Another troublesome problem for counselors is the parent who insists that his child prepare for an occupation which the child and the counselor agree to be inappropriate. The parent may refuse to discuss the wisdom of his choice but be eager to help his child to learn more about the occupation; in this process, the parent may discover what the counselor wanted to tell him, or he may find an acceptable and more appropriate related occupation. This approach will not always work, but it is sometimes worth trying when every other approach has failed.

The modest counselor, of course, will not be hasty about deciding that his client cannot get and hold a job in his chosen occupation. There is at least one case on record of a student who graduated at the head of his class in one of our best engineering colleges who would never have been admitted to most schools of engineering. More than one slow student has acquired a professional degree by spreading his college work over a longer period of time and has subsequently done a creditable job in his field.

Changing occupations. The problem of changing jobs in the hope of finding more satisfaction, higher earnings, or better opportunities for advancement is essentially similar to the problem of the client who has two tentative choices, and the checklist in Chapter 3 may be used to compare the present and prospective jobs.

Sometimes a person who has been less successful than he had expected contemplates a change of occupation in the hope that he may do better. When the person is better qualified for a different occupation or seems likely to find more satisfaction in the work itself, such a change may be desirable. There are cases, however, in which a person really likes his work, is well qualified for it, is even reluctant to leave it, but feels that perhaps he should change because someone has told him there is more money in another field or because his friends or relatives are making more money in other occupations. In such cases it is sometimes helpful to raise the question "If this new job offered you exactly the same salary and the same opportunities for advancement as your present job, would you change jobs?" If the answer is no, then the most careful scrutiny of the proposed occupation is indicated, in order to see if it really does offer anything better than the client's present field of work. Also helpful in discussing proposed changes may be the question "Where do you hope to be ten years from now?" The answer to this question often reveals goals not indicated in previous conversation.

When a person is forced to change occupations because his own has become obsolete or for some other compelling reason, a closely related occupation may offer him a better prospect of prompt employment with less sacrifice in earnings than would a change to a wholly new occupation. Related occupations may be discovered by following the directions in the *Dictionary of Occupational Titles*, volume II.

For more on changing jobs see Lowen [311]. Although the jacket blurb on this book is extravagant, the book itself contains some good, blunt advice from the experienced owner of an employment agency, including when *not* to change jobs.

Recruiting workers for shortage fields. As this book goes to press, there is increasing pressure on counselors to encourage students to enter occupations in which a shortage of workers is regarded as a threat to the welfare of the nation. There is an acute shortage of teachers, so educational associations and teachers colleges entreat all teachers and counselors to urge their best students to consider teaching as a career. There is a shortage of engineers, mathematicians, and scientists, so the patriotic motives of the counselor are enlisted to recruit more students for these areas in preparation for World War III.

The history of occupational choice and distribution clearly reveals that when an acute shortage of workers occurs, certain events follow. Wages and salaries increase. The shortage and the increased incomes are widely publicized. Large numbers of new workers move into the shortage fields or into preparation for them. The shortage is overcompensated, and a surplus develops. Sometimes these events occur in rapid succession, as when huge numbers of workers moved into munitions factories in the early days of World War II. Sometimes it takes years for the supply to catch up with the demand, but it always does unless some artificial obstacle is imposed. By frequently raising the standards for medical education, the medical profession has restricted the number and size of medical schools and the number of new competitors who could enter the field. Labor unions achieve the same result by restricting admissions to the union. Where there is no such restriction and the supply does not increase, the demand is less acute than it appears to be. Thus there is a widely publicized shortage of workers in the subprofessional health occupations, but the demand is not yet great enough to raise the earnings of these workers above the earnings of workers in more popular occupations for which the same workers can qualify.

How should the counselor respond to requests for aid in recruiting workers for shortage fields? If the counselor does everything that he is asked to do, he will soon find that he is successfully recruiting workers who will, in his judgment, be neither successful nor satisfied in the jobs to which he has enticed them. Is this his function? If not, should he do selective recruiting and lure only those who seem to have appropriate qualifications? This procedure would certainly be better than indiscriminate recruiting. But suppose the client would be even more successful and happy in some other field? Or suppose he is equally qualified for two fields which are both short of workers? Should the counselor encourage the client to go where he thinks he will be most successful and best satisfied or where the recruiting officers are busiest at the moment?

To the author of this book there can be only one acceptable answer to these questions. The counselor is not a recruiting officer, and he should never permit himself to become one. Employers, training institutions, and professional associations can be depended upon to publicize any genuine shortage and to urge all qualified candidates to apply. The nation will survive without the counselor's adding his influence. Under the seductive blandishments of the recruiters, the client needs one competent person whom he can trust to put the client's interest first and to help him to think clearly about what *he* wants to do. The counselor who permits any other interest to creep into his activities has ceased to be a counselor.

The counselor need not become belligerent on this point. He can respect the convictions, the motives, and the integrity of sincere recruiters. He can help them to make accessible to his clients the factual information about supply and demand which his clients need in order to appraise their own prospects of employment. He can accept the literature which is offered and even distribute some of it. He can invite recruiting officers to answer questions in group conferences *which the counselor will attend.* But every time the counselor does one of these things, he assumes an obligation to find and to verify and to present to his students or clients an equal amount of pertinent data regarding the disadvantages of doing what the recruiter has proposed. Such data may include distasteful aspects of the work, earnings in the lower half of the distribution, hazards, unfavorable working conditions, and the possibility that by the time the client has completed his training, the demand for workers may have been met.

So long as the United States remains a democracy, so long as we value the welfare and the freedom of the individual above the planning functions of the state, the counselor must do his counseling in terms of the needs and values of his client. The needs of society function in counseling only to the extent that the client values them and wishes to consider them in reaching his own decision. The counselor who intentionally permits his own values or the values of a professional group or of a government agency to take precedence over the values of his client has not only done his client a disservice, he has also undermined the foundation of freedom—the right of the individual to the pursuit of happiness as *he* chooses to pursue it.

Military occupations. Military service is an occupation. In vocational counseling it should be treated as such. There are certain obvious differences between military and civilian careers. The person who is eligible to be drafted has lost much of his freedom of choice, unless he is prepared to suffer certain unpleasant consequences. The soldier may be called upon to risk his life. He is given a certain limited license to inflict pain and death in ways that would be considered illegal or immoral without the license. Nevertheless, the differences between military and civilian occupations are not greater than the differences between various civilian occupations, and they do not require different treatment by the counselor. Policemen also have a limited license to inflict pain and death. Firemen also risk their lives. Family pressure can restrict freedom of occupational choice as effectively as legal pressure.

It is the responsibility of the counselor to make available to his clients the same kind of information about military occupations that he provides about civilian occupations, and in much the same ways. The head of enlisted classification in the United States Navy [92] has said in print that ". . . it is not the place of civilian counselors to augment the recruiting forces of the Armed Services." Nor is it the function of the counselor to dissuade the client who proposes to enlist. Neither patriotism nor pacifism justifies the counselor in substituting his values for the client's values. Nor can the counselor escape his responsibility for helping his client to get *all* the pertinent facts before the client decides what to do. Ask any group of veterans how their own military experience compared with the glamorous recruiting literature of the military services, and the question is usually answered by laughter.

Current practice in counseling on military occupations leaves much to be desired, because so much of it is based upon information received from, or presented by, recruiting officers, who can hardly be considered unbiased sources of information. There appears to be a feeling among some counselors that military service is now inescapable and that any discussion of resistance to it may be unpatriotic. But there are still more than 100,000 Quakers in the United States, plus a substantial number of Catholics, Jews, and other Protestants, who believe that war is morally wrong and who will not participate in it under any circumstances.

In the presentation of information about military occupations, the existence of such conscientious objectors to war is generally ignored. If an idealistic client has some doubts about war as a means of resolving conflicts, he is likely to be reminded of his patriotic duty. But the military services do not want conscientious objectors, and the law provides alternate service opportunities for them.

The counselor who really believes that he should present to his clients *all* the opportunities that are available to them should at least inform himself and his clients about the provisions which the Congress has made for conscientious objectors. These provisions are *not* restricted to members of the historic peace churches. Briefly, the law provides that any person who is conscientiously opposed to war, by reason of religious training and belief, and who can convince his draft board of his sincerity, may be assigned to certain designated forms of civilian service in lieu of military service. The counselor may obtain more detailed information about these provisions from, or he may refer his client for information to, the Central Committee for Conscientious Objectors, 2006 Walnut Street, Philadelphia, 3, Pa., and to the National Service Board for Religious Objectors, 15 St. and New York Ave., N.W., Washington, D.C.

Many religious denominations offer help to their own members who are conscientious objectors. Information about the beliefs of conscientious objectors can be obtained from the Fellowship of Reconciliation, Box 271, Nyack, N.Y., and from the national headquarters of several religious denominations.

Recruiting officers and recruiting literature are available to any counselor on request. They can be useful in providing factual information about the requirements of the various services. Since they are employed to encourage the enlistment of desirable prospects, they cannot be expected to say very much about the disadvantages of the service they represent. Among the better methods of acquainting students with military occupations are follow-up studies of alumni now in military or alternate service, group conferences with servicemen and veterans, including those who have chosen alternate service, and tours of military installations and of veterans' hospitals. In collecting or presenting information about civilian occupations, most counselors agree that both employers and employees should be used; this principle applies with equal force to military occupations.

Occupational information in psychotherapy. Reference was made in Chapter 7 to the relationship between emotional and vocational maladjustment and to the possibility that either might cause the other. When the psychotherapist suspects that an inappropriate occupation is either causing or aggravating an emotional disturbance, he may wish to review his patient's occupational choice and perhaps help him to find a more congenial field of work. Even though the change may not solve the whole problem, it may bring temporary relief that will facilitate therapy.

The author is indebted to one of his former students for the report of a client who had an excessive fear of disease and an aversion to filth and who found intolerable his work as a clinical laboratory technician, in which he was called upon to examine specimens from persons who were seriously ill. Before undertaking therapy for the fears, the counselor helped his client to choose a new occupation and to find a new job as a polisher of newly made dentures, in which activity his aversion to all blemishes became a vocational asset and his work brought recurring satisfaction.

The psychotherapist who wishes to become a vocational counselor to his patient or the counselor who is called in as a consultant to a therapist may find some help in the following suggestions:

Explore as thoroughly as possible the patient's feelings about his job, and try to determine whether the aversion is to some essential and inescapable part of the occupation itself or to some characteristic of the present job which might not be present in another job in the same occupation. Sometimes a person who is upset will be so anxious to get away from the frustrating situation that he will be inclined to change his occupation, when all that he really need do is to change his job. An unnecessary change of occupation may be undesirable, because it may involve discarding valuable and marketable experience and starting over again at a beginner's salary. The resultant financial strain may add new aggravations to the emotional problem. An occupation is only a name for a group of jobs which have many things in common. Even in so well-defined an occupation as that of the registered nurse, there is great variety of activity, environment, supervision, and responsibility, which depend in part upon whether the nurse works in a home, a hospital, a school, or an industry. In each of these locales there is great variety in jobs from one employer to another. Sometimes the aversion to a job is caused by tyrannical supervision or intolerable working conditions or hours of work or distance from home or some other characteristic of the particular position, which could be remedied simply by finding a more acceptable job in the same occupation.

If it appears that no change of this kind will achieve the desired result and that a change of occupation might, then the counselor and his client may examine lists of occupations, select those which seem to have possibilities, and review them as suggested above in the section on "The Tentative Choice." Obviously, in their review, they will pay especial attention to the things which have most disturbed the client in his last job. In so doing, there is some danger that equally irritating but different characteristics of the new job may be overlooked. It is, consequently, imperative that the review of occupations be preceded or accompanied by a thorough examination of the client's needs and values, likes and dislikes, abilities, limitations, and anxieties. The review should include the most meticulous scrutiny of all the duties that may be involved in any contemplated occupation, of the kinds of surroundings in which they are performed, and of the client's feeling about every aspect of the occupation. Failure to examine the occupation in sufficient detail may result in a new choice that will be no better than the old occupation, and this unhappy result may lead, in turn, to the erroneous conclusion that no change of occupation would be helpful.

THE BASIC PROBLEM

Stated in the simplest possible terms, the basic problem in all vocational counseling is to help the client to find out what he hopes to get from his job, what he has to offer in exchange for what he hopes to get, and in what occupations he will have the best chance of getting what he wants.

Finding out what the client most wants from his job is sometimes the most difficult task of all, because consciously even he may not know. He may have a strong urge to be conspicuous or to dominate, or he may seek other satisfactions which he has been told are socially unacceptable and which he cannot admit either to himself or to his counselor. But the desire may nevertheless be there, and it may be strong enough to cause the rejection of a choice that would otherwise be logical. Faced with apparently illogical rejections of logical choices, the counselor will do well to look for goals not yet revealed.

Because of the difficulty, sometimes perhaps the impossibility, of bringing all emotional needs and desires to the conscious intellectual level, the client will sometimes make what is for him a wise choice, although it may appear unwise to everyone, including himself. Strong feelings are sometimes a better guide to action than strong intellects.

To the beginning counselor a final word of reassurance may be welcome. A great deal has been written about counseling, but not much is really known about it, despite the impressive technical language in the literature. Basically, a counselor in any organization is just a person who has been given a little extra time so that he may try to do better what the other members of the staff have always tried to do as well as they could. A counselor does not have to be omniscient in order to be useful. Anything that he can do better than the average professional worker in his organization may represent an improvement in service to the client. At the very least, the counselor can listen longer than his colleagues. He can take more time and more care in trying to find out what the client needs and wants. He can spend more time in trying to meet the client's needs. And he can devote more time to making himself more competent to do this job.

The counselor will not always be sure what will best serve the client's needs. As long as the counselor lives, he will face this kind of uncertainty, no matter how competent he becomes. At times he will feel as bewildered as the client. At such times, it may help him to remember that the function of the counselor is not to solve the client's problem for him. It is to make available to the client all the help that the counselor can provide. If with this help the client still cannot solve his problem, the failure is not necessarily the fault of the counselor or of the client either. Man's knowledge of how to solve human problems is still incomplete. It is possible that there may be problems which cannot be solved. The justification of the counselor's existence is found, not in his ability to solve all problems or to help all people, but in his ability to give enough help to enough people to be worth what he costs.

REVIEW QUESTIONS

1. Do you agree or disagree with the author's statement of what the purpose of counseling is and is not? Why?

2. How would you use occupational information in counseling the client who has no occupational preferences, the client who has a tentative choice, the client whose choice is unrealistic, the client who is thinking of changing his job?

3. Where can you find a list of occupations arranged by industry?

4. Were you surprised to learn how many different occupations there are in banking, in printing and publishing? Does this affect your opinion of counselors who talk with clients about banking as if it were one occupation?

5. For what different purposes can you use the different volumes of the D.O.T. in counseling?

6. When everyone agrees that too many or too few persons are preparing for an important occupation, what do you think should be done about it? Why? How?

7. What would you do if your boss asked you to put on a campaign to recruit more students for science and mathematics courses?

8. A psychiatrist asks you to help him as a consultant in his work with a patient who wants to change his job. What suggestions will you offer to the psychiatrist?

9. Do you agree that strong feelings may sometimes be a better guide to action than strong intellects? Why? Why not?

10. Where does the discouraged counselor find the justification for his existence?

11. How can you use what you have learned from this chapter?

11
The Use
of
Occupational
Information
in
Counseling—Answering
Questions

One of the most common uses of occupational information in counseling is to answer questions raised by clients. Many persons who come to counselors want nothing more than accurate factual information, on the basis of which they intend to make their own decisions without further help. Others want some interpretation of the facts in relation to their own objectives. Where to get the facts has already been discussed in Chapter 4. The significance of these facts in occupational choice and some of the ways in which they may affect the job satisfaction of the client are discussed in the following pages.

By this time the reader may be a bit surprised at the repetition of section heads in Chapters 3, 4, and 11. The three chapters could have been combined; for some purposes combination would be desirable. But when the reader wishes to use these chapters for later reference, he may find it more convenient to have them separated. The author suggests that the beginner in counseling underscore those parts of Chapter 11 which are new to him and which he wishes to remember and that he review this chapter from time to time until these parts are permanently incorporated in his professional resources. The author suggests that Chapter 3 be used as a checklist with clients in those interviews in which the client seeks help in examining prospective occupations and that Chapter 4 be used mainly for reference when additional information is needed. Chapters 4 and 11 should not be used as interview guides, because they do not include all the specifics listed in Chapter 3.

Employment prospects. At certain times and in certain occupations, the demand for workers is so much greater than the supply that even substandard applicants have excellent prospects of employment. This was true of the demand for social workers in the early days of the Roosevelt-Hopkins relief program of the 1930s, for machinists and machine operators in the early 1940s, for stenographers and elementary school teachers in the early 1950s, for engineers in the early 1960s.

If a person is looking for temporary employment, he may find a job more readily and he may make more money in one of these shortage areas than in an occupation for which he is better qualified, but if he seeks a permanent job, he may be wiser to choose a field in which he will be able to compete when the demand returns to normal or when the supply approaches and perhaps exceeds the demand. If a person is well qualified for a shortage area, the excessive demand for workers may enable him to advance more rapidly than he could in another field.

Conversely, an excessive supply of applicants may well discourage the average or substandard candidate but need not force the superior applicant to look elsewhere. Even in a crowded occupation there may be room for the person whose qualifications place him in the top 1 or 2 percent. The person who chooses the overcrowded field should, however, have more than youthful optimism to support his judgment of his own superiority.

Shortages of workers may occur because the occupation is poorly paid. Comparison of earnings in occupations which require the same level of training sometimes reveals surprising differences.

For the person whose entrance to the occupation will be delayed by some years of preparation, current supply and demand may be less important than the forecast of employment prospects for the time when he expects to enter the labor market. For more on this see Chapter 4.

Long-range growth prospects in an occupation or industry, of course, mean greater opportunities for continuous employment, advancement, and increasing income. How much industries may differ in their rate of growth is indicated by the following figures on the increases and decreases in the number of employees in different fields from 1947 to 1964:

	Percent
Bituminous coal mining	−68
Railroads	−51
Meat products	+14
Finance, insurance, and real estate	+69
State and local government	+102

There is currently much concern about the effect of automation in displacing workers. Technological improvement often causes employment to decline in some occupations and concurrently to increase in others. The automobile industry, for example, helped to reduce the employment of blacksmiths by about 200,000, while it created jobs for 750,000 automobile mechanics [524].

The more the counselor can learn about the probable future growth or decline of the major industries and occupations in his employment market, the more helpful he can be to the persons he serves.

Nature of the work. Popular impressions of the work done in many occupations are so erroneous that this item warrants the most diligent and exhaustive investigation. Often the client's consideration of an occupation will terminate as soon as he gets the full picture of the work that it involves and of the amount of time devoted to different tasks.

The reader is invited to pause at this point and ask himself how many things he has to do in his job that he did not anticipate when he took it. There are few if any jobs in which a person never has to do anything that he dislikes, but the amount of time that one will spend in distasteful activities can be affected considerably by the choice of an occupation. One of the best investments the counselor can make of his time is in learning exactly what people do in the occupations that interest his clients and how much of their time they spend in doing it.

Work environment. To a Steinmetz or an Edison, engrossed in his work, the surroundings in which he works may be negligible. To others environment is far more important. Excessive heat, cold, humidity, dust, dirt, noise, or offensive odors are in themselves sufficient reasons for some persons to leave a job or to discard an occupation from further consideration, while an air-conditioned office, attractively furnished, in a good neighborhood for lunch-hour shopping may tip the scales in favor of one job over another. The fact that some of these considerations are unimportant in the counselor's scale of values, if they are, does not mean that they are unimportant to his clients. And the counselor who takes his class in occupations to visit a bakery, a laundry, a foundry, a forge, a meat-packing plant, a fertilizer factory, a cement plant, and a boiler shop may change some of his own ideas about the importance of environment.

If there is anything unusually attractive or repulsive or hazardous about the work environment, this fact should be noted and discussed in counseling and in terms of the client's values. At least one person has said he wanted "a greasy job." One group of garbage collectors was once reported to have a deficient sense of smell. Before any occupational choice is considered final, the client should visit several places in which the work is done, so that he may see, hear, feel, and smell the surroundings. Visiting several places is desirable, because the environment may vary from one company to another.

To a young woman who is looking for a husband, the presence of eligible males may be a major consideration. Other persons prefer to work alone. One taxi driver quit his job three times, but he returned to it each time in order to escape the close supervision that he encountered in other jobs.

Not the least important part of the environment is the kind of people with whom the client will work if he chooses this occupation. Are they people that he will understand and like, with whom he can and will establish cordial working relationships? Or are there substantial differences in background or in values that will be a barrier to comfortable human relations on the job? Will the client find in this occupation the kinds of people with whom he wants to spend the largest part of his life? Because in many jobs human relationships are so important, this factor may have a significant bearing upon success as well as satisfaction.

Some of the best information on the social climate in different occupations is found not in the books and pamphlets prepared for counselors and their clients, but in the reports of occupational sociologists. The following excerpts are from the *Abstracts of Sociological Literature on Occupations* [1]:

> A set of unofficial . . . work rules exists among the letter carriers, many of which are in direct violation of the official regulations. . . .
> The official job description is devised so that it will take the carrier exactly eight hours to sort and deliver the mail. . . . Usually, however, he alters the order in which he is supposed to deliver the mail; he may walk criss-cross, skip certain loops in his walk, make frequent stops at the relay box, cut across lawns, or devise other short cuts. He may also violate the official rules by holding over some of the mail for the next day's delivery in order to "even out" the differences in the amount of mail on the various days. The carrier then may spend the left-over time in a number of ways: he may go home and return to the station at the officially prescribed time; he may go shopping; he may join fellow carriers at a nearby tavern; he may sit in his car and read; or he may extend his lunch period beyond the official 30 minutes. . . .
> The carrier is not to return early too frequently. If he does, the supervisor will interpret the situation as one which indicates that the route is too short.

The norms also prescribe that the regular summer substitute for a given route should always return somewhat later than the prescribed time. Admonitions such as "Don't kill the route" are given to the substitute to emphasize the unofficial role expectations. If the substitute should violate this important norm, the group will penalize him by withholding needed information or deliberately interfering with the rule breaker's activity. For instance, when a substitute who is known to deviate from the unofficial norms is assigned a new route and asks about details of the route, he will be told that he can find all he needs to know in the Order Book. His questions about particular hazards on the route—such as vicious dogs—will remain unanswered. At times, the deviant may find that labels on the mail bundles for his route have been deliberately mixed up. . . .

The mass-mortuary . . . is characterized by impersonality. . . . "Time, not rapport, becomes the essence." . . .

The mass-mortuary often draws its clientele by mass advertising from the large trade area extending beyond a single community. . . .

The establishment's relationship to the survivors is analogous to the buyer-seller type of contractual relationship. . . .

In contrast to the mass-mortuary, "the local funeral home operates on the premise that the clientele . . . should receive personal, . . . sympathetic understanding, in a social, or status-connected relationship to the funeral director." . . .

"The local funeral home is organized so that the clientele can always feel certain they will have their funeral services handled by THE funeral director, whom they know personally." . . .

"If you don't have the kind of personality that will permit you to give comfort and sincere sympathy to the people, you just don't stay in the game," remarked one funeral director. . . .

The business goal of the local funeral home is defined according to community attitudes. These attitudes usually permit profitable operations so that the funeral director can live a comfortable, middle-class, quasi-professional existence. "Should it appear . . . that the funeral director is 'profiteering in sorrow,' community sanctions in the form of withdrawal of trade and 'talk' will either force his operations into an approved form, or eventually he will be out of business."

In many instances, the local funeral home performs services at a loss; in other instances, it may make up the differences. There may be charity cases for which the funeral director never sends the bill. In contrast, mass-mortuary practices approve the use of collection agencies to collect from survivors—a practice which not only collects the debt but includes, as well, interest on the unpaid balance.

Fifty-one per cent of the ministers and forty-one per cent of the priests believed the funeral director exploited or took advantage of a family's grief.

For the most part, clergymen did not meet with funeral directors socially, even though there was continuous contact throughout the years, and even though there was associational contact. This absence of social contact suggested that the clergy do not perceive of funeral directors as status equals.

Qualifications. See Chapter 4 on qualifications, physical demands, aptitudes, interests, legal requirements, discrimination, apprenticeship, capital.

In appraising aptitude for any occupation, beginning counselors are sometimes disturbingly naïve. So, too, are some experienced counselors and some psychologists. The beginner may assume that a test which is called a test of mechanical aptitude must be a test of mechanical aptitude. Actually it may be only a test which its author and publisher hope will measure mechanical aptitude. The trained counselor and psychologist have learned to look for coefficients of validity as evidence of the degree to which a test does measure what it purports to measure, but too frequently they accept a low coefficient as evidence of acceptable validity, or they assume that a high coefficient, obtained against criteria of success in one occupation in one company, justifies the use of the test to measure aptitude for related jobs in the same company or for similar jobs in other companies.

Actually, very few tests have been adequately validated for use in individual vocational guidance, and those which have been seldom purport to measure even half of whatever determines success in the occupation. This is not a book on aptitude testing, and there is not room here for adequate explanation and illustrations, but every counselor who expects to use the results of aptitude tests should scrupulously examine the evidence of the validity of his tests for the purpose for which he proposes to use them and be guided accordingly. For more on this see Super and Crites [470].

The counselor should also look for information about critical scores for employment and for success in the occupation and if possible in the company his client is considering. Regrettably, such scores are seldom available, and without them test interpretation for vocational guidance is dubious at best.

This does not mean that aptitude tests should not be used in vocational guidance. They should be used, and the counselor who uses them should know enough about the tests and enough about occupations to help his client to interpret the results for what they are worth, and no more.

Unions. Although the Taft-Hartley Act prohibited the closed shop in companies under Federal control, the closed shop can still be found in many places that are not subject to Federal regulation. If the closed shop predominates in the community in which the client wants to work and if he would rather change his occupation than change his home, the ability of the client to gain admission to the union may be the most important consideration of all. Many unions restrict the admission of new members, and some admit only the relatives of union members. It is imperative that the counselor be adequately informed about union entrance requirements in his community, that his information be up to date, and that this aspect of occupational choice be fully discussed with the client in order to determine how it may affect his ability to get a job.

The client who is willing to change his home can find several states in which the closed shop is illegal. In rural areas and in small towns there are often no unions.

Discrimination. Although one may find little discrimination in one occupation and much in another, there are few, if any, occupations which have not been successfully entered by at least a few members of every minority. Thus there are successful Negro architects who serve wealthy white clients and Negro school administrators who supervise white teachers. A single large company may have employment policies which vary from one plant or department to another.

Many large corporations recently have undertaken active recruiting of Negro college graduates. The recruiting has not been so extensive as to guarantee a job for every Negro senior, but it has proceeded far enough to produce a book on *How to Recruit Minority Group College Graduates* [52] in which Calvert warns employers that the demand for outstanding students already exceeds the supply.

Counselors, therefore, should not be too ready to discourage the competent young person who wishes to compete in a field where he will be subject even to widespread discrimination. It is the counselor's responsibility to help his client to get as much accurate information as possible about the nature and the extent of the discrimination that the client will probably encounter; it is not the responsibility of the counselor to decide how the client should act in the light of this information. Courageous persons who take long chances and succeed help to lower the barriers of discrimination for those who will come later, but the individual should know the chance he is taking when he takes it and be prepared to face the risks. He should not be shoved into a situation that he would rather avoid just because his counselor wants vicariously to fight discrimination, nor should the client be discouraged from taking risks that he recognizes just because his counselor is cautious. As a private citizen, the counselor is, of course, free to follow his own conscience; he may even have a civic obligation to work toward anything that he believes will improve the community, but he must not substitute his own values for those of his client in the counseling situation.

The harsh facts of discrimination are threatening enough to scare anyone who has to face them. In the slum areas of some cities, where the population was mainly Negro, Conant [98] found that 60 to 70 percent of the young men between the ages of sixteen and twenty-one were out of school and unemployed.

Weaver [505] suggested that

> In addition to finding out whether there are any employment opportunities for him at all in the field of his choice, a minority youth will need to look for answers to these questions: If there is discrimination, is it national, or is it confined to a particular locale? If minority workers are hired in this field, what is the degree of acceptance by co-workers on the job? What is the degree of acceptance by unions or professional organizations in the field? Once he is hired, can he expect reasonable equality of working conditions and opportunities for advancement? Is there a pay differential? What has been the past history in the field with reference to dismissal policy: Are the minority workers the first to go, regardless of merit and length of service?

Preparation. School counselors, who should be experts on preparation, make some of their worst mistakes in this area. Because we people in school business are so convinced of the value of education, we tend to confuse that which is desirable and that which is essential. Perhaps without meaning to do so, we place undue emphasis on preparation that may be desirable but is not indispensable. Thus we discourage clients from considering certain occupations unless they can get all the preparation that we recommend. One college student gave up his consideration of the ministry when told he would have to study Greek and Hebrew, but one of his friends became a lay preacher without ever going to college at all. Latin is no longer required or even recommended by most medical schools. It is imperative that counselors know and explain to their clients the difference between essential and desirable preparation and the many ways in which both kinds of preparation can be obtained through scholarships, work-study programs, apprenticeship, night school, on-the-job training, etc.

Where legal requirements must be met, the counselor has an obligation to see that the schools which his client considers entering have been approved and accepted by the legal board which issues the licenses. The author recalls two students who had completed a full year of graduate study in a school that was not accredited and were forced to repeat the same courses in an accredited university before they could be certified for public school counseling. Another student had two years of post-high-school study at an institute which was not accredited; both years of work had to be repeated before he could get his degree from an accredited university.

Employers' standards may be either higher or lower than licensing requirements, depending on the state of the labor market. In depression periods, much more than the minimum legal training may be needed to get a job. When workers are scarce, emergency certificates may be issued to applicants who do not meet the legal standards.

Advancement. Clients differ greatly in the value which they place on advancement. Some will risk everything for it. Others dislike responsibility and will refuse a promotion that is offered to them. Some prefer an assured though moderate advancement in earnings and status to the more spectacular advancement which they might achieve by taking more risks.

The cautious ones can often find what they seek in very large organizations, where promotion from within is company policy, where union contracts provide for increased earnings and privileges as one acquires seniority, and where there frequently may be found a bureaucracy not unlike that in the civil service and in public education. For an enlightening discussion of this topic see Caplow [58]. The risk takers are more likely to find their opportunities in small companies which are growing rapidly, in new industries, and in the volatile industries which are discussed later in this chapter. Caplow notes that individual earnings in medium-sized businesses are often larger than in huge corporations and that persons who have reached the top managerial level in a small business sometimes move successfully from one type of business to another at the top level.

The most rapid upward movement is more likely to be found where success depends upon the personal characteristics of the worker rather than upon his training and experience. Actors, athletes, authors, and salesmen, if they are good enough to reach the top, can often do so in much less time than actuaries, metallurgists, pharmacists, and railway conductors. The worker who goes into business for himself, whether as a barber, printer, funeral director, or real estate broker, can increase his earnings as rapidly as his own abilities and taxes will permit. He can also lose his shirt.

Pitt and Smith [378] have called attention to one aspect of advancement that is seldom mentioned in the literature on occupations:

> For example, great merchandising organizations such as Procter and Gamble require a number of chemists. But the major emphasis in such an organization is on sales and promotion. The young man who chooses chemistry as a career should realize that in such organizations the top executive jobs are almost invariably filled from the sales, merchandising, and advertising departments. . . . However, should a young man's interests include both chemistry and a desire for administrative responsibility, he had best look for employment in some of the basic chemical companies, such as du Pont or Olin-Mathieson, where the working chemist can aspire, with greater possibility of success, to a top administrative post.

Pitt and Smith noted how the same principle applies in other industries to engineers, purchasing agents, psychologists, etc.

In general, opportunities for advancement tend to be overemphasized in choosing an occupation. Our American culture places such a high value on financial success and we talk so much in school about our land of opportunity that we tend to leave students with the expectation that all, or nearly all, of them will advance to positions of prestige, influence, and affluence. Actually, most of them will remain at, or near, the level at which they get their first jobs. Salary schedules may provide modest increases in earnings as the years go by, but regardless of the economic system, one can have only a limited number of corporation presidents or cabinet ministers or commissars.

We might do our clients a better service if we concerned ourselves less with advancement and concentrated our efforts on increasing the probability that our clients would choose occupations in which they would be reasonably effective and reasonably happy in the entry job. Superior performance in the first job offers about as good a prospect of advancement as one may reasonably expect. Of course, if two occupations are equally attractive otherwise and one is growing while the other declines, there is no need to choose the poorer prospect.

Earnings. Grube [194] asked high school students to estimate the weekly earnings of beginning workers in several occupations. The estimates for some of the occupations were: laboratory assistant $30 to $200, plumber $25 to $220, teacher $40 to $200, typist $10 to $100.

Not infrequently the client's expectation of his own earning power is based upon what he has read or heard about the exceptionally high earnings of a few individuals. Unless he can get and accept a more realistic view of his prospects, he may persist in choosing an occupation for which he is poorly equipped or in which earnings are actually very low just because this is the occupation in which the impressively high earnings of a few persons were reported to him. By presenting the best reports on the entire range of earnings in the occupation and especially on the median earnings and on the earnings of the middle 50 percent, the counselor can help correct such false impressions.

One of the best ways in which to help students to get a realistic appraisal of their probable earning power is to have them conduct a follow-up study through their course in occupations and thus to see for themselves how much the former students of their own school are now making. Some of the author's interviews with prospective graduate students who thought of leaving well-paid business jobs in order to become school counselors have terminated as soon as earnings figures from follow-up studies were produced. Accurate figures on median earnings may also help the client when he is offered a job and must decide to take it or wait for something better.

In some occupations, earnings are higher in some parts of the country than in others. Teachers, for example, are paid much more in certain large cities and wealthy suburbs than in less affluent communities. It is sometimes important to inquire into local salaries in the territory in which the client wishes to work. One of the author's students, who is a New York City teacher, has wanted for several years to live and work in the South but has not yet found a job that pays anywhere near his present salary.

Sometimes earning prospects can be enhanced by a simple shift from one branch of an occupation to another. At times, for example, certain types of office-machine operators have earned much more than typists or even stenographers, despite the fact that their work required less training and simpler skills. The counselor needs to know rates of pay in different branches of an occupation and in different local companies, as well as in the occupation as a whole. See Chapter 4 for sources.

Number of workers. The more persons there are employed in an occupation and the older they are, the better are the prospects that some vacancies will exist whenever an applicant is looking for a job. Despite the rapid growth of some occupations, most vacancies in most fields result from the resignation, retirement, or death of employees. In a very small occupation, one may wait months for a suitable vacancy to occur. In a large occupation, hundreds of vacancies occur every day. The person who wants to insure himself against unemployment may find the larger occupations more attractive.

Distribution of workers. Some occupations are concentrated in certain areas. A person with a strong aversion to living in these areas may be severely handicapped if he chooses one of these occupations. Even if he likes the area, should health or other considerations ever force him to move, he may be forced to change his occupation. Other occupations are practiced almost everywhere and permit their workers to live wherever they choose. This fact can be of especial importance to a woman who hopes to continue working after marriage.

Television and theatrical entertainment are centered in New York and Hollywood. A mining engineer may be sent to foreign countries but may also find himself far from the conveniences of the large city. Advancement in some large companies may require moving to distant places. Accountants, automobile mechanics, bill collectors, bus drivers, carpenters, county farm agents, dentists, electricians, nurses, plumbers, stenographers, and teachers can find employment in every state in the country.

Even when employment is nationwide, there may be geographical differences in the occupation. Specialization in medicine is easier to arrange in a large city than in a country village. Veterinarians in wealthy suburbs treat more pets than pigs.

Likes and dislikes. Few things can so quickly change one's impressions of an occupation as asking several persons who are in it to say what they like and dislike about it. A mass of useful occupational information can be picked up by asking this question of friends and acquaintances as a part of casual conversation. Certainly no review of a potential occupation, in a counseling interview, should be considered complete until the counselor or his client has asked this question of several persons engaged in the occupation. Then comes the question the client must face: "How do you think you would feel about these things?"

Hours. The girl who has to work evenings, while her girl friend entertains her boy friend, is not likely to be wholly satisfied with her job, but the student who hopes to work his way through college may find an evening job that suits his needs exactly. There are individual differences in the hours that people prefer to work, and there may be excellent reasons for the preferences. There is almost endless variety in the hours at which work must be done, and the counselor who knows occupations can be of real service to some of his clients simply by making them aware of the occupations which will permit them to work at the hours which facilitate the kinds of lives they wish to live.

More of the world's work than most of us realize is done at unusual or irregular hours. Perishable food comes into the big city during the night, is auctioned to wholesalers and resold to retailers while the rest of us sleep. Bread is baked, milk is bottled, and pastry cooks arrive at restaurants before the sun rises. Truck drivers pound the highways at high speed throughout the night, while policemen, ambulance drivers, and interns pick up the pieces of the celebrants who drink and drive. Telegraph operators convey the urgent messages; postal employees sort and forward the millions of letters picked up in the evening collections. Subway motormen and taxi drivers take us home from the theater and return with others who are on their way to work. Electric linemen repair broken wires in midnight blizzards, while short-order cooks in all-night restaurants stand ready to serve them when they can take time to eat. Radio, television, and theatrical stars work when the rest of us wish to be entertained, as do the ticket sellers, ushers, stage hands, electricians, projector operators, and popcorn salesmen. Music and drama critics and newspaper reporters cover the news when it occurs; editors, compositors, pressmen, and newsboys bring it to us at breakfast. Many of these jobs require Sunday and holiday work, with off days during the week, sometimes on a rotating schedule and sometimes not.

Some editorial workers on weekly magazines work thirty-five hours in two days and have the remainder of the week off. Some railway trainmen work long hours on long runs and then lay off for a day or two. Some bus drivers and telephone operators work split shifts during the morning and evening rush hours with time off in between. Some jobs which must be covered twenty-four hours a day have rotating shifts, so that an employee works from 8 A.M. to 4 P.M. one week, from 4 P.M. to midnight the next, and from midnight to 8 A.M. the next. Some similar jobs put all beginners on the less popular shifts and let the employees with seniority choose their shifts. Some jobs, like night clerk in a small hotel, require the employee's presence but involve little actual work, which makes them ideal for students, who can use the quiet hours for study. Some department stores employ a special staff to work only on Sunday afternoons, taking telephone orders for merchandise advertised in Sunday newspapers.

Florence Broadley has suggested that such odd-hour jobs may relieve some handicapped workers of the difficulties which they experience in traveling during rush hours.

Vacations. Some teachers, perhaps some counselors, would frown upon a student who proposed to choose his career in terms of vacations offered, but the same teachers would think twice before giving up their own free summers and their Christmas and Easter holidays. When the vacation arrangements in an occupation are unusually attractive or unattractive, this fact should be noted in counseling and considered in terms of how important vacations are in the client's scale of values.

Stability of employment. Anyone who has found himself out of work in a period of economic depression knows how very important stability of employment can be. Yet this consideration may be overlooked by the optimistic young person who has never been close to the misery of unemployment. Even here the counselor should not substitute his own scale of values for that of his client, but the counselor does have a responsibility for making certain that the client, who is about to choose an occupation in which jobs are not steady, knows what he is letting himself in for.

Some persons are cautious and prefer a steady job even at the expense of higher earnings and more rapid advancement. Others are more inclined to take risks and to look for their security in their own ability to survive whatever calamities may befall. It is not the function of the counselor to convince the client that he should be either more or less cautious than he appears to be; it is the function of the counselor to help his client to find out just what kind of security he wants, how much he wants it, and where he can get it.

One of the author's acquaintances resigns from his job each spring and finds a new job each fall, so that he may devote his summers to coaching the young amateur ballplayers of his community and managing their teams, meanwhile earning a bare subsistence by umpiring the weekend games of semiprofessional teams in the vicinity. He is unmarried. Baseball is his major interest in life. He has not found a way to make baseball support him, but he has found a way in which he can support baseball; he is happy and useful leading the kind of life that he wants to lead.

Occupations differ even more than most of us realize in the continuity of employment which they provide. In general, the least stable occupations are those which provide goods or services the purchase of which can be postponed for months or years. Among these are luxuries, such as furs, jewelry, entertainment, and vacation travel, and the capital goods or "hard" goods, such as buildings, machinery, automobiles, refrigerators, washing machines. In general, the more stable occupations are those which provide goods or services the purchase of which cannot or will not be postponed for very long. These are found in the consumer goods or "soft" goods industries: the grocery stores which stock our daily supplies of food; the utilities which provide us with water, gas, electricity, communication, and transportation; the barber shops, beauty parlors, candy and cigarette counters, which we could get along without but won't; the public schools, police and fire departments, and other government services.

Because many occupations may be practiced in any of several different industries and companies, the place where one finds employment may have as much bearing on stability as the occupation in which he seeks it. Stable companies can usually be identified from their past record of earnings and employment. Such a company may be entered at almost any time a job is available, without much concern about the stage of the economic cycle. Volatile industries and companies can also be identified from their past record, but it is much more difficult to determine whether the current trend is up or down or about to change. Prediction of changing conditions is always precarious. Such help may be obtained by talking with persons in the industry, by reading business and financial publications and the reports of investment-information services. These publications may be found in the libraries of schools of commerce, in the business and economics sections of public libraries, and in the offices of banks and brokers. Librarians are usually glad to help the reader to find what he wants.

Sometimes one needs only a little common sense to anticipate what will happen. No crystal ball is needed to predict that employment in the manufacture of military equipment will rise and fall with military appropriations. In January, 1941, before World War II, the Grumman Aircraft Engineering Corporation at Bethpage, New York, had 2,116 employees. In the midst of wartime production, in September, 1943, the same company had 25,527 employees. After the war, employment dropped to 4,670 in January, 1946. Volatile industries of this kind provide phenomenal opportunities for rapid advancement of the person who has what it takes and who is employed at or near the start of the upswing. They may also provide comparably rapid demotion or separation when the boom ends, except for those who have made themselves so valuable that they become an essential part of the permanent staff.

Within the same industry or company there are sometimes substantial differences in stability of employment. In one period of only three months, in the metalworking industries, unemployment increased by 95 percent among the unskilled and by only 8 percent among the skilled workers [524]. Even professional workers are not exempt from the threat of unemployment. The cancellation of a single government contract for military equipment has caused the immediate layoff of 11,000 workers including 1,000 engineers.

In conclusion. It is now, perhaps, apparent why the author of this book insists that the counselor cannot discharge his responsibilities by referring his client to the library for occupational information. There are too many things the client needs to know that he will not find in any library. There are too many things that may affect his success and satisfaction which he may be unaware that he should even consider.

There is more to vocational counseling than aptitude and interest testing. There is more to vocational counseling than psychotherapy. There is more to vocational counseling than the choice of next year's courses. The client who comes to a professional counselor for help in choosing a career has a right to expect that the counselor will be competent to help him, and will help him, to clarify the needs that he hopes his occupation will meet, to find out what occupations are available to him that may meet his needs, and to compare these occupations in terms of his probable success and satisfaction in each.

Service to the client may include psychotherapy if he needs it. It may include aptitude and interest testing if there are appropriate tests available. It may include educational guidance if he is ready for it. It must also include, if the client desires, a careful review of all the considerations that may affect his choice and of all the pertinent facts about himself and about the occupation. To purport to offer vocational counseling, to accept a fee or a salary for doing so, and then to deliver only educational advice, psychometrics, or psychotherapy raises some questions about either the competence or the integrity of the counselor.

REVIEW QUESTIONS

1. What kind of client may be wise to choose an occupation which is not the one for which he is best qualified?
2. For what kind of client is current supply and demand less important than future supply and demand?
3. Why is it so important to explore in detail the nature of the work in a contemplated occupation?
4. What are some of the characteristics of the work environment that may affect job satisfaction?
5. Why should a client see his contemplated occupation in several places of employment before making his choice final?
6. Why is it imperative that the counselor be as well informed about union entrance requirements in his community as he is about college entrance requirements?

7. Do you agree or disagree with the author's statement about over-emphasis on advancement?

8. What is one of the best ways to help students get a realistic appraisal of their probable earning power?

9. Why should the size of an occupation be considered before choosing it?

10. How may the geographical distribution of workers affect occupational choice?

11. What are some of the occupations which have odd hours that you have not previously thought of in this connection?

12. Which occupations tend to provide stable employment?

13. Why do some workers in an occupation have stable jobs while other workers in the same occupation are frequently unemployed?

14. Will anything in this chapter affect your future thoughts and actions? What? How?

12
The
Teaching
of
Occupations

The first known course in occupations was taught in 1908 at Westport, Connecticut, by George H. Boyden, high school principal, at the suggestion of Superintendent William A. Wheatley [42]. The first known college course in occupations was offered a few years later at Middlebury by E. J. Wiley [515].

Hutson [250] has noted that in 1916

> The course in vocations was given national standing by its acceptance as an element in the program of studies recommended for secondary schools by the Committee on Social Studies of the Commission on the Reorganization of Secondary Education of the National Education Association. The Committee called the course "vocational civics" and recommended it for the ninth grade. They expressed the belief that pupils of that age are ready to consider their choice of vocation and that such a course would minister to that need. They felt that it might induce pupils and parents to see the economic value of high-school education and thus influence length of stay in school. More important than its meaning for vocational guidance, however, in the minds of this committee, was its possible contribution to civic attitudes and understandings. . . .

> The recommendation of the Committee on Social Studies must have had some influence. The output of textbooks for the course on occupations was considerable during the '20s and the '30s, suggesting that a market must have developed. On the other hand, vocational civics must be reckoned the youngest member of the social studies family and the one with least prestige. It is not supported by any college department, such as history, political science, economics, or sociology. . . . Any subject with a pedigree so obscure must have some difficulty in becoming established.

There are fewer textbooks for high school courses in occupations today than there were in the 1920s and 1930s. In many schools a course in vocational civics or in occupations has been introduced and later dropped. Why?

The most likely explanation appears to be that many teachers were assigned to teach the course with no preparation in how to teach it and with no desire to teach it. For example, the author of this book once received a letter which read in part: "I am a Latin teacher. Next year I have to teach occupations. Please tell me what to do." Such teachers understandably did a poor job. They and their students and their supervisors were disappointed in the results.

Despite a discouraging start, the course in occupations has persisted. Each year some schools drop it, others introduce it. Although no figures are available, there appears to be increasing interest in the course at the college level. Where a counselor really believes that a course in occupations is needed, the course is likely to appear. If the counselor moves to another school or college and his successor has other interests, the course is likely to be dropped.

While the full-semester or full-year course struggles for acceptance, short units on occupations are included in many social studies courses. The units vary in length from one week to ten or more. Apparently it is easier to introduce a new unit than a new course. Once introduced, the unit is less conspicuous and hence perhaps less likely to be dropped. Since most social studies teachers have had no preparation for teaching such units, there seems little reason to expect that they are superior to the earlier courses in vocational civics. In a few schools the counselor teaches the unit on occupations, with presumably better results.

A unit well taught may have real value. The evidence to date suggests that a course has more. For a summary of research on the teaching of occupations in units and in courses see Chapter 25. For further discussion of units and how to teach them see the section on "Presenting Occupational Information through Other Subjects" in Chapter 20.

The Vocational Education Act of 1963 has revived interest in the course in occupations. With the aid of Federal funds and a new group of pioneers, some states are now experimenting with pilot programs in ninth, tenth, eleventh, and twelfth grades. With state supervisors assigned full time to develop and improve these programs, and with in-service training under way, we may hope to see gradual improvement in the quality of the teaching.

As this book goes to press, North Carolina has 209 teachers of a ninth grade course called Introduction to Vocations. Five State Supervisors of Introduction to Vocations are assigned to help the teachers. Clary and Beam [90] have described the program. Further information may be obtained from T. N. Stephens, State Supervisor of Introduction to Vocations, Division of Vocational Education, State Department of Public Instruction, Raleigh, N.C.

New Jersey currently has a more varied program in which two State Supervisors of Introduction to Vocations are assigned to help 175 teachers of Introduction to Vocations in the ninth and tenth grades of 27 school districts. Further information on this program may be obtained from Margaret Blair, Director, Introduction to Vocations, Vocational Division, State Department of Education, Trenton, N.J.

We shall get good courses in occupations only when they are taught by teachers who are as well informed in the subject matter and as well trained in methods of teaching this course as the teachers of other subjects are for courses in their fields. Perhaps it is time to think about setting some certification standards for teachers of occupations.

REASONS FOR TEACHING OCCUPATIONS

It saves time. Part of the counselor's time is devoted to answering questions of clients. Many of these questions are matters of common interest; they come up again and again. When the counselor finds that he is using thirty interviews to give thirty clients substantially the same information, he can save time by getting the thirty together and giving the facts to all of them at once.

It provides a background of related information that improves counseling. A course meeting five periods a week for a full semester provides time for both student and counselor to study and discuss problems of common interest to the group. By the simple arithmetical process of dividing the number of students into the number of hours which the average counselor has free for interviews, it becomes at once apparent that the average student in the average school or college is lucky if he gets as much as an hour or two a year of the counselor's time. In the occupations class he may be in direct contact with the counselor as much as sixty or more hours.

The economies of time inherent in teaching occupations make it possible to provide the student with a background of factual information against which to discuss the individual aspects of his problem. In the interview itself the time usually spent on presenting general information may be devoted to the applications of this information to the problems of the client.

It gives the counselor an opportunity to know his clients better. One of the axioms of guidance is that the counselor must know and understand the clients whom he counsels. A course in occupations will not provide the counselor with all that he needs to know. But when the counselor spends half his time in counseling and the other half teaching occupations, he has many opportunities in the classroom to observe his students and to get acquainted with them before and after they come to see him individually.

It focuses collective judgment on common problems. Some problems are matters of common interest. Large numbers of students have to make inquiries and decisions on these problems at about the same time. They like to talk about the issues involved. They ought to talk about them. A course in occupations provides an opportunity for students to compare opinions and judgments, not only with one counselor and a few friends, but also with a group of perhaps thirty other students facing the same problem. Members of the group may contribute to one another and to the counselor new ideas and new information that the individual interview would not produce.

It provides some assurance that the problem cases will not monopolize the counselor's time. It is the normal student who needs only a little accurate information and a little related counseling in order to solve his own problem with whom the guidance worker has the highest probability of successful results. It is this normal student who gets the least attention in the school that tries to do all its guidance by individual counseling. Despite the best of intentions on the part of both the counselor and the administrator, the problem case always seems to be more urgent. Without a course in occupations the counselor may find that he is investing most of his time where he has the least chance of success.

It can be provided without increasing the school budget. If occupations is introduced into the curriculum as a substitute for some less important subject, no addition to the instructional budget is required. This has been done in some states by direction from the state department of education. Some large high schools and colleges have simply made occupations an elective subject and let the students, by their choice of subjects, determine which other courses would have fewer sections.

It may permit a part-time counselor to spend full time on guidance and thus to become more competent. By including occupations in the instructional program and assigning the counselor to teach the course, it is sometimes possible to relieve the counselor of a teaching assignment in another subject. Thus are provided both the opportunity and the incentive for the counselor to make himself as competent in his field as the teachers of other subjects are in theirs.

It keeps the counselor up to date. One of the great weaknesses in the guidance programs of many schools is the fact that the teachers and counselors know so many things about occupations that are not true. If the course in occupations includes plant tours and group conferences, as described later in this book, the participating counselor has his own knowledge of occupations automatically checked and revised every term.

Counselors recognize the need for it. Hyde [251] got more than four hundred counselors in New York State to list the duties which they regarded as most important. When forty-two separate duties were arranged in rank order of importance, according to the judgment of these counselors, "group guidance on occupational information" and "group guidance on high school education" were ranked number nine and ten, respectively. Preceding them in the list were individual counseling with students on six different kinds of problems and conferences with parents and with other members of the school staff. All other duties of counselors—testing, scheduling, compiling cumulative records, program making, supervising student activities, committee work, discipline, forwarding transcripts, correspondence, faculty meetings, reports, etc.—were considered less important than group guidance on occupational information and on high school education.

When the counselors and other guidance workers in Hyde's study were classified by grade level, type of school, etc., in eighteen smaller groups, sixteen of the eighteen groups said they thought they should be devoting more time to "group guidance on occupational information." No group thought they should give less time to it.

SHOULD IT BE REQUIRED?

Opinions differ as to whether occupations courses in high school and college should be required or elective. Bedell and Nelson [19] reported that 87 percent of 311 high school educators ". . . feel that occupational information should be a required part of the high school curriculum." Reports of current practice may be found in a series of articles by Calvert, Carter, Gorman, Hardenbergh, Hoppock, Lowenstein, Murphy, Sinick, Stevens and Tuxill [53, 67, 68, 222, 235, 237–239, 313, 432–

441, 458–460]. In general, courses in occupations which are offered at the junior high school level appear to be required more often than they are elective. Courses offered in senior high school and college appear more frequently to be elective.

However good the theoretical argument for the required course, the author is convinced that every course should begin as an elective. Too few teachers know how to teach occupations effectively. Too many of the present courses are of little or no value. Keeping the course elective keeps the teacher on his toes. If his course dies, the students will bury it. When the students who have had the course vote overwhelmingly in favor of making it a required subject, there may be reason for doing so, but when they do that, compulsion probably will not be needed.

SHOULD CREDIT BE GIVEN?

Credit toward graduation is given for occupations courses in many schools and colleges today. Current practice is reported in the articles by Calvert and others mentioned above. In general, the more common practice appears to be to give credit for courses in occupations on the same basis as for other academic subjects. The author is aware of no valid reason why credit should be withheld.

HOW TO FIND SPACE IN THE CURRICULUM

No one who really hopes to see education improved is much impressed by the argument that no new subject can be added because the curriculum is already filled. To accept this argument is to accept the premise that the best subjects are those which got into the curriculum first. If we accepted this premise, we should still require four years of Greek for high school graduation. A new elective subject can be added to any curriculum no matter how crowded when the responsible authorities want to add it. When they do not want to add it, the full curriculum provides a convenient excuse.

Even college-preparatory students usually have room for a few free electives, and Lowenstein [312] has now shown us that college freshmen who had a course in occupations as high school seniors made better grades in college than students from the same school who did not have the course. Some college admissions officers will accept occupations as an academic subject for full academic credit if it is offered by the school as a part of its social studies program and is listed under social studies on the high school transcript. If, however, the transcript classifies occupations with the courses in woodworking and industrial arts, the admissions officer may treat it as a shop course for which he will allow less credit or none.

When Thomas E. Christensen, director of guidance at Worcester, Massachusetts, wanted to add a new elective course in self-appraisal and careers to the high school curriculum, he wrote to the admissions officers of several New England colleges and asked if they would accept this new course as an appropriate academic elective subject for admission to college. Brown, Dartmouth, Harvard, and MIT said they would.

Some schools, of course, may find it easier to introduce a new subject in the general curriculum than in the college preparatory. General-course students certainly need vocational guidance as much as anyone. If pioneer counselors can learn to do a really effective job of teaching occupations in the general curriculum, time will ultimately be found for similar work in other programs.

Stiles [462] described a summer course in career exploration, provided for seventeen high school upperclassmen:

> Students were selected on the basis of counselors' opinions and students' acknowledged interest in such a course. . . . The first two weeks of the program were taken up with classroom work involving career choices. . . . The class viewed films. . . . Speakers from . . . personnel departments [and the] California State Department of Employment . . . talked with the students about . . . looking at an occupation. The manager of the . . . Employment office . . . arranged for the class to take the GATB . . . and to receive individual interpretation of the test results. . . . Field trips were taken to the University of California, St. Mary's College, the Chevrolet Assembly plant, and the Fibreboard Research Laboratory. . . . The final portion of the course was the "on-the-job" experience. . . . The student was placed in the field of his choice, and . . . participated in many of the routine functions of a specific job.

WHEN TO TEACH OCCUPATIONS

One accepted principle of educational psychology is that the best time to learn anything is just before we are going to use it. It is then that our interest is highest; it is then that there is the least danger that our knowledge will become obsolete before we use it. The appropriate time to teach occupations is, therefore, just before or at the time that large enough numbers of persons will need and want substantially the same kinds of occupational information, specifically, during the last term preceding the point at which substantial numbers of students terminate their full-time schooling. Local statistics on dropouts provide the best basis for locating this point. Likely points are:

Last term preceding attainment of compulsory school age
Last term of elementary school
Last term of junior high school
Last term of senior high school, whether academic, vocational, or comprehensive
Last term of college, junior college, technical institute, business school, etc.
Last term of graduate school

There may be two or more points in any school at which the dropout rate is high enough to warrant a course in occupations.

It is sometimes suggested that a high school course in occupations for students who expect to graduate should be offered in the eleventh grade or the tenth or the ninth, so that the course may help the students to choose their other courses. Certainly students should have all the help they need in planning their high school programs. Some consideration of broad occupational objectives is probably appropriate at this time, but we cannot expect most ninth-grade students, at the age of fourteen, to make occupational choices that they will not want to change before they graduate.

Anyone who has counseled high school students knows that they make plenty of occupational choices in the eighth and ninth grades. The same students continue to make more and different occupational choices in the tenth grade and in the eleventh grade and in the twelfth grade. The student who graduates from high school and goes immediately to work is more likely to act on his most recent occupational choice than on the choice that he made one or two or three years before.

The first job determines the kind of experience a young person will have to offer when he goes to look for a second job. The first job determines the field in which he will make many of the personal contacts that may lead to the second job. The first job, therefore, may influence the choice of the second job more than anyone realizes. In the same way, the second job may influence the third, and so on, until at the age of forty a good many persons find themselves trapped in occupations in which they never intended to remain more than a few months. Because of the crucial importance of the first job, it is desirable that the course in occupations be offered at the time when this first job is most likely to be chosen, and that time is when or just before the student goes out to look for a job.

In vocational and professional schools. Most occupations include a variety of jobs among which a choice must be made at the point of placement. A civil engineer may choose between companies which build highways, bridges, dams, and buildings and companies which do not specialize. He may work for the government, for industry, or as a teacher in school or college. Some of his potential jobs are stable; some are not. Some are hazardous; some are not. Some provide opportunities for rapid advancement; some do not. A carpenter, plumber, or electrician may work in building construction where he will be paid at the top union scale and be frequently unemployed, or he may choose a maintenance job in a large retail store or university and be steadily employed at a lower union rate.

In any vocational or professional school may be found seniors who are only vaguely aware of the variety of opportunities available to them and of the effect which their choice among these opportunities may have upon their future lives. Here also may be students who have decided not to enter the field for which they are trained and who need much the same kind of vocational guidance as the seniors in liberal arts colleges and in the general courses of the high schools. Hence courses in occupations belong in the senior years of vocational and professional schools as well as in other schools and colleges.

Failures due to wrong timing. Failure to recognize the principle that the best time to learn anything is just before we are going to use it has been responsible for the failure of some attempts at teaching occupations. Historically, vocational guidance was introduced into the public schools of the United States at a time when large numbers of students dropped out of school at the end of the seventh or eighth grade. At that time courses in occupational information were wisely placed in these grades. Today large numbers of students finish high school before they go to work. They need occupational information in the twelfth grade. They get it in the twelfth grade in some cities. But other schools still teach occupations in the eighth or ninth grade to students who plan to finish high school and then wonder why the students show no interest in it.

Elementary and junior high school courses in the better schools today focus their attention on the problem of educational planning, on the choice of high school subjects; occupational information is introduced only as it is related to this immediate problem. Occupational objectives are not ignored; they are kept as flexible as possible. The emphasis is on a comparison of the broad groups of occupations to which the different high school curricula may lead. Students are helped to compare these groups rather than the specific occupations within the groups. Attention is focused less on the distant objective and more on the immediate decision regarding next year's program. Students, parents, and teachers all can see some sense in this.

Even this plan cannot be blindly copied. The principle is the thing. If large numbers of students still leave one school at the end of the eighth grade, then there is need in that school for occupational information in the last half of the eighth grade.

At the college level the same principles apply. The student who will spend four years in college may need some occupational information in the freshman year as a partial basis for planning his college program. He will need more in his senior year when he is about to look for a job. Courses are currently offered at both points.

Faul [150] described one of the most comprehensive college courses in vocational planning, ". . . designed particularly for the student . . . unsure of his vocational goal." The course included self-appraisal, laboratory study, visits to various occupational programs offered by the college, guest speakers from local business and industry, practice with job application forms and letters, practice job interviews which were tape-recorded and played back, interviews and meetings with the college placement counselor.

An excellent review of college courses in careers appears in Morse and Dressel's stimulating book on *General Education for Personal Maturity* [341]. Four chapters describe the courses at four colleges in some detail. A perceptive appraisal is provided in a concluding chapter by Borow. Other college courses have been reviewed in a series of articles by Calvert, Carter, Gorman, Hardenbergh, Hoppock, Lowenstein, Murphy, Stevens and Tuxill [53, 67, 68, 222, 235, 237, 239, 313, 458, 460].

While the author of this book favors semester or year courses at strategic points, not everyone agrees. Some high schools have offered a four-year program of group guidance taught by the school counselors and meeting one, two, or three periods a week.

Weaver [505] has proposed that

> . . . occupational instruction be provided in each of the four high school grades and that general orientation to the world of work be provided in the last year or so of elementary school. . . . Time can be allocated in segments of increasing length . . . two weeks in the ninth grade, three weeks in the tenth, four weeks in the eleventh, and eight weeks in the twelfth. With allowances made for holidays, the total would be 17 weeks, or the equivalent of one semester.

For college students, Crosby [109] has proposed that

> Vocational guidance should begin in the freshman year and continue through college. It is desirable if it can be designed as a regular course with students meeting once a week, with attendance required, at least until the individual has demonstrated that he is capable of making wise vocational plans and carrying them out. Work during the first two years should include a general introduction to the field, a survey of the various occupations of interest to college graduates, problems involved in self-analysis, and finally a comparison of both subjective and objective factors considered important in choosing a vocation. During the last two years students should concentrate on preparation for placement, first in a general way by exploring employment possibilities, studying company policies, job requirements and duties, salary scales, and promotional opportunities. By the senior year students should register for placement, assemble references, write letters of application, prepare for interviews, and ultimately choose the job which seems to offer the greatest number of satisfactions as well as the best opportunity for personal growth.

The research on vocational development by Super, Tiedeman, and others, discussed in Chapter 7, has certainly lent support to the view that occupational information should be presented to students continually rather than periodically. With such a program I have no quarrel, *provided it does include* adequate exposure to facts about jobs at those strategic points at which the student is most likely to act on his preferences rather than just to dream about them.

If we could give students accurate information about jobs whenever the students show an interest in their own vocational development, whether this be in kindergarten or in graduate school or in every grade between, we could surely increase the probability of wiser decisions when the student finally goes to look for a job.

Super and Overstreet's [471] research on the vocational maturity of 105 ninth-grade boys in Middletown, New York, confirmed many of the conclusions which experienced teachers and counselors had drawn from their work with ninth-grade students. For example:

> Preferences expressed at the ninth-grade level should not be viewed as definite vocational objectives. . . .
> Vocational objectives should be kept as general as possible early in the student's experience. . . .
> The task of the vocational counselor in the ninth-grade is essentially a matter of furthering vocational development rather than of fostering specific vocational choices.

In their recommendations Super and Overstreet did not mention the prospective dropout who will quit school and go to work at the end of the ninth grade. Despite his vocational immaturity, the dropout must make immediate decisions as to where he will look for a job and whether or not he will take a specific job that is offered to him. These are vocational choices of a highly specific nature and of great potential impact on the future vocational development of the individual. In work with prospective dropouts, helping them to make specific vocational choices is very much a part of the counselor's job.

In discussing the implications of their research for the curriculum, instruction, and orientation, Super and Overstreet suggested that helping the ninth-grade boy

> . . . to get a better understanding of the currently preferred field is not sufficient; he needs to know about other types of occupations which may in due course appeal to him more, and particularly to develop a perspective on the world of work which will enable him to orient himself more quickly to unfamiliar occupations. He needs to know what to look for, where to find out about it. . . . He needs a general framework of occupational information, plus knowledge of how to fill in the details of any part of that framework.

COMBINING EDUCATIONAL AND VOCATIONAL GUIDANCE

At some points in the school program, one group of students may need educational information more than vocational, while another group in the same grade needs vocational information more than educational. For example, in a twelfth-grade class of 100 students, 35 may be going to college and 65 may be looking for jobs. In a large school there should be separate classes for these two groups. Undecided students should have the privilege of attending both classes. In small schools it may be necessary to treat both problems in one class. Where this is done, the teacher must clearly recognize that he is teaching two separate subjects, focused on two different problems, and he must be extremely careful not to confuse them in his own thinking and planning. He may have to use some of the techniques of the one-room rural teacher who has eight grades in a single class.

SEPARATE COURSES FOR BOYS AND GIRLS

There are, of course, many values in coeducation. Not many modern educators would recommend a return to the separate boys' high schools and girls' high schools of an earlier day. But the values of coeducation need not be lost by separating the sexes for a few classes. Some schools have provided separate courses in occupations for boys and for girls because few boys are interested in learning about opportunities in nursing, home economics, and other occupations in which women predominate and few girls show much enthusiasm over the prospect of becoming plumbers or mechanical engineers. The principal argument against separate classes appears to be the administrative difficulty of providing them in the smaller schools. Some persons have suggested that it will not harm a girl to know something about plumbing, because some day she may marry a plumber. Others point out that there are male nurses and female plumbers. The latter argument appears more logical than the former, but it is still unconvincing. There will not be time in any course to study all the occupations that all the students may possibly enter; the occupations selected for study should be those in which the largest numbers of students will probably find employment. This selection certainly excludes female firemen and male manicurists. If boys and girls are to be taught together, some of the techniques described later in this book will minimize the difficulties. In the order of their appropriateness for mixed groups the author suggests the follow-up, plant tour, case conference, and laboratory study.

COURSES FOR DROPOUTS

As long ago as 1940 Bergstresser [25] described a course in occupations for prospective dropouts:

> In the attempt to meet the special needs of the *pupils* who indicate their intention of *leaving school* at the age of sixteen, the *Providence* schools have inaugurated a new type of course which is called a *pre-employment class*. The teachers of these classes are called pre-employment counselors; they have all had special training in guidance and are especially qualified by experience and interest to deal successfully with the type of young people enrolled in these classes. The pre-employment counselors have these pupils for all of their school work excepting shop courses. In the pre-employment class the counselor devotes a great deal of time and effort to giving the pupils specific, practical preparation for meeting their individual problems of occupational and social post-school adjustment. The counselor also attempts, however, to give the pupils a certain amount of modified instruction in English and social studies. The counselors are given a very free hand to experiment with teaching materials which will function successfully with the pupils, all of whom are, of course, poorly endowed with academic and reading ability.

More recently Flynn and others [160] described a similar course taught to ninth-grade students in Huntington, New York, following which nearly all the prospective dropouts decided to stay in school.

The U.S. Department of Labor [6] has described one public school in which

> Each early school leaver, employed or unemployed, is assigned to a general orientation course to aid him in exploring the occupational possibilities of this community. This course also helps him to develop or to clarify his ideas concerning his own vocational objectives, and to relate these objectives not only to the abilities, aptitudes, and interests which the tests have revealed, but also to the occupational information he has acquired concerning job opportunities in his community. All instructors in this orientation course are trained counselors. At the end of every semester each boy and girl has a conference with the instructor of the occupational course in which he was enrolled. This provides the young people with an opportunity to evaluate their progress, as well as to reconsider the wisdom of their choice of occupational goals in the light of their progress and their developing interests.

Gardner [174] has proposed that the school extend its services to dropouts and graduates after they have terminated their formal education.

> Once the young person has left school . . . his educational or vocational future . . . is not usually regarded as a responsibility of the school. But it should be. We should not simply turn these boys and girls out on the streets. They need advice. They need jobs. They need to be helped to think constructively about their own abilities and limitations, about job opportunities, and about their further learning and growth. Bright youngsters are not directed to a library and told to get their own education; they are given guidance. Similarly the young people who go out into the world after high school—and even more urgently those who drop out before graduation from high school— should be helped in order to assure that the years immediately ahead will be years of continued self-development.
>
> To be specific, every high school in the land should provide *continuing* vocational and educational counseling for all who leave school short of college. These services should be available until the boy or girl reaches the age of 21. As things stand today the high school does not provide such follow-up.
>
> The personnel responsible for this service should be professionally equipped to appraise the young person's potentialities. They should be fully acquainted with the kinds of training available outside the formal system, and thoroughly informed on opportunities for work in the area.

Conant [98] has strongly endorsed the Gardner recommendation: "To my mind, *guidance officers, especially in the large cities, ought to be given the responsibility for following the post-high school careers of youth from the time they leave school until they are twenty-one years of age.*"

Schreader [419] described a start in the direction recommended by Gardner. The Detroit Job Upgrading Program

. . . is to help unemployed young people, 16 to 21 years of age, who have left school before graduation. . . .

Approximately thirty young people are enrolled in each of the seven Job Upgrading units at any one time. These groups meet with their teacher coordinator for three hours each morning Monday through Friday. . . .

Individual conferences, group discussions, filling out application blanks, practice interviews, field trips, educational movies, and parties make up the training. In all activities getting along with others, good manners, good grooming practices, promptness, and care in the completion of each assigned task are stressed as a necessity to becoming a successful worker. . . .

For the young people who need more intensive training . . . there is a six-week subsidized work experience in the afternoons. . . .

Every effort is made to help these young people obtain full time jobs. An important phase of the program is the follow-up service for the first six months they are in private employment.

Slotkin [445] described a similar experimental project which

. . . provides a concentrated pre-certification, pre-employment course of at least 20 days duration to boys and girls who are ready to leave school but are not employed. The objective here is to help students achieve clear, realistic vocational goals; prepare them for entrance employment; and screen them for further guidance and referral.

Upon successful completion of the course, students are placed in employment by the New York State Employment Service. The school counselor visits each boy or girl on the job about once a month until the young person reaches age 17. Those who lose their jobs are required to return to school for further job placement, or for return to full-time or part-time school.

In a later article on the same project Slotkin [443] reported

The course emphasized job finding . . . techniques and some minimum skills in such things as stock taking, wrapping, typewriting, and traveling about New York City. . . . Stress was placed on the importance of attaining a clear, realistic goal, and the ways in which this can be accomplished. . . .

Since this project dealt with the most alienated and least capable boys and girls, it was to be expected that the first work experience for many would be unsuccessful and disappointing. Patience and persistence were the two principal elements of the post-course follow-up. . . . The record for patience and persistence was established in making seventeen job placements for one boy in a three-month period, the seventeenth being successful.

In the two years since its inception several hundred boys and girls have been served. . . . The unemployment rate of the "graduates" has been checked on four different occasions. . . . At its highest the unemployment rate was less than half that of all sixteen-year-old dropouts, and at its best it was half that of the general population.

GROUP GUIDANCE FOR ALUMNI

Although most modern schools probably would accept the idea that their responsibility to the student and to the community does not end when a student drops out or graduates, relatively few schools have done anything to help their former students during the difficult period of transition and adjustment to work. Some vocational schools provide coordinators who call on young workers and their employers during the first few months of employment. Evening schools and continuation schools serve those who come to them. But the graduate or dropout from the average high school is usually ignored.

Someday, perhaps, a three-year senior high school which now has three counselors, each of whom follows one class through its three years in the school, will add a fourth counselor and then have each counselor follow each class for four years, including the year after graduation. Then, perhaps, we shall have an evening course in occupations, meeting once or twice a week, to which the young alumni and dropouts will be invited and in which they will have opportunity to discuss their common problems of adjustment to work. Topics for discussion may include how to find a job; how to get along with the boss and with fellow workers; whether or not to join a union; when, how, and if one should ask for a raise; how to make suggestions; whether or not to continue education on a part-time basis and where and how to do so; how to build a new social life around community activities to replace the life formerly centered around the school; how to budget, spend, and save money; how to invest savings. Included in the program for this group may well be some social activities to help them maintain old friendships and old contacts during the disconcerting period in which they are learning how to make new ones in a strange environment.

GROUP GUIDANCE FOR ADULTS

Cronin [108, 465] conducted the Seven College Vocational Workshops over a period of four years at Barnard College. Nine successive workshops drew a combined attendance of 422 married women graduates of 123 colleges. Ages ranged from 29 to 70, most of them between 35 and 50.

Each workshop met from 10 A.M. to 2 P.M., once a week for ten weeks. The programs varied, but each included speakers who described the opportunities for mature college women in a wide range of occupations, such as education, social service, science, health, library work, personnel, research, publishing, finance, and public relations; plus opportunities for volunteer work in social and political organizations, how to prepare a résumé of one's qualifications, how to write a letter of application for a job, techniques of job hunting, and what to do during a job interview. Most of the speakers donated their services. After the first workshop three or four "alumnae" from previous workshops were included in the program. Their "true-life stories were encouraging . . . to the students who had begun to acquire know-how and confidence but who were still daunted by the thought of actually braving 'the real world.' "

Follow-up returns from 319 participants revealed approximately 30 percent in paid employment, 30 percent in volunteer work, and 25 percent enrolled in some kind of formal education.

The Seven College workshops have been widely copied and adapted by other colleges, by adult schools, and by community agencies. Programs have varied from one-day sessions to full-semester courses. Commenting on these Cronin wrote

It is our conviction that the ten (or perhaps twelve) week vestibule type of course such as ours is infinitely more effective than the quick-shot career days type of program. . . . For the first four to six weeks SCVW women responded slowly and timidly, though enthusiastically. During the second half of each Workshop they showed that they were getting their bearings, evaluating facts and eliminating fantasies, developing self-knowledge and confidence. Most significant, perhaps, was the inestimable value of the interaction of group members on one another. They derived great comfort from recognizing the similarities in their viewpoints and needs, and a warm *esprit de corps* developed within the ten weeks. There seemed to be no competition among them but instead there was great reciprocal admiration of individuals' courage and potentialities. It was fascinating to observe this recurring phenomenon.

Somewhat similar courses have been offered under such titles as Career Horizons for Women, Gateway to Careers, Career Planning for Women, by Barbara A. Dank, Robert O. Johnson, Sylvia Kaplan, Marcia B. Singer and others at Hofstra University, New York University, the Evening College of the State University Agricultural and Technical College at Farmingdale, N.Y., and the public schools of Baldwin and Port Washington, N.Y. Some courses have been open to anyone, male or female, who wished to learn more about the opportunities for full-time, part-time, or volunteer work.

Gardner [175] described a project undertaken by the National Board of the Young Women's Christian Association in five cities. One full-day forum meeting was held in each city. Mature women who were interested in paid or volunteer employment were invited to lectures and discussions designed to help them to "explore their potential and relate it to opportunities available to them." The initial forums were followed by counseling and other activities which varied with the community. Two cities offered four or five session courses for prospective volunteer workers. One arranged a career day with workshops in five categories.

Hefter [213] described a course of five meetings for mature women who sought employment. The program included two speakers, practice job interviews, and much group discussion. Five of the nine participants got jobs.

Logie, Humiston, and Ballin [306] described a course in group guidance for adults which met two evenings a week for six weeks. Approximately two hundred persons participated; they met in groups of about twenty-five each. The program included lectures and discussions of "What is educational and vocational guidance? What can it—and what can it not do for you? The use and value of tests and measurements. Major trends in occupations today. How to study occupations." Included also were the preparation of a self-appraisal, an occupational screening report, a writing workshop for the preparation of letters of application, a reading workshop in the occupational library, individual interviews with all participants, and an unsigned evaluation of the program by each person. The evaluations indicated a generally favorable response and a desire for more individual counseling and information.

Logie and Ballin [305] subsequently reported that six months after completing the course, 41 percent of the employed participants had changed jobs, all who had changed reported their new jobs to be "more satisfying"; the most frequently mentioned reason for the changes was "occupational information acquired in class."

Lapidos [286] reported bringing together a group of refugees ". . . for occupational orientation . . . as to what to expect from the American job scene, pay scales, role of unions, training facilities for English, obtaining of social security cards and other basic facts."

Excellent source material to use in a course for women seeking part-time jobs may be found in Schwartz [421], a report based upon 155 interviews with employers in New York City.

Group instruction and other activities, designed to help adults and others to learn effective job hunting techniques, are described in Chapter 20; see the sections on "Practice Job Interviews," "Job Clinics," and "Practice on Employment Application Blanks."

Suggestions for group guidance activities related to the employment problems of older workers may be found in Chapter 13 of *Services to Older Workers by the Public Employment Service* [424].

GROUP GUIDANCE FOR RETIREMENT

Groups of retired men and women have been brought together for periodic meetings by social agencies, libraries, and other community organizations. Many of the programs have been planned primarily for entertainment and fellowship, but some have considered the problems of adjustment that accompany the transition from employment to retirement. Some large companies provide preretirement counseling services and arrange occasional group meetings.

Perhaps, also, someday, some counselor or some agency specializing in the counseling of older persons will experiment with group guidance for those who have just been retired from active employment. The experience of counselors who work with this group has indicated already that they frequently feel unwanted, useless, and frustrated. Perhaps someone will show the rest of us how to use the techniques of group guidance, including the case conference, the group conference, the tour, and the follow-up, to help the formerly busy person to adjust to a new life of freedom.

The frontiers of group guidance are yet to be explored.

WHAT TO INCLUDE

The content of the course in occupations will vary with the purpose, the grade level, the school, the counselor, and the students. No course of study, however perfectly it may function in one school, should ever be adopted in another without critical review by teacher and students to see if it really does meet their own needs better than any other course. Every course of study should be custom made to fit the needs of the group that it is to serve. Every course should be reviewed annually by teacher and students to see how it may be improved for the next group that is to get it.

We educators are always setting out to reform the world in one semester. One of our worst mistakes is our attempt to do too much. Some of our programs are a hodgepodge, thrown together in the pious hope that if we try enough things, something will probably work, and after all "it won't do the students any harm, will it?"

If our teaching of occupations is to be effective, we must face the fact that some things cannot be done in groups. For some students guidance is a highly individual matter, requiring individual attention in individual interviews. No teaching job is perfect. Some students always miss some points. Some will need facts that are not of sufficiently common interest to warrant inclusion in a group program. Additional information will still have to be given out in the interview. The limitations of the group technique must be clearly recognized. Then we must slough off the things we cannot do and concentrate our efforts on doing well the things that we can reasonably hope to accomplish.

The first rule in planning a course, therefore, is *don't try to do too much.*

The second rule is to *let the students help to plan the course.* Explain to them the general purpose. Describe and list for them some of the things that may be done. Let them suggest others. Let them indicate in some way which items they want most to have included. Then plan the course. We do not have to let the students make the final decision, but if we are going to help students with their problems, certainly we should let them tell us what the problems are.

Following are listed some topics that may be included and some questions that may be answered in courses in occupations. From this list the teacher may select and suggest those which appear to be of probable interest and value to his students. The important thing is to find out what problems the students have now, which of these are of common interest, what factual information will help to solve them, and how best to get and present that information. This is a job for real teachers and for counselors who know their business. It is a job that cannot be done by buying a textbook and following it mechanically.

Because educational planning and occupational planning are so closely related, they are often combined in the same course. Suggested topics in the area of educational guidance are therefore included.

Educational guidance. We teachers are so familiar with our schools and their programs that we sometimes forget how little our beginning students know about them. John Brewer used to tell of the boy who wanted to know what "al-jib'er-a" was. Biology, geometry, and physics are strange and meaningless words to students who have not encountered them before and, perhaps, to parents of limited education.

College students have their troubles, too. A boy elects astronomy because he thinks it will be fun on a clear night to point out Mars, Venus, and Saturn to his admiring girl. He expects to learn interesting conversational facts about the heavens; he anticipates a pleasant, not-too-difficult experience, something like an extended visit to a planetarium. Too late, perhaps, he discovers that the course may be just a very advanced study of mathematics.

Because students do not know the nature of subjects nor the goals to which subjects lead, they need and seek information and help in choosing their courses. Some of the information students need concerns their own individual problems and may best be given in individual counseling. Some of it is purely factual and of interest to all and may more economically be given in group guidance.

The strategic times for educational guidance are just before important choices must be made. In large cities with numerous, specialized, four-year vocational high schools, the last half of the eighth grade is the key spot.

The application of this principle is less clear in the choice of a college because of some uncertainty as to when the final choice will be made. No one would question the convenience, to all concerned, of a choice made in the eighth or ninth grade and not subsequently altered. No one would deny that even in schools with good guidance programs, many students reconsider and change their choices in the senior year. Arguing about the undesirability of this procrastination will not change the fact that many students never make final decisions until they must.

It seems desirable, then, that some general consideration be given to types of colleges and to differences in college entrance requirements, in the eighth- or ninth-grade course on educational opportunities, and that this problem be reviewed in more detail in the eleventh or twelfth grade for the students who are reconsidering their decisions at this point. The latter course should be open to any students in the tenth grade who feel a need for it.

Questions. The group presentation of educational information may save the time of the counselor in answering such questions as the following:

> *About possible choices:* What is the choice that must be made now? Is it between subjects, between curricula, between schools, or between colleges? What are the alternatives?
> *About the nature of each possible choice:* What is a curriculum? How many curricula are there? What subjects do they include? Suppose I don't like the one I choose: may I change?
> What does each subject involve? What do you do in the classroom? What kind of homework do you have? What do you learn? Do you have to be bright to learn it?
> What is a liberal arts college, a business college, a junior college, a technical institute? How do they differ? What colleges should I know about and consider? Which ones can I get into? What courses do they offer? What do they cost? Can I get a scholarship?
> *About where the choices lead:* If I take this course, what will it get me? If I study typewriting, can I get a job in an office? If I take home economics, can I be a hospital dietitian? What courses do I need to become a nurse? What is the difference between the general course and the commercial? Will I get a job in an orchestra if I go to the High School of Music and Art? If I take the commercial course now and find out later that I can go to college, will I be able to get in? If I take the college course and find I can't go, will I be prepared for a job?
> If I go to college, will I get a better job? What else will a college education give me? What kinds of jobs do liberal arts graduates get, engineering graduates, technical institute graduates? Is a coed college a good place to find a husband?

Some schools have provided courses in which students surveyed possible sources of information about colleges, made trips to colleges, visited college classrooms and laboratories, and discussed fraternities and sororities with college students.

Perhaps one of the most urgent responsibilities we have in educational guidance is to warn students about gyp schools, which employ high-pressure salesmen but which are not accredited. Further discussion of this problem appears in Chapter 20.

No matter how many questions are anticipated, there will always be others. Ample time must be provided in the course to consider any pertinent problems that the students wish to raise. Some will be common problems that are appropriate for group discussion. Some will be questions of fact, easy or difficult to answer. Some will be personal and will require individual counseling.

Because many educational choices are made in the light of ultimate occupational objectives, questions about jobs are certain to be raised.

This sometimes leads to confusion of purpose and procedure, especially in courses offered at the eighth- or ninth-grade level for students who expect to finish high school. For these students, at this point, the immediate choice is between curricula and elective subjects; it is only indirectly a choice between jobs that may or may not be obtained later. To teach this course well we must keep our own attention and that of our students fixed clearly on the immediate objective.

Facts about jobs should be brought into this course only when and only to the extent that they have direct bearing upon the immediate choice to be made. In the ninth grade it makes little difference whether a boy will be an engineer or a chemist. In either case he will take the college preparatory course and, probably, the same electives. It makes considerable difference, though, whether a boy plans to be a bookkeeper or a mechanical engineer and whether a girl hopes to be a psychometrician or a stenographer.

In the average high school one objective will lead to the college preparatory course, another to a shop course with related mathematics, and a third to business education. Each of these curricula leads to a whole group of occupations, and it is between these groups rather than between specific occupations that the choice must be made. So long as we discuss only the major differences between the groups of occupations to which the various courses lead and discuss specific occupations only when they have some clear relationship to the immediate choice of curricula or electives, so long will we keep the discussion realistic and so long will our students see some point in it. When we begin to teach occupational details that have no bearing upon the student's immediate problem, then we begin to lose student interest and to wonder ourselves if the course is worth the effort.

It is obviously unrealistic to try to teach eighth- or ninth-grade students occupational facts that they will not use until they are high school or college seniors. By that time the facts they learn now may no longer be facts. Even if they were, we could hardly expect the students to remember them accurately or to take much interest in learning them so long in advance. An earlier statement will bear repeating: the best time to learn anything is just before we are going to use it, not three or four years before.

Vocational guidance. The primary purpose of courses and units in occupations usually has been to provide a background of information about occupational opportunities. It has been assumed that the probability of wise occupational choice would increase with the student's knowledge of the jobs he might get, and much of the experimental evidence lends support to this assumption. The evidence is reviewed in Chapter 25.

If we may assume that the job of educational guidance has been properly done and that related occupational information has been introduced as needed, then the proper time for orientation to occupational opportunities is just before the student goes out to look for a job. For prospective graduates this means the last half of the senior year. For prospective dropouts it means just before they drop out. In small schools prospective dropouts may be invited to join the course planned for seniors. In larger schools separate courses may be organized for those who expect to leave before graduation. The same basic principle applies to elementary schools, secondary schools, colleges, graduate schools, and institutions in the field of adult education. If large numbers terminate their education and go to work at the end of the twelfth and fourteenth grades, then these are the grades in which to teach occupations.

The course in occupations undertakes to save the time of the counselor in answering such questions as the following:

> *What jobs are open to us?* What jobs did previous dropouts and graduates get? Where? What places hire the largest numbers of young people? In what kinds of business can I be my own employer?
>
> *What do you have to do in them?* What is a typical day's work? How does it differ from what most people think it involves?
>
> *What does it take to get them?* Are there rigid requirements of age, sex, height, weight, vision, marital status, and union membership? How much discrimination is there against Jews, Negroes, nonveterans, pacifists, and others? What aptitudes are essential and desirable? Must you have a license? How do you get it?
>
> *What preparation is required?* How much? What kind? Do I have it?
>
> *What of the future?* Which occupations and which businesses are growing? Which are declining? What are the opportunities for advancement?
>
> *What do they pay?* At the beginning, after five years, after ten? Is the work steady, or are there layoffs in slack seasons and in depressions?
>
> *What do the workers like and dislike about them?*

These few questions expand rapidly into dozens of others related to them. A detailed outline for the study of any one occupation appears in Appendix G.

The occupations selected for study should include the following, in order of importance:

> 1. The occupations in which substantial proportions of former students have found employment

2. Other major occupations in the geographical area in which drop-outs and graduates look for jobs

3. Other occupations of interest to the students

It is not uncommon practice to begin with the occupations in which the students are most interested. There are obvious psychological advantages in this procedure, provided it does not prevent a reasonable allocation of time to the occupations which most of them are likely to enter.

Numerous studies have revealed the sharp contrast between the occupations in which high school seniors express an interest and the occupations in which follow-up studies show them to be employed a year later. It becomes, therefore, the responsibility of the teacher to see that they learn something about the occupations in which they are most likely to find employment. Half of the students in any class will be below the median ability level of the group. Approximately half of the occupations studied should accordingly be occupations open to students below this median level of ability.

Another important caution for the teacher of occupations is to keep attention focused on beginning jobs. High school students do not choose jobs as bankers, buyers, and fashion designers. They may think they do, but what they really choose are beginning jobs as bank clerks, sales-clerks, and alteration workers. They may hope some day to reach the top, but cold statistics indicate that very few of them do. No amount of education, no amount of inspiration, and no amount of vocational guidance will change the fact that the great bulk of human workers must always be employed on the lower levels. The reader has no doubt heard remarks about organizations which had too many chiefs and not enough Indians.

Because most of our students will remain in, or near, the jobs at which they begin, it is imperative that most of our attention be given to such jobs. Opportunities for promotion need not be concealed, but they should not be overemphasized. If we are going to be realistic and truthful and if we are not going to contribute to future frustration, we must abandon the inspirational ballyhoo that any boy can be president, and we must encourage our students to choose occupations in which they may hope to be reasonably contented if cherished promotions do not materialize.

An excellent example of the kind of realistic occupational information that students need and that schools can supply may be found in Christensen's resource units [81], from which the following excerpts are taken:

Since many of our present students will find employment in Worcester either after high school graduation or post high school education they should become acquainted with Worcester's occupational opportunities. . . .

In recent years about one-half of Worcester's high school graduates have gone into full-time jobs.

The majority of boys who go to work after high school graduation are employed in manufacturing or related trade industries.

Most girls who go to work immediately after high school graduation do clerical work.

For the past few years, most of the girls who go into clerical work have begun work in finance, insurance, or real estate industries.

Some girls also go into offices of manufacturing plants, and into stores to do clerical work.

Entry jobs in the factory itself for both boys and girls include bench assemblers, scraper hands, and foundry helpers, also stock boys. . . .

More people in Worcester find work in the metal-working industries than in any other area of industry.

Metal-working industries include many skilled and semi-skilled jobs.

In the metal-working industries, there are opportunities as electricians, machine tool operators, machinists, moulders, pattern makers, sheet metal workers and structural workers.

Training for some of the jobs in the metal-working industries must be acquired either through long apprenticeship or in the Worcester Boys' Trade High School and for others, through on-the-job training. . . .

There are opportunities for clerical workers and library workers in the public library and its branches as well as in the various school, college, industrial and museum libraries.

The public schools, private schools, business schools, and colleges in Worcester employ over a thousand teachers and administrators, as well as many clerical workers and custodians.

The many stores in Worcester employ hundreds of sales clerks, cashiers, office workers, stock clerks, shipping clerks, and maintenance men. . . .

There are hospitals and clinics in Worcester as well as the many individual doctors and dentists who need laboratory workers, technicians, and other types of medical workers.

The city itself hires many workers to care for the city's business, as health, welfare, recreation, and social services. . . .

There are a number of printing companies in Worcester which offer opportunities for those who have had some training in printing at Boys' or Girls' Trade High Schools.

The telephone directory, newspaper want ads, State Employment Office offer sources of Worcester job information.

The recreational organizations in the city employ professional workers who are trained in group leadership. . . .

High school graduates without clerical training have been employed as general clerks, file clerks, messengers, office machine operators and telephone operators.

The follow-up study of the Guidance Departments each year shows the number of graduates entering the various Worcester industries. . . .

Four out of five persons remain in Worcester to earn a living. . . .

Follow-up studies of Worcester schools reveal that about .5% of our female graduates from Worcester high schools enter semi-skilled jobs, while 98% enter clerical jobs, with no girls entering skilled jobs.

Follow-up studies also indicate that of our male graduates about 4% entered skilled jobs, while 18% went into semi-skilled jobs, 18% unskilled, 48% clerical and 2.9% agricultural jobs.

Most craftsmen learn their skills through apprenticeship under the supervision of a journeyman.

Carpenters, construction laborers, painters, and plumbers in manufacturing and construction industries lead the number of skilled workers.

Some other skilled workers mentioned are:

Bricklayers	Opticians
Bus drivers	Shoe repairmen
Cabinet makers	Tailors
Electricians	Watchmakers
Foremen	Weavers
Jewelers	

Most semi-skilled work is routine, but it appeals to many workers for they like to work with machines and find satisfaction in being able to see what they have done for the day.

Operative work requires little physical strength, because most machines are controlled by levers. Those who enter operative occupations must be able to stand the routine work and must have patience and coordination to learn to operate a machine fast enough to earn good wages.

Both men and women work as operatives or semi-skilled workers, but there are three times as many men as women in this group.

In some lines such as laundry, canning and preserving industries, more women than men are employed.

Selling is not a typical entry occupation for young people. Only about 1% of the female graduates enter selling occupations and 4% of the males. . . .

There are about two women to every man engaged in office or clerical occupations. . . .

A secretary's position is very seldom a beginning or entry occupation. . . .

Caution should be shown in gaining impressions about clerical and service jobs from glamorized television dramas. . . .

While ninth grade pupils tend to be more realistic in their occupational plans than in their occupational aspirations, their plans are frequently still out of line with occupational realities. . . .

Professional occupations which demand an examination before entering are: Physician, dentist, nurse, lawyer, and certified public accountant. Teaching is the most recent addition to this group. In Worcester and in many other areas, an examination is required for appointment in the teaching profession. . . .

It is not easy to prepare for and enter professional work. For most of these occupations, one must complete long periods of training and study in competition with the brightest students.

Applicants are not accepted for professional training unless their school grades are high. Employers generally give preference to graduates whose grades in professional school place them high in their class. . . .

Women professional workers are still concentrated in a few fields, —teaching and nursing.

In other fields, such as engineering and the sciences where there have been personnel shortages in recent years, women have been finding increasingly favorable employment opportunities. . . .

Those interested in entering a profession should consider the trend toward requiring more and more educational preparation for professional positions. Moreover, this trend is likely to expand as more and more college-trained workers become available.

After entering the profession, a professional worker must continue his research and education in order to keep up with new developments in his work. . . .

The semi-professions include many workers such as technicians who assist engineers, scientists, physicians, and other personnel.

Some of these technicians include draftsmen, engineering aides, electronic, laboratory, or x-ray technicians. . . .

Approximately two years of formal training is required for semi-professional occupations. Training can be obtained in technical institutes and junior colleges. . . .

Because of the great number of college students graduating today, we shall have many more business administration graduates seeking executive positions in industry in the future.

There will continue to be opportunities for persons without college degrees, however, especially in small self-managed businesses. . . .

A survey of the Worcester job conferences revealed that a majority of the students were interested in and attended conferences on professional occupations, yet only 9% actually enter schools for professional training. . . .

There is one large category of employment frequently omitted from courses in occupations. It is the area of self-employment. Every town has its independent grocers, clothing merchants, barbers, beauty-parlor operators, shoe repairmen, small building contractors, plumbers, electricians, etc., who are their own employers. Most of them have a certain aptitude and skill in the management of their own affairs. It is just as much the job of the counselor to reveal opportunities for the utilization of this aptitude as it is to reveal opportunities for musical, artistic, or any other talent.

In self-employment the danger of failure and the rewards of success both tend to be higher than in other kinds of work. The risks should not be minimized; the opportunities should not be overlooked. If the class in occupations is to tour large local industries, it should tour small plants too. If personnel directors from large companies are invited to meet with the class to discuss employment opportunities in their companies, the proprietors of little one-man businesses should be invited to discuss their occupations. If occupational pamphlets are to be displayed, the display should include pamphlets which describe the opportunities in self-employment.

Negroes, Jews, and members of other minority groups may sometimes circumvent discrimination by choosing an area in which they may be their own employers. So also may handicapped workers. Helpful information is provided on request by the U.S. Small Business Administration, Washington, D.C.

Teachers and counselors who wish to help students explore the possibilities of self-employment may write to Junior Achievement, 51 W. 51 St., New York, for information on a youth program in this area.

Some colleges are now offering courses in how to get a job. Some instruction of this kind is included in many group guidance programs. More of it may be expected as more educators learn that most people do not get jobs through employment agencies.

Despite individual exceptions in the cases of some well-organized school and college placement services, many studies have shown that more than half of the people who get jobs obtain them through relatives and friends and by direct personal application to the employer. The effectiveness of these employment channels is due not so much to nepotism as to the fact that many small employers hire the first well-qualified applicant who applies and also show a distinct preference for applicants recommended by persons known to the employer. Relatives and friends can help the job applicant to learn about vacancies before they are advertised and can recommend him to employers who will place some confidence in the recommendation. The function of instruction in this area is to make students familiar with the more effective techniques of job hunting, including how to use relatives and friends ethically and effectively. These techniques are described in numerous books on the subject, available in most libraries.

Cuony [111] included job-finding techniques in his successful experimental course for high school seniors, which is described briefly in Chapter 25.

College courses in job-seeking techniques were briefly described by Calvert, Carter, and Murphy [53]. Lansner [284] described a short course in job-hunting techniques offered to college seniors by the college placement director. Keegan [270] described a similar course. Reeves [391] surveyed the ways in which job-getting techniques were presented to college students and reactions to these presentations. She found 60 colleges with courses in job finding, among 426 institutions which gave substantial assistance of some kind. An appropriate text for college courses in job finding is *Planning Your Career* by Calvert and Steele [54].

Other activities and other references designed to help students and adults to find jobs are described in Chapter 20; see the sections on "Practice Job Interviews," "Job Clinics," and "Practice on Employment Application Blanks."

Special classes for children with retarded mental development often include instruction in the nature of the jobs open to them, how to get a job, and what to do when they lose their jobs. The criterion of success for this group is to keep out of jail and off the relief rolls. If similar instruction were provided for more of our brighter children, we might find fewer of them in jail and on relief.

In some states students who go to work before the age of eighteen are required to have working papers and should be familiar with some of the child labor laws. All students who are about to go to work should learn something about workmen's compensation, unemployment compensation, and social security. The education departments and the labor departments of several states have prepared bulletins for students and for counselors, summarizing essential information about employment certificates and related labor legislation. A letter to the state capital will bring samples. The U.S. Department of Labor also has published useful pamphlets on this subject.

Ross [403] has reported the concepts of occupational information, essential in the general education of secondary school students, selected by a jury of educators from an original list of 720 items.

There is still some difference of opinion among the textbook writers as to whether the major emphasis of the course in occupations should be on current facts about jobs or on the technique of discovering such facts. Some writers have maintained that it is more important to teach the technique than to teach the facts, because the facts will go out of date while the technique will remain effective and because it is impossible to teach all facts about all occupations in any reasonable time. Certainly it is desirable for anyone to know where and how to get facts about jobs. But learning the sources of occupational information need not preclude learning immediately useful facts about current occupational opportunities. On the contrary, one of the best ways to learn the technique is to practice using it. The teacher who wishes to place the major emphasis upon sources of information and upon the methods of choosing an occupation will be particularly interested in the chapters on "Case Conference," "Laboratory Study," and "Self-measurement" in this book. If any further argument is needed for including facts about jobs, the answer to their becoming obsolete is to teach them just before they are to be used, and the answer to the impossibility of teaching everything about all occupations is to do what we do in every other subject, namely, select the more important facts and teach them.

Whether we place major emphasis upon facts about jobs or upon how to get the facts, any course in occupations should include somewhere some consideration of common errors in choosing an occupation, such as hero worship, overestimation of one's abilities or of employment opportunity, misconception regarding the nature of the work, other mis-information or lack of information about the occupation, and reliance upon recruiting literature and other biased sources of information.

Williamson [518] has noted several errors of thinking which may lead to unwise occupational choices. Among these are:

> . . . the *attractiveness of the remote*. . . . The grass on the other side of the road always seems greener—until we have crossed the road. . . .
>
> The tendency to *glorify the unusual*. . . . Enraptured youths believe that all a lawyer does is to deliver soul-stirring pleas for the innocent and oppressed; forgotten are the tedious days most lawyers must devote to writing briefs and telling the clients the meaning of their used-car contract. . . .
>
> *The white collar illusion*. . . . One need not be a doctor to be well thought of in the community, or practice law to attain financial security. . . .
>
> Students often . . . imagine that there exists somewhere *a perfect niche* for them. . . .
>
> There is no one perfect niche, but rather many opportunities for a happy balance between what an individual can do and what the job demands. Consequently a student should plan his occupational future in terms of *broad fields of work* rather than in terms of narrow and specific jobs. . . .
>
> *Misreading the signs* is the mistake made by those who jump to the wrong conclusions. A supposed liking for mathematics and science courses and a *dislike* for English are often judged to be signs pointing straight to a dazzling success as an engineer. The truth is that, in so far as these particular likes and dislikes mean anything occupationally, they indicate equally well some of the qualifications useful to the farmer, engineer, chemist, dentist, architect, mathematician, physician, physicist, and psychologist. . . .
>
> Many students hesitate to make a choice for fear that they will get into a blind alley job. These timid souls suffer from *fear of the closed mind*. . . . As new experiences yield more facts about abilities and interests . . . early choices may be reconsidered. . . . No student should expect to make an exact blueprint of his life for the next thirty years. . . .
>
> Indolent students resemble *sparkless motors*. . . . It is time we were rid of the popular . . . conviction that only the stupid have to study. . . .
>
> The *fallacy of occupational labels*. . . . A young man, fascinated by the front-page exploits of "G" men, discovers that they are engaged in activities quite unlike those he has read about. . . .
>
> The *fallacy of the added cubit* . . . comes from the passage in The Sermon on the Mount which contains the question, "which of you by taking thought can add one cubit to his stature?" . . . Adjustment of

ambitions to *achievable* vocational goals is the proper way to make a vocational choice.

The *fallacy of perfectibility*. . . . All of us like to believe that we are *potentially* capable of greatness in all things. . . . Nature has set pretty definite limits to what any of us can do. . . .

The assumption of *equal ability* for many occupations. . . . No two people have quite the same native weapons for the battle of life. . . .

The *phrenological fallacy*. . . . There is no known relationship between aptitudes for jobs and bumps on the head, shape of the features or any other anatomical characteristic. . . .

The fallacy of *sequential training* is the pitfall of those who think that they should spend no time on studies which are not in the direct sequence leading to the job they have chosen. Such students . . . miss the rich experiences to be gained from wandering in the bypaths of education.

Borow [33], in a thoughtful article, has suggested conditions under which college courses in vocational planning function most effectively.

1. *When the student, at the time of entrance into the course, is highly motivated to develop a workable plan for vocational life*. . . .

2. *When the student is free from persistent emotional involvements*. . . .

3. *When the student is furnished opportunities for counseling at crucial stages in the sequential development of his course experience*. . . .

4. *When the student is oriented to the purpose and nature of counseling in advance of his series of interviews*. . . .

5. *When a self-history or autobiographical approach is used to lead the student through the initial stages of vocational exploration*. . . .

6. *When the student is freely permitted to explore his subjectively expressed job interests and to reject, if he wishes, those occupations inferred from test results or other data*. . . .

7. *When the student is given abundant opportunity to penetrate the occupational universe symbolically and to correct and enlarge his image of how the world of work is ordered*. . . .

8. *When the student is encouraged to relate his findings about occupations to those facts and impressions he has gathered about himself*. . . .

9. *When the student is encouraged to investigate more than one occupation*. . . .

Redefer and Reeves [388] have included an excellent chapter on how to teach college courses in career planning in their book on *Careers in Education*.

For additional suggestions on what to include in a course in occupations the reader may wish to review Chapters 2 and 3.

WHO SHOULD TEACH IT?

In the best schools courses in occupations are taught by persons as well trained for this job as the teachers of chemistry, geometry, and French are for theirs. Once in a while a superior English teacher or social studies teacher does a brilliant job of teaching occupations—as the same superior teacher might do a brilliant job if assigned to trigonometry. But the miserably dull courses in school after school have long since demonstrated the futility of trying to get good instruction in occupations from teachers who have not been specifically trained for this work.

Not homeroom teachers. The reasons have been well stated by Warters in the first edition of her book [501].

> Surveys show that the home room is a frequently used medium for group guidance. The surveys also show that, in the main, it is an ineffectual medium. Because all students are assigned to home-room groups, usually all teachers are expected to serve as home-room teachers whether they are qualified or not. Teachers who give instruction in academic subjects are asked to give also guidance concerning life needs. They are not, however, asked to perform the two functions with the same students at the same time; and they are given much less time for performing the second than for the first. Consequently, the second is considered a less important function and is often neglected for better performance of the first.
>
> Under such conditions, the average home room has little chance of being a satisfactory medium for group guidance. The work is usually assigned to the teachers as an extra without their being trained for the work or willing to do it. Lack of understanding and training makes many teachers feel inadequate to the work. Feelings of inadequacy and of insecurity create feelings of resentment; and resentful teachers, like resentful pupils, seldom put forth much effort in support of a disliked project. Some teachers may try to avoid the new responsibility by converting the guidance period into a study period and may justify this procedure by calling attention to the scholastic records of some home-room members. If because of an administrative decree they must use the period as an "activity period," then they demand to be told what to do and how to do it. The administrator usually appoints a committee to provide assistance through recommended programs. The committee members may soon discover that others have done this work for them, that there are books which contain home-room programs outlined in detail, that through the purchase of one book alone they can supply the teachers with a hundred guidance lessons. Thinking and planning are thus reduced to a minimum for everyone.
>
> When home-room programs are planned according to some such stereotyped lesson plan, the home-room period is not used by students

for exploring some purposeful, student-suggested topic, based upon their common concerns. Instead, it is a class rather than a conference period, adult-programed rather than student-programed, and concerned more often than not with some subject uninteresting to the students because it is outside their experiences and inappropriate to their educational level. And students complain that when home-room periods are conducted according to such procedures, they are more often "preached at" than guided.

Unless teachers are trained and willing the home-room plan is doomed from the start.

McKown [325] in his *Home Room Guidance* said flatly, "The study of occupations is a very highly specialized subject and cannot be adequately handled by the average home room sponsor."

Lincoln [301] in her measurement of the results of instruction in vocational information found the homeroom less effective than separate classes.

The homeroom teacher who is reading this book because he has been assigned to teach occupations as part of his homeroom program need not give up in despair. He will find his work more difficult than if he had a separate course in occupations, but if he really wants to do a good job, he can find plenty to do. Most of the teaching methods described later in this book can be used in homerooms. Other helpful suggestions will be found in Ross [405].

Not teachers of other subjects. In lieu of a course in occupations, some schools ask all teachers to include in their other courses some consideration of occupations in which these courses are useful. When well done by a teacher who wants to do it, this kind of teaching may have real value. At best, however, it is only a supplement to, and never an adequate substitute for, a course in occupations. Too many important occupations are not clearly connected with any academic subject. For more on this topic see the section on "Presenting Occupational Information through Other Subjects" in Chapter 20 on "Other Methods of Getting and Using Occupational Information."

Counselors trained for the job. The twenty-fourth yearbook [418] of the American Association of School Administrators recommends one full-time counselor to every 200 students in the secondary school. Most states now require counselors to be certified in guidance. Such certification usually requires training in occupational information and how to present it. The counselor thus trained is the person to teach the course in occupations. His individual counseling interviews reveal the problems which are common to the group. His class discussions lead some students to seek individual interviews. When these students come to him, he has already had some acquaintance with them. Thus each part of his job reinforces the other.

Lapidos [286] has observed that ". . . from the point of view of the counselor, this approach enables one to observe the individual in a group setting, to evaluate his social responses, and ability to function in the interpersonal relations area. This opportunity for observation is rarely available to the individual counselor."

Christensen [82] described the course in self-appraisal and careers offered in the high schools of Worcester, Mass., which was taught only by professionally trained counselors. Each teacher of the course served also as the counselor for the students in his section and had released time for individual counseling with each student.

Fox [166], Kenyon [273], and Sutherland [473] have described other high school and college courses taught by counselors.

Throughout the remainder of this book it is assumed that the school counselor will be the teacher of occupations, and the words "teacher" and "counselor" are used interchangeably.

Full-time teachers of occupations. Some counselors will never teach occupations, because their major interests are in other aspects of guidance. Where this is the case, occupations may be better taught by a classroom teacher who wants to teach it and who will take the trouble to learn how to teach it.

A counselor can always find plenty of excuses for not keeping his own occupational information up to date. When he fails to do this and he makes no provision for anyone else to do it, students frequently receive misinformation, based on what the counselor thinks is true or what was true three years ago or what the student or client can dig out for himself from a file which is always partly obsolete.

Students would get much better occupational information if there were one person in each school and college whose *major* job were to be an expert on the major occupations which the school's alumni usually enter, specifically a full-time teacher of occupations, hired and retained and promoted mainly because of his knowledge of the subject and his skill in teaching it.

With such a person on the faculty, a student could go to a teacher of occupations and get as good information about jobs as he can now get about chemistry from a teacher of chemistry.

Somehow, if we are ever to do a good job of vocational guidance, we must provide an elective course in occupations in every high school and college, taught by a teacher or counselor who is as competent in this area as the teacher of Latin is in his.

PROTECT TIME ASSIGNED FOR COUNSELING

When the teaching of occupations is assigned to counselors, the administrator must be careful to see to it that the total hours available for individual counseling are not thereby reduced. Every hour that the counselor spends in class releases for one hour a teacher who would otherwise be instructing the same students in some other subject. The hours thus saved should be reserved to replace the counseling time which the counselor now devotes to teaching.

To illustrate how this may be done, imagine the following: In a high school five periods of classroom teaching per day constitute a normal load. The school has had two full-time counselors and no group guidance. The school now proposes to introduce three elective sections of a course in educational planning for freshmen and two elective sections of a course in occupations for seniors. The total of five sections will be divided among the counselors. These five sections will replace five sections of other courses that were formerly taught by other teachers. The teaching time thus released is five periods, the equivalent of a full load for one person. This released time is used to add a third counselor to the guidance staff. These three counselors now divide the five group guidance sections among them.

The net effect of this arrangement is that five periods of group guidance have now replaced five periods of other subjects, three persons are assigned to guidance instead of two, these three persons now divide the responsibility for individual counseling and for group guidance, the hours available for individual counseling remain unchanged, and the budget has not been affected at all.

For another illustration, imagine a small high school which has had one part-time counselor giving three periods a day to counseling and two periods to teaching English. Two periods of group guidance are introduced to replace two discontinued sections of some other subject. Teaching assignments are shifted so that the counselor now teaches the two sections of group guidance while someone else teaches the two sections of English. The counselor can now devote his full attention to guidance and gradually become as competent in guidance as he formerly was in English. The time available for individual counseling is unchanged, and the budget is not affected.

The school which is too small to have even one full-time guidance person will have to struggle along with part-time service. Expected results should be cut about 50 percent. A teacher who has to keep up to date in two fields obviously can do only about half as much in each as the full-time specialist. Virginia Hartman has well expressed the difficulties.

> I find that being a teacher-counselor creates more necessity for added preparation even though my class load is lessened, because essentially the same procedures must be followed to do an effective job of teaching and in addition and at the same time I have to learn and assimilate all the information and techniques I can to do an effective job of counseling. I desperately need more time for organization and over-all planning for both jobs, and the days just aren't long enough.

COMPROMISE PLANS

Various compromises have been tried on an interim basis. Some schools have had the counselor take over certain homeroom or social studies periods for group guidance work. Others have asked all homeroom teachers to try group guidance for one year, selected the teacher who was most successful, created a full-time job for this person, and asked him meanwhile to prepare for the job in summer courses.

Compromise plans which move in the direction of competent full-time service are good to that extent. Those which serve as half-hearted substitutes tend to defeat their own purpose.

Absolute minimum training for any person undertaking to teach occupations for the first time should include the following:

> One course in principles and techniques of guidance
> One course in facts about jobs and where to get them
> One course in methods of teaching occupations

To this minimum should be added promptly the essential background courses for all counselors, as required by the state department of education.

METHODS OF TEACHING OCCUPATIONS

No two teachers can teach equally well by the same method. Every good teacher must experiment until he finds which techniques work best for him. Techniques which various teachers of occupations have tried and liked are described in the next several chapters. Most of these techniques can be used in any course or unit on occupations. Some can be used for one day and repeated or not. Some require continuity over a longer period. Some car be and have been used for a full-semester course.

The beginner is perhaps more likely to try too many methods than too few. He is advised, therefore, to select one method which appeals to him, to plan his first course largely around this method, and to introduce other methods during his first term only to provide variety when he feels variety is needed. He should keep all his plans flexible and have a second and a third method ready to substitute if the first proves unsatisfactory.

Principles and techniques of working with groups in general have been well presented by Glanz [182], Kemp [272], Lifton [298], Mahler and Caldwell [316], Miles [330], and Warters [500].

REVIEW QUESTIONS

1. Of the reasons offered for the teaching of occupations, which do you find most convincing? About which are you skeptical? Why?

2. Do you think courses in occupations should be required or elective? Why?

3. Are courses in occupations ever accepted for college entrance credit? Do you think they should be? Why? Why not?

4. What basic principle should determine when the course in occupations will be taught?

5. Is there a place for a course in occupations in a vocational or professional school? Why or why not?

6. In what order of importance should occupations be selected for study?

7. Why should attention be focused on beginning jobs?

8. What large category of employment is frequently omitted from courses in occupations?

9. Through what media do most people get jobs? What are the implications of this fact for the teaching of occupations?

10. Do you agree or disagree with the author's position on the teaching of facts about jobs versus teaching how to get the facts? Why?

11. Who should teach the course in occupations? Why?

12. Will anything in this chapter affect your future thoughts and actions? What? How?

13
Students
Follow
Up
Alumni

The follow-up technique of teaching occupations may be handled in a variety of ways. It has the advantage of human interest, live material, and direct contact with original sources. It has been used by the author with both high school and college students; both groups have been enthusiastic about it. It may be used for an entire course, a part of a course, or a club program independent of any course. A similar procedure was used by one of the author's students on a group of Federal prisoners who followed up the "alumni" of their institution.

PURPOSE
Many high school and college students have only vague and limited knowledge of the employment opportunities which they may expect to find when they are ready to look for a job. As a result, their occupational plans are often vague, unrealistic, and restricted to the few occupations with which they are familiar. Their concepts of beginning jobs are reflected in the popular caricatures of the college graduate who wants to start as an executive. Their salary expectations are based on rumors they have heard about the fabulous earnings of an atypical few.

The major purpose of the follow-up study is to give the students a more realistic picture of their future by helping them to find out what has happened to those who have preceded them. A considerable variety of additional information may be picked up incidentally but should be regarded as useful surplus rather than as a primary objective. Don't try to do too much.

PROCEDURE

Any project of this kind, which involves public relations, should first be discussed with, and approved by, the counselor's immediate superior. There are many different ways to conduct a follow-up study and to use the results. For the sake of simplicity in description, one method will be suggested; the reader should not hesitate to vary the procedure in order to suit his own and his students' purposes and preferences.

Preparing the questions. The teacher describes the project to the class and invites them to suggest questions which they would like to ask former students about their present jobs. As questions are suggested, they are written on the blackboard *in the words of the students* who suggest them. If a student has trouble in wording a question, the teacher may help. If the student's words are hopelessly ambiguous or confusing, the teacher may try to frame the question in simpler form and ask the student if this expresses his idea. But so far as possible, teacher editing of questions should be avoided at this point. There will be plenty of opportunity to edit the questions later. The task now is to encourage the students to think about what they want to know and to formulate their own questions. Public correction of a student's errors in composition may discourage other students from offering their own contributions lest they be similarly corrected. If someone gets facetious or asks an offensive question that the teacher would be unwilling to include in the study, he may omit the question as graciously as he can, but he should avoid censoring questions if at all possible.

Each question is numbered as it is written on the board. When the students exhaust their ideas or the teacher feels that enough time has been spent on them, he stops the suggestions and invites the students to consider which of the questions are most important to them. He explains that too many questions will reduce the number of persons who will respond. He asks each student to select the five questions which are most important to him and to write the numbers of these questions on a piece of paper.

The teacher announces that he reserves the right to add a few questions of his own and to edit the questions selected, but he assures the students that their preferences will be considered in the final choice of questions to be asked. Students usually do not mind a little teacher participation in the class if they are permitted to make some of the decisions themselves.

The teacher then asks how many students chose question number one. He asks a student to count the raised hands and another student to write the total on the board beside the question. The teacher repeats this process with each question. Each student has chosen five questions, so each student may raise his hand five times, but not more than five. Some students like the idea of having five "votes."

When the votes for all the questions have been tabulated, the teacher announces that the five most popular questions will be included in the study and repeats that he will add a few of his own. If the teacher sees that the sixth and seventh most popular questions are ones which he would include as his own, he may accept them in lieu of some that he would ask.

The teacher announces that these questions will be incorporated in a letter which will be sent to all last year's graduates and dropouts. He assigns two or more of his best students to copy the names and addresses of these former students from the school records. Each name and address should be put on a separate card.

Preparing the letter. The teacher drafts a letter including the students' questions and his own. The following form is suggested as a guide:

> Dear _____
>
> Our class in occupations is writing to former students in order to learn something about the kinds of jobs that may be open to us when we finish school. I am a member of the class, and I am writing to ask if you will be kind enough to tell us something about your own experience.
>
> What we would like best would be a letter, telling us as much as your time permits about the answers to these questions:
>
> What is your present job?
>
> Just what do you do?
>
> How did you get your job?
>
> How much do you earn? Or what do jobs like yours usually pay?
>
> What do you like about your job?
>
> What do you dislike about it?
>
> What advice would you give to one of us who wants to do what you are doing?
>
> If the answers to any of these questions are confidential, will you please tell me how far I may go in reporting them to the other members of the class? Replies which are not confidential will be shown to other students in this and in future classes.
>
> I am sure you know how grateful we will be for any information you may send us. We do want to know what we are getting into. You who have gone before are the ones who can tell us best.
>
> Sincerely yours,

Mailing the letters. The letters are duplicated and brought to class, along with the cards containing the names and addresses of the former students and an adequate supply of envelopes and stamps. The names, the letters, and the envelopes are evenly divided among the students. Students who wish may be permitted to choose the names of their friends from those on the cards. Each student takes the first of his cards, addresses an envelope to this person, fills in the salutation on one of the duplicated letters, signs his own name, and puts the letter in the addressed envelope. He does not seal the envelope yet. He repeats this process with each name. He puts his own name and the date on the back of each address card to provide a record of who wrote to whom. Then he addresses an equal number of return envelopes to himself, in care of the teacher, at the school. When all the student's letters and envelopes are ready, he shows them to the teacher, receives the necessary stamps, puts one stamp on each return envelope, inserts it with the letter in an envelope addressed to a former student, seals and stamps this envelope. When all his letters are ready to be mailed, he returns them to the teacher, who sees that they are mailed. A committee of dependable students may be assigned to mail the letters.

It is important that the letters be addressed in class and mailed at once. Experience indicates that when this task is assigned as homework, too many students postpone it too long. It is also important that the return envelopes be addressed to the student in care of the teacher at the school; if they are addressed to the student at his home, too many students forget to bring the replies to school.

Discussing the replies. Replies will not arrive the day after the letters are mailed. For five or ten days the teacher must plan interim activities for the class. Sometime in the second week there will usually be enough responses to provide material for a class session.

When the replies do come in, the teacher takes them to class, unopened, and gives them to the students, who immediately open and read them. The teacher then invites one student at a time to read his letter to the group. The students are invited to interrupt at any time they wish to raise a question or to make a comment. The teacher takes the real responsibility for selecting statements in the replies that are worth discussion. Whenever such a statement appears, the teacher interrupts and raises a question for discussion, emphasizes the importance of the statement just read, or, possibly, disagrees with it. When the letter is completed, the teacher inquires if anyone wishes to raise any question or make any comment, then calls on someone in another part of the room to read one of his replies. Sometimes two or three letters are read with no questions and no comments. At other times an entire period may be devoted to discussing one or two letters.

Some of the author's students have suggested that the discussion periods might be more profitable if the instructor would begin each period by inquiring what jobs were represented in the letters at hand and then selecting the letters to be read so that a good sampling of jobs would be presented.

Students have suggested also that the instructor be alert to opportunities to draw all the students into the class discussion. For example, when salaries are mentioned, the instructor may interrupt to inquire how many others have letters from persons in similar jobs, what they earn, how many have letters from people earning more money, what jobs they have, etc.

At the end of the class period all letters are returned to the teacher, who may collect separately those which have been discussed and those which have not. The discussion continues for as many days as letters are available or until the class or the teacher decides that further discussion would not be beneficial.

After the letters are discussed, they may be given to a class secretary or a committee who will compile a statistical summary. At the end of the course each student receives a mimeographed copy of the summary; it indicates the kinds of jobs in which these former students found employment, the number and percentage in each, the range of salaries, the most frequently mentioned things that the respondents liked and disliked about their jobs, the ways in which they got them, and the employers who hired them.

In most of the discussions the teacher seeks first to draw comments from the class. After giving them ample opportunity to state their own ideas, the teacher contributes additional comments of his own, sometimes agreeing with and emphasizing a point made by one of the students, sometimes gently disagreeing, and sometimes adding information from his own experience. The teacher may be surprised and encouraged by the frequency with which the students themselves will draw from the letters the very inferences and conclusions which the teacher would otherwise call to their attention. The advantage of this procedure as a teaching technique is, of course, that the student having thought of an idea himself, having publicly expressed it, and heard it publicly approved is more likely to value it and to remember it than if it had been presented to him in lecture form. In a lecture, if he were a bit inattentive, he might not even hear it. In the rapid-fire conversation of a class discussion it is difficult not to pay attention.

The alert teacher can find in the responses of former students live human-interest material on which to base discussions of many kinds. The arrangement of topics discussed will follow no nicely logical syllabus, but what is lost in logic may be more than made up in the use of material that is interesting and vital to the students because they can see it functioning in the lives of former students who are doing now what the present students hope to be doing the following year. Beginners who have had little experience in leading discussion groups may find helpful suggestions in Appendix B.

The request for a response in letter form is imperative if the teacher plans to use the responses as a basis for class discussion. Respondents who write letters express opinions and relate experiences which invite discussion, as the brief responses to printed questionnaires do not. The number of responses will be smaller when a letter is requested, but the quality will more than compensate. One study of this kind at the college level brought responses from 32 percent of the former students. This is 8 percent less than the national average return for questionnaire studies using only one request. A higher percentage response can be obtained by sending additional letters at intervals of two weeks to the persons who have not responded. If the follow-up study is made in order to collect statistical data rather than to provide provocative material for class discussion, the conventional questionnaire will probably bring a larger proportion of returns, with the data in more convenient form for tabulation.

The eagerness with which students open and read the replies will convince any teacher that it really is important to have the letters addressed to them. This procedure and the active part which the students have in determining what questions will be asked give them the feeling that this is really their project. Natural human interest is reinforced by the fact that some of the respondents are close personal friends of the students, and they mix highly personal communications with replies to the questions. In such cases, the students may be permitted to withhold the personal parts and to copy on a separate sheet the replies to the questions. This sheet may be given to the secretary instead of the entire letter.

In Appendix D appears the transcript of a demonstration discussion conducted by the author for a group of counselors in training.

Teachers sometimes ask, "What's the use of trying to follow up students now when they are all in the army? How are you going to reach them? And if you do, what good will the information be?" An actual reply from an alumnus will indicate the material that can be obtained for use in orientation of students about to enter the service:

Question: What advice would you give to this year's seniors who will be in the service next year?

Answer: Prepare yourself for a terrific physical and mental readjustment!!! Forget right now all the movies you've seen, all the storybook glamour you've heard about the army—the air force in particular. There is no glamour other than that of damn hard teamwork. You must learn to live, eat, and drink with all kinds and conditions of men and to get along with them all. You must be prepared to lead a life in which you as an individual will cease to exist save as a number on a filing card.

The following questions have been used in various follow-up questionnaires sent to alumni in military service:

What branch of the service are you in?
What do you like best about it?
What do you like least about it?
On what basis were you given your present assignment?
How soon after induction did you get it?
If you were going through the classification procedure again would you do anything differently? What? How?
What was your occupation before induction?
What use have you been able to make of your previous education and experience?
What in-service training have you had? Will you be able to use it later in civilian life?
What advice would you give to persons about to enter the service?

Summarizing the data. The students should have a part in deciding which items will be included in the statistical summary. Among the items which they may wish to consider are the following:

A list of employers who hire dropouts and graduates, with each employer's address, the jobs for which former students were hired, and the number of persons hired for each job category, for example:

Lord & Taylor, Manhasset, N.Y.

Salesclerks, temporary	25
Salesclerks, permanent	4
Stock clerks, permanent	2

A list of occupations in which the former students are now employed, the number employed in each, and the range of beginning wages, with the occupations arranged in descending order of numbers employed, for example:

Retail salesclerks ($51–$64)	40
Stenographers ($66–$80)	15
Automobile service station attendants ($45–$67)	10

A similar list of occupations in which the respondents are employed, with their employers listed under each occupation. Employers and wages should not be shown in the same table unless the counselor first verifies the data. A few unfortunate errors may antagonize employers whose goodwill the counselor wants.

Expressed likes and dislikes of workers in different occupations represented by five or more former students, for example:

Retail salesclerks like
  Meeting different people
  Air-conditioned store
Retail salesclerks dislike
  Standing all day
  Disagreeable customers

Suggestions made by dropouts and graduates, which the class has discussed and which a majority of the class considered to be sound, for example:

Be very neat and careful in filling out application blanks; if you do this poorly you may not even be interviewed for the job.
If you want to be a reporter, learn to typewrite.

Methods by which former students got their jobs, with the number who reported each method, for example:

Relatives	35
Direct applications to employers	25
Friends and acquaintances	20
Employment services	6
Civil service examinations	5

Some teachers may wish to have each student keep a notebook in which to make his own statistical tabulation as the replies are received. Others may prefer to assign this responsibility to a committee. The author has always used the latter method in order to reserve class time for discussion.

When the statistical summary has been completed, some of the interesting discoveries may be selected from it and included in a news release prepared by the class, by a committee, or by the teacher. This release should be submitted to the principal for approval and then sent to the local newspapers.

Bias of incomplete returns. Baer and Roeber [14] in their second edition reviewed several researches on bias in follow-up returns. These researches suggest that incomplete returns are likely to be weighted with proportionately more replies from certain groups which tend to respond more readily than their opposites. The groups which tend to respond in larger proportions are graduates as opposed to dropouts, recent graduates as opposed to older graduates, girls as opposed to boys, and students near the top of their class in school grades as opposed to students near the bottom.

Because of these biases, careful research workers try to get as nearly complete returns as possible.

Ganley [172] achieved an average return of 98.5 percent in six annual follow-up studies of high school graduates. He got responses from about 70 percent of the group by mailing two letters in succession. The remainder were reached through brothers and sisters still in school or by visits to homes and places of employment.

Christensen [80] got a 98 percent response by means of postcards and telephone calls.

Mooren and Rothney [339] mailed personalized, handwritten letters and personalized questionnaires to half of 688 graduates of four Wisconsin high schools. Mimeographed form letters and standard questionnaires were sent to the other half.

> Ninety-five percent of the subjects had responded by the end of the fourth mailing period. . . . Replies were eventually obtained from *all* the subjects. . . .
>
> The *personals* answered slightly more promptly. . . . The differences are very small. . . . [The] increased work of writing personal appeals and constructing personalized questionnaires . . . would not be justified unless a difference of from one to four percent in returns was very important to the investigation. . . .
>
> Although girls tended to answer about 10 percent faster than boys, initially, the difference had disappeared by the fourth mailing. . . .

The counselor whose time and facilities do not permit such persistent research should not let this fact deter him from getting such data as he can by follow-up. Despite all the inaccuracies that may creep into his results, even a small response will bring him useful, interesting, and sometimes surprising information.

Lanson [285] sent letters to 100 high school dropouts and received only ten replies, all from boys, ". . . although a fourth of the dropouts were girls." Eight of the ten respondents answered the question "What advice would you give to students who want to quit?" with variations of "Don't do it." Lanson concluded that "Letters and questionnaires are obviously not the way to get information on early school leavers," but she found the advice to potential dropouts "useful in counseling."

The counselor who must rely entirely upon returns by mail will do well to keep his questionnaire short. Baer and Roeber [14] in their second edition reported that ". . . a short questionnaire, such as that on a postcard" was the only one in thirty-five follow-ups to produce a 100 percent return. Postcards or envelopes for the future follow-up may be addressed by seniors to themselves just before graduation. The seniors may also be invited to suggest questions for inclusion in the question-naire which they will receive; the more they participate in preparing for the follow-up, the more likely they may be to respond when the time comes to do so. An offer to send a summary of the results to those who respond, with present addresses of all who reply, may help to increase the number who respond.

Felician [153] sent a postcard follow-up to 143 recent graduates of a Catholic high school and got a 36 percent response. He then enclosed the postcard in a letter written by a student and sent this to another 117 graduates in the same class. This time he got a 72 percent response.

Several years ago 200 schools cooperated with the National Associa-tion of Secondary School Principals in testing a variety of procedures for conducting follow-up studies. Forty of the schools were visited by mem-bers of the project staff. What was learned from this experiment has been ably reported by Beery, Hayes, and Landy [20]. Their report is still one of the best of all references on follow-up work.

Business firms experienced in direct-mail advertising have found that they can profitably use as many as ten or more different letters in series on the same prospects. From carefully controlled tests these firms have found that return envelopes of pink or goldenrod paper produce slightly more returns than those of white, blue, or green.

Other persons experienced in follow-up work report that a covering letter, separate from the questionnaire, usually brings more replies than a letter which is made a part of the questionnaire and that a letter en-closing a return envelope brings more replies than one without it.

When accurate data are imperative, the questionnaire must be care-fully prepared to avoid ambiguity. When earnings are to be reported, the question should indicate whether hourly, weekly, monthly, or annual earnings are to be recorded and whether take-home pay or earnings before deductions are desired. Part-time work should be distinguished from full-time by some clear definition; full-time has sometimes been defined as employment for more than twenty hours a week.

The graduates and dropouts to be approached in any follow-up study should include those whose separation from the school occurred approxi-mately a year earlier. Some schools also include graduates and dropouts of former years. Some follow up all former students at intervals of 1, 3, and 5 years; some at intervals of 1, 4, and 7 years; some at intervals of 1, 5, and 10 years. As noted in Chapter 2, high schools need to follow up their alumni after they have completed college and military or alternate service in order to find out where these former students got their first jobs. Without this information the vocational and educational guidance of prospective college students can be sadly unrealistic.

One important purpose of the follow-up project in the teaching of occupations is to help students to decide what they will do the next year. Plans projected beyond that time are best regarded as tentative—they change with disturbing frequency. A follow-up of the last preceding class brings in the most up-to-date information about conditions likely to face the present class. It has the added interest of including many persons known to present students. Follow-ups after more time has elapsed may add valuable information but should not be substituted for the one-year study.

The one-year study should be made every year on the preceding year's dropouts and graduates. Conditions change; a series of studies will reveal the changes. In a small school one year's group may be too small to provide a comprehensive picture of the major opportunities, but a series of one-year studies will soon fill in the gaps. To get a comprehensive picture sooner, the first study might cover all dropouts and graduates of the preceding five years.

The counselor who is making his first follow-up study may wisely keep it as simple as possible. After some experience, he may serve his colleagues and improve his staff relations by asking teachers and administrators if they would like him to include some questions of special interest to them. To avoid embarrassment, it may be necessary to explain at the start that space may prevent including everything desired but that the interests of the staff will be considered to the extent that space permits.

Seven of the author's graduate students have tried follow-up projects with their own students, following the procedure described in this chapter. Four reported enthusiastic student reaction; two had only average success; one tried harder than all the others but never quite managed to put it across. The kind of impromptu discussion described above requires a teacher who is a good discussion leader and who is alert and skillful enough to recognize and select good topics for discussion from the letters as they are read to the class. Such a teacher can do a superb job with surprisingly little effort.

The teacher who has misgivings about his ability to lead this kind of discussion need not forgo the follow-up study as a class activity. With no discussion at all, the students can learn much if the responses from alumni are passed around the class so that each student is permitted to read each response. On one occasion the author used this procedure with his own students, and every student in the class said that he had learned something worth the time devoted to reading the replies.

VARIATIONS

The possible applications and variations of the follow-up technique are innumerable. Any kind of organization that offers vocational guidance may follow up its former members, find out what has happened to them, and make their experiences available to present members as a glimpse into their own future. Alumni in military service may be followed up for a report on their experiences, which may include some items not mentioned in military recruiting literature. Alumni in college may be asked about things not mentioned in the college catalogues.

The follow-up may go to all alumni or to a small sample; it may be detailed or brief; it may ask for statistical data or for personal experiences and comments. Alumni may be reached by letter, by telephone, by personal interview, or they may be invited to return to the school to meet with present students. The study may be conducted by counselors, students, an office staff, or the alumni themselves. The results may be reported orally, in mimeographed or printed form, on film, or in person by the alumni themselves. Class discussion of the results may be directed by the teacher, the results may be used to begin a session in which all discussion will proceed nondirectively, or replies may be circulated around the class for all to read with no discussion unless the students start it.

A follow-up of prison "alumni." Ruderman [409], when he was educational officer at the Federal Correctional Institution, Danbury, Connecticut, handpicked a group of fifteen inmates and asked if they would like to participate in a follow-up study of Danbury "alumni." Questionnaires were mimeographed and mailed with a covering letter. The percentage of responses was not high, but the quality was excellent. Two of the respondents implored that any future letters be mailed in plain envelopes, not bearing the corner card of the U.S. Department of Justice. Among the questions suggested by the inmates were the following:

> Have you had difficulty finding a job because of your past record?
> Were you asked about conviction of crime?
> Did you have to explain your case in detail?
> Did being on parole prevent you from getting a job that you were otherwise qualified to fill? Please explain.
> Were you unable to gain admittance into a union?

Has a change of attitude developed toward you since your release from the institution on the part of your family?

The replies indicated a wide variety of experiences. Some employers had said in effect, "I'm glad you told me. Now let's forget it. Start where you are." One respondent said, "Everyone in the industry wanted to know all about it. They probably expect to arrive there any day now!"

Ruderman's complete report of the investigation contains numerous quotations from the replies; they make fascinating reading, even for one who hopes not to have personal use for the information.

Sondern [450] described how a judge brought successfully rehabilitated former probationers to his court to meet and talk with first offenders currently on probation.

Schools, colleges, and community agencies. One third-grade teacher had her students write letters to the fourth-grade students in order to learn what kinds of educational activities to anticipate in the year ahead. The fourth-grade teacher cooperated by having the letters answered.

One junior high school sent a selected group of its own students to the elementary school, where they answered questions about junior high school asked by sixth-grade students.

Group guidance classes in another junior high school prepared a questionnaire which they sent to tenth-grade students. See Cuony [112].

One eighth-grade English teacher invited three of her classes to suggest questions they would like to ask former students about their experiences in high school. The ten most popular questions were selected. Each student interviewed one, two, or three former students and reported the results to the class.

In one high school the senior problems class made a follow-up study entirely by personal interview. In another, a guidance club completed a follow-up under the direction of the school counselor. In some schools the counselors and the office staff do all the work of the follow-up study and then discuss the results with the students in class.

In the high school at Boonsboro, Maryland, Ferdian [154] follows up all graduates and dropouts one year after they leave the school. Those who enter college are followed up five years after high school graduation. In grade 12 a unit on occupations is focused on the occupations which most alumni enter.

To supplement the usual follow-up by mail, Ferdian posted in the high school corridor a large bulletin board reading: "WANTED. Information about Graduates, Boonsboro Hi School. Please drop information in box below. . . ."

Hoyt [246] and his students prepared a mimeographed report of the results from their follow-up of high school alumni. Two copies were placed in every homeroom. Additional copies were used for discussion in social studies classes. The report included in one table the job title, duties, employer, and business address of each employed respondent and in a separate table the job title, salary, and what the respondent liked best and least about his job. For each college attended the report quoted what the students liked and disliked about it.

The Denver schools published a twenty-four page booklet on *Vocational Opportunities in Metropolitan Denver* [495]. It included some of the results of ". . . interviews with recent graduates of the Denver Public Schools now employed in the Denver metropolitan area." Charts indicated that 66 percent of the employed graduates were in retailing, public utilities, manufacturing, real estate, insurance, and banking. The two largest job categories were clerical, 57 percent, and unskilled, 21 percent. The booklet closed with a list of 226 employers who had hired Denver graduates.

Nolfo [359] described how a high school followed up its graduates of the preceding five years and reported the results in a display during American Education Week.

> The display consisted of a listing of companies and firms, under which the names of Haldane graduates appeared. . . . A map of New York State with colored pins showed the location of plants that hired local graduates. . . .
>
> The display was personalized by adding a notice and a sheet of paper for comments, asking viewers of the display to make corrections or additions to the list of first jobs. Quite a few people contributed corrections. . . .
>
> Before the survey, the writer was under the impression that the local boys and girls found it difficult to obtain jobs in the home community. The survey proved how wrong this idea was.
>
> Out of 140 graduates (five-year period), 42 obtained "first jobs" in the home town and 98 obtained "first jobs" within a 25 mile radius of the town. To other Haldane staff members, too, this was startling; it has since caused them to be more careful about predicting where local graduates will find work.

One teacher prepared a follow-up questionnaire in two parts. While still in school the students answered part 1, in which they recorded their occupational choices and salary expectations. Some time after leaving school they answered part 2, in which they recorded the jobs they got and the salaries they earned. This kind of questionnaire makes it easy to compare expectations with achievements; the discrepancy between the two may be embarrassing to some of the alumni and tempt them not to reply. Any question which embarrasses a respondent may reduce the number of responses; such questions should be included only after consideration of this possibility.

Several high schools have invited their alumni who were in college to return to high school during their Christmas or spring vacations to meet with the high school students who were choosing colleges. In one case an informal afternoon tea was arranged with no formal program. In another, an evening meeting was arranged for parents and students, at which questions from the audience were answered by a panel of college students. In other schools, the alumni were seated at separate tables in the cafeteria during the lunch period. Each table was marked with the name of the college represented. Students were free to roam and ask questions.

Hayward [209] arranged an alumni day in which thirty-nine former students spoke for one or two minutes in a morning assembly and then met with students in smaller groups. The program was planned for the day before Easter vacation. It began with a breakfast for the alumni. One alumnus left college at 3 A.M. in order to participate. "The program was exceptionally well received by the students and the faculty. . . . Teachers expressed surprise at the manner in which alumni held attention and controlled groups. . . . The reunion breakfast gave the opportunity to keep abreast of conditions at the schools which our students attend."

Jackson and Rothney [254] compared responses given by the same fifty persons to the same questions asked on a questionnaire and in a recorded interview five years after graduation from high school. They found that

> For every dollar spent for the mailed questionnaire study, approximately $60 was spent on the interview procedure. . . .
> Interviews elicited significantly more complete answers. . . .
> Each . . . procedure elicited evidence . . . which did not appear on the other.

One girls' vocational high school invited to a special assembly alumni who were currently employed in dressmaking, garment-machine operation, beauty culture, millinery, tearoom management, and interior decorating. After each guest spoke briefly, the students were invited to ask questions. One purpose of the assembly was to help girls who were nearing their sixteenth birthdays and who were undecided whether or not to quit school. Among the questions asked were the following: "Does the school really train you for the job?" "What was your greatest difficulty at your first job?" "If you didn't know what to do, whom did you ask?" "How did you advance to your present position?"

During a severe economic depression, one superintendent of schools found five of his young alumni who had avoided unemployment by creating their own jobs and going into business for themselves. He brought them back to the high schools to tell the seniors how they did it.

One teacher found a young alumnus who had applied for a civil service job as stenographer. He had rented a typewriter, taken the competitive examination, and been called in for an oral interview. At this point he was turned down because he was only seventeen years old and the announcement of the examination had specified a minimum age of eighteen. He had not read the announcement carefully. At the request of the teacher he told his experience to the students in an assembly program as a warning to read announcements carefully. The same assembly group heard another warning from a student who had signed a contract to pay $92 tuition to a gyp civil service school.

A business school posted daily on a bulletin board in the school corridor the names of students and graduates who obtained new jobs, with a notation of the nature of the job and whether it was permanent or temporary. Students watched the bulletin board closely for news of their friends and incidentally learned the kinds of jobs that were open to graduates of the school.

Another school posted two new photographs of alumni on its bulletin board each week, with brief accounts of their activities in school and since graduation.

The public schools of at least three cities have made motion-picture films showing high school graduates at work on the kinds of jobs most frequently obtained. One film was accompanied by a script to be read by the teacher; the script described each student's job, how he got it, what he earned, and where he went to school.

Many high schools and colleges now make annual follow-up studies of recent graduates and prepare mimeographed reports which are distributed to faculty and students. The reports include job titles, employers, and school or college majors. Some include salaries; others include the students' names. Excerpts from some of the reports are published in student newspapers. The following excerpts illustrate different forms in which the results are presented.

From Wellesley College:

Category: Advertising and Publicity
Job Title: Typist-Trainee
Organization: Copywriting Dep't.   Young & Rubicam, NYC
Major: English

From the Averill Park, New York, High School *Guide to Parkers:*

Barbara Robinson, employed by the State Income Tax Department
as an IBM Key-Punch Operator
Phil Worrell has been employed since June as substation mainte-
nance man with Niagara Mohawk Power and Light Company
Jill Dooling has been a receptionist and clerk-typist at Travelers
Insurance Company, Albany, since May

From the Fashion Institute of Technology:

Apparel design

Graduates of course	97
Number reporting	96
Employed	88
In fashion industries	86
In other industries	2
Personal plans	2
Housewives	3
Attending full-time college	3

Occupations

Designer	33	Samplehand & Assistant in publication	1
Designer-Dressmaker	1		
Assistant Designer	24	Assistant Patternmaker	3
Asst. Designer & Pattern-maker	1	Assistant Milliner	1
		Model	1
Asst. Designer & Sample-hand	1	Model—Sales	1
		Sales	1
Asst. Designer & Secretary to manager	1	Fashion Co-ordinator & Designer	1
Sketch Designer	1	Assistant Fashion Director	1
Sketcher	4	Assistant Fashion Co-ordinator	1
Sketcher & Comparison Shopper	1	Assistant Production Manager	2
Artist	2	Photo Studio Trainee	1
Stylist	2		

Industries

Women's & Junior Dresses	14	Children's Underwear, Nightwear, Robes & Housecoats	4
Custom Dresses	2		
Children's Dresses	10		
Women's & Junior Sports-wear	5	Furs	1
		Shoes	1

Children's Sportswear	9	Shoe Ornaments	1
Knitwear	5	Men's Shirts	1
Women's & Junior Blouses	1	Boys' Wear	3
Children's Blouses	3	Rubber Products	1
Women's & Junior Coats		Fashion Design Studio	2
& Suits	3	Pattern Company	1
Bathing Suits	1	Buying Office	3
Women's Underwear, Night-		Retail	2
wear, Robes & Housecoats	10	Publication	1

The State University Agricultural and Technical Institute at Farmingdale, New York, has published a series of reports on placement and progress of graduates. For each department of the institute, these publications report the number of graduates, the number employed in the field for which they were trained, the number in military service, the number continuing their education, the number in other activities, the average weekly salary, typical placement situations, and current employment prospects.

If all colleges would make comparable data available to prospective students and their counselors, the problem of choosing a college would be simplified for some students, and some of the poorer colleges would receive fewer applications. Perhaps it is time for counselors, students, and parents to begin asking other colleges for information of this kind.

A major breakthrough in this direction has been achieved by Hoyt [245] with the publication of his 35 S.O.S. Guidance Research Information Booklets. Based upon data collected from 5,000 students and 2,000 graduates of 35 different training programs in 20 trade, technical, and business schools, these reports reveal the kinds of jobs which the graduates of each program actually got, where the jobs were located, what they paid, and many other facts of interest to prospective students. The data are presented in easy-to-read charts, amusingly illustrated.

Positions held by the graduates of several curricula were listed with the curriculum descriptions in the annual catalog and bulletin of Southern Technical Institute [70].

Moyer [343] wrote to college alumni and asked for detailed accounts of their occupational experiences since graduation. The replies were filed by occupation and by employer and were made available to future students who wished to read them.

Radcliffe College [382] published a series of four-page leaflets "based on the activities of the graduates of the Harvard-Radcliffe Program in Business Administration." Each leaflet contained a general comment on the opportunities for women in one occupation, followed by four or more profiles in which alumni described "My Typical Workday" and "The Qualities Most Needed for Success and Enjoyment in My Job."

Sutherland [473] invited recent college graduates to give brief talks to students in a freshman course unit on vocational opportunities.

One engineering college built a careers course for the junior class around a series of lectures in which alumni described their own jobs.

One academic department in a graduate school invited some of its alumni to return in groups of three and four for occupational group conferences with students.

One of the most readable of follow-up reports is *Peacocks on Parade: A Survey of the Alumni of Saint Peter's College* by Grady, Malnig, and Tuleja [188]. Covering the alumni of eighteen years, this report includes average income by occupation, methods used in obtaining employment, relation of jobs to expectations, occupational distribution of graduates by major fields of study, and percentages of satisfied and dissatisfied workers by occupation. Appended is one of the best questionnaires this author has seen; it is comprehensive, easy to answer, and coded for machine tabulation.

Lichliter [293] followed up the alumni of Lindenwood College over a period of ten years. Her report included a table showing the major occupations of Lindenwood graduates by categories and also the specific entry jobs with names and addresses of employers.

Stevens [457] compared the occupational choices of 217 entering freshmen at Diablo Valley (Junior) College with the jobs held four years later by sixty-nine respondents to a follow-up inquiry. Twelve percent chose business at entrance. Forty-six percent were in business jobs four years later.

Davenel [115] described how a college placement office organized four hundred alumni to report on job openings in their companies and on developments in their occupations. The alumni served also as sources of occupational information for students and helped the placement office to set new records in a depression year.

In a recruiting brochure, the New York State College of Agriculture at Cornell [490] included thirty-eight photographs of alumni in thirty-eight occupations, each accompanied by a few sentences about the alumnus and his job.

Simmons College devoted one issue of its *Bulletin* [429] to a selected list of beginning jobs obtained by Simmons graduates. Addressed "To the Director of Guidance" it read in part:

> With a conviction that high school girls may be helped by reviewing a sampling of specific positions held by college graduates, we

have asked Miss Anna M. Hanson, who is director of placement at Simmons College . . . to list a few of the widely varied positions to which Simmons graduates have gone. We hope that this presentation will prove interesting to some of your students as they begin to think about career possibilities.

Several other colleges have published collections of articles on different occupations, prepared by their own alumni, and have distributed the publications to their students and prospective students. As an informational service to students, such publications can be useful and interesting. As recruiting literature they may suffer from the desire of the recruiter to present an attractive picture. The success stories of superior alumni have been flagrantly misused in the recruiting literature of the accredited as well as the gyp schools.

One state employment service made a follow-up of all high school dropouts and graduates who had registered with the service under the cooperative high school program. The results were reported to each high school in the program.

The Corpsman [102], a periodical for the men and women of the Federal Job Corps, published a series of articles describing the jobs of some of its graduates. Sample headlines: "Job Corps Graduate Is Electrician's Aide"; "Kilmer Graduate Is Typewriter Repair Trainee."

One Altrusa Club arranged a two-day vocational conference at which high school graduates of the preceding three years told high school students about the problems which these alumni were meeting in their work.

An occupational therapist in a hospital got former patients to return and tell others of their experiences in achieving successful vocational rehabilitation. The patients asked questions eagerly.

The Urban League in Pittsburgh, Pennsylvania, once prepared a motion-picture film showing Pittsburgh Negroes at work in more than thirty occupations, including the professions, business, industry, and personal service.

The counselor or teacher who can do none of the things suggested in this chapter but who wants to get some of the benefits from follow-up returns can begin by writing informal personal letters to his former clients or students at the rate of one a week, just to inquire about what they are doing now. If some of his alumni are in the same town as his institution, he can make the same kind of inquiry by telephone or in person and learn much more. Anyone can do this, and anyone who will do it regularly for a few months will be impressed by what he learns from the replies.

COMMENT

As noted above, the primary purpose of the follow-up technique described in this chapter is to give the students a more realistic picture of what is ahead of them. Other methods of occupational research show what jobs are available to all the workers in a given geographical area; from these data the jobs that will be available for the present seniors can only be inferred. A survey of local employers may reveal what jobs the employers think they will have available for young graduates, but no employer can be blamed for hiring the best-qualified applicant, and when the time comes to do the hiring, there may be experienced workers available. Only the follow-up study has these two advantages: (1) It has no geographical limits; it goes wherever the alumni go, and it maps the true geography of the employment market for this group; (2) it reveals the kinds of jobs that the alumni have been able to get in the open competition of the employment market. In addition, the follow-up study provides current occupational information on the student's own level of understanding and interest, obtained directly from original sources by means of student activity. It dignifies the student who is conducting his own segment of the survey, the respondent who is being interrogated as an adult worker, and entry jobs, which no matter how unimpressive become the subject of group analysis and discussion. If well done, the project may help to build good alumni relations. Incidentally, the results may facilitate curriculum revision.

As a technique of teaching occupations, the student-made follow-up is not perfect. It is not foolproof. Employment conditions change from year to year; there may be desirable opportunities not discovered by former students; a single former class may be too small to provide an adequate sample of available employment opportunity; the information supplied by alumni may be inadequate or inaccurate because of ambiguous questions, omissions, errors in recall, or intentionally false replies. The class discussion is almost wholly dependent upon the returns and what the teacher can make out of them. Provocative, profitable discussion results only under a skillful discussion leader; consequently, not every teacher can use this technique with equally good results. However, no technique known to this author does a better job of bringing down to earth the naïve and unrealistic vocational expectations of the average group of high school and college students.

Most of this chapter has been devoted to the follow-up study as a technique of teaching a unit or a course in occupations. Follow-up data, of course, have other uses.

The good counselor follows up his clients to the point of job placement and beyond, in order to learn what happened as these clients tried to follow the plans which the counselor helped them to make. The counselor thus learns how realistic or naïve he was in what he tried to do with and for his clients.

The counselor who does not do this kind of follow-up never knows how much he helped or hindered the clients who sought his aid in choosing or in reaching their occupational objectives. In ignorance of the results of his work, this counselor may go on confidently making the same mistakes for the remainder of his professional life.

The counselor who is planning career conferences, or buying occupational books, or arranging plant tours, or interpreting vocational interest inventories needs to know not only what occupations are of interest to his clients. He needs even more to know what kinds of jobs his former clients have been able to get, and what kinds they did not get despite his counsel and their persistent efforts.

Perhaps the greatest weakness in vocational counseling today is the widespread counselor ignorance of what has happened to former clients, and the consequent repetition by counselors of their own mistakes.

REVIEW QUESTIONS

1. What is the major purpose of the follow-up study in a course in occupations?

2. Why should the teacher accept suggested questions in the words of the student?

3. Why should letters be addressed in the classroom rather than at home?

4. Why should the class not use a long questionnaire?

5. Why should the replies be addressed to, and opened by, the students?

6. What are some of the topics suggested for the statistical summary?

7. What is the highest percentage return that others have obtained on follow-up studies?

8. Of the various kinds of follow-up projects described which most appeals to you? Why?

9. What two advantages are peculiar to the follow-up study?

10. In Appendix B on "Suggestions for Discussion Leaders," did you find anything new to you that you can use? Did you find anything with which you disagree?

11. What technique of teaching does the best job of bringing unrealistic vocational expectations down to earth?

12. You have just been hired as a counselor in the high school or college that you attended. There have been no follow-up studies. Your boss asks you to make one. How will you proceed?

13. Is there anything in this chapter that you can use to improve your work? What? How?

14
Plant
Tours

The plant tour provides a painless way of getting students to absorb information about occupations other than the one they currently expect to enter—an important objective with students whose ambitions exceed their abilities. It comes nearest of all to the author's definition of perfect teaching—a situation in which everyone learns, everyone enjoys learning, and no one feels that he has been overworked. An entire course or unit may be taught by this technique alone, it may be used to add variety to a course taught by other methods, or it may be used independently of any course.

PURPOSE

The purpose of the plant tour is to give students an opportunity to see, hear, feel, and smell the environment in which they may work if they choose any of the occupations observed. Additional information will be picked up en route; it should be welcomed, but the teacher should not be too eager to teach every possible fact. Again, don't try to do too much. Enjoy the trip. Let your students enjoy it.

PROCEDURE

Because schools have different policies regarding student tours, the counselor's or teacher's first step should be to discuss policy with his immediate superior.

Where to go. The first places selected for visits should be those in which large numbers of former students are employed. These are most likely to be the places where the present students ultimately will work, regardless of where they now think they will work. When these tours have been completed, the less important places may be included as time permits.

If no follow-up studies have been made and the teacher has no information about the present employment of former students, the following potential sources of employment should be considered:

Retail stores
Restaurants and hotels

> Telephone company
> Railroad and bus companies
> Garages and service stations
> Electric light and gas companies
> Cleaning and dyeing firms
> Building and general contractors

These businesses are usually found even in small communities, and they frequently account for a substantial proportion of beginning jobs.

Many small communities also have one or more factories that are well known to everyone. The new teacher coming in from another community may quickly learn about them at the local bank, chamber of commerce, or library. The local office of the state employment service could be the best source of information about potential employers, but it is sometimes reluctant to release employers' names. The teacher should, nevertheless, visit the local employment office and get all the information he can. The employment services have a great deal of information on related topics which they are usually eager to share with school counselors.

How to get in. After an industrial plant tour the author's students often ask, "How do you make arrangements for these tours? How do you get the companies to let us come?" Students seem to feel that supersalesmanship must be required. Actually most employers need no persuading. In general, they are as willing to do another person a favor as are other human beings. Most employers are parents; they are interested in their children and in what the schools are trying to do for them. Many of them recognize that effective vocational guidance may help to reduce labor turnover, which is one of their persistent problems. Some employers are subject to government regulation and therefore especially eager to cultivate public goodwill. In periods of labor shortage, some employers welcome the opportunity to show what they have to offer to prospective employees. Others see potential future customers in any tour group. And nearly all of them have had twelve years of indoctrination in which to form the habit of doing anything that a teacher asked them to do.

For the reader who wants specific directions, the author's usual procedure is to telephone the company office and say to the person who answers, "Could you tell me the name and the exact title of your personnel director? . . . Will you connect me with him please?" And when the personnel director answers,

> Good morning. This is Robert Hoppock. You don't know me. I'm a professor at New York University and I'm calling to see if you would

like to do us a favor. May I tell you what we want? . . . We are trying to do a job here that may have some long-range effect upon the kind of people who come to you to apply for work. My part of this is in helping to train the school and college counselors to whom students go when they want help in deciding where they will look for a job. As a part of this training, we try to get them out of the classroom and into industry where they can see what a job looks like. I'm calling to inquire whether or not we could arrange sometime to take this group on a tour of your plant.

Usually, there follows a short conversation in which the personnel director inquires about the size of the group, what we wish to see, and when.

Sometimes a little preliminary conversation with the telephone operator or with the president's secretary is necessary when the company has no person whose title is similar to personnel director, and we have to identify the person who hires high school graduates and dropouts. Sometimes the personnel director's secretary asks who is calling and about what. In rare cases, the secretary will handle all arrangements; sometimes she will relay the request to her superior; usually, she puts her boss on the wire immediately. An occasional employer finds it impossible or inconvenient to arrange a tour; most employers have responded favorably; many of them cordially.

If the reader wishes to arrange tours for high school students, the approach may be revised as follows:

Good morning. This is Fred Lange. You don't know me. I'm a teacher at the high school, and I'm calling to see if you would like to do us a favor. May I tell you what we want? . . . We are trying to do a job here that may have some long-range effect upon the kinds of people who come to you to apply for work. We are trying to help our students to learn a little more about the kinds of jobs that may be open to them when they finish high school. In order to make this part of their education more realistic, we want to take them on some plant tours. I'm calling to inquire whether or not we could arrange sometime to take them on a tour of your plant.

Some teachers hesitate to ask for permission to tour a plant, because they fear their presence will distract the workers, lower production, and thus increase the employer's costs. The author has found no evidence on the effect of student tours, but Wright [529] reported that when the Rockbestos Products Corp. set aside a Family Day for their workers' relatives to tour the plant, ". . . production went up 15 per cent."

Preliminary arrangements. It is desirable for the teacher to make a preliminary visit himself in order to determine whether the trip will be profitable, to explain to the host just what he wishes to accomplish, and to select important points for emphasis. In practice some busy teachers omit this step. It is perhaps better to omit it than not to take the class on any trips.

In making the preliminary arrangements, whether by visit, letter, or telephone, the teacher should do the following:

Explain clearly the purpose of the trip.

Determine into how many groups of what size the class will be divided and thus how many guides and assistant teachers will be needed. Try to keep the groups small enough for everyone to hear what the guide says during the tour of the plar.t; the ideal number probably is between five and ten students in each group. Do not insist on small groups if the host finds it difficult to provide for them. In the author's experience, hosts have often preferred to divide the class into small groups and to provide a guide for each group. On one trip to a hospital, each student in the class was provided with a nurse as a guide. On other occasions, a class of seventy-five has had to get along with one guide.

Fix the starting and closing times.

Find out where the group should report and to whom.

If possible, arrange for a question period in a quiet room before or after the tour; in large groups only a few students may hear what the guide says during the trip. If a question period can be arranged, see Chapter 15 of this book for suggestions on how to conduct it. Inquire whether or not it will be feasible to include a representative of the union or one or two young employees in the question period.

Provide a sufficient number of assistant teachers to keep the groups together and in order; these assistants may be recruited from parents or older students or from the class itself.

Arrange transportation.

Secure the parents' consent if necessary.

If company literature is available for distribution, try to distribute it to the class a day or two before the tour. There is likely to be more student interest in reading it before the trip than after. The impending visit provides motivation for prompt reading plus an opportunity to ask questions which may be provoked by the publications.

The experience of the author and his students suggests that if the question period comes after the tour, the students will have more questions to ask and less time in which to ask them than if the question period precedes the tour. Few guides seem to be able to stick to a time schedule. If the tour comes last and the guides know that the class will depart at a certain time, they cover more ground in less time. Most plants of moderate size can be *seen* in forty-five minutes or less. They could not be fully explained in forty-five days. The major purpose of the tour is to see, hear, feel, and smell the environment in which the work is done; this purpose can be accomplished on a fairly rapid tour. The author suggests that the teacher try arranging his own tours both ways until his own experience indicates which arrangement is better for his purpose. Sometimes the question period cannot be provided, because the host has no conference room large enough to seat the class.

Preparing the students. The students may be told that the trip has two major purposes. For those who think they may someday like to work in the place visited, the trip will provide an opportunity to see the surroundings in which they may work and the kinds of jobs to which they may be assigned. For the others, it will provide an unusual and a pleasant opportunity to learn something about how other people make a living— an important part of anyone's cultural education. The students may be invited to suggest other purposes which the trip may serve.

How to behave. Before the first trip the group should be told explicitly how to behave during the visit. Even well-bred children are often thoughtless. Even thoughtful, conscientious children may not realize the importance of not doing in a factory things which are permissible, perhaps even encouraged, in the classroom. Emphasis should be placed upon the status of the group as guests and upon the importance of acting like guests.

Reed [389] suggested several do's and don't's for counselors who visit industry. The following items have been selected from her list. Some of these suggestions apply mainly to counselors and to teachers; others apply equally to students and should be discussed with them.

Have an objective and a plan for its realization.
Be a welcome guest and a courteous one.
Maintain the attitude of the scholar and guest.
Be appreciative. It costs time and money to entertain you.
Be humble. Most counselors are grossly ignorant of business principles, practices, and problems.
Arrive on time and leave on time.
Show appreciation for courtesies received by a "thank-you" letter.
Observe absolutely any safety precautions relative to dress, handling material, touching machinery, etc.
Avoid visits during busy seasons or on days known to be especially busy.
Don't force yourself in if you are not wanted.
Don't be late and don't change a date and hour once set unless absolutely necessary.
Don't act like a censor of business ethics or a labor inspector.
Don't ask impertinent questions.

Don't ask too many questions; look and listen.

Don't give advice gratis.

Don't jump at conclusions.

Don't scatter your opinions around promiscuously.

Don't betray confidences. It is an unpardonable sin.

Don't interrupt work. Talking to employees on duty may cause accident, destroy teamwork, or lower piece-rate wages.

Don't introduce unpleasant or controversial topics.

Don't expect free lunches, boxes of candy, a bag of doughnuts, a dish of ice cream, or a sample pair of hose.

Don't comment on what you have observed in other plants. Most of all avoid comparisons.

Don't take along uninvited guests. It is bad manners and bad policy.

Don't presume to rate employer policies and training programs for publication. When educational systems have learned how to rate their own employees and training programs, it will be time enough to attack the same problems in industry.

Don't try to educate or socialize employers.

Don't argue. It will not help in attaining your objective.

To Reed's suggestions may be added:

Don't smoke on tours without first asking if smoking is permitted.

Don't lag behind the group. You may lose them or you may be suspected of pilfering.

Suggestions for acceptable behavior should be reviewed briefly before each subsequent trip until they become habitual practice with the students.

Further discussion of plant visitation may be found in Reed's book on pages 122 to 125 and 242 to 244.

What to observe. Perhaps the most important caution of all is to keep attention focused on the workers rather than on the process. Otherwise, the class may learn much about the manufacture of vacuum cleaners but relatively little about the workers who manufacture them. The students should be asked to look at every worker and every job with three questions in mind: If I wanted to do that job, would I have what it takes? Would that job meet my needs? Would I enjoy doing it?

They may be asked, instead or also, to select the one job they see which they think they could do best and the one they could do least well.

Class discussion after the tour. At the next class session these points may be discussed and a blackboard or notebook list made of the abilities the students think would be required in the jobs they observed and the things they think they would like or dislike about such jobs. These lists should give the alert teacher an opportunity to correct misunderstandings and to initiate discussion of abilities, aptitudes, interests, and job satisfaction. The beginner who feels lost in exploring these topics need not abandon trips on this account; all this information is surplus value, incidental to the main purpose of giving the students the opportunity to see, hear, feel, and smell.

If the class saw too many jobs to discuss all of them, preference should be given to those which offer the largest number of opportunities to beginning workers.

If time permits, the class may be taken to visit two or more places of employment in the same line of business. In this way they may learn more effectively than from any lecture that opportunities, requirements, working conditions, etc., vary from employer to employer and that what one person says about an occupation should never be considered final until it has been compared with what others have to say. Classroom discussion on the day following such visits may focus on which company the students would prefer to work for if they were offered jobs by both, and why.

Before and after each trip, news releases regarding it may be prepared by the class, by a committee, or by the teacher, submitted to the host for correction, approved by the principal, and sent to the local newspapers. A letter of thanks should go from the class or the teacher to the host.

VARIATIONS

Sidewalk superintendents. Nearly everyone likes to watch other people work. Students should be encouraged to observe people on the job at every opportunity and always to ask themselves the same three questions: If I wanted to do that job, would I have what it takes? Would that job meet my needs? Would I enjoy doing it? They may be asked to report their observations, orally or in writing, daily or weekly. The teacher who likes to glamorize activities may organize a Sidewalk Superintendents' Club.

A day in industry. White [513] arranged an Occupational Orientation Day, on which fifty-eight local employers were hosts to several hundred high school seniors in order to give graduating students a better understanding of the occupational opportunities of the community. Each student was assigned to one workman with whom he spent the entire workday. Wherever possible the student participated in some of the work.

Advance preparation included written instructions to each student, as follows:

Please report to (workman) at (firm and address) Thursday, April 28 at _____ A.M. for the activities of Occupational Orientation Day. This person will have been notified of your assignment and is asked to report on your punctuality and cooperation during the day. Keep this slip as an introduction to the supervisor who will outline your program for the day.

Final letters to the cooperating companies read as follows:

Gentlemen:
Thank you for your willingness to cooperate with the high school in our plan for Occupational Orientation Day, Thursday, April 28.

A list of the students who will report to your firm is enclosed. We hope that these boys and girls will make a favorable impression and receive a fund of knowledge and experience from the contact with your staff.

Each student should have a slip of introduction. If convenient, will you return these slips with personal notations regarding punctuality, conduct, apparent interest and the like. This material may be used in future counseling with the boy or girl.

We appreciate your cooperation and hope that definite benefits will materialize from the activities of this day.

Cordially yours,

White reported that in five years of conducting such programs, not one unfavorable report had been received, which suggests that there must have been careful matching of student interest with work assignment and effective indoctrination of students on how to behave. White suggested that, in making assignments, one should

Avoid assigning a student to a place where he has been or is employed in a part-time capacity. There is apt to be nothing new in the experiences of the day unless this is avoided.

Do not assign all the good or poor students in any category to one or two firms. Spread the good, average and poor as widely as possible.

Avoid assigning known cliques of students to the same firm.

Student comment on the experience included the following:

I was sent yesterday, along with Harriet Redding, to the First National Bank in Lake Forest, Illinois. It proved to be a most interesting and thrilling experience. . . .

Machines—I never did see so many different kinds before. One machine typed in capitals and added and subtracted too. This was used for the ledgers and journals. Other girls there were busily balancing their own records and also the statements that are sent out to their customers at the end of the month. They let us cancel a few of the checks. . . .

We were allowed to photograph the checks, which is done twice a day, and also to stamp them with the bank seal. The switchboard operator showed me how to operate the switchboard too. We were also shown how to operate an addressograph—a machine that typed out the addresses on envelopes. One of the girls there even took us up to the attic, where old journals, etc., are kept for years. . . .

Harriet and I had a wonderful day. Neither of us had thought there was so much work connected with a bank, but now we know.

Thank you, Mr. White, for sending me there. I appreciate it very much.

Dorothy Hironimus

The American Steel and Wire Co. reported its experience with Occupational Orientation Day in its own house organ, from which the following excerpts are taken:

> Maybe you know all there is to know about your job. If you think you do, just let a young high school student spend a full day at your elbow asking what you're doing and how, when, where, and why you're doing it. . . . There are more questions in the average high school senior than in a barrel of radio quiz programs. . . .
>
> O.O., we might explain, stands for Occupational Orientation, a flossy term for what Fibber McGee would call, "finding out all about what goes on in a particular job and how you're gonna like it if you should decide to take it up and all like that there."

Wilson [519] arranged a program of fifty-one visits for 422 students and teachers in a single day. All students above grade 9 participated. In preparation for the visits, each student was given a list of eighty-four common occupations, invited to add others and then to mark his first, second, and third choices. First-choice visits were arranged for 96 percent of the students. The Board of Education chartered buses to take students to seven nearby communities. Students who had participated in a similar program the year before and who elected the same occupation a second year were taken to a different place of employment in which to see the same occupation, even if this required transporting them to another city. Each visit included a tour of the facilities, a lecture, and a discussion period.

Nursing was the most popular occupation. One group of thirty-seven students visited the local hospital, where student nurses took them on a comprehensive tour of the plant, demonstrated various phases of a nurse's work, and produced a play illustrating various types of nursing service. A second group of twenty-eight students, who had visited the local hospital the year before, traveled to another community where they toured the wards, diet kitchen, laboratory, classrooms, and nurses' residence and saw the film "R.N." Refreshments were served to both groups.

Most of the groups were much smaller; more than half of them consisted of fewer than five students, and ten consisted of one student each. The occupations observed included advertising, agriculture, architecture, art, accounting, automobile mechanics, banking, beauty culture, bookkeeping, bricklaying, cabinetmaking, carpentry, chemistry, dentistry, dietetics, drafting, chemical, civil, electrical, and mechanical engineering, electrical installation and repair, fire fighting, floristry, forestry, foundry work, insurance, interior decoration, jewelry, journalism, laboratory technology, library work, machinist work, music, nursing, optometry, occupational therapy, office work, patternmaking, personnel work, pharmacy, photography, physical therapy, printing, psychology, retailing, secretarial work, shoe repair, social work, stenography, teaching, telegraphy, telephone line work and switchboard operation, textile technology, veterinary medicine, and YMCA work.

From his experience with this project Wilson reported: "Every report received from students, teachers and hosts favours continuance of the visits (90% returns). For the third year in succession no one refused to act as host to a group. . . . Every host indicated willingness to talk with individual students from time to time as requested by the school."

The Career Insights Program [63] provided two weeks of plant tours during the 1965 summer vacation for students about to enter the senior year of high school in Rochester, New York. Participants were selected from interested applicants, each of whom was required to obtain the written approval of two teachers and one counselor from his school. The selected students were divided into five groups of six to twenty persons each, according to their expressed interests in chemistry, engineering, business operations, marketing, and production. An experienced counselor or teacher led each group. The program was "sponsored by the Genesee Valley School Development Association in cooperation with the Industrial Management Council, Rochester area industries, and area high schools." The project provided opportunities for students to observe and talk with workers in many different jobs within the fields of their major interest. The project coordinator was Charles M. Achilles of the University of Rochester.

Losi [309] and others arranged a Job Visitation Program in which 400 high school seniors each spent one day observing one worker at his work.

DuBois [138] arranged plant tours for high school students as part of a career-day program. Seven groups of students were transported in seven school buses. Each group went to two or more plants. The buses left the school at 9 A.M. and returned before 3 P.M., so that the plant tours did not interfere with the normal bus transportation of pupils to and from school.

Washville [502] described a similar program in a smaller community as follows:

Have you ever had the opportunity to be an overnight guest at a hospital, witness an operation and tour the entire institution? Have you ever done any sports announcing over a radio station? How would you like to be a secretary to the city's mayor? Have you ever observed a salesman close a five-hundred dollar sale? How would you like to attend a State Police cadet class and experience an on-the-spot arrest for a highway violation? These are a few of the many situations students of Central High School of Hopewell Township, Pennington, New Jersey, experienced on their "Job-for-a-Day." . . .

This technique placed each individual in his chosen field of work for one day's observation. . . .

An occupational questionnaire was distributed to each student to be completed after his day-on-the-job. The information gathered from this survey has been used to give the students of the high school a picture of jobs and requirements on the local scene. . . .

Sixty-seven students participated in the project that included thirty-two different occupational fields. . . .

The conclusion from the follow-up showed that 100% of the students considered the day was beneficial, and 14% stated that they would change their occupational goal as a result of their day-on-the-job. All of the students are in favor of continuing the project, and they felt the day had more to offer than listening to vocational speakers.

The project helped to further public relations between the school and the community and a growing number of prospective graduates have already received offers of employment.

Bley [29] reported several similar programs:

One way of acquainting youngsters with the world of work and its requirements is to give them a closeup view of the inner workings of their community's business and industrial firms. Recognizing this, a number of schools, businesses, youth-serving agencies and civic clubs have developed special programs that bring youngsters behind the scenes to see first-hand how trained and experienced employees handle various aspects of their daily jobs.

One such program in Philadelphia, Pennsylvania, co-sponsored by the Chamber of Commerce and the Board of Education is "Retail Executive for a Day." On that day, groups of high school seniors assigned to 30 cooperating stores, appeared at 9 in the morning, were greeted by company executives and oriented briefly on store policy, general merchandising, retailing and personnel procedures.

Each student was then assigned to an administrative official whose activities he observed through the day. At noon, the boys and girls lunching with the firm's top executives, took part in a question and answer period on store procedures.

Participating students later prepared papers on their observations for presentation to their high school classes. Those writing the best reports were invited to a follow-up luncheon held two weeks later by the Chamber of Commerce and the cooperating firms. Also invited were the student's high school principal and sponsoring teacher.

A similar program, "A Day on the Job with an Optimist," developed by the Optimist Club of Peoria, Illinois, utilized the business and professional experiences of club members. Lists of these members and their occupations were drawn up and matched with names of students expressing related vocational interests.

Each youngster spent the entire day with the Optimist member, joining him for lunch at the Optimist Club where he was introduced to the group's civic activities. As follow-up, youngsters were asked to fill out questionnaires on their day's observations.

In New York City, the Manhattan Boy Scout Council has been successfully conducting a "Community Leadership Day" for the last five years. For this program 150 Explorer Scouts are selected. Each spends a full working day with a business or industry executive.

Besides observing the executive at work, the Scout takes a tour of company premises and lunches with his sponsor. . . . In one case an executive, impressed with a Scout's potential, financed the boy's college training.

Cavitt [72] reported that one YWCA invited senior girls from forty-five high schools in neighboring small towns to come to the city for one day, tour local industries, observe workers, ask questions, see the YWCA residence, and talk with business girls who lived there.

McKinney [324] described a program which was arranged to give high school students

. . . a day's experience on a job under conditions which would be just as realistic as possible. . . .

Each student was to appear on the job at whatever starting time was required of the other employees. He was to remain throughout the day and work as a regular employee. His noon hour was of the same nature as his employer's. If the employer ate at the local drug store, the student would do the same; if the employer brought his lunch, so would the student. In this manner, it was hoped that the student would gain an understanding of the daily routine of the occupation and of such related factors as rest periods, slack times, contacts with salesmen, and both the drudgery and glamour involved. Students were to dress for the job so that the receptionist, the hairdresser, the forest ranger, the secretary, the welder, and the printer could all participate in whatever activities might accompany the regular day's work.

After the initial contact with the prospective employer was made by a committee member, the remaining interviews became the responsibility of the student. He was informed of the name and telephone number of his employer. It was then necessary for him to make a contact and request an interview in order for him to secure the necessary information about working hours, lunch arrangements, dress, and other appropriate details.

Each employer was informed as to the purposes of the preliminary interviews and was furnished with a suggested outline of points which might be covered. The outline was developed from suggestions made by students during discussions held as a part of senior problems class. Publicity was the major responsibility of one of the committee members. The nature of the activity made it easy to develop a series of progress reports over a period of three or four weeks and these, along with appropriate pictures, were used in the local paper. . . .

Several telephoned to ask about paying their students even though it had been agreed that no payment would be made. The employers were asked to abide by the original arrangements. . . .

Several students were given regular employment as a result of contacts made during the day. The preliminary interviews proved to be excellent learning experiences as they provided many of the young people with their first opportunity for a contact which was similar in many ways to a typical job application interview.

Both the students and their employers were asked to evaluate the day's activities. Students consistently reported that the actual experience on a job, even for a single day, gave them information which was helpful in making occupational plans. A few individuals who were unable to work at jobs representing their first choices felt that the experience was less valuable than it could have been for that reason. Employers reported that student participation was sincere, courteous, and cooperative, and that the experience was of sufficient value to the students to justify the time required. Several suggestions as to possible improvements were offered by employers who were unanimous in their opinion that the same arrangements should be tried for another year.

Hawes [207] reported a "Day-at-Work-with-a-Kiwanian" project in which thirty-nine Kiwanis members took 105 eleventh-grade students into their businesses for one day of work.

One county medical society got 150 physicians to agree to take students from thirty-eight high schools on their rounds with them for one day.

The Heart Association of Maryland arranged and financed a weekend at Johns Hopkins University for fifty high school juniors and seniors who had demonstrated an interest in medicine or medical research but who were not definitely committed to a medical career.

Englander [148] got mathematics teachers to select 120 high school students "who showed sufficient promise to warrant the exploration of teaching mathematics as a career." The students were invited to spend a day on a college campus where "A new approach to the learning of mathematics was demonstrated by a professor," and the students saw a motion picture in which the hero was a teacher. In groups of twelve the students met with college counselors to discuss mathematics teaching as a vocation.

Wintman [523] described a career week in which ". . . 350 visitation appointments were made and kept by the students," who went in small groups to see local places of employment. Several of the students were invited to return for individual employment interviews. Student comments included: "Now I really have an idea of what these jobs are really like" and "I didn't know that there were so many opportunities right here. . . ."

Extended visits to industry. Bley [28] also reported:

> A more extensive program along these lines is "Employee for a Week" developed by the Anderson, Indiana Urban League. Here the League contacted business and industrial concerns in that community, requesting that they employ a Negro boy or girl for one week without pay in a job related to the youngster's vocational choice. The League felt that the opportunity to try out in the field of job interest was intangible pay, worth much to each boy and girl.
>
> After employer contacts were made and various clerical and retail jobs listed, students were registered, interviewed, screened and counseled. Those selected for the program reported at their "jobs" on Monday morning.
>
> To publicize the project, pictures were taken of the youngsters at work. Newspapers provided additional publicity and radio stations beamed promotional spot announcements from 10 to 20 times daily.
>
> Evaluation sheets prepared by the Urban League for students and employers covered: adaptability of students, performance, customer reaction, fellow-employee reaction and managerial appraisal of the experiment.
>
> At the end of the week, a dinner was given for participating students, with each relating his or her own experiences on the job.

Highlights [422] reported that

> Each year senior and junior boys majoring in mathematics and sciences at Mynderse Academy, Seneca Falls, can take a course conducted at Gould Pumps, Sylvania Electric and Seneca Falls Machine

Company. The boys are screened by representatives from industry and assigned to one of three groups depending on their interests in engineering or related fields. The boys report to the assigned plants at 7 A.M., one morning a week, for eight weeks. One morning is spent in each of the divisions of the plant to which they are assigned. They keep a diary of their observations of and their discussions with the workmen to which they are assigned.

Carl B. Rogers, Jr., guidance director, reports the following values derived from the three years the program has been in operation: (1) industries, as well as the workmen, are enthusiastic about the program; (2) many boys have decided on careers in engineering, tool design or drafting as a result of their experiences; (3) several boys discovered that engineering holds no interest for them.

Heathcote and Hayter [210] took small groups of boys from a British secondary school on "extended visits to industry" during the Easter holidays. In two days at the Davy and United Engineering company the boys visited production departments, did some supervised work in the training school, heard lectures, and saw films. In three days at the National Coal Board they toured a colliery, the apprentice training school, and area workshops; they also spent some time with classes of new entrants. At Hadfields Ltd. they spent four days with the Easter intake of trainees, visiting production departments, and hearing lectures on safety, wages, training, hygiene, and industrial relations. After the visits "about one third" of the boys "changed their choice of employment to some extent."

King [276] described two programs of industrial visitation in the United Kingdom:

Industry and commerce in an age of full employment and a shrunken birthrate have encouraged instructional visits from the schools, if only with an eye to recruitment, at all levels. Among the more elaborate examples in the writer's experience there is the "Week in Industry" plan under which during either term or vacation, a group of senior pupils studies an industrial concern or group under the surveillance of works staff. . . .

At Leggatt's Way Modern School, Watford, boys in their last year have been given two weeks in factories in jobs selected by themselves. They make notes on processes, tools, and materials, as well as on conditions, hours, wages, and welfare. It is reported that, as a result, 85 per cent have been helped to decide, and 48 per cent have changed their original choice. . . .

For college students. One college arranged an annual program, cosponsored by the local Rotary Club, in which 350 seniors visited thirty local firms, inspected operations, and talked with managers and supervisors.

One school of nursing took its students on field trips to see the opportunities for employment of nurses in industry.

One medical college [526] invited students and their advisers from seven undergraduate colleges to spend a day on the medical campus. The program included observation of a clinical conference in which a panel of physicians discussed a patient, a tour of the Medical Center and research laboratories, a lecture on "Medicine as a Career," and a question period.

Miller [335] described a college course in which the students visited twenty different industries. "The assumption behind the 'Study of Industry' course is that . . . the opportunity to see men and women . . . carrying on occupational processes day after day, will tend to encourage students to think more realistically about their own career choices."

Tours for counselors and teachers. For several years the Dutchess County Guidance Association in New York [252] scheduled one day a year on which teams of two or three counselors visited different plants. The chairman of each team prepared a written report. All reports were edited by a project chairman, then duplicated on loose-leaf paper and distributed to each member school for insertion in a reference notebook.

Believing that the "more complex the local industrial community, the bigger the counselor's job," counselors in the suburban area of Philadelphia, Pennsylvania, applied "the principle of college visitation . . . to the area of vocational guidance." To learn at first-hand about working conditions, placement procedures and personnel, job requirements, salaries, and opportunities, the Montgomery County Personnel and Guidance Association dropped its after-school meetings in school buildings. With the help of the Manufacturers Association of Montgomery County, luncheon meetings were arranged at nine different industrial establishments. After each meeting, the host company provided a guided tour of the plant. Tour leaders were "asked to emphasize such things as jobs, opportunity, training, and placement practices rather than to focus on the product." Summary data on the company were mailed to all members of the counselors' association. For details see Hughes [248].

The six counselors of one junior high school took turns making weekly visits to local shops, offices, and industries, and sharing their information with each other.

Barrett [17] described how thirty counselors made a summer tour of thirty-four North Carolina colleges, in state cars, with financial aid provided under the National Defense Education Act.

Clark [88] and other counselors have made their own plant visits in order to learn more about local jobs for their students and alumni.

Many counselor educators arrange plant tours for their students. Sinick [430] had his rehabilitation counselors in training use the following outline to report their observations:

AN OUTLINE FOR REPORTING OBSERVABLE
ASPECTS OF A BUSINESS OR INDUSTRIAL FIRM

  I   The business or industry
     A Name and address of firm
     B Products or services
     C Major operations performed
 II Physical features of the environment
     A Transportation to and from firm
     B Mobility on premises
       1 Location of parking lot, access to buildings
       2 Location of cafeteria, washrooms, fire exits
       3 Space for movement, condition of floors
     C Lighting, heat, humidity, ventilation
     D Sanitation, orderliness
     E Noise, vibration
     F Health and accident hazards
     G Other physical features
III Psychosocial features of the environment
     A Characteristics of employees
       1 Predominant age range
       2 Male vs. female
       3 Minority group members
       4 Physically disabled
     B Interpersonal relations
       1 Isolated task vs. joint operation
       2 Opportunity for conversation
       3 Close vs. occasional supervision
     C Other psychosocial features
 IV Physical demands of work performed
     A Sitting vs. standing
     B Limbs required
     C Visual acuity
     D Color vision
     E Other sensory requirements
     F Finger dexterity
     G Weight lifted
     H Other physical demands
  V Psychological demands of work performed
     A Range of intelligence

      B   Memory and other mental demands
      C   Precision and other pressures
      D   Repetitiveness vs. variety
      E   Adaptability
      F   Other psychological demands
  VI   Psychological rewards of work performed
      A   Autonomy, freedom of behavior
      B   Responsibility vs. lack of responsibility
      C   Exercise of initiative, judgment, creativity
      D   Direct or indirect service to others
      E   Other psychological rewards

"Business-Industry-Education (BIE) Day" has now become a popular annual activity in many communities. It has been widely sponsored by local industries. On one day the schools are closed, and all the teachers tour local industries as guests of the management. Each teacher chooses the company he wishes to visit. Each company arranges the day's program for its own guests. Further information may be obtained on request from the National Association of Manufacturers, 277 Park Ave., New York.

One superintendent of schools arranged for his teachers to make eight visits on eight different days to eight different local industries. A mimeographed history of the industry was prepared by each company and distributed to the teachers prior to each visit. The visits were usually scheduled from 3:00 to 5:00 P.M., partly on school time. The parties were divided into very small groups, so that everyone could hear the explanations made by the workers who conducted the teachers through the plants. One of the participating teachers had been in the school system for thirty-one years and had never been inside one of the plants before.

Three types of plant tours are described in *Trends in Education-Industry Cooperation* [477] as follows:

> At San Francisco, Calif., 34 high school principals and vocational counselors were taken on a two-day tour of industries in that area by the local office of the National Association of Manufacturers.
>
> The visitors questioned company representatives in each plant on the minimum qualifications necessary for employment and received suggestions for assisting high school students in obtaining jobs and advancing in their chosen fields.
>
> Questions asked by the educators indicated that they were interested in devising better methods of screening students for prospective jobs in industry. . . .
>
> The plants visited during the tour were the California Packing Corporation, Standard Oil of California, Tea Garden Products Company,

Friden Calculating Machines Company, General Electric Company, Sunshine Biscuits, Inc., and General Motors.

A second NAM-sponsored two-day tour in the same area took 19 college editors and reporters on a trip investigating job opportunities in industry for college graduates. . . .

Colleges represented on the tour included University of California, Stanford, Santa Clara, San Jose State College, College of Pacific, University of San Francisco, St. Mary's, and San Mateo Junior College.

Plants visited included Crown Zellerbach Corporation, The Emporium, Lilli-Ann Manufacturing Company, Sunshine Biscuits, Inc., General Electric Company, Marchant Calculating Machine Company, and The Paraffine Companies.

At Toledo, Ohio, 1,000 students enrolled in the Macomber Vocational High School were taken on a tour of the Spicer Manufacturing Division of the Dana Corporation.

Seven buses were chartered to shuttle back and forth from the high school to the plant all forenoon. A carefully planned schedule was put into effect and the school authorities established a departure time of each class and also for the return of each group.

As each group boarded buses, the students received copies of a special "Welcome to Spicer" folder containing a letter of greeting from R. E. Carpenter, executive vice president of the corporation, in which the hope was expressed that "This plant tour will be helpful to you in your school work and may inspire in you the desire to qualify yourselves to some day take your place in this or some other plant to assist in carrying on the American tradition of craftsmanship that has earned for this country the reputation of leadership in the manufacturing world."

Sabbaticals for counselors. Some school systems have arranged for one or more of their counselors each semester to spend a "sabbatical" working in the junior division of the state employment service. The employment service, in turn, sent one or more of its interviewers to serve as school counselors. The counselors learned more about jobs open to their students; the interviewers learned more about the kind of information they could get from the school. Valdez [491] described a program of this kind conducted in San Francisco.

Tours of schools and colleges. Substantially the same procedures used for tours of industrial plants may be used for tours of schools and colleges. It is now fairly common practice for high school counselors to spend from two to four weeks each year visiting the colleges to which their students have gone or to which future students may go. The trips are made on school time at the expense of the board of education. The counselors see classrooms, laboratories, libraries, dormitories, and other physical facilities. Some counselors take photographs, which they use to illustrate subsequent lectures to students and parents. They talk with admissions officers about entrance requirements and with placement officers about the kinds of beginning jobs which former students have found. The counselors also talk with their own alumni at each college to get student reactions at first hand and to follow up on the counseling that took place in high school. For a report on the experiences of two counselors who visited several colleges see Dolan and Yates [133].

More and more counselors are finding ways to take their students on similar tours of nearby colleges. One high school put all its seniors in school buses and took them to visit five colleges in one weekend; the colleges were happy to provide meals and lodging at their own expense. Another school took forty students on a three-day trip to visit eight colleges. Two faculty members and two parents chaperoned. The cost per student was $42.50. The experience of one school in conducting and improving such trips was described by Santolo [414].

A simple, readable pamphlet for students and parents on *How to Visit Colleges* [242] may be obtained from the National Vocational Guidance Association, 1605 New Hampshire Ave., N.W., Washington, D.C.

Wilson and Bucher [520] have an excellent chapter on "How to Visit a College," with twenty suggested questions to ask.

Lippman [302] found that her seventh-year students in a special service school ". . . showed little concern for the future." She took them to tour a vocational high school in which two former students from her school were enrolled. "The trip was a social success. My children had been accepted and liked in a new situation, outside the realm of school. For some it was a practical demonstration of a future possibility, which made sense."

Elementary schools take their students on tours of the junior high schools. Junior high schools take theirs to visit senior high schools. Senior high schools and colleges arrange for their students to visit classrooms and observe activities in elective subjects before choosing their electives. For a brief account of an eighth-grade visit to a high school see Mason [321].

Other variations. One high school arranged with local service clubs for students to attend weekly club meetings for four weeks. Students were assigned to club members engaged in occupations of interest to the students. Each student reported to his host's place of business before lunch, went to lunch with him, and returned to work with him after lunch for the remainder of the school day.

The Rotary and the Soroptimist Clubs of another city cooperated with the schools in arranging for small teams of interested twelfth-grade boys and girls to visit leaders in business, industry, and the professions at their factories and offices. The students went by themselves, usually in groups of five or six, seldom more than ten.

At one high school a group of twelfth-grade students undertook to make a motion picture on how to get a job. To collect material for the film, they interviewed personnel directors and filled out application blanks. Although the project was commenced during the economic depression of the 1930s, all those who wanted jobs had been hired before they finished the film, and the film was never completed.

At another high school girls in the practical-arts class were sent to the school dental clinic in groups of three for instruction by the dental-hygiene teacher in the sterilization of instruments, care of equipment, and preparation of the patient for the dentist. The purpose was not to prepare the girls for dental-hygiene work but to show them something about one more occupation that might be open to them.

COMMENT

No amount of reading and talking about jobs in a chemical laboratory will leave the lasting impression of one whiff of hydrogen sulfide. No amount of discussion in a comfortable classroom will give one the sticky feeling of the high humidity in the rooms in which certain industrial processes must be completed. The noise of a boiler factory, the heat of a hotel kitchen, the cool comfort of an air-conditioned retail store—these are important considerations to some persons in the choice of an occupation. The plant tour provides one means of finding out about them in such a way that they are not likely to be overlooked or forgotten.

One of the author's students has commented on this point as follows:

> During my first years in public health nursing, I had to visit a button factory and look for health hazards. I was amazed to learn the conditions under which people worked and to smell a terrible odor coming from a place where cows' hoofs were being processed for the making of the buttons. The smell was awful, but the visit educational and memories of it will remain with me for the rest of my life.

After a class tour of a garment factory a counselor wrote:

> What hit me was the speed at which most of the women and men worked. I had heard and read of piece work but I had never seen it. . . . Not ever for me, I thought.

After taking a class of high school seniors to tour two insurance offices, one teacher of secretarial subjects reported their reactions in these words:

They noticed that one of the firms has a very lovely building with a spacious green lawn that looks like a velvet carpet. However, on the inside, the offices are generally dark and gloomy. There is no cafeteria; all the firm has for eating facilities are sandwich machines. People ate and smoked at their desks; the place was blue with smoke. The atmosphere was, on the whole, quite depressing. At the other firm, which does not boast of such an impressive exterior, the offices are cheerful, with plenty of light. There is a cafeteria where one may buy a hot lunch at a nominal fee. No one is allowed to smoke or eat at his desk. The atmosphere was efficient and businesslike, but at the same time, one of harmony and cordiality.

One high school junior commented:

I always wanted to be a fireman. In fact it was one idea I had since I was a kid. Our social studies class took a trip to the New York Fireman's School. After I saw what went on I changed my mind.

One can read about working conditions; one can talk about working conditions; one can recognize and acknowledge them intellectually; one can even memorize them and retain them long enough to pass an examination. But the visitor who has seen them and heard them, felt them and smelled them, has learned them emotionally as well as intellectually. He never forgets them.

The conducted tour to observe occupations presents important, factual information in a way that is easy and pleasant to absorb. The trip adds zest to any class that is getting tired of the traditional classroom. It provides excellent motivation for later study and discussion. It gets the teacher out of the classroom into the community and brings his own occupational information up to date. The information is obtained from primary sources and is presented to students simultaneously; errors due to intermediate communication and to obsolescence are thus reduced to a minimum. The information is more likely to be accurate, up to date, and pertinent to local conditions than is information obtained from most other sources. The visit also establishes and maintains employer contacts which may be useful in counseling, in placement, and in public relations.

In a study of 15,109 students in twenty-eight Catholic boys' high schools, Julius [263] found that

Over two-thirds of the seniors and lesser numbers in the other classes were interested in visiting places of work to see how various jobs appealed to them. Strangely enough, the parallel survey of the guidance services available in these same schools indicated that this opportunity is offered least to seniors and most to freshmen. . . .

Findings indicate that programs which administrators ranked high were ranked low in general by students, and those which administrators ranked low were ranked high by students.

Problems of time and transportation. Like all techniques the tour has its disadvantages too. If the trip is made on school time, students may miss classes in other subjects; if it is made after school, it may conflict with extracurricular activities or other responsibilities of the students. Sometimes there are transportation difficulties and expenses. These problems of conflict and of transportation are probably best solved as two high schools have solved them. In these schools the course in occupations was scheduled to meet for two or three consecutive periods two or three days a week. Nothing else except a study period was scheduled for these students in the afternoon session of the days on which the class met. School buses were not in use at this time and were used to transport students to and from the plant tours. The class returned to school by the end of the last period. The buses were then available for their usual duty and the students were free for their after-school activities. Using this plan, the class in occupations from one school toured thirty different plants in one year. At the end of the year the students and the teacher really knew something about the world outside the classroom.

In large cities with thousands of seniors and potential dropouts, popular employers may be reluctant to receive so many visitors, but in Detroit, Michigan, the Institute for Economic Education [390] over a fifteen-year period arranged plant tours for 53,347 teachers and 228,197 students.

The places visited may not be typical. Superficial impressions may be mistaken by teacher and student for adequate knowledge of opportunities and requirements. If the group is large, only a few students may hear what the guide tells them. Hosts may conceal facts that they prefer not to have widely known.

Though the tour is fun for the students, it is work for the teacher. Making advance arrangements takes more time and trouble than assigning another chapter in a familiar textbook. Occasionally, the tour is not welcomed by the prospective host, though this is unusual.

The most serious disadvantage is the danger of physical injury to a student and a subsequent suit for damages. In some states teachers are protected by law from such suits; in other states, insurance protection is available. The cautious teacher will discuss this aspect with the proper school authorities before arranging the first trip.

The teacher who has a public liability insurance policy on his home may be able to add protection against damage suits by students for a small additional charge.

Kearney [269] reported that

> Most attempts to collect damages from teachers do not fare well in court. . . . The courts are inclined to hold that if teachers exhibit the kind of care and concern that would normally be used by prudent parents, they are not negligent and hence not liable for damages. . . .
>
> So far as the author knows, there have been no lawsuits based upon things that have occurred on field trips.

Despite these disadvantages the author used tours when he taught his first high school class in occupations in 1927; he is still using them to give counselors in training realistic, up-to-date facts about occupational and educational opportunities and requirements. A class of his own graduate students who were taught mainly by tours and group conferences (see Chapter 15) voted overwhelmingly in favor of tours, even when they had to spend three extra hours in traveling and saw nothing more than the general offices of an advertising agency. They said that the tour gave them the "feel" of the organization and that employers talked more freely on their own premises than when they were guests at the school.

Comparison with the group conference. To compare the tour and the group conference techniques, the author invited the director of nurses of a nearby hospital to attend his class for a group conference. The instructor and the students spent an hour and a half asking her questions about nursing as a vocation. The following week the class toured the hospital. In a third session they listed things they had learned from the tour which they had not learned from the group conference. Some of the items listed were:

> Institutional nurses may spend considerable time supervising student nurses.
>
> Philosophical attitude of nurses toward their hours of work.
>
> Opportunities for part-time work for high school girls as nurses' aides.
>
> Opportunity to choose specialization within the hospital after some experience.
>
> Enthusiasm of student nurses.
>
> Hazards: anesthetics are explosive.
>
> Duties of nurse in operating room: sterilizing instruments, washing gloves, folding linen.

Duties with child patients: preparing food, entertaining them, playing with them.

Student nurses must make up time lost because of illness.

How troublesome patients can be.

Nurses dislike obstetric and maternity cases because their duties are mainly "maid service," cleaning up, etc.

Physical surroundings.

Odors.

Importance of habitual routine in emergency cases.

Need for good feet.

Nursing is not a glamorous occupation.

Nurses say the work is not hard.

Opportunity to teach student nurses.

Mental strain.

Difficulty of required studies.

The caste system and the way it is changing.

Some of the facts listed above could have been learned in the group conference, but they were not learned in the group conference despite the fact that everyone had ample opportunity to ask questions and most of the questions usually recommended for occupational studies were asked. Apparently, there are some questions one doesn't think of asking until he sees actual conditions. Apparently also, there are some things one can learn in no way except by firsthand observation.

REVIEW QUESTIONS

1. What are the four purposes of the plant tour?
2. What are the first places to be selected for plant tours? Why?
3. How would *you* arrange a plant tour for a group of your students or clients?
4. What valid reason may be given to students for touring plants in which they never expect to work?
5. What are some of the suggestions that may be made to students regarding their behavior on plant tours?
6. What questions should students be asked to think about as they look at each job?
7. Could *you* use the day-in-industry idea? Where? How? Why not?
8. If you were a director of guidance, would you try to arrange "sabbaticals" for your counselors? Why? Why not?
9. What does a plant tour do for the teacher?
10. How can you avoid the difficulties that arise when students have to miss other classes in order to go on tours?
11. Can plant tours be arranged in large cities?

15
Group
Conferences

When tours are not feasible, the group conference may be substituted. Like the two techniques already described, this one also may be used for an entire course, included within a course taught largely by other methods, or conducted as an independent project. The group conference resembles a press conference. In place of reporters there are students seeking information for their own guidance. Their questions are answered by one or more persons who have the information the students want. This technique may be used to get information about occupations, employers, unions, schools, colleges, and other subjects. It may be used for a single class, club, or assembly session; for a series of weekly career conferences; or for an entire unit or course in occupations.

PURPOSE
The purpose of the group conference is to provide the students with information which the counselor may or may not possess, to get this information at first hand from primary sources, to do this in a way that will arouse and maintain student interest and attention and not require the resource person to prepare or to make a speech.

PROCEDURE: OCCUPATIONAL CONFERENCES
The procedure described below includes steps to be taken when one or more group conferences are to be arranged as independent projects. Some of these steps may be omitted when the group conferences are included in the course in occupations. For example, if conferences are to be held after school hours and attendance is to be voluntary, it is imperative that the counselor first learn how many students plan to attend; otherwise he may find himself embarrassed with a guest and no audience. If conferences are to be included as part of a course and held during the regular class session, the teacher will still wish to consider the interests of his students, but he can present guests of his own selection without fear of losing his audience.

Tabulating student interests. The present interests of the students are ascertained from a mimeographed or dictated questionnaire which includes such items as the following:

> Considering what you now know of your own abilities, interests, and opportunities, what occupations do you think you are most likely to enter when you finish school?
>
> What other occupations are you seriously considering?
>
> What others would you like to enter if you could?
>
> Would you like to have more information about any of these occupations? Which ones?
>
> Would you attend, after school hours, group conferences with persons employed in these occupations?
>
> If you expect to continue your education after graduation, which colleges or other schools are of interest to you?
>
> Would you attend, after school hours, group conferences with representatives of these schools?

When the interests have been tabulated, the teacher examines the list. If important occupations or institutions have been omitted, he may prepare a list of these and inquire how many students would attend conferences on them.

Selecting resource experts. When the final list has been determined, a tentative schedule is prepared. Every conference is held on a different day in order that any student may attend as many as he wishes and the counselor or teacher may attend all.

The teacher then looks for good representatives of the most popular occupations, who may be invited to confer with the interested students. A good representative has had sufficient experience to know his field. He is temperamentally disposed to take a balanced attitude toward it and to state frankly both the advantages and disadvantages as he sees them. He is preferably not a recruiting officer. Employment managers and personnel directors usually have more of the desired information at their fingertips than do general managers and corporation presidents.

As noted in Chapter 5, employers and employees do not always agree about the advantages and disadvantages of employment in certain occupations, companies, and industries. It is, therefore, desirable to hear from both. Separate conferences may be arranged, or two guest experts may be invited to the same conference. If both are to participate in the same meeting, they should be so informed when they are invited.

If the same occupation is well represented locally in both large and small companies, both should be represented. In one community the small employers were neglected and resented it.

Minimum attendance. No representative should be asked to come unless the teacher is absolutely certain of a minimum attendance of five students. There should be indications of interest and promises of attendance from ten to fifteen students. Experience will indicate the proper ratio. Twenty or twenty-five is probably a desirable maximum; if the group is larger, there may not be opportunity for all of them to ask as many questions as they wish. Except for this limitation the technique can be used with groups as large as the teacher can manage. The author has held group conferences frequently in college classes of fifty and seventy-five. Working with high school students, Rubinfeld [407] ". . . discovered that a group of over a hundred could be handled without any difficulty and with the informal atmosphere still maintained."

Rubinfeld also found that

> When subject-matter teachers in fields relating to the particular conference requested their students to sign up, attendance was better than when the announcements were made in the homeroom. . . . For example, when we first advertised an engineering conference in the homeroom, we had 80 youngsters signed up, and only 55 in attendance. When we developed our new approach and advertised this conference in all of the science and mathematics classes, 125 students signed up and there were 120 in attendance.

Diamond [121] also ". . . tried sending information notices to the subject teachers most closely related to the career under discussion. . . . Although the original registration was quite substantial, only about half of those who signed up attended the conference. . . . Attendance *was* somewhat improved by sending the students reminder notes just prior to the conference." Diamond got better results by announcing each conference daily for two weeks over the school's public address system. "A colorful sign and registration sheet is placed on the guidance bulletin board. . . . The meetings are always held in the same room at the same time and always on the same day of the week. . . . Although the number of students who sign up is comparatively smaller than it was originally, at least 85% of those who sign up attend."

Inviting the guests. The teacher telephones or writes to the representative and invites him to come. The teacher explains the purpose of the conference and says in effect, "Please don't bother to prepare a speech. We prefer an informal conversation. The students and I will have plenty of questions to ask you." The teacher says also, "The purpose of the conference is not to recruit students for this field nor to discourage their entering it but to provide them with some of the facts they should have before they decide either way."

The author has found many guests more willing to come when informed that a speech was not desired. At the conclusion of several conferences, the author has asked the guests whether they would have preferred to make a speech. Almost invariably, they have expressed a preference for the group conference. They like to know that they are talking about something that is of interest to the audience.

One school has reported considerable difficulty in getting guests for conferences which were held during the first period of the school day. The author has encountered reluctance of some guests to leave their suburban homes and come to New York for Saturday morning conferences but has had no trouble getting guests for conferences at 4:15 and 6:15 P.M.

Guests from large organizations sometimes bring free literature for distribution. If this can be obtained and distributed a day or two before the conference, some students will read it in advance and ask questions about it during the conference. Employers, if asked, will sometimes supply copies of their employment application forms.

What to ask. If the students are meeting periodically as a class, they may be given a part in suggesting and selecting the basic list of questions to be asked. Otherwise the teacher prepares the list. In either case the list should be long enough to keep the guest talking if he is disposed to answer all questions briefly.

In Chapter 3 appears a detailed list of possible questions, based upon the basic outline for occupational studies prepared by the National Vocational Guidance Association. In group conferences, the author uses a much shorter list, which is reproduced below:

Do you employ dropouts? High school graduates? College graduates?

Do they all start in the same job?

Do you have any part-time or summer jobs?

What are the principal job categories in which beginners start? About how many beginners did you hire last year for each of these major job categories? Do you expect to hire more or fewer next year?

(From here on most of the questions are focused on the one or two categories which take the largest numbers of beginners.)

What are the starting salaries? About how much may the average worker expect to earn after five years? After ten years?

What does a person do in this job? What is a typical day's work?

What are the minimum qualifications for getting a beginner's job? Minimum and maximum age, height, weight? Sex? Other physical requirements? Do you require a physical examination? On what physical deficiencies would an applicant be rejected? Do you hire married women? Do you fire single women if they marry? Does the worker have to have a license? Where does he get it? What are the requirements for getting it? Must he supply his own tools? What do they cost? What aptitudes do you look for in new applicants? Do you give aptitude tests?

Must the beginner belong to a union? What are the chances of getting in?

Must the worker be a citizen? Must he live in the city or state in which he works?

Do you have any Negroes working for you now? Jews? Do you give preference to veterans? What chance does a nonveteran have?

Does a beginner need capital? How much? [This question is used only when the guest is self-employed.]

What preparation is required? What is the minimum you would accept? What do you prefer? How much time is required to get it? What does it cost? What subjects are included? Can you tell us where to get a list of approved schools? What subjects do you prefer to have an applicant study in high school?

How does the beginner get a job? To whom does he apply? Where? When?

What are the opportunities for advancement?

What are the future prospects? Is the occupation or the business expanding or contracting? How does the current number of applicants compare with the number of vacancies?

What are the hours? Are they regular or irregular? Is overtime required? Optional? Do you work Sundays? Holidays? Evenings?

Is the job steady or seasonal? What happened to the workers during the last depression? Does advancing age make the worker more or less valuable? What is the retirement age? Are pensions provided?

Do you ever have any accidents? What kind? What are the hazards?

Is the marriage rate among your girls higher or lower than average?

What do you think the workers like most about their jobs? What do they like least?

Do people generally have any mistaken ideas about this occupation?

Is there anything else we should have asked you?

Is there anything you would like to ask us?

For classroom use, even this list may be abbreviated to a few key words which serve to remind the teacher of the questions to be asked. This abbreviated form may be mimeographed as a checklist and each item crossed off as a student or the teacher inquires about it. In this way the teacher can keep track of the questions which have been asked

even though they did not come up in the order in which he has them
listed. The key-word-reminder form which the author currently uses is
as follows:

Explain purpose and method.
Do you employ dropouts, H.S. grads., college grads.?
Start in same jobs? Summer or part-time? Principal job categories?
How many hired last year? Next year?
Starting salaries? 5 years? 10?
Nature of work?
Qualifications? Age? Sex? Height? Weight? Other physical? Mari-
tal status? Tools? License? Aptitudes? Unions? Citizen? Residence?
Discrimination? Veterans? Capital?
Preparation? Minimum? Desirable? Time? Cost? Content? Ap-
proved schools? Preferred H.S. subjects?
Entrance? Advancement? Future prospects? Supply and demand?
Hours? Regular? Overtime? Sunday and holiday? Evening?
Steady or seasonal? Effect of depressions? Advancing age? Retire-
ment age? Pensions?
Hazards? Marriage rate?
What workers like? Dislike?
Mistaken ideas?
Anything we should have asked? You ask us?
Thanks.

Although the word "discrimination" appears on the key-word-reminder
form above, the question is always asked in the words which appear in
the longer form. By asking whether or not the employees include any
Negroes or Jews and how many, the counselor can get at the same topic
with less embarrassment to his guest and therefore with a better chance
of getting a truthful answer. The same approach may be used with
labor unions by asking how many union members are Negroes, Jews,
or belong to other minorities.

The question about the nature of the work is frequently extended into
a series of questions as follows:

Would you mind telling us what time you came to work this morn-
ing?
What was the first thing you did?
How long did that take?
What did you do next?
How long did that take?
What did you do next?
How long did that take?
[These questions are repeated as often as necessary to cover the
entire day.]
What time did you quit?

Did you do anything yesterday that was different from what you did today?

How about the day before yesterday? Last week? Last month?

What else do you do on your job?

Of all these various duties, which ones occupy the largest share of your time?

The author's experience indicates that these questions often elicit important information that would otherwise be missed. They consume considerable time, sometimes to the exclusion of some of the other questions, but what they reveal is frequently so surprising as to be well worth the time. The reader is urged to try these questions a few times and draw his own conclusions.

When the guest expert is a former student being questioned about his own job the following questions are used:

What schools did you attend?

Did you graduate? Drop out? When?

What was your first job? How did you get it? What did you like best about it? Least? How long were you there? Why did you leave?

What was your next job? Same questions as above. Repeat for all subsequent jobs.

Regarding present job, ask also

What time did you go to work this morning?

What was the first thing you did?

How long did that take?

What did you do next?

[Repeat through the entire day.]

Did you do anything yesterday that was different from what you did today?

How about the day before yesterday? Last week? Last month?

What else do you do on your job?

Of all these various duties, which ones take most of your time?

What is the usual starting salary in jobs like yours?

What qualifications do you need to get the job? Age? Sex? Height? Weight? Other physical? Marital status? Tools? License? Aptitudes? Unions? Citizen? Residence? Discrimination? Veterans? Capital?

Preparation? Minimum? Desirable? Time? Cost? Content? Approved schools? Preferred subjects?

Supply and demand for workers? Outlook for the future? Advancement?

Hours? Regular? Overtime? Evening? Sunday? Holiday?

Steady or seasonal? Hazards? Marriage rate?

Anything we should have asked? You ask us? Thanks.

Physical arrangements. The teacher arranges a comfortable place for the meeting. Small conferences may be held in the boardroom, in the counselor's office, or in the living room of the home economics practice house; larger ones, in the library or in another room of appropriate size. If possible, he seats the group around one large table or several tables pushed together to give a round-table effect.

The teacher notifies the interested students several days ahead and reminds them on the day of the meeting.

Arrangements are made to have the guest graciously received and taken to the meeting place. The guest is seated at one end of the conference table; the teacher at the other. If it is necessary to use a classroom, the guest may be seated at the teacher's desk, and the teacher may sit in the rear of the room. The important point here is to make the physical arrangements suggest an informal conference rather than a lecture. It is desirable that all students be between the teacher and the guest, so that as they talk to each other they have to speak loud enough for all to hear. After the conference is well under way, the teacher may move about the room.

If a classroom is used, the teacher writes the guest's name, title, and business address on the board. If there is to be more than one guest, the names are placed on the board so that each guest's name appears above the chair which that guest will occupy. Students then find it easier to direct their questions to individual guests and to call them by name.

Encouraging student questions. The teacher repeats, in front of the group, the purpose of the meeting and says to the guest, "We want to ask you questions, all kinds of questions. I shall begin them, and the students will interrupt whenever they feel like it. If we ask for any information that is confidential, just tell us it's none of our business, and we will go on to the next question."

The teacher then begins to ask his list of questions; he is alert for any indication that a student is ready to ask a question, and he encourages any such signs. The more questions the students ask, the better. The purpose of the meeting is to give them what they want; the teacher's list is just a crutch to lean on if the students do not respond. Sometimes the students will carry the whole meeting; at other times no one but the teacher will ask a question. After a series of weekly group conferences with high school students Rubinfeld [407] reported that "One of the things observed at later conferences was that students who had attended earlier had developed a framework of questions which they could fire in rapid succession without going off on tangents."

Student questions can be stimulated by a preliminary meeting, in which each student is given a question to ask, but this is likely to make the conference less spontaneous, the meeting more formal, and the students more reticent about injecting very important questions which arise in their minds during the conference.

During a high school career day at Port Jervis, New York, H. Townsend Carpenter gave a list of suggested questions to students in some of the group conferences and not to those in the others. The questions were not assigned to individuals. He reported that the students who received the suggested questions appeared to be more interested in the discussion and kept their guests longer than did the students who received no suggestions.

Questions can also be stimulated by a preliminary meeting or a "warm up" period in which members of the group are asked to suggest possible questions. If no response results from this invitation, the group may be divided into committees of five, asked to discuss for five minutes the kinds of questions they would consider appropriate, and then to report to the group.

The author recommends that the beginner experiment with any of these procedures that appeal to him and see which seem to work best with his students.

The kinds of questions that students will sometimes ask when left to themselves are indicated in Appendix E.

The teacher also should be alert for any sign that the guest is about to launch a speech and should head him off. If the guest brings notes and suggests that he open the meeting with a few remarks, the teacher may ask if he is willing to delay the speech until the teacher and students have had a chance to ask their questions. Then, if the questions have not brought out all the things that the guest thinks important, the group will be glad to have him make whatever additional comments he considers appropriate. To cover this, one of the teacher's last questions should be, "Is there anything else we should have asked you?"

An occasional guest will insist on making his preliminary speech, even if he has to do it in response to the first question. When this happens there is little the teacher can do without being rude. Fortunately, it does not happen too often to be tolerated.

The teacher listens carefully to every answer and inserts whatever additional questions may be needed to clear up any vague statements or to follow up any interesting leads. He interrupts with a new question whenever it is necessary to keep the speaker and the students reasonably on the subject.

At the close of the meeting teacher and students individually express their thanks. If it can be arranged, there may be some advantage in closing the formal part of the meeting a few minutes early in order that shy students may come forward and ask questions less conspicuously.

Follow-up. On the day following the conference there should be opportunity for the students and teacher to discuss any further questions that either may wish to raise. If necessary, the teacher may stimulate discussion with such questions as "How many would like to enter that occupation? How many would not? Why? Why not?" "How many think you have what it takes? How many do not? Why? Why not?" Or the teacher may give a short test on the information brought out during the conference, let the students correct their own papers, and then discuss differences of opinion regarding correct answers.

After each group conference a news release may be prepared by the class, by a committee, or by the teacher. It should include the name and position of the guest and some of the interesting things he said. It should be submitted to the guest for correction and to the principal for approval, then sent to the local newspapers. A letter of thanks should go from the class or the teacher to the guest.

PROCEDURE: CONFERENCES WITH UNION OFFICERS

In some communities labor unions control admission to certain occupations. Union contracts affect promotion, tenure, and other conditions of employment. Even where unions are not in control, they are often excellent sources of information. Union officers and employers sometimes see things differently, and each may contribute information which the other would not volunteer. It is therefore often desirable to arrange group conferences with local representatives of the major unions, at their headquarters if convenient, otherwise at the school.

After a group conference with James Clark, an officer of the Building Service Employees International Union, the author's students were asked what they had learned that they did not know before and how they felt about the conference. Among their responses were the following:

I never realized that there *was* such a Union or that salaries for these jobs were so high. The time was certainly worthwhile!

The building service trades are relatively stable sources of employment.

Minimum starting salary is much higher than I imagined.

The best time to get a job in the building service industry is during April, May, June. . . . This session was one of the most informative.

I learned the difference between a closed shop and a union shop I learned that the union expects the employee to do his work, and may even agree to the firing of a shirker.

I learned what a "union book" is.

Unions are another source of information about jobs which I had not given much consideration to.

Excellent source of employment for dropouts.

Education is *not* prerequisite for a job in the building service field.

The best lesson and lecture I have ever seen.

Salaries are much higher than I had thought.

Extremely interesting and informative.

Mr. Clark was "down-to-earth" in the answers he gave.

One of the most interesting sessions of the semester.

The most impressive material we have had from a guest speaker.

Enjoyed the class! *Do it again.*

What to ask. The following questions will help to start the conversation:

With which occupations or industries is this union concerned?

In which of these are the largest numbers of union members employed?

In these occupations or industries, what proportion of the employees are union members?

Must a person be a union member in order to get a job?

If not, must he join the union in order to keep his job?

Is there any limit on the number of new members who will be admitted to the union? If so, who gets in?

How does one become a member? What does it cost?

Is there an apprenticeship program? How long is it? What does it include?

What other advantages are there in belonging to the union?

Are there any disadvantages?

Is there anything else we should have asked you?

Is there anything you would like to ask us?

To these questions may be added most of the questions suggested above for occupational conferences.

PROCEDURE: CONFERENCES WITH PLACEMENT OFFICERS

Some of the most realistic, most interesting, and most compelling information about occupations can be obtained from school and college placement offices, from the state employment services, and from commercial employment agencies. If visits to these offices can be arranged, the students may enjoy seeing what such places look like. Students who have been there once may feel less uneasy when they come later to register for placement or to be interviewed for a job. If visits cannot be arranged, group conferences with placement officers may be held in the classroom.

What to ask. At either location, such questions as the following may bring out the desired information:

Which occupations account for most of your placements? What other kinds of job orders do you handle?

Where are beginning workers most in demand today? In which occupations is it hard for a beginner to find a job?

Where are experienced workers in demand? In surplus?

Among the occupations and industries with which you work, which provide the steadiest jobs? Which are least stable?

Can you venture any guess as to the occupations in which beginning workers will be in demand four years from now? In surplus?

Which occupations are predominantly male? Female?

What are some of the mistakes that people make when they are looking for a job?

Can you tell us about any successful applicants and what they did when they were looking for work?

Who may use your service? When? How? What does it cost the applicant?

Is there anything else we should have asked?

Is there anything you would like to ask us?

If time permits, two conferences with the same placement officer may be arranged, one at the beginning of the course, another at the end. The second conference will sometimes reveal the rapidity with which employment conditions change and the need to keep one's occupational information up to date.

PROCEDURE: SCHOOL AND COLLEGE CONFERENCES

What to ask. The procedure for these is identical with the procedure for occupational conferences except that the questions are changed. The teacher's list may be compiled from such topics as the following:

What is the purpose of your school? What do you try to do for the students who attend? What do you expect them to do for the school?

How do you achieve this purpose? What curricula are offered? What degrees are conferred? What courses are required? What electives are available? In what year does specialization begin?

What happens to your alumni? Where do they go? What do they do? What kinds of jobs do they get? How much do they earn? Do you have a placement service?

What is the cost of tuition? Other fees? Books? Board and room? Fraternities and sororities?

Are scholarships or student loans available to freshmen? To others? In what amounts? How many of each? What determines whether or not you obtain one? What are the opportunities for part-time employment?

Is the school accredited? By whom?

What is the student-faculty ratio? What are the minimum, maximum, and average faculty salaries?

What living accommodations are available? Are dormitories adequate, or must some students rent rooms in private homes? How many students live on campus? Off campus? At home? Is there a college commons or cafeteria? If not, where do students eat?

Is there an infirmary on campus? A resident physician? A registered nurse?

Is the college in a city, a small town, or open country? What cities are nearby? What other colleges?

What proportion of the students belong to fraternities? Sororities? What kind of social life is provided for those who are not invited to join fraternities or sororities?

Is this a rich man's college? A poor man's school? A religious institution? Has it any church connections? What proportion of the students enter from private schools, from public schools? Is the proportion of students in any category larger than in the average institution? What is the geographical distribution of the student body?

What is the average enrollment? Are minority groups represented? To what extent? Is the school coeducational? What is the ratio of men to women? What restrictions are placed on women students? What are the regulations regarding smoking and drinking? How strictly are they enforced?

What does the school pride itself on doing exceptionally well? What are its weak spots? What do you wish you could do better?

What are the major and minor sports? Are athletic scholarships available? In what amounts? On what basis? To what extent and in what ways are intramural sports encouraged? What are the other principal student activities? Which of these are most popular? Least? What is the nature and extent of hazing?

How many persons applied for admission last year? How many did you admit? When must applications be filed? Is an interview required? When are applicants notified of your decision?

How bright do you have to be to enter? Graduate? What proportion of freshmen flunk out? What are the entrance requirements? Class rank? Examinations? Subjects? What exceptions are made to these and under what conditions? What kind of student do you welcome? What students have been admitted from our school? How did they do?

What do your students like best about the college? What do they dislike?

What else should we have asked you?

Is there anything you would like to ask us?

With a few variations and omissions the same list of questions may be used for junior high school conferences with representatives of senior high schools and for senior high school conferences with representatives of nursing schools, junior colleges, technical institutes, and other post-high-school institutions.

Teachers of elective subjects within the school may be invited to class and asked about their subjects. Possible questions include:

What is the purpose of the course? What do you learn in it? How do you learn it? What do you do in class? What kind of homework do you have? How much? May anyone take this course? If not, who may? What abilities do you need? How can you find out whether or not you have them? What do the students in the course like best about it? What do they like least? What else should we have asked you?

VARIATIONS

A school superintendent in Oregon found that his counselors knew little about occupations and arranged with local service clubs to send two businessmen each week to spend an afternoon with the counselors.

If desired, interested parents may be invited to join the students in questioning the guests.

Lipschitz [303] compiled a list of occupations on which parents expressed a desire for more information. She then recruited alumni employed in these occupations and arranged a group conference at which the parents queried the alumni. The parents asked that a similar program be arranged for their children.

One high school set aside one full day a week for special activities. During this time, forty groups of students, interested in different occupations, held conferences with workers in the fields of their interest.

If there is a good stenographer or note taker in the group, a summary of the information presented may be prepared, submitted to the speaker for correction, distributed to interested students, and placed in the library for future reference. Business education students in a Connecticut high school took notes on occupational talks given by local businessmen. At three o'clock of the same day each speaker received a copy for correction. The speakers were pleased.

The author's students once inquired whether or not the group conference could be used successfully in the early elementary grades. No one knew the answer. Heayn [211] thereupon tried it with a kindergarten group of five-year-olds and reported that "Only two questions were asked by the pupils—they were more interested in expressing themselves by statements rather than by questions." A teacher of third grade found her students enthusiastic when she took the time in advance to help them plan the questions they would ask.

Tape recordings. Some schools have made tape recordings of their group conferences and filed them for later use. One guidance director found that student interest was much lower when the class could only listen to a tape than when they were actively participating as questioners of a live guest. The author has seen no reports of counselors using the tapes as they would use books, to provide information to individual students who are curious about a specific occupation or company; perhaps there are possibilities here to be explored.

Alumni as guest experts. High schools and colleges frequently use their own alumni as guest experts. Present students may be more interested in the experiences of former students than in those of other guests, and alumni relations are strengthened for the school. One graduate school offered a course on employment opportunities in guidance and personnel work, in which every class session consisted of a group conference with from one to four alumni or students currently employed in the field. At one session three high school counselors answered questions about their jobs, at another three college counselors, then four counselors from community agencies, three placement officers, three industrial personnel officers, three personnel officers in government service, an assistant superintendent in charge of guidance, and two city directors of guidance. The students were enthusiastic about the results, and the instructor learned some things he had not known.

Forte [165] reported a high school assembly program in which five recent graduates and their employers answered questions asked by a panel of students. After the assembly the guests visited senior classrooms where they met the students in smaller groups and where anyone might ask questions. The students asked to have the program repeated with additional former students and their employers.

Students as guest experts. In a survey of work experience among 721 high school seniors in Oakland, California, Marion Brown found one or more students experienced in 102 different occupations. Such a wealth of occupational contact might well be tapped in any senior class in occupations by utilizing experienced students as guests in group conferences. They would not know all the answers, but they would bring to the conferences a point of view sometimes strikingly different from that of the employer. Every teacher of occupations and every counselor should explore the recent occupational experiences of the students and faculty in his own school before he looks outside. Too frequently we overlook the extent to which students can educate one another and sometimes even teach us a few things we do not know. Little and Chapman [304] suggested that ". . . taken together, pupils in almost any secondary school probably know more about the work and the workers of that community than even the best informed teacher or counselor."

Einbinder [144] arranged a series of after-school meetings in which senior students described their part-time jobs to other interested students, then answered questions. Topics discussed were how they got their jobs, work done, earnings, opportunities, and training required. Occupations represented included model, dental assistant, apprentice automobile mechanic, nursery work, and retailing.

Minkin [337] used juniors and seniors, who had just returned from their two months of student teaching, as resource persons in a series of group conferences for other students in a teachers college. She

> . . . occasionally pointed out significant facts that had been mentioned, but there was very little that [she] had to do to elicit all the details which needed to be covered. . . . The girls were asked to vote on whether they wanted to continue the discussion the following week. There was a unanimous affirmative action taken for two consecutive weeks after the first session although the girls knew that if they didn't vote to meet, they would have a free period. . . . There was also a unanimous vote to have such discussions each year after practicum.

Parents and others. Similarly, counselors and teachers may well catalogue and utilize the occupational experiences of the parents and other close relatives of students, most of whom welcome an invitation to help the school.

Rauschkolb [385] described a group conference arranged by a student club with the father of one of the members. The guest ". . . was delighted to know that it would not be necessary to prepare a speech." A checklist of suggested questions was given to some of the students, who were instructed to cross off each question as it was asked and to ask the other questions whenever there was a lag in the discussion. The club members asked questions for forty minutes. At the conclusion the guest invited the students to apply to him for summer employment after they started college. On anonymous appraisals of the conference, some of the student comments were "Great! On any industry." "Much more beneficial than a prepared speech." "I want more!!!"

School employees may be valuable and handy resource persons. The

secretaries and other clerical workers in the school offices, the maintenance personnel, the cafeteria staff, and the administrative officers
may answer questions about their own occupations. In one school, the
janitor was also part owner of a radio store and supplied students with
firsthand information on the work of the radio repairman.

Dingilian and others [127] reported that their staff ". . . systematically inventoried its own work experience so as to provide a
'built-in' consultant service which tapped first-hand knowledge of over
100 different occupations."

Greenberg [192] found that several of his fellow teachers held additional jobs outside the school. The students in his group guidance class
prepared questions which they would like to ask the teachers regarding
their outside jobs. Class representatives were sent to interview some of
the teachers and to report the answers to the class. "While the interviewers showed strong interest in the project, the rest of the class was
not overly enthusiastic about it." Greenberg then arranged a group conference with a teacher chosen by the class. "The discussion was lively,
interesting and highly informative. An overwhelming majority preferred the group conference technique."

Glamour magazine and the John Wanamaker store in Philadelphia
[259] arranged a "career-vacation week" during which women employed
in six different occupations were available for conferences with Wanamaker customers.

In cooperation with the heads of academic departments, Dittersdorf
[132] arranged a series of group meetings between interested students
and workers in occupations related to different school subjects. The
meetings were held during the last period of the school day. Attendance was voluntary. One result was improved relations between counselors and faculty.

The American National Theatre and Academy and the New York
City YMCA jointly sponsored a series of theater job counseling seminars, held in the evening at monthly intervals, with successful theater
people as resource persons.

Some counselors and some students have written letters to employers
and others, asking some of the questions that might be asked in a group
conference. The replies have been bound or filed and made available to
other students. The counselor who does this should remember not to
ask so many questions that he discourages replies.

One high school district [425] arranged a series of ten evening meetings for former students who were seeking employment. At each meeting a panel of personnel directors and other executives described occu-

pations in one of the principal local industries. Topics covered were typical jobs, duties, future prospects, present opportunities for dropouts and for high school, vocational school, and college graduates, training desirable, and how to apply.

At Dartmouth College, Placement Director Donald Cameron [55] conducts orientation meetings for seniors who are interested in possible jobs with any of the employers who recruit liberal arts and science majors. One week before the recruiter arrives, all interested seniors are invited to attend a fifteen- to thirty-minute meeting, at which the placement director describes the company and its jobs, and answers questions. "Specific information outlined in the particular company's brochure is not covered save by questions, rather, an attempt is made to describe in general terms the impact and nature of the work, the responsibilities one might expect as his time with the company increases, and intangibles which may loom important from the student's point of view."

At the conclusion of this meeting, the names of interested students are placed on the recruiter's schedule of interviews. Students who do not attend the orientation meeting can get on the interview schedule only if there is room for them after all who did attend have been scheduled.

During one year as many as 170 such orientation meetings have been held. On occasion there have been five or six meetings in succession on one afternoon. An undecided student may attend as many of these meetings as he wishes. He can thus get the equivalent of an extensive course in occupations.

COMMENT

The group conference at best is only a substitute for a visit that cannot be made. Practically anything that can be done in a group conference at school can be done in a group conference at the factory or college immediately following a tour of the plant.

Advantages. The group conference does have certain advantages over other techniques when the visit is impossible. It provides direct, first-hand contact with primary sources of up-to-date information. Like the tour, it helps to bring the teacher's information up to date, it establishes and maintains contacts which may lead to placement, and it may help shy students to overcome their fear of employers by getting to know a few. Most students find it more interesting than reading a book or listening to a lecture.

The informal, conversational question-and-answer technique keeps a wandering speaker on the subject. Every change of voice wakes up the student who would otherwise be asleep if the speaker were dull. Every student has the opportunity to participate in class activity. The question-and-answer technique also reduces to a minimum the danger that teacher and guest both may guess wrong about what will interest the group. The author has used the group conference repeatedly in college and graduate courses and is enthusiastic about the results; the students seem to like it, too.

The advantages of the group conference, as here described, over the common career conference and college night are described in Chapter 20.

Disadvantages. The group conference has its disadvantages also. The guest may be dull or poorly informed. He may be biased by limited experience, prejudice, age, success, or failure. He may oversell or undersell his field. If he has a charming personality, he may quite unintentionally recruit poorly qualified students who want to be like him and who think they will be if they follow his occupation. If he is offensive, he may repel even those who should enter the field.

Students will always be subject to influences of this kind as they meet workers from various fields and talk with them. Such workers turn up as relatives and friends, family doctors, tradesmen, etc. *There is no educational isolation from facts about jobs.* The group conference provides an opportunity to bring these casual conversations into the schoolroom, to expand them into systematic interviews in the presence of a trained counselor who can clear up misunderstandings, counteract bias, and follow through later with individual interviews.

The biases and the personality influences may be to some extent canceled by arranging subsequent conferences with two or three other persons in the same field, with employees and union representatives as well as with employers, with young workers and with persons of only average success as well as with the distinguished. The author has tried having two or more guests from the same occupation in the same session; it can be done, but it requires skillful handling and extra time. Such guests have occasionally challenged and disagreed with each other, but they have invariably done so good-naturedly. Perhaps this is because no sharp clash of personal interest has yet arisen. Beginners may be safer starting with one guest at a time.

Fortunately, most of the guests who have appeared in the author's classes have been willing to cooperate in any way that promised to help the students. One, but only one, insisted upon making the ten-minute speech he had prepared despite instructions not to do so. On a few occasions, one guest has been more eager to talk than the others and has threatened to consume much more than his share of the time. When this happens, the counselor who is running the conference can direct more of his questions to the other resource persons, who will often say what the loquacious one was about to say. The eager one can usually be depended upon to interrupt if he has anything important to add.

Another disadvantage, if the conference is part of a course, is that some students will not be interested in the occupation discussed. The conversational method, however, makes it less difficult for the students not personally concerned to accept the information presented as part of their cultural background.

The group conference will not do the whole job of guidance any more than any other technique of group guidance. It will not always bring out all the desired information. In Chapter 14 reference was made to one of the author's graduate classes which participated in a group conference on nursing and later visited a hospital. Following both these experiences, four members of the group interviewed four nurses from other hospitals and reported that they learned the following things which had not come up in either the group conference or the visit:

Contrary to statements made in the group conference, some private-duty nurses will go into homes even when a shortage of nurses makes it easy for them to get hospital cases.

The nurse has more responsibility in home nursing than in the hospital. She carries all of it herself. There is no one around to consult. In emergencies she must decide whether or not to call the physician and the family.

Some families turn off the heat at night and leave the nurse to sit up in a cold house.

Some hospitals exploit student nurses. It is imperative to choose an accredited school.

Nurses dislike giving baths, changing beds, arranging flowers, waiting on convalescents. They regard these activities as maid service and are eager to turn them over to subsidiary (practical) nurses.

Many have overcome an initial fear of gore.

A head nurse needs some teaching skill.

No matter where you train, you must take state board examinations which are "three days of hell."

Small schools sometimes provide inadequate instruction.

Nurses in training resent being treated like children.

The overambitious teacher who hopes to present a complete picture of an occupation in one group conference will nearly always be disappointed. The teacher who seeks only to add something to his own and his students' store of information will often be gratified with the results. Despite its imperfections the group conference does provide a means of obtaining some information which students and counselors badly need and would otherwise lack.

In Appendix E appears the transcript of a demonstration group conference in which the author and a class of twenty high school seniors quizzed three employers. The advantages and disadvantages of the group conference technique were discussed by the participants and the audience immediately after the demonstration; this discussion is included in the transcript.

REVIEW QUESTIONS

1. What are the characteristics of a good guest expert?
2. How large a group can be handled in a group conference?
3. What is the best way to ask about discrimination?
4. By what series of questions can you get the best description of the nature of the work?
5. Where should the guest and the teacher be seated?
6. How did Carpenter increase student interest?
`7. What should be one of the teacher's last questions?
8. Which of the following should be used as guest experts: personnel directors, union officers, placement officers, alumni, students?
9. What are some of the advantages of the group conference?
10. How can guest bias be counteracted?
11. In what ways do you find the group conference reported in Appendix E to be superior or inferior to lectures followed by questions?
12. How can you use what you have learned from this chapter?

16
Students
Survey
Beginning
Jobs

Most high school graduates and dropouts get their first jobs close to home. This happens even in many suburban communities, despite popular impressions to the contrary. Follow-up studies reveal the same to be true for the dropouts and graduates of some community colleges and urban universities and for the "alumni" of some community agencies. In such institutions it is imperative that the counselor and his clients be familiar with the major employment opportunities of their community.

A few minutes of browsing through the classified telephone directory will quickly reveal to the average counselor how little he knows about the occupational life of his community. After this experience one of the author's students commented, "It surprised me to find out how little I knew of the small community I was born in and lived in for twenty-one years. I never realized that there are so many places of employment in our community. . . . This report opened my eyes to something I was completely unaware of." Follow-up studies, plant tours, and group conferences compile and convey information about only those occupations which are known to alumni, students, or teachers. Good employment opportunities may be overlooked by students and clients because they and their counselors are unaware of the possibilities.

Planning, conducting, and reporting the results of a survey is more than a one-day job. This project is appropriate for a unit or a course in occupations, for an interested social studies or homeroom group.

PURPOSE
The purpose of the student survey is primarily to help prospective graduates and dropouts to find jobs, incidentally to facilitate vocational

choice. To this end the survey is designed to inform the students and
the counselor about employment opportunities which they might otherwise overlook, to reveal where most of the local job opportunities are
likely to be found, to provide each student with a list of employers who
may have vacancies for which he could qualify, to make the student a
little more realistic in his expectations about the kind of job he may
hope to get and how much he may hope to earn, to provide some training and experience in interviewing employers, and to relieve some of the
anxiety which some students may feel about approaching employers.

PROCEDURE

The teacher and students together discuss and select the territory to be
covered. In a small community this may be the whole town; in a large
city it may be the school district. It should be within the employment
market area for the school and should not be too large to be covered
thoroughly by the class.

A local street map is purchased from the city offices, or a committee
of students may prepare one. The teacher and the class discuss and
decide whether the students are to work individually or in teams. The
map is divided into a number of sections equal to the number of individuals or teams. Allowance must be made for the greater concentration of employers in business and industrial zones, and the size of the
sections adjusted accordingly. Each section is numbered and assigned
to one student or one team. The map and the list of assignments are
posted on the bulletin board.

In a discussion session the students suggest the questions that they
wish to ask employers. The final list is decided by vote, subject to approval by the teacher. The list should be brief and the questions simple.
Ten questions are probably enough for the first attempt; five might be
better. Among the final questions may be such as these:

> Do you expect to have any jobs open for our graduates this June?
> About how many?
> What will the jobs be?
> What will they pay?
> What qualifications would we have to have to get one of them?
> Will they be permanent or temporary, steady or seasonal?

An interview blank is prepared and mimeographed with space for the
name and address of the employer, the nature of the business, the person interviewed, the interviewers, the date, and each of the questions
to be asked. Ample space is left for replies. This form is not given to

the employer to fill in but is used by the students to guide the interview and to record their notes.

Practice interviews. Several class sessions are spent in teaching the students how to approach the employer and how to conduct the interview, what to do and what not to do to secure the facts pleasantly. The teacher may prepare for these lessons by reading appropriate sections of *How to Interview* [27].

As a part of this preparation several practice interviews are staged in the classroom with the teacher or a student acting the role of the employer. At the conclusion of each practice interview the other students and the teacher discuss two questions: What was good about this interview? How could it be improved? For the first practice interview, one student may be asked to do everything wrong. This sometimes produces a hilarious session which dramatically emphasizes mistakes to be avoided. It serves also to give the other students a little confidence— surely they can do better than this. After a few practice interviews it may be possible to find an employer who will take an hour off to attend the class and to participate in some final practice interviews. He may add his own comments to those of the class and the teacher.

Letter to employers. While this preliminary training is going on, the employers are approached by letter. The purpose of the project is explained, and their cooperation is solicited. Service clubs and chambers of commerce may help by sponsoring the project.

A sample letter follows.

Mr. Harry Green
Bridge and Union Streets
Lambertville, N.J.

Dear Mr. Green:
The students in our senior class will be looking for jobs within a few months. They are eager now to learn something about the kinds of jobs that may be open to them when they graduate. The purpose of this letter is to inquire if you would be willing to help them.

Specifically, would you be willing to have one or two of our students call on you sometime to ask you some questions about employment opportunities and requirements in your organization? Will you please indicate your reply in the space provided below and return this letter in the enclosed envelope?

Sincerely yours,

Counselor

Would you be willing to have a student call?   _____
What time of day is most likely to be convenient
for you?   _____
Would you like us to telephone in advance for an
appointment?   _____

Public relations. Depending upon the extent of the teacher's interest in public relations, he may or may not wish to approach employers in other ways. Public acceptance and interest in the survey may be increased by appropriate publicity and by inviting a sponsoring committee to help plan the study. Potential sponsors may be invited to a few preliminary meetings for the exchange of ideas; the committee members may then be chosen from those who show the most helpful interest at the preliminary meetings. Potential sponsors include the board of education, the superintendent of schools, the state supervisor of guidance services, the state employment service, the state board for vocational education, the chamber of commerce, civic clubs, businessmen and -women, labor unions, teachers, student-body officers, student groups, parent-teacher organizations, newspapers, radio and television stations. As noted before, any extensive public relations activity should first be discussed with the teacher's immediate superior. Many successful surveys have been made without publicity or sponsorship of this kind.

If the territory to be covered includes any establishments which the teacher or the community consider hazardous to the morals of young persons, these places may be omitted from the survey. When in doubt the teacher may find it wise to discuss such problems with his supervisor. One blast of righteous indignation from a powerful community leader could wreck a community survey overnight.

When the teacher is satisfied that the students will be a credit to the school and that they will be courteous, tactful, and appreciative, the actual interviews begin. A few of the more tactful students may be sent out first and then asked to tell the class about their experiences. After this each student or team calls on all the employers in the section assigned. Each day the students report results orally to the class and file their interview records with the class secretary for the final composite report. Interesting points are discussed informally in the classroom as they come up.

Discussion of results. Discussion procedures may be varied to suit the preferences of the students and the teacher. The author's students have enjoyed the following: At the beginning of the period the class is divided into buzz groups of four to six students. Each group chooses its own chairman. Each person reports to his group the most interesting things that he has learned about beginning jobs since his last report. The group selects the three most interesting items to report to the class. The small group discussion is allotted five to fifteen minutes, depending on the teacher's judgment of how much time seems to be needed. Then each group chairman is asked to report one of the three items his group has selected. After each report the teacher invites questions and comments. If time permits, each chairman is asked to report a second item and then a third.

Final report. When all the returns are in, the class secretary or a committee prepares a composite report, listing the places where jobs are expected to be available and such additional data regarding them as may have been collected. This report is mimeographed and given to each student as an aid to job hunting. Copies also may be placed in the school library for reference by future classes undertaking similar projects. If there are other prospective graduates or dropouts who were not enrolled in this class, copies may be offered to them or the composite report may be posted on homeroom bulletin boards or published in the school paper.

For descriptions of this technique in practice see Engen [147] and Dresden [134].

For a more extended discussion of community surveys and job analysis see Chapter 11 in Norris, Zeran, and Hatch [361].

Dempsey and Begnoche [118] described a survey undertaken by eighth-grade students who expected to go to work within the next one to four years. A member of the guidance department went with the students to each interview. With the permission of the employers, pictures were taken. These were developed by the photography club. Students prepared an illustrated booklet of local job opportunities and presented a copy to each eighth-grade class. Several employers expressed approval of the project.

Krieg [281] organized a volunteer group of high school juniors and seniors to survey local jobs for graduates and dropouts.

A map of the city and a list of businesses were obtained from the Chamber of Commerce, and the New York State Employment Service gave us suggestions. The questions to be asked of the employers were decided upon, practice interviews were staged, divisions of the city were assigned and canvassed by teams of two, and results were tabulated and discussed in class. A form letter which was made from suggestions of the members of the group was sent to employers to explain the project before the canvassing started.

Most of the people were non-academic, a few were really quite slow academically, and some of them could properly be called "culturally deprived," but everyone was interested and enthusiastic. The employers were enthusiastic, too, and have since inquired about some of the interviewers in regard to jobs after they finish high school. The youngsters knew surprisingly little about the different kinds of jobs available in the community. The experience was valuable not only in respect to learning about jobs, but it also gave these students poise and confidence in meeting people. This is very important I think for such people—it might make a difference in getting the job in the first place and in either keeping the job or in being considered for promotion later on.

Clark [89] undertook her own survey

. . . in the belief that counselors should make themselves aware of vocational opportunities in their own local area, and that the most effective way of doing this is through personal visits to local firms. . . .

All of the companies except one seemed genuinely delighted to have evidence of the school's interest. Personnel managers were generally most cooperative in answering questions, in providing literature, and in conducting extensive tours of company operations. Most expressed a real desire for greater contact with educational circles. Occasionally, it was necessary to assure the personnel department that information concerning such matters as specific salaries would not be distributed to students. In the one instance where a tour was refused, necessity of meeting a work deadline was given as the reason. An invitation was extended, however, for a tour at a more convenient time. . . .

I have found especially useful the sample application blanks and questionnaires which some firms volunteered to give me and in future plan to request these myself. Examining such forms gives students tangible proof that most companies really do ask for information on high school marks, attendance records, and teacher evaluations before hiring an applicant.

VARIATIONS

The teacher who wants to get a little information in a short time can do so by asking each student to interview the members of his family regarding jobs for beginners at the places where they work.

Some schools have asked local employers to supply lists of jobs for which they have hired school dropouts and graduates without experience. These lists have then been duplicated and distributed to students.

Clark [87] took her tenth- and twelfth-grade classes ". . . for a walk to observe the various occupations which might be open to them. They took pictures of most of them, and thoroughly enjoyed the trip. We had no idea that so many . . . occupations were so close to us."

In one school [527] students selected help-wanted advertisements from the local newspapers and wrote to the employers, explaining that they were students who were not applying for the jobs but who would like to have more information about them to supplement their study of occupations. Many personnel directors answered their letters fully.

Dresden [134] reported that Totheroh sent a student recorder with each student interviewer. His students also prepared news releases for the school and community newspapers, provided speakers to describe the project and its results to local clubs which requested them, and broadcast a radio program.

Flax [157] had his students come to class one day dressed as they would be for their interviews. On another day a local businessman came to the school and let several students practice interviewing him, after which he commented on the interviews and answered questions. Flax found that letting the students go in pairs for their initial interviews seemed to increase their confidence; after the first day they went alone. After graduation some of the participants reported that the confidence and skill acquired in these interviews helped them later when they went to apply for a job.

Cox [107] described a Negro high school of 1,300 students in South Carolina which had a heavy dropout rate because many students needed money for themselves and their families. From leads supplied by the faculty, the counselor contacted employers and prepared a list of those ". . . who needed students for part-time and eventually full-time employment." The list was given to all the teachers, who then referred to the counselor all students who wanted part-time jobs. Dropouts caused by financial difficulties declined by 97 percent.

Where there are no jobs. Preston [381] described how a job survey grew out of a discussion in a social studies class in a little lumber town from which

> . . . almost all of its young people have moved away as soon as they finished high school because there were no jobs open to them in the community—or so they believed.
> We got to talking about this one day in my senior problems class. My original intention had been to have the mill owners come in and talk about the lumber industry and answer students' questions about

what it offered them. But we decided instead to go talk to the mill owners and everyone else who employs help in . . . our region. . . . So what was originally planned as a three-week classroom activity turned out to be a *three months* community job survey!

The survey included six mill owners, mill foremen, "woods" crew bosses, 14 groceries or markets, five cafe owners, county road crew superintendents, two federal forest service offices, the state forest service office, five service stations, the telephone office, the superintendent of schools, ranch owners, the post office, two banks, three department stores, a butcher shop, four garages, the power and light company, the water company, a dress shop, three tourist "packers" (guides), fire-wood choppers, and a hardware store. The students went in pairs. . . . When the data were in, we edited the material and published a 60-page booklet. . . . We thought this would not only give us a summary report of our findings but also be valuable to future classes.

We spent the rest of the period in class discussing the project and what it meant to us. This proved to be very stimulating and opened up many avenues for further investigation and for individual projects.

In larger cities. In another community [99] selected students from the commercial departments of three senior high schools interviewed all of the 3,200 employers in the city. The students were excused from afternoon classes and worked until 5 P.M. Ninety percent of the employers were covered in five days. Most of the others were reached in a second week, but a few selected students worked eight weeks to make the survey complete. About 250 employers, fewer than 10 percent, refused to be interviewed on the first call; one establishment was visited twelve times before replies were received.

In regional high schools. Janney [255] prepared an occupational map of the adjoining communities of Lambertville, New Jersey, and New Hope, Pennsylvania. Each place of employment was indicated by a key number which could be used to identify the name and nature of the business. With a combined population of less than ten thousand, the two communities yielded 339 places of employment. The map was used to show students in the South Hunterdon Regional High School the variety of local employment opportunities open to them. The economics and general business classes also used the map in studying the community. The school office used it in assigning bus routes. The yearbook staff consulted it for advertising prospects. And the city-planning board examined it at one of their meetings.

Ames [10] described how one high school surveyed the occupations of fifteen nearby communities with a population of 17,500 at a total cost of $306.10.

Contacts with employers were made through mailed questionnaires, student interviews, and telephone calls. The employment pattern of the area was also revealed by a study of the occupations of the employed members of family groups represented in grades 7–12. For this, survey forms were distributed in grade 7–12 classes, filled in by the students, and taken home for completing and checking by the parents. . . .

Wide publicity was given to the reports. A junior student wrote a series of articles for the local papers. . . . Talks were presented to civic and business groups. . . .

Graphs and charts, prepared by the art department of the high school, made these talks more colorful.

Hints for interviewers. DuBato [136] and his twelfth-grade students prepared and duplicated a series of "hints to the interviewer" for their own use during their survey. The hints included:

Appearance

1. GIRLS: Skirt, blouse (or sweater); clean socks; shoes polished; neat hair; conservative makeup; clean fingernails. GUARD AGAINST HALITOSIS AND BODY ODOR!

2. BOYS: Slacks, cleaned & pressed; sport shirt (tie NOT required); or business shirt (tie is required); presentable windbreaker or sport jacket; shoes polished; hair combed; clean fingernails. GUARD AGAINST B.B. AND B.O.!

3. No gum chewing!

Steps

1. Introduce yourself.

2. Present card of introduction.

3. ASK FOR PERSON-IN-CHARGE.

4. Explain reason for visit.

5. If employer is busy, ask when you may return (RECORD NAME & ADDRESS OF ESTABLISHMENT ANYWAY. MAKE NOTE OF TIME YOU MAY COME BACK.)

6. When interview is over, thank employer, and leave.

7. If employer is unfriendly, be courteous and make a quick exit. (MAKE NOTE OF EMPLOYER'S ATTITUDE ON YOUR QUESTIONNAIRE. RECORD NAME & ADDRESS OF ESTABLISHMENT ANYWAY.)

8. DO NOT SIT DOWN, unless invited to do so.

9. DO NOT LEAN, OR SLOUCH.

Remember!

1. DO NOT CALL ON doctors, dentists, lawyers, or other professional persons.

2. DO NOT CALL ON large concerns (20 or more employees) without Mr. DuBato.

3. YOU ARE AN OFFICIAL REPRESENTATIVE OF ROSLYN HIGH SCHOOL. CONDUCT YOURSELF ACCORDINGLY AT ALL TIMES AND UNDER ALL CIRCUMSTANCES.

4. The employer is NOT doing YOU a favor. *Both you and the employer are performing a public service of benefit to the rest of the school and the community.* This should be your attitude and frame of mind when you approach each establishment.

Surveys by college students. Fick [155] described how 700 teachers and 500 junior college students canvassed all homes and businesses of one school district in a single day and recorded on 75,000 cards the collected data about occupational pursuits and opportunities.

Leis [289] used eighty-four students in a college psychology class to interview 210 local manufacturers. Devoting to the project an average of less than six hours per student the class obtained a 70 percent response, after which Leis took over and got reports from all but two of the remainder.

Surveys by community agencies. Bley [28] described five projects in which community organizations undertook local occupational surveys for the benefit of young job seekers:

In one community, members of an adult service club called on local employers and solicited Christmas jobs for teenagers. Local radio stations publicized the program, and the local office of the state employment service cooperated. Young people were placed as salesclerks, gift wrappers, cashiers, and checkers.

In another community, a local social agency organized a door-to-door canvass of employers in order to find summer jobs. Members of a youth group helped to formulate the plans and did the interviewing. Each interviewer was provided with an identification card and with a card form on which to record information regarding possible jobs. Also included was space for the interviewer's impression of the employer as friendly or hostile.

The entire teaching staff of one city was assigned for a day to make an occupational survey of the community. Following months of preparation and publicity, each teacher called on five or six employers.

A local parent-teacher association sent a questionnaire, through the homerooms, to high school students. Included was a checklist of possible summer jobs, on which each student was asked to mark any jobs that he would like to have if available, for example, mowing lawns, washing cars, baby sitting, working in a retail store. After the replies were tabulated, the school placement officer helped the PTA to develop plans for approaching prospective employers.

In another city, the Police Athletic League sponsored a survey of local employers to discover after-school jobs for teenage boys and girls. Volunteer members of precinct youth councils made the initial employer contacts. Newspaper publicity urged all employers to notify their police precincts of any vacancies.

Lapidos [286] reported a job survey undertaken by a Jewish youth council in its own neighborhood, which was primarily a retail business district of a large city.

> The cooperation of the local Chamber of Commerce, congregations, parent organizations, and other interested Jewish adult groups were solicited and the program was advertised through the local community newspaper. . . . 75 young members of the council volunteered to go out as "job solicitors" and a regular block-by-block campaign was worked out. Prior . . . orientation sessions were held on such topics as, how to approach the prospective employer, interview technique, follow-up, etc. . . . After these sessions, the students verbalized greater feelings of confidence and security in job seeking. The 75 participating students brought back a substantial number of part time leads (approximately 60) as well as a number of full time leads. . . . Employers have continued to call in when they have needed temporary or part time help. . . . 40 actual placements resulted.

Williams [517] described how the manufacturers of one city ". . . decided to try education as the means of showing the new generation the opportunities in their home town." Technical research work was done by four field workers who were loaned to the project on a part-time basis by the state division of employment security. The report was published in a 192-page book illustrated with more than a hundred pictures of jobs in local plants. Fifty-nine local companies paid for 7,000 copies of the book, which were given to the local schools for classroom use with high school freshmen.

Many communities have made local occupational surveys at considerable expense and have published the results in a format which discourages student reading. A superb example of survey data reported in appropriate terms for use in vocational guidance may be found in Brochard, Beilin, and Thompson [44]. Zapoleon's *An Outline of the Steps to Be Taken in a Community Occupational Survey* [536] contains seventy-one concise, specific suggestions.

COMMENT

Students whose occupational plans are based upon starry-eyed visions of glamorous careers, in fields about which they know very little, sometimes need an opportunity to look at the realities of the employment market. Participation in a survey of beginning jobs will not correct all the unrealistic dreams, but it may help a few students who want to be realistic to find out what the realities are.

The author assigned a graduate class of experienced teachers and counselors-in-training to undertake a short survey of the kind described in this chapter as part of a training course in group guidance. The students called on several employers in their home communities and inquired about employment opportunities for high school graduates and dropouts. After this experience the class listed what they considered to be the advantages and disadvantages of the student survey as a group guidance technique for use with high school seniors. Among their comments were the following:

> It reveals some information not otherwise available. It provides a realistic way of learning. It provides insight into the philosophy of the employer. It makes students more aware of qualifications for employment. It will "larn 'em humility." Students may be discouraged by unpleasant experiences with gruff employers. Students may bring back misinformation. The technique may improve or injure public relations, depending upon how well the project is conducted.

The guidance values of this technique are those of forcing the students to face realistically what will and will not be locally available to them and what they will be expected to offer in exchange for the jobs they want. Not all their reports will be accurate. An occasional student may even report wholly fictitious answers from an interview that he did not find time to arrange. The teacher should be prepared to verify statements that might be seriously misleading if false.

To reduce the dangers from misinformation, Edna Fredericks, one of the author's students, made the following suggestions:

> Since a great deal of trouble might arise from a student's careless inaccuracies as well as from willful misrepresentation, might not the interview blank have a little space at the bottom to be initialed or signed by the person being interviewed? The student might say, "This is the information I am taking back to my classmates. Will you take a minute to glance over it and sign your initials here if I have the information correct?" Students sometimes take notes in such a fashion that they themselves can't read them later. This check might make them more careful in recording the information, more conscious of the necessity of accuracy.

Another of the author's students, Earl J. Bailey, noted that

> A great deal of adverse criticism was leveled at one of our social studies teachers who sent out eighth-grade pupils to make a study of

the community stores and places of business, as the people thought the questions asked were too personal and none of the business of the teacher. It might be stressed that great discretion should be exercised in formulating the questions to be asked, especially in a small community.

This technique provides a quick way of covering considerable territory. It may reveal some employment possibilities previously unsuspected. It may injure public relations if poorly done or improve them if well done. From the results of the survey the more promising opportunities may be selected for further study by visit or group conference.

REVIEW QUESTIONS

1. What is the purpose of the student survey of beginning jobs?
2. How are students prepared for interviews?
3. What are the guidance values of the survey?
4. You are teaching a twelfth-grade course in occupations. You have time to do either a follow-up study or a survey of beginning jobs, but not both. Which will you do? Why?
5. How would you conduct a survey if you were a counselor in the high school that you attended?
6. You are a counselor in a settlement house in a poor section of a large city. Your club members need and want part-time jobs. How will you organize a survey of beginning jobs to help them?
7. You are a graduate student in a course for counselors. You and the other students in your class want to know more about beginning jobs for counselors. How will you organize and conduct a survey?

17
Case
Conference

The case conference has long been used as a device for training counselors and for pooling information and judgment on difficult problems. It is here adapted to another purpose. It may be used for orientation, educational guidance, or vocational guidance and for any length of time from one period to an entire unit or course.

PURPOSE
The purpose is the old, old ideal of education, so frequently sought, so seldom achieved—to teach students how to think. But this time they are not to learn how to think in the abstract in any and all situations by some irrelevant exercise in mental calisthenics. Instead they practice thinking about problems of orientation, educational guidance, and vocational guidance by trying to solve actual cases from the past experience of the counselor. It is hoped that after practicing on others the students may approach their own problems more effectively.

PROCEDURE

Selecting the cases. The counselor selects from his past experience the case of some student who faced a fairly common problem. He changes enough unimportant facts to disguise identities and then presents the case to the class. He says in effect, "If you faced this problem what would you do? What do you think this person should have done?" For example:

Robert will have to earn most of his college expenses. He thinks he should get a job for the first year after high school, save as much money as he can, and start to college the following year with some cash on hand. One of his teachers has suggested that if he does this, he may lose his desire to go to college before the year of work ends. What do you think he should do? Why?

Julia is a sophomore in high school. Her brother, who has been supporting the family, is to be married in April. Julia's mother has just told her that she will have to quit school in April and go to work. Julia wants to be a stenographer and has made a brilliant start in the commercial course. What can she do?

Anne is a college sophomore. She has not been invited to join a sorority. She feels greatly disappointed, and she regards her college career as a failure. Someone has suggested that she transfer to another college where she might be invited to join a sorority. What should she do?

Dick has been offered two jobs, very much alike except that one is in the small town where he lives, while the other is in a large city a hundred miles away and pays $25 a week more. Which should he take?

Martin is shy, awkward, and uneasy in the company of strangers. He greatly admires his uncle who seems to be confident, poised, and cordial to everyone. The uncle is a traveling salesman. Martin thinks that if he becomes a traveling salesman, he will become more like his uncle. What do you think?

The beginning counselor, who has no cases of his own, may select a case from some good book such as Allen [7, 8] or Kitch [278], or he may find case material in the recollection of problems that he and his friends have faced, or he may invent a case and tell the students that the case is hypothetical. Students also may be invited to invent and submit typical cases; some students may seize this opportunity to submit their own problems in disguise.

Christensen [81] has proposed the following cases:

John B. is a boy who likes to make things out of wood. He sometimes draws his plans and then constructs his object. His best grades in school have been in the shop courses, mechanical drawing, and art. After graduation from high school, however, John plans to take a business administration course in a local junior college and apply for a job as an office manager.

John says, "I don't know whether I will like working in an office or not, but I think you have to have a 'white-collar job' today to be a success."

Do you agree with John? Why? Can any job guarantee success? What would you do if you were John?

David S. was an excellent student and had high scholastic ability. He was the only son of a physician. His father encouraged him to study medicine, also, but David was undecided. When he graduated from high school, David still did not know what to do. He knew very little about occupations and so entered college in the premedical program because his father was a physician. He soon found out that he disliked his choice but did not know what to do. Finally, he decided to stay and continue with his study of medicine because "no one really enjoys his work anyway."

Do you agree with David? Why? How successful do you think David will be as a physician? Could David have avoided this situation?

Bob is a tall, fine looking student in high school. He is excellent in athletics and has had good grades in mathematics and mechanical drawing. He has thought of drafting as an occupation and has decided to attend a technical school where he can get professional training in this field. Some members of his family and some of his friends advise him to forget about drafting. Bob is colored and his friends feel that he would be unable to get a job in his home town in his particular field. They tell him he should accept the job his uncle can get him in a local restaurant, but Bob does not want to become a kitchen worker.

a. What would you advise Bob to do under the circumstances? Be sure to explain *why* you think as you do.

b. What information does census data give about relative opportunities for Negro and white workers?

Tom has just graduated from college where he majored in physical education. He has been offered a job as a teacher-coach in a small high school in a New England town. The salary is $4,000 a year in the beginning. Tom has refused the job because he feels he should be able to get at least $6,000. He has had no experience as a teacher or as a coach, but he says he thought "such jobs" paid better salaries.

a. What are the average beginning salaries for teacher-coach in New England today?

b. What do you think was wrong with Tom's planning when he began the study of physical education as a career?

c. What advice would you give Tom about this job? Give your reasons.

Jim's mother wants Jim to have a "white-collar" job. She says "There's prestige to a 'white-collar' job. I don't want him to have a job where he'll be getting dirty all the time. I want him to wear good clothes and be with nice people all the time. I know he hasn't liked high school and that his marks have been poor, but I think if he got to college, he would work harder and do well. I want him to be a lawyer or a doctor. He wants to be a machinist or an electrician. He says he'll make more money as a skilled worker, but I tell him he's got to be something we can be proud of. He's got to go to college and be something."

a. Why do you think Jim's mother feels as she does about the "white-collar" jobs? Is she unusual in her feelings on this subject?

b. If you were Jim's counselor, would you agree with or disagree with his mother? Demonstrate how you would talk with her about this problem.

c. What do you think about the statement, "He hasn't liked high school and his marks are poor, but I think if he got to college, he would work harder and do well"?

d. What would you tell Jim's mother about the salary and working conditions of a machinist or electrician?

Rosalie has wanted to be a teacher ever since she was a little girl who used to play "school" whenever she could get the other children to be the "pupils." Now that she is finishing high school, she is planning on entering State Teachers College, but recently an elderly friend of the family advised her strongly against teaching. He said it was an overcrowded field and that she had better think about something "new and growing" like radio or airline work.

a. What evidence could you give Rosalie to prove that teaching is either an overcrowded or an expanding field at the present time? Be sure to tell Rosalie where you found this information.

b. Why do you think the family friend felt as he did?

Christensen has also suggested a hypothetical case into which the student may project himself:

If you had planned to become:

1. a doctor or
2. a registered nurse or
3. an engineer or
4. a teacher or
5. a clergyman or
6. a judge or
7. a scientist or
8. a manager of a printing shop or
9. a banker or
10. an airline pilot

and found it impossible to enter that occupation, what other occupation might you enter? Why is it important to consider alternate occupations?

Belen [22] presented the following case to a ninth-grade class of thirty college-preparatory boys with an average IQ of 102:

Fred is a ninth-grade student. He would like to go to college, but he is not sure that he can raise the money. He wonders which course he should take in high school. What do you think he should do? Why?

At first, the class responded very slowly. Nothing like this had been done with them before this time. As questions were asked, the boys began to question one another as to the validity of their suggestions. My most difficult problem at this point, was controlling their enthusiasm. I then divided the class into seven buzz groups. As I walked around the room, I noticed interest kept mounting. Each suggestion submitted by the chairman of the group was sound, and well planned. The groups then began to question one another as to the reasons for their answers. At this point, the bell rang. The class did not want to stop. Interest was at a peak.

Leading the discussion. While the students discuss the problem, the counselor acts as chairman. Difference of opinion is encouraged. Students are assured that it is all right for them to change their minds during the discussion, to favor one approach at one time and later to favor a different approach, because we are all searching for the best approach, we are all trying to help one another to think logically about the problem, and we should all be as willing to receive new ideas as to contribute them. This cooperative approach to a problem may be at first a little strange to some students; if so, it is perhaps time they become acquainted with it.

The counselor expresses no opinions but supplies additional information if requested and injects pertinent questions if the students do not think of them. As the discussion of various possibilities is completed, the class may vote on them or not, as the counselor thinks wise. If they do vote, the counselor points out that a majority judgment is not necessarily a correct judgment and that the vote is taken merely as a matter of human interest and as a further means of comparing ideas.

When the discussion ends, the counselor reports what the former student actually did and mentions that this was not necessarily the best solution. The class may or may not wish to comment upon the decision. When they finish, the counselor makes any comments that he considers appropriate and then goes on to the next case.

In presenting the case, the counselor gives just enough facts to start discussion. His entire presentation takes no longer than a minute or two. Obviously, in this time, he cannot present all the information that one should have before making an important decision. The presentation is inadequate; the inadequacy is intentional. The purpose of this intentional inadequacy is to give the students practice in thinking for themselves about what additional information they should have before they reach a decision. They may go a long way toward one decision before someone asks for information on a relevant point, and when this information is presented, they may see at once that they were on the wrong track. After a few experiences of this kind they begin to ask pertinent questions before they try to make decisions. This habit of inquiry is exactly what this technique is intended to develop.

Live cases. After some experience on disguised cases the teacher may invite members of the class to submit problems of their own on which they would like to have the help of the class. From the problems submitted the teacher may select those which he believes can be discussed with profit to the class and without injury to the individual who submitted the problem. The experienced teacher-counselor who knows his class will quickly recognize some problems that should be discussed only in private, lest the blunt comments of tactless youth crush the feelings of the subject. Other problems are so relatively free of emotional context that they can be discussed with little danger. When the students know that they are discussing a real problem and that what they say may affect someone's decision, class interest approaches a new high. The person whose problem is discussed sometimes gets help, too. After such a discussion one of the author's students, who had offered her own problem for demonstration use, wrote, "I can't express in words how grateful I am . . . for the help that you have given me. Thanks a million."

In a college course on choosing your vocation, Hewer [215] devoted each of several class meetings

> . . . to the discussion of the vocational problem of a different member of the group. The name of the member under discussion was not divulged to the group, but the member himself had been informed that he would be the one discussed. His test results, personal data and grades were available for the discussion.
> Observations of the groups indicated that the students became increasingly adept at requesting and utilizing data relevant to a vocational choice. The students also demonstrated the ability to acquire and use educational and occupational information in the small class setting. As a result of their discussion, the group generally arrived at several useful vocational suggestions for the person whose problem was under discussion.

DuBato [135] has described

> . . . an adaptation of the case conference wherein the individual student appears before his contemporaries for help and suggestions. The only adult participant is the classroom teacher or guidance counselor. . . .
> In the beginning, most students will shy away from discussing their problems in front of the class. The most desirable class size is ten to fifteen. Larger classes lose some of the intimacy, informality, sincerity, and mutual trust that a successful case conference requires. . . .
> It is sometimes wise for the inexperienced leader to conduct his initial case conferences outside the classroom with small informal groups of, say, three to six close friends. . . .

Kagan [266] has observed that "resistive clients who tend to fear or distrust school personnel often become very communicative in group counseling situations. . . . There is a certain security in observing that the counselor is outnumbered. . . ."

The counselor who has had little experience in leading informal discussions may find helpful suggestions in Appendix B. The transcript of a demonstration case conference appears in Appendix F.

What students learn. To demonstrate this technique in a graduate course the author asked two classes to discuss the case of an experienced counselor who had been offered two jobs, one as a city director of guidance, the other as a college professor teaching training courses for counselors. The question posed was which job she should take. Both classes were asked at the end of the discussion to list what they had learned from it. Their answers included the following:

> College professors have more free time than public school administrators.
> Nature of tenure in college teaching.
> Incomes of college teachers.
> Extent to which advancement may be limited by age of superiors.
> Administrators lose direct contact with students.
> Probationary period in college teaching.
> Retirement provisions for college teachers.
> I'm sure I never realized that there were so many things to consider and weigh when making such a choice.
> A person must make the decision *himself*, but before doing so, he should consult with others for the purpose of completely evaluating each alternative.
> University positions carry more freedom.
> University job has higher maximum salary than high school.
> Because of college enrollment slump, professors may be discharged.
> I personally find I get too confused talking it over too much.
> Heretofore completely ignorant of university tenure.
> Much thought and meditation required prior to choosing between jobs.
> Careful evaluation necessary before making decisions.
> College professors have more freedom with regard to how they use their time and plan their work.
> Didn't know that university didn't have legal tenure.
> Didn't think of the internal politics that the director might have to cope with.
> I didn't realize that school and university jobs paid so similarly.
> In selecting your position, you should think of the contributions each job will make to the community. Not always thinking of myself alone.
> Discuss with others the pros and cons of the position—a larger number of people than I would have consulted before having learned of this technique.

All I learned that would be of value to me is how very complex such a problem is. It teaches me fully to explore the issues. This problem is presenting itself to me within a month.

Also I see the desirability of consulting those who know basic information.

Discuss problem with others in order to bring out the good and bad points of both positions.

Useful contribution to my education the point that working in the school brings security by means of a pension.

Knowledge re "pension refund" when teachers leave public school system for another job.

Possible pension rights under the university.

Value of considering every pro and con.

I learned that it is impossible for an outsider to determine the course to be taken by an individual no matter how much of his background is known.

I did not learn anything I did not know before I came to this class.

Need for thoroughly investigating the pros and cons of each situation in every respect for present and future possibilities.

The only thing I learned was that even graduate students will change their minds as a result of the type of discussion we had; before I didn't think anybody here would change his initial opinion.

Freedom in the classroom for college professors.

Discussion on the pros and cons of the young lady helped me to clarify my own thoughts on the situation. As something was mentioned it seemed to stimulate me to thinking.

I realized how many arguments pro and con there are in a situation of this kind and how one would have to think before making an important decision.

I was faced with a similar problem six months ago and reviewed all questions presented in class as well as many more that apply to nursing.

I learned that college instructors can absent themselves for a day or two "without anyone batting an eyelash."

I also found out what the expression "retiring on the job" means with regard to college professors.

VARIATIONS

Fink [156] invited his students to submit their own problems for class discussion and reported:

I have used a variation of the case conference and this has been so successful it has become a Friday morning feature of every week. We discuss problems of the kids in the class. At first it was slow getting started and the problems were of a minor nature or were about "friends of mine." Since then it has become a real problem solving period and the class is not at all reluctant about admitting the problems are personal. The only part I play is to decide whether the problem could be best demonstrated by role-playing or discussion and from then on the class takes over. No attempt is made to try to reach an answer or to solve the problem; I only want the problem brought out and want the class to see that all problems have some degree of universality and that there are many possible solutions.

Baer and Roeber in their second edition [14] described two ingenious variations of the case conference:

The guess-who and guess-what technique. In order to show the necessity for a thorough study of personal traits, one teacher used a series of cards on which he had placed data concerning a particular but unidentified twelfth grade student. In a class session, he presented the first card, which gave only a fictitious name of a real student in the class. He then asked the students what occupational field the unidentified student should enter. The students naturally indicated complete ignorance and confusion. Next the teacher showed the second card which told the student's age, the third card which showed the student's height, the fourth card which showed the student's weight, the fifth which gave his hobbies, and so on. The teacher, of course, had to present many such cards before the students were able to identify the student in their class—and still more cards before they had any suggestions of possible and promising occupations for that student. Through this series of interest-arousing activities, students saw the need for all types of such information if they were adequately to study themselves.

The teacher employed a similar procedure to show students the kinds of information needed in studying an occupation. After he displayed each card containing information about one occupation before the group, he asked each student to indicate whether he would like to do the work. The first card gave the yearly salary. Next came cards giving the hours of work, the working conditions, related school subjects, and so on. Through this series of activities, the teacher aided students in seeing the importance of viewing an occupation from every pertinent angle before making any vocational choice. The skills thus developed by students helped them with their immediate problem of choosing a vocation. These skills were of even greater value when, as, and if John or any of his classmates wished to make another vocational choice.

Greenberg [191] used flash cards to impress his students with the desirability of getting all the pertinent facts before selecting an occupational objective.

To try it out on an average ability seventh grade class, I prepared the following five flash cards:

1. $110.00 salary per week
2. outdoor work

3. physical work
4. college is not required
5. most people in this field are employed by the city

After showing each card I asked how many would accept the job knowing only what was on the card. Five out of thirty wanted the job upon seeing card #1, seven more joined in upon seeing card #2 and by the time I got to card #5 twenty students had accepted the job. I then informed the 20 that they were all hired as garbage-men. . . . By the time we had played the game several times, most of the students had formulated a series of very sophisticated questions which they wanted answered before committing themselves to a job.

Christensen and Burns [83] suggested cases in which the students could be asked to identify the values illustrated and to compare them with their own values. Among the cases were these four:

A man refused to expand his successful furniture repair shop, saying "I like to do the work myself. . . . I like money, but I don't need a lot of it."

A contented salesman said "I don't want responsibility for bossing other people. I like my job."

A teacher declined a business job because "I enjoy working with young people. . . . I wouldn't feel I was doing anything worthwhile."

A young man quit his job in the post office and explained "I thought security was everything; I thought I wanted it above everything else but I don't."

Super [467] has indicated how group opinion may influence a student's choice of a college.

The relevant values are primarily social in origin and significance: Siwash is tops among colleges, Johnny wants to be thought tops, and so Johnny wants to go to Siwash. The fact that Johnny may not be able to get into Siwash is discussed in the orientation class. As the class is attitude-conscious, and the teacher is aware that he is dealing with facts which may have emotional significance, Johnny's disappointment becomes manifest and the implications of these facts for him are discussed. Several new facts and attitudes emerge: the class thinks that a number of other colleges are really about as good as Siwash, Johnny's record is good enough so that he could probably be admitted to some of these other colleges, and several respected local citizens, all of them considered tops by the class, went to these less selective colleges. Supported by the group's interest in his plans, finding that the group considers other colleges acceptable and status-giving, and made newly aware of the fact that others have achieved status without going to Siwash, Johnny finds it relatively easy to scale down his college ambitions. The group has given a positive emotional tone to facts to which, unwittingly, it had in the past given a negative emotional tone. In this example the attitudinal orientation method used was group *discussion*, discussion not so much of Johnny and of Johnny's problems, but rather of colleges and of people who went to them. The facts dealt with in attitudinal orientation are more social than personal. . . .

As the need to make decisions heightens the emotional value of facts, formal orientation activities provided at the choice points of development need to be not only factual, but also *attitudinal*. There must be time for members of the group to express their attitudes toward the facts encountered, to work through their related feelings, and to modify their attitudes to make them fit the facts.

A technique similar to the case conference has been used in several group efforts to teach job-hunting techniques. Individual students have presented to a group their own statements of qualifications, their letters of application, etc., for suggestion and criticism. Case histories revealing how other persons chose jobs, planned campaigns to get them, and got them have been discussed.

Other job-hunting courses have included practice job interviews before a class, followed by class discussion of good and bad practices displayed. This variation will be discussed further in Chapter 20.

COMMENT

An alert class that likes to argue will bring out most of the important elements in any case. They will quickly catch the fallacies in each other's thinking and will improve as they go along. A slow class or one accustomed to docile acceptance of whatever teacher says may require more help and a longer time to get under way. Some cases readily provoke profitable discussion. Others do not. The teacher must expect considerable variation in the quality of class sessions until experience indicates which are the most stimulating cases.

The teacher who likes to encourage students to think for themselves, who enjoys provoking discussion, and who has had some success at it will do better with this method than the teacher who prefers to tell them how to do things, though the latter teacher, if he can manage to keep reasonably quiet while the students are discussing, will find his audience more attentive than usual when he starts his lecture.

The author's experience, reported above and in Appendix F, seems to indicate that the technique does result in making students more conscious of the variety of considerations that should influence vocational decisions.

In Appendix F appears the transcript of a demonstration case conference at the graduate level. Following the transcript is a summary of what the students said that they learned from the conference.

The technique of the case conference is developed in more detail in two books by Richard D. Allen, *Case-conference Problems in Group Guidance* [7] and *Common Problems in Group Guidance* [8]. Although both books are now several years old, they are still excellent.

REVIEW QUESTIONS

1. What is the purpose of the case conference, and how is this purpose achieved?

2. In opening the case conference, how much information does the teacher offer? Why?

3. Does the counselor express his own opinions?

4. Does the counselor raise questions?

5. What are the values and the dangers in using live cases from the class?

6. How may group opinion influence a student's choices?

7. In what ways is the case conference superior to instruction on the same topics? In what ways inferior?

8. Where and how could you use the case conference in your present or future work? For what purposes? What would be its values and limitations in this situation?

9. What do you like or dislike about the case conference reported in Appendix F?

18
Laboratory
Study

The techniques previously described require all the students to study substantially the same thing at the same time. The laboratory study undertakes to provide for individual differences.

Though developed and used primarily for vocational guidance, this technique could be used for educational guidance in the choice of a school or college by the substitution of a different set of questions. The method may be used in either a unit or a course in occupations.

PURPOSE

The purpose is to give each individual an opportunity to study intensively one or more occupations of particular interest to him, to compare the requirements of these with what he already knows about himself, to prepare a summary of his present thinking that may facilitate profitable discussion in the counseling interview, and incidentally to learn where and how to get facts about jobs whenever he may need them in the future.

PROCEDURE

Students select occupations. Each student selects one or more occupations that he would like to study. The student who has no preference may be given a list from which to choose, or he may have an occupation assigned to him. The most comprehensive list from which to choose is in the *Dictionary of Occupational Titles* [123]. See Chapter 10 for suggestions on how to use the *D.O.T.* to help "the client with no preferences." If pressed for time, the teacher may use the classified section of the local telephone directory as a partial list of local employment possibilities.

Resources are provided. Books, pamphlets, magazines, and newspaper clippings on various occupations are moved from the school library to the classroom, or arrangements are made to conduct the laboratory study in the library itself. The students are asked not to deface library materials.

Each student is given one or more copies of an outline for the study of an occupation such as the one in Chapter 3 or the one reprinted in Appendix G.

The students are taught how to find and use the sources of information available to them: indexes, bibliographies, publications, and people. Most available printed material may be located through the indexes described in Chapter 4. The librarian may be asked to show the class what other indexes and materials are available locally and how to use them. The class may also visit the nearest public library for the same purpose.

The teacher gives a few simple suggestions on how to compare and appraise materials from different sources by noting copyright dates, authors' related experience and qualifications, biases to be expected in recruiting literature, etc. These suggestions are repeated later at appropriate times as the teacher helps individual students with the problems they bring to him. For more on this see Chapter 5.

Students may be encouraged also to visit the local office of the state employment service and to call on local workers and employers for information. Suggestions regarding visits will be found in Chapter 14. Additional suggestions regarding sources of occupational information may be found in Chapters 4 and 5.

Excellent suggestions for conducting a job information interview may be found on pages 93 to 96 of Borow and Lindsey's *Vocational Planning for College Students* [36].

The students next proceed to work individually on the occupations they have chosen. Each class period is used for independent study. The teacher is present as a consultant; he answers questions and makes himself generally helpful, but each student plans his own work and proceeds at his own pace.

Students report frequently and briefly. Occasionally the teacher calls the group together to compare experiences and to tell one another very briefly and informally, never in more than a few sentences, where they have found the most interesting and useful information. At these times each student is given an opportunity to ask the others if they know where he can find something that he has had trouble locating. The skillful teacher can use these sessions to develop a mutually helpful attitude that will make the class profitable and pleasant for all. A few minutes also may be devoted to exchanging interesting bits of occupational information that the students have picked up. These reports should be brief, never longer than a few sentences per student; they can become insufferably boring if each student is asked to tell all that he has learned. The author has obtained the best results by asking each person in turn two questions: What is the most interesting thing you have learned since your last report? Is there anything on which you want our help? Students who talk too long should be gently interrupted. For suggestions on how to do this see Appendix B.

The reporting procedure may be varied by asking each student to write one sentence stating the most interesting thing he has learned about any occupation or about sources of occupational information since his last report. The teacher may collect the papers and read each sentence to the class, pausing after each one to inquire, "Does anyone want more information on this?"

For further variety, the class may be divided into small buzz groups and asked to exchange with one another the most interesting things they have learned. Each group may also be asked to choose its own chairman and to report through him to the total group on the one most interesting item reported to the buzz group. Time for questions may be allowed after each report.

Students who complete the study of their preferred occupation before the rest of the class may be assigned to help others who are having trouble, or they may be allowed to begin the study of a second field.

The project terminates when the teacher feels that the students have spent as much time on it as will be profitable. This may be at the end of a few weeks or at the close of a semester.

There should be no final symposium in which each student has to suffer through long oral reports on occupations in which he is not interested. This mass review is a lazy man's way of teaching, and students justifiably resent it. If some kind of final review is desired, it can be arranged by announcing all the occupations that are being investigated and then inviting the students to ask each other any questions they wish.

VARIATIONS

One high school used substantially this technique, but with a shorter outline, in the occupational part of its course in self-appraisal and careers. The author never saw a better laboratory session than one conducted by this method in a class of general-course seniors. The room was equipped with a small library of occupational pamphlets. Books describing several occupations had been taken apart and the individual chapters separately rebound as pamphlets in order that several students could use them at once. Each student had a folder containing his own outline and notes. Each came into the room quietly, went to his desk, opened his folder, went to the library, selected his materials, brought them back to his desk, sat down to read and take notes. During the entire period the teacher talked with her two visitors; only two or three students came to ask for help. At the close of the period each student took his materials back to the library, put away his folder, and went on to his next class. As here described this procedure could suggest a lazy teacher, but the quiet, competent, interested students convincingly reflected the effective teaching that had gone before. Here were students, by no means above average in ability, who had learned and were learning to get what they wanted with a minimum of outside help. One could easily anticipate their continued use of similar techniques in adult life.

A high school in Wisconsin used a similar technique with younger students. A classroom was equipped like a library with bookshelves, tables, and movable chairs. The school collection of occupational books and pamphlets was moved in. Each student chose six occupations and arranged them in order of preference. Then each began with the occupation at the foot of his list and worked up.

In Wiley's [515] pioneer effort at Middlebury College each student investigated one occupation and reported on it to the class. There have since been innumerable repetitions and variations of this procedure in all kinds of institutions.

At one small New England high school, the five teachers invited the eighty students to state their vocational preferences. The teachers divided the more popular occupations among themselves, got all the information they could on these occupations, and made periodic oral reports to the students. Attendance at the report sessions was voluntary and close to 100 percent. In one year the five teachers reported on a total of thirty occupations.

At another school each teacher undertook to become an authority on one occupation and to report to the students on it. Each Tuesday the seventh period of the school day was reserved for these reports. Classes were rotated so that each teacher got a different class each week until all the students had heard all the teachers.

In one school each student was asked to interview the members of his family about their occupations and to make a brief report to the class.

Maye [322] found that his students gathered more information when they knew that another class would be invited to join theirs in order to hear their reports.

COMMENT

One of the author's students, S. R. Stinson, has suggested that

Since vocational guidance at this school level is primarily intended for those who plan to drop out or leave high school after graduation for full-time employment, the class in the study of occupations will be a selected group of those, for the most part, who do not have the ability or the perseverance to do college work. Included in this group will be most of the poorer students, academically speaking, who as a group tend to dislike book study and paper work. In addition, many or most of these students have no definite vocational plans but rather will be likely to take or accept any job that they are able to secure. Their occupational mobility is high once they do become employed, but the level is likely to remain fairly low. Yet, in order to use this technique, we are going to ask these students to carry on through their independent research a rather exacting type of study which, in order to be successful, will call upon them to do considerable book study and paper work. Generally speaking, it would seem to me that almost any of the other techniques we have studied would be more suited to this particular group of students and much more likely to gain their interest and participation.

Hutson [250] also has criticized the laboratory study:

Instead of having the pupil become acquainted with the whole array of occupations so that he will have a basis for choice, it serves to concentrate his attention on a narrow sector of the vocational horizon. It is true that he will make a report to the class and that he will listen to their reports, but the learning acquired from such experience is of doubtful quantity and quality.

The author has seen some of the best and some of the worst teaching of occupations done by this method. In the hands of a lazy teacher it can be a quick way of killing all interest. Under a good one it can be a stimulating experience in independent research.

Some students will do a superficial job of research, but even this can be helpful to the counselor, for the report will quickly reveal the nature and extent of the information upon which the student's occupational preferences are based; in two minutes a skilled counselor can learn from a completed outline what might easily require twenty minutes to draw out by oral questioning.

Students will pick up some misinformation; they will do this in any case. Some of it will be corrected by contradiction from other sources.

Some will remain to be corrected as the teacher reviews the outline, some will be corrected in the counseling interview, and some will get by. Nothing we do is perfect.

But students under a good teacher will learn by this method where and how to find the most reliable facts about jobs—a useful part of anyone's education. They will accumulate pertinent occupational information from a variety of sources. They can hardly escape comparing sources. They will have, in the blank form constantly before them, a reminder of the important kinds of information to be sought and considered. They may also have the experience of thinking somewhat systematically about the relation of occupational facts to their own needs, abilities, limitations, ambitions, and interests before they come to the counselor to discuss them.

REVIEW QUESTIONS

1. What are the purposes of the laboratory study? How is it conducted?

2. What are some of the methods that may be used to exchange information? Which do you prefer? Why?

3. Should each student report the results of his research to the group? How?

4. What are some of the advantages and disadvantages of the laboratory study?

5. If you were teaching a course in occupations would you use this method? Why? Why not?

6. If you had to choose between the laboratory study and the case conference, which would you choose? Why?

7. What do you like or dislike about the outline for the study of an occupation which appears in Appendix G?

19
Self-
measurement

Most teachers of occupations have tried in some way to help their students to consider their own fitness for the occupations in which they were interested. Many teachers and counselors have hesitated to give students the results of psychological tests, perhaps rightly fearing that they would be misinterpreted and misused and that bitter protests might follow from parents of children with low intelligence quotients.

Some years ago the late Richard D. Allen boldly proposed to surmount these difficulties by teaching students what tests do and do not mean, how to take them, how to score them, how to interpret and use the results. The implied assumption was that teachers, counselors, and psychologists are not the only ones who can learn such things. He wrote a book called *Self-measurement Projects in Group Guidance* [9] in which his proposals were implemented with suggested teaching techniques. A number of schools have since put Allen's ideas into practice in their courses in self-appraisal and careers. Some colleges have included discussion of test scores in vocational planning courses.

The technique has implications for educational and vocational guidance and, to some extent, for orientation. It may be used within a course or a unit, or as an entire course in itself.

PURPOSE
The purpose is to help students learn whatever tests may reveal about their abilities, interests, and limitations and to teach them how to interpret and use the results of such tests.

PROCEDURE
The students are given an elementary course in psychological testing, not unlike the training courses offered to future school psychologists and counselors in colleges and universities but adapted to the level of the students.

In this course they study the nature of individual differences, the theories of testing, the concepts of reliability and validity, the meaning of percentile ranks, the use of norms, and the interpretation and use of test scores in making educational and vocational choices.

The students then take a wide variety of tests of aptitude, interest, and intelligence; they discuss in turn what each one measures and fails to measure, what the results mean and do not mean. Each student gets his own scores; no one else sees them except the teacher. The students are not compared with one another, but each student is encouraged and helped to compare his scores on one test with his scores on other tests of similar and different characteristics in order to learn all he can about his own strengths and weaknesses. Each student has a folder in which he keeps a profile sheet. On this sheet he records graphically his percentile rank on each test, so that he can see at a glance those areas in which he is relatively strong and weak.

Class discussions of test results are always in terms of hypothetical rather than actual cases. The teacher never says, "John has a P.R. of 17; what does this mean?" but rather, "If you had a P.R. of 17, what would it mean?" Each student has a chance to hear his own score or one near it discussed as a hypothetical case and to ask any questions that he wishes without revealing his own score.

VARIATIONS

College preparatory students at a university high school, in a course called vocations and college life, visited several local places of employment, then took a battery of aptitude tests and compared their measured abilities with the requirements of the occupations they had seen.

Christensen and Burns [83] suggested that students be asked, "Have other people ever helped you to appraise yourself? If so, have you agreed with their opinions?" and that students be invited to "Name two or three jobs you don't think you could do. Give reasons for your answer. . . . Name the broad occupational group which you believe best matches your . . . abilities. . . . Pretend that you are an employer . . . about to hire several people. . . . Work out a list of personality traits which you consider important in your new employees."

One liberal arts college included a unit on self-measurement in its required course in freshman orientation. Whenever possible the students scored their own tests. All test scores, including intelligence quotients, were released to the students. The course was taught by a professor from the department of psychology to sections of twenty to twenty-five students each.

Other self-appraisal units in college courses in vocational planning are described in Chapters 13 and 16 of Morse and Dressel [341].

One college of education, which offered a course in personal and professional development, devoted the first quarter to the administration and interpretation of tests, to individual counseling and corrective instruction in reading, in computation, in written expression, in study skills, and in the budgeting of time, according to individual needs. Throughout this quarter, in both the classroom and the personal interviews, a continual effort was made to discover personal qualities that might handicap the student as a teacher, to overcome these handicaps if possible, and to redirect student ambitions if necessary.

The distribution of class time was approximately as follows:

Two weeks (six hours) of introductory discussion
Three weeks (nine hours) of test administration in the classroom
Three weeks (nine hours) of test interpretation
Three weeks (nine hours) of discussion of typical cases

Each student had two or more interviews each quarter with the instructor or with one of his assistants, who were graduate students majoring in guidance. Interviews dealt with individual problems indicated on a student-problem checklist, the extent to which the course was or was not serving the needs of the student, test interpretation, revision of occupational plans, choice of courses for the next quarter, and selection of a faculty adviser. Test scores were given to students at the discretion of the instructor and in counseling interviews after the class discussion of test interpretation.

Van Dusen [492] described an evening course offered to adults by an urban university as a part of its program in vocational counseling:

It is scheduled for a one-hour and forty-minute meeting weekly. . . . The enrollment is limited to about fifty students each semester. This arrangement permits as many as sixteen weeks to work through the problems which are brought to the counseling program, which is listed in the Bulletin of Courses as "Vocational Counseling."

The Counselors who serve these adult students are graduate students in Psychology, Educational Guidance, and students in a division of the Graduate School designed primarily for professional training in guidance and personnel work. At the present time, there are thirteen such Counselors, each serving four or five clients. . . .

The following week another group session is spent in administering the verbal part of a core battery of tests. The battery includes two intelligence tests, two interest inventories, and two personality inventories. We have found the information from this battery is helpful to most of our clients. It is needless to point out that by group administration we effect a considerable economy in testing time which can be used by the staff in ways we believe more profitable to the client. After the group finishes each test they again "buzz" in the smaller groups on the issue of what kinds of questions, pertinent to the counseling situation, the test they have just completed could possibly answer. At this point we have felt that a good many of the prevalent false impressions and false hopes held in tests are corrected. And we feel that having the clients explore, with each other in their small sub-groups and then with the discussion leader, the limitations of test scores, erroneous ideas concerning the usefulness of tests more quickly dissipate than is ordinarily accomplished through the counseling interview alone. At least it seems that in most instances, the client has a large headstart on understanding the tests when such issues arise in the interview.

Morelli [340] described how the Utah State Employment Service experimented with one, two, and three sessions of group counseling with the "hard core unemployed" from several occupational groups and with "high school seniors who had participated in the school counseling and testing program." No attempt was made "to resolve individual vocational problems." The high school seniors "were given their individual aptitude test profiles," and these were explained by the Employment Service counselor.

From two years of experimentation the following tentative conclusions were drawn:

Each group should consist of not less than 7 nor more than 12 individuals.

Sessions should be scheduled for 2-hour periods.

Individuals appear to gain more insight into their problems through personal interaction with the group than they do through an individual interview with the counselor.

Jolles [260] reported another variation of this technique as follows:

A formal course in Industrial Psychology was given to 10 prison inmates of at least above average mentality. During the course the students became interested in learning about their own vocational aptitudes, and they profited from a class discussion of their test results. At the end of the course the entire group had lost their hostile attitudes toward Psychology and the prison classification system. Many of the group wished to continue guidance on an individual basis. Finally, the technique is not only time saving but also makes it easier for inmates to seek help by enabling them to escape ridicule from fellow prisoners.

Hahn and MacLean [201] suggested that

The concept of the multipotentiality of any individual, and an introduction to the various methods of comparing oneself with various norm groups in which competition may take place, should play an important part in the materials presented. . . . Tentative choices of field and level of major interest should be made, and these should be discussed privately with the counselor while the group program is in operation. . . . Choices of vocational thresholds rather than finalities should be encouraged. This principle is important because occupational choices made in adolescent or early adult years are seldom predictive of the level ultimately reached in middle age.

Froehlich and Benson [169] suggested that

Group discussion of testing can be used to facilitate both testing and counseling. Three ways in which group discussion does this will be described.

As we counsel with pupils, it becomes apparent that they do not understand the basic concept of individual differences. They find it hard to believe that they cannot do everything equally well. Most pupils are aware of differences in scholastic aptitude, but somehow they forget that they fit into the picture too. It is hard for all of us to accept our limitations. If pupils have an opportunity to discuss test results, the counseling process has a base from which to start. It will not have to be interrupted to provide for instruction or setting the stage, before test results are considered in the interview. An effective means of handling these discussions is to present a summary of test results given in the school. A distribution of scores might be placed on the blackboard, and through group discussion, the following points developed:

1. *Scores have a wide range which reflects differences among individuals.* Questions such as these can be used to stimulate discussion: What is the difference between the highest and lowest score? How do you account for this difference? Would we get differences as large as this on another test? On measures of height or other physical traits? Can you think of any human characteristic where there are no differences among individuals?

2. *Most scores are found in average group.* The following questions are suggested. What 10 scores do most pupils get? How do you account for this bunching of scores? Does this make the extremely high score more significant than the average scores?

3. *Individuals have high scores in one test and low in another.* Why do not pupils get the same marks in all subjects? Is it because pupils have more ability along some lines?

Slotkin [444] described a method of teaching high school students to understand test norms.

Froehlich [168] and Hoyt [244] reported experiments in which group discussion of test scores produced as good results as individual counseling.

COMMENT

Many tests are good enough to be used in the rough screening of applicants for employment, but they are not good enough to predict the success or failure of any one individual.

Test scores may be spuriously high or low because of individual differences in cultural background and in previous education or because of errors in test administration.

Before any test score is given to any student, the teacher should be as certain as possible that the score is as accurate as can be obtained, and that both he and the student fully appreciate the possible errors of measurement.

But once the teacher and the student are satisfied that a specific test score will add useful information to the student's knowledge of himself, there is no more reason for concealing low scores on aptitude or intelligence tests than there is for concealing defective eyesight, poor hearing, or a weak heart. Sooner or later every human being must learn and accept his own limitations. One of the counselor's responsibilities is to help the student to discover both his assets and his liabilities, to accept those which cannot be changed, and to make wholesome emotional, educational, and vocational adjustments to them. The longer we delay revealing them, the more difficult the adjustments may become.

Warters [501] noted that

Because teachers of classes in group guidance fail to make clear the basic concept of the limitations of human capacity, students often gain wrong conceptions of their individual possibilities. . . . Students should not be led to believe that endless opportunities are awaiting them in adult life and that these possibilities are open to all who are ambitious and willing to work hard enough to attain them. . . . Making clear the basic concept of limitations helps to decrease neurotic tendencies, whereas failing to make clear this concept helps to increase them.

Emotional turmoil. Unquestionably, there will be emotional turmoil when some students discover their limitations, but emotional turmoil is not necessarily undesirable. Skillfully handled, it may even facilitate improved adjustment. The effective teacher will not ignore it nor minimize it; he will face it squarely as one of life's common occurrences. He will arrange counseling interviews whenever the need for them is indicated.

There is no simple formula for helping people to adjust to their newly discovered limitations. Sometimes group discussion will help. Sometimes individual counseling will succeed. Sometimes nothing seems to work. However, the inability of some individuals to face reality with equanimity is no reason for denying to others the opportunity to plan their own futures on fact rather than on fancy. The bluntness of this argument for giving students the truth is not intended to imply that the counselor should be blunt when he presents the facts. Indeed, there will be few times when the counselor will have more need for all the kindness, consideration, and tact at his command.

Although some students are disturbed when they learn of their limitations, others are relieved. To a frustrated student, the most welcome news in the world may be the discovery that his intellectual capacity is not equal to that of his competitors and that neither he nor his teacher nor his parents should expect his achievement to meet the standard previously set.

The teaching of occupations has been criticized on the ground that students learned about occupations beyond their own range of ability and thus acquired unrealizable ambitions. If the criticism is justified, the remedy is not to abandon the course in occupations. The remedy is to teach students all we can about the nature of individual differences in vocational aptitude—how to discover them and how to make appropriate vocational adjustments in the light of them. And we must stop being secretive about test results, which are more vital to the student than to anyone else who uses them. Not every test reveals a limitation. Students sometimes discover aptitudes and abilities of which they were unaware. The desirability of this revelation is seldom questioned.

One of the limitations of aptitude testing has been the general lack of cutting scores, without which the counselor cannot tell whether a mediocre score is too low for satisfactory work performance or high enough to permit the client to hold a steady job if he has the other essential qualifications. Christensen [79] reported a promising attack on this problem. A large manufacturer and a carpenters' union used the General Aptitude Test Battery for selection purposes and established their own cutting scores. High school seniors were ". . . referred for GATB testing early in their senior year. . . . Counselors may help . . . a . . . senior to estimate his chances . . . as a carpenter's apprentice since they know from past experience the approximate cut-off scores used for selection."

The author does not recommend that every beginning counselor rush out and buy the first tests he finds, administer them carelessly, have them scored without rescoring to check accuracy, and interpret them without reading the manual of directions! Certainly anyone who is to use tests and teach students to use them must be adequately trained in test administration and interpretation. The necessity of such training already is recognized in some state certification requirements for school counselors. If the beginning teacher of occupations has not had such training, he should get it as promptly as possible.

Although the self-measurement technique gets pretty close to individual differences, it is still not intended to substitute for individual counseling. It is intended to facilitate counseling by enabling student and counselor to discuss test results without the counselor's having to teach a thumbnail course on test interpretation in one interview.

Witnessing one of these courses in action, the author was amazed to hear general-course seniors discussing test interpretation with far more understanding than one finds in many meetings of beginning counselors and in most meetings of school teachers. High school students can learn psychology; it is high time we taught them some.

Public relations. Because some schools have established policies regarding the release of test scores, the teacher should inquire about such policies before undertaking a unit on self-measurement. The possible effect of the unit on public relations should be discussed in advance with the teacher's immediate superior.

The beginning counselor, who is using this technique of group guidance for the first time, may be wise to begin with tests that will create a minimum of disturbance, for example, tests of musical aptitude, spatial relations, vocational interest, clerical aptitude, etc., rather than tests of intelligence. Personality tests, if used at all, probably should be introduced last, and only when the counselor has time and skill to counsel individually and immediately those who may be greatly disturbed by their extreme scores.

Rothney [406] found that counselors who reported and interpreted test scores to 869 high school sophomores noted obvious disappointment in ". . . only 3 per cent of the cases."

REVIEW QUESTIONS

1. Do you agree that test scores should be released to students? Why? Why not? Under what circumstances?

2. If you were to conduct a self-measurement project, would you change the procedure described in the text? How? Why?

3. Do you agree with the author's comments on emotional turmoil?

4. Are students always disturbed by learning of their limitations? What did Rothney find on this topic?

5. If you were teaching a course in occupations, would you include self-appraisal in some form? In what form? Why? Why not?

6. Has anything in this chapter surprised, provoked, or challenged you? What? How?

20
Other
Methods
of Getting and Using
Occupational
Information

The methods of getting and using occupational information already described are not the only good ones, nor are they the only ones that have been widely used. This chapter contains brief descriptions of, and comments upon, some other techniques which appear to have merit and some which the author questions but which require comment because of their common use.

Audio-visual media. *Tape Recordings.* Kenyon [273] has reported how one high school, its staff and students, a radio station, and local industries cooperated to prepare recorded descriptions of local employment opportunities and requirements. All recordings were made at the factories and included the normal factory noises as sound effects. The expense was underwritten by the companies. The recordings were used in the course in occupations.

One school broadcast over a local radio station and recorded for later use a series of group conferences in which a counselor, a boy student, and a girl student questioned guests about their occupations. Another school reversed the process by recording group conferences in the occupations classroom and subsequently broadcasting the recordings over the school radio on a schedule that permitted other occupations classes in the city to listen.

One high school principal asked one of his alumni to speak to a student assembly and repeat some things the alumnus had said to the principal in conversation. The alumnus was reluctant to make a speech but willing to repeat the conversation and have it recorded. This was done, and the recording was later carried on the school's public address system. Radio commentators have made considerable use of recorded interviews with busy persons who could not be persuaded to come to a studio; perhaps counselors should make more use of their tape recorders in collecting and presenting occupational information.

Meagher [356] prepared colored slides of fifty local occupations and recorded on tape a synchronized commentary describing duties, training, and working conditions. Some of her students enjoyed finding their relatives and friends in the pictures.

The Picture Story. Some of the best visual aids are homemade. These show former students, both dropouts and alumni, engaged in their present activities at college or at work. There should be several pictures of each person in order to portray adequately all his activities. Emphasis should be on photographs of the worker at work in his work environment rather than on industrial processes and equipment. Students whose hobby is photography can produce surprisingly good studies of local jobs, schools, and colleges. All that is necessary is to explain clearly the desired results, suggest *Life* magazine as an example, and leave the rest to them.

The author once required a college class to present a photographic term paper, showing one worker performing all the duties of his job, with explanatory captions. Some of the results were mediocre, of course, but all were at least acceptable, and a few were really superb. One student presented the work of a barber, including everything from honing a razor to sweeping the floor, in thirty-three photographs so clear and simple that no captions were really needed. Another did an illustrated study of a medical laboratory technologist with a half page of explanation under each picture. Both were far superior to most of the textbook descriptions of these two occupations. The technique is good for what it teaches the person who makes the pictures; it is helpful in presenting facts to other students. The teacher who is a photographer himself and who wishes to do a really superior job will find helpful suggestions in *The Technique of the Picture Story* by Mich and Eberman [329].

Many schools have had students prepare "career books," in which they pasted clippings and pictures related to the occupations of their choice and in which they sometimes recorded whatever they learned about the occupations. The laboratory study method described in Chapter 18 is a refinement of this early technique; the picture and clipping notebook may still be used to supplement the laboratory study. Students should be instructed to give preference to pictures that show the worker at his work. They should be urged not to cut clippings from library references.

A teacher of retarded children clipped newspaper and magazine pictures of workers at their work. Each picture was mounted on a piece of cardboard. A few interesting facts about the work depicted were typewritten and pasted on the reverse side. Then the card was covered with cellophane. Sets of these completed picture cards were passed around the class. Considerable interest was reported.

The Burroughs Corporation [142] prepared a booklet for distribution to elementary and high school pupils who toured their plant. The booklet consists of ten photographs showing people at work in ten jobs. Above each picture is a one-sentence job description. Below each picture is the statement "This job requires a high school education." Three of the pictures include Negro workers.

Exhibits. Kenyon [273] got business firms to provide the high school with photographic murals, 40 by 60 inches, illustrating local job opportunities.

Kenyon also produced an "Opportunity Day Career Exhibit" for which local industrial, professional, and labor groups provided materials. The displays were housed in booths which varied in size from 8 by 8 to 16 by 60 feet. The entire exhibit was placed in the high school gymnasium. Students were invited to inspect it during free periods. Some teachers brought their classes. Evening hours were provided for parents and for visitors from other schools.

Forty-two separate displays, representing several hundred different occupations, were sponsored by such groups as manufacturers, office managers, cost accountants, sales organizations, a railroad, an airline, a trucking company, police and fire departments, an electricians' union, a painters' and decorators' union, a radio station, an employment service, a farm bureau, and professional groups of nurses, engineers, teachers, architects, dentists, etc. Each exhibitor was asked to provide a representative to answer the questions of interested students.

Wilstach [522] reported a ten-day exhibit similar to Kenyon's. This was seen by 40,000 persons from 140 schools, and 900,000 pieces of literature were distributed.

Churchill [85] and Crosby [110] described similar projects.

Musselman and Willig [349] described a vocational information center at a science fair. More than thirty thousand pieces of free vocational literature were collected from 200 sources and were distributed to the 10,000 children and parents who visited the fair during one weekend.

Parker [371] described an exhibit of local job opportunities, prepared by industry, housed in the school gymnasium, and opened to students and parents for one evening. Several schools cooperated; some brought their pupils by bus.

One state university placement office [11] sponsored a "Career Carnival," at which 14,000 students saw the exhibits of seventy-six potential employers and talked with their representatives about possible jobs.

Such exhibits add some of the values of visual education to other methods of presenting occupational information. When the exhibits are all shown on the same day and for one day only, they have many of the disadvantages of the career day, which is discussed later in this chapter. The counselor cannot be present in every booth to hear what goes on, so the student is dependent upon the ethics and integrity of the company representative. In a period of acute labor shortage, recruiters may be tempted to omit facts that might discourage prospective applicants.

Perhaps it is time someone experimented with a series of exhibits presented one at a time and at intervals which would permit the counselor to be present and to hear what is said to his students, just as he would at a group conference. This would obviously take more of the counselor's time—could it be better spent than in thus participating in the conferences in which his students are getting the information on which some of them will base their decisions?

Bulletin Boards. After an assignment to examine the help-wanted columns of a local newspaper, Thelma Meisner, a graduate student in the author's course in occupations, reported:

> I put these help-wanted ads on the bulletin boards, and I found that several of my students told me that they would never think of looking for a Secretarial position under Y for Young Woman wanted, or under A for Assistant to Manager wanted, or for G for Girls wanted for secretarial positions, etc. I shall certainly emphasize to all my classes that when looking through the want-ad columns, the students should make certain that they look through the entire want-ad section, rather than just particular sections that might apply to them. I feel that this is a point that should be brought out by all teachers who know that students are going to use the papers to find jobs. Since then these columns are tabulated as to the number of jobs offered, and the salary ranges, and placed on the board every Monday by volunteers.

Frosch [170] reported:

> Some of the things that we did with a bulletin board while I was at Brooklyn College, were to clip weekly from the newspapers, the

type of want-ads pertaining to a specific type of job—i.e. clerk, statistical typist, comptometer operator, steno-typist, typist, etc. Then, we would place on the bulletin board some pertinent pictures, or typed material regarding this type of job, the type of training necessary for that job. Of course, in order to have everything ready for each week's changing of the board, one or two girls would get the assignment on Friday to prepare for Monday the specific job to be dealt with the following week.

Since leaving the College, I now do the same thing with my high school class. I do all my teaching in one room which makes it very convenient. However, most of my students are low-average, therefore the scope of jobs open to them is quite limited unless they do have business background training. The bulletin board in this case has helped to show many students (even in so short a period) that they must have knowledges such as typing, clerical practice in filing, they must know how to be well-groomed, etc. One advantage in this high school, is that we can take one day a week to completely discuss any job they desire to prepare for the bulletin board. Again, one or two girls are responsible for the making of the bulletin board, and then, in addition to my grade, the class will grade them Satisfactory or Unsatisfactory in the preparation of the material. It is interesting to note how severe the students are with each other.

With one group that I teach, this occupational information is very interesting. This is a Work-Experience Group (one week work, one week in school). They are the best persons to come into the school and say that the job they now hold (such as messenger, page, etc.) would not be necessary, if they had done more studying in typewriting, or paid more attention in their English classes. Unfortunately, they go into this program during their last term at school when it is a little too late for them to back-track on their education. However, I find they are most anxious to improve their typing abilities so that they can get jobs as typists rather than continue as messengers or as they call themselves "lowly file clerks."

Counselors who plan to use bulletin boards to display occupational information may find the following suggestions helpful: Place the board where it will be seen and passed frequently by large numbers of students. Post only one item at a time. Change items frequently, at least once a week. Use short captions in big letters that can be read from a distance. Occasionally post something amusing—a cartoon, a joke, or an anecdote.

Slides. The Waukegan Township High School [511] in cooperation with the American Steel and Wire Company prepared a series of forty-eight slides from photographs taken in the Waukegan Works. One purpose of the slides was ". . . to present visually . . . the occupational opportunities of local industry." The slides were used in orientation, shop, commercial geography, and general English classes in the high school and also in training programs at the mill. Included in the series were pictures of recent high school graduates at work in the plant with such captions as

> Victor got the job, as you see here. He's learning to operate a Ditto machine and eventually he plans to learn all clerical duties in connection with his department.
>
> Among the young employees at Waukegan Works you'll find many of your friends and former classmates—girls and boys whose pictures appear among the graduating classes of Waukegan Township High School—girls like Lucille Martin here who got her diploma from W.T.H.S. Lucille is a stenographer in the accounting department. That smile suggests she knows her picture is being taken.
>
> Less than a month after she was graduated, Eleanore Rogala came out to the big lake-front wire mill. Eleanore has learned to operate the many different calculating appliance machines necessary to carry on the business of the world's largest and finest steel wire mill.
>
> Within a year, this young lady, Mary Anne Sedar, was graduated from W.T.H.S., hired as a typist and then promoted. She has many responsible duties now and among them is operation of the complicated addressograph machine shown here.
>
> Here—one of your former classmates—Stanley Chadwick (left) is learning the finer points about generators from instructor George Hagen. Stanley is an electrical apprentice and will receive practical training in electricity. He was graduated from this school.
>
> As a machinist apprentice De Forest Johnson is learning operation and maintenance of the many different types of machines required to maintain the wire mill equipment in the wire mill. Here young Johnson—who was graduated from W.T.H.S.—operates a turret lathe.
>
> Another machinist apprentice and former classmate of yours is Anton Urbancic. Here he is learning to operate the engine lathe and he has already mastered the operation of many other machines.

Mason [321] reported that

> Members of the photography club of the senior high school prepared colored slides showing various classroom and extracurricular activities which are a daily part of the school program. These pictures started with an eighth-grade graduation exercise and ended with a picture of senior-high-school graduation. Eighth-grade students and their parents were invited to attend an evening meeting at which these slides were shown. The showing was followed by a general discussion on the various courses offered in the senior high school. At the conclusion of the discussion time was allotted for questions from the floor.

Educational Motion Pictures—Homemade. Motion pictures of former students at work have been mentioned already in the chapter on follow-up. One school also made a film on beginning jobs and one on how to hunt a job. Students and teachers who have 8- or 16-millimeter motion-picture cameras may do likewise in their own communities. Further suggestions may be found in *Students Make Motion Pictures: A Report on Film Production in the Denver Schools* by Brooke and Herrington [45]. Peters and Brown [377] described the making of a motion picture of a local industry.

Cleland [91] described how three amateur photographers were temporarily released from teaching in order to produce a film showing twenty-three alumni at work in twenty-three occupations. Only one graduate and one employer declined to cooperate.

The student motion-picture club at one junior high school made a film which showed student clubs in action and other extracurricular and classroom activities. The film was taken to elementary schools and shown to students who would be entering this junior high the following year.

One senior high school prepared a similar film in which the physical plant, club activities, the guidance office, the placement service, and the work-experience program were shown to two entering students. The dramatic, music, and science departments cooperated in producing the film, which was then shown to students in the seven junior high schools.

Quick results have been known to follow the showing of some films. Wright [529] showed a motion picture about job opportunities in the telephone company and reported that ". . . many girls who were not particularly good in secretarial work, but were alert and with pleasing personalities, applied immediately for part-time operator jobs, and were accepted."

Educational Motion Pictures—Commercial. The most complete guide to all kinds of audio-visual materials on all aspects of guidance is the *Education Media Index, Volume 7: Guidance, Psychology, and Teacher Education* [143] and its supplements. The Index includes films, filmstrips, slides, pictures, phonotapes and discs, videotapes and kinescopes, models, mock-ups, charts, maps, and programmed instructional materials. There are subheadings in Volume 7 on occupations, vocation, and vocational guidance.

New audio-visual materials on vocational guidance are listed annually in the "Blue Book of Audiovisual Materials" [31].

For several years Saterstrom and Steph [415] have prepared an annual *Educators Guide to Free Guidance Materials*. This is a bibliography of films, filmstrips, and other materials, many obviously produced for recruiting or public relations purposes.

Some state departments of education have published lists of recommended films on occupations.

Because films are expensive to buy, there may be difficulty replacing them when they become obsolete. For this reason, rental is usually preferable to purchase. In Canada, film libraries are maintained by provincial departments of education located in the capital cities of the provinces, and lists of available films are supplied on request. In the United States, similar libraries are maintained by some city, county, and state departments of education and by some universities.

When industrial visits are impossible, pictures bring the student visual impressions of the working environment, materials handled, and duties performed. Students like to look at pictures; consequently, pictures are often used to broaden the occupational horizons of students. Incidentally, pictures may increase respect for some jobs of low prestige by showing vividly the need for knowledge and skill.

In general, visual aids are about as good or as bad as the pictures are appropriate and truly representative of typical conditions. Some industrial films are prepared for purposes other than guidance; they show processes and products but reveal little about the worker and his job. Some recruiting booklets from colleges, industries, and military services are lavishly illustrated with photographs that show only those facilities and activities which are most attractive; they give biased impressions that the counselor may find difficult to correct. All guidance materials should be critically previewed before they are exhibited to students.

Educational Television. In cooperation with local broadcasting companies, several schools and colleges have experimented with television programs. Interviews between a moderator and one or more guests have followed the general outline proposed for group conferences in Chapter 15. Some programs have been filmed at, or telecast direct from, places of employment in an attempt to provide some of the values of the plant tour discussed in Chapter 14.

Beachley [18] described a series of half-hour telecasts of occupational information to 8,000 junior and senior high school students.

Goedeke [184] reported the use of fifteen-minute television programs picked up in school classrooms, preceded and followed by fifteen minutes of class discussion. One program for high school seniors showed good and poor job interviews. Another, for ninth-grade students, showed activities in several vocational curricula at a local high school. Student and counselor reactions were favorable; evaluation data are included in Goedeke's report.

To date it appears that the principal advantage of educational television is in reaching a larger audience than can go on a plant tour or participate in a group conference. The principal disadvantage appears to be the lack of active pupil participation and the inability of the audience to ask questions of those who appear on the screen.

Entertainment Films and Television Programs. No one will ever know how many persons have based the choice of an occupation in part upon some bit of fact or fallacy picked up from a commercial motion picture or television program. A substantial proportion of these programs portray occupational conditions, activities, requirements, advantages, and disadvantages. The portrayal is often accurate so far as it goes but is frequently inaccurate in its effect because of the necessary emphasis upon dramatic situations. The effect upon emotional attitudes toward the occupation is frequently undesirable because the occupation is made to appear much more or less attractive than it is in fact.

Just as students need to be inoculated against biased information in recruiting literature, so they need to be warned about the danger of accepting the impressions they receive from entertainment programs on television and in the motion-picture theater. In some way we must develop in young people the habit of looking critically at all excessively glamorous and incomplete occupational presentations.

The teacher of occupations may do something about this by occasionally assigning his students to see a particular motion picture or television program and then to discuss such questions as "What occupations were shown?" "What impressions did you get regarding these occupations?" "Do these impressions truly represent the facts?" "What other facts would you want before choosing one of these occupations?" For students who do not have access to television sets and who cannot afford a trip to the movies, alternate assignments should be provided.

Museums. Trips to museums have been suggested for classes in occupations. The author cannot work up much enthusiasm for them. Even commercial and industrial museums show mainly industrial processes and products; they show very little about the worker and his work. A museum trip may not "do the students any harm," but it does consume time that might better be spent on a tour of some place where the students might later find a job. These comments, of course, would not apply if the purpose of the visit was to learn about opportunities for employment on the staff of the museum itself.

Dramatization. Several schools have had students write and produce one-act plays designed to teach something about guidance. The author has seen some very good dramatizations of the right and wrong ways to apply for a job. Both the performers and the audience appeared to enjoy the productions and to learn from them.

Dramatic radio programs in guidance are frequently duds. Elaine Stearn Carrington did a good one on plumbing once for the National Vocational Guidance Association and the American School of the Air over CBS. It was subsequently published in *Occupations* [64]. Commercial radio-script writers like Carrington are paid several hundred dollars per script. Those who do guidance programs usually get much less. The results reflect the difference.

Except for the kinds of productions described above, most of the guidance dramatizations that the author has seen or read about have been embarrassingly undramatic. Doubtless they provided motivation for the authors and performers to learn related facts, but they have not appeared effective as media of instruction or entertainment for the audiences. Some of the author's students insist that the dramatic medium has possibilities not yet realized. A series of scripts on guidance topics has been published in pamphlet form under the title of *Socio-Guidramas* [447].• Other scripts may be found in Richmond [394] and Weiss [506].

Role playing. Role playing is a kind of dramatization without a script, sometimes without an audience. Each actor is told to pretend that he is a certain character with certain problems, interests, motives, needs, or other characteristics and that he is to act as he thinks such a person would act in real life. Each actor improvises his own conversation as the action proceeds.

Role playing is often an effective way of arousing interest and starting discussion on any topic that can be dramatized. The action may take the form of an interview between a client and a counselor, a student and parent, a student and an employer or employee. Small-group discussions, such as a family conference, a teachers' meeting, an industrial staff conference, or a meeting of union officers, can be dramatized in the same way.

Role playing is sometimes used to help an individual to understand the thoughts and feelings of another person by asking him to assume the role of the other person in an appropriate situation.

Job attitudes. Beginning workers who want to do a good job are sometimes confused by the differences between education and industry. Students may be helped to anticipate some of these differences. As part of a survey of beginning jobs or as a separate assignment, students may ask employers for some of the reasons why they have promoted some workers and discharged others. On the basis of the answers received, selected students may role-play an employer promoting one employee and discharging another, in both cases explaining his reasons. Or an employee may ask for an increase in salary, and the role-playing employer may explain why the employee will or will not get it.

Practice job interviews. Role playing is often used to give students classroom practice in applying for a job, the teacher or another student playing the role of employer. At the conclusion of each interview the students and teacher discuss: "What did the student do well? What would you have done differently?" A transcript of one such practice job interview and the subsequent discussion appears in Appendix H. As with the practice interviews described in Chapter 16 interest and humor may be added to the practice sessions by having one student intentionally do everything wrong.

Some teachers have invited employers to participate in the practice interviews and then to tell the students which applicants they would hire and why if the applications and the vacancies were real. Some employers have subsequently hired students whom they discovered in such practice sessions. This technique was used and evaluated by Cuony [111] in a course which produced encouraging results in subsequent occupational adjustment. For more on Cuony's research see Chapter 25. Excellent case material for discussion may be found in *Why Young People Fail to Get and Hold Jobs* [514].

Chervenik [75] arranged demonstration employment interviews for men and women college seniors before groups limited to fifteen students. Local employers served as interviewers, and the interviews were recorded. The students and the interviewers discussed interviewing techniques after each interview. Chervenik reported increased demand for reference materials on interviewing and on companies after the demonstrations. A transcription of one interview is reproduced in her report.

The author and his students have observed that in a period of labor shortage, employers are frequently less critical than members of the class. One employer even said she would hire the girl who had tried to do everything wrong. The employers' comments have been enlightening and helpful on many items about which the students were in doubt.

Some employers have held practice interviews in their own offices and then come to the classroom to comment on the good approaches and to suggest improvements in the poorer ones. Kenyon [274] suggested that tape recordings be made of job application interviews at local plants.

Barbarosh [16] had each student in his course in occupations prepare a "job campaign folder" containing a letter of application in answer to a want ad, a letter inquiring about possible vacancies, an application blank completely filled out, a request for a letter of reference, a thank-you letter to a person providing a reference, and a letter thanking a personnel officer for an interview. He also used a tape recorder to let his students hear how they sounded during an interview.

Baer and Roeber [14] suggested that

> Among the best projects for teaching students good interviewee skills is to have them take all the steps in finding job openings and in landing jobs. In advance, a school official must contact local employers and arrange for their co-operation in carrying out the project. Each student can then pick one of the co-operating employers. He next writes a letter to the employer asking for an interview. As preparation for his interview, the student gathers and organizes information concerning himself and information about the employer, the company, its work, and its products. The student also briefs himself regarding what to expect in the form of questions from the employer, what to ask about the company and its policies, how to dress and groom for the interview, and how to act during the interview. After he is interviewed by the employer, the student reports back to his class concerning his experiences.
>
> The direct benefit of the foregoing project is the first-hand experience gained by the student in an interviewing situation. The indirect advantage is the possibility that through this project the student may actually find a job. Such a project has been used in an English unit at Jennings (Missouri) High School. According to reports, it has been an exceptionally fruitful experience for the high school seniors, many of whom actually found jobs thereby.

The tendency of counselors to think and act and counsel in terms of their own value patterns has been mentioned in Chapter 7. Berkowitz [26] has noted the ways in which the middle-class background of the average counselor may lead him into error in teaching some of his students how to apply for a job. The student who does not own a business suit, who does not want a white-collar job, who has a long experience of failure in paper-and-pencil activities may need a different kind of instruction from the prospective stenographer.

> A certain white-collar bias . . . seeps into school systems. The bias may be implicit in the wall-chart of the job-applicant in the blue-serge . . . the arrows approvingly point out: "clean shirt," "tie," "shoes shined." *No*-suit Lefty can only slink away, once again confirmed in feeling out-cast, with no hope of belonging. . . .
>
> In teaching how to fill out an application blank, do we neglect to add that it is quite possible to secure work without so doing? . . .
>
> The youngster who can get a suit may be ill-at-ease in the unaccustomed attire. The whole class will not be applying for the position of office boy. Yet school placement people have been known to send boys out as truckmen's helpers in their Sunday best for immediate work. . . .
>
> Rejection is a painful experience for everyone. The person who is already insecure needs to be prepared for many rejections. . . .
>
> It is not always safe to assume that the client knows how to get to the business section of the city. It may be wise to stress practical details of transportation, using a self-service elevator, and finding the man who does the hiring. . . .

Peagler [375] used the practice job interview with a group of seventeen retarded adults, few of whom had ever been gainfully employed.

> Yet their deepest desire is to get a job and become self-sustaining members of the community. . . . Each member of the group was eager to be interviewed and was very serious in acting the part of the interviewee. . . .
>
> I found it best to interrupt the interview to discuss a good or a bad point at the time it occurred. If I waited to the end most of the group had forgotten what had happened. . . .
>
> Whenever a word or a term proved difficult I listed it and after the interviews we studied the words and terms for future recognition.
>
> Retarded groups have a short attention span and to vary the technique one of the better class members would act as the interviewer and interview me. I then asked the class to watch for some of the intentional mistakes that I made. At times my performance would border on the burlesque but I wanted the mistakes to be obvious and the humor boosted the class morale.
>
> The first interviewers answered the questions self-consciously, mumbled answers, slumped in their chairs, and were confused by the vocabulary used and the intense questioning. As the interviews and discussions continued the majority of the class was able to relax and give clear complete answers. . . . Each class member began to build up a supply of information about himself . . . that could be called upon without hesitation during an interview.

Job clinics. Observing that colleges spend much time in preparing students for their careers but little time in teaching them where and how to get jobs, one college [149] held annual job clinics attended by 450 seniors. Employers were invited to the campus for a full day of open-panel discussions on how to get a job. Questions submitted in writing by students in the audience were discussed extemporaneously by the employers. At the end of the day, students and employers met in the college cafeteria for coffee and doughnuts while the students circulated from employer to employer and asked additional questions. The questions dealt mainly with where to look for a job, how to write a letter of application, how to dress properly for, and what to say during, the employment interview.

The sponsors of these clinics reported enthusiastic response from both students and employers. They noted two problems which the clinics did not solve: how to locate employers who have vacancies and how to prepare the college senior to answer effectively when asked what specific job he wants. "Certainly throughout the entire college training a more intensive effort must be made to familiarize the student with those businesses which may become prospective employers."

The sponsors observed also that the success of a clinic of this kind is affected considerably by the skill of the chairman who conducts the panel discussion.

Various community agencies have organized group activities to help adults improve their job-hunting methods. Among these are the Man Marketing Clinic sponsored by the Sales Executive Club of New York and the Job Finding Forum of the Advertising Club of New York. Directions for starting a job-finding forum may be found in Larison [287].

Ziegler [537] taught job search techniques to 1,000 unemployed and underemployed adults in small groups, each of which met for only two sessions of one-and-a-half hours. Of the 1,000 participants, 700 found jobs—half of them within two weeks. A readable description of Ziegler's work was prepared by Miller [334] for the *Reader's Digest.*

A good, brief reference on the job résumé and letter of application is *Pathway to Your Future* by Adler [5]. A good general reference on job finding is *How You Can Get the Job You Want* by Gardiner [173]. For adults, one of the best books ever written is *How and When to Change Your Job Successfully* by Lowen [311]. Although several years old it is still excellent.

How to use directories and other references to compile a list of prospective employers is explained well in Wasserman and Mason [503].

Practice on employment application blanks. Some teachers have asked local employers for copies of their employment application forms and for permission to duplicate them. The students in class have filled in the blanks, compared the completed forms, and submitted them to the teacher for criticism. Some employers have consented to review the blanks and then come to school and tell the students which applicants they would have selected to interview if the applications had been genuine and why they would have selected them. Teachers reported that they found plenty of room for improvement in the blanks submitted by students at the beginning of projects of this kind and substantial improvement later.

Coaching on how to apply for a job should not become too standardized. As an employer, the author has received identical letters of application from several seniors about to graduate from the same school.

Work experience. Work experience is sometimes arranged by schools and colleges, and it is accompanied by group discussions in which the students exchange experiences. Work experience is no substitute for a course in occupations, but it may be a valuable supplement to such a course. The primary guidance value of work experience is that it gives the student a realistic impression of what one occupation involves. It may also provide an opportunity for him to test his abilities on the job and to discover whether or not he likes the work and the environment.

Young [531] arranged five days of work experience with local employers for high school seniors. Among the comments of the students on this experience were these:

> I found out that I would not be capable of performing physical therapy.
> I found out that this is the type of work I would like.
> I learned that I would enjoy working in a neat and clean factory.
> Even though the buildings are old, the staff and employees were wonderful. I learned that a good place to work does not always include new and expensive buildings.
> Many of my former conceptions about engineers were cleared up. . . . I found out that mechanical engineering does not interest me very much.
> I learned more about engineering, especially electronic engineering, and I decided definitely not to go into engineering.
> This type of work is not for me.
> This is a job that I have never considered before and now that I have had a preview of what it would be like, I want to learn more about it.
> I now have definitely decided not to go into medical technology. As

with most jobs, it quickly loses its glamor and becomes the same old routine.

I found out definitely that I want to go into nursing.

It helped me decide for sure that I want to go into nursing.

I found out that I could never do physical therapy work. It does not fit my wants.

What group guidance may contribute to the work-experience program is suggested by the following quotation from Dillon [126]:

School personnel in most cities were aware of the fact that many workers lose jobs because the individual is unable to adjust to his new situation and not, as commonly thought, because he lacks proficiency in a given skill. Applying this to students going on work programs, the schools realized that these student workers would be confronted with a whole series of new experiences. It would be the first time that many of them would have to adjust to an adult environment; would be called upon to do a job without continuous supervision; would need to know about personal budgeting of money earned; would have to learn how to get along with their fellow workers; would face real work situations where the rewards were often promotion and increases in pay. Guidance personnel, in the cities visited, saw the need for group, as well as individual, counseling on the many problems like these that students would encounter for the first time. To meet this need, guidance workers outlined topics for group counseling, such as the following:

1. Educational implications of the job
2. Promotional possibilities of the job
3. Implications of the interview
4. Work opportunities in the community
5. Need for good employer-employee relationships
6. Processing of forms for placement on the program
7. Requirements of the job from the standpoint of the school and the employer
8. Common problems arising from the job
9. Adjustment problems of the beginning worker
10. Social security, unemployment deductions and income tax deductions
11. Budgeting of savings and expenditures
12. Budgeting of time
13. Job analysis as it relates to training needs
14. Business etiquette
15. Occupational information as it relates to the job

Slotkin [445] has described an experimental

. . . half-day school, half-day work program for 47 potential dropouts, age 16. . . .

Each student attends a daily group guidance session which stresses assessment of each individual's characteristics in relation to demands of the labor market. . . .

A guidance counselor is assigned to these 47 students and a New York State Employment Service worker assists in finding employment. The school counselor visits the boys and girls at their work to help them adjust to their jobs.

The Bureau of Guidance, New York State Education Department, is currently engaged in an experimental School to Employment Project which provides work experience for students on jobs in the school and in other public agencies, with stipends paid from a special fund supplied by the state. Jobs in private employment, for which no state funds will be supplied, are also to be sought. The program includes a daily group meeting of the participating pupils with the coordinator who supervises their performance on the job. *Developing Work-Study Programs for Potential Dropouts* [119] is a manual for teacher-coordinators in this program, based upon the experience of coordinators in Buffalo and New York.

The public schools of Newark, New Jersey, created a Diploma Squad of prospective dropouts for whom the L. Bamberger department store provided jobs that the students were permitted to hold only so long as they remained in school. Losi [309] reported that "it works." The program was described by Garrison [176].

Norris, Zeran, and Hatch [361] noted some of the potential disadvantages and limitations of work-experience programs.

Work hours keep students from participating in various school activities both during and after school hours. Jobs often are routine in nature and provide limited occupational experience. Full supervision cannot be provided on the job by many employers. With a limited number of staff assigned as coordinators, on-going class instruction is not tied together adequately with the job experience. Too much emphasis is placed upon the remunerative values of the experience rather than the life adjustment values. School and work hours prove to be too heavy a schedule for some students and the health of students is endangered. Some students may be too immature to gain the benefits which should accrue from work experience. Teachers report that students use work as an excuse for not attending school or not performing certain duties. The program causes too many interruptions in an organized and smoothly operated school schedule.

Youngberg [532] found that fewer life insurance agents quit their jobs in the first six months if—before they were hired—they had some actual contacts with prospective purchasers of life insurance, either by telephone or in joint calls with an assistant manager.

The reader who wishes to know more about work-experience programs in secondary school and in college will find excellent descriptions of them in Burchill [49], Dillon [126], Hunt [249], and Wilson and Lyons [521].

Work experience for counselors. Fountain House [327, 481, 489], a center for the rehabilitation of former mental patients in New York City, achieved "a reduction of almost forty percent in the mental hospital readmission rate" by means of a program which included the gradual introduction of patients into employment in carefully selected jobs. Before any patient was placed in a job, the counselor worked in the job himself for a day or longer in order to be sure just what the worker would have to do and under what conditions.

Some universities and industries have cooperated in arranging summer work experience programs for counselors. One such program, conducted by San Diego State College, is described in *Viewpoint* [493].

School and agency publications. Among the most useful publications are those prepared locally, by counselors and by students under counselor supervision, to describe local employment opportunities. Smith [496] prepared a summary of local wage scales and employment opportunities in the specific occupations for which her school offered training. Kenyon [273] and White [512] prepared local textbooks, one of which is described later in this chapter.

One high school yearbook [95] included five pages of pictures of seniors at work on their part-time jobs. Rohr and Speer [401] described how one high school used the school newspaper to present information related to guidance problems.

At the request of the principal, a faculty committee at Abraham Lincoln High School in Brooklyn, New York, prepared the *Lincoln Directory of Career Information* [300], a thirty-eight-page document containing lists of occupations in which workers were expected to be in demand, career books and directories of vocational training, two-year colleges and their terminal programs; suggestions on where and how to start the search for a job; employment application forms and résumés; and questions from civil service examinations. Copies of the directory were distributed at a careers assembly. Perks [376] reported that "not one directory was left behind, nor has a single copy been found left in any part" of the school building. "Students from the few classes which missed the assembly came clamoring to the office in search of copies."

The Corpsman [102], a periodical for the men and women of the Federal Job Corps, published a series of articles describing some of the jobs open to its graduates. Sample headlines: "Automation in Bowling Creates New Jobs"; "Many Jobs Open for Local and Interstate Drivers."

Library tour. Students may be more likely to use a library if they know that it contains something they want and if they are acquainted with the personnel and with the procedure for using the library's resources. It is, therefore, not uncommon for teachers to take students on library tours.

The following suggestions are from a lesson plan prepared by Agnes Higgins and reproduced by Forrester [164].

> Arrange to take the Occupations Class to the school library during a class period. With the assistance of the school librarian, show the class the shelves where the occupational books, occupational pamphlets, indexes, and bibliographies are located. Point out, also, the location of books giving information about several occupations and those describing specific fields of work.
>
> After the class is seated around library tables, provide each pupil with one of the bibliographies or occupational books. . . . Explain that at the end of four minutes, a signal will be given and the books should then be passed to the pupil immediately to the right. In that way, each pupil will have an opportunity to look at several books during the remaining part of the period. If in the course of the rotation of books, a pupil looks at some book which he would like to read on the second visit to the library, he may make a note of it.
>
> On the second visit to the library about a week later, each pupil may be permitted to go to the shelves to select his reading material on some vocation of interest. This is called a browsing period and he may return a book to the shelves any time he thinks he is not interested in it and select another book. The teacher and librarian both will assist pupils to find books and pamphlets of interest, or books which will widen their vocational horizons.
>
> Only short informal comments about the books or pamphlets surveyed should be called for during the next class period. The importance of consulting several sources of information and of getting several people's points of view should be emphasized. If a pupil inquires about the selection of some material for later reading, the use of indexes, guides, and the card file may be explained.
>
> Pupils may be reminded that they may use a study period for further reading or they may borrow material at the close of school for over-night use or, if desirable, for longer periods.

Brooks [46] described how one high school set aside one week for special emphasis on the use of the library in vocational guidance. The guidance director spoke to the senior class, reviewed library materials on occupations, and told the students how to use them. Books and pamphlets on occupations were placed on browsing tables at one end of the school library, with a different counselor in attendance each period and after school. Parents were invited. The senior guidance classes contributed a display of their notebooks containing surveys of local industries. Teachers cooperated by making related assignments. Average daily visitors to the exhibit numbered 141.

Writing the gyps. Counselors in training, who are struggling through three years of graduate work to earn an Ed.D. or a Ph.D. at a cost of several thousand dollars, will be pleased to learn that there is one "university" which, upon payment of $100 and the completion of one correspondence ". . . course in Counseling . . . grants the degree of Doctor of Psychology (Ps.D.) and wards [sic]a degree diploma (17 x 22 in.) which you will be proud to own and display as evidence of your study." The program ". . . consists of 29 fascinating assignments. . . . Text books, study assignments, testing material, lectures, etc., are included in the tuition fee without additional charge. . . . There are no hard and fast entrance requirements. High School, while helpful, is not required." The advertising circular does not mention that the institution is not accredited and that its degrees are not recognized by other institutions or by the legal agencies which certify counselors.

Every year thousands of former public school students become the victims of gyp schools, unscrupulous institutions that misrepresent their offerings, proffer extravagant assurances of employment for their graduates, and entice students and their parents into signing contracts to pay exorbitant tuition fees. One of the important guidance responsibilities of the public school is to warn its students and their parents to beware of gyp schools. Community agencies have the same responsibility to their clients. Some public schools have prepared and distributed bulletins warning their students about gyp schools.

How to identify the gyps is a difficult problem. Some are flagrant. Others are borderline. The least the counselor can do is to caution his students to beware of any institution that advertises in pulp magazines, promises employment at high wages after a short period of training, and employs high-pressure salesmen. The better correspondence schools have organized the Accrediting Commission of the National Home Study Council with offices in Washington to accredit schools that offer instruction by mail; it publishes a directory [129].

The U.S. Office of Education occasionally publishes a revised list of *Degree Mills*. A degree mill is ". . . defined as an organization that awards degrees without requiring its students to meet educational standards . . . traditionally followed by reputable educational institutions."

Information about other schools that are suspect can sometimes be obtained from the state department of education and from the Better Business Bureau of the state and city in which the school is located. Local employers may be asked if they have ever hired graduates of the school. If a local lawyer will examine the cancellation clause in the school's contract, his interpretation of its meaning may sometimes differ from that implied by the school's salesman.

The teacher or counselor who wants to inform his students about gyp schools may himself answer a few of their advertisements in pulp magazines. He will soon be able to display some gaudy sales literature, and to report some of the sales tactics to which his students may be subjected if they answer similar advertisements. Another approach is to find a cooperative parent, preferably a lawyer, who will permit his son or daughter to answer a few such advertisements and who will then join his child in reporting their experiences to the class. The same experiences might also be reported to a parent-teacher meeting. *Caution:* Do not give this assignment to *your* students without first doing it yourself, then warning your students and their parents to expect to see some high-pressure salesmen and to sign nothing without first discussing it with you.

The American Personnel and Guidance Association has published *Looking at Private Trade and Correspondence Schools, A Guide for Students* [308] which offers suggestions on how to distinguish the good schools from the gyps. Some of the good schools have objected to some of the statements in this document.

There are unquestionably some excellent private schools that do a better job than some public schools. The best basis for identifying the good ones is the kind of follow-up done by Hoyt [245] and described in Chapter 13.

Teaching the textbook. Teaching the textbook is the natural resort of teachers who have been trained in other subjects and assigned to teach occupations without training. It is one of the quickest ways to destroy student interest unless the teaching is superb. There are some good teaching ideas in textbooks. Judiciously used, they can be helpful. But to be effective the teaching of occupations must be related to local problems. To be interesting the course must be taught by methods adapted to its peculiar purposes. It cannot be taught by the traditional method of chapter assignment, reading, and recitation.

Some of the better textbooks, workbooks, and other teaching materials are:

For colleges: Borow and Lindsey [36], Calvert and Steele [54], Gates and Miller [177], Magoun [315], Martinson [319], Pitt and Smith [378], Smith [446], and Zapoleon [535].

For secondary schools: Belanger and Lifton [21], Belman and Shertzer [23], Christensen [81], Christensen and Burns [83], Gilles [179], Goldberg and Brumber [185], Hill [218], Houghton [240], Katz [267], Lifton [296], Lifton and Williams [299], Parmenter [372], *Resource Units in the Teaching of Occupations* [392], Sinick [431], Spiegler and Hamburger [452], Splaver [455], Turner [484], Wolfbein and Goldstein [525], Zapoleon [535].

For elementary schools: Carson and Daly [65], Carson and Tyler [66], Goldberg and Brumber [185], Lifton [295, 297], Lifton and Williams [299]. Some of the materials prepared for junior high schools are also appropriate for the upper elementary grades, for example, Christensen [81], and the *Resource Units in the Teaching of Occupations* [392] prepared for use with Puerto Rican children in New York.

For slow readers: Carson and Daly [65], Carson and Tyler [66], Goldberg and Brumber [185], Turner [484].

There have been several attempts to publish periodicals that would present current information about a variety of occupations and that could be used in courses in occupations. Most such ventures have failed. One publication which has survived for several years is *Your Future Occupation* [534].

Kenyon [273], who used a variety of teaching methods, also prepared his own textbook on local occupations. We would have better teaching of occupations if more teachers would follow his excellent example.

White [511, 512] prepared a forty-one-page mimeographed booklet describing the products, processes, and employment opportunities in forty-seven local manufacturing industries. The booklet was used as assigned reading in general English and in orientation courses and as optional reading in other courses. The following excerpts from the descriptions of different companies indicate the kind of information presented.

Abbott Laboratories. . . . The women perform capsule filling, packaging, inspection, and filling operations. Finger dexterity is important for these employees and the work techniques generally must be acquired through training in the plant. . . .

Arwell, Inc. . . . provides hospitalization, surgical and medical, health and accident group life insurance—and a liberal Pension Plan for all its employees. All annual premiums are paid for *in full* by the Company. . . .

Blatchford Calf Meal Co. . . . Approximately forty to fifty men are employed in production processes. They perform general mill labor, some machine operations, and the loading and unloading of cars. This work does not require special knowledge or skills and the methods and nature of the operations are learned on-the-job. . . .

Bunting Publications, Inc. . . . Approximately fifteen men are employed as type-setters, compositors, lock-up men, pressmen and plate-makers. These are specialized skills which may be learned in school shops or on-the-job. The program of training offered in the Vocational Print Shop of WTHS is good preparation for work in the printing trades. . . .

The Bunting Publications, Inc. has an excellent record of employee-employer relations. They have had no lay-offs since 1914 and each employee is guaranteed fifty-two weeks of work a year. A bonus based upon fifteen percent of the corporation's net profit is distributed to the employees at the end of the year. The firm has had a forty-hour work week, with paid holidays, since 1921 and a thirty-five hour week for office workers since 1945. The progressive nature of these policies is a matter of company and community pride. . . .

Johns-Manville Products Corp. . . . The office force of Johns-Manville is made up of approximately 400 men and women employed in a wide range of positions. These jobs are generally open to high school graduates who have had training in typing, shorthand, book-keeping, office machines, and the like. The office is large, air-conditioned and a pleasant place in which to work. . . .

Modern Pattern Works. . . . Accident prevention is stressed by this firm. They are proud of the fact that no time has been lost because of accidents since the firm was organized in 1932. . . .

National Division, U.S. Envelope Co. . . . Many opportunities are available for women interested in production as hand and machine operators. The work for women is attractive since the raw material is necessarily clean and there are no objectional dusts, odors, grime or dirt. High school education is an advantage to women employees although the necessary skills must be learned on the job during the training period.

Publications of this kind are invaluable resource materials in vocational guidance, even where they are not used as textbooks. And if textbooks are to be used, there is certainly merit in producing textbooks which describe the important local employment opportunities.

Presenting occupational information through other subjects. Some teachers try to show the occupational uses of their subjects to their students, some teachers refuse to do so, and some do so perfunctorily under compulsion. Some teachers know more about occupations in their own fields than do counselors, some teachers know less, and some know many things that are no longer true. Bedell and Nelson [19] found that less than 40 percent of 311 high school educators ". . . feel they are qualified to present occupational information in the subjects they teach."

The school that depends on the teachers of other subjects for the teaching of occupational information will get some very good information on some occupations and some very bad misinformation on others. Many occupations will not be described at all, because they are not obviously related to any one subject in the curriculum.

Should subject teachers then be excluded from the presentation of occupational information? Certainly not. The teacher who has or will get accurate information about employment opportunities in his own field can be a real asset to the ingenious counselor, both in and out of the teacher's own classes. He can help to arrange and he can participate in tours and group conferences. He can give his own advanced students more detailed information than should be included in a group guidance program for all students. He can relieve the counselor of trying to keep up to date on details in the fields that the teacher can and will cover.

Students can and should have the benefits of all that the interested teacher will do for them. Students should not have to depend for occupational information upon teachers who will not undertake to keep their own information up to date. Subject teachers who are interested in guidance should be used to supplement the group guidance program but not to replace it.

A counselor can extend his service to his colleagues by informing teachers each time he receives a new occupational book or pamphlet that is related to their fields. Some teachers will not be interested; others will be grateful and will help to call the publications to the attention of their students.

Munson [345] prepared five pamphlets on *Guidance Activities for Secondary School Teachers* of English, foreign languages, mathematics, science, and social studies. Each pamphlet includes a chapter on occupations related to the subject field, with a list of occupations, suggested instructional activities, related references, films and filmstrips. The English pamphlet includes a chapter on "Locating and Getting a Job." The social studies pamphlet includes an outline for a ninth-grade unit on career opportunities and requirements in general.

Ritzman [395] described a "subject career day" in which each teacher was encouraged to present the career possibilities of her own subject. Evaluations of the program were made by students, teachers, and administrators. They recommended that future programs be held early in the school year, that they be spread over two days to cover morning classes on the first day and afternoon classes on the second day, and that departments plan programs which would not overlap and which would give more complete coverage.

Further suggestions may be found in Tennyson, Soldahl, and Mueller's pamphlet on *The Teacher's Role in Career Development* [475].

Some schools have introduced occupational information units into social studies and English classes instead of establishing separate courses in occupations. From the evidence available to date, the results appear to have been disappointing more frequently than they have been encouraging.

Toporowski [480] reported impressively favorable results from a unit in social studies. Lincoln [301] reported that a course meeting five times a week produced better results than a unit in an English class, although the unit did better than a course meeting only once a week.

In New York State occupational information units were for several years included in the course of study approved for social studies classes. Here Hartley [205] reported that twenty-one of thirty-three schools with counselors had occupations units in social studies.

> In most schools visited, the guidance units were left to the indi-
> vidual teachers and were taught according to their interest in the
> subject. In only a few cases, did counselors indicate that they ever
> visit these classes or work with the teachers concerned. . . . The
> question of how effective guidance units in social studies are was
> raised by a number of persons interviewed. One system had estab-
> lished guidance laboratories as a substitute for these units and an-
> other had established laboratories in addition to them. Many coun-
> selors were only partially satisfied with the occupations units in social
> studies and some of the teachers of the units indicated they passed
> over them as quickly as possible. In one system, the social studies
> supervisor was suggesting that teachers eliminate the unit.

How the teachers of these units feel about them is revealed in Hamel's study of 389 schools in New York State [202]. He found that the prevailing practice in these schools was to offer a unit on occupations. The unit was taught daily for one to ten weeks in the ninth-grade citizenship education classes by a citizenship education teacher who had little or no training in guidance and who followed the *New York State Citizenship Education Syllabus* for the unit.

Although the teachers of these units felt that the subject of occupations was worthwhile, they were not satisfied with present arrangements for teaching it. They recommended that the time devoted to the teaching of occupations be extended up to twenty or forty weeks, that occupations be offered as a separate course in the eleventh or twelfth grade, and that it be taught either by the guidance counselor or by a teacher especially trained and hired to teach occupations.

Hoy [243] found that in schools where units on occupations were included in other subjects, 40 percent of the principals expressed satisfaction with the results; in schools that had separate courses in occupations, 76 percent were satisfied.

How to Teach a Unit on Occupations. The classroom teacher who has been asked to include a unit on occupations in his subject or who wishes to do so need not give up in despair. The poor results reported may be caused by lack of interest, which retards the teacher from doing the work required to produce better results. The really interested teacher who wants to do a good job may find some help in the following suggestions.

Do not try to do what you know you cannot do, even if the syllabus or the textbook seems to imply that you should.

Do not waste your time giving your students an overview of the world of work which is so superficial that it gives them nothing which they do not already know.

Scan Chapter 2 of this book on "What the Counselor Should Know about Occupations," and ask yourself "Are there things here that my students should know and that we could learn together?" Do the same with Chapter 3 on "What the Client Should Know about Occupations."

Take your class to visit your school or college placement office or the nearest office of your state employment service, or ask the placement officer to visit your class. At either place, conduct a group conference as described in Chapter 15, using the questions suggested there for conferences with placement officers.

If your school has made a recent follow-up study of the occupations of former students, present the results to your students. Let your students select the jobs they would like to know more about. Bring in former students as guest experts for group conferences on their occupations. See Chapter 15.

If your school has not made a recent follow-up study, consider whether or not you and your students will have time to make one and to discuss the results. You might wish to follow up just the students who majored in your subject. See Chapter 13.

With the help of your students, do a quick tabulation of the present jobs of the members of their families and of the students who have part-time jobs. Let your students select the jobs they would like to know more about. Bring in students and parents as guest experts for group conferences on their occupations. See Chapter 15.

With or without your students' help, examine your local classified telephone directory. Select some of the major businesses and companies of your community. Take your class on plant tours or arrange group conferences with representatives of these companies. See Chapters 14 and 15.

As a class project make a quick survey of beginning jobs. See Chapter 16.

Ask some local employers to help you, and run several sessions of practice job interviews as described above.

For additional suggestions see DuBato [137], Munson [346], and Chapter 22 of this book.

Career clubs. Most high schools have a club program. Some club programs include a career club, which is, in effect, a course in occupations on an extracurricular basis. Under exceptionally favorable circumstances, with a superior club leader, a career club can be good. As a permanent substitute for a course in occupations, it is about as effective as an algebra club would be if it were substituted for an algebra class.

Several of the teaching techniques described in this book can be used in career clubs and in other clubs that wish to devote one or more club meetings to occupational or educational opportunities. Particularly appropriate are the tour and the group conference.

For an interesting description of a good career club in action see Orrico [367]. For a related program, with emphasis on learning how to run a business and with tryout experiences in a variety of activities, write to Junior Achievement, 51 W. 51 St., New York. See also Kenyon [273].

Career day. The career day is an inferior but common variation of the group conference described in Chapter 15. Twenty or more guest speakers are invited for the same day and assigned to as many classrooms. Each guest makes a speech and then answers questions about his occupation. Students choose which meetings they will attend. The career day is inferior to the series of group conferences, spread over several weeks and months, in the following ways:

Students can attend only one or two meetings in one day. They may be interested in more. They can attend any number of group conferences held on different days.

The counselor can be present in only one meeting at a time. What goes on in the others is either unsupervised or supervised by teachers who are mostly amateurs in guidance. In a series of group conferences the counselor can attend all, can clear up on the spot any statement which he thinks may be misunderstood, can learn things about his students from the questions they ask, and can subsequently go to the counseling interview with the same background of information as the student. Incidentally, the counselor may have his own occupational information brought up to date.

The career day must be held on the day announced. It is always difficult to get twenty good speakers who are all free on the same day. If one speaker withdraws, a substitute must be found quickly. Too frequently these problems result in the counselor turning to a vocational training school which has a selfish interest in recruiting students and which will gladly send a speaker. Some of the worst guidance is done by such recruiting officers. The group conference can be postponed if the scheduled speaker cannot come.

The career day creates a bulge in the demand for individual counseling that is greater than most counseling staffs can meet before student interest has been attracted elsewhere. A series of periodic group conferences spreads the demand for counseling and permits the staff to see the students promptly.

The career day is popular with educators who do not have a course in occupations and who are annoyed when the desire of their students for knowledge interferes with the smooth routine of the curriculum which they have provided. Plummer and Ingram [379] disposed of their students' needs in this area with dispatch:

> In a single package labeled "College-Armed Forces-Career Day and Carnival," we gave 7000 teen-agers in our community a look into their futures.
> It had been our experience that considerable school time was being lost through interruptions during the year by college, armed services, and career groups for interviews, assemblies, trips and demonstrations.
> Last fall we combined all these into one comprehensive program.

Recognizing the limitations of the career day, several of the better schools and colleges have extended it into a series of periodic meetings. As far back as 1928 Wright [528] described a series of seventy-eight small group conferences, spread out over a semester and divided among six Minneapolis high schools. These conferences covered twenty-eight occupations, described by fifty-two speakers who were provided by the Kiwanis Club Vocational Guidance Committee. The meetings were attended by interested twelfth-grade students during their last term in school.

Mosback [342] reported a series of seventeen evening conferences, at weekly intervals, to which parents as well as students were invited. Jointly sponsored by an evening school and a Kiwanis Club, each program included a vocational-guidance motion picture, two or three minute talks, and a question period. Bradford [38] brought to the versity of Toronto campus, in one three-day period, all the recruitm officers who wished to interview prospective graduates in engineering.

After experience with both the single career day and with a series of group conferences, Rubinfeld [407] reported ". . . the story of the development of a weekly career group conference" for high school students:

> These conferences were mainly conducted in the library. . . . For each conference the librarian put up a display. . . . Speakers were introduced, and after a brief introduction merely awaited questions posed by the students and the moderator. The speakers had previously been notified that no formal speeches were required, and if we failed to ask certain questions they could fill in the void at the end of the conference. . . .
>
> Students . . . who had previously undergone . . . a regular career day were emphatic in their praise and appreciation of the informal group technique as opposed to the regular career day program. Speakers . . . invariably stated that they would welcome the opportunity to return. . . .
>
> There was no longer question of lack of control over the conferences, since some member of the guidance council was in charge and could detect any flagrant mistakes in the talks—in one instance we called in students who had attended a conference, in order to correct an erroneous idea implanted by one of our guests.
>
> Since we did not have to schedule all speakers for one special day, we were able to be far more selective, and rarely had a guest who could not do a satisfactory job. . . .
>
> Interests of the small groups could now be considered, and we were thus able to conduct conferences on such careers as foreign language secretary for a group of 11, private piano instruction for a group of 8, and ballet dancing for a group of 15. . . .
>
> We had ample time to find speakers who were still on the ground . . . floor of their occupations.
>
> Occupational conferences were now a regular part of the school routine, and it was no longer necessary to have several members of the guidance department forsake all other work for four to six weeks to prepare for the one day three-ring circus. . . .
>
> Speakers found it a pleasant experience, and willingly consented to come again. Sometimes after a regular career day in the past, speakers who were personal acquaintances had candidly begged us not to call on them again because of the obvious lack of interest on the part of some students in attendance at the conference.
>
> From a public relations standpoint our individual conferences proved far superior to the standard career day. There was now ample time to meet with each speaker . . . answer any questions . . .

and extend the many courtesies that are almost impossible during the hustle and bustle of a regular career day program. . . .

One major defect that has yet to be overcome is the failure of some students to attend any conferences throughout their 3 years in our school. . . . Some interested students . . . have attended as many as 15 conferences, and many of our students have participated in at least 10.

Chervenik [76] prepared a helpful booklet for college students who wish to plan career conferences.

Feingold [151] prepared detailed, specific suggestions with sixty pages of sample materials for any community agency that wishes to plan and conduct a career day.

Citizen counselors, Dutch uncles, etc. Many counselors have arranged for students or clients, who were curious about specific occupations, to interview persons engaged in these occupations. Organized programs of such interviews are sometimes arranged in cooperation with local service clubs.

There are obvious values in getting up-to-date information from a primary source. There are less obvious dangers in getting such important information from only one person, whose experience may be limited or atypical and who may function as a very biased but very persuasive amateur counselor.

The author recalls a school superintendent who had wanted to be a physician, until he discussed the profession with a physician who was very unhappy in his work and who persuaded the boy to change his goal. Not until he had gone too far to turn back did the boy discover that he had been given a grossly distorted view of the medical profession. In middle age he still regretted that unfortunate interview.

An overly enthusiastic person, on the other hand, may recruit for his occupation many persons who would be better placed elsewhere.

Some counselors try to prevent such unfortunate results by careful selection of their resource persons and by urging them to present a balanced picture of advantages and disadvantages of the occupation. The reader may judge how effective such admonitions may be.

Youngberg [532] found that prospective life insurance agents, who discussed the job with other agents before deciding to undertake it, were just about as likely to quit their jobs in the first six months as were agents who did not have such preliminary conversations. A taste of work experience, as noted earlier in this chapter, did reduce the termination rate.

The author and a few of his counselors-in-training have tried three-way interviews, in which the counselor and client together went to interview the resource person. Reports from those who have tried this have been encouraging. The counselor has an opportunity to see if an obviously biased picture is presented. He can help the client to get the information he wants by rephrasing ambiguous questions, by asking for clarification of answers, and by injecting important related questions not asked by the client. He can help the client to learn how to conduct such interviews himself. Incidentally the counselor has some of his own occupational information brought up to date, and some of his misinformation corrected. This, of course, takes time. But it is time well invested.

College night. This is another twenty-ring circus in which college recruiting officers describe their institutions and answer questions. It is even worse than the career conference, because every speaker has a selfish interest in the outcome. Even when colleges are crowded, every institution is looking for more students of the type it prefers, and some recruiting officers are paid in proportion to the number of acceptable students whom they recruit.

Honest college representatives do have a place in high school guidance programs. The good ones are really helpful. But they can meet students and parents just as well in a series of group conferences at which the counselor can be present to see what goes on.

Ross [404] suggested that "If the college-day type of activity is to be held in the school, it should be broadened to the extent that all types of training situations should be included. Students should learn about trade training, apprenticeships, and business schools as well as about colleges and universities." The same suggestion should be followed in arranging a series of group conferences.

Assembly speakers. Assembly speakers are sometimes used to present information about schools, colleges, and occupations. This technique is another inferior substitute for the group conference. It requires too many students to sit through lectures in which they are not interested. It allows the counselor no opportunity to interrupt if the speaker gets off the subject. If the speaker is dull, the students become restless.

Debates. The teacher who likes to promote formal debates or informal arguments will find plenty of controversial issues in the area of occupations. The relative desirability of two occupations for a person equally qualified for both can be discussed repeatedly by changing the occupations. Students may be assigned in advance to one side of the argument or assigned to one side for half of the class period and then reassigned to the other. Some students will study much more enthusiastically in preparation for a debate than for other purposes. Contrasting points of view may serve to emphasize individual differences in values and help the students to see the desirability of making their own choices in terms of their own values.

Cooperation with employment services. School and college placement offices and local offices of the state employment service are among the best sources of up-to-date occupational information. As such they have been mentioned frequently in this book.

Many college counselors and faculty advisers are unaware of the resources available in the better college placement offices. The *College Placement Annual* [94] is given free to college seniors who seek the services of their college placement offices for career guidance. It is a directory of approximately two thousand United States and Canadian employers who recruit on college campuses. It indicates the jobs for which these employers expect to hire college graduates during the year ahead. The companies are arranged alphabetically and indexed geographically and by major job categories. Also indexed are companies that recruit for foreign employment, those that offer summer jobs, and those that recruit holders of doctoral degrees and experienced college alumni.

The occupational listing of employers can open the eyes of the college student who has no idea of what he wants to do. In addition to suggesting many jobs that may not have occurred to the student, this list also indicates how many employers are recruiting for each occupation and thus gives some indication of the probable demand for workers. One issue, for example, listed only two employers who planned to hire interior decorators but sixty-five who would be recruiting dietitians and home economists. Engineers were sought by twenty-five times the number of companies that wanted liberal arts graduates. The companies recruiting mechanical engineers were ten times as many as those recruiting mining engineers. There were twenty companies recruiting salesmen for every one company hiring public relations personnel.

Also available for students and faculty to consult at college placement offices are periodic salary surveys [413] prepared by the College Placement Council. These surveys report the monthly salaries currently being offered to college seniors in different curricula by various types of employers.

In several communities cooperative arrangements have been developed between the state employment service and the public schools. These arrangements vary greatly. They have included the following:

Lists of typical beginning jobs and wages for high school dropouts and graduates have been prepared by the employment service for duplication and distribution by the schools.

Employment-service representatives have met with classes in occupations and with other student groups for group conferences on employment opportunities, supply and demand for workers in different fields, and related topics. Conferences have been held at the school and at the employment service.

Employment-service interviewers have gone to the schools to interview and register students who were about to graduate and look for work.

Employment-service counselors have become job counselors to prospective graduates, at the request of the school, long before graduation.

An employment-service counselor has been assigned to work full time in a high school, registering all seniors, placing them in part-time jobs during the school year and in full-time jobs thereafter. Follow-up visits to employers have been made by teachers under the direction of the employment-service counselor.

The employment service has administered its General Aptitude Test Battery to high school students, scored the tests, and reported the results to students and counselors. Tests have been administered individually at the employment service and to groups of students at the schools.

School counselors have made available to employment-service counselors the cumulative records of students who were applying for work.

Employment-service counselors and school counselors have exchanged jobs for a semester, each remaining on his own payroll and each learning much that would increase his understanding of future clients and their problems.

In one community, the social agencies, schools, and state employment service jointly arranged and sponsored two meetings for young people who wanted summer jobs. At the first meeting, a personnel director discussed how to get a job and how to hold it. At the end of this session 349 attendants registered on the spot with the state employment service. At the second meeting the participants were divided into ten groups to meet with speakers who discussed opportunities for summer employment in various fields such as construction, restaurants, service stations, hospitals, baby sitting, and lawn care. The joint committee solicited job orders from employers; letters were mimeographed by the state employment service and mailed by the community chest. Of the 349 participants in the project, 267 found summer jobs.

The counselor who wishes to make some similar arrangement should discuss possibilities with the placement officer of the school or college or agency in which he works and with the manager of the nearest local office of his state employment service. Most managers welcome such inquiries.

During the school year 1964–1965, representatives of the local public employment service worked with 9,942 high schools in the United States. They registered 633,019 seniors who were looking for work, counseled 333,356, and placed 101,954. The employment service also registered 72,882 dropouts and placed 19,175 of them. In addition, 8,372 potential dropouts were helped to find part-time and after-school jobs to help them stay in school. For more detail, see Goodwin [187].

REVIEW QUESTIONS

1. Of the methods described in this chapter, which would you most like to try? Where? With whom? Why?

2. How have tape recordings been used to present occupational information?

3. Are homemade visual aids good or bad?

4. How have help-wanted advertisements been used to present occupational information?

5. What possibilities do you see in the use of tape-recorded television programs?

6. How may entertainment films and television programs be used in teaching occupations?

7. What kind of dramatization has proved effective?

8. How did practice job interviews affect the demand for reference materials among Chervenik's college seniors?

9. Do employers appear to be willing or reluctant to help schools and colleges to present occupational information?

10. What do you think you should do about the white-collar bias of teachers described by Berkowitz?

11. What can *you* do to protect your students or clients from gyp schools?

12. Would you build your first course in occupations around a good textbook? Why? Why not?

13. What do you think of White's booklet on local industries? Could you prepare and use something like this in your work?

14. To what extent and in what ways should subject teachers participate in presenting occupational information? What are the limitations of this approach to the teaching of occupations?

15. Do you think Hartley's report on occupations units reveals any neglect on the part of counselors? If you were a high school counselor, what would you do about it?

16. If you were a classroom teacher of your favorite subject and

were asked to include a six-week unit on occupations in your course, what would you do?

17. What are the disadvantages of career days and college nights?

18. How do career days affect the demand for counseling?

19. What do you think of Plummer and Ingram's carnival?

20. Did Rubinfeld's students prefer the career day or the weekly group conference?

21. Did Rubinfeld find any need to correct misinformation presented by guest experts?

22. Did Rubinfeld find the career day or the weekly group conference better for public relations?

23. What are some of the ways in which state employment services and other placement offices cooperated in presenting occupational information to students?

24. What would you do differently from the way the instructor did it in Appendix H?

21
Occupational
Information
in the
Elementary
School

Between the ages of five and ten, many children spontaneously announce vocational choices. Adults correctly expect many of these choices to change as the children mature. No one wants to urge or even to encourage children to make decisive vocational choices before such choices must or should be made, but this does not mean that occupational choices in early childhood should be ignored. Occupational choices and the interests that they reflect provide teaching opportunities the alert teacher will be quick to utilize.

How the teacher responds to the child's announced "decision" may help to determine whether the child will come to regard the choice of an occupation as important or unimportant, as something that he may properly discuss with his teacher or as something in which the teacher is not interested, as something that the child should investigate and think about realistically or as something just to dream about in fantasy.

The teacher's response to the child's expressed occupational choice may help to determine the child's attitude toward different occupations. If the teacher regards some occupations as preferable to others, he will probably be unable completely to conceal his own feelings. He should, however, be acutely aware of the fact that whenever he does reveal his feelings, he thereby risks substituting his own values for the values of the child. The substitution may not always be desirable. The teacher who has never thought much about his own attitudes toward different occupations may do well to examine himself with care to see how frequently his prejudices are showing and whether or not any of them should be revised.

The teacher's response to the child's early occupational choice may affect also the child's attitude toward himself. Many other influences come to bear here, of course, but it is always possible that the teacher's attitude toward the child's choice will be interpreted by the child as an indication of the teacher's attitude toward the child himself and that this, in turn, will affect the child's own attitude toward himself.

As the child approaches the end of the elementary school program, his current vocational choices become more likely to affect his future. If he will go on to high school, he may have to make an immediate choice among various vocational and academic high school courses, and his choices will often be influenced by his occupational objective. If he will not continue his formal education, he faces the immediate problem of where to look for work.

The time for concentrated doses of occupational information and for formal courses in occupations has already been suggested in Chapter 12. Except in rare cases, this is not in the early years of the elementary school. However, regardless of our plans and intentions, children do pick up a great deal of occupational information and misinformation during their years in the elementary school. They become aware of many occupations which were unknown to them before. They acquire impressions of the work people do in these occupations, of the kinds of people who do it, of the compensations it offers, and of the abilities that are required for acceptable performance. On the basis of these impressions they enthusiastically embrace some occupations as possible careers for themselves, and they firmly reject others from either present or future consideration.

Hill [217] has reviewed some impressive evidence:

> Awareness of adult occupations and their status emerges at least by the mid-elementary school grades among boys, and perhaps a little earlier among girls, according to Simmons. Davis found that status attitudes regarding occupations were well under way in their formation among third-graders. . . . Nelson has demonstrated that children as low as grade three have well-formulated status attitudes regarding occupations and level of education. His finding that children start as young as eight and nine to reject some occupations as of no interest to them is especially significant since this rejection tends to harden as age increases. He concluded that "the process of narrowing the range of occupations considered favorably by children was definitely begun prior to third grade." . . .
> Earlier characterizations of the vocational thinking of younger children as largely in the realm of "fantasy" no longer seem defensible. If "realism" is the quality of occupational planning that brings plans into harmony with abilities, values, and opportunities, the occupa-

tional thinking of children by grade six has been shown to be surprisingly realistic. . . .

Units of instruction on education and work should be planned and taught beginning no later than the third grade.

How much these early impressions affect later occupational choices we do not yet know, but the potential effect appears to be considerable. To the extent that the information which children receive is accurate, the probability of good choice increases. The elementary teacher has as great an obligation as the counselor to see that the occupational information incidentally presented in his classroom is accurate information.

The occupations to which elementary school children are most frequently exposed are not the occupations that they are most likely to enter. Lifton [294]

> . . . requested cooperation from some 400 teachers at all grade levels. Each teacher was asked to consider which occupations they could use as illustrative of classroom concepts. To insure real occupational sophistication on their part, they were restricted to only those jobs for which they knew training requirements, salary levels, and job opportunities. . . . As a group, teachers knew most about professions. This was followed by sales and clerical jobs, with skilled trades barely being mentioned. This proportionate distribution of jobs, representing teachers' knowledge about occupations was *in almost exact reverse* to the distribution of jobs resulting from census data.
>
> Using another approach, teachers were asked to go through all the books they used in their classes and to make a list of occupations used for illustrative purposes in the texts. . . . In the primary grades there was a heavy emphasis on service occupations—firemen, policemen, and so on. There was then a rapid shift in the upper grades to the professions, with the skilled trades again being barely represented. In other words, from both their teachers and their texts, youngsters were receiving a distorted picture of the importance and types of jobs available. . . .

Although we now have several books on elementary school guidance, there are only two on occupational information in the elementary school, one written in 1923 by McCracken and Lamb [323] and one in 1963 by Norris [360]. Kobliner [280] reviewed the literature in 1955.

"Lessons on Specialists at Work," "What We Need to Go into the Baking Business," "The Clothing Business," "The Building Business," and "What I Want to Be" are among twenty-eight lessons in elementary economics prepared by Senesh [423] for children in the first grade.

An inexpensive text-workbook for grades 3 and 4 and a teacher's manual to go with it have been prepared by Lifton [295, 297]. In the text, orientation to occupations is emphasized, and the child is encouraged to consider "What do you think you could be"; "What do you do best"; job families; "What kinds of work can you do now"; and what makes jobs different.

Teaching materials for grades 7 to 9 are provided in the *Widening Occupational Roles Kit* [299] that includes 400 job briefs, five color filmstrips, five junior guidance booklets, thirty-five student workbooks, and a teacher's manual.

Two workbooks about jobs for slow learners have been prepared by Carson and Daly [65] and by Carson and Tyler [66].

The *Rochester Occupational Reading Series* [185] provides occupational information for "the slow and reluctant learner" in grades 6 to 10.

Resource Units in the Teaching of Occupations [392] was prepared and used in New York City with Puerto Rican children. Although used in ninth and tenth grades, the units are also appropriate for overage children in the elementary school.

Of course, all that has been said above applies not only to teachers, but also to counselors in elementary schools which have counselors.

PURPOSES

At least eight specific purposes in presenting occupational information to elementary school children have been identified. They are:

To increase the child's feeling of security in the strange new world outside the home by increasing his familiarity with it. To timid children, the unknown is always fearful. As they become better acquainted with their communities and the people in them and find these people friendly, their fears tend to decrease.

To encourage the natural curiosity of young children by helping them to learn the things they want to learn—and to enjoy learning them. In *The Psychology of the Elementary School Child* [12], Averill observed that "Growing children . . . are intrigued from their earliest days by man's occupations; by his adventures and his machines; by his ships and his mills and his factories and his skyscrapers; by his farms and his mines and his technologies."

To extend the occupational horizons of the child, so that he may begin to think in terms of a wider range of possible future occupations. Discussing vocational guidance in grade 1, Duffy [139] suggested, "It is not so important that students choose careers during the early years, as that they discuss various occupations and become acquainted with many." McCracken and Lamb [323] pointed out that "When the time comes for the child to select an occupation . . . if he knows about two occupations only, he will choose one of them, simply because of his ignorance of another."

To encourage wholesome attitudes toward all useful work. To this end, a unit on community helpers is found in most elementary school curricula. Among the many comments on this purpose are those of Bailard [15], "The elementary grades, too, are the ideal levels at which the child should learn about the dignity of work"; Lee and Lee [288], "The community around the elementary school pupil plays an important part in his life. His contacts outside of school time with the corner grocer, the policeman, the fireman, the postman, can be utilized and expanded to increase his knowledge and understanding of the value of each community helper"; and Super [467], "Thus, orientation to unskilled and semiskilled occupations, which tend to be looked down on after financial and social status values become attached to them in the eyes of children, might best take place in the elementary school. At that age they would be judged less by monetary and prestige returns, and more by the intrinsic nature of the activity; strength, speed, skill, tools, and the social contribution of the worker would be among the determinants of which the child was aware. At this stage of his development, he would be able to take in facts which would serve as the basis for a more tolerant and accepting attitude toward unskilled and semi-skilled work as he grew older. . . ."

To begin developing a desirable approach to the process of occupational choice. Chamberlain and Kindred [73] suggested that "Vocational planning should start from the time a child enters school. Even though most elementary pupils . . . are too immature to make satisfactory vocational choices, nevertheless the problem of selecting and preparing for future employment should be made a conscious part of their thinking."

Cavanaugh [71] described the purposes of vocational guidance in the elementary schools of Denver, Colorado: "Vocational guidance helps pupils and parents develop understandings and attitudes about the world of work. It concerns itself with an early identification of vocational interests and aptitudes by giving pupils vocational awareness. . . . A background for vocational choice is developed."

By appropriate suggestion as opportunities arise, the alert teacher can gradually help his students to become more aware of the personal needs that they are seeking to meet through their occupational choices and of the desirability of considering their abilities and their employment opportunities as well as their interests when they are thinking about what they will do for a living. As in other subjects, so in the area of occupational information, children can be taught where and how to get facts and what biases to beware of. Final choices, of course, will come later, but they may be better choices if the child's early attention has been directed to reality as well as to fancy.

One of the painful experiences of many young persons comes when they find that no employer is prepared to hire them at the lucrative salaries they expect or for the kind of work they wish to do. The elementary teacher can help students to face reality before it becomes painful to do so by letting his students see the kinds of jobs that beginners get and by answering his students' questions with accurate information about beginning salaries and the median salaries of experienced workers. To explore the need for such information, one eighth-grade teacher asked his students what occupations they expected to enter and what they expected to earn at the start and after ten years. He found that most of them expected "fabulous salaries."

To help students who are dropping out of school and going to work. There are still some elementary schools from which large numbers of graduates go to work. Most school systems have at least a few retarded children who never reach the high school. These students need occupational information on which to base their immediate decisions about where to look for work, just as do high school and college seniors who will not continue their education.

To help students who face a choice between different high schools or high school programs. Some large cities have a bewildering variety of specialized vocational high schools that some students must choose from at the end of the eighth grade. Other communities have only one high school but a variety of curricula. If the student faces a choice of this kind, if his choice will be based in part upon his occupational objective, he may need occupational information. If he needs it, his school has an obligation to help him to get it.

To show children who really need money how they can get it without stealing. In the poorer sections of some cities this is a real problem, and teachers make it their business to help their students to get and to exchange information about part-time jobs.

ACTIVITIES

Most of the methods of presenting occupational information that have been described in this book have been used in elementary schools.

Plant tours. Among the most frequently mentioned are class tours of local places of employment. These may begin as early as the kindergarten. They are frequently included in the social studies program as a part of learning about the community and about how people in an organized society help each other. The first places visited may be within the school. In the words of one first-grade teacher,

> We visit school helpers. We watch the school fireman shovel coal into the furnace and haul away barrels of ashes. We watch the clerk use the typewriter and the adding machine. We watch the dental hygienist sterilize instruments. We watch the lunchroom helper cut sandwiches and portion out soup. We watch how Bill cleans the windows, his body secured by a safety strap. At the pet shop we watch the storekeeper clean fish tanks and take out dead fish.

Other places frequently visited include firehouses, police stations, post offices, public libraries, banks, restaurants, newspaper plants, dairies, bakeries, retail stores, garages, and local industries. One group of students who were about to drop out of school made regular visits to a neighborhood employment agency to study the kinds of jobs available. Some teachers have taken their classes on "walking tours" to observe several kinds of outdoor workers at work.

One of the author's students, Pierce Palmer, reported his experiences in taking his students on tours as follows:

> My section of the sixth grade is made up of sixteen students with an IQ range of 46 to 92. Two are Puerto Rican children who entered this country in October and know very little English.
> The first visit was to the telephone office. I called the manager on Monday and made arrangements to visit on Wednesday. My first mistake: that was my only contact; I made no further arrangements. I explained to the class that the visit was being made to acquaint them with possible future jobs. I told them to watch for anything that interested them.
> When we arrived at the office we were met by the manager (a personal friend), who immediately broke the group in half, put each half in charge of a conductor, and hustled me off to a midmorning snack.

The groups were halfway through their tour before I got back to them. The children were asking questions and receiving good answers—but mostly on operating procedures, not about jobs. The tour consisted of the switchboard room and the cable-contact room—no outside work. As soon as the tour was over, we left. One point to the good here: all concerned told me how well behaved and polite the class was. The manager gave each child a little book for phone numbers.

We arrived back at school just at lunchtime, so discussion had to wait until after lunch. I then asked what anyone had gained from the visit. One girl said that she had asked the operator supervisor how to get a job in the office and was told that a high school diploma was almost a necessity. "I'll never get that," she said. A chorus of "me either" followed, and I knew it to be only too true. As far as occupational opportunities are concerned the visit was an utter failure. . . .

I felt I had only one way to go: I couldn't do any worse. You had mentioned in class that the reason for visits was not to understand the process involved but to learn about jobs. This was my goal.

I visited the manager of the local knife factory and asked a few questions. I learned they employed 173 women and 76 men. There are jobs available for all levels of ability. He would be pleased to show the class around, as it would be good public relations and it might help him out in the future.

I explained that I was not interested in the class learning how knives are made. I wanted jobs explained, wanted to let the class find out what is expected of each worker. I also asked him to please concentrate on beginning jobs. We then made a rapid tour of the plant, and he pointed out the beginning jobs and explained a few of the simpler machines.

The next day I asked the class what they would be most interested in if looking for a job. Pay, time off, and liking the work were most often mentioned. I explained our next visit and briefed them on what they would see. I cautioned them to examine what each job entailed, not just watch how the knives progressed.

The class was divided into three groups, each to be shown the same things. This time I spent one-third of my time with each group. The conductors had been well coached by the manager. The plant is divided into departments, and the groups were started on the beginning job in each and worked on up, with the main emphasis on beginning work. (I had asked for office and administrative positions to be omitted.) The plant tour was very successful, and in about two hours we gathered outside and walked back to school. During the walk back, I realized a big omission: no session with the manager after the tour.

We had time to talk before lunch, and what I expected happened. We didn't know anything about pay scales, and I also pointed out fringe benefits. During the noon hour I called the manager and got this information. But there were still other questions brought up the answers to which I did not know.

We wrote a letter of thanks to the manager, including the conductors and workers in our thanks. The mother of one of my boys works in the plant. She told him the letter was posted on the employees' bulletin board for all to see. We had a return letter of favorable comment on the behavior of the class and the interest shown.

I believe that this was a very successful visit in spite of my omission. The class was enthusiastic. Nearly all had seen at least one beginning job he liked. My 46 IQ boy had seen a man pushing a cart around picking up waste material to be reused and thought that job to be ideal—incidentally, it would be for him.

The Wood Novelty Works came next. I used the same procedure for this visit as for the knife factory but added one step: the owner agreed to answer questions after the tour. The day before the visit the class formulated a list of questions to be asked.

The plant setup was different, and the class was divided into only two groups, but results were still good. The class asked good questions, adding many not on our list.

It has occurred to me that perhaps a first visit without questioning at the plant may be advisable with a class such as mine. I can then help them formulate better questions with more class participation.

My supervisor has received favorable comments (unsolicited) from all three of the places concerned, and the two weekly newspapers have printed notices of the visits.

I have planned several more visits. . . .

Student Reactions. Palmer took another sixth-grade class to visit a television-antenna plant employing about five hundred men and women. This class had IQs ranging from 114 to 142, with an average of 121. After the tour, he asked the students to write their answers to these questions: "What did this trip do for you as far as helping you decide what you want to be? Did it help you in any way?" Among the students' replies were the following:

> I wouldn't like to do that kind of work, because it must get very monotonous doing the same thing over and over again.
> I thought most of the jobs were very boring, because you do the same thing all the time. . . . When we took a trip to the Telephone Company I saw the job I wanted.
> The jobs there wouldn't please me because of the noise, and most of the work is so monotonous.
> That kind of a job I would like to do to raise money for college.
> It increased my want to be a electrical engineer because I saw some of the things I might be trying to improve. . . .
> One thing I didn't like about it was the noise. I don't think I could ever stand it. When I grow up I want a cleaner job.
> I would like to work in the factory if there wasn't so much noise. . . . One thing I didn't know was that women worked in a factory like this one.

I would not like to do welding . . . because of the noise, it is very dangerous, and in the summer it would be very hot.

I wouldn't like to work there, because it is so noisy.

I would like to work in the cafeteria. . . .

I don't think I would . . . like to work there because of the noise and to do the same thing over and over. . . .

One thing did hold my interest. I liked the cafeteria. I wouldn't mind working there. . . .

I don't think I would like to work on a machine because of the monotony and noise.

The trip . . . really did give me something . . . it showed me what I didn't want to do.

If you're not careful, you can easily get hurt.

It made me even surer that I wouldn't want to work in a factory. I think I would find the work monotonous.

The noise in the factory was deafening. . . . I think it is a horrible job.

I enjoyed the offices, because I want to be a private secretary.

I did get something from our visit. . . . I couldn't work at the factory because of the danger of being hurt. . . . I want to be a doctor. Now I know how much a doctor would be needed in a factory like this.

I wouldn't like welding, because if you weren't careful you could get pieces of things in your eyes. . . . I would like a much cleaner job.

Other methods. Another frequent activity is some kind of survey of the occupations of the children's parents, other relatives, and friends. Sometimes the children are asked to interview their parents and report to the class. Sometimes parents come to the classroom to describe their occupations and to answer questions. Sometimes the class visits the parent at his place of business. One fifth-grade teacher reported that her children "fight to have their fathers come in to tell us about their work." On this subject one of the author's students, Colin S. Baron, has suggested:

An understanding teacher would employ tact and show respect for the child's feelings when setting out to do this. He would not rush into this but prepare the ground by finding out first: What do most fathers work at? Or brothers, mothers, sisters? What issues have to be handled carefully to avoid embarrassment to children—who hasn't got a father or whose dad is unemployed, etc.? What are the local resources of the community which can be utilized by the children themselves to find out about a particular job? To be more positive, how can the child be made to feel good about some of the jobs in which members of his family are engaged, even if they lack "prestige value" from a middle-class point of view? After studying a particular job, can people—fathers, etc.—who actually do this be brought into the study and be questioned by the class—or junior high school students come into the sixth grade to tell them and answer questions about their school?

To avoid embarrassing the child whose parents are dead or unemployed, the teacher may refer instead to "some member of your family, some other relative, or neighbor, or friend."

Jesmur [256] asked her sixth-grade pupils what occupations they thought they would be most likely to enter when they were ready to start working and whether they would like to learn more about any of these occupations. All but one said yes. The class decided they would each interview a relative, friend, or neighbor about his occupation. Together they prepared the questions they would ask. Later the students were asked what they had learned from the interviews. Among their responses were:

> You need to be good in math.
> You need three years of apprenticeship.
> I was surprised at the many different things he did.
> He made more money than I thought.
> The job is more dangerous than I thought.
> It takes more education than I thought.
> You have to live in or near a large city.
> You need to travel a great deal.

Of twenty-eight pupils, twenty-three thought they learned something from the experience; ten thought they had what it takes to do the job they investigated, eight thought they had not; thirteen thought the job would meet their needs, ten thought it might not.

Field trips were arranged for the class to observe four of their resource persons at work. Several of the informants came to class for group conferences.

A county judge came to the class and also arranged for the pupils to see a trial and to tour the county courthouse. After these experiences, the class discussed the jobs they had seen. Three thought they would like to be judges, twenty-seven thought they would not. Eighteen were interested in some kind of work they had seen, twelve saw no job that interested them. Everyone thought the trip was worthwhile. Everyone discovered some occupation of which he was unaware before the trip.

One elementary teacher got a shoemaker, a cabinetmaker, and a watchmaker to visit her class, bring their tools, and show the children what they did in their work. She found the students keenly interested.

Group conferences have been arranged in the upper grades, with workers from a variety of occupations and with representatives of vocational high schools. One fifth-grade group prepared a list of questions and sent its members out to get the answers from workers in the community.

Children have collected pictures of workers at their work and displayed them on bulletin boards or in scrapbooks. Some pupils have taken their own photographs of workers at their jobs. All the usual visual aids have been employed.

Stories of workers are frequently included in the reading program. Children sometimes role-play workers in different occupations performing their usual duties. One class played a game in which one student pretended to be engaged in a certain occupation and described his duties while the class tried to guess his occupation. One fourth-grade teacher asked her students to state the occupations they liked and why and those they disliked and why.

Instruction about working papers and child labor legislation is given to prospective dropouts. One school provided tryout experiences within the school for any of its fifth- and sixth-grade students whose occupational interests made this possible; participants included prospective librarians and secretaries.

One eighth-grade teacher of mentally retarded children spent almost the entire year on occupational information. For most of his pupils this was to be their last year in school. Because of their low reading level he presented much of the information himself. Attention was focused on the kinds of jobs these students could get, the nature of the work, earnings, deductions, how to find vacancies, and how to dress for, and how to behave during, a job interview.

Kaback [265] described occupational information projects developed by three elementary teachers. In grade 1 the children repaired a broken chair, discussed abilities needed to do the job, and went on to explore the work of carpenters and of various school employees. In grade 2 they prepared a "newspaper" in which each pupil reported his occupational preference and his reasons for it. In grade 4 the class visited a housing project under construction.

Kaback [264] also described how one teacher undertook to encourage her Negro pupils to overcome the obstacles they may expect to encounter:

A sixth grade teacher recently reported the following experience about providing occupational information to a group of socially disadvantaged children. Acting on impulse, she called the Urban League in her city and asked whether they could send several people to talk to her pupils about the hardships they had encountered before they entered their present occupations. Six men, representing the professions and the trades, responded eagerly. As she told it, some of the teachers were moved to tears as the children sat enraptured at the personal and occupational information spread out before them. The men too were so enthusiastic about the response from the children and the type of questions asked of them that they have since called the school to ask when they might come again.

In Hawaii, Tsugawa [483] taught a one-month unit on occupational information to her fourth-grade children who

> . . . telephoned and interviewed relatives, friends, and other resource people in the community. . . . We know that elementary school children cannot realistically choose their occupations, but we believe that it is our responsibility to set the stage to enable our children to get a preview of as many occupations as possible before the time comes when they must seriously select their life-work.

Kaye [268] taught a unit on occupations to fourth-grade students. The class and teacher developed an outline for individual reports, which included ". . . what my father does, what I want to be, and an interview with someone who does what I would like to do." The children were encouraged to talk with persons in different jobs and to consider "What do you like about their jobs? What don't you like?" Other suggestions included:

> Take your camera and take pictures of people doing their work. Think of all the different occupations you have come into contact with all day. Are all of them necessary and important? Write a report on everything you have learned. Be sure to include pictures, interviews, and whatever else seems interesting to you. . . .
> In class, role playing helped illustrate what to do and what not to do in interviewing. . . .
> In art the children made pictures of people doing different jobs. . . .
> Some fathers visited school and told the children about the nature of their work.
> The most important thing the children learned was to respect other people and the work they do.

The following are excerpts from the children's reports:

> Without laundry men, germs would get in our clothes and many people would get sick.
> We could not live without garbagemen.

The children became more realistic about their future goals and more respectful of their fathers. One boy who wanted to be a policeman ". . . discovered the hard training and work involved and changed his mind." Another began to work harder when he learned that he would need a good school record to get into the college of his choice. The unit made the children ". . . more aware of their future and how much planning it entails."

Breiter [41] discussed with her fifth-grade class the possibility of interviewing some workers and arranging some group conferences. The children suggested and voted on the questions they would like to ask. One girl who was about to go to Bermuda for a spring vacation volunteered to interview an airline stewardess. Two boys called on the veterinarian who was treating their dogs. One girl telephoned a laboratory and arranged to interview a bacteriologist. Group conferences were arranged with a pediatrician, a school nurse, a lawyer, and a chemist. Among the things the pupils said they learned were these:

> I found out that some branches of medicine require longer working hours than others.
> Television glamorizes the doctor's job. It is not realistic.
> I have learned that a doctor needs more preparation in school than many other jobs do.
> I never knew that nurses could work in industry as well as in doctor's offices, hospitals and schools.
> I have learned about bacteriologists and what they do. I never even heard of one before.

Grell [193] has suggested several ways in which elementary teachers may present occupational information to their pupils. "One approach is to study whole industries. . . . By selecting an entire industrial field, it becomes possible to emphasize vocational and industrial skills at various levels and at the same time present a realistic picture of jobs available in a given locality."

Buell [48] offered a suggestion for curriculum directors:

> Each school should list available material for use in each occupation that might be touched upon. Such a reference list would include pertinent textbooks, reference books and fiction; trips to various places would be suggested; an annotated list of motion-picture films and still-films with their distributors would be given; when there are pictures and clippings for illustration a record of these would appear; in short, a complete file of information for each topic would be kept for use of the teachers.

Paul [374] prepared a 112-page book on local occupations for prospective dropouts, for use in the elementary schools with average pupils of fourth-grade reading level.

The National Association of Guidance Supervisors and Counselor Trainers [351] surveyed guidance practices in elementary schools in nineteen states. In the kindergarten, 19 percent of the schools made some use of occupational information. This percentage increased from two to six points each year and reached 49 percent in the eighth grade.

A social studies curriculum focused on occupations. One public school system [78] built its entire elementary social studies program around occupations. The program began in grade 1 with workers in the home, workers who come to the home, and workers in the school. In this grade, said the teachers' committee ". . . we must begin to lay the foundation for . . . deep appreciations of . . . workers and what is expected of them in their occupations." Grade 2 studied other "workers in our community," specifically the postman, dentist, fireman, barber, policeman, community nurse, doctor, druggist, grocer, and librarian. Here, said the teachers, "It is essential that . . . our Social Studies program provide for our children an evaluation of various . . . occupations . . . in relationship to their everyday experiences and the environment they are studying."

In grades 3 to 6 the committee said,

> The traditional program in social studies stresses *environment* principally, and *man* incidentally. Since we recognize the importance of the individual child, we . . . propose that this *guidance-generated* social studies program *reverse* the procedure, emphasize the study of man and his contributions to the general development of civilization, and be concerned in the elementary grades with the orientation of children into the world of work and workers. . . . It must be presented in a spiral program . . . repeated under a variety of circumstances. . . .
>
> Thus while we . . . are preparing the child gradually as he grows, for a realistic choice of an occupational field, we are at the same time, helping him to develop as a potential citizen and to develop a comprehensive understanding of himself, his environment, and his relationship to it. . . .
>
> The emphasis in grade four should be on the development of a global picture of the world and its people . . . a realization that people live and work in different ways in different kinds of places. . . .
>
> The world grows smaller . . . because of the great advances in . . . transportation. . . . The fusion into this global study of transportation workers and their impact upon the lives . . . of people . . . should culminate with a thorough investigation of . . . vocational opportunities . . . in water, air, rail, and highway transportation together with an analysis of the physical, mental, social, and educational demands upon the individual. . . .
>
> The program in grade six will comprise a study of our relationships here . . . with our Latin American Neighbors and emphasize our

dependence on people in these lands for raw materials. These raw materials will be manufactured into useful commodities by workers in our city and distributed all over the world.

The purposes for grades 7 and 8 include:

To give the child a broad understanding of the purposes, functions, and relationships of local industries and to help him explore the vocational opportunities in his own community. . . .

To guide the child to a wise choice among the varied curricula offered by the high school. . . .

WHAT TO DO

One cannot do everything at once, so where should one start? What are the things that every teacher can and should do?

Listen. When a child wants to talk about his occupational choice, let him. And listen attentively. Let your attention indicate to him that this is important, that you think the discussion is worth your time and his, and that you are glad that he feels like telling you about it.

From kindergarten to about third grade, let the children dream. The child-development people tell us that these are the ages during which fantasy is a good thing, when many children do not clearly distinguish between fantasy and reality.

Somewhere around the fourth grade many children learn to make this distinction, and they reject fantasy. This is the time to start facing the realities of supply and demand, suggesting that children consider not only would I like this occupation and would it meet my needs, but also do I have what it takes and can I earn my living at it. This is the time to encourage children to investigate every occupation that interests them, to keep their plans flexible, and always to have alternate plans in case the preferred plan proves later to be less attractive or feasible than it now appears.

If the child wants information, help him to get it. Use your own professional skills to find the best information available. Use the sources described in Chapter 4. Help him to learn where and how to look for facts about jobs. Appraise what you find as suggested in Chapter 5.

Critically examine your own comments on occupations. Do they reflect the values of your social class? Are you saying things that will make it harder for your students to feel satisfied with honest work in occupations which you consider menial? Are you tossing out bits of misinformation about occupations because you have not bothered to verify your casual impressions or to bring up to date the information you acquired some time ago?

Check your facts. Introduce occupational information into your teaching only to the extent that you consider appropriate. When you do introduce it, be sure it is as accurate as you can make it. Give a reasonable portion of the time to local occupations and to the entry jobs in which young beginners start. Help them to learn about jobs you know they can get as well as about the glamorous ones that have caught their attention.

Take your pupils on tours of places where some of the workers are former pupils of your school. **Arrange group conferences** with dropouts and graduates of your school who are now employed. The inclusion of former students is important for several reasons. It increases the probability that your pupils will be exposed to occupations in which they *can* get jobs. It reassures some pupils that there really are jobs for people like them, which can be especially important for children who face the discouraging prospect of racial discrimination. Review the teaching methods described above and in Chapters 13 to 20. Use the methods which seem most appropriate to your group, which you and they will enjoy.

If your school includes grades seven and eight, if your students must choose between specialized high schools or curricula or elective subjects before they leave you, or if some of them reach the age at which they can and do drop out, review Chapter 12.

REVIEW QUESTIONS
    1. How may the elementary teacher unintentionally influence his pupils' future occupational choices?
    2. What are some of the purposes of presenting occupational information to elementary school children? Which of these make most sense to you? Why?
    3. What workers in *your* school or college or organization could profitably be visited and observed by your students or clients?
    4. What were some of the things that Palmer learned from taking his sixth-grade students on plant tours? What did some of his students learn?
    5. Of the other methods described in this chapter, which do you like best? About which are you skeptical? Why?

6. Roughly what proportion of elementary schools now make some use of occupational information?

7. What seem to you to be the advantages and disadvantages of the elementary social studies curriculum built entirely around occupations?

8. What are four things that every elementary teacher can and should do? Should *you* do them, too?

22
Suggestions
for
Beginners

This chapter is for the teacher or counselor who has never attempted to teach occupations or who has had the author's early experience of trying it with no startling success. The following outline includes, in the most elementary form and in consecutive order, some of the steps that may help to put the neophyte on the right track.

Identify the group to be served. What is their present grade level? How much longer will they be likely to continue their education?

Identify the major purpose of the work you are about to undertake. Is it to help students to choose occupations or to help them to plan their education, or is it something else? Discuss this with your immediate supervisor, and be certain that you both clearly understand and agree upon what you are going to try to accomplish.

Prepare a written list of the problems that you think are common to most of the students in this group and that you think your course might help to solve. Arrange them in order of importance. Show the list to your supervisor and others. Ask for comments and suggestions. If possible, ask a number of present and former students.

Decide which you think are the one or two or three most important problems that you can really do something about. For your first year concentrate on these and forget the others. Don't try to do too much. What you do, do well.

Get your supervisor's approval on your final choice.

For your own guidance, put down in writing exactly what you really expect to accomplish by the end of the term. Keep it modest. State it in terms of things that you know you can do. You can provide an opportunity for students to learn certain things. You cannot be sure they will learn them. On the contrary, you can be pretty sure some of them will not. Hold yourself responsible only for what you know you can accomplish.

Prepare a second statement of additional things you *hope* to accomplish. Do all you can to accomplish them, but do not consider yourself a failure if your first attempt falls short of all you wish.

Review Chapter 12 of this book. See if you have overlooked anything that you think you ought to consider. Revise your plans if necessary.

Review Chapters 13 to 20, and select the method of teaching that you think will be of most help in achieving the goals you have set yourself. Consider your own emotional response as well as your intellectual judgment. If you enjoy your teaching, the students will be more likely to enjoy their learning. Choose the technique you think you could use most easily and effectively.

Select two alternate techniques that you can introduce for variety when you feel that variety is needed and that you could turn to for the whole course if the first one should prove a failure.

If you feel a bit overwhelmed by the problem of choosing from techniques of teaching that you have never tried, if you would feel more comfortable following another teacher's choices on your first attempt, then try the following. These suggestions may be used for courses or units in occupations in school or college, or for a series of group sessions with clients in a vocational rehabilitation or other community agency.

Begin with a simple follow-up study. Explain to the group that the purpose of this is to help them to discover where they will have good prospects of finding a job; to help them to be realistic rather than naive in their vocational planning. With the help of the group, compile names and addresses of former students or clients of the same institution. Develop with the group a project designed to discover the present occupations of these former students or clients. Do as much as possible of this by personal interview between present and former student or client. As replies are obtained, discuss them in class. For more detailed suggestions see Chapter 13.

After the follow-up is under way, get as many former students or clients as you can get to meet with your group as resource persons in group conferences. Invite only one resource person to each class session. Inquire in detail about the nature of his job. Ask also what he likes best and what he likes least about his work. Ask how he got the job, and what advice he would give to a present or former student or client who wants to get a job like his. Invite the members of the class to ask any questions they wish. Provide them with a suggested list of questions, or help them to develop such a list in preparation for the first group conference. For more detailed suggestions see Chapter 15.

Provide practice in applying for a job. Ask local employers for sample copies of their job application forms. Ask permission to duplicate these for class use, unless the employer will provide enough copies for the whole class. Have the students fill in one of these application forms in class. Invite the students to raise for immediate discussion whatever questions arise in their minds while they are filling in the forms. Ask local employers to review the completed forms, then to visit the class and suggest how the students can do a better job. If you cannot get local employers to do this, do it yourself. Repeat with the application form of another company. Stage a series of practice job interviews. At first, let the students role play both employer and applicant. Later ask local employers to role play themselves as interviewers. Ask the student applicants to come to class dressed as they would dress to apply for a job. Ask the employer to comment on each interview after the class has discussed it. For more detailed suggestions see the section on "Practice Job Interviews" in Chapter 20.

To supplement the three major activities described above, or to provide additional variety, consider one or more of the following:

A survey of beginning jobs. See Chapter 16.
Group conferences with employers and unions. See Chapter 15.
Plant tours. See Chapter 14.
Practice in writing letters of application. This may be a joint project with the teacher of English composition.

Get your supervisor's approval on the methods selected. When you have had more experience, you will not bother your supervisor with every detail, but in the beginning it is imperative that you understand exactly what assignment has been given you, what you are expected to accomplish, and how. You can be certain of this only by discussing your plans with the boss.

One of the author's students developed a follow-up project with her junior high school class after obtaining her principal's permission. When the class was about to mail the letters, the superintendent of schools stepped in and forbade the whole project on the ground that only the senior high school principal should authorize a follow-up of graduates. Hence it may be well to ask your immediate supervisor's permission to discuss new projects with others whose approval is either necessary or desirable.

Tell your students in general terms what you are going to do and why. Let them participate as much as you and your supervisor think wise in making the final plans. Keep perfectly clear in your mind and theirs that you are teaching the course and making the final decisions. You are inviting them to help by contributing ideas and suggestions, but if you and they disagree, you will still be carrying the responsibility for the course, and you will have to make the final decisions. Do not apologize for this attitude. Do not be officious about it. The students will respect you as long as you do your job conscientiously and considerately, even if they disagree with you. They will not respect you if you are afraid of them.

Adapt the suggestions in Chapters 13 to 20 to fit your own local needs and purposes. Do not think that because you are new, you cannot improve on them. Think always about what your students need and want and how you can give it to them in ways that will be profitable and enjoyable for all of you.

Halfway through the course ask the students to write for you the answers to these two questions: "What have you liked best about this course so far? How do you think we might improve it?" Repeat these questions at the end of the course.

When you need more help than you can get at home, write to your state supervisor of guidance. He is there to help you.

If you think the author of this book can help you, write to him.

If you use any of the information or ideas in this book, the author will be grateful for a brief report of your experience and your own judgment of the results. If you have any suggestions for the next revision of this book, they will be welcomed. Revisions always raise questions about what should be retained, deleted, or added.

REVIEW QUESTIONS

1. Summarize the most important points in this chapter. Try to do it in not more than five sentences.

2. What might be the different purposes for teaching occupations to different groups?

3. Select the group of students or clients of most interest to you. What would be your purposes in teaching occupations to them? Be as specific as you can. What are you sure you could do for them? What teaching methods would you use?

4. Would you discuss your plans with your supervisor as frequently as the author suggests? Why? Why not?

5. To what extent would you let your students participate in deciding what the class will do? Just how would you provide for this participation?

23
Suggestions
for
School
and
College
Administrators

Most school and college administrators now feel reasonably convinced that a good program of education must include some provision for guidance, but they are not at all certain just what that provision should be. They have heard enough extravagant claims of guidance enthusiasts to be wholesomely skeptical. They have seen enough failures to make them uneasy.

The administrator who examines this book will do so, presumably, in the hope of finding some acceptable answer to the question "What should I be doing about occupational information?"

Here is a suggested minimum program:

A MINIMUM PROGRAM OF OCCUPATIONAL INFORMATION SERVICES FOR AN ACCREDITED SCHOOL OR COLLEGE

An annual follow-up of the dropouts and graduates of the preceding twelve months, and of others who have been gone long enough to have completed their higher education and military service and to have obtained full-time employment. Tabulation of the present occupations and employers of all respondents. Distribution of this tabulation to all students and staff. See Chapter 13.

An annual survey of entry jobs expected to be available to dropouts and graduates in the year ahead. Tabulation of job titles, employers, and employers' addresses. Distribution of this tabulation to all students and staff. See Chapter 16.

Plant tours to principal sources of employment as revealed by follow-up studies and surveys of entry jobs. At least one tour a month,

arranged and conducted by the school counselor, the college placement officer, or the teacher of occupations. See Chapter 14.

Group conferences with employed alumni in a wide range of occupations. Admission open to all interested students, staff, and parents.
At least one such conference a week, arranged and conducted by the
school counselor, the college placement officer, or the teacher of
occupations. See Chapter 15.

Tape recordings of all group conferences, indexed by occupation,
industry, and employer, with the date of the conference recorded on
the tape itself and clearly labeled on the container. Tapes filed with
occupational books and used as a source of occupational information
in counseling. All tapes removed from current use when five years
old.

An occupational information file in which no publication is more
than five years old and all publications have been reviewed and approved by someone employed in the occupation. All recruiting materials labeled as such. See Chapters 4 to 6.

An elective course in occupations for terminal students and prospective dropouts, taught by a person who has been adequately trained
to teach this subject. See Chapter 12.

Appointment of an experienced counselor as Supervisor of Occupational Information, with a roving commission to do everything he
can to improve the accuracy and adequacy of the occupational information made available to students by counselors, teachers, librarians, placement officers, psychologists, social workers, and all other
members of the school or college staff. In school systems that are
large enough to have full-time supervisors of other subjects, such
as music, the supervisor of occupational information should have no
other responsibilities.

Occupational information services are frequently poor because the demands for
other services are more insistent. Most students, parents, and counselors
do not know the difference between good and bad occupational information; so no one urges anyone to provide anything better than the misinformation currently distributed.

A few attempts have been made to provide better service.

Detroit, Michigan, is experimenting with full-time "guidance con-
sultants" whose "specific duties" include working with classroom
teachers "to help effect a process whereby children's individual understanding of educational and occupational opportunities will be broadened"; stimulating "exploration of the educational-occupational world
. . . through all-school activities"; arranging "weekly field trips . . .
to cooperating industries"; and working "with parent group to help
inform them of educational and vocational training opportunities" [292].
Trained and experienced counselors in the public schools have been
assigned to work on this project under the direction of George E. Leon-

ard of Wayne State University. Each consultant serves one high school, with other specialists in the elementary and junior high schools from which its students come.

Scherini and Kirk [417] described provisions made by the University of California Counseling Center at Berkeley to keep counselors informed of changing occupational opportunities and requirements. One full-time specialist in occupational information maintained a library, visited public and private employment agencies, reported at weekly staff meetings on new opportunities and trends. Counselors went on plant tours, met with the staff of the University Placement Center, served internships in the Placement Center, and had weekly seminars with specialists in different occupations.

What to do. The college or school administrator who wants to improve the occupational information available to his students can probably make his greatest contribution in five minutes—by designating one competent person to make occupational information his major responsibility. If finances preclude the creation of a new position, a realignment of the present staff may serve. What is imperative is that one person clearly understand that his worth to the institution is henceforth to be judged by the accuracy and the adequacy of the occupational information that the students receive.

Someday, perhaps, we shall see occupational information as a field of specialization for experienced counselors who have demonstrated both interest and competence in this area, who will be certified for this work at an advanced level as are specialists in other professions, and who will be paid accordingly.

REVIEW QUESTIONS

1. Summarize the minimum program in fifty words or less.
2. If you were free to do whatever you thought wise, which parts of the recommended minimum program would you introduce and in what order? Why?

24
Suggestions
for
College
Teachers

This chapter is for the instructor in a counselor education program who intends to use this book as a text. The chapter reflects the author's philosophy of education and describes the procedures that he has found useful in teaching a graduate course in occupations to counselors in training. The description of the author's practices is not intended to imply that he has found the only or the best way to teach a course of this kind. He has never taught the course twice in exactly the same way and will probably be doing something different by the time this book is printed. This chapter is intended only to provoke in the mind of the beginning instructor some ideas of his own for doing something better than conducting recitations and examinations.

Teacher education. The purpose of teacher education is not to indoctrinate willing or resistant students with the contentions of the author or the convictions of the instructor. It is not to turn out teachers who will be uniform, interchangeable units, stamped with the brand of the institution from which they come. It is, rather,

> To orient beginners in a new field
> To tell them what we think the purposes of our work should be
> To acquaint them with past and present practices and ideas and research
> To encourage them to try their own ideas whenever they think they see a way to do things better than we have done them
> To encourage them to challenge our thinking at every point and to evaluate the results of their own activities

We have had very little research on the uses of occupational information in counseling or in teaching. None of us really knows very much about it. If we are to develop and improve our service to high school and college youth, we must be modest about our own limited knowledge and never lose our respect for the student now in our own classes who will someday show us how to do a better job. Although this book can be used in the conventional manner of assignment, recitation, and examination, the author does not recommend such use. At our present stage of development, it is more important to start students thinking than to have them memorize what someone else has thought or done.

Teaching methods. The author has used in his own college classes a variety of methods which may be employed independently or in combination. In Appendix Y will be found a series of lesson plans, some of which may be helpful to the instructor who is teaching this course for the first time. At least one plan is provided for each chapter in the text. Additional assignments will be found in Appendix Z. The author does not suggest that every student be asked to do everything suggested in these appendixes but that the instructor select the projects that appeal to him, add his own ideas, and try them. If he will invite his students to help him evaluate his work as suggested below, he will soon find which projects work well for him and his students and which do not.

The methods which the author currently uses most frequently are demonstration and discussion. The lesson plans in Appendix Y call for demonstration counseling interviews by students and demonstrations by the instructor of the techniques of teaching occupations. In practice the instructor has done some demonstration interviews, and the students have demonstrated some of the teaching techniques. Some student demonstrations have been brilliant; some were excellent examples of what not to do. There is real value even in poor demonstrations; in addition to providing material for discussion, they may encourage timid members of the class to say to themselves, "I could do better than that."

Experiments in the author's classes have indicated that demonstrations produced better results than class discussions based upon questions brought in by students, that demonstrations by the instructor produced better results than demonstrations by the students, and that the students preferred to have some demonstrations done by the instructor and some by students rather than to have all done by either. For more on these experiments see Hoppock [231, 232]. For other methods of teaching occupations to counselors see Goldman [186], Hoppock [228, 229], Rundquist [410], and Wellman [509].

Discussion of student demonstrations. After student demonstrations of interviews and of teaching techniques the author frequently asks the class to discuss two questions: "What did he do well? What would you have done differently?" The author's students are never asked nor permitted to say that what another student did was "wrong." The reason for this distinction is the author's desire to build in the class a spirit of mutual helpfulness which may permit a student to accept new ideas rather than a competitive atmosphere of captious criticism which threatens the demonstrator with loss of status and puts him on the defensive. What the demonstrator did well is always discussed first in order to assure him that he can do some things well and that his achievements are recognized and accepted before any changes are suggested.

How to lead discussions. Several of the lesson plans provide for class discussions. When the topic is one of great interest to the group, a student leader may preside and conduct what looks like a good session. Actually it may be only a session in which a few aggressive students staged a hot argument. Leading and developing a good discussion, extracting from it the maximum value for the group, is a job for a skilled professional. It is in this kind of class leadership that the instructor earns his salary. Students may be invited to lead discussions when the instructor wishes to demonstrate what an amateur can do with a technique that is being studied or when the instructor is willing to sacrifice the welfare of the class in order to provide practice for the one leader; but the instructor who wants his class discussion to contribute maximum learning to the total group will develop his own skill as a discussion leader, and he will use it. The beginner will find some suggestions for discussion leaders in Appendix B.

Buzz groups. Several of the lesson plans mention buzz groups. These are small groups of four to six students each, into which a larger class may be divided for various purposes. The group is usually asked to select its own chairman and secretary. The function of the chairman is to see that everyone in the group gets a chance to talk. The secretary takes notes and makes the kind of report requested by the instructor. The groups usually remain in or near their usual seats in the classroom.

Buzz groups are used to give the timid student an opportunity to express himself in circumstances that he may find less threatening than the usual class discussion, to arouse interest in a topic which the instructor wishes the entire class to discuss later, to exchange more information than can be reported to the whole class, to summarize quickly data collected by the class or the ideas of all the students.

Buzz-group discussion may continue as long as the groups are interested and the instructor considers desirable. Usually the discussion is terminated after five or ten minutes. If brief reports are desired, it is imperative that the instructor word the question for discussion so that it can be answered in one or two sentences, for example, "What is the *one* most interesting item reported in your group? What does your group consider to be the *one* strongest argument on either side of this question?"

External motivation. The author has taught in some universities in which he was warned to be careful how much work he assigned, because the students would do it all. In such institutions no external compulsion to work may be either necessary or desirable. In other institutions, students are subject to so many demands on their time that even the better ones are tempted to neglect work which is entirely voluntary. Most students who enroll for courses want to learn something and intend to do a reasonable amount of work outside class, but many of them need a little external motivation to get them started and to prevent them from postponing much of their reading until just before the final examination. Several of the author's students have confirmed these impressions and thanked the instructor for providing the motivation.

As a further check on these impressions the author once compared two sections of the same course. In one section the final examination was given in weekly quizzes on each week's assignment. The other section, which met later in the week, was given identical quizzes but assured that the results would not affect their grades. The percentage of correct responses in the first group was substantially higher, and more of the students in the first group said they had done each assignment.

It is the present opinion of the author that some kind of frequent quiz or written report is a necessary evil for many students and that it should be designed to direct the attention of the student to those of his own needs which may be met by the work assigned. Examinations on useless trivia are often convenient to score but frustrating to students. They may be used occasionally if the instructor explains that their sole purpose is to determine whether or not the student has done the work and if the question is one that every conscientious student should be able to answer easily. But significant questions that reinforce the purpose of the assignment are certainly preferable to the memorizing of details that serve no purpose of the student.

The author has no objective evidence but has seen many indications that some students will work more industriously if they are assured that quiz questions will be taken from a list provided in advance. The review questions at the end of each chapter have been used in this way by the author.

Student reports. In lieu of quizzes the author has from time to time asked his students to report orally or in writing on how they proposed to use what they were learning in the course. Some students have stated bluntly that they could see no use for it in their jobs. Others have been surprisingly ingenious in applying the principles and techniques to a great variety of situations in and out of school. Excerpts from a few of the better reports follow:

> My class for expectant mothers continues to benefit from this course. . . . A review of . . . techniques decided us on a planned visit to the home of a former student, now mother of twin girls. The students were oriented as to purpose, future possibilities for discussion and need for cooperation.
> The alumna demonstrated care of the infants (handling, bathing, dressing, feeding, etc.) and explained methods and even need for improvising in the home. The students asked practical questions. The next class showed the benefits of the visit in increased questions, enthusiasm and optimism in their own ability.

> This course has given me the courage to put on a marionette show called "Who Gets the Job?" It is simple enough to bring out the proper and improper way of applying for a job and since the mentally retarded must have everything presented to them in an objective manner, I believe I have succeeded in arousing their interest in occupational education and vocational guidance.

> The material in the text . . . was used in planning a more effective visit to a hospital recently made by a small group of seniors. An informal experiment was carried out by discussing with half of the group such things as the purpose of the trip, what questions should be asked, etc. The group which discussed these items was more interested, asked more intelligent questions, and in general appeared to profit more from the visit.

> The discussion and demonstration of . . . techniques . . . has now opened up for me some excellent possibilities for group guidance in my homeroom period. This past Tuesday I used the "resource visitor" technique in the homeroom period by inviting the custodial engineer of the school to talk on the possibilities of employment in his field. The students and the visitor had an informative and stimulating discussion that ran well into the next regular period. Since the beginning of the course, I have also taken my students to the local fire station, both as a lesson in civics and with a view to questioning the fireman assigned to us on employment possibilities in the department. This was followed by two periods of evaluation of the visit when the class met the following day.

Student comments. As a quick, rough means of evaluating his own teaching, the author frequently asks his students to use the last two or three minutes of the class period to write one sentence of comment on the session just ending and not to put their names on the papers. The papers are collected by a student at the door and given to the instructor.

In conclusion. The instructor who believes that his students cannot tell good teaching from bad, who thinks that they do not want to learn the things they should, who is convinced that he can teach better without their help than with it will have little interest in student comments on his teaching, and in many of the teaching methods described in this book. There is room for difference of opinion in education and for a variety of teaching methods. Any of us could be wrong, and we may be grateful that our colleagues who disagree with us provide some insurance for the student against our mistakes.

The evidence to date seems to this author to suggest that most students do want to learn, that they welcome the teacher who will show them what they need to know, help them to learn it, provide a moderate amount of external motivation when they need it, consider their wishes and their preferences when it is feasible to do so, adapt course content and methods to their needs, and try to make learning a pleasant experience. Educational institutions exist primarily to find out what students want to learn and to help them learn it, effectively and enjoyably. Education should be fun. Education should leave the student with the feeling that what he got was worth the effort.

REVIEW QUESTIONS

1. Why does the author suggest discussing what the students would have done differently rather than what the demonstrator did wrong? Do you agree?

2. Do you agree or disagree with the author's views on student discussion leaders?

3. What is a buzz group, and what purposes does it serve?

4. How can the instructor encourage brief reports from buzz-group secretaries?

5. To what extent do you agree or disagree with the author on external motivations?

25
Evaluation

Up to the present time most of what has been done in counseling and guidance has been done because it seemed like a good idea. Only in rare instances has anyone attempted to find out whether or not the anticipated results were in fact achieved. A few of the rare attempts to evaluate the formal and informal teaching of occupations are reported in this chapter. The results are summarized under two headings: "General Conclusions" and "Specific Results."

Other research on the teaching of occupations has been reviewed in a series of articles by Sinick and Hoppock [432–441].

General conclusions. Sweeping generalizations based upon a few research studies frequently are upset by later research. The reader is urged to regard the following conclusions as tentative. They *appear* to be justified by the research to date, but any or all of them may have to be revised if future evidence contradicts rather than confirms the pioneer studies. From the research which the author has found to date, the following inferences appear to be reasonable:

Courses in occupations measurably increased the subsequent job satisfaction and earning power of the students who went to work and the academic success of the students who went to college.

Courses in occupations reduced unemployment among both graduates and dropouts.

Courses in occupations measurably increased the range of occupations in which students were interested and their interest in specific occupations.

Courses in occupations increased the ability of students to answer questions about occupations by as little as 0 and by as much as 217 percent.

Courses in occupations, with emphasis upon local opportunities for employment, brought occupational choices into closer harmony with employment opportunity but failed to bring them into closer harmony with measured abilities. Psychological testing plus individual counseling brought occupational choices into closer harmony with the measured abilities of the students but failed to bring them into closer harmony with employment opportunity.

Courses in occupations plus individual counseling produced better results than either one alone.

Courses in occupations increased the demand for individual counseling.

Separate courses in occupational information, which met five times a week for one semester, were measurably more effective than homeroom programs or English courses as mediums for the presentation of occupational information.

Students in different institutions found courses in occupations both more and less interesting and useful than other subjects.

More high school principals were satisfied with the results of courses in occupations than were satisfied with occupational units in other courses.

With college freshmen, plant tours were more effective than occupational films.

With high school students, speakers and visitations were more effective than pamphlets and films.

Preliminary group sessions facilitated subsequent counseling.

Small-group meetings were as effective as individual counseling and more economical.

One day spent in observing a worker in the student's preferred occupation, and two weeks of work experience in the preferred job, both led to changes in expressed occupational goals.

Intensive instruction in how to find a job produced quick results.

Turnover among new employees was reduced by improving the accuracy of the job description given to applicants for employment.

Conflicting results from different studies indicated encouraging success in some cases and dismal failure in others. Apparently the success or failure of a course in occupations depends upon one or more factors about which at present we can only speculate. Presumably these factors include the competence of the instructor, the appropriateness and accuracy of the instructional materials, and the interest and ability of the students. In some cases the research results appear to have been influenced by the quality of the tests used to measure results.

Specific results. The conclusions stated above were drawn by the author of this book from the results of research by several different investigators. The specific results which led to these conclusions are summarized below. Also included in the summary are the results of other investigations.

Research results frequently are qualified. These qualifications may be indispensable to accurate understanding and interpretation of the investigator's report. In the brief paragraphs that follow, qualifications have been omitted in order to make the summaries concise and intelligible to the beginner. The reader again is urged to read with caution and to base no important decision upon any of these results without first reading the complete report of the original research. Names and numbers in brackets indicate the references in the Bibliography in which the complete reports may be found.

Cuony taught a course in job finding and job orientation to an experimental group of thirty-five high school seniors in Geneva, New York. One year after graduation he compared them with an equated control group from the same class of the same school. The students who had had the course were better satisfied with their jobs than those who had not had the course. The combined annual earnings of the experimental group exceeded those of the control group by $7,719; the course cost $1,542. [Cuony, 111]

Five years after graduation Cuony again compared the two groups. During the fifth year the students who had had the course were still better satisfied with their jobs, were unemployed less frequently, and again earned more money than those who had not had the course. All differences were greater at the end of the fifth year than at the end of the first. During the fifth year the combined annual earnings of the experimental group exceeded those of the control group by $14,226. [Cuony and Hoppock, 113]

Rosengarten followed up two groups of graduates of the high school at Roslyn, New York, over a four-year period. The experimental group had had a course in occupations in their senior year; the control group had not. Differences in time employed, in job satisfaction, in merit ratings by employers, and in earnings favored the experimental group; but only the difference in earnings was statistically significant. Average weekly earnings of the experimental group exceeded those of the control group by $7.75. Total earnings of the experimental group exceeded those of the control group by $23,992. The cost of the course was $6,274. [Rosengarten, 402]

Kutner took one experimental group of seniors at the Technical and Vocational High School in Paterson, New Jersey, on a series of eight plant tours. Another experimental group took ten tours. One year after graduation both groups were compared with equated control groups on job satisfaction, weekly wages, number of jobs held, number of weeks employed, and employer ratings. Although most of the differences favored the experimental groups, the differences were not statistically significant. [Kutner, 283]

Toporowski selected three experienced social studies teachers who agreed to add eleven weekly lessons on occupational planning and job finding to their twelfth-grade course of study for one-half of their pupils. Six months after graduation he compared these pupils with a control group taught by the same three teachers. The students who had had this unit on occupations were better satisfied with their jobs, earned more money, and suffered less unemployment than the students who had not had the unit. [Toporowski, 480]

Weitz compared two groups of life insurance agents to see if he could reduce the percentage who terminated their jobs within the first six months. Before they were hired, the experimental group received an illustrated booklet that described the typical activities of an agent and the time spent in each activity. The control group did not receive the booklet. Turnover within the experimental group was 30 percent lower than in the control group. [Weitz, 507]

In a similar experiment in another company, the experimental group received a recruiting booklet that presented both the advantages and the disadvantages of becoming a life insurance agent. The booklet clearly and candidly stated the disappointments and frustrations an agent faces and asked "How would you react to problems like these? Could you take them in stride?" The control group in this experiment received the usual type of recruiting literature that emphasized the positive aspects of the agent's job. Turnover in the first six months was 33 percent lower in the experimental group. [Youngberg, 532] Subsequent follow-up at six-month intervals revealed that the experimental group continued to show fewer terminations over a total period of two years. [Youngberg, 533]

Actual contacts with prospective purchasers of life insurance—either by telephone or in joint calls with an assistant manager—also increased the probability of survival, but conversations with life insurance personnel were of doubtful value. [Youngberg, 532]

Skahill found a group approach more effective than individual interviews in recruiting college seniors for industrial employment. Recruiting officers visited campuses, interviewed students, selected the students who would be offered jobs, invited all such students to visit the plant on the same day. On this day the students toured the plant, saw a film, lunched with company executives and met with them in small groups for questions. The acceptance rate increased from one-third to one-half. [Skahill, 442]

Exposure to an enjoyable demonstration of "a new approach to the learning of mathematics," to the French motion picture *Passion for Life,* and to small group discussion with college counselors, all in one day on a college campus, increased the number of high school students who included teaching among their three preferred vocational choices. [Englander, 148]

Ziegler taught job-search techniques to 1,000 unemployed and under-employed adults in small groups, each of which met for two sessions of one-and-one-half hours each. Of the 1,000 participants, 700 found jobs —half of them within two weeks. [Miller, 334] [Ziegler, 537]

When a list of employers ". . . who needed students for part-time and eventually full-time employment" was given to all teachers in a Negro high school, dropouts caused by financial difficulties declined 97 per-cent. [Cox, 107]

A one-month course for prospective dropouts in several New York City schools emphasized job finding techniques, minimum skills, and realistic goals. The unemployment rate of the "graduates" was checked on four occasions. At its highest, the unemployment rate was less than half that of all sixteen-year-old dropouts. [Slotkin, 443]

Lowenstein taught a course in occupations to college-bound seniors at James Madison High School in Brooklyn, New York. One year after graduation he compared them with an equated control group from the same class of the same school. The students who had had the course made a higher grade-point average during their freshman year in col-lege, despite the fact that they reported spending less time in study. More of the experimental group participated in extracurricular activi-ties. [Lowenstein, 312]

A course in occupations was taught to twenty-six high school sopho-mores and juniors, whose failing grades were believed to be related to unrealistic career goals. One year later only four of the twenty-six were still failing. [Leonard, 291]

At the University of Minnesota, Stone found that one year of residence in college, without either individual counseling or a course in occupa-tions, increased the percentage of students who were judged by coun-selors to have poor occupational choices in relation to their measured abilities. One year in college, plus individual counseling, increased the percentage of poor choices. One year in college, plus a course in voca-tional orientation, increased the percentage of poor choices. Only the course in occupations plus individual counseling reduced the percentage of poor choices. The students who had the course plus individual coun-seling also improved measurably in social adjustment while other stu-dents did not. [Stone, 463]

When the occupational plans of high school students were compared with certain items of information about the students and their preferred occupations and when the appropriateness of occupational plans was judged by the investigator, the students judged to have the best plans were those who had had both a course in occupations and individual counseling. Next best were students who had received counseling without the course; poorest were the students who had received neither. [Lincoln, 301]

When the measured mental ability of high school students was compared with the estimated mental ability required in the occupations of their choice, the students whose choices appeared to be most appropriate were those who had received individual counseling plus group instruction in educational and vocational information in classes which met five times a week. Next best were the students who received counseling without instruction, next were the students who received neither, and last of all were the students who received counseling plus instruction once a week. [Lincoln, 301]

The occupational choices of ninth-grade students who had had both a course in occupations and individual counseling included nearly twice as many different occupations as did the choices of students who had received individual counseling without the course and the choices of students who had received neither. [Lincoln, 301]

High school juniors and seniors of low mental capacity who had been planning to go to college changed their plans after a combined program of testing, counseling, and homeroom guidance. Each student was given his own test scores and his rank in the class on each test. [Hedge and Hutson, 212]

Of sixty-seven high school students, each of whom spent one day observing a worker in his preferred occupation, 14 percent said they would change their occupational goals as a result of this experience. [Washville, 502]

When boys in their last year of formal schooling spent two weeks in factories in jobs selected by themselves, 48 percent of them changed their original occupational choices. [King, 276]

The occupational plans of eleventh- and twelfth-grade students were brought into closer harmony with employment opportunities when information about local employment opportunities was presented to them through school assemblies and through group and individual conferences. [Nick, 357]

A self-appraisal program of homeroom guidance for ninth-grade students, which included testing and subsequent interviews, did not bring about closer harmony between the distribution of the students' occupational choices and the distribution of employment opportunity in the community. [Boyer, 37]

Boys who had had courses in occupational information while in high school excelled, in tenure of employment after they left school, boys who had not had such courses. Girls who had had similar courses did not show similar superiority. [Long, 307]

After five years, boys who had received a variety of guidance services, including group guidance, through the Worcester Boys' Club, were superior to boys who did not receive the services, in the proportion of those still attending school or college, in the percentage of out-of-school youth employed, in stability of employment, in average earnings, and in job satisfaction. The proportion of adjudicated delinquents was smaller in the experimental group. [Cole, 93]

University of Minnesota students who took a vocational orientation course made better scores on a test of occupational information than students who did not take the course. [Stone, 463]

New York University students after a course on employment opportunities in guidance and personnel work, taught by the follow-up method described in Chapter 13, correctly answered more questions about the subject than comparable students who had not had the course. [Hoppock, 223]

On tests of occupational information given before and after courses in occupations, two classes of New York University students scored 28.5 and 27.3 before the courses and 82.4 and 86.6 after the courses. These gains are respectively 189 and 217 percent of the original scores; they are the largest gains in occupational information reported to date. [Warren, 499]

Although several reports of current practice have indicated that units on occupations are found in more high schools than are courses in occupations, Hoy found that where units were used, 40 percent of the principals expressed satisfaction with the results; where separate courses were taught, 76 percent were satisfied. [Hoy, 243]

High school students in courses on educational and vocational information which met five times a week learned more than students in similar classes which met once a week. The latter group learned more than pupils who studied educational and vocational information in homerooms. [Lincoln, 301]

High school students who received instruction in educational and vocational information as part of a course in English added more to their knowledge of education than did students who received such instruction in homerooms and in separate classes which met once a week. They added less than students in separate classes which met five times a week. [Lincoln, 301]

High school students who received instruction in educational and vocational information as part of a course in English added more to their knowledge of occupations than did a control group of students who received no instruction. In another study they added less. [Flowerman 159, Lincoln, 301]

During a ten-week course in occupations, ninth-grade students gained about twice as much in their knowledge of occupations as did eighth-grade students who did not have the course. [Jessup, 257]

At the beginning and at the end of a nine-week unit on occupations, taught in an industrial arts course, experimental and control groups of ninth-grade boys were asked to "list all the jobs they could think of and tell something about each one." At the end of the unit, the experimental group listed 138 percent more occupations than they had listed at the beginning. The control group listed 23 percent fewer. [Guerra, 196]

Tenth-, eleventh-, and twelfth-grade students who had a course in occupations in the ninth grade were not measurably superior to comparable students who did not have the course when the two groups were compared on the Kefauver-Hand Tests of Occupational Information, False Guidance, and General Educational Information; on the proportion of students who had made occupational choices; on the percentage of students who planned to graduate from high school; on the mean intelligence quotients of students who planned to go to college; on reasons given for planning to graduate from high school or for choosing a particular occupation; and on the Symonds-Block Student Questionnaire designed to measure how the student feels toward his studies, his teachers, and his environment. [Kefauver and Hand, 271]

High school seniors, after studying occupations that they liked, changed their attitudes toward related occupations that they had previously said they disliked. [Recktenwald, 387]

By ten minutes spent in reading an *Occupational Abstract*, experienced counselors increased by 96 percent their correct answers to important questions about one occupation. [Hoppock, 224]

University of Minnesota students preferred the *Occupational Survey Outline* by Hahn and Brayfield [200] to the original form of the *Outline for the Study of an Occupation* by Hoppock. After the Hoppock outline had been revised in the light of the students' comments, in an effort to incorporate the best features of both original forms, the students preferred the revised Hoppock outline which is reprinted in this book in Appendix G. [Borow and Hoppock, 35]

High school juniors, seniors, and graduates gained, respectively, 38, 77, and 34 percent in correct answers on a test of occupational information after reading a book on which the test was based. [Charters, 74]

High school juniors, seniors, and graduates expressed greater interest in retailing as an occupation after reading a book on opportunities in retail stores. [Charters, 74]

Reading a pamphlet on farming as an occupation changed the answers of some students to the question "Would you like to be a farmer?" In a small-town high school in a rural county an equal number of students changed their answers from Yes to No and from No to Yes. In a New York City continuation school the number of yes answers decreased. [Hoppock, 226]

A "readable" description of an occupation increased high school students' knowledge of the occupation by an amount exactly equal to that contributed by an "encyclopedic" presentation of the same information. More students reported the readable description to be interesting, and more of them decided to enter the occupation after reading it than after reading the other. [Hoppock, 227]

University of Minnesota students who were asked to list their current courses in order of preference rated vocational orientation in second or third place from the top. [Stone, 464]

In comparison with other courses taken, University of Minnesota students rated a course in vocational orientation above average. [Stone, 464]

In different high schools as few as 6 percent and as many as 39 percent of the students in group guidance classes felt that there was no point in what they were doing. [Sachs, 412]

In two high schools students were asked to list the courses in which they had learned a great deal that was of present or probable future value to them; group guidance received a smaller percentage of possible mentions than did other courses. [Sachs, 412]

Sixty percent of eighth-grade students said they had been interested in their group guidance work and had enjoyed the class. [Lincoln, 301]

Ninety-eight percent of high school girls in grades 9 to 12, after an eight-week unit on occupations, said it ". . . should become a part of the regular curriculum." [Walker, 487]

When high school dropouts and graduates were followed up eight years after they had taken a required ninth-grade course in occupations, 80 percent of the respondents said the course should be retained as a required subject. About half of the graduates recommended that the course be moved to the eleventh or twelfth grade, while most of the dropouts thought it should remain in the ninth. Suggestions for improvement included more plant tours plus qualified and interested teachers. [Rubinfeld and Hoppock, 408]

After a group guidance course in which ten inmates of Indiana State

Prison were given intelligence and achievement tests and in which their test scores were discussed in class, seven of the ten inmates requested vocational guidance interviews with the instructor. Five of the ten also brought up some of their personality problems. [Jolles, 260]

College freshmen preferred plant tours to occupational films. [Miller, 336]

Plant tours were more effective than occupational films in reducing the number of college freshmen who had no occupational choice. Each was more effective than neither. [Miller, 336]

Dierkes [125] reported that in one year of the Careers Unlimited Program 5,669 students from twenty-two Detroit senior high schools visited seventy-eight host organizations. Ninety-four percent of the students said the trip had been "valuable" or "very valuable." Among the student comments were "Gives you a chance to see the job—learned much more than through books about the occupation"; "I would like to visit more than one organization"; "I want to attend every year."

Edmiston and Scrivner [140] compared four methods of presenting occupational information to high school students. Using tests of occupational information as the criterion, they found the order of efficiency of the four methods to be speakers, visitations, pamphlets, films.

University of Minnesota freshmen who were exposed to a fifty-minute lecture and discussion session on the aims and methods of vocational counseling demonstrated "better understanding of the counseling process" and fewer "points of dissatisfaction" with subsequent counseling interviews than did comparable students who were counseled without the preliminary group session. There was no significant difference in the clients' "over-all ratings of the value of the interview." [Richardson and Borow, 393]

Hoyt compared the effectiveness of group meetings and of individual counseling on freshmen at the University of Minnesota. His criteria were the increase in percentage of realistic vocational choices, certainty of vocational choice, and satisfaction with it. Thirty-four hours of counselor time in group sessions with twenty-five students produced as good results as thirty-nine hours spent in individual counseling with fourteen students. [Hoyt, 244]

Hewer used Hoyt's criteria to compare Minnesota freshmen who had a course in occupations with other freshmen who were counseled individually. She found no difference between the groups on certainty of, and satisfaction with, vocational choice. Realism could not be measured, because the judges disagreed. [Hewer, 214]

Brief comments on selected studies. The reader who wishes to read some of the original researches may be interested in the following additional comments.

The report by Charters and others [74] is probably the most comprehensive extant on methods of evaluating occupational literature.

Cole [93] used more ultimate criteria than anyone else to date. His is the only one of the researches here reviewed that included delinquency as a criterion. In his unguided group, 11 percent became delinquent; in his guided group, only 1 percent.

Cuony [111] offers one of the best examples of careful equating by alphabetic random sampling, extensively pretested. It is one of the few studies to use ultimate criteria and to demonstrate the financial profit that may accrue to a community and its workers from effective work in vocational guidance. The full report includes a fairly detailed description of the course in job finding and job orientation which produced the impressive results in job satisfaction and in earnings.

Cuony [111], Long [307], Toporowski [480], Weitz [507], and Youngberg [532] all reported less unemployment or longer duration of employment following the presentation of more or better occupational information. When and if we have another severe economic depression, we may have more research using this criterion.

Lowenstein [312] used a table of random numbers to set up his groups and pretested his method of equating fourteen times. Despite the fact that the students in his pretests went to several different colleges, in no case did random sampling produce groups with significant differences in freshman grades.

Stone's [463, 464] is one of the few studies to compare the effectiveness of counseling plus instruction in occupations with the results of each one alone. It is the most intensive evaluation of a course in occupations at the college level. It has been frequently cited in support of the belief that group guidance without counseling is ineffective. Less frequently mentioned is Stone's report that individual counseling without the course in vocational orientation was also ineffective. All of Stone's results are dependent upon his use of an intermediate criterion and the assumption that counselors can determine which of their clients' choices are good and which are poor.

Nick [357] used one of the simplest of research designs and produced some of the most impressive evidence of the impact of occupational information on occupational choices. After learning about employment opportunities in their hometown, the percentage of his students who chose some overcrowded occupations was cut in half, while the percentage who chose some of the shortage fields was doubled. Any teacher or counselor could use his procedures without any training in statistics.

Weitz [507] and Youngberg [532] produced some of the most impressive evidence of the direct effect of occupational information alone on subsequent job satisfaction. With no difference between experimental and control groups except in the nature of the printed recruiting brochure, both found that turnover among new workers could be reduced by 30 percent when the accuracy and adequacy of the job description were improved. We do not yet know whether the better job description led different persons to accept or reject employment, or whether it simply led to more realistic expectations and hence fewer disappointments and frustrations. But either way, the better job description did produce better job satisfaction for the worker and impressively lower turnover costs for the employer.

Ziegler [334, 537] demonstrated how much can be done in a very short time when a skillful teacher meets people who really want to learn how to get a job. Many teachers and counselors would dismiss as superficial any attempt to produce impressive results in only three hours, but few teachers and counselors have ever equalled Ziegler's results even in thirty hours. One is reminded of Parkinson's Law: work expands to fill the time available for its completion.

How to tell how well you are doing. Teachers often fear evaluation, sometimes with good reason, because the results may be influenced more by the prejudices of the evaluator than by the quality of the teaching. No one, however, need fear his own evaluation of his own work if he begins it quietly, in a small way, for his own information, and without the publicity which might encourage unfriendly critics to demand the results.

There are several different ways in which a teacher may seek to learn whether or not his work is producing the results that he hopes it is. The beginner may start with the simplest and easiest methods and progress to the more complex as his own interest and competence grow. Every professional worker owes it to himself and to those he serves to try at regular intervals to learn as much as he can about how well he is doing.

Described below are some of the ways in which teachers try to evaluate their results. Some of these methods are used also to evaluate the results of individual counseling and of other activities in guidance, in education, and in other kinds of work with people.

Teacher opinion. Perhaps the most elementary method of evaluation is for the teacher frequently to ask himself, "How am I doing? Do I seem to be getting the results I expected?" Every good teacher does this almost automatically. Every good teacher should do it. And every good teacher should recognize that this kind of evaluation can be far from accurate. The research worker calls this kind of evaluation highly "subjective," because the results depend so much upon the judgment of the person who makes the evaluation.

Student appraisal. A slightly higher level of evaluation is reached when the teacher asks the students to express their opinions of the program. The expression may be oral or written, formal or informal, anonymous or not. This method also is subjective, because it depends so much upon the judgment of the persons who evaluate the program. It is perhaps less fallible than the teacher's judgment, because the number of judges is increased and the personal welfare of the judges is less affected by the outcome. The teacher who asks his students for really candid comments on anonymous reports will sometimes get surprisingly frank appraisals of his work. One second-grade child said, "I hate arithmetic and you can't teach it." One ninth-grade student, when asked why he took a course, replied, "So you wonder too!"

Measurement. Another type of evaluation may be employed when the objectives of instruction can be measured. For example, if one objective is to reduce failures or dropouts, the number of failures or dropouts can be counted. If one objective is to increase the average earnings of the participants, the average earnings can be computed. Similarly amenable to quantitative treatment are such criteria as lapse of time between school leaving and employment, percentage of time employed, scores on tests, and rating scales.

Pretest and retest. There are various ways of using measurements in evaluating any course. One may be called "pretest and retest." For example, a test of information about occupations may be prepared and given to the participants before and after the course. If there is a marked increase in scores on the test, one may conclude that the course produced the increase. This kind of evaluation is called "objective" because the results depend very little upon the judgment of the person making the evaluation. Two different evaluators could give the same tests to the same groups at the same time, and they would presumably get the same results. But even this kind of evaluation may produce erroneous conclusions. For example, any person's knowledge about occupations is continually increased by his everyday conversations, reading, and observations. The pretest-retest technique provides no way of determining whether the measured increase was caused by the course in occupations or would have occurred from other causes if there had been no course.

Control group. Another way of using quantitative data is often called the "control-group experiment." This requires the use of two groups of people, groups which are as nearly identical as the evaluator can make them. One group is called the "experimental" group; the other group is called the "control" group.

A test of occupational information is given to both groups at the beginning of the experiment. Then the experimental group is exposed to the course in occupations while the control group is not. At the end of the experiment both groups are measured again; if the experimental group has shown a greater gain than the control group, we may conclude that the difference was caused by the course. We may still be wrong if the two groups were not truly equated in the beginning or if the experimental group had superior opportunities to learn about occupations aside from the course. But there is less danger of error in the carefully controlled experiment of this kind than in the kinds of evaluation previously described.

In the same way, experimental and control groups may be compared on average earnings one year after graduation, on percentage of time unemployed, on self-estimates of job satisfaction, etc.

Criteria. The basis on which we finally compare experimental and control groups, in order to determine the success or failure of an experiment, is called the "criterion." No evaluation experiment is better than the criterion or criteria employed.

Intermediate criteria. One of the weaknesses in several evaluations of counseling and guidance has been the use of an intermediate rather than an ultimate criterion. For example, one of the ultimate aims of counseling is to help people find their way into jobs in which they will be reasonably successful and reasonably satisfied. We think that they will be more likely to reach this objective if they are well informed about occupational opportunities and requirements. Hence we teach facts about jobs, and the acquisition of such facts becomes an intermediate objective on the way to the ultimate objectives. Because the acquisition of facts can be measured more readily than subsequent success and satisfaction, some investigators have used this intermediate criterion to evaluate courses in occupations. The use of this intermediate criterion makes the entire evaluation dependent upon the truth or falsity of the original assumption that people who acquire a knowledge of occupations will subsequently achieve more vocational success and job satisfaction than those who do not acquire such information. If this assumption is true, the evaluation may be a good one. If the assumption is false, the evaluation may be misleading.

Intermediate criteria employed in other evaluations include ratings of students' vocational plans as good or poor in relation to what the counselor knows about the students' ability or about employment opportunities.

The use of intermediate criteria does not necessarily invalidate an evaluation, but it does make the experiment dependent upon the truth or falsity of the assumed relationship between the intermediate criterion and the ultimate objective.

Among the few researches using ultimate rather than intermediate criteria are those of Cole [93], Cuony [111, 113], Kutner [283], Long [307], Rosengarten [402], Toporowski [480], Weitz [507], Youngberg [532], and Ziegler [334, 537].

Equating experimental and control groups. If valid conclusions are to be drawn from control-group experiments, the two groups should be similar in all respects at the time the experiment begins. They should remain similar throughout the experiment, in all respects, except that one group is exposed to a course in occupations while the other group is excluded from it.

For example, in Cuony's research the persons who had had the course in job finding and job orientation were found to be better satisfied with their jobs than the persons who had not had the course. If most of the persons in Cuony's experimental group before the experiment were cheerful, happy-go-lucky, and easily satisfied with life in general and if most of the persons in his control group before the experiment were morose, anxious, and hard to please, then we might expect the persons in the experimental group to be better satisfied with their jobs even if they had not had the course. Under these circumstances we could not tell whether the course did or did not contribute to their job satisfaction.

In order to have a valid experiment, Cuony had to be reasonably sure that his groups were equated on all the things that might affect their job satisfaction. Since he also wanted to measure the effect of his course on earnings, he had to be reasonably sure that his groups were equated on all the things that might affect their earnings. Job satisfaction and earnings might be affected substantially by mental health and motivation and work habits and personality; these are extremely difficult to measure.

The best way that we know to equate groups on characteristics that we cannot measure is to choose both groups from the same population by means of sampling. This may be done by taking names at regular intervals from an alphabetic list, or it may be done by using a table of random numbers.

For most experiments in counseling and guidance, it is better to use alphabetic or random sampling than to equate the groups on such things as age, intelligence, achievement, and other characteristics which can be measured. To equate groups adequately on specific variables we must assume that we know all the variables which might affect our criteria and that we can equate on all of them. Since we can seldom make this assumption, we can seldom feel confident that our groups are properly equated. The inherent weaknesses in this kind of equating have been well stated by Travers [482].

We do know, however, that if we use large enough samples, we can equate on practically anything by means of random sampling. We can also pretest our equating procedures to see if they do produce equated groups. Cuony's and Lowenstein's experiences in pretesting suggest that random groups may not have to be prohibitively large in order to serve our purposes.

Pretesting equated groups. A method of pretesting equated groups in order to see if they are free of contaminating differences has been described by Hoppock and Cuony [234] and applied in the researches of Cuony [111] and Lowenstein [312].

How statisticians can help. The careful research worker wants to be as sure as possible that the results of his experiment mean what he thinks they mean. The careless investigator can deceive himself as well as others. Statisticians have devised ways of helping the research worker to determine whether the results of his experiment might have been caused by certain errors of chance.

The counselor or the teacher of occupations who wants to do precise research will take a good course in educational statistics as soon as possible. The counselor or teacher who does not expect to do statistical research himself should nevertheless study statistics so that he can understand the reports of research which appear in his professional literature and can judge their importance to him. The reader who has not yet had a course in statistics may find some help in the following brief explanation of some statistical terms and concepts frequently used in evaluation studies.

Errors of sampling. Experimental and control groups are frequently samples of a larger group. Because human beings differ from one another in many ways, no sample composed of human beings is ever a perfect sample of the total group from which it was drawn. The careful research worker tries to select his experimental and control groups so that they will both be representative of the larger group from which they were drawn and therefore also similar in all characteristics which might affect the outcome of the experiment. However, he knows in advance that there will always be small differences between any two samples before he even begins his experiment.

Conceivably a difference observed between the experimental and control groups at the end of an experiment could have been caused by these original differences between the groups rather than by the experiment itself. We would then say that this observed difference was due to errors of sampling.

The research worker who finds a difference between his groups at the end of an experiment naturally wants to know whether the difference is so small that it might have been caused by these errors of sampling or so large that it can only be reasonably explained by concluding that his experiment caused it. There is no known way of computing the probability that a difference observed at the end of an experiment was caused by the experiment. There is a way of computing the probability that errors of sampling might produce a difference as large as that observed by the research worker at the end of his experiment. How this probability is computed is too involved to explain here, except as follows:

The first result of the computation is a figure which is called "the standard error of the difference." The research worker divides the observed difference by the standard error of the difference. The result of this division is another figure, with which the research worker then refers to a statistical table. From this table he learns what is the probability that errors of sampling alone might produce a difference as large as the difference that he has observed.

If there is only 1 chance in 100 that errors of sampling might produce such a difference, the research worker has more confidence in his results than he would have if there were 10 chances in 100 or 50 chances in 100.

In current research literature these probabilities are often reported in such phrases as "significant at the 1 percent level" or "significant at the 5 percent level." What these phrases mean is that there is only 1 chance in 100 or only 5 chances in 100 that errors of sampling might produce a difference of the size reported.

Some research workers report their results in other terms. Instead of saying there is 1 chance in 100 that sampling errors might produce a difference as large as the difference observed, they say there are 99 chances in 100 that the observed difference is a "true difference." Instead of saying there are 5 chances in 100 that errors of sampling might produce a difference as large as the observed difference, they say there are 95 chances in 100 that the observed difference is a true difference, etc. Some statisticians object to this practice.

Significant differences. Other research workers apply the term "significant difference" to any difference that is three or more times as large as its standard error. When a difference is three times as large as its standard error, there are only 13 chances in 10,000, or 0.13 chance in 100, that errors of sampling might produce a difference as large as the difference observed.

Differences which are only slightly less than three times as large as their standard errors are not called significant differences, but they should never be called insignificant. There is very little practical difference between 13 chances in 10,000 and 14 chances in 10,000. It would hardly make sense to call one of these differences significant and to call the other insignificant because "insignificant" is a word which means "trivial, immaterial, meaningless." In order to avoid confusion over what is significant and what is not significant, many research workers and statisticians now prefer the terms "significant at the 1 percent level" or "at the 5 percent level," etc.

The statistical significance of observed differences may be computed not only for differences between experimental and control groups but also for differences between test scores obtained by the same group before and after a course and for many other differences.

Abbreviations. To save space in research reports the capital letter D is often used to designate an observed difference and the small Greek letter σ is used to indicate the standard error of the difference. D / σ or $D \div \sigma$ indicates the ratio between the difference and its standard error. This ratio is often called the "critical ratio." If $D \div \sigma$ equals 3 or more, the difference is "statistically significant." In order to distinguish the standard error of the difference from other standard deviations which are also designated by σ, some statisticians prefer to add a subscript such as σ_{diff} or σ_D.

Errors of interpretation. Some research workers make mistakes in interpreting the results of their own research. One reason a good counselor learns statistics is to avoid being misled by such mistakes. For example:

Some research workers report as insignificant any difference which is not significant at the 5 percent level. They may say correctly that no significant differences were found, but they go on to imply that the observed differences are trivial and unimportant. They may even go so far as to conclude that an experiment was a complete failure because there are 6 chances in 100 that errors of sampling might produce a difference as large as the difference observed.

Some research workers err in the opposite direction. Having concluded that their experiment made one group superior to another and that the difference between the groups is statistically significant, they assume that everyone should be greatly impressed and should immediately begin to reform education along the lines they suggest. They are bewildered and hurt to discover that weather-beaten superintendents of schools are still skeptical and even other research workers are annoyingly calm about the whole thing. The explanation is simple.

If an experiment involves enough persons, a difference as small as one or two points in average test scores can be statistically significant. It can indicate a genuine superiority, which almost certainly was not caused by errors of sampling, but most administrators would correctly regard such a small difference as educationally unimportant, however genuine it might be. In terms of the labor involved in any educational activity such a small result would not be worth the effort. A difference of this kind might be called statistically significant but educationally insignificant.

The beginner should never forget that a single experiment proves only that in one situation certain results followed certain events. If we conclude from one experiment that a repeat experiment in the same or a similar situation would produce similar results, we may be right, or we may be wrong. The conditions surrounding two experiments are never identical. If the repeat experiment is conducted in a different location, under a different teacher, by means of different teaching methods, or in different grades, the results may be entirely different. The fact that Stone obtained a statistically significant result at the

University of Minnesota does not prove that Hoppock will be able to obtain a similar result at New York University nor that Borow will obtain a similar result at the University of Minnesota nor even that Stone will obtain a similar result at Minnesota if Stone repeats his experiment. In any repeat experiment, similar results may or may not be obtained. We never know until we try. Stone's success gives us hope; it does not give us proof that we will be equally successful. This is why every teacher and every counselor should in some way continually evaluate the results of his own work.

Where do we go from here? In common with other aspects of guidance and in common with nearly all aspects of education, what the teaching of occupations needs most is more and more evaluation of results. We have had enough research now to know that certain desirable results can be produced and measured if the conditions are right. We do not yet know what the right conditions are. In time we may find the right conditions if enough teachers will do whatever they can to evaluate their work.

We need an almost infinite variety of studies to evaluate the teaching of occupations to different groups, for different purposes, at different age and grade levels. We need evaluations of courses taught by teachers with different kinds and degrees of preparation who use different methods under different conditions. Bit by bit we shall learn what we need to know until someday we can say with some assurance what are the essential conditions for the effective teaching of occupations. Meanwhile, we must find out empirically whether or not the courses in occupations that we have introduced are producing the results that we anticipate.

This book was written for beginners. Therefore, what can the beginner do about evaluation? Here are a few suggestions:

> Formulate a concise, written statement of your objectives. Whenever possible, state these objectives in terms which will permit you to find out whether or not the objectives have been achieved, for example, to increase the students' knowledge, to reduce the percentage of students who transfer from one curriculum to another, to reduce the percentage of students who fail in school or who drop out of school, to reduce the amount of time that graduates are involuntarily unemployed or the number of jobs from which they are discharged or the rate of job turnover among them, to increase average earnings during any period you wish to investigate, to increase job satisfaction.
>
> Let your students help you. At the end of each course ask them what they liked about it and how they think it could be improved.

Compare every class with itself before and after your course. If you are teaching facts, prepare an examination before you begin to teach. Give this examination at the beginning of the course; repeat it at the end.

Seize every opportunity to set up controlled experiments. Try one technique with one class, a different technique with another, and compare results. Make the two classes as much alike as possible in every respect except the one that you wish to investigate. Use ultimate rather than intermediate criteria.

Read one or more good books on how to do research, such as Borg [32].

Include in your professional preparation a course in educational statistics and a course in how to do research. Before you enroll for either course, ask the instructor if it will help you to evaluate your own work.

Why do research? If you follow these suggestions, you will do more work than the average teacher. Why bother? You will not be paid extra for it. You will not be given a lighter teaching schedule. You may even have to finance the research yourself. But if you are a real teacher, you would not be in this business unless you had a little missionary zeal, a genuine desire to help the people you serve and to leave your small corner of the world a little better because you were here. If you are modest, you do not talk much about this. In some circles you may even hesitate to admit it. But at times you know that your greatest satisfaction comes from this kind of service.

You will, then, undertake research because it will help you to improve your own work and thereby to be of more service to those you are trying to help. You will undertake research because it will stop you if you are wasting your time on laborious procedures that do not produce results. You will undertake research because it will contribute to improving the techniques by which other teachers will help future students long after your work is done. Incidentally, your investment of time and money in research need not be wholly unselfish. If you have what it takes to become a leader in your profession, one of the quickest ways to establish your leadership is to do good research on significant problems and to publish your results in the better professional journals. You might try it once, just for fun. You might find a thrill in discovering something that no one in the world ever knew before.

REVIEW QUESTIONS

1. Of the various research results reported in this chapter, which did you find of most interest? Why?

2. How have courses in occupations affected job satisfaction, earning power, and success in college?

3. How have courses in occupations affected the demand for individual counseling?

4. Were more high school principals satisfied with courses in occupations or with units on occupations in other courses?

5. Was Cuony's course a good financial investment for his community? What was the yield on the investment?

6. What did Hoyt find about the relative effectiveness of group and individual counseling?

7. What did Cole find about the relationship between guidance and delinquency?

8. What did Nick learn about the effectiveness of occupational information in making occupational choices more realistic?

9. Of the methods of evaluation described in this chapter, which could *you* use now to evaluate your work? Which would you like to use in the future? Why? How?

10. What is the difference between intermediate and ultimate criteria? Which is better? Why?

11. For experiments in guidance, why is sampling preferable to other methods of equating experimental and control groups?

12. What is the difference between "not significant" and "insignificant"?

13. What are some of the errors of interpretation made by research workers?

14. Why should *you* do research?

appendix **A**

Principal
Publishers
of
Occupational
Pamphlets

The following are the principal publishers of pamphlets containing information about different occupations, prepared specifically for purposes of vocational guidance. In general, the quality of their publications is at least as high as the average of occupational literature. This does not mean that all their publications are free from error or that each is the best publication on the occupation that it describes or that the pamphlets of any publisher are of uniform quality.

The reader is urgently advised not to order complete sets of any of these publications without first getting the copyright dates on all the publications in the set. Most publishers do not include copyright dates in their advertising. The prospective purchaser will have to request the information and insist upon getting it. The addresses given were correct at date of publication. Anyone using the list should check.

Bellman Publishing Co., P.O. Box 172, Cambridge, Mass. 02138
B'nai B'rith Vocational Service, 1640 Rhode Island Ave., N.W., Washington.
Careers, Largo, Fla.
Chronicle Guidance Publications, Inc., Moravia, N.Y.
Guidance Centre, University of Toronto, Toronto, Canada.
Henry Z. Walck, Inc., 19 Union Square West, New York.
Institute for Research, 537 S. Dearborn St., Chicago.
Occupational Outlook Service, U.S. Bureau of Labor Statistics, Washington.
Personnel Services, Inc., Jaffrey, N.H.
Richards Rosen Press, 29 E. 21 St., New York.
Science Research Associates, Inc., 259 E. Erie St., Chicago.
U.S. Women's Bureau, Washington.
Vocational Guidance Manuals, Inc., 800 Second Ave., New York.

The list above includes only those publishers who produce pamphlets in series, with each new title covering a different occupation. On request, most of these publishers will add the counselor's name to their mailing lists to receive announcements of new publications as they appear. A longer list of pamphlet publishers, including many professional associations that cover only their own occupations, may be found in Forrester [163].

appendix **B**

Suggestions for Discussion Leaders

Teachers who are just learning to lead student discussions may find the following suggestions helpful:

Select, for discussion, topics that you think are of vital interest to students, topics on which you think they are likely to disagree with one another and with adults.

Formulate provocative questions about these topics, questions that you think will draw an immediate response from someone in the class.

Whenever possible, prepare in advance twice as many topics and questions as you expect to need. Then if one fails to provoke discussion, drop it and go on to the next.

If the group seems unresponsive, give them a question, ask them to think about it for sixty seconds, then call on someone to express his opinion. Then call on another and another. When you find difference of opinion, ask the first speaker to respond to the challenge. Or divide the class into small groups of four, five, or six students. Ask them to discuss the question four, five, or six minutes among themselves. Then ask each group to select one person to summarize its discussion for the class. After all reports have been heard, invite further comment. During the reports and the comments, look for supplementary questions that can be used for further discussion in the small groups.

When the members of the group start to talk, encourage them. Never express disapproval if you can avoid it; it will discourage the student from participating voluntarily again. If you feel that a contrasting point of view needs to be presented, ask, "Does anyone disagree?" or "What do you think of this idea? Some people think . . ."

When several persons raise their hands at once or when you are calling on individuals to report, start with a person in one corner of the room. When he finishes, select someone in the opposite corner, then someone in the middle, etc. If students in one part of the room seem to be monopolizing the discussion, students in other parts will feel left out.

If the group is really talkative, aggressive, and not easily discouraged, you may find it desirable sometimes to take the unpopular side of a debatable issue, be the devil's advocate, and invite the group to attack your position.

Welcome every bit of humor. A hearty laugh will wake up drowsy students and add zest to the whole discussion.

Occasionally summarize the discussion so far. Note points of agreement and disagreement. Thus help the group to see that they are making progress, if only in learning where they disagree.

Sometimes you can encourage further comment by summarizing what one student has just said, e.g., "You feel that . . . ," "It seems to you that . . . ," "You wonder if. . . ." For more on this technique see Cantor [57].

When the discussion veers off the topic, let it go for a few minutes. Wait to see if one of the students will bring it back. If no one does and the diversion is not profitable, bring the group back to the topic, e.g., "I think we're getting a little off the subject. What do you think about . . . ?"

If you have to express disapproval, include yourself in the group disapproved, e.g., "*We* have talked long enough on that question. *We* are getting off the topic. *We* are forgetting our respect for individual differences." Do not do this when it does not seem natural; your students will soon recognize insincerity. But make yourself one of the group in every sincere and dignified way that you can.

If you have to restrain a student who talks too much, try to do so in ways that will not discourage others from participating. Conceal your annoyance. When you invite comments from volunteers, ask them to raise their hands; then call on the volunteers who have participated least. When the loquacious one gets the floor, watch for an opportunity to interrupt him by agreeing or disagreeing with something he has said; then, while you have the floor, invite someone else to comment on the same topic or introduce a new topic. If necessary, speak to the offender privately. Tell him you appreciate his help in keeping discussion active, that recently he has contributed so much that some of the other students have not had time to make their contributions. Would he please try to limit himself to about the same amount of time that others use or raise his hand and let you decide whether or not it is his turn. If nothing else works, you may have to interrupt him in class and say,

"Forgive me for interrupting you; I think it is time we heard from some of the others." You may not always feel like being so considerate of his feelings, but if you are less so, you will discourage some of the timid students from participating in the discussion. You can get maximum participation only when the most timid person feels safe to say what he thinks without fear of being either reprimanded or ridiculed.

Do not expect inexperienced, untrained students to make good discussion leaders. Let them try occasionally, if you wish, for their sakes. But do not expect them to do your job for you.

Above all, maintain a friendly, permissive atmosphere. A good, lively discussion should be an enjoyable experience for everyone. Enjoy it yourself. Help your students to enjoy it.

appendix C
Forms Used
in
Follow-up
of
Alumni

Department of Guidance and Personnel Administration
School of Education, New York University

Two forms are reproduced on the following pages. In both of them the letter appeared on page one of a four-page folder, and the remaining material was on pages two, three, and four. For related discussion see Chapter 13.

NEW YORK UNIVERSITY
SCHOOL OF EDUCATION
WASHINGTON SQUARE, NEW YORK, N.Y.

To Former Students in Guidance
and Personnel Administration
at New York University:

The members of our class in Occupations are undertaking a follow-up study of recent alumni of our department. Would you, as a former N.Y.U. student, help us to get a picture of what happens to our graduates?

Would you be kind enough to answer the questions in this form and return it to me? If any of your answers are confidential, please tell me how far I may go in reporting them. Replies which are not confidential will be shown to students and possibly filed in the library.

I am sure you know how grateful we will be for any information you may send us.

Sincerely yours,

Please return to:

68 M South Building
New York University
New York, New York

1. Your name _____

2. Your title _____

3. Employer _____

4. Address _____

5. Highest N.Y.U. degree held _____ 6. When conferred _____

All things considered which of these statements comes nearest to expressing the way you feel about your job?

7. _____ I like it.

8. _____ I am indifferent to it.

9. _____ I dislike it.

10. What do you do in your job?

11. What do you like best about your job?

12. What do you dislike most about your job?

13. Were you in your present job before you began to study at N.Y.U.?

_____

How did you get your job? Please check all correct answers.

14. _____ By examination

15. _____ By promotion within the same organization

16. _____ Through an employment agency, teachers' agency, bureau of appointments, etc.

17. _____ Through the recommendation of a relative

18. _____ Through the recommendation of a friend or acquaintance

19. _____ By personal application, preceding any recommendation

20. _____ In some other way. Please describe _____

_____

21. What were your earnings (salary before deductions) from your job during the last twelve months? (In a residence job, please add to your earnings the estimated value of board, room, etc.)

21. _____

Do you feel that your training at N.Y.U. was a good investment?

22. _____ Yes, unqualified

23. _____ Yes, with reservations

24. _____ No

25. Would you be willing to talk with N.Y.U. students who hope to work in your occupation, your city or your organization?

25. _____

NEW YORK UNIVERSITY
School of Education
WASHINGTON SQUARE, NEW YORK, N.Y. 10003
AREA 212 777-2000

To Former Students in Guidance
and Personnel Administration
at New York University:

Carlene Feldstein and I are undertaking a follow-up study of recent doctoral alumni of our department. Would you help us to get a picture of what happens to our graduates?

Would you be kind enough to answer the questions in this form and return it to me? If any of your answers are confidential, please tell us how far we may go in reporting them. Replies which are not confidential will be shown to students and possibly filed in the library.

I am sure you know how grateful we will be for any information you may send us.

Sincerely yours,

Robert Hoppock
Professor of Education

Please return to:

Robert Hoppock
778 CF Education Building
New York University
New York 10003

1. Your name _____

2. Your title _____

3. Employer _____

4. Address _____

5. Highest N.Y.U. degree held _____ 6. When conferred _____

All things considered which of these statements comes nearest to expressing the way you feel about your job?

7. _____ I like it.

8. _____ I am indifferent to it.

9. _____ I dislike it.

10. What do you do in your job?

11. What do you like best about your job?

12. What do you like least about your job?

How do you feel now about the graduate education you received at New York University? How would you change it? What would you keep?

appendix **D**
Discussion
of
Returns
from
Follow-up[1]

On one occasion, the author was teaching a graduate course in group guidance to a class of approximately seventy-five teachers and counselors in training at New York University. The technique of the follow-up study had been discussed. By way of demonstration the instructor had asked the class to imagine that they were twelfth-grade high school students in a class in occupations. Together in class the students and the instructor developed a list of questions for a hypothetical follow-up study. Each student was then asked to interview one recent high school graduate or dropout, get the answers to the questions, and bring a written report of the answers to class for a demonstration discussion.

The following week the instructor again asked the class to imagine that they were twelfth-grade students while the instructor demonstrated how he would conduct a class discussion of the answers brought to class. At the end of this demonstration the advantages and disadvantages of the follow-up technique were under discussion when a ninth-grade teacher of occupations said, "This all looks very nice when you demonstrate it here with us. But we're not high school students. I'd like to see you do this with my students."

The instructor asked the class, "How many of you would like to see a demonstration with actual high school students?" The response was unanimous. "How many of you could bring one or more high school students with you next week?" Several hands were raised.

The following week approximately thirty high school students were present. According to the teachers who brought them, they ranged in IQ from about 70 to 130, in age from eleven to seventeen, in grade level

[1] For related discussion see Chap. 13.

from the seventh to the twelfth. Approximately half were boys and half, girls. Approximately half expected to go to college and half did not. The demonstration class was seated in the front of a large class room. The New York University graduate class was seated in the back of the room. Three graduate students who were majors in business education took shorthand notes on the discussion. The following transcript has been produced from their notes:

Instructor: First of all, I want to thank all of you people for coming in this morning. We have about thirty of you; that's a pretty good class. You are making it possible for us to do something that all these people in the back appreciate very much.

Let me tell you what we are trying to do. You, perhaps, have heard the remark, "Those who can, do; those who can't, teach; those who can't teach, teach others to teach." Well, my job is to teach others to teach. I have been trying to teach those teachers back there how they can give you some help in planning your immediate future. Some of you are in ninth grade. For you, the immediate future is planning your high school program. Some of you are seniors. For you, the immediate future is either the choice of a college, the choice of a job, or the choice of the place where you are going to look for a job.

Now the technique which we have been teaching these teachers is a technique of getting information from students who have gone where some of you are going to go—getting information from some who are in college, some who are at work, and bringing that information back into the classroom so that you people can have a chance to see what has happened to some of the people who may have gone where you are going. We have, up to this point, gone out and interviewed some people who were in various jobs. Several people here have, I hope, papers on which they have the answers to some questions that they have asked recent high school graduates and dropouts.

(Will you people in the back, who have answers with you, pass your papers up front? Mr. Lifton, will you collect them please?)

While Mr. Lifton is getting the papers for us, let's find out what kind of group we have. How many of you are in the twelfth grade? Eleventh? Tenth? Ninth? Eighth? Seventh? Below the seventh? We have you all the way from the seventh grade to the twelfth. We have about an even number of boys and girls. How many of you at the present time would say you will probably go to college when you finish high school? Go to work? Well, you are about evenly divided on that too.

Now we have the papers. I'll give one to each of you. Read them as you get them, please, so you will have some idea what's on them. (Pause) Now, if you have read enough of your paper to have some idea what's on it, let me tell you what we are going to do.

We want to see if you can learn anything from these papers that will be of help to you with your plans for the future. I am going to ask you to read from these papers. From time to time I will stop you, and we will discuss various points which arise. Will all of you please pay strict attention to these papers as they are read and keep asking yourselves this question: "Is there anything there I would like to know more about?" If so, raise your hand, and we will see if anybody knows the answer. Or maybe there is a question in your mind to which you don't think we have the answer, but you would like to know what we think about it. Let us know and we will tell you what we think about it. If the paper suggests something to you that you know and that you think the rest of us would like to know, raise your hand. What we are trying to do is to help each other make plans. Don't be afraid of these people in the back. They are not going to give you any grades on this morning's lesson.

Does any one of you have a paper on which you found something particularly interesting? Somebody like to read one to us? (*A student raises his hand.*) Good! If any of you can't hear, just let us know.

Student: (*reading*) What is your job? Just what do you do?

I am an automobile mechanic. I grease cars, repair carburetors, generators, starters, ignition systems, and the braking system.

How did you get your job?

My uncle owns a large auto repair shop, and, ever since I can remember, I have spent most of my spare time in his shop learning the business. When I graduated, he gave me the job.

Instructor: There are two things you can learn from that. One is that a great many people get their jobs through relatives and friends. We have had several studies made of how high school graduates get their jobs, and usually from one-half to three-quarters of them get jobs either by direct personal application or through relatives and friends. Now that doesn't mean that you must have a rich uncle to get a job, but it does mean that your friends and relatives are often in a position to tell you about a vacancy. The most important thing of all when you are looking for a job is to get there before anybody else gets there. Obviously, a businessman is not going to hire you unless you are the kind of person he wants, but if you are and somebody else is and you get there first, you probably will be the one who gets the job. Friends and relatives can help you to get there first, especially when vacancies occur in the places where they work. So the first thing to do when you are looking for a job is to tell all of your relatives and friends what kind of job you are looking for.

Will you please read again that question and answer, "How did you get your job?"

Student: (*reads it again*).

Instructor: Now, here is a boy who has been working for a good while in an auto repair shop. Suppose his uncle could not have hired him, would he have been able to get a job in some other repair shop? How many think so? How many think not? That suggests an idea. It's a good thing to work on a job after school or on Saturday even if you have to work for nothing. There are two reasons for this. First, you have a chance to find out whether or not you can do the work and how well you like it. Second, if you decide later to look for a job in the same occupation, you can offer the employer some experience.

Student: (*resumes reading*) What are your usual weekly earnings?

Instructor: What would you guess that this boy is earning?

Student: Between $40 and $60.

Instructor: Who would have a different guess? Well, there is a good deal of spread between $40 and $60. How many guess it would be nearer $40? $60? About half each way.

Student: (*resumes reading*) Well, that depends on how long I wish to work, but I would say a good average is between $50 and $60 a week.

How many days and hours do you put in at that salary?

Five days a week, nine hours a day.

Instructor: Five days a week, nine hours a day. How many of you know somebody who works at some kind of job? How many hours a day does this person work?

Student: Six.

Student: Five.

Student: Eight.

Student: Eight.

Student: Seven.

Student: Six.

Student: Eight.

Student: Eight.

Instructor: This boy works nine hours a day. That's a little more than most people do.

Student: (*resumes reading*) What are the opportunities for advancement?

I may be able some day to work myself up to chief mechanic, or open a business of my own.

Instructor: There is an important thing. He is in a line of work which would make it possible for him to go into business for himself. If you think that some day you would like to go into business for yourself, it may be possible for you to pick some line of work where you would not need too much money to start a business.

Student: (*resumes reading*) Was a high school education adequate for this job?

Well, that is a hard one to answer. In my case I believe it was, for I gained most of my practical experience in my uncle's shop. However, if a fellow wanted to become a mechanic, I think he would be better off in a vocational high school.

Instructor: Let's take that last question. This boy says for him high school was all right because he had an opportunity to learn the business in his uncle's shop, but for others a vocational high school would be better. Ask yourself what course would be best for you to take if you wanted to be an automobile mechanic.

Student: General.

Student: General.

Student: General.

Instructor: How many of you are in the same school as those who have answered? Is there anybody in that school who thinks a different course would be advisable? (*No response*) In that school what courses have you that deal with auto mechanics? (*No response*) Now tell us why you would pick that course.

Student: In the commercial, you would have nothing to do with mechanics, nor would the college preparatory.

Instructor: Your point is that the general course does at least include some shopwork?

Student: In the college course in our school, they have a science class, but in the general course, they have more shop.

Instructor: Do the people in the general course have a chance to study the same science as in the college course?

Student: Yes.

Instructor: Would some of you from another school tell us what would be the course to take in your school?

Student: General.

Instructor: Any other courses?

Student: Scientific.

Student: College preparatory.

Student: Academic.

Student: College preparatory.

Student: Business education.

Instructor: Tell us why you think the general course would be best.

Student: In the general course, they have more about automobiles than in the college preparatory course.

Instructor: Any other reason?

Student: Shop, too.

Instructor: Anyone in that school who feels differently about it?

Student: Well, you can take shop with any course in our school.

Instructor: Do you think another course would be better?

Student: In the business education course, you could learn something about business too.

Instructor: What do the rest of you think about that? In the general course would you have more shop than in the commercial?

Student: Not in my school.

Student: In our school they have general mathematics in the general course.

Instructor: Is there something of that sort in your school?

Student: Yes.

Instructor: Do you know whether that includes the kind of bookkeeping you would need for a garage?

Student: No.

Instructor: There are two sides to this, probably. If you are going into this occupation, you are going to begin working as a mechanic, and then after some time you may want to open your own business. Would you need bookkeeping at the start or later?

Student: Later.

Instructor: Do you all agree?

On the basis of this situation, suppose a boy wants to go into a garage and is looking forward to opening his own garage later. Should he learn bookkeeping in high school, or should he wait until just before the time he is going to need it and learn it then? How many think in high school? How many later? Now, we have a good division of opinion. Somebody tell us why he holds his opinion.

Student: I think he should wait, because he might never get advancement in his job and never use what he had learned.

Student: I don't think he should take bookkeeping, because he should utilize all his time in learning the trade.

Student: I think he should take it, because bookkeeping always comes in handy.

Student: Don't you think a time will come when he is going to need bookkeeping?

Instructor: If he does not start the business at once, could he take the bookkeeping when he does?

Student: Yes.

Instructor: Where?

Student: At night school or college.

Instructor: There are two ways he could learn bookkeeping: now, in school, or five years later. Which is better?

Student: In school.

Instructor: Why?

Student: Well, if he learns it in school, five years later he would not have any trouble. He would have more time for himself later on.

Student: I think if he learned it in high school and had no chance to apply it for five years, he would not be proficient.

Student: I think he should take it while he has the chance.

Student: It could very well depend on whether he is going to be a success or just a plain mechanic. How is he going to know whether he will be a success or not?

Instructor: Have we any answer to that one?

Student: I think that if his heart is set on it, he will try and try until he does get it.

Instructor: Those last two or three remarks bring us into another problem that is tremendously important. It is the problem of how you can get some idea of whether or not you are likely to succeed in whatever you try to do. Before we discuss that, let's finish the other topic. Most of you have agreed that if a boy wants to be an automobile mechanic, he should take the general course. He should have shop and some science on the study of engines if he can get it. Do we all agree? How many think so?

There is some difference of opinion among you on this matter of bookkeeping. Let's see if we can get any general agreement. How many of you think that at some time he ought to study bookkeeping? You were divided as to where he should study the bookkeeping. How many of you think in high school? Afterward? We might talk about this a good bit longer, and maybe some of you would convince some of the others. Sometimes you can argue a long time and not get anywhere. I think it might be profitable to spend more time talking about that, but I will pass on because this is a demonstration rather than a class. If it were really a class, I think we would spend more time on it. Let me try to repeat what I think were the principal arguments you did bring out.

The reasons for studying while in school were he has the time; even if he has to study again later on, it will be easier; he is going to need it some time.

The reasons for studying it later were if he takes it now, he may have forgotten it before the time comes to use it; since he does not know whether he will be successful enough to open his own business, he should wait and see.

Have I summarized fairly accurately?

Student: In many schools, you cannot take both shop and bookkeeping.

Instructor: If you were in such a school, how many of you think you should take shop? All of you. Let's shut off the discussion on that.

Now we can get started on this other question. Someone said our mechanic should take bookkeeping because he is going to need it later, and then someone asked how he could tell that he would be successful enough to need it, and then you said if he really wants to be a success, he will keep on trying until he is. How many of you think that anybody who really wants to be a success can be? How many would not say so? Why?

Student: You may not have the natural ability, mechanical ability.

Instructor: What is mechanical ability?

Student: Some people just don't have the knack of putting things together and taking them apart.

Instructor: I am one of them.

Student: That was my point—good aptitudes.

Instructor: What is an aptitude?

Student: I think it is the ability to do different things naturally. It doesn't have to be taught.

Instructor: Let me see if I can put your idea in other words. How many of you have seen a basketball game this winter? How many of you have seen at least one basketball player you thought was pretty good? Pretty poor? Do you think the difference between the good and bad player was entirely a matter of how hard they tried, or was it something else?

Student: I know somebody who practices very hard, and still he is no good.

Instructor: Did any of you ever try and try to do something and still find you could not do it well? What was it?

Student: Paint a picture.

Student: Occupations and citizenship! I never get a good mark in it.

Instructor: Like me, I flunked history in college. Have any others had that experience? Let's see what the subjects were.

Student: Math.

Student: Algebra.

Student: Art.

Student: English.

Student: History.

Student: French.

Student: Science.

Instructor: You see what a variety of courses we have here in which people have tried hard and didn't get anywhere. What subjects have you found that come easily?

Student: Algebra.

Student: Electrical wiring.

Student: English.

Student: Mathematics.

Student: History.

Student: Science.

Student: Chemistry.

Student: Biology.

Instructor: Did you notice that some of the same subjects were mentioned as easy and as hard? People differ a great deal. Some of us, without any great effort, can learn algebra very easily. Some of us have to work and work, and we still can't do very much with it. Suppose there is an occupation in which a knowledge of algebra is very important—for example, insurance actuary. If algebra is easy for you, then that is one reason why you might be a success as an insurance actuary or like being an insurance actuary. Now, there may be other reasons why you would not be a success. On the other hand, knowing that being an insurance actuary requires all this knowledge of algebra, how many of you know now that you don't want to be that? Well, you have learned something this morning!

Engineering requires mathematics, and many boys discover they do not have what it takes to learn all that mathematics. They might be wonderful at other jobs, but they can't master the mathematics. How many of you would take the chance and try to become an engineer? O.K. How many would not? Well, you have learned something else this morning.

That is what we mean by aptitudes—the ability to do things better than the average person without putting out any great effort. A person who has an aptitude for something sometimes finds that it is so easy to do this thing that he doesn't think it is very important. It doesn't seem to him that there is any great credit to him in being able to do it, so he may prefer to do something else. You know—you always tell a beautiful girl she has brains and a smart one that she is beautiful.

Just the other night I had dinner with a man who had always wanted to be a college professor, but he never got to be one. Instead of that, he took a job as supervising principal in a little country town in New Jersey and has stayed in that job for twenty-nine years. He took a little country school there and built it up so that it offers practically any course you would want. He has done a really wonderful job but to him that doesn't seem important at all. He has an awfully good aptitude for running a school system, but he still wishes he were a professor of German.

Sometimes we make the mistake of going off and trying to do the thing that we can't do. I remember having a professor of economics in college who said that everybody in choosing an occupation chooses either the thing for which he is best fitted or the thing for which he is least fitted. A salesman, if he is a good salesman, is usually pretty successful at getting along with other people. If you are going out to buy something, you would rather buy it from somebody you like. Now, let's suppose that you don't get along well with other people, and then you see three or four different salesmen, and you notice that all of them have a lot of friends, so you think, "I will be a salesman. Then I will make friends." What would happen?

Student: You would be a failure.

Instructor: See how you might choose an occupation for which you are not at all fitted? Let's suppose you are very good at math and no good at getting along with people. You might be so concerned with your failure to get along with people that you might not think your ability at math was important, so you might rush off and spend the rest of your life doing the things you were not very good at. If you find yourself going off and doing the things you are not very good at, think it over and talk it over with your teacher or counselor. Does any of this discussion raise any questions in your mind?

Student: I think if you are not wanted and you go around with some people, you might find out why you are not wanted and correct the weakness.

Student: If people do not like you, you could not go around with people.

Instructor: How are we going to get out of that jam?

Student: Maybe somebody will tell you his frank opinion.

Instructor: Well, that happens sometimes. How many of you have had someone tell you something he didn't like about you? Suppose you are not very good at getting along with people, what could you do about it? Let's suppose I am no good at it. I can't get a girl to go to the dance with me.

Student: Ask a teacher.

Student: Ask them what is wrong.

Student: If you are not liked, ask yourself why not. For instance, in playing a game, you may not be a good sport.

Student: If nobody tells you off, you can compare yourself with other people.

Instructor: Do you think you might go wrong on that?

Student: The other person might be better or worse than you in certain fields, and you would mistake the reason for his superiority.

Instructor: I did that once. I noticed that a very popular boy often made insulting remarks, so I insulted people, and it didn't get me anywhere.

Student: Suppose you act tough in imitation of some popular boy, you might get your head handed to you.

Instructor: What else could you do?

Student: If you have a special thing in which you are interested, try to find someone else who is interested in the same thing.

Student: If you have—I have some oil paints—share it with others.

Instructor: Be reasonable about sharing.

Student: Don't always keep on wanting others to give you something, and never give things yourself.

Student: Mind your own business.

Instructor: That's tremendously important in getting along with people. (*The instructor here told an anecdote of his college days, illustrating this point.*) Let me give you one other suggestion. All of you try this as a kind of assignment for the next twenty-four hours. Try in every contact you have with somebody else to ask yourself how you would like to be treated if you were he, and then act that way. It's a very hard thing to do, but try it. You may be surprised at the results.

Student: Suppose a person likes to be treated some way that you don't like to be treated.

Instructor: Very important. So you ought to ask yourself how he would like to be treated rather than how you would like to be treated if you were he.

Student: Suppose he likes to be treated rough, and you are afraid of him?

Instructor: You'd better modify this assignment enough to keep your health.

Now, from this one paper that you read to us, we have talked for nearly an hour on several different subjects—courses for auto mechanics, aptitudes, human relations. We are a long ways from auto mechanics—maybe not, though.

Will someone read from another paper?

Student: (*reading*) What job do you have?

My first job was filing checks to help me become familiar with the signatures of the customers and the titles of accounts. I was then moved to the Transit Department. There the work sent up from all of the tellers is sorted, proved, photographed, and bundled to be sent to the bank to which it belongs or to our own bookkeepers to be posted. After learning this I was moved to the Statement–Safe Deposit and Adjustment Department. Here we prepare the sheets for the bookkeepers, give the statements to the customers at the end of the month, help them balance their checkbooks to prove it with the statement, and explain the method of determining service charges which we figure during the month. We also let the safe-deposit customers have access to their boxes, and print names on "Special Account" checkbooks.

Instructor: Before this was read, how many of you would have said that people who work in banks spend most of their time handling money? Doing paper work? In contact with other people? From this one person's description, how many would say that he spent most of his time putting things on paper? You can learn this: there are some jobs in banks which involve a great deal of paper and pencil or typewriter work.

Student: (*reading*) How did you get the job?

I was told of the opening, left an application in the personnel office and received the job. . . .

Student: (*reading*) How many days and hours do you work?

I work five days from 9 to 4 and one night from 6:30 to 8. I average thirty-five or forty hours a week.

Instructor: You remember the boy who worked in the garage? How many hours did he work?

Student: Forty-five.

Instructor: How many of you would very much prefer a job where you can keep clean? How many a dirty job? See the difference? That is why some people are happy in garages who would not be happy in banks and the other way round.

Well, our time is up. Thank you all very much for coming in to help us this morning. I appreciate it, and I know those people in the back of the room appreciate it, too.

appendix **E**

Demonstration
Group
Conference [1]

The following demonstration was presented at a meeting of the Mid-Hudson Branch of the National Vocational Guidance Association, held in the auditorium of Arlington High School just outside Poughkeepsie, New York. Seated on the left side of the stage was a class of approximately twenty high school senior boys and girls. Seated on the right side, behind a table, were three industrial employers. Seated between the two groups, slightly to the rear, behind a small table, was the author, who conducted the demonstration. Seated in the orchestra were counselors and teachers who came to watch the demonstration. The following transcript was prepared from shorthand notes taken by Laurence E. Prendergast. It is not a verbatim transcript, but it is correct in all parts essential to the demonstration. Since it has not been submitted to the participants for correction, it should not be used as a source of occupational information.

Hoppock: (*to audience*) What we are going to try to do this afternoon is to demonstrate for you one technique that can be used to do something that all counselors are trying to do—to provide for students accurate, up-to-date information about job opportunities. This is not the only means that can be used, but it is one means. We call it the group conference. It is, perhaps, most similar to the career conference technique with which several of you are familiar. It differs from the career conference in these respects.

The career conference usually involves about twenty different talks at the same hour. That means that students can get to only one or two such talks. Group conferences, such as we shall demonstrate today, are usually scheduled at intervals throughout the year so that a student can attend as many as he likes.

The usual career conference procedure is to have a speaker on each

[1] For related discussion see Chap. 15.

occupation and to have him talk from twenty to forty minutes. The technique that we are going to demonstrate this afternoon provides for no speeches. The whole conference is conducted by questions and answers. The reason for this is that the average personnel man is a good personnel man, but he is not a good teacher. He is not a brilliant speaker. A poor speaker will put an audience to sleep. If this group over here (*pointing to students*) doesn't go to sleep on me, none of you will go to sleep. I promise you that.

Another difficulty is that the speaker will talk about what he *thinks* the students are interested in. Maybe he guesses right, and the students are interested; maybe he guesses wrong, and the students are bored. Maybe he gets off the subject and talks only about what interests him. In the group conference that we shall demonstrate, if one of our guests starts off the subject, I will wait until he pauses for breath and then ask him another question.

Another disadvantage of the career conference is that the counselor, as well as the students, can hear only one or two of the speakers. One of the most important advantages of the group conference technique is that the counselor gets educated in the process, and counselors, I regret to say, need occupational information almost as much as students.

The students here had never seen me until five minutes ago. They have had no instructions. We people on the platform have had no preparation.

Now to you folks (*turning to students*), you are here this afternoon primarily to put on a good show. However, I hope that you will receive more benefit from this than just the satisfaction of having been gracious people who helped to put on a show. This is the sort of thing that might be done any day in any school to help the students get information about the kinds of jobs that will be open to them when they go out to work.

The only limitation on the questions you may ask is that the questions must have something to do with jobs. Ask as many questions as you like.

Now, to our panel, we are grateful to you for giving up an afternoon to help us. You have heard me tell the audience what we are not going to let you do. If they or I ask you any question that you don't want to answer, just tell us it's none of our business.

(*To audience*) I have a hunch that this class is a little scared, that they are going to need a little warming up. One way would be for me as instructor to start asking questions. However, under these circumstances, I think I might still be sitting here asking questions half an hour from now. If they were a class in school, we would know each other and we would be ready to go right to work. If they were a new class, we would have spent all of yesterday getting ready for today.

If you have to take a group that is cold and may go dead on you, there is a simple technique that you can sometimes use to warm them up. It is to break the group up into very small groups and let them talk to one another about the kinds of questions they want to ask. I hope it works!

(*Hoppock here divided the class into groups of five.*)

For the next two or three minutes, you will please talk with your own group about this question: "What questions do you think we ought to ask these people?" Here are three personnel managers from three different companies. What questions do you think we ought to ask them in order to get as much valuable information as we can about jobs?

(*Interval of five minutes during which students talked and Hoppock conversed with the three guests.*)

Now will you stop your discussion and pick one person out of each group to report for the group. Go ahead—back in your huddle to decide who's going to report for you.

Ready? Have you decided? O.K. Let's start with this group in the middle. Will the chairman of each group do this? Tell us what are some of the questions your group mentioned.

Student: What are the requirements you need to get in? What subjects do you prefer students to have taken? What is the pay? And the vacations? (*Laughter*)

Hoppock: That's all right. Don't let these people laugh at you. They are all school teachers, and they like long vacations, too.

Student: (*continuing*) Pensions and chance for advancement?

Hoppock: Now let's take the group back in the corner.

Student: I don't think we had anything different. If anyone went to a business school, would he have a preference over a high school graduate?

Hoppock: Now this group.

Student: Would a person with previous business experience have an advantage over one going directly from high school?

Hoppock: And this group.

Student: We had nothing different.

Hoppock: All those questions are good. That's the sort of thing we want to get at. Now, I am going to ask you to let me have the first few minutes. When we resume questions, don't leave it to the chairman of your group, but all of you pitch in. We want to put on a good show, and it will be a good show if we have a lot of questions.

Mr. Duel is personnel manager of International Business Machines, which is a large company with about twenty-four hundred employees. Mr. Peters is with Frederick Hart Manufacturing Company, which employs about four hundred people. Mr. Becker represents the Fargo Manufacturing Company, which has about eighty-five employees.

Will you tell us, Mr. Becker, when your company hires people who are just out of high school, do you hire them for several different kinds of jobs, and, if so, for which jobs do you hire the largest number.

Becker: The largest number that we hire are either for office work or, in the case of boys, for machine-shop work where they go on to learn to be machinists. For the starting office jobs that we have, we find that the commercial-course high school diploma is adequate.

Hoppock: Mr. Peters?

Peters: At present, it's more in the shop itself, both in the machine shop for machinery operations and some assembly operations. We hire a great many girls for assembly operations; we do not have women in the machine shop itself. We have started a number of girls in the office. We have started them in the shipping department, typing, filing, etc.

Hoppock: It's principally either clerical work or assembly work? And Mr. Duel?

Duel: We prefer a high school graduate for any job—of course, until you get up into some jobs that need more than high school training.

Hoppock: What is the largest single group of occupations in your plant?

Duel: Well, I believe clerical, if you consider it clerical. In our definition, it will run factory-clerical, which would include automatic-press operators, dispatchers, stock clerks, etc.; in the office, purchasing and office services.

Hoppock: Other than clerical, what would be the next largest category?

Duel: Assembly.

Hoppock: (*to class*) Now you have the picture. Here are three plants. All have clerical jobs, and all have machine-shop jobs. Let's take the clerical first. Who has a question?

Student: In my case, I have taken a straight college course and one year of typing. What chance do I stand of getting a job?

Duel: To answer that question, I would have to know a lot more. She would have a chance in a great many jobs that do not require a lot of typing.

Hoppock: The fact that she had only one year of typing would not disbar her? Mr. Peters?

Peters: That would be perfectly satisfactory. It is not necessary in some cases to be able to take dictation in shorthand. We expect that with practice in the plant, they will become very competent.

Hoppock: Mr. Becker?

Becker: In our setup, I am afraid she would be out of luck. In a small plant, there is less flexibility. She would have to know both shorthand and typewriting.

Hoppock: Would you think that that was generally true of small plants?

Becker: Yes.

Student: In my case, I have had two years of shorthand and typing. I am interested in receptionist work. What are my chances of getting it? I would prefer to work in the personnel department.

Hoppock: Assuming that the girl is otherwise satisfactory, would two years be sufficient training to get her a job as a receptionist in your personnel department?

Duel: For me, our personnel department is a promotion. We do not hire people directly for that department. They are people that come in the plant somewhere else and merit promotion.

Becker: Just the reverse. Our starting girls' jobs include taking dictation, typing, and certainly as a receptionist.

Peters: We follow somewhat the system of Mr. Duel, using the personnel department as a promotional opportunity. If a person starts off narrowing down the job so closely, in a city the size of Poughkeepsie the opportunities are limited.

Hoppock: In a small company, you are likely to have broader jobs. Mr. Peters made a very important point. It would be less true, but it would still be true in a city the size of New York. If you decide before you go out for a job that this is the one thing that you want and you are very specific about it, you will find that your opportunities will not be so numerous as they would be if you were less narrow in your aim. Next question?

Student: I take straight secretarial work and some bookkeeping. Would I have to start at the lowest-level office job, or would my training get me a better starting position?

Becker: In our particular case, she would start taking dictation immediately. We have recently acquired a young girl from this school, and the first thing she started off with was taking dictation. She is sort of a roving stenographer. This girl travels through several offices.

Hoppock: Does that mean you have a secretarial pool?

Becker: She is our pool. (Laughter) She does very well.

Peters: We would employ her as a stenographer. Naturally, when we get a person with secretarial experience, even if it is only study in school, we are not going to put her in the shop, because that is a wasteful way of operating.

Duel: She would probably start on straight typing. There might be some dictation. She would not start on secretarial work. In our production-engineering department, there are girls who do typing and are occasionally called on for dictation.

Hoppock: (*to student*) Does that answer your question?

Student: Yes. I have another one. Would I have to work with ten or fifteen or twenty others, or could I work by myself? Would I have to read back shorthand notes of other people?

Hoppock: When you say work by yourself, do you mean having a private office?

Student: No. I mean would I be responsible for carrying through a job, or would several girls be put on it and have to read back each other's notes?

Hoppock: In any of your places, would she have to read back someone else's notes?

(*All three said no.*)

Student: How would a young man start? Would there be any chance for him without office training?

Duel: Well, there are many different jobs for which he would be eligible—dispatcher, shipping department, receiving department, stores, etc. There are any number of different jobs.

Student: Could you advance from those jobs, or would you have to stay there the rest of your life?

Duel: That would depend entirely on you.

Becker: Our procedure would be first of all to acquaint the young man with our machine setup, hoping that he would be a machinist. Then he would be sent to the shipping department. From there, there is a likelihood of going into the front office. However, front-office jobs are usually jobs held by technicians.

Student: Would there be any opportunity for a person to get into mechanical drawing? I have had three years of mechanical drawing, four years of mathematics, and one year of shop.

Peters: Well, that's very difficult to say. It depends upon our requirements right at the moment. We have four students that exchange. They spend ten weeks in the Rochester Institute of Technology; they are in college ten weeks, and they spend ten weeks in the plant. They are taking up a regular engineering course, and they will eventually become diesel designers, product designers, etc. But the opportunity for a fellow to come cold out of high school and get into our extremely technical engineering department is very limited.

Hoppock: Any place for this boy at IBM, Mr. Duel?

Duel: We have hired in the past occasionally a boy with those qualifications, but I would say it was the exception rather than the rule.

Hoppock: Mr. Becker?

Becker: I would say that he was starting too early. I would certainly recommend a school like Rochester or one of our state schools. If a boy came to us with that background, we would be pretty well stopped right there.

Hoppock: With two more years of training, could he go further?

Becker: Yes. Four years would be more desirable.

Hoppock: The answer seems to be generally no. Do you men happen to know if there are other places around Poughkeepsie where this boy might get technical work?

Becker: I don't know of any plants where he could get such work.

(*The other two personnel men nodded agreement with his statement.*)

Hoppock: What it amounts to is that with a high school education he is going into a job where he will be competing with college graduates.

(*Peters and Becker nodded agreement.*)

Duel: There is another way around that. If this boy has the inclination and the other necessary requisites to go into our toolmaker's school, he could work his way up to a responsible position.

Student: A girl starts at a clerical position. If she does her work well, can she advance?

Becker: Even in a small plant, the answer is yes.

Peters: That depends entirely upon a review of the girl's progress which we make at short intervals to determine advancement.

Duel: The answer would be the same if I understand the question correctly. The young lady is talking about promotion. Does that promotion mean in responsibility or financially?

Student: In responsibility.

Duel: Promotions of that nature in our plant are earned. We hire nobody directly for better positions; we prefer to fill them from our own ranks.

Student: How would you go about applying for a job and getting a job?

Peters: Usually, they come in and ask if we have one, and, of course, it is impossible to say, "Yes, we do have one." So we have them fill out an application, and then we talk to each and every individual who comes in. We try to get from them information regarding their education, skills, hobbies, the things they want to do to earn their bread. We discover a lot of latent talent in some individuals. Never apply for a job by phone. That's terrible, and it happens every day, all day long. We do like young people to come in and talk to us, and we try to help them in every way we can.

Hoppock: Suppose a boy comes to your plant, would he ask to see you?

Peters: In our case, we are very fortunate. We are right on Main Street, and our entrance is very clearly marked.

Hoppock: What does it say over the entrance?

Peters: It says, "Personnel Department."

Hoppock: Mr. Becker?

Becker: Well, he comes to our main office and is met by our receptionist. If the applicant is applying for a job in the shop, then he talks with our plant manager. There our program is the same as Mr. Peters's. We talk the whole situation over with the applicant. If it is a question of a job in the office, then I am called in.

Duel: We are not as handy. We are not right on Main Street; we are four miles below the city. The procedure is pretty much the same. The applicant comes to our personnel department. The receptionist will ask if he is a new applicant. If so, he fills out an application. Everyone who comes down is interviewed. We try to work it so that if a person comes down twice, the second time he is assigned to a different interviewer. It is my suggestion that when you go into a place to apply for a job, have a plan in mind. Have a path that you want to follow for your life's work. Don't say, "I will take anything." That's most discouraging to us. Apparently, from the questions you have been asking here this afternoon, I don't think you are of that type.

Peters: I discovered something about that type. As far as young people are concerned, they come out with that "I will do anything" answer because they don't know what we have for them to do. If I find it in the case of a person who has fifteen or twenty years of shop experience, then I know he is a floater. But with young people, I think it is a matter of not knowing what jobs there are.

Hoppock: If a young person does not get a job as a result of his first application to you, is it a good idea for him to go back again?

Duel: Frankly, when a person comes into our plant and we haven't anything for him, we want to look him over a little. After the interviewer has talked with him, if he determines that he is good material for a certain kind of work, his application is coded for that work. When we get a requisition, we go to our file and pick out the applications that have been coded for that kind of work. We select eight or ten that look best.

Then the manager of the department selects the one he wants. Our personnel department does not hire. The manager of the department that needs the help makes the choice.

Hoppock: Should he just wait, or would he gain anything by going back to see you?

Duel: That would be according to what the interviewer coded him as. The interviewer may have in mind some opening he thinks is going to exist. He may tell the applicant, "Come in the latter part of next week." In that case, he should come in. Otherwise, he accomplishes nothing by coming back too soon.

Hoppock: Suppose a boy likes IBM, and he comes in June and you haven't anything, and the interviewer doesn't have any prospect for him. If he gets another job and he still wants to work for IBM, what are the chances of his getting a call from you?

Duel: His application remains in our active file for six months.

Becker: In our case, we like to have people keep coming back. It doesn't mean anything as far as we are concerned to say, "Nothing yet, come back next week." There are distinct advantages to working for a small company and to working for a large company. If a person keeps coming back, he sort of sells the idea to us that maybe he prefers a small company.

Peters: We follow something of the same procedure as IBM. At the end of six months, we destroy the application. We assume that they have a job somewhere else.

Hoppock: Next question?

Student: Would you rather have experienced help or someone just out of high school that you can teach yourselves?

Peters: It depends on what the opening is. For instance, we hire every month two or three young people who are completely inexperienced. We start them on quite a low level. The foreman watches their progress and sees how they handle equipment and machinery. If they show that they are adaptable to that kind of work, we will promote them to a small bench job. We find that is a very good way to start young people off.

Student: What are the age requirements? Would it be advisable to apply before getting out of school?

Hoppock: Suppose we take those separately. First, about age requirements?

Becker: Only as controlled by the law.

Hoppock: Which is what?

Becker: Sixteen with working papers; eighteen without.

Peters: Our minimum is eighteen.

Duel: Eighteen except in the apprentice school.

Hoppock: Should he apply now or after graduation?

Becker: The sooner, the better.

Peters: We would accept his application now.

Duel: We would accept it, but we wouldn't do anything until he got out of school.

Student: Could Mr. Duel explain what he means by the apprentice school?

Duel: We have a three-year toolmakers' apprentice school for high school graduates, who can pass the entrance examination, that starts them right out at the bottom to learn the toolmaker's trade. They go off into tool design, etc. They work in the job for a certain number of hours —I think it is four hours a week that they have in class, tool design, metallurgy, etc. After the boy gets through with school, he is not a graduate engineer, but for our money he has got an excellent basis to get ahead. We look to that school for a lot of our management.

Student: If you had completed that course, what value would it have in another factory?

Becker: It is a well-recognized course.

Student: Would there be any disadvantage in taking a part-time job while you are waiting to hear from a company?

Becker: I should say you should immediately accept whatever employment was offered, so long as it was respectable, and await an opportunity to get into the company of your choice. You will find all employment is related. Even the fact that you get up in the morning and go to a plant—you learn about safety—that's work experience, and it is all valuable.

Hoppock: Suppose he took the other job. If you heard that he had taken it, would you take his application out of your file?

Becker: No.

Hoppock: Would there be any advantage in the person's writing you a letter, telling you what he had done?

Becker: Well, it's nice to know that people think that way of our particular organization, and such correspondence would, of course, be attached immediately to the person's application.

Student: Do the other gentlemen see any disadvantage in working for another company while waiting to hear from the company of your first choice?

Duel: I think these questions are being tossed at me. I had better give you the whole story. We are in an expansion program, and everybody in the United States east of the Mississippi River knows it. We have in our file right now ten thousand active applications. Probably three thousand of these are from people who are within a radius of thirty-five miles of our plant and who are unemployed at the present time. We are giving most of our employment opportunities to these people.

Student: Are there any opportunities for girls other than in clerical work?

Duel: We have girls in the assembly department, inspection work, cafeteria, etc.

Hoppock: Do they need any special training for those jobs?

Duel: Someone asked a question before regarding work experience. We prefer to have brand-new people with no experience. We want them with some technical education, but more than that we want them to be socially competent. We want them to be good citizens. We want them to be able to get along with people. We want them to be honest. We want them to be able to think. If they can do these things, we can teach them to do the job.

Student (girl): I have had four years of science and four years of mathematics. I would like to be able to use this training somewhere without a college education. Is there any chance of my getting a job which would give me this opportunity?

Hoppock: Does that training have any value?

Peters: I have seen some very competent draftsmen—female. It would be difficult in this area to get the kind of work you probably want. In our plant, your opportunities would be clerical, assembly, and storekeeping and in our production control office. Your opportunities are quite limited.

Hoppock: Do you have girl apprentices, Mr. Duel?

Duel: We have not. The school was originally founded about twenty-five years ago, and, when the book was written, it said young boys who are high school graduates. Why we don't have girls, I don't know.

Hoppock: Do you think the rule might be changed?

Duel: I doubt it very much, because the nature of the work requires physical strength.

Hoppock: Mr. Becker, have you any use for a girl with this training?

Becker: It seems a shame, but I don't think we have.

Student: I would like to ask if there is anything in the salesmanship line or purchasing for a high school graduate?

Duel: Speaking for our company, the sales end is a different division. We have nothing to do with it. I do know that they prefer college graduates.

Hoppock: How about purchasing?

Duel: He might start in any clerical job and work into that.

Hoppock: If that were a boy's ambition and he wanted to be transferred there later, would you be able to take him with that understanding?

Duel: We wouldn't promise him that he would be transferred, but it wouldn't hurt him to ask.

Becker: All our sales are made to public utilities or telephone companies. That immediately calls for trained engineers. As to purchasing, that also calls for great technical training because of the nature of our business.

Peters: We are only now beginning to form the nucleus of our sales organization, and since we deal in the sort of technical equipment we manufacture, sound recorders, it is necessary that we have technically trained men. We also do the bulk of our business with the state and Federal governments. A man who sells must also be able to design technical installations. We have placed two young people, neither one of whom has had much technical training. It's a very, very long program which will take a number of years to complete, but in the main you can't go out and sell without a great deal of technical training.

Hoppock: We have been at this now for more than an hour. Suppose at this point we stop the demonstration and discuss the technique. (*To audience*) If we were interested primarily in teaching these young people rather than in demonstrating a technique, I would have asked more questions. I have a list of questions here which I have not used. If you are using this technique, it's a good idea to be fortified with such a list of questions.

First of all, would any of you like to ask any of the students here about their reaction to this as a technique of getting information?

From the audience: Do the students feel let down when they find out that most of these jobs start low, and they have to have some training —when they learn the facts from personnel men rather than from teachers?

Student: I feel that it's all right to start at the bottom and work up, but I feel that we are getting less chance to do so. I think they prefer people with college education, and the competition is getting keener, and without a college degree you have very little chance.

Hoppock: How many have a letdown feeling? None. How many feel more encouraged? None. It's about a neutral reaction. (*Laughter*)

From the audience: Why have the students not asked about salaries?

Student: We feel that maybe these companies have different salary rates and wouldn't like to talk about it so much. (*Laughter*)

Student: I figure that you are going to have to start at the bottom anyway.

Student: I feel that most of us have a better idea of what we want to do than what we are going to get paid.

From the audience: Do they feel that somewhere in their guidance they have been misguided in high school? (*No answer from students*)

Duel: Maybe that's because the direction of these young people's thinking is to a professional level. I don't think that today these young people have more competition in seeking a job than they did years ago. When we speak of college people, they come in at a different level. There are plenty of openings where young people can begin. We hope we are on an expansion program and that we will need machine operators, etc. From these people we will have to develop supervisory personnel. We promote from within.

Student: I feel that we were not misled if we stick to a certain course, but I think you can misguide yourself by jumping from course to course in the middle of your high school.

Hoppock: How many would say that you have had provided for you by your school something that you would call vocational guidance? (*All students raised hands.*)

In the light of what you have learned today, how many would say your guidance was realistic? (*Most students raised hands.*)

From the audience: When records are sent to the various firms, the student should fully realize that his attendance, punctuality, and extracurricular activities are almost as important as a good set of grades. Is that correct?

All employers: Yes.

Student: Would the men suggest that it would be better for a high school graduate to work a couple of years in a smaller place before applying to a large firm?

Duel: I think he has got it in reverse.

Becker: There's another slant to it, too. In a small shop, everyone has to be flexible. In a sense, that is our training program.

From the audience: I would like to have the students show the reaction as to their preference of this type of presentation of job information over a formal approach.

Hoppock: Would you rather get your information this way than by having these three people make a speech? How many would? (*He counts.*) How many would not? Nineteen say yes; two say no. Why?

Student: In a formal address, he would tell you more of what he has got for you, whereas this way we have to pull it out of him.

Hoppock: Who feels differently and why?

Student: I think it makes you feel more free in asking questions. You can put it over better, and you can put the employer sort of on the spot.

Student: Couldn't you ask questions after the speech was made?

Student: After sitting and listening to them speak, you are not in a mood to ask questions.

From the audience: Would the students feel more satisfied with a combination of the two? (*The speaker went on to describe such a combination at some length.*)

Hoppock: We spent about an hour on this. How many think it would have been better if we had had three ten-minute speeches and a half-hour of questions? (*He counts.*) About four and a half. (*Laughter*)

Suppose we ask the employers. Do you feel that you would have done a better job if you could have made a speech?

Duel: If I had made a speech, I could not have covered nearly all the different opportunities we have. Here I knew they were interested in clerical opportunities, and they had a chance to ask specific questions. I think we can get much more across to you this way than by standing up and frothing at the mouth for twenty minutes.

Peters: I agree.

Becker: I personally like this setup.

From the audience: Isn't it important to know what product is manufactured in each of these gentlemen's plants?

Hoppock: *Touché.* I proceeded on the assumption that that was known to everyone here. Let's find out!

Duel: IBM's plant here makes business machines, mainly electric typewriters.

Peters: Frederick Hart makes sound recorders, film and wire recorders, food mixers, and does job shopwork.

Becker: Fargo manufactures wire connectors. They are used by the public utilities to join different types of transmission wires. We also make railroad-signal equipment and aircraft parts.

From the audience: Has industry in this area prepared job summaries of the opportunities in their plants which they refer back to the schools? If not, would they welcome cooperation from the schools on such a project?

Peters: In our case, I would say that such a survey might be effective if it hit us at certain times when we had job opportunities. Generally, I don't feel that we could be particularly helpful in trying to assist you in making such a survey.

Becker: If such a survey were made, we would be very willing to cooperate. I don't know that we could promise anything definite in the way of openings if that is what the question was intended for.

Duel: I feel the same way.

Hoppock: Suppose this group of counselors were to go to you and ask you questions about job opportunities in your plants, would you welcome that kind of thing?

All employers: Yes.

Hoppock: Suppose we give our guests a chance. Would you three people who have been answering questions all afternoon like to ask anything?

All employers: No.

Hoppock: We are very grateful to you. I know I speak for the audience in telling you how much we appreciate what you have done for us. And the same goes for our student group. You've done a good job.

appendix **F**

Demonstration
Case
Conference [1]

The following is approximately a verbatim transcript of a demonstration case conference in the author's course in group guidance at New York University.

Instructor: This morning we are going to do another demonstration. This is to be a demonstration of the technique of the case conference described in Chapter 17. Those of you who have your texts—will you get them out and take a quick look at Chapter 17 now. How many of you have read that chapter? All right, those of you who have not read it are going to see the technique in operation before you read about it. I suggest that those of you who have read the chapter read it again during this next week, because I think some things in it will mean more to you after you have seen the demonstration.

Briefly, this is a technique in which we attempt to give students some practice in thinking about the kinds of decisions that a number of them are likely to have to make at some future time. We take cases out of the previous experience of the counselor, or we may take cases out of the current problems that members of the class are facing, and the group discusses these problems. One such discussion obviously would not teach a person a great deal, but going through a series of such discussions, we think, will give a person practice in thinking about such decisions and will give him practice in developing a technique of attacking similar problems. It may help him sometime to make a better decision than he otherwise would. So much for theory.

Now, we can use a case out of my counseling experience or out of yours, or perhaps some one of you has a problem. If it is a very simple problem where your own emotions are not greatly involved, it might be interesting to you, and more interesting to the rest of us, than some

[1] For related discussion see Chap. 17.

problem in which we have no personal interest. Are there any of you who are facing a decision on which you would like to have our help?

Student: I have been wondering how I could apply what I am learning. I am a physical therapist. I can see how the basic principles apply, but I would like to know how I could give group guidance to a group of spastics.

Instructor: Anyone else who has a problem?

Klopp: A man approached me this morning and asked if I would be interested in a particular type of job. I don't know much about the job, since I could talk about it for only a moment.

Instructor: (To student who volunteered first problem) If you don't mind, I will take this problem rather than yours, because it is better fitted to what I want to use this demonstration for.

Let's take Mr. Klopp's case. We have a real-life issue before us. All you know at the present time is this: Mr. Klopp has been offered a job and doesn't know whether or not to take it. We are not going to tell you anything except what you bring out by your questions. What do you want to know before you venture an opinion?

Student: What is his present position? What position is he offered?

Klopp: Administrative assistant at Scott High School, East Orange, New Jersey. I teach one class a day, and the rest of my time is spent in guidance.

I know very little about the other question. My adviser here at New York University saw me this morning about my curriculum and asked me to fill in a card. He said he would be willing to recommend me for a job in some research study in consumer education.

Student: Are you satisfied with the job you have now?

Klopp: Yes.

Student: Do you know whether this is going to be a permanent position?

Klopp: My adviser said it is definite for one year and would lead on to a permanent job.

Student: Why do you think he selected you for consideration for this job?

Klopp: That's a good question, because I told him I am no expert in consumer education. I have done a lot of other work for this adviser such as reading, grading papers, and preparing special bibliographies.

Instructor: Let me interrupt at this point to do some incidental teaching. This is a nice illustration of the kind of thing that happens over and over again. There are very few things that can contribute so much to the job opportunities open to you as a reputation for doing things well. People who set themselves a very high standard and hold themselves to it are extremely rare. When you discover one of them, if you are in a position to recommend people for jobs, you don't forget him very quickly. I find myself doing what this adviser apparently has done —saying to prospective employers, "Well, this man does not have the experience you are looking for, but he has the qualities you want." In looking for someone to do a job for me, I have a strong preference for those who I have seen do top-quality work.

By way of illustration, if you are majoring in nursing education, what you do in my course is relatively unimportant, but in your nursing education courses you should exert every effort to impress the professor with the quality of your work. Conversely, if you are majoring in guidance, what you do in my class is very important.

What else do you want to ask Mr. Klopp?

Student: Would it be possible for you to obtain a temporary leave of absence?

Klopp: That was suggested to me, and I would try to do it.

Student: Do you think that you would be as happy in a research job as in your present job? You seem to be the type of person who prefers working with people rather than things. Your present job involves working with people. Wouldn't the new job be mostly working with things?

Klopp: I know very little about the new position, but it is headed by some professor in the city, and no doubt he would be doing all the creative work, and the assistants would be doing routine work. I don't think I would be very happy doing routine work.

Student: I don't think we should continue this discussion until we are able to get more of the facts regarding this new job. Let's take it up again next week when we have all the necessary information.

Student: I would be interested in knowing the basic thinking about why you thought about leaving your present job.

Klopp: Well, there was a chance to jump up close to $2,000 immediately, whereas it would take me—well, $150 into $2,000, whatever that is. (*Laughter*)

Student: Should you decide not to go on with this job after a trial, would it help you when you return to your present job?

Klopp: That's a dangerous question. It could stymie me if the people were narrow-minded, but on the other hand, it could help me.

Student: How much will your past education help you in the new job? What opportunity will you have in the long run to do better in the new job?

Klopp: The work I am doing now is directly in line with both jobs. I am interested in guidance which involves some research.

Student: Would taking the new job mean breaking up your home and moving elsewhere?

Klopp: No.

Student: On the basis of interest and satisfaction, do you think this increase in salary would be enough to force you to make the change?

Klopp: If other things are equal.

Student: I am under the impression that the job you have now involves dealing with people and the other with figures. It seems to me that one big choice is whether you prefer to work with people or in small groups. I think satisfaction with a job is more important than money.

Student: What is this research project you are going to do?

Klopp: I don't know much about that. It is a research study in consumer education, and it sounds to me as if there will be some polling in it, such as the Gallup Poll. Dr. Hoppock may know something about it.

Instructor: I know of such a project. I don't know enough about it to even guess what this job might be. It is not, as far as I know, tied up to any institution. From what I know about it, I would guess that the exact nature of your job is probably not known at the present time, even to the person who is hiring you, and that it will be determined by what develops from year to year.

Student: Too many people expect school teachers to derive all their satisfaction from the job. I think there is a very important satisfaction in a good pay check.

Student: Do you know anything about consumer research?

Klopp: Never did it, but I like to read about it. I think those people are on the right track. It is an idealistic movement.

Student: Have you any idea as to hours in the job?

Klopp: No.

Student: Have you investigated what it might do to your physical well-being?

Klopp: No.

Student: He is going from an overcrowded field and going to a new one. If he makes good, there is an open road ahead, and he can step on the accelerator. He is throwing away security, but every pioneer has to take that chance.

Student: In spite of the promise made, this new position is precarious, since he has no definite assurance as to the future. So I would say, "Sit where you are."

Student: Until we know something about the job, what problem has he?

Student: How many years have you been in your present job?

Klopp: Two years.

Student: How far can you go in this position?

Klopp: That's another thing that is puzzling me. It's all a guess how far I can go.

Student: The only thing I get out of all this is that the gentleman reminds me of "Old Man River." He don't say nothing. I don't see how we can get anywhere in the absence of more material about the job.

Student: I think we can be helpful by suggesting to the subject what questions there are.

Instructor: Let me call to your attention as counselors-in-training what I should also call to your attention if you were a class of high school students. This discussion is bringing out the desirability of getting all of the facts before you make a decision. That has been repeatedly pointed out. If you learn nothing else except just to be impressed again with the importance of getting all of the facts, then the discussion may have been worthwhile.

Let's go on and see what help we can give Mr. Klopp on the basis of such facts as we have, and what his next step would be in terms of the kinds of information he should ask for.

Student: Have you tenure?

Klopp: I do not have tenure.

Student: Will you get tenure in another year?

Klopp: Yes, a year and a day.

Student: I think it depends on what security means to him—whether he should stay and get tenure or make a change.

Student: Do you expect to get tenure?

Klopp: Yes.

Student: In my mind, we have learned something now that I think may be helpful. I think basically, there are two things he can go ahead on. One is knowing himself, and the second is knowing the job. In the first category, I would suggest our subject take a personal inventory. The second is knowing the job. I think he should make an organized effort to ascertain what the job is, the nature of the duties involved, etc. Then by having this knowledge of knowing himself and knowing about the job, when he gives it to us for appraisement, we will be able to bring him to the threshold of objective viewpoint where he will be able to make the decision for himself.

Instructor: You have made an important point. A decision of this kind sometimes forces one to go back and examine one's basic philosophy. We must ask, "What do I want most?" Sometimes we deceive ourselves on this point. If you examine back for a period of years, you may find that there have been occasions when you could have secured what you think you want, but you didn't avail yourself of that opportunity. Let me illustrate. You may think you want independence more than anything else. You may not realize that you also want security. That's because you have security and not independence. But if you look back over the previous decisions you have made, you may find that you have had the choice and that you chose security without independence rather than independence without security. If you find that to be true in your own past history, you had better ask yourself, "Am I kidding myself about what I want?" None of this is intended to apply to Mr. Klopp. Just don't you ever forget how very necessary it is to examine your own scale of values.

Student: So far a number of people have hinted at various possibilities, and it goes back to getting more definite information. One of these problems is the leave of absence. If he went to his school and asked some of the very pertinent questions, I think he might be jeopardizing his position. Does that apply in his situation?

Klopp: I don't think so.

Student: Why doesn't he ask his wife? (Laughter)

Instructor: I think that's another thing we should keep in mind. Another person who has had an opportunity to observe you in a good many different situations may be able to draw some inferences about you that have never occurred to you at all, and yet, as soon as he suggests them to you, you see a certain logic in them. Certainly, you don't want to accept someone else's judgment in preference to your own, but you want to learn all you can from it.

Klopp: I gather there are two points of view. Are there any here who would give an immediate answer, "Not interested," this afternoon?

Instructor: How many? (He counts.) About seven out of a class of seventy-five. How many would be ready to say yes? Three out of seventy-five. That's about ten who are ready to make a decision now. Do you want any of these people to explain why?

Klopp: Yes, especially those who say refuse it.

Student: I know he is interested in people, and I don't think he would be emotionally happy in a job dealing with figures.

Student: The state of New Jersey law does not allow a leave of absence until a teacher is on tenure. Therefore, a leave of absence is impossible for him.

Student: The job is too vague and places no demands on his present capabilities.

Student: From the discussion I take it that the gentleman has two things to the good: he likes the increase in money, and he is pretty much indifferent to the job. I feel that the increase in money is not really what he wants. He may be thinking in terms of a new home or automobile. I don't think it is any basis to take a job without interest better than he has shown.

Student: The security reason. Any teacher, once he gets his tenure, is set. He will get his yearly increase. It's steady. The other is very speculative.

Student: How long has it been since you have thought of your life's goal? What is it? Will you obtain it if your superior should retire?

Klopp: I have been in this business a long time. I think my primary goal is happiness. If money or the job is a way to that happiness, I will settle for it. The people who said no don't help me too much because of my past living. One man said not to investigate further because it is too vague. Many of the best jobs I have ever had started as very vague things.

Security! I am not a great believer in security and tenure. I think the tenure law has advantages and disadvantages, and the disadvantage is the false security it develops. When I took my present job, I thought I was secure. While you are trying to be helpful to me in stressing security, you only upset me a little. (*Laughter*)

Instructor: It has been suggested that you make sure you have all the pertinent information. In your textbook, you will find a list of questions. As your assignment for next week, you might take this job and analyze it.

Student: How many years have you been in public school work?

Klopp: Seventeen.

Instructor: He has been in this work seventeen years, and at the present time, he has been in his present job only two. So apparently tenure has not been highly prized by him in the past. How many changes of job have you made during your teaching career?

Klopp: Three.

Instructor: That seems to indicate that in his scale of values tenure is not too important.

Klopp: Having tenure did not help during the Depression. Teachers were fired, tenure or not, by abolishing positions, etc.

Instructor: Let's not be diverted to a discussion of tenure. Our concern is, "What should he do, feeling as he does about tenure?"

Student: Let's take a poll and see how many of the class are security-minded.

Instructor: Let me restate the question. The question is how many would label yourself as security-minded. (*He counts.*) Twenty-two. How many would not? (*He counts.*) Twenty-six.

Student: If you had not been approached for this job, would you have thought of making a change?

Klopp: That's a hard question. I would not think of putting an application with an agency right now, but after I get my degree, if I get it, my services would be on the market.

Student: I believe we are concerned with Mr. Klopp's personal problem. I take this view. I am constantly trying to arrive, and when I have reached a goal, I push my goal higher. If he remains in this job, he will become stagnant.

Student: This problem of tenure can't be so easily dismissed. Tenure has kept wages down and kept people from making changes. I think his attitude is much more healthy.

Instructor: I think we have spent as much time on this one individual case as we should for demonstration purposes. Let me ask you to vote once more. Suppose you had to make a decision on the basis of the information you have now. Suppose Mr. Klopp were called out of this classroom and told he had to give an immediate answer. How many think his answer should be yes? (*He counts.*) Thirteen. No? (*He counts.*) Thirty-two.

Of those people who said you would keep the old job, how many of you think that if you had time to get all the facts, there is at least a fifty-fifty chance you would take the new one? (*He counts.*) About twenty-nine or thirty out of thirty-two. So your problem is not solved yet, Mr. Klopp.

Now we will leave Mr. Klopp and discuss the technique. Will you please take a sheet of paper. Will you put the following things on this paper? At the top of it, will you put Case Conference Demonstration, Mr. Klopp, and your own name. Now will you list on this sheet briefly, but as clearly as you can, anything which you learned from this morning's discussion that you think would be helpful to you if at some time in the future you were faced with a decision about changing your job.

(*Class writes.*)

Let's compare ideas and see what you have learned.

Student: (*reading*) I have learned that if you are going to derive any benefits from counseling, you must have an impersonal and unemotional attitude.

Student: (*reading*) An individual can solve a problem more readily if he discusses the points involved with a group of individuals who can advise him and help him understand his problem by being able to recognize the information he must know before making a decision.

Student: (*reading*) Others will be involved in the decision. Others can give valuable advice.

Student: (*reading*) The relative importance of the security of my present job would have to be evaluated and compared with all the advantages that the new job may have.

Student: (*reading*) Review all elements of old and new. Consider both in relation to desired achievement. Does it answer your basic need?

Student: (*reading*) Importance of appraising and reevaluating my personal set of values, my philosophy and outlook of life. The inventory of myself should help me obtain sufficient insight as to my own physical and mental limitations, past achievement, previous scholastic and job experiences, and interests. This search would serve to help me evaluate the problem confronted with a greater degree of adequacy.

Student: (*reading*) What would I gain in this new job? What would I lose in giving up my present job?

Student: (*reading*) The class discussion reinforced an operational belief that I've been carrying round for a few years—that it is a good idea to investigate and to get *all* the facts before making the plunge. It's pleasant getting an operational belief reinforced.

Student: (*reading*) Before making a change, I would take the time to get all important facts possible to obtain and consider them carefully.

Instructor: In the time that we have left, I would like to get your reaction to this as a technique to be used in a group guidance situation. Specifically, what do you think is good and what do you think is bad about this technique? First, the things you like.

Student: The democratic technique of having students solve the problem.

Student: This technique could be applied to several situations.

Instructor: Could you give me an illustration of that?

Student: In a history class a child is having trouble, and perhaps the older children could help him.

Student: Interest is a problem in getting people to discuss. This was personal and hence aroused interest.

Student: The large number of people who participated.

Student: It helped me to solve a personal problem. I'm facing the same kind of choice right now.

Student: It's an advantage over the follow-up study in that the individual is right here to tell you his reaction and add further information.

Student: The respect for others shown by all.

Instructor: That's something you will have to watch. The atmosphere of the discussion will be pretty largely a reflection of your attitudes. You must build the proper atmosphere. More than anything else, however, it is a reflection of your own attitude.

Student: The idea that in a class like this every point of view is expressed and the subject makes his own decision, whereas in individual counseling, the guidance counselor tends to make the decision for the person.

Instructor: Some of you are interested in nondirective counseling. What you have seen this morning is also partially a demonstration of the application of nondirective techniques to a teaching situation. Cantor's book on the subject is a fascinating work. This was not a pure demonstration of nondirective teaching, but to some extent it involved that.

Now let's have the difficulties and disadvantages you noticed during the demonstration.

Student: In this type of teaching, I think there is a great possibility of getting off on tangents. The teacher must be careful of that. Here it was pulled back in every instance, but with a new teacher using the technique the danger would be tremendous.

Instructor: That's one of the great differences between what I did this morning and completely nondirective teaching. I had a goal this morning, but the nondirective teacher seldom cuts off discussion.

Student: How effective would this method be with a shorter class period?

Instructor: I don't know. Will you try it for us and tell us next week?

Student: No. I don't try anything any more.

Instructor: Who is willing to try it for us and give us a report? (*Two students volunteered.*)

Student: The problems may be too personal.

Instructor: Yes. When you begin with this, I think you would be smart to use dead cases. For instance, I tried this with a supposedly dead case two years ago, but actually the person involved was sitting in the room. Some of the things said were pretty rough. Adolescents can be brutal. That's all for today.

As noted above, at the end of this demonstration the instructor asked the students to write their answers to this question, "What, if anything, did you learn from this discussion that you think would help you if you were offered a new job that you were not sure you wanted?"

Fifty-three students answered this question immediately, with no opportunity to consult each other or to discuss their ideas.

Twenty-eight of the fifty-three papers contained some equivalent of the following statements:

The importance of gathering all the facts.
Learn all facts about job before making a decision.
Make sure that you have all the facts before trying to make a decision.
In order to arrive at a logical decision, a person must have sufficient facts.

Twenty-three of the fifty-three papers contained some equivalent of the following:

Make sure of what you want out of life.
Evaluate this new job in terms of my goals in life.
Evaluate yourself to know what real life goals are.
The vital importance of a reevaluation of what I desire to achieve in life.
It made me stop and evaluate me.
I began to list my own values and standards.

Mentioned less frequently, in addition to the comments included in the transcript, were the following:

Seek help from those who know one's personal faults and good qualities.
It reassured me that my idea of not trusting snap judgments about important problems was not altogether on the wrong track.
I was pleased to learn that personal satisfaction and happiness in one's position was considered to be more important than monetary returns. This point reassured me in my own thinking.

Mr. Klopp, whose problem the group discussed, replied as follows:

That one's emotions must be assayed equally as deeply as one's ambitions.
That I should know more about legal (state) angles before making a decision, e.g., tenure and leave of absence.
That my goal in life should affect the present decisions.
That security can be an anchor as well as a shield.
That to guide others, I should remember that about one-seventh of professional persons (at least in this class) will make a quick decision without looking for half the facts.

appendix **G**

Outline
for the
Study
of an
Occupation [1]

by Robert Hoppock
New York Universtiy

PART I QUESTIONS

The questions listed below are intended to help you in your search for the kinds of facts you will want to get before you decide whether or not to choose a particular occupation as a career. If any question does not apply to the occupation you are studying, ignore it. If any question would require excessive work in order to get information that you are sure would have no effect upon your occupational choice, ignore it. Use this outline, not as a blueprint of rigid specifications, but as a checklist, to be sure you do not overlook any item of importance to you. Use it also as a guide in taking and in arranging your notes for any reports you may prepare.

You may find it convenient to cut one copy of this outline into its various major sections, to paste each section at the head of a page in your notebook, and to record below and after each pasted heading all your notes on the appropriate questions.

To find answers to these questions consult the chapter on "Sources of Occupational Information" in the latest edition of *Occupational Information* by Robert Hoppock, published by the McGraw-Hill Book Company, New York.

Introduction

Interesting facts about the service which workers in this occupation render to other people, about the origin and history of the work, etc.

---

[1] For related discussion see Chap. 18.

Future prospects

Are workers in demand today? Give evidence. Is employment expected to increase or decrease? Much or little? Why?

Nature of the work

Begin by quoting the *Dictionary of Occupational Titles,* if its definition seems appropriate. Supplement this, if necessary, by more detail on divisions of the work; other occupations with which it may be combined; tools, machines, and materials used; etc. Be sure to state as clearly as you can just what the worker does, for example, "opens letters, reads and sorts mail, takes dictation, transcribes letters, answers the telephone. . . ."

Check your description of the work against the following list of words to see if you have told all that you should. Must the worker:

Walk	Kneel	Reach	Handle
Jump	Stand	Lift	Finger
Run	Turn	Carry	Feel
Balance	Stoop	Throw	Talk
Climb	Crouch	Push	Hear
Crawl	Sit	Pull	See

Is the work done inside, outside, or both? Is it done under abnormal conditions of high, low, or changing temperature? Is the place of work likely to be dry, humid, wet, dusty, dirty, noisy, cramped, inadequately lighted or ventilated, malodorous? Is the work done with others, around others, or alone?

Qualifications

Age. What are the upper and lower age limits for entrance and retirement?

Sex. Is this predominantly a male or female occupation? Are there reasonable opportunities for both? Is there any more active demand for one than for the other?

Height and weight. Are there any minimum or maximum requirements? What are they?

Other physical requirements. Are there any other measurable physical requirements, e.g., 20/20 vision, freedom from color blindness, average or superior hearing, physical strength? Be specific. Don't generalize about "good health" and other desirable qualities needed in all occupations.

Aptitudes and interests. Has there been any research on aptitudes required? Has any vocational interest test been validated on workers in this occupation?

Tools and equipment. Must these be supplied by the worker at his own expense, as a physician must equip his office? What is the average cost?

Legal requirements. Is a license or certificate required? Where and how does one get a statement of the requirements? In general, what are they?

Unions
Is the closed shop common or predominant? If so, what are the requirements for entrance to the union? Initiation fees? Dues? Does the union limit the number admitted?

Discrimination
Do employers, unions, or training institutions discriminate against Negroes, Jews, others? What is the evidence? If you find unsupported assertions of discrimination and similarly unsupported denials, say, "It has been both asserted and denied that. . . ."

Preparation
Distinguish clearly between what is desirable and what is indispensable.

How much and what kind of preparation is required to meet legal requirements and employers' standards?

How long does it take? What does it cost? What does it include?

Where can one get a list of approved schools?

What kind of high school or college program should precede entrance into the professional school? What subjects must or should be chosen?

What provisions, if any, are made for apprenticeship or other training on the job?

Is experience of some kind prerequisite to entrance? Describe.

Entrance
How does one get his first job? By taking an examination? By applying to employers? By joining a union? By registering with employment agencies? By saving to acquire capital and opening his own business? How much capital is required?

State types of places in which the worker may find employment.

Advancement
What proportion of workers advance? To what? After how long and after what additional preparation or experience?

What are the related occupations to which this may lead, if any?

Earnings
What are the most dependable average figures you can find on earnings by week, month, or year?

What is the range of the middle 50 percent?

Pay most attention to beginning wages and average wages of all workers. Avoid misleading emphasis on the exceptional worker who is highly paid.

Include extra earnings from tips, commissions, free board and room, expense allowances for auto, travel, etc. Mention deductions for uniforms, union dues, pension and insurance plans, etc.

Are earnings higher or lower in certain parts of the United States or in certain branches of the occupation?

Number and distribution of workers
According to the United States census how many were employed at this occupation? Avoid *labor force* figures: get the number employed. Divide the total population of the United States by the number employed to show how many persons there were in the total population to each one in this occupation.

How many were men? Women? Negroes? Of other races?

If there are any better figures than those in the census, use them and state the source.

Are the workers evenly distributed over the United States in proportion to population, or concentrated in certain areas? Where? Why?

Can a person practice this occupation anywhere that he may wish to live?

Do conditions in small towns and rural areas differ materially from those in urban centers? How?

Advantages and disadvantages
Here list what workers say they like best and dislike most about their jobs.

Are hours regular or irregular, long or short? Is there frequent overtime or night work? Sunday and holiday work?

What about vacations?

Is employment steady, seasonal, or irregular? Does one earn more or less with advancing age, e.g., professional athletes? Is the working lifetime shorter than average, e.g., models?

Are the skills acquired transferable to other occupations?

Is the work hazardous? What about accidents, occupational diseases?

Is the worker exposed to:

Vibrations	High places	Explosives
Mechanical hazards	Danger of burns	Radiant energy
Moving objects	Electrical hazards	Toxic conditions

In comparison with other occupations requiring about the same level of ability and training, in what ways is this one more or less attractive?

Include here anything important not covered under other headings.

Related occupations

What are the related occupations that might prove acceptable to the person who thought he wanted to enter this one but who finds either himself or the occupation lacking something?

Sources of further information

Names and addresses of major professional associations and other organizations from which you got helpful information.

Bibliography

Best references for further reading. Annotate each one. Arrange in order of merit.

PART II WHAT ARE YOU GOING TO DO ABOUT IT?

The purpose of this section is to help you compare what you now know about this occupation with what you know or can learn about yourself. You are to fill in the blanks which follow. This will involve some repetition of facts that you have already recorded elsewhere. This repetition is necessary in order to help you to select and bring together the most important facts, so that you can get a good look at them and decide what your next steps should be.

1 **Duties.** List here all the things you would have to do in this occupation that you think you could do well AND enjoy doing.

_____
_____
_____
_____
_____
_____
_____
_____
_____
_____
_____

2 List here all the things you would have to do in this occupation that you think you could not do well OR that you would dislike doing.

_____
_____
_____
_____
_____
_____
_____
_____
_____
_____

3 **Physical requirements.** List here any physical requirements that you must meet in order to enter this occupation, for example, height, weight, 20/20 vision, freedom from color blindness.

_____
_____
_____
_____
_____
_____
_____
_____
_____
_____

4 List here any of these requirements that you think you might find it hard to meet.

_____
_____
_____
_____
_____
_____
_____
_____
_____

5 **Aptitudes.** List here any aptitudes in which you must be better than average in order to do satisfactory work in this occupation or to get the training necessary to enter it, for example, mechanical aptitude, clerical aptitude, scholastic aptitude, finger dexterity, pitch discrimination, reaction time.

_____

_____

_____

_____

_____

_____

6 List here the names of any tests you have taken to measure these aptitudes and the results of the tests and any other evidence of the aptitudes you possess. List also the results of any tests you have taken to measure your interest in this occupation and any other evidence of your interest in it.

_____

_____

_____

_____

_____

_____

7 **Preparation.** List here the number of years of high school and college training that you must have to enter this occupation.

High school_____College_____

8 List here the number of years of high school and college training that you think you have the ability, the money, and the desire for.

High school_____College_____

9 **Earnings.** List here how much money you think you could earn in this occupation.

First year $_____

After five years $_____

After ten years $_____

10 List here how much money you think you would have to earn in order to feel that you were doing about as well as you have a right to expect.

First year $_____

After five years $_____

After ten years $_____

11 **Other requirements.** List here any other requirements that you must meet in order to enter this occupation, for example, license requirements, examinations, union membership.

12 List here any of these requirements that you think you might find it hard to meet.

_____

_____

_____

_____

_____

_____

_____

_____

_____

_____

13 **Number of jobs.** List here how many persons are employed in this occupation in the community in which you wish to work.

14 List here the best estimate you can get of how many jobs in this occupation become vacant each year in the community in which you wish to work.

_____

_____

Job satisfaction. Ask several persons now working in this occupation what they like best and dislike most about it.

15 List here the things that most of them say they like most.

_____
_____
_____
_____
_____
_____
_____
_____
_____

16 List here the things that most of them say they dislike most.

_____
_____
_____
_____
_____
_____
_____
_____

17 **Miscellaneous.** List here any other reasons why you think this would be a good occupation for you to enter.

_____
_____
_____
_____
_____
_____
_____
_____

18 List here any other reasons why you think this would NOT be a good occupation for you to enter.

_____
_____
_____
_____
_____
_____
_____
_____

SUMMARY

Go back over the things you have written on the preceding pages and

19 List here the most important reasons why you think this would be a good occupation for you to enter.

20 List here the most important reasons why you think this would NOT be a good occupation for you to enter.

---

21 **Tentative decision.** If you had to decide today whether or not to enter this occupation, what would you decide, and why?

Demonstration
Practice
Job
Interview[1]

The following is approximately a verbatim transcript of a demonstration of the practice job interview. It was presented in the author's course in group guidance at New York University.

Instructor: We will try to demonstrate a practice job interview for you this morning. Do we have in the class anybody who is at the present time in a position where he does hiring? No. Is there anybody here who has been in such a job? No. All right. Is there anybody here who would enjoy taking over the role of an employment interviewer for a demonstration this morning?

Lifton: I will do it if no one else will.

Instructor: All right.

Are there some of you here who expect at some time in the future to have to apply for a job and who would like to have this opportunity to try out your interview technique and get the benefit of the suggestions of the people here on what you did well and what you could do better? (*Miss Brennan raises her hand.*) All right, what kind of job would you like to try out for?

Brennan: Teacher.

Instructor: Of what?

Brennan: Social studies.

Instructor: What kind of school?

Brennan: Secondary.

Instructor: What type of area?

Brennan: Suburban.

Instructor: What size?

Brennan: About a thousand in a senior high school.

[1] For related discussion see Chap. 20.

Instructor: All right, Mr. Lifton is the superintendent of schools. You have been recommended by New York University. Your papers have been sent to him. He is in his office, sitting at the desk. You arrive at the front door of the school. You're on your own!

(*To class*) Will all of you keep a pencil and paper handy and note what Miss Brennan does. Don't pay any attention to Mr. Lifton. He's just an accessory. Make note of anything she does that you think is good —anything that would make a favorable impression on you if you were the employer. Also, anything that you would do differently.

Brennan: Good morning, Mr. Lifton.

Lifton: Won't you come over here and sit down? I have received the information from the New York University employment bureau. I would like to know a little bit more about you. Are you at all familiar with our school?

Brennan: Well, no.

Lifton: Tell me how your students have reacted to you as a person.

Brennan: I have never taught before, but I am very much interested in working with young people. I have worked for the Red Cross, teaching first aid.

Lifton: Were those all boys or all girls?

Brennan: Mixed groups.

Lifton: How old?

Brennan: Twelve to seventeen.

Lifton: Why do you feel you would like to work with that age group?

Brennan: I like to work with young people. They show right in their faces how they feel toward you.

Lifton: Unfortunately, we have some young people in our school who are rather mischievous. Can you handle that type of situation?

Brennan: I think so. I might have a tendency to be a little dictatorial.

Lifton: You think you would enjoy teaching despite its difficulties?

Brennan: I don't mind it.

Lifton: That's a sort of negative way of saying things. Do you like it?

Brennan: Yes.

Lifton: Have you found yourself usually the leader or a follower in groups you have been a part of?

Brennan: When I have been working with young people where I was oldest, I was the leader, but in the case of college work I was one of the group.

Lifton: Do you think you would be able to go into the classroom and teach where the students were asked to do their own work? We have a progressive school and use the project method.

Brennan: I have no experience, but I know something about that from my courses at the university.

Lifton: Have you given any thought to living problems—where you will live if you should teach here?

Brennan: I am sure I can take care of that.

Lifton: Have you ever lived alone before?

Brennan: No.

Lifton: Have you any questions you would like to ask me about the work here?

Brennan: I would like to know what advancement I could achieve here outside of regular teaching.

Lifton: I don't quite understand.

Brennan: I am interested in guidance work. Could I work in that department or assist a counselor? Later on, could I work into guidance work?

Lifton: That's a lot of questions at once. In our system here, we like to feel that all our teachers are counselors, but we have specific opportunities for guidance work. As far as a specific job in guidance goes, there are not many in our school system. It would be a case of waiting for a person to leave, and then you would have to compete with other individuals for the job.

Brennan: I understand.

Lifton: Have you any other questions?

Brennan: How active is your PTA here?

Lifton: Well, I think that's something we could stand improvement on.

Brennan: In some systems, it has a tendency to be political.

Lifton: Would that bother you?

Brennan: Yes. As an individual, I would expect free exercise of my political beliefs. I would want no one to tell me how to vote. That's one thing I don't like to work with in a PTA, because I know they do have that tendency.

Lifton: I see. I notice your subject matter is social studies. How would you attack the problem of presenting to your students the various parties and what they stand for?

Brennan: I would present the facts. I don't think the teacher should present her own point of view. On the other hand, I think she should present the facts. Under our constitution we have a democracy in this country and full information on the part of the electorate is essential to the successful functioning of a democracy.

Lifton: You say that since we have a constitution, we have a democracy in this country?

Brennan: Not completely.

Lifton: How would you try to help your students see what a pure democracy is?

Brennan: I think I would try to separate the students into various legislative groups and show them how laws are made. If we have clubs, you can work a great deal through that medium.

Lifton: You feel, then, that if you have the formal aspects that would provide for democratic expression, you would have a program that would train the pupils in democracy?

Brennan: Yes. Of course, you would not have them separate from their home environment. But at least you have an opportunity to present it to them.

Lifton: You feel, then, that to carry this message across, you would have to talk to the parents about your own philosophy?

Brennan: Well, it might help, but I really haven't thought it out that far.

Lifton: Do you believe it is proper for a teacher to have viewpoints which she presents in class as her own?

Brennan: No, not in my subject.

Lifton: Let's assume you are getting a class right out of grammar school. Do you think those children are in a position to make a choice?

Brennan: I'm sorry, I don't understand.

Lifton: Would you feel those children at that point had a sufficient background to make a decision?

Brennan: Not at that point. I think that they would have to be exposed a little more to life.

Lifton: Would information alone permit this understanding?

Brennan: Not information, but understanding.

Lifton: Are there any other questions?

Brennan: I can't think of any offhand. Do you have regular increments?

Lifton: Yes. Before you leave today, I would like you to make a round of the classrooms and be introduced to the teachers. You will have a chance to evaluate our school, and our teachers can evaluate you. This is a procedure we follow with everyone we are considering hiring.

Brennan: Have you any clubs?

Lifton: Yes. Suppose you look through the school, and I will see you at the end of the day. If you have any questions then, I will be glad to answer them.

Instructor: Thank you both very much. (*To class*) If you were the superintendent, how many would hire her? (*He counts.*) Forty-two. You got forty-two jobs for yourself. How many would not? Five. Now, what do you want to ask?

Student: In the beginning, don't you think she should have sold herself more?

Student: I think it might be interesting to find out how many believe a superintendent would have hired her.

Instructor: How many of you, trying to imagine what a superintendent would do, think he would hire her? Twenty-seven. Apparently you think superintendents do not have as good judgment as you have. Let's take your notes now in this order. First, those of you who saw Miss Brennan do something that you liked, tell us, so she can know what she did that created a favorable impression on you.

Student: She showed interest in the job. She showed what I call a remarkable piece of psychology. She admitted that she had a tendency to be dictatorial. She admitted that she would need assistance from the administration. Telling the truth in this way is bound to make a good impression on an interviewer.

Student: Most superintendents do not regard a school as a correctional institution for their teachers.

Student: I feel she showed remarkably poor psychology in making a statement about her deficiency. I think the gentleman is being far too charitable about superintendents of schools. I don't think they would consider the confession on the part of the teacher as intelligent.

Instructor: Let's restrict our discussion for a moment to additional comment on this one point.

Student: I liked the atmosphere of self-confidence but at the same time of self-appraisal.

Student: Some supervisors, perhaps, would not think of that as a weakness. We have a situation within our school which calls for dictatorial action on the part of the teacher.

Student: I have heard some administrators say that the people coming out today let the class run away with them.

Student: At one place she talks about democracy in the classroom, and on the other hand she talks of herself as dictatorial. As such, I would think she was only trying to make an impression when her own personal characteristics are in opposition to what her beliefs are.

Student: It might be interesting to have a vote on whether it was good or bad.

Instructor: We will when we finish getting the comments.

Student: I am probably wrong . . . (*Laughter*)

Instructor: At least you are modest.

Student: (*continuing*) I think a good many people like to think they are dictatorial. Maybe she isn't. I don't think Miss Brennan or anyone else can make such a statement. I don't think we can decide for ourselves whether we really are dictatorial or not.

Student: I once applied for a job as an instructor. I had a tendency to conceal certain things about my personality. He asked me point-blank, "What's the matter with you? Isn't there anything about yourself that you don't like?" He said, "I am sure there is not a person living who doesn't have any weakness." He was displeased.

Instructor: Let's take a vote on this. Before we vote, let me caution you, Miss Brennan, not to pay too much attention to the vote. The majority has been known to be wrong, and you do what you think best.

How many think her statement went beyond what you would consider good procedure on her part? (*He counts.*) Twenty-six. How many feel that she did not? Twenty-six. (*Laughter*) How many of you did not vote either time? Seven. Now, how many of you feel that to some degree, which you yourself would determine, it is desirable to be candid, frank, and open about your limitations if you are asked about them? It looks unanimous. It was except for one. How many of you feel that it is better to say nothing about your limitations unless you are asked about them? (*He counts.*) Twenty-four. How many of you feel that it is better to volunteer such information? Nine. How many did not vote either way? Twenty-six. A good many of you are undecided on that point.

If you don't mind, I would rather not spend any more time discussing that point. What other things did she do that you liked?

Student: I think the superintendent of schools would have been thrilled by her question, "Could I assist anyone in the guidance department?" I think those were fine questions.

Student: I think she was well dressed.

Student: He asked several questions which were rather vague. She asked him to clarify them. I think that showed intelligence on her part.

Student: I think she was very assertive. In order to get the job, she did not fall on the superintendent's desk and agree with everything.

Student: I think she was very clever in not divulging her political stands.

Instructor: Now, what would you have done differently?

Student: I think he left her wide open, and she jumped right in when she asked a few questions, particularly in regard to politics. People are very sensitive to these points today. As she went on, he just led her further and further on. Well, I happen to agree with everything she said, but that type of answer and the continued questioning would assure her not getting the job. There must be a point where an applicant can maintain his self-respect and yet earn a living.

Student: She made no statement as to her position.

Student: I disagree with that last statement. For any person to say, "I don't want my vote to be dictated," puts you on record as being a progressive individual.

Student: I would not be quite as direct in answering that question. She might just smile. (*Laughter*)

Student: For any teacher to introduce any controversial issue is poor diplomacy. For example, a superintendent told me that in interviewing a teacher, he asked her, "What do you think of the governor's stand on teachers' salaries?" She happened to look up and saw a personally signed picture of the governor on the wall. She did some very quick thinking, and although she disagreed with the governor's stand, she still said, "Well, I am very much in favor of the governor's stand."

Student: (*interrupting*) That's a lie.

Student: (*continuing*) Wait a minute. She was not hired and made some inquiries about the superintendent. She found he comes from Kentucky, is a rock-ribbed Democrat in politics, and basically was opposed to the governor's program. The point I am trying to make is that there is a distinct danger in discussing such matters, and it is foolhardy for the applicant to bring them up herself.

Student: Coming back to Miss Brennan's remarks, I take it that she was going to present both sides of the story to her students. Last week I attended the alumni luncheon. The governor of Connecticut spoke on "The Teacher in Politics." His ideas were nearly identical with those of Miss Brennan.

Student: I'm afraid that most of us, being human, can't present any issue where we have a particular viewpoint objectively.

Instructor: Assuming the truth of what you say, what should Miss Brennan have done differently?

Student: I believe she should never have brought in the issue of the PTA. She should not have tried to explain her views on politics.

Instructor: Let's have your collective views on this. How many feel that in an employment interview, you should not be the one to introduce a discussion of what you would do on controversial issues? Practically unanimous. If the subject is introduced by the employer, how many feel the wisest thing for you to do is to state candidly and calmly your own feeling about how you ought to handle the thing? About half. How many of you feel that you should do something other than that? Eight. Those eight persons, tell us what you think we should do.

Student: I would parry.

Student: I would hedge.

Student: I would give an impersonal answer.

Student: I would give a middle-of-the-road answer.

Student: Same thing.

Instructor: Let's drop that topic and go on to anything else that Miss Brennan did that you would have done differently.

Student: I don't think that if the superintendent of schools asked her what she meant by the constitution, she should have answered the question.

Student: I think that a person applying for a job has every right to go armed with a certain battery of questions. The teacher should go with a certain amount of feeling that she is interviewing the superintendent to see if that's the kind of job she wants. I am amazed to find a certain percentage of people here who feel you have to fawn on the superintendent in order to get a job. I feel that no one in the profession should ever approach a job from that viewpoint.

Instructor: When I am interviewing candidates, that's one of the first questions I ask them, "What questions would you like to ask me?" I do it not only because I want the person to know all about the job, but also because I think I can learn a good deal about the individual just by observing the kinds of questions he asks and whether his questions all deal with "What am I going to get out of the job?" or with "What is the nature of the situation here, and what have I to offer to the job?"

It's a little difficult for me to illustrate that type of question. (*Pauses*) Let's imagine candidate A saying: "What is the salary? What are the salary increments? How soon can I be promoted? How many hours do I work? Do I have to serve on committees, etc.?" Candidate B says: "Tell me something about the kind of students. What do they most need to learn? What things do you think you need in your training program that are not there and that you think I can contribute? What is your general philosophy of teaching?"

You see the difference between A and B.

Student: What would your reaction be to the teacher who asked you, "Is the PTA in your community politically controlled?"

Instructor: I would be unfavorably impressed both by that and by her insistence on freedom to vote. After all, voting is secret, and the mere asking of the question would indicate at least a chance of some past experience of political trouble on her part. I don't want to hire teachers who get in jams, because they get me in jams. Therefore, I would have pursued that a little further than Mr. Lifton did. All my other impressions were highly favorable. I got the impression that her very manner contradicted her statement that she was dictatorial. But I still had my fingers crossed, because I have had some very unpleasant experiences with people who argue very bitterly for what they say are matters of principle but what to me are matters of hurt feelings.

Student: I feel that she knew the community where she was applying, and evidently it was a politically minded community. She might not want the job if he indicated he would go along with the PTA.

Instructor: I would go right along with you. If, as a candidate, you are not sure that you want the job, even if it is offered to you, then you may very well ask a great many questions it would be unwise to ask if you definitely know you want the job. But don't overlook the possibility of postponing those questions to a second interview. This interview is for him to determine whether he wants you. I have had candidates take my time asking me questions long after I have made my decision not to hire them.

In the initial interview, you can let the employer ask the questions. Then wait and see if he offers you a job. If he mails you a contract, call him up and thank him. Tell him you would like to come over to talk to him. Then you can ask all the questions you want.

I am expressing dogmatic opinions. If you disagree, come on back at me and tell me so. Anybody want to disagree with any of these things? Don't be afraid to. It won't hurt your grade.

Student: I think the majority of people have the attitude that superintendents are old fuddyduddies, just waiting for a chance to catch the applicant in a trap. He wants to find out something about the applicant. If he sees the applicant on his guard, he concludes the candidate is hiding something.

Instructor: I think I agree with you completely on that. I think your attitude should be, "If I do not have what this employer wants, then I don't want the job." If you can afford to do it, it is far better to take the attitude that this is a cooperative interview in which the employer and you are trying to decide whether you want each other. I think you are quite right in saying that you create a much better impression if you are frank, open, and candid unless you are such a clever actor that you can avoid questions and still give the impression of candor. I still think there is no point in the first interview in dragging in on your own initiative things that jeopardize your chances of getting the job.

Student: The candidate's economic situation may be such that he must get the job. This may not be so often true today, but during the Depression it certainly was usually the case.

Instructor: I think we would all agree that you may find yourself in a situation where you want a job desperately. Then it becomes a question of "Is it better to hedge or to be candid?" I don't believe you can give a general answer to that. It depends greatly on the situation, and there is no way you can be sure you are sizing up the situation accurately. I know a superintendent of schools who would be perfectly delighted with the answers Miss Brennan gave. I know others who would not touch her with a 10-foot pole. If she can afford to do it, her problem is to find the superintendent who feels as she feels.

Student: I think you should look up the man.

Instructor: If you want the job enough to take the time, it certainly pays to find out everything you can about the prospective employer. Find out what he has written and read it.

Student: You can hire a detective agency. (*Laughter*)

Student: I felt she didn't ask enough about the job and didn't tell the superintendent what she had to give this group.

Instructor: Miss Brennan, would you think out loud for us for a minute or two, and tell us, for our benefit as students of group guidance techniques, what are your feelings after being gone over by this group? I think we should all know as much as we can about this. Do you feel you have been all torn apart? Do you feel you have learned something helpful?

Brennan: I was wondering if you could be inside my mind and see what I was thinking as I answered. He raised the discipline question. I wanted him to know that I could discipline a class if necessary. I wanted him to know that if he should ever observe me disciplining a class, I would look tough to him.

When he asked me about the constitution, I was irritated. He could watch me teach a class. I was trying to make believe that I was a teacher without any experience. He should have known it would be difficult to answer such questions without having any experience in the classroom situation.

Instructor: Have you learned anything that you think is going to be of help to you in your next employment interview?

Brennan: Yes, not to ask questions on the personal level. I might have been hurting his feelings when I mentioned the PTA.

Instructor: Well, we will let you rest for a moment. Will the rest of you examine your reactions and let us know what you have learned from the demonstration interview and our discussion of it?

Student: I think I have learned the importance of a more carefully planned approach on the part of the individual. Before a person goes in to see an interviewer, he should know all the questions he wants to ask.

Student: I have learned that most teachers like to carry on the belief that they can be independent, like doctors, lawyers, and members of other professions. I have learned that in applying for a job, I am the same as any other worker.

Student: I have learned the importance of explaining to the applicant about intangible things, such as dress and deportment.

Instructor: Yes. That's one of the things, I think, that most teachers do not realize and that most placement people have impressed on them over and over again. I know that in my own experience, placement workers have asked me over and over again, "Why don't the teachers tell these young people how to dress when applying for a job, how to act in that situation?" I know we think we are doing a lot in that direction, but reports on our results indicate it is a matter to which we will have to give more and more attention. We must be sure we are doing the job, and we must reexamine our techniques to see if we can't do it more effectively.

That again is one reason I am this morning demonstrating this technique to you. It's one of the methods you can use to get some of these things across. You can do it as we did, or you can stage the thing. You can coach the children so that in two interviews one does all the wrong things and another all the things you think are good. Let the class see them both. Then be prepared to have your class tell you that your "correct" pupil did one or two things wrong, too.

It does make good discussion material. There hasn't been anyone falling asleep here this morning. What else did you learn that you can use?

Student: In going after a position that you really want, to study the interviewer as much as you possibly can.

Instructor: O.K., that's all for today.

appendix **I**

Chronological History of the Teaching of Occupations

The first nine items have been selected from the *History of Vocational Guidance* by John M. Brewer [42].

1836 Edward Hazen in *The Panorama of Professions and Trades,* a book published in Philadelphia, recommended including a course on occupations in the schools.

1841 *The Book of Trades* published in Glasgow reported that Saturdays had been used for school visits to factories and shops.

1899 John Sidney Stoddard wrote a book on *What Shall I Do?* ". . . in the form of reports on a series of imaginary school classes in which the advantages and disadvantages of fifty different occupations were studied."

1908 Westport, Conn. George H. Boyden, high school principal, at the suggestion of Superintendent William A. Wheatley, taught the first organized course in vocations.

1910 Louis P. Nash in Boston proposed "a course of study on occupations." The proposal was included in the 1911 annual report of the superintendent of schools.

1913 The Boston School Committee established a vocational information department which sent to the schools ". . . a plan for a course in vocational information one half hour per week, open to all graduating classes from the eighth grade and all others thirteen years old or over."

1915 The first issue of the *Vocational Guidance Bulletin,* now *The Personnel and Guidance Journal,* was published. W. Carson Ryan, Jr., was the editor. He was also secretary of the National Vocational Guidance Association. The longest item in the first issue ". . . commented on an article by Supt. W. A. Wheatley of Middletown, Conn., 'A Course in Vocational Information in a Small City' " from the March, 1915, *School Review.*

1915 Vermont. By legislation the state board of education ". . . was directed to arrange for a course of study on vocational opportunities to be given in all junior high schools."

1916 Ginn and Company, Boston, published *Occupations* by E. B. Gowin, instructor in economics at Wesleyan University, and Superintendent W. A. Wheatley. This was the first textbook for classes in occupations to achieve widespread use. It was written for boys' classes; it was later revised by Brewer and extended to cover mixed classes of boys and girls.

1923 Earliest known report of a college course in occupations, taught by E. J. Wiley at Middlebury College [515].

1925 New Haven, Conn. "Marie McNamara began an intensive attempt at guidance through the home rooms of a junior high school. . . ." The program included carefully prepared lesson plans, demonstration lessons by the supervisor, observation, and supervision. "It was early discovered, however, that occupational information could not be given effectively by home-room teachers, and special regular classes in that subject were provided."

1938 The public schools of Chicago introduced their elective course in self-appraisal and careers for high school seniors, to be taught only by teachers trained in guidance.

1949 The U.S. Office of Education reported 158,098 students enrolled in courses in occupations from grades 7 to 12.

1952 The public schools at Worcester, Mass., introduced their elective course in self-appraisal and careers for high school juniors and seniors, to be taught only by certified counselors who had time reserved for individual counseling with the students in the course. Harvard, Brown, Dartmouth, and MIT accepted the course for college entrance credit.

1953 Cuony [111] reported that high school alumni who had had a senior course in job finding and job orientation were better satisfied with their jobs and earned more money than comparable students who had not had the course.

1955 Lowenstein [312] reported that college freshmen who had had a high school course in occupations made a better adjustment to college than comparable students who had not had the course.

1957 Cuony [113] reported a five-year follow-up of the students who had his course in job finding and job orientation. They were still superior in job satisfaction and in earnings to comparable students who had not had the course. During the fifth year the students who had had the course also suffered less unemployment. All differences between the two groups were greater at the end of the fifth year than at the end of the first.

1959 The Academy of Teachers of Occupations was organized at the annual convention of the American Personnel and Guidance Association in Philadelphia.

1963 The State of North Carolina developed Introduction to Vocations as an elective course in the ninth grade of forty-five high schools and appointed the first State Supervisor of Introduction to Vocations to help the teachers. As of 1966 there were five state supervisors helping 209 teachers of this course.

appendix **J**

Some Other
Aspects of
Occupational
Adjustment

Job rackets. Counselors and teachers of occupations will want to warn their students about the racketeers who sometimes exploit job seekers. Students should be warned to read everything on an application blank before they sign it; racketeers may conceal in fine print a contract that will obligate the applicant to deposit a cash bond or to pay for uniforms or for tools or materials or for an expensive training course. The "employer" may then disappear with the money. Any proposal that the applicant lay out any cash or assume any financial obligation in order to get a job should be investigated thoroughly. The proposal may be legitimate, or it may not. Ask the state employment service and ask other employers in the same business whether or not the proposed payments are customary and reasonable. If the prospective employer is unknown to the applicant and to the counselor, it may be wise to ask the employer for a bank reference and for one or two credit references and then to ask these references what they know about the integrity and the financial responsibility of the employer.

Is ambition a symptom of maladjustment? Teachers and counselors are moderately ambitious people; they are likely to assume that their students are or should be equally ambitious and to let this assumption affect their counseling. The assumption is debatable. If a person is useful enough to support himself and his family and to discharge his generally accepted obligations without injuring others, if he is sufficiently contented so that he feels no urge to do more, who is to say that he should and on what grounds? Is the reformer, the do-gooder, the teacher, or the counselor justified in believing that his values, his ideals, his ambitions are more commendable than those of his less ambitious neighbor or student? May not his student counter with the assertion that ambition is only a symptom of maladjustment, anyway, and may he not find some evidence to support this challenge?

The easily satisfied, not very ambitious person may be a source of irritation to those who develop stomach ulcers in their frantic urge to achieve things. He may not contribute greatly to the progress of the human race. But neither is he likely to become a tyrant, a demagogue, a vicious criminal, or a bellicose, belligerent, obnoxious boor. There is something to be said for him, even if he does not fit neatly into our American culture pattern of success at almost any sacrifice.

The case for the unambitious was amusingly stated by Robert Louis Stevenson in his delightful "An Apology for Idlers" [461]. The philosophy of the little man, who is content to remain a little man, was neatly expressed by Pat, the meat cutter, in the Columbia motion picture, "The Marrying Kind," from which the following excerpt is quoted by permission:

> Look, I got a job. One thing, it's steady. Up, down, come or go, one thing people gotta—is eat. All right. Twenty after eight in the morning I give that Emily a good bite in the neck an' I'm off. Ten minutes to nine—sometimes five—I'm here. Good ventilation—clean working conditions. Twelve o'clock I go have lunch—take a little walk around —look in the windows—come back. Five-thirty—we close that door, no matter what. Half hour clean up—ordering—whatever. Six o'clock —hot or cold or Wednesday—I'm out. Ten minutes to seven—maybe five—I'm home. And here's the thing: Once I cross that door going out I don't care about the shop or the store or the business again until I hit it the next day. From the time I leave this store the only animal I worry about is Emily. I don't want to be a big man. Listen—aroun' Twenty Eleven Thirty-fifth Avenue, Jackson Heights, I'm the biggest man there is. That's the only place I want to be a big man. So what's wrong with my point of view? All right. So I'm a stick in the mud— no ambition—but for my kind of type, I got married to Emily who's the right kind of type for my kind of type—an' she don't push me. She don't tell me what the woman next door got for Christmas. That's it. Live an' let live.

A suggestion for beginners. Ask each student in your class to write on separate file cards the names of all the occupations in which he has ever held a part-time or full-time job, the name of his employer, the last year in which he worked at each occupation, and his name. File these cards by occupation, and refer to them whenever you want information about any of the occupations represented. The information you get from your own students will sometimes be more up to date and more representative of local conditions than anything you can find in print. Your students may enjoy the novelty of teaching you and of learning from one another.

Ask your students to prepare similar cards for the occupations in which the members of their families are currently employed. On each card, record the name of the occupation, place of employment, current date, name of employee, home address of employee, relationship to student, and name of student. Example: Plumber. Middletown Co. 1963. Joseph Ryan. 16 Webster Ave. Father of Mildred Ryan. Use these cards to locate additional sources of firsthand information about local occupations. Most parents welcome an opportunity to help the school in this way.

One quick way to give your students an idea of the variety of occupations that may be open to them is to list on the blackboard the names of all the occupations in which the students and the members of their families are or have been employed.

Occupational information is powerful stuff. News about high wages in a rapidly expanding industry will move thousands of workers across a continent. Depending upon the training required, it will lead students to quit school or workers to return for more education. It will cause the introduction of new courses into schools or colleges, the hiring of new teachers, and the promotion of old ones.

Conversely, evidence of overcrowding in an occupation will precipitate sharp declines in related college enrollments and put panic in the hearts of professors who want to keep their jobs. This panic, in turn, will affect the judgment of the professors regarding the fact of overcrowding and persuade otherwise honorable teachers to stretch the truth a little in their recruiting programs.

Tryout cures truant. Forkner [162] has reported:

A specific case of a young lady in a mid-western high school illustrates a number of aspects of guidance that took place when the school and industry co-operated in helping her make decisions that would be suitable to her. We shall call her Mary.

Mary had reached her junior year in high school. She was unsettled about her future—in fact, she was unwilling even to discuss her plans with anyone. She had been a constant source of worry for the guidance office not only because she was frequently a truant but also because she was failing in her courses. She was attractive, intelligent, and self-possessed. She had informed her parents and the school counsellor that she was leaving school as soon as she reached her seventeenth birthday, since that was the age when she could legally withdraw.

As a last resort the counsellor asked her if she would rather be working than going to school. Mary replied that she certainly would.

In fact, it turned out that the failure to have money like her associates was one of the chief causes of her difficulties. The counsellor told her that she would not be able to get her a full-time job, but if she was willing to go to school regularly in the mornings she could take one of the work-experience jobs the school had in the afternoons. . . . Mary asked what kind of work it was and was informed that the school would try to find her a job in a department store. She was not very enthusiastic about store work, but agreed to try it.

The department store where Mary was placed had a personnel director who took her job seriously. She acted on the premise that her job was not to hire and fire, but rather to discover the potentialities of people and then capitalize on them for the benefit of the individual and the employer. After Mary had spent about a week behind the counter, the department head of the section in which Mary worked reported to the personnel director that the girl was impossible. She was discourteous to customers, she did not get along with the other girls in the section, and she was frequently late and away from her station. The personnel director called the school co-ordinator of the work-experience programme and asked her to come down for an interview about Mary.

After some discussion about her problem, they called Mary in for a talk. They told Mary that apparently she was not suited to the work of selling goods and to working with others, but that they would like to see if there was something in this large store that she would like to do. They proposed to Mary that she spend the next three days just walking through the store. She was to be free to talk to whomever she wished about their work. The store had among its service facilities a lunchroom, a dispensary where those who were ill were given temporary care; it had a large staff of office workers, change makers, a shipping and receiving department, an art and advertising-layout department, a claims department, and a personnel department. Mary was told a little about each department and then given a note by the personnel director to the effect that Mary was a student at the "X" High School who was making a survey of job opportunities for young high school graduates, and that it would be appreciated if each person to whom she talked gave her as much help as possible.

Mary was told to report back to the personnel director at any time that she found something that seemed to be of interest to her. About the end of the third day the head of the advertising and art department called the personnel director on the telephone and asked her to come up to his office. When the personnel director got there she found Mary and the department head talking, and she suspected the worst. But, on the contrary, the department head held up a large sketch which Mary had just completed of a dress the firm was getting ready to advertise in the papers over the weekend.

The sketch was done with flowing lines. There was decisiveness about her strokes. The details stood out in bold relief. The impression was striking. By its side, he held the sketch done by one of the girls who had been with the company for several years as a top artist. Mary's sketch was far more eye-catching and appealing.

Mary herself was aglow. At last she had something that she herself had discovered. No one had told her to be an artist. No one had told her that she ought to do this or that. She had made a remarkable discovery, too—that it was exciting to create something. She discovered for the first time that she had something that many others do not have—the ability to create.

Mary turned to the personnel director and asked her if it would be possible for her to redeem herself by working in the art department. Assured that she might do so, she asked if she might return to school, even though it was late, to see if she could find the work-experience co-ordinator and her counsellor and tell them the good news.

Mary finished her junior year and spent the senior year carrying four subjects in the morning and working every afternoon and on Saturday in the art department of the store. Her truancy ceased entirely. Her school marks put her on the honour roll for the last semester of the junior year and throughout her senior year. . . .

Upon the completion of Mary's high school work the store that helped her discover herself gave her a full-year scholarship with all expenses paid to attend one of the famous schools of fashion design. She is now one of the top designers in her field.

One-third of students have jobs. According to Hollis [221],

> In a recent survey . . . in one hundred nineteen public secondary schools . . . one-third of the pupils in these schools were gainfully employed while attending school. . . .
>
> No longer can we . . . say that placement and work experience are not factors in the educational program. We of the school system must be interested in job placement of our pupils.

Frustrations of the freshman employee. The following suggestions for young college graduates were prepared by Sam N. Wolk, Chief of the Career Service Division, U.S. Civil Service Commission. With only slight revision they could well be given to any person about to enter his first job, whether he be a retarded dropout, a brilliant young Ph.D., or a fledgling counselor.

THE FACTS OF LIFE

Graduation day is approaching. You'll soon begin your work career. Some of you may enter industry or commerce, others will gravitate toward government or education. No doubt all of you are intelligent and ambitious. You probably all will be full of enthusiasm and vigor as well when you first begin to work. Too soon, however, many of you will become disillusioned and discouraged because you expect more from your first job than any beginner has a right to expect.

Our civilization is characterized by bigness and complexity, and our organizations reflect that fact. If you have elected to start your career with an organization, prepare yourself to meet and deal with the frustrations of organizational life. These frustrations can be particularly irritating to one who is exposed to them for the first time. Here are some of the things any young man or woman should be mindful of if he or she wants to avoid the morass of disappointment and the pangs of ulcers.

1. Expect to encounter delays occasioned by channels of communication or chains of command. Organizational structure may seem cumbersome, but it serves a useful purpose. It prevents those at the top from being bogged down with details and frees them for the planning and directing job they're being paid to do.

2. Expect to attend seemingly interminable conferences and committee meetings. Boring many of them may be, and some may result in only a decision to hold another meeting. However, no other device has yet been invented which is a more efficient medium for communicating ideas and arriving at operationally sound decisions.

3. Expect to spend drab hours reading dull letters and memoranda composed by others while, at the same time, your sprightly prose is being blue-penciled by some idiot upstairs.

4. Don't expect to be formulating policy six months after you start work—you will be most unusual and successful if you're doing it six years from now. You'd really better plan on sixteen.

5. Don't lose sight of "the big picture." But, on the other hand, don't be so enamored of it that you neglect to master the details of your part of the canvas. To be blunt—learn your job and learn it well. You will never be of value to any organization otherwise.

6. Expect to.be assigned occasionally to tasks below your dignity and capabilities. When it happens don't become convinced that your talents are not appreciated. It's just that those jobs have to be done from time to time, and they historically have been assigned to "the new man."

7. Expect to have your suggestions for improvement turned down firmly and not always politely. Don't form the opinion that your superiors are bumbling idiots of no vision who reached their positions of eminence either through sordid conniving or through the grace of an otherwise intelligent God. They just possibly may know more and have better judgement than you think. They may also have learned through bitter experience that the sweeping changes you advocate might bring the organization to the brink of embarrassment, if not of disaster.

8. Develop a sensitivity to your supervisor and the organization. It is far easier to make adjustments than it is to re-shape people's attitudes or organizational inertia.

The points cited above are not written with any intent to frighten you away from an organizational career. They are mentioned only to alert you to their existence. Once you are aware of them, it will be easier for you to adjust to them, and put those minor trappings of the workaday world into proper perspective. Once you accept the fact that there are frustrations as well as satisfactions to be found in any job, you will be of more value to your organization and to yourself. Keeping that realization in mind will make your chances for success in your career considerably better.

Some ethical considerations.

A counselor should never encourage a person to enter or prepare for a specific occupation or field of work if the counselor has not recently inquired about the opportunities for employment.

A counselor should never rely upon his own impressions as a source of occupational information without verifying the accuracy of his impressions.

A counselor should never recommend a piece of occupational literature which the counselor has not examined for evidence of accuracy.

A counselor should never refer a person to a library for occupational information without warning him to examine the copyright dates of all publications before reading them.

A counselor should never refer a person to recruiting literature from employers, unions, educational institutions, military services, etc., without warning him that recruiting literature frequently exaggerates advantages and minimizes disadvantages.

Teen-agers and the quit-school dilemma. Bley [30] discussed this problem as follows:

> Teen-agers tussling with the quit-school dilemma in one California community can now talk things over with adults who once grappled with similar problems and then decided to drop out.
>
> These adults however are outstanding examples of drop-outs who returned to school, earned their diplomas and then made good in their chosen fields. While some are high school graduates, others have completed college. Several have even acquired advanced graduate degrees. These ex-drop-outs also represent a varied cross-section of occupational levels.
>
> In cooperation with the school, each of these adults meets informally with a potential drop-out. He encourages the youngster to talk about himself and his problems. In turn he describes his own related experiences, giving special emphasis to the reasons that prompted his return to school. In this way, he enables the youngster to understand what might be in store for him if he drops out. Through his own success, the adult also serves as a positive illustration of the values of finishing school.

Academic vs. vocational high schools.

The first results of a nationwide study are in. The American Institutes for Research . . . examined a cross section of vocational and academic graduates who have been out of school from two to eleven years. Some of the things they found:

Vocational grads usually get their first full-time job after high school in less than six weeks. . . . Academic grads take much longer. . . .

Academic grads who don't go to college have much less job security. . . . They also earn less. . . .

As for their general education, vocational grads do not appear to be at a disadvantage. A comparison between them and academic graduates without a college education shows no difference in leisure activities, affiliation with community organizations, or even conversational interests. *Changing Times* [141].

Occupational exploratory groups attract superior students. Fletcher [158] reported:

On an experimental basis last year, we asked for volunteers from about 1,200 first-quarter freshmen in the College of Arts and Sciences. About 200 volunteered. I'm not going into details of how we got the volunteers. We merely described the program to the freshmen. We told them we were going to form occupational exploratory groups on an experimental basis. We wanted only those to volunteer who were definitely interested in going through with the complete program. About 200 volunteered. We wanted about 70 to form six groups of twelve each. We narrowed the 200 down by putting up certain barriers of coming to special meetings, etc., so we would get the most highly motivated of them in the group. We carried the program through for one quarter and got some interesting results from it. The main thing I want to point out here is the nature of the group that volunteered. They were the best students. Almost all of them were above the 50%ile on the Ohio State Psychological Examination. Twenty-five percent of them were above the 90%ile. Only a handful were below the 50%ile. Furthermore, those who were in the lower percentiles tended to drop out of the program during the first few weeks, apparently because the groups were too high level for them. They seemed rather frightened. The higher ability students were talking above their level and about things that apparently did not interest them. That result is important because in counseling I think all of us worry and we should worry, about the fact that we tend to concentrate on the poorer students too much. I'm not saying that we should not deal with the poorer students and the problem cases, but when you look at the total point of view of returns to society, it is the good people who can really return things to society if they get in the right area and are properly adjusted. We tend to neglect them from the counseling standpoint. I am inclined to feel that the group approach may be the only way of getting at the better students. We all know that forcing guidance and counseling upon individuals is not a very satisfactory technique. Counseling should be voluntary to get the best results. Well, here is one way, one of the few ways I know of, of apparently attracting the higher level people into a guidance situation.

Tryouts for stenographers and typists. An unusual opportunity for realistic job exploration is provided for stenographers and typists by some of the specialized employment agencies that are listed in the larger classified telephone directories under the heading of "Office Help—Temporary." During a summer vacation a stenographer may be employed for periods that vary from a few days to a few weeks in several different jobs with several different employers, to whom she may be referred by such an agency.

Helping the handicapped. The vocational guidance of the physically, mentally, and emotionally handicapped worker is a specialized field in which the beginning counselor will do well to seek expert assistance. If you are trying to help a handicapped person, write to the U.S. Vocational Rehabilitation Administration, Washington, for the name and address of the vocational rehabilitation office that serves the area in which your client lives, then write to this office and ask it what kinds of help it can provide for you and your client. If your client is a veteran, send a similar letter to the Veterans Administration, Washington. Specialized services are provided by voluntary associations and government agencies that have been formed to help persons with a specific handicap, for example, local tuberculosis and health associations, state commissions for the blind, for crippled children, etc. The names and addresses of such organizations can be found with the help of your local or state council of social agencies or department of public welfare or with the help of directories available at your local or state library. Try also the classified telephone directory.

Do not ask a physician who has not specialized in vocational rehabilitation to decide whether or not your client can safely enter a specific occupation. Physicians know little more about the physical demands of most occupations than do other laymen. If you must use the services of such a physician, be sure that you first determine the physical demands of the job, give a list of these physical demands to the physician, and then ask him to determine whether or not your client can meet them. Information about the physical demands of a specific job can best be obtained from local employers and employees engaged in the occupation;

more general information can be obtained from the *Dictionary of Occupational Titles* [123], the United States Employment Service, and the United States Civil Service Commission, Washington. (See Appendix O, "Using Occupational Information with the Handicapped.")

Situation wanted. Bley [30] reported that

In Independence, businessmen financed five full pages of unusual want-ads in the local newspaper. These ads appearing in a Sunday edition late in May were headed: "Can you employ one or more of these students? The Reporter with splendid cooperation from the business firms of Independence prints here a complete employment section. Listed on these pages are young men and women who would like to have work in Independence."

Seventy-eight separate want-ads were featured. Each was 4" by 5" and contained a good-sized photograph of the applicant, his name, school and a brief description of his training and special interests. One ad for a girl read: "Will not attend college. Would like permanent work in Independence. Majored in typing. Prefers office work." An ad for a boy ran: "Plans to attend Junior College. Would like summer and part-time work next fall. Majored in metal work. Would prefer outside work."

The name of the sponsoring business firm appeared at the bottom of the ad. Sponsors included dairies, florists, hotels, theatres, auto suppliers, hardware and paint stores, farm equipment, insurance, construction and lumber companies.

Readers interested in hiring any of these 78 youngsters were urged to contact the school or the Independence office of the Kansas State Employment Service.

Guides to good referrals. The following list is taken from *How to Make Referrals* [241]:

1. Check to see if the school has used all its own available resources in helping the student before looking outside the school for help. Perhaps there are other steps which should be taken before referring the student to an outside agency or specialist.

2. Try discussing an incipient problem with an agency or specialist before its referral is urgent. Many agencies are willing to work in cooperation with the school in the area of prevention.

3. Try to discover what persons have had contact with the parent or student in regard to the problem, and what results were obtained from these contacts before making a referral. A case conference may result in the early and appropriate use of resources in the school and community, and will also serve to bring together information about the student in usable form, and to coordinate the efforts of the total school. Let your right hand know what your left hand is doing.

4. Designate one person to be responsible in working with the

parent and student in developing a referral. All others will then keep that person informed of new developments.

5. Learn whether a community agency is already working with the family, for a consultation with that agency is the proper first step in considering a referral in such cases.

6. It is unwise and impractical to refer a student to community agencies without the knowledge, consent, and cooperation of his parents. Many child guidance agencies will not accept students for treatments unless parents cooperate fully and are willing to present themselves for help, too. Check on the policy of your local agencies in this regard.

7. Keep in mind when telling students or parents about available services, in the school or in the community, that the teacher should explain both the functions and the limitations of these services. Do not give the impression that any specialist or agency has all the answers and can work wonders.

8. Do not coach a student or parent regarding how they might "wangle" hard-to-get services. Such "coaching" is not professional.

9. Let the student or his parents make their own arrangements for service whenever possible. Do not "spoon feed" the student by being more "helpful" than necessary.

10. Remember that in some cases, however, help may be needed by very immature, dependent, or ill students or parents in arranging an appointment or even in arranging transportation to the agency.

11. Secure a signed consent from the student's parents before releasing information to a social agency. This is a wise precaution in most cases.

12. Help the agency or specialist by indicating which person should be the point of contact representing the school. This person will supply additional information as needed, and will receive agency reports which he in turn will share, as seems indicated, with others on the school staff.

13. Call attention of the specialists within the school system to students who seem to need their help the most. This may not be thought of as a referral, but rather as a way of helping the specialists use their energies in the proper directions.

14. A school can expect a report from a referral agency regarding its general plans for working with a case. A school cannot expect to know the details of treatment, nor to share in confidences given by parents or students to agency personnel.

15. Share information about the student with the new service working with him, but do not violate the confidence of the student except under very unusual circumstances. In passing along information, distinguish between professional sharing of information and gossip. Facts, not your evaluation of facts, will usually be most valuable.

16. All agencies, public or private, have their own eligibility requirements and accepted procedures. Do not expect them to suspend rules for you.

17. Expect to be asked to work cooperatively with the specialist or agency during the treatment period. In some cases this will be an important part of the treatment.

18. *Respect the individual!* The basic attitude in the referrals, as in all counseling, is a fundametnal respect for the individual and a fundamental belief that it is best for him to work out his own problems in his own way. Schools and agencies are helpers in this process, not directors.

19. Get acquainted with the people working in community agencies in your area. There is no substitute for personal respect and friendship in building smooth and effective school-community cooperation. Try inviting them to a faculty meeting to tell of their service and to meet the staff. Visit them at the agency to get the "feel" of their service.

20. Remember that a parent's great emotional involvement with his child may make it difficult for him to recognize that a problem exists.

21. Do not expect immediate help for particular symptoms. Usually basic attitudes and feelings are involved in behavior, and these attitudes and feelings may change very slowly. Do not expect miracles to be worked on cases you refer.

The tyranny of words. According to Grunes [195],

Another striking class difference exists in the meaning of the word "engineer," which is usually interpreted as referring to a professional by the higher status groups, and as a skilled mechanical worker by the lower.

The counselor unaware of such class differences may have difficulty communicating with members of other classes than his own. . . .

If, instead of the usual questions about what he wants to be, we ask, in turn, for the student's "dream job," the job he is "really trying for," and the job he "expects to get," we can begin to see which job to counsel him about, for we force him to think realistically. When we used these questions, we found that white collar dreams are far more comon than white collar expectations.

Suggestions on choosing a career. To students beginning a course in occupations:

Within a few months or years, you will be earning your own living. You will be working several hours a day at something you either like or dislike, at something that is either easy or hard for you to do, at something that you do well or do poorly.

You will be happy and contented or miserable and frustrated or somewhere in between. Which you will be will depend partly on the kind of person you are and partly on the job you hold. The job you get will depend partly on luck, partly on whom you know, partly on your training and experience and other qualifications, and partly on how wisely you choose and seek the kind of job you want.

This course will not do much to change the kind of person you are; it will not do much to change your luck or the persons you know or your qualifications for a job. This course may help you to choose an occupation in which you will have a good chance to find a job that you can do well and that you will enjoy doing. No one can guarantee your success and happiness, but you can do much to contribute to them if you do a good job of choosing the area in which you will look for work.

As you acquire information about occupations in which you might find employment, as you think about which occupations offer the best prospects for you, you may find it useful to consider some of the following suggestions:

Do not expect to find a job in which you will never have to do anything that you dislike.

Do not stay permanently in a job in which you dislike most of the things you have to do.

Choose an occupation because you like the work, not because of the rewards in money or prestige.

Do not choose an occupation because you admire someone else who chose it.

Choose an occupation that will use the abilities you possess.

Avoid occupations that require abilities you do not possess.

Do not confuse interest and ability. You may have one without the other.

Choose an occupation in which there is likely to be an active demand for workers when you are ready to go to work.

Before making a final choice of an occupation, find out what are all the things you might have to do in it. Find out which of these will take most of your time.

Beware of recruiters. They may tell you only part of the story.

Beware of biased information from other sources.

Take all the advice that is offered; then act on your own judgment.

Characteristics of a good occupation. The best occupation for any person is, of course, the occupation which best fits his needs and his abilities, the occupation which offers him the most of what he wants and to which he can offer the most of what it demands. There are, however, certain characteristics of occupations which are so generally regarded as desirable that most persons will wish to consider them when choosing an occupation. Among these are the following:

A large number of vacancies at all times. This is desirable in order to provide good prospects for initial employment and for reemployment in case one's employer goes out of business. The number of vacancies that occur in any occupation is determined more by the size of the occupation than by any other factor, including growth. Other things being equal, therefore, the larger the occupation, the better.

Stability of employment. As noted in Chapter 1, employment in some occupations is chronically irregular; in others it is almost always continuous during satisfactory performance. Other things being equal, the more steady the job, the better.

Growth. At first glance, stability and growth may appear to be contradictory. Sometimes they are. The most rapid growth frequently occurs in the least stable industries, such as the manufacture of aircraft, which depends mainly upon military appropriations. In contrast is air transportation, which has shown remarkably consistent growth in both depression and prosperity and thus has offered continuity of employment plus growth. A growing industry has a continually increasing demand for new employees, who must have new supervisors who are usually chosen from older employees. Thus growth means more opportunities for advancement. Other things being equal, the more rapidly an occupation is growing, the better, provided this growth is not periodically followed by sharp declines in employment.

Safety. Some persons relish danger. Most persons do not. Some occupations have abnormally high accident rates. Some are plagued by occupational diseases. Other things being equal, the safer the occupation, the better.

Normal hours. Some persons like irregular or unusual hours. Most persons do not. Most of us have a life outside the job as well as in. Irregular or unusual or extra long hours interfere with family and other social life. Parents see less of their children. Girls see less of their boy friends. Other things being equal, the more normal the hours, the better.

Average or better earnings. Some occupations have been underpaid for decades and appear likely to continue so. Money isn't everything, but the author knows of only one person who ever chose a job *because* it was underpaid. It is, of course, true that some worthwhile apprenticeships require a financial sacrifice at the beginning, but many other low-paid jobs offer no better prospects for advancement than jobs that pay better. Other things being equal, the more the job pays, the better.

Earnings increase with age. Occupations differ greatly in the effect of age upon earnings. Professional athletes and actresses frequently earn less in their advancing years. Public school teachers almost invariably earn more. Someone once defined an adequate standard of living as "fifteen percent more than you have now." The person whose income is moving in this direction is more likely to feel satisfied with his job than the person whose income is declining. Other things being equal, the better occupation provides a reasonably good prospect of a steadily increasing income.

appendix **K**
The
Influence of
Automation on
Occupational
Guidance[1]

Is automation the greatest blessing or the worst calamity ever to befall the human race? Either way, what should a good American high school do about it? Specifically, how will automation affect the guidance program?

Will we discard all vocational and professional education on the ground that there will be no jobs?

Will we discard all educational and vocational guidance and send everyone to the liberal arts college to prepare for a life of leisure?

Will we still have jobs, but will they change so rapidly that no one can any longer anticipate and prepare for a career?

John Snyder, co-chairman of the Foundation on Automation and Employment, Inc., says that "automation is a major factor in the elimination of 40,000 jobs per week." He believes that "we face a national catastrophe that will make the Great Depression of the 1930s seem like a humorous anecdote."

On the other hand, the United States Bureau of Labor Statistics reports that our rate of unemployment in 1964 was slightly lower than in 1954. If the catastrophe of mass unemployment is coming, it has not yet arrived.[2]

There are, unquestionably, individual catastrophes in the lives of adults who have been displaced. There is hardship and bitterness among non-white, teenage boys, whose unemployment rate is four or five times the national average. There will be frustration and anxiety among high school and college graduates if we encourage

---

[1] This appendix appeared first as an article in *The High School Journal*, February, 1966. It is reprinted here by the kind permisison of the Journal.
[2] There will certainly be another recession or depression someday. When it comes, unemployment will rise and automation will be blamed. Before jumping to conclusions about causes, we may get nearer the truth if we will compare rates of unemployment with what they were in the depression of the thirties, before anyone had heard of automation. At that time, we were blaming "modern technology," the technology which subsequently helped to give us the longest and greatest period of prosperity in our history.

them to prepare for occupations in which there will be no jobs for them.

In the face of this mixture of certainty and uncertainty, what can the high school do to prepare its students for the unpredictable occupational world of the future?

We can do nine things.

I

We can recognize that the future is not wholly unpredictable, and we can stop talking as if it were. In some areas we can make some reasonably good estimates. When we know how many children were born in 1965, we can predict about how many teachers we will need to staff the elementary and high schools from 1970 to 1982. When we know how many freshmen are in our colleges, we can predict a surplus or a shortage of teachers four years hence. Our estimates will not be perfect, but they will be far better than the naive expectations of uninformed high school and college students.

As high school administrators, teachers, librarians and counselors we can purchase and circulate an adequate number of copies of the *Occupational Outlook Handbook,* replace them each time a new edition appears, and make sure that our students and their parents see them and use them.

II

We can reassure ourselves and our students that there will still be *some* life careers open to the person who will choose carefully, considering both his abilities and the probable supply and demand for workers at the time when he will enter the labor market.

Does anyone seriously believe that fifty years from now there will no longer be any policemen, firemen, barbers, beauty operators, cooks, gardeners, photographers, letter carriers, jewelers, salesmen, inn keepers, waiters, plumbers, carpenters, electricians, dietitians, nurses, hospital administrators, chemists, physicists, engineers, librarians, statisticians, sociologists, architects, accountants, meteorologists, surgeons, foresters, lawyers, tax collectors, politicians, teachers, or high school principals?

III

We can give more attention to stability of employment as a consideration in educational and occupational planning. In the past we have sometimes acted as if stability were of no consequence, or as if it were the same for all occupations, and we have often ignored it in counseling.

Automation has made us more aware of the risk of unemployment. Now we can, and perhaps will, do what we should have done before, that is, inform ourselves and our students of the relative stability of employment in the occupations that they are considering.

The student who is about to prepare for an occupation in which he may be frequently or permanently unemployed should be aware of the risks he is taking. The student who wants a steady job in a stable organization can find it with our help, if we do our job.

IV

We can make an annual follow-up study of all our former students who graduated or dropped out during the past year. We can find out what kinds of jobs they were able to get in spite of automation. We can ask them to tell us their observations of the effects of automation on them, in their search for work and in their present jobs. We can ask them what they have learned of the probable future effects of automation on employment in the places where they work.

We will not interpret their reports as the final pronouncements of experts, but we may get some leads that will merit further exploration. And we will learn more than we know now about how automation affects *our* students.

V

We can make similar follow-up studies, five and ten years after high school graduation, of those who go on to college and graduate school. Thus we can learn how automation has affected these alumni; and how it may affect our present students who are now choosing colleges to prepare them for the occupations which they confidently expect to enter.

VI

We can consult the executive secretary of the local chamber of commerce, the president of the central labor council for the city, and the local manager of the state employment service.

We can ask each of these persons to tell us what he has observed of the effects of automation on employment in the local industries in which most of our students will seek their first jobs. We can ask what other effects of automation these persons anticipate. And we can ask them to suggest other persons whom we might consult for further information.

Among these other persons may be individual employers in automated industries, officers of local unions whose members have been affected, and occupational analysts in the state employment service. We can ask each of these persons to suggest others, and we can pursue this inquiry as far and as long as the results appear to justify the effort.

VII

We can prepare and distribute two reports of what we have learned.

A detailed report can be filed in the principal's office, in the school library, and in the guidance office. This report can be cross indexed by occupations and industries in the school file of occupational information.

A brief, *readable* summary report can be duplicated and widely distributed to the entire school staff—administrators, teachers, counselors, librarians, attendance officers, social workers, psychologists, coaches, custodians, and bus drivers—each of whom is sometimes approached by students who seek information, and each of whom may make offhand comments that influence pupils. The summary report can be distributed also to all high school students and their parents and to local newspapers.

If either report includes statements about specific local employers, or quotes the statements of individual resource persons, the report may be shown to them for the correction of any inaccuracies before it is duplicated. Somewhere in each report we can put an index of all occupations and industries discussed in the report, with appropriate page references. In each report we can mention the other and tell how copies of it may be obtained.

We can arrange a conference of the teachers of all the courses in which either report might be used as an assigned reading or reference, or discussed in class. In this meeting we can provide for appropriate classroom coverage without undesirable duplication. Included in this conference may be the teachers of courses in occupations, senior problems, college planning, social studies, industrial arts, business and vocational education; also the curriculum director, the director of audio-visual materials, the librarian, and the counselors.

VIII

We can make all of these research activities a part of our annual school program, for the data collected this year will be out of date a year later. If a complete repetition seems unnecessary, we can at least telephone our principal sources of information, inquire what changes have occurred since last year, and then decide how much updating needs to be done.

IX

We can adjust the occupational guidance of our terminal students to what we learn about the effects of automation on employment in the local industries in which most of them will look for work. We can adjust the educational guidance of our college preparatory students to what we learn about the effects of automation on employment in the broader geographical area in which they will look for work.

Our follow-up studies of both groups of students will indicate the industries and the locations with which we will be most concerned. Although some high school graduates move far away, most of them begin their careers in or near their home towns and many remain there. Although some college graduates journey to the ends of the earth, far more of them remain within five hundred miles of their home towns.

We have all been a little too readily frightened by the alarming reports of what automation has done to jobs in the industries that have been most affected. Sometimes we have not paused long enough to reflect, and to ask how many of our former students have ever sought work in those industries.

The nation as a whole must be concerned about what happens to all of its people. But the individual high school must be far more concerned about what happens to its students. What is important to the high school in Lambertville, New Jersey, is what automation is doing to jobs in Lambertville, and across the river in New Hope, and in nearby Trenton, rather than what automation is doing to jobs in Detroit, Des Moines, or Dallas.

Suggestions for Opening a Counseling Interview

1. Listen. Let the other person tell you whatever he wants to tell you. If he asked for the interview, let him open it. Let him direct the course of the conversation. At this point do *not* ask questions.

2. Try to understand how all this looks to him. In your own words, summarize what he has told you, including the feelings he has expressed. In this way help him to tell his story.

3. If he has a problem, restate the problem as he sees it.

4. If he wants help from you, restate in your own words what he has said he wants you to do.

5. Revise your restatements until he agrees that you now understand

> His problem as he sees it
> How he feels about it
> What he wants you to do

At this point, ask questions if you need to.

6. Find out what he has done already in his own efforts to solve his own problem.

7. If you can do what he wants, and there is no good reason for not doing it, do it.

8. If you cannot do all that he wants, tell him what you can and cannot do.

9. Let him accept or reject your services.

10. Do what you can to help him in the way that he wants to be helped.

11. When you have done this, and not before, offer any additional services that you wish to offer, and let him accept or reject them.

appendix **M**

Assignments
for Observers
of Interviews

Below are several sets of questions. One set will be assigned to you. Please watch the interview carefully. Look for the answers to your questions.

One purpose of this experience is to help you to become more aware of, and more sensitive to, the things that can help or hinder you in achieving your purposes in any interview that you conduct. Another purpose is to help the interviewer.

At the end of each interview we will discuss these two questions: What did the counselor do that you liked? What would you have done differently?

We will depend on you for any appropriate comments related to the specific parts of the interview that you were asked to observe. We will not ask you for all of your observations. We will ask what you liked and what you would have done differently.

In your comments on the interview, please do not say, "He should not have done that" or "He should have done this." Instead, please say, "I think I would have done it this way."

Part I

General Questions

1. How did the counselor open the interview? How did he close it? What effect did his action at these points have on the client? Did the counselor structure the interview? Did he set any limits on what the client might say or do? Was the counselor flexible in changing his plans and his behavior as the situation changed?

2. Were these two persons trying to help each other, or were they opposing each other? Was either of them maneuvering for a favorable position? Was either of them on the defensive? Did either one try to put the other on the defensive? Did either one do anything that helped

the other to avoid feeling defensive? Did either one try to hold off the other, keep him at a distance, set up a barrier between them?

3. What kind of relationship did the counselor try to establish in this interview? Did the relationship improve or deteriorate during the interview? Did the atmosphere of the interview change at any point? Did it become more or less comfortable or strained? Why?

4. What feelings could you detect in the client? What feelings did he express in words, in tone of voice, in facial expression, in any other way? Did the counselor sense these feelings? How did he respond to them?

5. What feelings could you detect in the counselor? What feelings did he express in words, in tone of voice, in facial expression, in any other way? Did the client sense these feelings? How did he respond to them? Was the client's response the kind of response that the counselor wanted? Was it the kind of response you would have wanted if you had been the counselor?

6. If you had been the client, how would you have felt during this interview?

Comfortable?	Cooperative?
Anxious?	Resistant?
Relaxed?	Friendly?
Tense?	Belligerent?
Eager?	Soothed?
Apprehensive?	Irritated?

What would have made you feel this way?

7. Did the counselor try to satisfy the needs of the client or the needs of the counselor? How much time did the counselor give to helping the client to discover and to satisfy the client's needs? Was the counselor sensitive to the client's reactions? Did the counselor notice them, respond to them, or ignore them?

8. Did the client express himself freely? Did he seem to feel free to do so? Or was he afraid to do so? If you were the client, would you have felt free to do so in this interview? Why? Why not? Did the counselor interrupt or cut off the client at any time? Was this desirable or not?

9. Did the counselor make the client feel relaxed and comfortable? How did he do it? Did he overdo it? Did he say anything that was not quite true? Did the client sense this? Will the client discover the falsehood later and resent it?

10. Was the counselor relaxed? Comfortable? Tense? Nervous? Fearful? Why? Were his feelings apparent to the client? How did the client react to them? Could the counselor do anything to make himself more comfortable? What?

11. Was the counselor solicitous, protective, or paternal? Would you have been more or less so?

12. How often did the counselor direct the course of the conversation? How often did he follow the lead of his client? Please count the responses that fall in each of these two categories. Ignore responses which you cannot put in either category.

13. Did the counselor really listen? Did he really try to understand what the client said and how the client felt? Or was he impatiently waiting for the client to stop talking so the counselor could express himself? Did the client sense the counselor's feelings and respond to them better than the counselor sensed and responded to the client's feelings?

14. Did the counselor permit or encourage the client to interrupt him in order to ask questions or to react to the counselor's comments; or did the counselor tend to lecture without interruption? If you had been the client, how would you have responded to the counselor's behavior?

15. Did the counselor reveal any expectations on how the client would or should respond? Was the counselor looking for conformity, independence, resistance, action, submission, gratitude, anything else? Did he get what he was looking for? How did the counselor's expectations affect the client's behavior?

16. Did the counselor feel any hostility? Did he reveal it? Did the client detect it? How did the client react to it?

17. Did the client feel any hostility? Did he reveal it? Did the counselor detect it? How did the counselor react to it?

18. Did the counselor try to sell anything? Did he succeed? Did he reveal any bias? Did he operate in the framework of his own values or of his client's? Did the counselor respect the right of the client to be himself?

19. Did the counselor want to be fair? Did the client know how the counselor felt? How were the counselor's feelings expressed? Did the counselor reveal his ability or inability to keep confidences?

20. Did the counselor express himself clearly? Did he use words that the client might not understand? If so, was this necessary? Did he explain them? Did the client really comprehend what the counselor said? Was the counselor intentionally vague?

21. Did the counselor take any notes or record any information during the interview? How did the client react to this? How would you have reacted to it?

22. Did the counselor present any information? Was it accurate? Are you sure? Was he sure? Was the client ready for it? How did the client react to it?

23. Did the counselor use any written or printed documents, or any other materials? Would you have used the same, or more, or fewer, or others?

24. Did the counselor offer any appraisal of the client? If so, was the appraisal well documented? Was it fair? Did it reflect the values of the counselor? Was it presented at the best time? Was the client ready for it? How did the client react to it? Did the client have sufficient opportunity to appraise himself before the counselor appraised the client?

25. Who did most of the talking? The counselor? Or the client? Try to keep an approximate record of the number of seconds and minutes that each one speaks. Would you have talked more or less?

26. Did these two agree on any future action? On anything else? Was the agreement genuine? Was it a comfortable agreement for both? Was it a compromise acceptable to both? Was it imposed by one on the other? Was it resented by either? Will it strengthen their future relationship? Will it be a source of future irritation?

Part II

Questions Relating to Occupational Information

27. Did the client seek help in judging the appropriateness of a tentative occupational choice? If so, did the counselor help the client to examine all pertinent aspects of the occupation? Did the counselor or the client use a checklist? What important considerations were not considered?

28. Did the counselor overestimate the client's ability to solve his own problem? Did the counselor assume that the client can choose an occupation wisely without adequate occupational information? Did the counselor adequately protect the client from obsolete, biased, glamorous, or otherwise misleading occupational information?

29. When the counselor was asked for information that he did not have, how did he respond? Was he embarrassed? Did he parry the question? Did he ignore it? Did he offer his own vague or casual impressions of the occupation in lieu of specific factual material from a good source? Did he offer to get the information? Did he offer to go with the client to the best available sources of the desired information and help him to get it?

30. Did the counselor refer the client to any other source of occupational information? Was it a good referral? To a good source? Will the client be able to use this source effectively without help? Did the counselor offer to help?

31. Did the counselor approve or disapprove of the client's occupational choice? If so, did the counselor have adequate basis for judgment?

32. Will this client have a hard time finding the kind of job he wants? Was the supply and demand for workers discussed? As of today? As of the time when this client will look for work? Did the counselor have the facts? Was the probable future expansion or contraction of employment in this occupation considered?

33. Did the counselor find out how much the client knew about the real nature of the work? Did their discussion include both the pleasant and unpleasant aspects of the work? Did it get down to the realistic details? Is the environment in which this work is done likely to affect the worker's health or satisfaction? Were the pertinent facts considered?

34. Were all important qualifications reviewed? Age? Sex? Height? Weight? Vision? Color blindness? Hearing? Dexterity? Skill? Aptitudes? Tools? License? Union membership? Discrimination?

35. In discussing preparation, did the counselor distinguish between what is desirable and what is indispensable? Were certification requirements considered? Were employers' standards? Were apprenticeship and other kinds of training on the job reviewed? Was the distinction between accredited and nonaccredited schools explained? Was the client warned of gyp schools?

36. Did the client know how people get jobs in this field? Should he? Are the client's expectations of advancement realistic? Does he know what proportion of workers advance and to what?

37. What did the counselor say about earnings? Did he give unwise emphasis to the highest or lowest earnings? Did he give some indication of average earnings? Did he state the source of his information? Was it a good source?

38. Is this a large or a small occupation? Are jobs available everywhere, or is the worker geographically restricted? Should these topics have been discussed? Were they?

39. Should any of these topics have been discussed? Were they? Hours? Stability of employment? Effect of age on earnings? Hazards?

40. Did the client know what workers in this occupation like and dislike about it? Should he? Did the counselor? Should he?

appendix **N**

Report on
Observation
of a
Counseling
Interview

How well do you think the counselor did each of the following? Grade each item A, B, or C. Did the counselor:

1. Listen? Let the client talk? Help him to state his problem as he saw it?

2. Restate what the client wanted the counselor to do, and revise this restatement as often as necessary until the client agreed that this was what he wanted?

3. Find out what the client had already done in his own efforts to solve his own problem?

4. Tell the client what the counselor could and could not do? (If he could not do all that the client wanted.)

5. Let the client accept or reject the services which the counselor could provide?

6. Do what he could for the client?

1_____

2_____

3_____

4_____

5_____

6_____

What do you think the counselor did well?

What would you have done differently?

What questions would you like to raise for group discussion?

appendix **O**

Using Occupational Information with the Handicapped[1]

by Daniel Sinick

Knowledge of the world of work is often especially important for students and clients with disabilities. The mentally retarded, the blind and partially seeing, the deaf and hard-of-hearing, the orthopedic, and cardiac have typically been deprived of the fairly constant contact normally experienced with work and workers. This deprivation results from reduced mobility, sensory or mental impairment, or prolonged medical treatment. Specific ways teachers and counselors can enhance the handicapped's familiarity with occupational information are suggested in this article.

Two basic points should first be made. One is that occupational information is only in part occupational literature; the printed word must be transcended and supplemented in every way possible. The other point is that the same principles and practices generally employed with the non-handicapped are applicable to the handicapped. Certain selected emphases on content, however, seem desirable, as well as selection or adaptation of particular methods.

Content emphases that apply broadly to variously disabled individuals—because of their circumscribed contact with life—include knowledge of work in general, of the workaday community (including transportation to places of employment), of job-finding techniques, and of job interview skills in particular.

Among methods of general value are those which provide personal knowledge of work and work situations: not only visits to places of work but actual employment, whether paid or unpaid, in the school or in the community. This can be accomplished through a work experience program or through part-time, temporary, or volunteer work. Methods that bring workers into the school are also useful: career speakers might include "handicapped" as well as non-handicapped alumni, and educational television might be adapted to this

[1] Revised and reprinted from the *Vocational Guidance Quarterly*, Summer, 1964, pages 275–277, by permission of the author and publisher.

general purpose. Toward job-hunt knowhow, practice is needed in obtaining and pursuing job leads, while role playing provides practice in the conduct of job interviews.

The Physically Handicapped

For the physically handicapped, two additional emphases on content suggest themselves. One has to do with physical requirements of occupations. These must be regarded imaginatively, however, and not narrowly or superficially; strict adherence to the findings of job analysis would rule out occupations actually engaged in by severely disabled individuals. Another natural area of emphasis, because of hiring difficulties encountered, is that of self-employment opportunities. A teaching and counseling aid in the first area is the *Dictionary of Occupational Titles*, prepared by the United States Department of Labor; excellent self-employment information is available from the Small Business Administration, Washington, D.C.

Additional methods in using occupational information with the visually handicapped include records and tape recordings, optical aids, large-print materials, brailled materials, special chalk and chalkboards, and persons to serve as readers. Recordings and other materials may be either purchased or prepared.

Three general sources of materials and related information are: American Foundation for the Blind, 15 W. 16 St., New York; American Printing House for the Blind, 1839 Frankfort Ave., Louisville, Ky.; and National Society for the Prevention of Blindness, 1790 Broadway, New York. Large-print materials are easily prepared with large-type typewriters, available from most manufacturers. An example of preparation of other materials is the taping of a suitable radio program for later playback.

For the hearing impaired, methods involving visual aids are especially appropriate. Such techniques as demonstrations, charts, pictures, and posters can achieve significance without sound. Also effective are *captioned* slides, filmstrips, and films. Captions can be separately prepared, then coordinated with the presentation, a procedure equally applicable to educational television. A useful device in dealing with the deaf or deafened is an overhead projector, which allows the teacher to present material visually while facing the class, thus maximizing the opportunity for lip-reading (better called speechreading).

The orthopedic, the cardiac, and others with neuromuscular or circulatory limitations, can profit from teachers' or counselors' use of opaque projectors, adjustable reading stands, automatic page turners, and home-to-school telephone. Books, pamphlets, and magazines are inserted directly into an opaque projector for ready reading. Reading is facilitated as well by inexpensive stands that hold material in any position desired; electrically operated page turners, while rather expensive, serve to expedite reading. For the homebound, a telephonic system can be installed for the communication of occupational and other information.

The Mentally Retarded

As for the mentally retarded, a number of content areas and methods need emphasis. Occupations requiring broadest coverage are at the service, semi-skilled, and unskilled levels, where the retarded find most of their jobs. Toward finding jobs, these students and clients need practice in using the telephone and completing application blanks. Telephone use includes the directory, dialing, and the etiquette of telephone talk.

Application blanks obtainable from employers for practice are normally expected to be completed by job applicants themselves, whereas friends and relatives may help with letters of application. To hold their jobs, the retarded require particular attention to work attitudes, habits, and standards; they must recognize the importance of co-operativeness, persistence, punctuality, and work quality.

Methods with the mentally retarded, who have been characterized as "here-and-now persons," are best geared toward immediate and tangible learning outcomes. Concrete materials and activities, when accompanied by demonstration, extra repetition, and drill, can be effective. Special occupational materials are needed at a reduced reading level, in regard to both vocabulary and conceptual content.

A few such materials are currently available [1–4].[2] Pictures, slides, filmstrips, and films are useful, films more so when run at a slower pace. Of two suitable sets of filmstrips now available, one [6] was designed specifically for older mentally retarded pupils, and the other [5] for the upper elementary and junior high grades.

In summary, this article has suggested content areas and methods requiring emphasis in teachers' and counselors' use of occupational information with the physically handicapped and mentally retarded. These students and clients need added exposure to the realities of jobs and work situations, if their typical under-exposure to such realities is not to develop into blurred vocational plans.

REFERENCES

1. Carson, Esther. *Teen-agers prepare for work.* Books I and II. Castro Valley, Calif. (18623 Lake Chabot Road): Author, 1960.

2. Goldberg, H. R., & Brumber, Winifred T. (Eds.) *Rochester occupational reading series.* Chicago: Science Research Associates, 1961.

3. *Handbook for the custodian's assistant.* Hayward, Calif. (224 West Winton Ave.): Hayward Union High School District, 1961.

4. Lifton, W. *What could I be?* Chicago: Science Research Associates, 1960.

5. Lifton, W. *Foundations for occupational planning.* Chicago (1345 Diversey Parkway): Society for Visual Education, no date.

6. *Occupational education.* Jamaica, New York (146–01 Archer Ave.): Eye Gate House, no date.

---

[2] In this appendix, numbers in brackets refer to references at the end of this appendix.

appendix **Y**

Lesson Plans
for a
Graduate
Course in
Occupations for
Counselors[1]

Most of the lesson plans in this appendix include assignments which are intended to be announced to the students in advance of the sessions in which the lesson plans are to be used.

In the lesson plans the assignments are first identified by numbers. The numbers refer to numbered items in Appendix Z, in which all the assignments are reproduced. The purpose of this arrangement is to make it convenient for the instructor to make his assignments by number and for the students to find the assignments easily by referring each time to the same appendix.

In nearly all cases, the assignments are also printed in full with the lesson plans, so that the instructor need not refer to Appendix Z. There are a few exceptions in cases where the assignments are unusually long. Such exceptions are noted in the lesson plans.

[1] For related discussion see Chap. 24.

Lesson plan 1   Getting acquainted

Purpose. Even at colleges where it is traditional for everyone to speak to everyone else, there are shy students who will not go beyond a simple hello without some encouragement. In large summer sessions and in urban universities, students have been known to sit through an entire course without ever speaking to the students in adjoining seats. The timid souls sometimes welcome a little help in getting acquainted.

The students who do talk freely with everyone sometimes report that they learn as much from each other as from the instructor. Most instructors probably wish to encourage such learning. Helping students to become acquainted is one way of encouraging it. Students sometimes feel more comfortable with an instructor whom they know something about. The purpose of this plan is to help students to become better acquainted with one another and with the instructor.

Procedure. There are several ways of breaking the ice. The frequently employed practice of asking each student to introduce himself to the group is probably the least desirable. It embarrasses the shy student, and it does little to start conversation.

Perhaps the simplest and quickest way to start students talking is to say to the group, "Will you please reach over and shake hands with the persons on each side of you and in front and in back of you. Tell them your name, your nickname, where you come from, what you do, and why you are here." In the author's classes this usually starts the group buzzing even before the instructor finishes speaking. Conversation continues until interrupted by the instructor's calling the group to order and inquiring, "Does anyone object if I now pronounce you all properly introduced to everyone else in the class?" To date no one has objected.

Another method is to ask the class to suggest what they would like to know about each other, list the suggested items on the board, then ask them to converse until each person is prepared to introduce to the class the person in the next higher numbered seat. When all are ready, the introductions are performed. Students seem to find it less embarrassing to introduce others than to introduce themselves. This method may consume too much time to permit its use in large classes; it has worked well in small ones.

Both the latter methods start students talking with each other immediately. Once started, they frequently continue.

Students are sometimes curious about the instructor but hesitant to ask him personal questions. To overcome their reluctance they may be invited to form small groups of four to six students each and to formulate any questions they wish to ask the instructor about his education, experience, or anything else. By designating one of their group to ask all the questions, they can conceal the identity of the interested person and thus relieve him of any anxiety about the instructor's reaction to his question. Questions directed to the author have ranged all the way from "What other jobs have you held?" to "Are you married?"

Lesson plan 2   Teachers observe own comments on occupations

Purpose. To make classroom teachers aware of the fact that they do influence the attitudes of their students toward occupations even if they do not intend to.

Assignment. Number 28.

For one week observe yourself. Notice every remark you make to any-one about any occupation. Observe the frequency and the content of your remarks, and ask yourself: What effect might these remarks have on the attitudes of these persons toward these occupations? How might these remarks influence the future occupational choices of these persons? Are my remarks based upon accurate knowledge of the facts? Do I want to change what I have been doing? How?

Activities in class. Divide the class into buzz groups of four to six students each. Ask each group to select a chairman and a secretary and to exchange their reactions to this assignment. After five or ten minutes ask each secretary for an oral summary of the discussion in his group. As each report is received, invite questions and comments from the class. Near the end of the period, summarize the discussion and add your own comments.

Lesson plan 3   How occupational choice affects life off the job

Purpose. To emphasize the importance of occupational choice.

Assignments. Numbers 1 and 29.

Read the Preface, Contents, and Chapter 1.

For one week, take a detached look at your life. Notice and list all the ways in which your job affects your family and your own life off the job. At the end of the week review your list and reflect on what it reveals about the importance of occupational choice.

Activities in class. Divide the class into buzz groups of four to six students each. Ask each group to select a chairman and a secretary and to exchange information on ways in which they have seen the choice of an occupation affect the worker's life *off* the job. Ask each secretary to take notes and to select the three most interesting instances reported in his group.

After five or ten minutes, ask each secretary to report orally one of the interesting items he has selected. After each report, pause long enough to permit questions or comments. If time permits, continue with a second and then a third round of reports from each secretary. Interrupt the reports when the end of the period approaches or when the class appears to have heard enough.

Make any summary comments that you wish to make to emphasize the importance of occupational choice.

Lesson plan 4   Group conference with alumnus

Purpose. To show to the students the kinds of information that can be obtained from alumni. To demonstrate one way of getting it. To add a little to the counselor's store of useful occupational information.

Assignment. Number 30.
Bring to class some questions that you would like to ask any young alumnus of any high school or college about his job.

Preparation. Arrange in advance for a young, employed alumnus from some high school or college to serve as guest expert in a group conference. In preparation for this, review Chapter 15.

Activities in class. Explain the purpose of the session. Describe the procedure to be followed. Introduce the guest, and conduct the group conference as suggested in Chapter 15.

Lesson plan 5   Group conference with placement officer

Purpose. To show to the students the kinds of information that can be obtained from placement officers. To demonstrate one way of getting it. To add a little to the counselor's store of useful occupational information.

Assignment. Number 2.
Read Chapter 2.

Preparation. Arrange in advance for a placement officer from a school or college or from a local office of the state employment service or from a private employment agency to serve as guest expert in a group conference. In preparation for this, review Chapter 15. The conference may be held at the placement office if space permits.

Activities in class. Explain the purpose of the session. Describe the procedure to be followed. Introduce the guest, and conduct the group conference as suggested in Chapter 15.

Lesson plan 6   Group conference with union officer

Purpose. To show to the students the kinds of information that can be obtained from union officers. To demonstrate one way of getting it. To add a little to the counselor's store of useful occupational information.

Assignment. Number 3.

Read Chapter 3.

Preparation. Arrange in advance for an officer of a union local to serve as guest expert in a group conference. In preparation for this, review Chapter 15. The conference may be held at union headquarters if space permits.

Activities in class. Explain the purpose of the session. Describe the procedure to be followed. Introduce the guest and conduct the group conference as suggested in Chapter 15.

Lesson plan 7   Students exchange occupational experiences

Purpose. To add a little to the students' store of useful occupational information by helping them to learn from one another's work experiences. To demonstrate a method which some of them can use to help their students to exchange information about their part-time and vacation work experiences.

Assignment. Number 4.

Read Chapter 4.

Activities in class. Ask each student who has been employed in some occupation other than teaching, at any time during the past five years, to name one such occupation, to state one thing that he liked about it and one thing that he disliked. Then invite the other students to ask any questions they wish to ask about the occupation. For some occupations there will be no questions. For others there may be so many that a time limit will be desirable. Continue until all students have had an opportunity to report or until the end of the period approaches. Then mention to the students that one accessible source of occupational information is the students in their own classes who have had part-time or vacation work experience, and suggest that they try a class session like this one.

Lesson plan 8   Students plan occupational library

Purpose. To give students some practice in using what they have learned. Specifically, to help them to plan the beginning of an occupational library.

Assignments. Numbers 5, 31, 32, and 33.

Because of the length of these assignments, they are not reproduced here in full. Briefly, they instruct the student to read Chapter 5, examine several references, then:

Assume that you have just been hired as the first counselor in a new high school. The principal tells you that you may order $50 worth of books to begin the school's collection of occupational information. What will you order? Prepare a list with prices and bring it to class.

Activities in class. Invite the students to report orally the titles they have selected and the price of each. Ask one student to write the selections on the blackboard as they are reported and to leave a margin in which votes can be recorded later. Accept only one title from each student until all who volunteer to contribute have had an opportunity to do so; then invite further contributions from anyone.

When all or most of the selections have been reported, ask the class to look at the blackboard and to make any changes they may now wish to make in their own selections. Then read the first title from the board and ask all students who have this title on their revised lists to raise their hands. Have a student count the hands, and report the count to the blackboard secretary. Ask the secretary to record the count opposite each title. Repeat with all the titles. Then ask the secretary to draw a circle around the number of votes for the most popular titles until the cost of the titles so designated comes to $50.

Invite the students to compare the titles so marked with the titles which they selected individually, to tell each other what they would delete from the blackboard list and what they would substitute and why.

Lesson plan 9   Comparison of filing systems

Purpose. To give the students some practice in thinking about the advantages and disadvantages of different plans for filing occupational information. To provide an opportunity for them to submit their judgments to the appraisal of their colleagues and the instructor.

Assignment. Number 6.

Read Chapter 6.

Activities in class. Select from Chapter 6 one of the review questions which asks the student to decide how occupational information will be filed in a specific situation. Divide the class into buzz groups of four to six students each, and ask them to compare their ideas on the question for five minutes. Then invite the class as a whole to discuss the same question. For suggestions on leading the discussion see Appendix B.

Take your own notes on the discussion. Summarize the discussion for the group. Add your own comments. Repeat with another question.

Lesson plan 10   Comparison of theories of vocational choice and development

Purpose. To encourage the students to formulate their own theories of occupational choice and to compare and to revise them.

Assignments. Numbers 7, 35, and 36.

Read Chapter 7.

Review the theories described in Chapter 7. Prepare to attack those with which you disagree and to defend the others.

From all the theories of vocational choice and development with which you are now acquainted, select the parts that make sense to you, add your own ideas, and state your own theory in your own words. Compare your theory with the phenomena you have observed in your own life and in your own work with other persons, and see how well it serves to explain your actions and theirs.

Activities in class. Invite the students to suggest and to vote on the theories they would most like to discuss and on how much time they wish to spend on each. Start with the theory that gets the most votes. Invite those who disagree to open the discussion by attacking this theory. Then invite its defenders to respond. Continue the discussion until the time limit has expired or until discussion lags. Summarize what has been said, add your own comments, and repeat with the next theory.

Lesson plan 11   Students examine own needs

Purpose. To clarify the composite theory for counselors described in Chapter 8. To arouse the interest of the students by relating the theory to their own personal experiences. To increase their own understanding of themselves and others.

Assignments. Numbers 8 and 34.

Read Chapter 8.

Review the occupational choices that you have made in the past. Note particularly the decisions that you made when you had to take some action, such as accepting or declining a job. Try to identify the needs that influenced your decision. Consider how these needs have affected your own job satisfaction and job performance. Prepare to share some of your thoughts with the class.

Activities in class. On the chalkboard write:

> Job Choice
> Job Satisfaction
> Job Performance

Divide the class into buzz groups of four to six students each. Ask each group to select a chairman.

Ask each person to recall, during one minute of silent meditation, how his own needs have affected his own job choices, his own job satisfaction, and his own performance in the jobs he has held, and ask him to select one such recollection that he will share with his group.

Ask each buzz group chairman to invite the members of his group to share their recollections with each other and to ask each other any questions they wish. Allow five to fifteen minutes for this, depending on how animated the discussion appears to be.

Terminate the group discussion. Provide another one minute of silent meditation; ask each person to formulate one question he would like to raise or one comment he would like to make.

Invite volunteers to ask their questions or make their comments. Add your own comments if you wish.

Lesson plan 12   Demonstration client-centered interviews

Purpose. To let the students see what can happen when a client seeks occupational information from a nondirective counselor. To provide an opportunity for the students to compare their ideas on the use of client-centered counseling in this kind of situation.

Assignment. Number 9.

Read Chapter 9.

Preparation. Ask two or three students to prepare to do demonstration interviews before the class and an equal number to act as clients seeking occupational information. Ask the counselors to be as nondirective as the circumstances permit.

Activities in class. Have the first counselor and client conduct their interview before the class. If the interview runs too long, interrupt it when you think it has served its purpose. Then ask the class to discuss two questions: "What did the counselor do well? What would you have done differently?" Summarize the discussion, add your own comments, and repeat with the next interview.

Lesson plan 13   Discussion of the use of occupational information in counseling

Purpose. To give the students an opportunity to compare and to revise their ideas about the proper use of occupational information in counseling.

Assignments. Numbers 10 and 26.
Read Chapter 10.
Bring to class one written question that you would like to have discussed in class.

Activities in class. Invite the students to vote on which of the questions they would most like to discuss. Start with the question which gets the most votes.

Divide the class into buzz groups of four to six persons each. Ask each group to select a chairman and a secretary and to discuss the question for five minutes. Then ask each secretary to summarize in two or three sentences the remarks of his group that he thinks are most likely to interest the class. After these reports, invite further comments from the class as a whole. Summarize the discussion, add your own comments, and repeat with the next question.

Or skip the buzz sessions, invite open class discussion of each question, summarize the discussion, add your own comments, and repeat with the next question.

Lesson plan 14   More demonstration interviews

Purpose. To give the students another opportunity to compare and to revise their ideas about the proper use of occupational information in counseling.

Assignment. Number 11.
Read Chapter 11.

Preparation. Assign two pairs of students to demonstrate counseling interviews on some of the kinds of problems described in this chapter. The assigned counselors may select their own problems, or the teacher may choose them. The interviews may be rehearsed or not.

This procedure may be varied by announcing only the nature of the client's problem and asking everyone to prepare to be either the counselor or the client if called upon.

Activities in class. Have the first counselor and client conduct their interview before the class. If the interview runs too long, interrupt it when you think it has served its purpose. Then ask the class to discuss two questions: "What did the counselor do well? What would you have done differently?" Summarize the discussion, add your own comments, and repeat with the next interview.

Lesson plan 15   Counseling by college faculty advisers

Purpose. To encourage students to think about the proper use of occupational information by amateur counselors. To give them an opportunity to compare and to revise their ideas.

Assignment. Number 37.

You have just been appointed as the first dean of students in a co-educational liberal arts college of 1,000 students. You have no assistants. There is no college placement office. During your first week on the campus you are asked to meet with a group of faculty advisers. One of them asks you how they should respond to student requests for occupational information. Write your reply on one page and bring it to class.

Activities in class. Divide the class into buzz groups of four to six students each. Ask each group to choose a chairman and a secretary to compare their answers to the assignment and to select the one best answer from the group. If the group cannot agree, ask the secretary to make the choice.

Ask the persons chosen by the group to read their answers to the class. Ask the class to discuss which of these is the best answer and to choose one of them.

Encourage the expression of dissenting opinions. Help the class to express all their ideas and to compare them. Help them to see where they agree, where they disagree, and why.

Summarize the discussion, and add your own comments.

Lesson plan 16   Counseling by homeroom teachers

This plan is identical with the one preceding except for the assignment, which is number 38.

You have just been appointed as the first counselor in a new high school of 500 students. You have no assistants. During the first month you are asked to meet with a group of homeroom teachers. One of them asks you how they should respond to student requests for occupational information. Write your reply on one page and bring it to class.

Lesson plan 17   Counseling by group workers

This plan is identical with the one preceding except for the assignment, which is number 39.

You have just been employed by a national organization as its specialist in vocational guidance. At the annual convention you are asked to serve as the resource person in a section meeting of group workers. Most of them are paid professionals, with some training in social work but none in occupations. They are employed in boys' clubs, settlement houses, YWCAs, etc. The group asks you how they should respond to requests for occupational information. Write your reply on one page and bring it to class.

Lesson plan 18   Discussion of plans for the teaching of occupations

Purpose. To give the students an opportunity to compare and to revise their ideas about the teaching of occupations.

Assignments. Numbers 12 and 40.

Read Chapter 12.

You are a counselor in the high school or college that you attended or in another school that you know well. Your supervisor asks you to recommend where courses in occupations should be offered, what they should include, and who should teach them. What will you recommend? Write your reply on one page and bring it to class.

Activities in class. Ask for a volunteer, or select one of the better students, or appoint buzz groups and ask each of them to select one of their group to report his plan. Ask the selected student to take your place at the front of the class, to describe briefly the school or college that he has chosen and the program that he would propose for the teaching of occupations in this institution. Limit him to five or ten minutes. Then ask the class to comment on two questions: "What do you like about this proposal? What would you do differently?" When the discussion lags or you feel that it has served its purpose, interrupt it, summarize it, add your own comments, and repeat with another student.

If time permits, the answers to the assignment may be written and collected a week in advance. Then the best papers may be selected for class discussion and returned to their authors at the next meeting.

Lesson plan 19   Demonstration discussion of follow-up returns

Purpose. To demonstrate one way in which the returns from a follow-up study may be used for class discussion. To show the class some of the things that can be learned from follow-up projects. To add a little to the counselor's store of useful occupational information.

Assignments. Numbers 13 and 41.

Read Chapter 13.

Prepare five or ten questions that you would like to ask the alumni of some school or college, or the former clients of some counseling agency, or the former members of some club or other group. Find three such persons, ask your questions, and bring the replies to class.

Activities in class. Invite volunteers to read their questions and answers. Invite the other students to ask questions or to comment on the reports. Comment on them yourself when you feel inclined to do so.

As the reports are made, suggest to the class, or ask them to suggest, ways in which the items reported could be used to develop useful discussions in high school or college classes.

Or divide the class into buzz groups of four to six persons each. Ask the students to tell each other what they learned from their inquiries and what they think we ought to do about it. After ten or fifteen minutes invite questions, comments, and open discussion.

Lesson plan 20   Demonstration plant tour

Purpose. To demonstrate how to conduct a plant tour as described in Chapter 14. To show the class some of the things that can be learned on a tour. To add to the counselor's store of useful occupational information.

Assignments.

For the first tour. Number 14.

Read Chapter 14.

For subsequent tours. Number 42.

You are soon to go on a plant tour. The instructor will tell you where. Go to as many libraries as you can, and read everything you can find on occupations in the industry to be visited. Review Chapter 4 on "Sources of Occupational Information," and use any sources that might help you to learn more about these occupations.

Try to find someone who is now employed in the place we are to visit, or in similar work elsewhere. Ask him what he likes best and what he likes least about his job. Ask him what are *all* the things he does in his job.

Ask your students, family, and friends for any questions they would like you to ask on the day of the tour. Formulate the questions you wish to ask.

During the tour, assume that the jobs you see are the only jobs open to you and that you really need a job. Select the job for which you would apply. Consider your ability to do the job or to learn to do it. Consider how well the job would meet your most important needs.

Activities in class. Conduct the tour as described in Chapter 14, with such modifications as may be necessary or desirable to fit local conditions.

At the next class session after the trip ask the class:

> Has anyone ever worked at the place we visited? At any place like it?
>
> Did you observe anything different from what we saw on our tour?
>
> Does anyone have any questions or comments?

Lesson plan 21   Demonstration group conference

Purpose. To demonstrate how to conduct a group conference as described in Chapter 15. To show the students some of the things that can be learned in group conferences with guests of different kinds. To add to the counselor's store of useful occupational information.

Assignments.

For the first conference. Number 15.

Read Chapter 15.

For subsequent conferences. Number 43.

Go to as many libraries as you can, and read everything you can find on the occupation or industry to be covered in the next group conference. Review Chapter 4 on "Sources of Occupational Information," and use any sources that might help you to learn more. Bring to class any questions that you would like to ask the guest expert.

Activities in class. Conduct a group conference as described in Chapter 15. If time permits, devote several class sessions to group conferences with different kinds of guests, including an employer, an employee, an apprentice, a self-employed proprietor, a parent, and a student. Group conferences with an alumnus, a placement officer, and a union officer have been provided in previous lesson plans. After some experience, try having two guests at one time, then three or four.

Lesson plan 22   Demonstration survey of beginning jobs

Purpose. To demonstrate some of the ways in which the information collected by the students may be exchanged in class discussion. To give the students a few of the experiences that their students will have if they undertake a student survey as described in Chapter 16. To add a little more to the counselor's store of useful occupational information.

Assignments. Numbers 16 and 44.

Read Chapter 16.

Prepare five questions that you would like to ask employers if you were participating in a survey of the kind described in Chapter 16. Interview three employers, and ask them the questions you have prepared. Submit a one-page report that could be duplicated and given to the staff and students of a school or college, or to the staff and clients of an agency.

Activities in class. Divide the class into buzz groups of four to six students each, and ask each group to choose a chairman and a secretary. Ask each person to tell the others in his group the one most interesting thing that he learned from his interviews. After five minutes or more of discussion in the small groups, ask each group secretary to report to the whole class the one most interesting discovery made by his group. Encourage any discussion that the report may inspire, but do not force it. Continue until each secretary has reported one item. Then ask each to report a second item. Continue until all the items have been reported and discussed or until the class period nears its end. Then ask each student in turn, "Would an assignment and a class session like this be of any value to the persons with whom you work, or hope to work? Would any variation of it help them? Tell us the kind of group you work with and how you would use or vary this technique with them." Again encourage questions and discussion if time permits. If much time remains for this part of the class session, ask the class to form buzz groups and to discuss this topic before they report to the whole class.

Lesson plan 23   Demonstration case conference

Purpose. To demonstrate how to conduct a case conference as described in Chapter 17. To show the class some of the kinds of topics that come up for discussion during a case conference and how the conference may be used to give students practice in thinking about vocational choice.

Assignment. Number 17.
    Read Chapter 17.

Activities in class. Select from your own experience a case of vocational choice in which occupational information was important. Select two alternate cases to use if the first one fails to provoke discussion. Present the first case to the class, and conduct the case conference as described in Chapter 17. If time permits, repeat with additional cases.

Or explain to the class that you are about to demonstrate a case conference and ask: "Are any of you now facing a decision about whether or not to accept a job that you can have if you want it? Is there such a person who would not be embarrassed or hurt by the questions we might ask or the comments we might make if we used you and your problem for our demonstration case conference?" If you get any volunteers, choose one of them and let the class ask questions of him and then express their thoughts on whether or not he should take the job and why. If you get no acceptable volunteer, use one of the cases you brought to class.

Lesson plan 24   Demonstration laboratory study

Purpose. To give the students some of the experiences that their students will have if they undertake the laboratory study of one or more occupations as described in Chapter 18. To demonstrate one way in which the information collected by the students may be exchanged without a series of boring oral reports. To add a little more to the counselor's store of useful occupational information.

Assignments. Numbers 18 and 45.

Read Chapter 18.

Select an occupation about which you know very little but that you might consider entering if you were to leave your own. Learn everything you can about this occupation, following the suggestions in Chapter 4. Record what you have learned and your reaction to it by filling the blanks in the "Outline for the Study of an Occupation" which appears in Appendix G. Consider whether or not some experience of this kind would be helpful to your students or clients. Come to class prepared to exchange information on the two or three most interesting things that you have learned from this experience.

Assignment 45 may be made several weeks in advance. It may be used as a term project. It was once used by the author as the basis for an entire course in sources of occupational information; a report of this experience, with the students' evaluation of it, may be found in Hoppock [228].

Activities in class. Ask each student to write one sentence stating the most interesting thing he has learned from this experience about any occupation or about sources of occupational information. Ask each student to read his one sentence to the group. After each sentence is read, ask the class, "Does anyone wish to ask Mr. Blank for any more information on this topic?" After a few times this query may be shortened to "Anyone want more information?" or "Any questions?" Do not be surprised if the first few sentences evoke no questions. Encourage discussion, but do not force it. Make any comments you wish to make on the information reported and on the class discussion. If time permits, call on each student for a second or third report.

Continue until the class period nears its end. Then invite the class to discuss "What seem to you to be the values and the limitations in this method of teaching occupations?"

Lesson plan 25   Demonstration self-measurement

Purpose. To demonstrate how aptitude tests may be administered, scored, and discussed in class.

Assignment. Number 19.

Read Chapter 19.

Materials needed. Enough copies of one vocational aptitude test to supply all the students and the instructor. An equal number of test manuals and scoring keys. The test selected should be one that can be administered to a group and scored by the students. If the instructor wishes to devote only one period to this lesson, the test should be one that can be completed and scored in not more than half of the available time. For teaching purposes, the manual should include several validity coefficients, obtained against different criteria, and tables of norms for several different populations. The author has found the hand-scoring form of the Revised Minnesota Paper Form Board convenient for demonstration purposes.

Activities in class. Explain the purpose of the demonstration. Distribute and administer the test, following the directions in the test manual. When the test is completed, distribute the scoring keys and have each student score his own test. Then distribute the test manuals. Invite the students to ask questions about the meaning of various scores for various purposes. In answering their questions, call attention to the validity coefficients for various criteria; invite the students to comment on, and to ask questions about, what these coefficients reveal about the validity of the test for various purposes. Call attention to the tables of norms, and ask the class to answer questions that you ask about how a person with a given score would compare with various groups and about which norms should be used for various purposes.

Suggest to the class hypothetical cases in vocational choice, and ask how certain scores on this test might affect such choices. Near the end of the period ask the class to discuss the values and the dangers of this kind of class session for high school and college students, assuming that several successive periods would be devoted to it and several tests taken and discussed.

If you wish to devote more than one period to self-measurement, the tests may be scored and the test manual studied between classes. Obviously, one cannot teach a semester or a year course in statistics, in test administration, and in test interpretation all in one class period. It is assumed that any counselor in training who proposes to use this technique with his own students will have had or will soon take adequate training in testing.

Lesson plan 26   Group conference with a counselor or teacher
                 of occupations

Purpose. To inform the students about some activity that they may wish to adapt to their own purposes.

Assignment. Number 20.

Read Chapter 20.

Preparation. Invite to the class a counselor or teacher of occupations who is doing something that you believe will interest your students. Such a person will sometimes be found among the students in the class.

Activities in class. Conduct a group conference as described in Chapter 15, but substitute such questions as the following:

What was your purpose in undertaking this project?
How did you proceed?
What results did you get?
What did it cost?
Did you make any mistakes?
If you were to do it again, would you change anything?
Have you any suggestions that might help us if we were to try something similar?
Is there anything else we should have asked you?
Is there anything you would like to ask us?

Lesson plan 27   Occupational films

Purpose. To show the students the kind of occupational information that is available on film. To give them a little practice in appraising occupational films.

Assignment. Number 46.

Review the sections on films in Chapter 20.

Preparation. Select two or three occupational films from one of the film catalogues, rent them, and arrange to show them during the class period.

Activities in class. Tell the class that they are about to see a film that contains some occupational information. Ask them to view it critically, to identify its good and bad points, to decide whether or not they would show it to the students or clients with whom they work or hope to work. Explain that an occupational film is not intended to present a complete picture of an occupation; it is intended to extend the range of occupations of which the student is aware, to add something to his knowledge, and to arouse enough interest to start a profitable discussion.

Show the film.

Ask the class, "From this film, what did you learn that you did not know before?" Have a student write the answers on the blackboard, so the class can see how much new information the film did convey.

In buzz groups or in open class discussion ask the class to list the reasons why they would or would not use this film, and to suggest how it might be used to start discussion. Summarize their discussion, add your own comments, and repeat with another film.

Lesson plan 28   Demonstration practice job interview

Purpose. To demonstrate one way in which students may be prepared for employment interviews. To add a little to the counselor's knowledge of how people are hired.

Assignment. Number 47.

Review the section on "Practice Job Interviews" in Chapter 20.

Preparation. Invite a local employer to attend the class, conduct the interviews, and participate in the discussion. Select three students and assign them to apply for the kind of job for which the selected employer hires workers. Invite two of the students to do one or two things that they think are wrong. Ask the third student to do nearly everything wrong.

Activities in class. Introduce the guest, and explain that he will interview three students from the class just as he would if they were genuine applicants for work. Ask the other students to focus their attention on the applicant and to take notes on what the applicant does well and on what they would do differently if they were in his place. Do not ask or permit the students to say that what the applicant did was "wrong." Urge them to try to help one another by comparing ideas of how to do things well, but not by sniping criticism. Tell them that each applicant will do some things that he thinks are correct and may do some that he thinks could be done better. The purpose of this is to lessen embarrassment for both the applicants and the critics; no one knows which things the applicant did wrong intentionally.

Ask the guest not to concern himself about time limits. Tell him that you will interrupt the interview after five or ten minutes, depending on the length of the class period. Seat the guest at a desk at the front of the room. Provide an extra chair for the applicant. Ask the first applicant to leave the room and reenter as he would if the room were the employer's office. The interviewer greets the applicant as he enters, and the interview proceeds without previous rehearsal.

At the conclusion of the interview ask the class to comment on what the applicant did well. Ask this question first in order to bolster the applicant's morale before any changes are suggested. Encourage discussion. Add your own comments if you wish. Then ask the students what they would have done differently. If students start to criticize the interviewer, remind them that the purpose of this session is to help the applicant, who may expect to meet all kinds of interviewers, and ask them to restrict their comments to the applicant. Encourage discussion as before. Assure the applicant that he need not defend what he did, that he is to accept only those suggestions which appeal to him and to ignore the others. He may ask questions if he wishes.

At the conclusion of the students' discussion, invite the applicant and the guest to comment on both the discussion and the interview.

Repeat the process with the two remaining applicants. Hold the one who does everything wrong until the end, as a relief from fatigue and repetition. His performance usually provokes much laughter; it serves to dramatize and reinforce some points by exaggeration.

The procedure may be varied by having high school students or undergraduate college students serve as applicants.

Lesson plan 29   Gyp schools

Purpose. To make the students aware of the kind of sales pressure to which their students and clients may be subjected when they respond to the advertisements of gyp schools.

Assignments. Numbers 48 and 49.

Review the section on "Writing the Gyps" in Chapter 20.

Buy the gaudiest pulp magazine you can find. Scan the advertisements, and answer three which seem to you to represent gyp schools. Bring to class some samples of the recruiting literature that you receive. *Caution:* Do not give this assignment to *your* students without first doing it yourself, then warning your students and their parents to expect to see some high-pressure salesmen and to sign nothing without first discussing it with you.

This assignment should be made at least two weeks in advance.

Activities in class. Invite volunteers to report their experiences with school salesmen and to read excerpts from the sales literature.

Divide the class into buzz groups of four to six students each. Ask each group to choose a chairman and a secretary and to discuss what they should do to protect their students and clients from gyp schools. Ask each secretary to report the one best idea his group can devise.

As each report is received, invite the class to comment on the values and limitations of the action proposed and to offer suggestions for improvement. Summarize the discussion, and add your own comments.

Tell the class how to terminate the sales pressure to which they have been subjected by school salesmen. No method is guaranteed to end it, but the following have helped: Write to the school, saying, "I have enrolled at [Blank University] and am no longer interested in your school. Will you please remove my name from your mailing list." Give the same message to salesmen who call or phone. If this fails, return all mail to the post office, unopened; on the face of the envelope write "Refused." It will then be returned to the sender at his expense.

Lesson plan 30   Course units on occupational information

Purpose. To encourage the students to think about a problem which some of them will face. To give them an opportunity to exchange and revise their ideas.

Assignments. Numbers 50 and 51.

Review the section on "Presenting Occupational Information through Other Subjects" in Chapter 20.

You are the counselor in a small high school that has no course in occupations. The social studies teacher has offered to devote ten weeks of class time to a study of occupations if you think this desirable. The teacher asks you: "Should we do this? In what grade? What should we cover and by what methods of teaching? Who should teach it?"

Write your reply on one page and bring it to class.

Activities in class. Present to the class, for open discussion, the questions in the assignment. Take one question at a time. Encourage expression and comparison of all shades of opinion. Allot class time so that all the questions can be discussed. As you approach the end of the time limit for each question, summarize the discussion and add your own comments.

Lesson plan 31   Discussion of occupational information in the
elementary school

Purpose. To give the students an opportunity to compare and to revise
their ideas about the use of occupational information in the elementary
school.

Assignments. Numbers 21 and 52.

Read Chapter 21.

Interview three elementary school teachers. Ask what they do to make
their students more familiar with the ways in which people earn their
living. Bring to class a composite list of the things that these elementary
teachers do.

Activities in class. Divide the class into buzz groups of four to six students
each. Ask each group to choose a chairman and a secretary and to tell
each other what they learned from their interviews with elementary
teachers. Ask each secretary to report the things which his group found
elementary teachers to be doing. As these reports are made, ask a class
secretary to compile on the blackboard a composite list of all activities
reported.

Ask the students to imagine that they are members of a board of
education that has been asked to approve these activities and to tell the
teachers which of these activities they would prefer to have provided
for their children if some have to be omitted. Ask each student to select
the one activity that he considers most valuable and to argue for it as
if he were in a board meeting. Near the end of the period, vote on which
activities should be given priority.

Lesson plan 32   Discussion of plans for beginners

Purpose. To give the students an opportunity to compare and to revise
their plans for using what they have learned from this course.

Assignments. Numbers 22 and 53.

Read Chapter 22.

Quickly review the entire text to this point. Formulate a plan for one
thing that you intend to do in your present or future job as a result of
the things you have learned in this course. Prepare to describe your plan
to the class if you are asked to do so.

Activities in class. Ask for a volunteer, or select one of the better students, or appoint buzz groups and ask each of them to select one of their group to report his plan. Ask the selected student to take your place at the front of the class to describe briefly the plan he has prepared. Limit him to five or ten minutes. Then ask the class to comment on two questions: "What do you like about this proposal? What would you do differently?" When the discussion lags or you feel that it has served its purpose, interrupt it, summarize it, add your own comments, and repeat with another student.

If time permits, the answers to the assignment may be written and collected a week in advance. Then the best papers may be selected for class discussion and returned to their authors at the next meeting.

Lesson plan 33   Discussion of plans for administrators

Purpose. To give the students an opportunity to look at guidance from the point of view of their superiors and to begin thinking about what they will do when and if they become administrators.

Assignments. Numbers 23 and 54.

Read Chapter 23.

Imagine that you are the top administrative officer in the organization in which you now work or hope to work. Formulate a plan for one thing that you would do about occupational information in your organization. Prepare to describe your plan to the class if you are asked to do so.

Activities in class. Same as in Lesson Plan 32.

Because Chapters 22 and 23 are short, the lesson plans based on them may be combined, and the students may be given their choice of the two assignments.

Lesson plan 34   Appraising the course

Purpose. To give the students an opportunity to help improve the course, to compare and revise their ideas on how it should be taught. To help the instructor to learn more about the student response to his efforts.

Assignments. Numbers 24 and 25.

Read Chapter 24.

If you were to teach this course, what would you do differently? What would you retain from the content and methods of the course as it has been taught this year? If you prefer to make some comments anonymously, put them on a separate sheet without your name on it.

Activities in class. Divide the class into buzz groups of four to six students each. Ask each group to select a chairman and a secretary and to select the one best suggestion for improvement that has been proposed by its members. Ask the secretaries to report these suggestions. As each proposal is reported, invite questions and comments from the class. Ask the class to vote on each suggestion. How many agree? How many disagree? How many did not vote either way?

Repeat with the things they would like to retain from the present course.

Lesson plan 35   Faculty meeting on occupational information

Purpose. To encourage the students to think about how they can use what they have learned in this course or to arouse their interest at the beginning of the course.

Assignment. Number 56.

You are a teacher in a high school that has never done much to inform its students about occupations. Your principal calls you to his office and says, "I think we ought to do something to make our students better informed about occupations. I'm looking for ideas. How do you think we ought to go about it?" Write your reply on one page and bring it to class.

Activities in class. Divide the class into buzz groups of four to six students each. Ask each group to choose a chairman and a secretary and to decide what is the first step they would suggest to this principal. If time permits, ask them to list subsequent steps in sequential order.

After five or ten minutes, ask each secretary to report the first step suggested by his group. List these steps on the blackboard.

Ask the class to imagine that they are high school teachers in a faculty meeting and that the principal has asked them to decide which of these steps should be taken first. Invite discussion. Try to reach amicable agreement. When you think the discussion has continued long enough, take a vote.

Ask each secretary to report the second step suggested by his group. Add these to the list on the board. Ask the class to discuss and vote on what the second step should be.

Continue with subsequent steps until near the end of the class period. Then summarize the discussion and add your own comments.

Lesson plan 36   Discussion of plans for evaluation

Purpose. To encourage the students to think about evaluating their work. To give them an opportunity to compare and revise their plans for doing so.

Assignments. Numbers 25 and 57.

Read Chapter 25.

Formulate a plan for evaluating something that you now do or plan to do. Prepare to describe your plan to the class if you are asked to do so.

Activities in class. Same as Lesson Plan 32. This plan also may be combined with the plans for Chapters 22 and 23, and the students may be given their choice of three assignments.

Lesson plan 37   Comparison of current activities

Purpose. To give the students a glimpse of the occupational information services provided by the schools and colleges represented in the class.

Assignment. Number 58. This assignment should be made at least two weeks in advance.

Prepare a one-page summary of the occupational information services provided in your school, college, or counseling agency. If you are not so employed, choose a school with which you are or can become familiar. Include the following information: name and address of institution; grades included; number of boys, girls, teachers; number and nature of guidance staff; past and present occupational information activities that you think (1) have worked well, (2) are of doubtful value.

Make enough copies of this report so that each member of the class may have one. Bring these to class on the date that this assignment is due.

Sample report

High School, Somewhere, New Jersey, Grades 9–12. 200 boys. 200 girls. 16 teachers. One full-time counselor who teaches courses in occupations.

Occupational information activities that have worked well:

1. Course in occupations for seniors

2. Form for requesting interviews
3. Bulletin board for new books
Occupational information activities of doubtful value:
1. Career day

Activities in class. Have the mimeographed reports distributed so that each person has a complete set.

Invite the students to read the reports silently and to ask questions of one another when they want more information.

Lesson plan 38   Discussion of journal articles

Purpose. To encourage students to read professional journals and to look for information and ideas which they can use in their own work. To help them to improve the tentative plans that they formulate from such reading. Incidentally to help some of them to become acquainted with journals that they have not read before.

Assignment. Number 59.

Browse through the back issues of any of the journals listed below. Find and read five articles that discuss some aspect of occupational information. Look for ideas that you can use in your present or future work. Submit a report on two pages: (1) your plans for using anything that you learned from this assignment; (2) full bibliographic data on the articles that you read.

Start page 1 with the words "I intend to . . ." If you cannot get one good idea from the five articles, continue reading additional articles until you do get results.

Journals
American Child
Bulletin of the National Association of Secondary School Principals
Clearing House
Employment Security Review
Journal of College Placement
Journal of College Student Personnel
Personnel and Guidance Journal
School Counselor
Vocational Guidance Quarterly
The journals in your own specialty, e.g., vocational rehabilitation, vocational education, industrial arts, nursing, social work, industrial personnel work.

Activities in class. Collect the papers. Tell the class that you will read them aloud. Ask them to try to help one another by contributing additional information and ideas. Read the first paper. Invite discussion by asking such questions as "Have any of you ever tried anything like this? Have you ever seen anyone else try it? How did it work? How many of you like this idea? What do you like about it? Does it have any disadvantages? Is there any way in which it might backfire? Can you suggest any improvements?"

Add your own comments to those of the students.and go on to the next paper. Do not be surprised if the students have no comments on some of the papers. If you need help in encouraging discussion, see Appendix B.

Lesson plan 39   Question, comment, and discussion

Purpose. To give the students an opportunity to ask questions about anything in their reading which puzzles them or arouses their interest. To let them express and compare their reactions to what they read.

Assignment. Number 60.

Any chapter in the text or any other reading the instructor may choose, accompanied by the following instructions:

Read the material assigned. As you read, note anything which is not entirely clear to you, anything you do not understand, anything that seems to you to be unsound or debatable, anything you would like to challenge, anything about which you would like to ask a question, or anything that you would like to have discussed in class. Note also any suggested activities that you have seen in operation, with which you have had experience that you could report to the class, or on which you would like to comment. Whenever you encounter anything of this kind, stop reading and write your question or comment. Put each question or comment on a separate sheet of 8½- by 11-inch paper. In the top left corner put the number of the page in the publication which provoked your response. In the top right corner put your name and seat number. Hand these sheets to the class secretary at the beginning of the class period.

Activities in class. Select a student for class secretary, and seat him near the door of the classroom. As students arrive and hand their papers to him, have him sort them by page number. By the time you have completed announcements and other preliminaries, the secretary should have most of the papers sorted. If the sorting is not completed, start with the top paper and let the secretary finish the sorting during the early part of the class period. The sorting process is not imperative; it merely saves some time by grouping together the questions and comments which relate to the same topic.

Open the class session by asking the secretary to read the first paper. If this contains a question, answer it, or ask the class what they think about it, or both. If the paper contains a comment, express your agreement or disagreement, or ask the class to do likewise, or simply thank the contributor and go on to the next paper. If questions arise which you cannot answer, say simply, "I'm sorry, I don't know. Does anyone else?" If the question is important enough, take it home, and try to find the answer before the next session. Some questions can be answered in a sentence. Some could be handled adequately only by writing a book. Appraise each one as it comes up, in terms of its probable interest to the class as a whole, and allocate time accordingly. If some papers have not been read by the end of the period, take them home, read them, select a few of common interest to be handled during the first few minutes of the next class period, and answer the others by writing comments on the papers and returning the papers to the students at the next class session. If all the papers are covered before the end of the period, ask the class, "Is there anything else you would like to discuss?" If there is no response, dismiss the class.

The procedure is informal. Your answers are extemporaneous. There is no preliminary selection of questions to be discussed and no advance preparation of replies except in the case of holdovers as noted above.

Questions could be collected at one session and discussed at the next. This procedure would permit more selection and preparation, but it would postpone the discussion until after the students had read another assignment and written another set of questions and comments. The author prefers to discuss the comments and answer the questions while the subject matter is as fresh as possible in the minds of the students, even at some sacrifice in selection and preparation. The obviously unrehearsed classroom procedure assures a spontaneity which the students seem to like, too.

Lesson plan 40   Discussion by interest groups

Purpose. To give students with common interests an opportunity to ask each other questions, to exchange information, ideas, and experiences.

Assignment. Number 107.

Bring to class one or more questions that you would like to ask other members of the class whose present or future work is in some way similar to yours.

Activities in class. Divide the class into interest groups, e.g., elementary schools, junior high schools, senior high schools, colleges, rehabilitation, others. Send each group to another room. Instruct the students in each group to ask each other any questions they wish, continue as long as they feel the discussion is productive, then prepare one question they would like to ask the instructor or the class, and return to the main classroom. Use the remaining time, if any, to discuss the questions brought back.

Lesson plan 41   Fillers for emergencies

Occasionally a teacher must conduct a class session for which he is wholly unprepared. An expected guest does not appear for a group conference. A well-planned lesson ends when the period is only half over. A colleague is taken ill, and someone must cover his class. In such situations the author has found the following procedures helpful, and the students have said they found them worth the time spent on them.

1. Ask each student to review what he has learned during the past few days or weeks from any source about any subject, to select one item that he thinks might interest this group, to state that item in one written sentence. When most of the students have written their sentences, invite volunteers to read theirs. If no one responds, call on them individually. After each item is read, invite the class to ask questions or to comment. Do so yourself, if inclined. Then go on to the next item.

In a large class this procedure may be varied by asking buzz groups to review the sentences that their members have written and to select the most interesting one to be read to the group.

Writing the items is not always necessary. It does, however, seem to produce results from some students who otherwise say they cannot think of anything to report.

2. Ask each student to write one question that he would like to have the class discuss for his benefit and to sign his name. Collect the questions; read them aloud. After reading each question, ask the class how many would like to discuss it, count the raised hands, record the number on the paper with the question. Assure the students that they may raise their hands as often as they wish.

Ask the class how much time they wish to give to each question, and let them decide.

Arrange the questions in order of popularity, and invite the class to discuss them in this order. Summarize the discussion on each question, and add your own comments.

appendix **Z**

Assignments
for use
in Counselor
Education[1]

Assignments can be given to students more accurately and in less time if they are printed or mimeographed and numbered. Then, instead of dictating a long paragraph to the class, the instructor can simply announce, "For the next session please prepare assignments 7 and 34."

The assignments below include all those which appear in the lesson plans in Appendix Y, plus additional assignments for enriching the course. Some of the assignments require very little time; some are long enough to be used as term projects; some can be long or short as the student or the instructor may desire.

Group I   Reading assignments in this book
1. Read the Preface, Contents, and Chapter 1.

2. Read Chapter 2.	10. Read Chapter 10.	18. Read Chapter 18.
3. Read Chapter 3.	11. Read Chapter 11.	19. Read Chapter 19.
4. Read Chapter 4.	12. Read Chapter 12.	20. Read Chapter 20.
5. Read Chapter 5.	13. Read Chapter 13.	21. Read Chapter 21.
6. Read Chapter 6.	14. Read Chapter 14.	22. Read Chapter 22.
7. Read Chapter 7.	15. Read Chapter 15.	23. Read Chapter 23.
8. Read Chapter 8.	16. Read Chapter 16.	24. Read Chapter 24.
9. Read Chapter 9.	17. Read Chapter 17.	25. Read Chapter 25.

Group II   Other assignments
26. Bring to class one written question that you would like to have discussed in class.
27. Prepare and submit a one-page statement of how the work assigned for this session has affected your thoughts, your actions, and your plans for the future. How can you use what you have learned?

[1] For related discussion see Chap. 24.

28. For one week observe yourself. Notice every remark you make to anyone about any occupation. Observe the frequency and the content of your remarks, and ask yourself: What effect might these remarks have on the attitudes of these persons toward these occupations? How might these remarks influence the future occupational choices of these persons? Are my remarks based upon accurate knowledge of the facts? Do I want to change what I have been doing? How?

29. For one week, take a detached look at your life. Notice and list all the ways in which your job affects your family and your own life off the job. At the end of the week review your list and reflect on what it reveals about the importance of occupational choice.

30. Bring to class some questions that you would like to ask any young alumnus of any high school or college about his job.

31. Examine the issues for the past three years of the several indexes listed in Chapter 4 under "Publications." Select one occupation, and compare the indexes to see which would be of most help to you in finding information on this occupation. Repeat with two other occupations. Decide which of the indexes would best serve your needs as a guide to the purchase of occupational publications for your library. Select and write for ten or more of the free publications listed in recent issues of these indexes.

32. Examine any of the following that you have not previously examined. Spend enough time with each to be reasonably sure that you know whether or not it contains any information of value to you. Read what interests you; skip what does not. Consider which references may be of value to your future students or clients. Take appropriate notes on those you wish to remember.

Occupational Outlook Handbook, Superintendent of Documents, Washington (see latest edition).

Occupational Outlook Quarterly, Superintendent of Documents, Washington.

Occupational Abstracts, monthly except July and August, Personnel Services, Inc., Jaffrey, N.H.

Dictionary of Occupational Titles, vol. I, Superintendent of Documents, Washington.

Dictionary of Occupational Titles, vol. II, Superintendent of Documents, Washington.

Directory of National Trade and Professional Associations of the United States, Potomac Books, Washington (see latest edition).

Encyclopedia of Associations, vol. I, *National Organizations of the United States,* Gale Research Co., Detroit, Mich. (see latest edition).

American Universities and Colleges, American Council on Education, Washington (see latest edition).

American Junior Colleges, American Council on Education, Washington (see latest edition).

33. Assume that you have just been hired as the first counselor in a new high school. The principal tells you that you may order $50 worth of books to begin the school's collection of occupational information. What will you order? Prepare a list with prices and bring it to class.

34. Review the occupational choices that you have made in the past. Note particularly the decisions that you made when you had to take some action, such as accepting or declining a job. Try to identify the needs that influenced your decision. Consider how these needs have affected your own job satisfaction and job performance. Prepare to share some of your thoughts with the class.

35. Review the theories described in Chapter 7. Prepare to attack those with which you disagree and to defend the others.

36. From all the theories of vocational choice and development with which you are now acquainted, select the parts that make sense to you, add your own ideas, and state your own theory in your own words. Compare your theory with the phenomena you have observed in your own life and in your own work with other persons, and see how well it serves to explain your actions and theirs.

37. You have just been appointed as the first dean of students in a coeducational liberal arts college of 1,000 students. You have no assistants. There is no college placement office. During your first week on the campus you are asked to meet with a group of faculty advisers. One of them asks you how they should respond to student requests for occupational information. Write your reply on one page and bring it to class.

38. You have just been appointed as the first counselor in a new high school of 500 students. You have no assistants. During the first month you are asked to meet with a group of homeroom teachers. One of them asks you how they should respond to student requests for occupational information. Write your reply on one page and bring it to class.

39. You have just been employed by a national organization as its specialist in vocational guidance. At the annual convention you are asked to serve as the resource person in a section meeting of group workers. Most of them are paid professionals, with some training in social work but none in occupations. They are employed in boys' clubs, settlement houses, YWCAs, etc. The group asks you how they should respond to requests for occupational information. Write your reply on one page and bring it to class.

40. You are a counselor in the high school or college that you attended or in another school that you know well. Your supervisor asks you to

recommend where courses in occupations should be offered, what they should include, and who should teach them. What will you recommend? Write your reply on one page and bring it to class.

41. Prepare five or ten questions that you would like to ask the alumni of some school or college, or the former clients of some counseling agency, or the former members of some club or other group. Find three such persons, ask your questions, and bring the replies to class.

42. You are soon to go on a plant tour. The instructor will tell you where. Go to as many libraries as you can, and read everything you can find on occupations in the industry to be visited. Review Chapter 4 on "Sources of Occupational Information," and use any sources that might help you to learn more about these occupations.

Try to find someone who is now employed in the place we are to visit or in similar work elsewhere. Ask him what he likes best and what he likes least about his job. Ask him what are *all* the things he does in his job.

Ask your students, family, and friends for any questions they would like you to ask on the day of the tour. Formulate the questions you wish to ask.

During the tour, assume that the jobs you see are the only jobs open to you and that you really need a job. Select the job for which you would apply. Consider your ability to do the job or to learn to do it. Consider how well the job would meet your most important needs.

43. Go to as many libraries as you can, and read everything you can find on the occupation or industry to be covered in the next group conference. Review Chapter 4 on "Sources of Occupational Information," and use any sources that might help you to learn more. Bring to class any questions that you would like to ask the guest expert.

44. Prepare five questions that you would like to ask employers if you were participating in a survey of the kind described in Chapter 16. Interview three employers, and ask them the questions you have prepared. Submit a one-page report that could be duplicated and given to the staff and students of a school or college, or to the staff and clients of an agency.

45. Select an occupation about which you know very little but that you might consider entering if you were to leave your own. Learn everything you can about this occupation, following the suggestions in Chapter 4. Record what you have learned and your reaction to it by filling the blanks in the "Outline for the Study of an Occupation" which appears in Appendix G. Consider whether or not some experience of this kind would be helpful to your students or clients. Come to class prepared to exchange information on the two or three most interesting things that you have learned from this experience.

46. Review the sections on films in Chapter 20.

47. Review the section on "Practice Job Interviews" in Chapter 20.

48. Review the section on "Writing the Gyps" in Chapter 20.

49. Buy the gaudiest pulp magazine you can find. Scan the advertisements, and answer three which seem to you to represent gyp schools. Bring to class some samples of the recruiting literature that you receive. *Caution:* Do not give this assignment to *your* students without first doing it yourself, then warning your students and their parents to expect to see some high-pressure salesmen and to sign nothing without first discussing it with you.

50. Review the section on "Presenting Occupational Information through Other Subjects" in Chapter 20.

51. You are the counselor in a small high school which has no course in occupations. The social studies teacher has offered to devote ten weeks of class time to a study of occupations if you think this desirable. The teacher asks you: "Should we do this? In what grade? What should we cover and by what methods of teaching? Who should teach it?"

Write your reply on one page and bring it to class.

52. Interview three elementary school teachers. Ask what they do to make their students more familiar with the ways in which people earn their living. Bring to class a composite list of the things that these elementary teachers do.

53. Quickly review the entire text to this point. Formulate a plan for one thing that you intend to do in your present or future job as a result of the things you have learned in this course. Prepare to describe your plan to the class if you are asked to do so.

54. Imagine that you are the top administrative officer in the organization in which you now work or hope to work. Formulate a plan for one thing that you would do about occupational information in your organization. Prepare to describe your plan to the class if you are asked to do so.

55. If you were to teach this course, what would you do differently? What would you retain from the content and methods of the course as it has been taught this year? If you prefer to make some comments anonymously, put them on a separate sheet without your name on it.

56. You are a teacher in a high school which has never done much to inform its students about occupations. Your principal calls you to his office and says, "I think we ought to do something to make our students better informed about occupations. I'm looking for ideas. How do you

think we ought to go about it?" Write your reply on one page and bring it to class.

57. Formulate a plan for evaluating something that you now do or plan to do. Prepare to describe your plan to the class if you are asked to do so.

58. Prepare a one-page summary of the occupational information services provided in your school, college, or counseling agency. If you are not so employed, choose a school with which you are or can become familiar. Include the following information: name and address of institution; grades included; number of boys, girls, teachers; number and nature of guidance staff; past and present occupational information activities that you think (1) have worked well, (2) are of doubtful value.

Make enough copies of this report so that each member of the class may have one. Bring these to class on the date that this assignment is due.

Sample report

High School, Somewhere, New Jersey. Grades 9–12. 200 boys. 200 girls. 16 teachers. One full-time counselor who teaches courses in occupations.

Occupational information activities that have worked well:
1. Course in occupations for seniors
2. Form for requesting interviews
3. Bulletin board for new books

Occupational information activities of doubtful value:
1. Career day

59. Browse through the back issues of any of the journals listed below. Find and read five articles that discuss some aspect of occupational information. Look for ideas that you can use in your present or future work. Submit a report on two pages: (1) your plans for using anything that you learned from this assignment: (2) full bibliographic data on the articles that you read.

Start page 1 with the words "I intend to . . . ." If you cannot get one good idea from the five articles, continue reading additional articles until you do get results.

Journals

American Child
Bulletin of the National Association of Secondary School Principals
Clearing House
Employment Security Review

Journal of College Placement
Journal of College Student Personnel
Personnel and Guidance Journal
School Counselor
Vocational Guidance Quarterly

The journals in your own specialty, e.g., vocational rehabilitation, vocational education, industrial arts, nursing, social work, industrial personnel work.

60. Read the material assigned. As you read, note anything that is not entirely clear to you, anything you do not understand, anything that seems to you to be unsound or debatable, anything you would like to challenge, anything about which you would like to ask a question, or anything that you would like to have discussed in class. Note also any suggested activities that you have seen in operation, with which you have had experience that you could report to the class, or on which you would like to comment. Whenever you encounter anything of this kind, stop reading and write your question or comment. Put each question or comment on a separate sheet of 8½- by 11-inch paper. In the top left corner put the number of the page in the publication that provoked your response. In the top right corner put your name and seat number. Hand these sheets to the class secretary at the beginning of the class period.

61. For students whose major field is guidance and personnel administration and who have not done this already in one of this instructor's classes: Prepare a brief autobiography covering anything that you think might help the instructor to be more helpful to you. What do you hope to get out of this course? Why? How do you hope to get it? If the instructor had unlimited time, how could he be of most help to you? If you have written a similar autobiography for another class and have a copy of it, this may be substituted.

62. Review the history of your own occupational preferences and of the information that influenced them. Recall the sources of this information. List all these sources, and compare them for probable accuracy and adequacy. Compare your own experience with what you know or can learn about the occupational preferences of the students or clients whom you serve and with what you know or can learn about the sources from which they get their information. Reflect upon what you might do to help them to get better information upon which to base their decisions.

63. Look back over your own educational and vocational experience, and try to recall any times when you were given vocational guidance by anyone. Select three of these occasions, recall the guidance you were given and evaluate it in the light of your subsequent experience. Then consider how your experience as a client may help you to improve your service to your clients.

64. Sometimes we grow so accustomed to our work that we do not notice how much it affects our happiness. For twenty-four hours, observe and record every aspect of your daily work that brings you feelings of satisfaction, pleasure, frustration, annoyance, or any other emotion. Compile a list of all the emotions associated with your work during this time, and of what aroused these emotions. Browse through Hoppock [225], noting particularly Chapters 1, 2 and 3 and the epilogue. Reflect upon what you might do to increase your own job satisfaction.

65. For twenty-four hours, think about the occupation of every person you see at work and of the persons in every place of business that you pass. Ask yourself what you think would happen to employment in these occupations in the event of a severe economic depression. Select the occupations that you think would be most likely to offer steady employment in periods of depression. Learn anything you can about what happened to employment in these occupations during previous economic cycles.

66. Identify five occupations in which you feel reasonably sure you could perform as well as, or better than, the average worker and five other occupations in which you think your performance would be so far below average that you would find it difficult to hold a job. For each occupation find one item of evidence to support your conclusion.

67. Find ten persons employed in ten different occupations, or ten persons all in the same occupations, or both. Ask each one, "What do you like best about your job? What do you like least about it?" See how often the answers surprise you. Consider making these questions a part of your daily conversation with other persons in other occupations to add to your store of occupational information and to give your acquaintances the pleasure of talking about themselves.

68. Ask your students what occupations they expect to enter when they go to work. Tabulate their responses. Consider what your community would be like if all of its workers chose these same occupations in these same proportions.

69. Examine Mahoney [317]. Read the list of items considered essential to the basic preparation of a counselor, select those that you want to know more about, copy each selected item at the top of a blank page in your notebook, look for the information you want throughout this course, and record the information in your notebook as you find it.

70. Appraise the adequacy of your own occupational information about the employment opportunities for the students or clients that you now serve or hope to serve. From the suggestions in Chapter 2, select some things that you can do to extend your own knowledge of these occupations and start doing them.

71. Select one occupation that you have sometimes thought you might like to enter but in which you have had no experience. Read the checklist in Chapter 3 with this occupation in mind. Consider what additional information you should have if you were seriously thinking of changing to this occupation.

72. Ask some of your students or clients to read the checklist in Chapter 3 and then to tell you what additional information they would like to have on the occupations they are considering.

73. Ask your students what they would like to know about occupations. Select several of their questions on which they need help that you would like to give them. Go and get the information. If you need help, ask for it in class.

74. Examine the books and pamphlets on occupations in your school, college, agency, or public library. Appraise some of them by the criteria suggested in Chapter 5.

75. Go to any library that has both a collection of occupational publications and the *Dictionary of Occupational Titles,* volumes I and II. Select several books and pamphlets, each describing a different occupation or group of occupations. Select the *D.O.T.* classification number under which you would file each publication. Decide how you would cross-index those publications that describe more than one occupation.

76. Visit each of the following:

The libraries where you work
The public library nearest where you live or work
The manager of the nearest office of your state employment service

Explain that you are a teacher, a counselor, or a counselor in training, and that you want to learn more about sources of occupational information for your students or clients. Ask the persons in charge to tell you and show you what kinds of information about occupations and about schools and colleges you can obtain at each place. Ask how they file occupational information and what they have found to be the advantages and disadvantages of their filing plans.

77. If you are now employed as a teacher, ask your students these two questions: "If you could have your choice of all the jobs in the world, what would you choose? Considering your abilities and limitations and opportunities, what occupation do you think you are most likely to

enter after you finish school?" Examine the responses, and see whether your students are more or less realistic than you expected. Consider whether or not you should do anything to make them more aware of reality.

78. In your next ten counseling interviews or in your casual conversations, be as nondirective as you know how to be and as the situation permits. See what happens.

79. Review your own counseling to see if you have been using occupational information in the ways that you now think you should. If you think changes are desirable, make the changes and observe the results as well as you can.

80. Ask all the students in your classes to answer this question: "If the elective courses in our school included a course on opportunities and requirements in different occupations and if you were free to take the course this year, would you take it?" See how much demand there is for a course in occupations in your school. Consider whether or not you should do anything about it. If you are not a teacher, omit this assignment.

81. Read "Training for Failure" in the March, 1938, issue of *Occupations*, pages 563 to 564.

Think about what *you* should do for those of your clients who might do well as proprietors of their own small businesses.

82. Find out whether your school or agency has ever made a follow-up study of its former students or clients. If it has, examine the results to see how many surprises you can find.

83. Using the procedures suggested in Chapter 13 and any others you can invent, learn as much as you can about the present occupations of the former students or clients of your school, college, or agency.

84. If possible take a group of your own students or clients on a plant tour. If this is not feasible, go on a plant tour yourself, and do the things you would ask your students to do if you were taking them.

85. Examine the classified section of your local telephone directory. Prepare a list of the larger business classifications that you think should be called to the attention of your students or clients as potential sources of employment. Add an appropriate title and introductory paragraph, so that your list could be duplicated and distributed to the persons you serve. Consider what else you could do to make your students or clients aware of the wide range of occupations in your community.

86. Go for a one-hour walk through the business section of the territory served by your school or agency. Observe the occupations that might be open to your students or clients. Bring to class a numbered list of all the occupations you found.

87. Each day for one week read carefully the business news in your daily newspaper, including the help-wanted and situation-wanted advertisements. See what you can learn about present and probable future employment opportunities for the students or clients you serve. Notice the kinds of jobs that are offered, what they pay, and what they require. Consider whether or not you should read such news regularly and whether or not an assignment like this would be of value to the persons with whom you work.

88. If you are a teacher, plan and conduct a lesson, a project, or other activity on employment opportunities in one or more occupations related to one or more of the subjects you teach. Use one or more of the teaching techniques described in Chapters 13 to 20. Repeat with other occupations and other techniques. Compare results, using one or more of the techniques of evaluation described in Chapter 25.

89. Attend meetings of the nearest local branch of the American Personnel and Guidance Association and related groups. Talk with the people you meet. Find out what they are doing. Look for ideas you can use.

90. Consult your local telephone directory and directory of social agencies. Find the organizations that have names like Career Clinic, Job Finding Forum, and Man Marketing Clinic. Visit one or more of them. See it in action. Learn what the sponsors are trying to do and why and how. Consider whether or not you should do something similar, now or in the future. This assignment may be repeated as many as five times if you wish to visit more than one of these.

91. Visit one or more employment agencies: public, private, school, or college. See "Employment Agencies" in the classified telephone directory. Explain that you are a present or future counselor or teacher and that you are trying to learn something about agencies to which you might refer applicants. Ask if they will tell you what kinds of applicants the agency registers, what kinds of jobs it handles, and what kinds of applicants are easiest and hardest to place. Inquire about fees. Ask for sample registration forms and contracts, and read them.

92. Find one way in which you can use something that you learned in this course. Use it. Evaluate the results. Submit a one-page report.

93. Write to all the organizations listed below, as indicated in these assignments. Examine the material that you receive. Write one page on your reactions to what you have received, in terms of its value to you and your students or clients, and how you propose to use any of it. The addresses were correct at date of publication. Anyone using the list should check.

In these assignments, "P and L" means write to this organization as follows: "Please send a list of your publications on occupational infor-

mation and vocational guidance to [your name and present address]
and send announcements of future publications to [your name and
future address]." Use your official letterhead if possible.

Whe   u receive the list of publications, order any that interest you,
and reau ..1em.

Write to:

The principal publishers of occupational information listed in Appendix A, for P and L.

U.S. Employment Service, Washington, for P and L.

Your own state employment service for P and L.

U.S. Bureau of Apprenticeship and Training, Washington, for P and L.

Your own state apprenticeship council for P and L.

U.S. Bureau of Labor Standards, Washington, for P and L.

U.S. Civil Service Commission, Washington; the State Civil Service
Commission in your home state; and the Municipal Civil Service Commission in your home town for announcements of all future examinations of interest to your students or clients.

U.S. Office of Education, Guidance and Personnel Services Branch,
Washington, for P and L.

Your own state department of education, Guidance Service, for P and L.

Your own state department of education and your own state department of labor for any free publications which describe the employment certificates issued to minors and the responsibilities of the school counselor in connection therewith. Read enough of what they send you to become generally familiar with your responsibilities in this area.

U.S. Vocational Rehabilitation Administration, Washington, for P and L.

U.S. Small Business Administration, Washington, for P and L.

Superintendent of Documents, Washington, for P and L.

The department of commerce of your own state, at the state capital, for P and L.

The chamber of commerce of your own state and your own city for P and L.

American Personnel and Guidance Association, 1605 New Hampshire Ave., N.W., Washington, for P and L.

College Placement Council, 35 E. Elizabeth Ave., Bethlehem, Pa., for P and L.

American Federation of Labor and Congress of Industrial Organizations, 815 16 St., N.W., Washington, for P and L.

National Association of Manufacturers, 277 Park Ave., New York, for P and L.

National Child Labor Committee, 145 E. 32 St., New York, for P and L.

National Urban League, 14 E. 48 St., New York, for P and L.

National Scholarship Service and Fund for Negro Students, 6 E. 82 St., New York, for P and L.

National Council of Technical Schools, 1507 M St., N.W., Washington, for P and L.

Federal Extension Service, U.S. Department of Agriculture, Washington, for P and L.

Family Economic Bureau, Northwestern National Life Insurance Co., Minneapolis, Minn., for annual review of university and college placements.

American Nurses Association, Inc., 10 Columbus Circle, New York, for P and L.

National Association of Social Workers, 2 Park Ave., New York, for P and L.

Director of College Recruiting:

Armstrong Cork Co., Lancaster, Pa.

E. I. du Pont de Nemours & Co., Wilmington, Del.

General Foods Corp., White Plains, N.Y.

General Motors Corp., Detroit, Mich.

Texaco Inc., 135 E. 42 St., New York

Ask for brochures on employment opportunities for college graduates.

Director of Employment:

Chase Manhattan Bank, 1 Chase Manhattan Plaza, New York.

Your local telephone company.

Ask for pamphlets on jobs for high school graduates and dropouts.

94. Find a client who needs and wants occupational information to help him to choose an occupation and who can work with you all term. Get the facts for him, and deliver them to him. Do a thorough job, using everything appropriate that you learn in this course. Discuss with your client the probable accuracy and adequacy of the information you get and his feelings about it. If you lose one client during the term, get another. Keep a complete record of everything you do. Hand in a one-page summary of what you did and of your own and your client's evaluation of it.

Do *not* refer your client to other sources of information. *You* go to the sources. *You* read the references. *You* get the facts. *You* compare sources to verify the information. *You* present the information to your client only when *you* are sure it is the most accurate and the most adequate information that *you* can provide. *Never* forget that if *you* make a mistake, your client may suffer for it for years to come.

95. From your own follow-up reports or from your own community survey or from your classified telephone directory or from volume II of

the *Dictionary of Occupational Titles,* compile a list of occupations that you want to learn more about. Arrange the occupations in order of their interest to you. Study as many of these occupations as your time permits, as thoroughly as your interest indicates. See Chapter 4 on "Sources of Occupational Information." Submit a one-page report, briefly describing what you did and listing some of the things you learned from this project.

96. Make a list of the occupations which appear in as many motion pictures or television programs or short stories or books of fiction as you have time to see or read before this assignment is due. Consider whether the nature of the occupation is presented accurately or not. Would a person get a correct or a false impression of the occupation from what you have seen? In your report, list the name of the picture or program or story and the occupations shown. Opposite each occupation write A, B, or C to indicate your rating of the accuracy of the impression conveyed.

97. Prepare a photographic follow-up report on the present jobs of ten or more of your former students or clients, with pictures of them at their work and a running commentary on what they do, what they earn, how they got their jobs, etc.

98. Do a photographic survey of ten or more jobs for beginners in the neighborhood of your school or agency. For each job, get pictures of workers at their work, showing their principal activities. Add such explanatory comments as you would want for your students or clients.

99. Visit ten or more placement offices or employment agencies— public, private, school, college, etc. To find them, look in your classified telephone directory under "Employment Agencies." Explain that you are a present or future counselor or teacher and that you may wish to refer applicants to the agency. Ask if they will tell you what kinds of jobs the agency handles and what kinds of applicants are easiest and hardest to place.

Submit a two-page report. On page one, list the agencies visited and star (*) those which were cordial and cooperative. On page two, summarize the most interesting things you learned.

100. Ask the instructor to assign you to a specific bibliography of occupational information. Write to all the publishers of free materials listed therein, as follows: "Gentlemen: Will you please send me any free publications of yours that contain facts about jobs for use in vocational guidance." Prepare and submit a list of the publishers who send you any free material that you think counselors would like to have, with the address of each publisher and the titles of the free occupational publications received from each.

101. From the *Occupational Outlook Handbook* prepare a list of occupations in which the employment outlook is favorable. From your list, select those that offer the most opportunities in your community. Check local sources of information, e.g., placement services, employers, unions, employees, regarding local opportunities. Compile a final list of occupations in which the outlook is good both locally and nationally. In not more than five pages, report what you did and what you learned and how this experience has affected your plans for the future. Give both reports to the instructor on the date assigned.

102. Examine all the books, pamphlets, and magazine articles you can find on elementary education published in the past two years. Select short quotations that summarize what these publications say about the use of occupational information in elementary schools. Put each quotation on a separate sheet of paper, and add full bibliographic data on the source. Bibliographic data for each reference should include authors' names and initials, title of book or article, copyright date, name of journal if an article, name and address of publisher if a book, page numbers from which you took quotations, the library call number, and the library in which you found the reference. On a separate sheet list the author and title of each book you examined that said nothing on this subject.

103. Same as assignment 102 but with books, pamphlets, and magazine articles on guidance, counseling, and interviewing, published in the past two years, to see what they say about the use of occupational information in counseling.

104. Interview the counselors and librarians of ten high schools or ten colleges. Get the best estimate you can of how much each school spent for occupational information during some recent period of twelve months and the best record you can get of what they spent it for. Find out how many students were enrolled in the school during the same period. Compute the expenditure per pupil per year for occupational information for each school and for the total group of schools. Submit a full report.

105. Using the *Education Index* as a guide, explore periodical literature on the uses of occupational information in counseling and in teaching. Look for ideas that you can use. Each time you get an idea, write a one-paragraph description of it. Add full bibliographic data on the source. Submit these notes as your report.

106. Find some way in which you can help some group of people who want occupational information to get what they want. The group may be a school or college class or club, a community youth group, a parents' association, or any other organized or unorganized group. You may use one or more of the methods of teaching occupations described in the text, or you may invent your own methods. Submit a one-page report summarizing what you did and your own and your group's evaluation of it.

107. Bring to class one or more questions that you would like to ask other members of the class whose present or future work is in some way similar to yours.

108. If you are a teacher, or counselor, ask the students or clients who are assigned to you: "In what occupations are you interested? What would you like to know about them?" Get the answers in writing. Read them. Select some of the questions raised, and help your students or clients to find the answers.

109. Take a group of your own students or clients on a plant tour.

110. Prepare a photographic report on *all* the duties of one person now employed *as a beginner* in any job that you might reasonably expect to be open to the persons with whom you now work or hope to work. If you are now employed in a school, college, or agency, use one of your former students or clients as a subject. Show the report to your present students or clients.

111. Using everything you now know about the sources of occupational information, find the best answers you can to the question or questions assigned.

112. Examine one or more of the following. Quickly scan the preface, table of contents, and index to see if the book contains anything of interest to you. Read as much or as little as you like. If you learn nothing useful in the first fifteen to thirty minutes, try another book.

Baer, M. F., and E. C. Roeber: *Occupational Information.* [14]
Borow, H. (ed.): *Man in a World at Work.* [34]
Isaacson, L. E.: *Career Information in Counseling and Teaching.* [253]
Norris, W.: *Occupational Information in the Elementary School.* [360]
Norris, W., and others: *The Information Service in Guidance.* [361]
Shartle, C. L.: *Occupational Information.* [426]

113. A boy was always collecting and caring for animals of all kinds. At age sixteen, a university psychologist tested the boy and reported that he had high-level aptitudes in English and in science. His high school average was ninety-six.

He went to a liberal arts college, majored in science, and became editor of the college newspaper. He spent each summer in camp, continuing his interest in animals.

In his senior year of college, he applied for admission to colleges of veterinary medicine. He was denied admission because he was currently failing in organic chemistry.

He asks you, "What other occupations are there for a person like me?"

Consult volume II of the *Dictionary of Occupational Titles*. Bring to class a list of possible occupations for this student to consider. Include the *D.O.T.* code number and title of each occupation. Arrange and number the occupations in order of their probable appropriateness for this student. Keep your list for use in class and for possible future reference.

114. If you work in a high school or college, find out if a unit or a course in occupations is taught there. Talk with the teacher, ask if you may visit and observe the class. If the teacher is cooperative, ask if you may take over one or more sessions and try your hand at a case conference, a group conference, a practice job interview, or a plant tour.

115. Arrange to spend all or part of one day talking with a person and observing his work in some job that you would like to have some day, or in some occupation that seems likely to be open to your students or clients, or in some other occupation that interests you.

116. Find one former student of your school or college, or one former client of your agency, who fits the following description:

> He has completed his formal education.
> He has completed his military or alternate service, or has not yet been called.
> He is now employed.
> He has been employed not more than five years since he left your school, college, or agency.

Arrange for a leisurely personal interview with him. In this interview, learn all that he is willing to tell you about:

> His present job:
> What are *all* the things he has to do?
> What does he like best about it?
> What does he like least about it?
> How did he get it?
> What suggestions would he offer to *your* students or clients if they wanted to get a job like his?
> His vocational development:
> What were his vocational choices at different times?
> When did he change them and why?

Before the interview, get all the information you can about him from the records of your school, college, or agency and from counselors and teachers who knew him.

Look for records of any discussion of vocational preferences in any counseling interviews and for records of any vocational aptitude tests or interest inventories.

Submit a summary of the most interesting things you learned from this experience. Maximum length, one page.

On the reverse side of the page, report how this experience has affected your thoughts, your actions, and *your plans for the future*.

117. Visit five, ten, or fifteen factories, stores, offices, and other places of employment where your students or clients might find jobs. See, hear, feel, and smell the environment in which people work. Observe what they do. Take your students or clients with you if you wish.

Interview the employer about opportunities and requirements in the jobs for which your students or clients might be hired. Interview union representatives or other employees if possible.

Try to include some places in which your former students or clients have found jobs, and interview them as well as the employer. You may find some interesting differences in the answers you get—not because either one is trying to deceive you, but because they see things from different points of view.

Before each visit, read any parts of the *Occupational Outlook Handbook* that cover occupations or industries that you might expect to see. You may then ask better questions and learn more of what you want to know.

Prepare a reference notebook that you will want to keep on your desk for your own use in teaching and counseling. If you type, please make a carbon copy that we may keep to show future students here.

118. From the assigned reading, copy and bring to class one or more of these:

1. One sentence with which you heartily agree
2. One sentence with which you disagree
3. One question you would like to raise for discussion

Hold your paper until the end of the period. Then give it to the class secretary.

Bibliography

1. *Abstracts of Sociological Literature on Occupations*, Vocational Guidance and Rehabilitation Services, Cleveland, Ohio, 1965.
2. *Accident Prevention Manual for Industrial Operations*, National Safety Council, Chicago (see latest edition).
3. *Accredited Higher Institutions*, Government Printing Office, Washington (see latest edition).
4. *Accredited Institutions of Higher Education*, American Council on Education, Washington (see latest edition).
5. Adler, K. R.: *Pathway to Your Future: The Job Resume and Letter of Application*, Bellman Publishing Company, Cambridge, Mass., 1964.
6. *After Teen-agers Quit School*, U.S. Department of Labor, 1951.
7. Allen, R. D.: *Case-conference Problems in Group Guidance*, Inor Publishing Co., New York, 1933.
8. Allen, R. D.: *Common Problems in Group Guidance*, Inor Publishing Co., New York, 1933.
9. Allen, R. D.: *Self-measurement Projects in Group Guidance*, Inor Publishing Co., New York, 1934.
10. Ames, D. A.: "Toms River Surveys Its Needs," *Personnel and Guidance Journal*, January, 1953, p. 227.
11. "Annual Career Carnival," *Journal of College Placement*, December, 1957, p. 95.
12. Averill, L. A.: *The Psychology of the Elementary School Child*, David McKay Company, Inc., New York, 1949.
13. Babbott, E.: "What Shall I Do This Summer?" *School Counselor*, March, 1964, p. 154.
14. Baer, M. F., and E. C. Roeber: *Occupational Information*, Science Research Associates, Inc., Chicago, 2d ed., 1958, 3d ed., 1964.
15. Bailard, V.: "Vocational Guidance Begins in the Elementary Grades," *Clearing House*, April, 1952, p. 496.
16. Barbarosh, B.: Memorandum to C. R. Losi, January, 1955.
17. Barrett, E. S.: "College Visitation Workshop," *School Counselor*, October, 1963, p. 48.
18. Beachley, C.: "Careers via Closed Circuit Television," *Vocational Guidance Quarterly*, Winter, 1958–1959, p. 67.
19. Bedell, R., and W. H. Nelson: "Educators' Opinions on Occupational Information Use in Rural High Schools," *Occupations*, December, 1950, p. 205.
20. Beery, J. R., B. C. Hayes, and E. Landy: *The School Follows Through*, National Association of Secondary School Principals, Washington, 1941.
21. Belanger, L. L., and W. M. Lifton: SRA Occupational Exploration Kit, Science Research Associates, Inc., Chicago, 1961.
22. Belen, E. D.: Memorandum to R. Hoppock, May 14, 1960.
23. Belman, H. S., and B. Shertzer: *My Career Guidebook* (with Coun-

selor's and Teacher's Manual), The Bruce Publishing Company, Milwaukee, 1963.

24. *Bennett Occupations Filing Plan and Bibliography,* Sterling Powers Publishing Company, 18½ Palmer St., Athens, Ohio, 1958.

25. Bergstresser, J. L.: "Counseling and the Changing Secondary-school Curriculum," *Bulletin of the National Association of Secondary School Principals,* May, 1940, p. 67.

26. Berkowitz, B.: "The 'Leftys' Make You Stop and Think," *Vocational Guidance Quarterly,* Autumn, 1955, p. 16.

27. Bingham, W. V., B. V. Moore, and J. W. Gustad: *How to Interview,* 4th ed., Harper & Row, Publishers, Incorporated, New York, 1959.

28. Bley, G.: "Job Surveys," *Youth and Work,* National Child Labor Committee, New York, Autumn, 1955, p. 1.

29. Bley, G. (ed.): *Youth and Work,* National Child Labor Committee, New York, Summer, 1955, p. 1.

30. Bley, G. (ed.): *Youth and Work,* National Child Labor Committee, New York, Winter, 1955, p. 3.

31. "Blue Book of Audiovisual Materials," published annually in *Educational Screen and Audiovisual Guide,* Chicago.

32. Borg, W. R.: *Educational Research, an Introduction,* David McKay Company, Inc., New York, 1963.

33. Borow, H.: "College Courses in Vocational Planning," *Vocational Guidance Quarterly,* Winter, 1960–1961, p. 75.

34. Borow, H. (ed.): *Man in a World at Work,* Houghton Mifflin Company, Boston, 1964.

35. Borow, H., and R. Hoppock: "Students Appraise Job Study Outlines," *Personnel and Guidance Journal,* October, 1953, p. 93.

36. Borow, H., and R. V. Lindsey: *Vocational Planning for College Students,* Prentice-Hall, Inc., Englewood Cliffs, N.J., 1959.

37. Boyer, P. A.: Letter to principals of junior high, senior high, and vocational schools, with enclosures, Oct. 5, 1945.

38. Bradford, J. K.: "CERP—The Toronto Experiment," *Journal of College Placement,* May, 1958, p. 26.

39. Brayfield, A. H., and G. T. Mickelson: "Disparities in Occupational Information Coverage," *Occupations,* April, 1951, p. 506.

40. Brayfield, A. H., and P. A. Reed: "How Readable Are Occupational Information Booklets?" *Journal of Applied Psychology,* October, 1950, p. 325.

41. Breiter, L. R.: Memorandum to R. Hoppock, July 5, 1963.

42. Brewer, J. M.: *History of Vocational Guidance,* Harper & Row, Publishers, Incorporated, New York, 1942.

43. Brill, A. A.: *Basic Principles of Psychoanalysis,* Doubleday & Company, Inc., Garden City, N.Y., 1949.

44. Brochard, J. H., H. Beilin, and A. S. Thompson: *Middletown Occupational Handbook,* a publication of the Career Pattern Study, Teachers College Press, Columbia University, New York, 1954. (Mimeographed. Obtainable from the Board of Education, Middle-

town, N.Y.) A superb example of a community occupational survey reported in appropriate terms for use in vocational guidance.

45. Brooke, F. E., and E. H. Herrington: *Students Make Motion Pictures: A Report on Film Production in the Denver Schools*, American Council on Education, Washington, 1941.

46. Brooks, A. B.: "Occupations Week," *Wilson Library Bulletin*, January, 1942, p. 364.

47. Brunner, K. A.: *Guide to Organized Occupational Curriculums in Higher Education*, Government Printing Office, Washington (see latest edition).

48. Buell, C. E.: "Occupational Guidance by the Elementary School Teacher," *Educational Administration and Supervision*, April, 1949, p. 242.

49. Burchill, G. W.: *Work-Study Programs for Alienated Youth*, Science Research Associates, Inc., Chicago, 1962.

50. Burianek, B., and W. Tennyson: "File It for Display Use," *Vocational Guidance Quarterly*, Winter, 1955–1956, p. 51.

51. Byrn, D. K.: *How to Express Yourself Vocationally*, National Vocational Guidance Association, Washington, 1961.

52. Calvert, R., Jr.: *How to Recruit Minority Group College Graduates*, Personnel Journal, Swarthmore, Pa., 1963.

53. Calvert, R., Jr., E. M. Carter, and I. Murphy: "College Courses in Occupational Adjustment," *Personnel and Guidance Journal*, March, 1964, p. 680.

54. Calvert, R., Jr., and J. E. Steele: *Planning Your Career*, McGraw-Hill Book Company, New York, 1963.

55. Cameron, D. W.: Letter to R. Hoppock, Oct. 10, 1961.

56. *Canadian Universities and Colleges*, Canadian Universities Foundation, Ottawa, Canada (see latest edition).

57. Cantor, N.: *Dynamics of Learning*, Henry Stewart, Incorporated, Buffalo, N.Y., 1946.

58. Caplow, T.: *The Sociology of Work*, The University of Minnesota Press, Minneapolis, 1954.

59. *Career Guidance Index*, published periodically by Careers, Largo, Fla.

60. *Career Guide for Demand Occupations*, Government Printing Office, Washington, 1965.

61. *Career Index*, published periodically by Chronicle Guidance Publications, Inc., Moravia, N.Y.

62. *Career Information Kit*, Science Research Associates, Inc., Chicago, 1965.

63. *Career Insights, Announcement Folder and Student Workbook*, Project Coordinator, Charles M. Achilles, University of Rochester, Rochester, N.Y., 1965.

64. Carrington, E. S.: "Working with Hands and Brains," *Occupations*, May, 1935, p. 694.

65. Carson, E. O., and F. M. Daly: *Teen-agers Prepare for Work*, book I, Esther Carson, Castro Valley, Calif., 1956.

66. Carson, E. O., and C. Tyler: *Teen-agers Prepare for Work*, book II, Esther Carson, Castro Valley, Calif., 1957.
67. Carter, E. M., and R. Hoppock: "College Courses in Careers—1952," *Personnel and Guidance Journal*, February, 1953, p. 315.
68. Carter, E. M., and R. Hoppock: "College Courses in Careers," *Personnel and Guidance Journal*, January, 1961, p. 373.
69. Cartter, A. M. (ed.): *American Universities and Colleges*, 9th ed., American Council on Education, Washington, 1964.
70. *Catalog and Bulletin*, Southern Technical Institute, Marietta, Ga., 1966–1967.
71. Cavanaugh, G. P.: *Guidance in the Denver Elementary Schools*, Public Schools, Denver, Colo., 1960.
72. Cavitt, E. B.: Letter to R. Hoppock, Feb. 25, 1955.
73. Chamberlain, L. M., and L. W. Kindred: *The Teacher and School Organization*, Prentice-Hall, Inc., Englewood Cliffs, N.J., 1949.
74. Charters, W. W., and others: *A Study of Techniques for Evaluating Occupational Literature*, Ohio State University Bureau of Educational Research, Columbus, Ohio, 1938. Available in large university libraries.
75. Chervenik, E.: "Demonstration Employment Interviews," *Occupations*, April, 1950, p. 433.
76. Chervenik, E.: *Planning a Job Opportunities Conference*, United States National Student Association, Madison, Wis., 1948.
77. Chervenik, E.: "Tempting Students to Sample Occupational Information," *Vocational Guidance Quarterly*, Winter, 1953, p. 39.
78. Chmura, S. J.: *Social Studies Outlines: Grades I to VIII*, Public Schools, Chicopee, Mass., no date. (In five volumes.)
79. Christensen, T. E.: "Helping Students Enter Industry," *Vocational Guidance Quarterly*, Autumn, 1954, p. 24.
80. Christensen, T. E.: Letter to R. Hoppock, Nov. 29, 1961.
81. Christensen, T. E.: *Resource Units for Junior High School Orientation Classes*, Public Schools, Worcester, Mass., 1961. (Not for sale. May be borrowed for one month from the author.)
82. Christensen, T. E.: *The Self-appraisal and Careers Course Helps Seniors Achieve Educational, Vocational, Personal Maturity*, Superintendent of Schools, Worcester, Mass., 1953.
83. Christensen, T. E., and M. K. Burns: *Resource Units in Self-appraisal and Careers*, Public Schools, Worcester, Mass., 1954. A handbook for teachers of Worcester's twelfth-grade elective course in self-appraisal and careers. (Not for sale. Directors of guidance may borrow a copy from Dr. Christensen.)
84. Chronicle Plan for Filing Unbound Occupational Information, Chronicle Guidance Publications, Moravia, N.Y., 1966.
85. Churchill, E. C.: "Community Career Day," *American Vocational Journal*, December, 1949, p. 10.
86. Clark, H. F.: *Economic Theory and Correct Occupational Distribution*, Teachers College Press, Columbia University, New York, 1931.

87. Clark, R. W.: Memorandum to R. Hoppock, Jan. 17, 1953.
88. Clark, V. M.: "A Local Occupational Survey," *Vocational Guidance Quarterly*, Winter, 1962, p. 115.
89. Clark, V. M.: Memorandum to R. Hoppock, Aug. 25, 1961.
90. Clary, J. R., and H. E. Beam: "Realistic Vocational Education for Ninth Graders," *American Vocational Journal*, May, 1965, p. 16.
91. Cleland, H. L.: "A Follow-up Survey through Visual Aids," *Occupations*, February, 1941, p. 331.
92. Clifton, R. S.: "Counseling Youth for Military Service," *Personnel and Guidance Journal*, December, 1955, p. 202.
93. Cole, R. C.: *An Evaluation of the Vocational Guidance Program in the Worcester Boys' Club*, Boys' Club, Worcester, Mass., 1939. (Out of print.)
94. *College Placement Annual*, College Placement Council. (Not for sale. Available at college placement offices affiliated with the council through regional placement associations. Available on request to subscribers to the *Journal of College Placement*.)
95. *The Colonial*, 1961 Yearbook of William Floyd High School, Mastic, N.Y., p. 38.
96. Combs, A. W.: "Non-directive Techniques and Vocational Counseling," *Occupations*, February, 1947, p. 261.
97. Comfort, A.: *Authority and Delinquency in the Modern State: A Criminological Approach to the Problem of Power*, Routledge and Kegan Paul, Ltd., London, 1950.
98. Conant, J. B.: *Slums and Suburbs*, McGraw-Hill Book Company, New York, 1961.
99. *Conducting a Job Opportunity Survey of Your Community*, State Education Department, Bureau of Guidance, Albany, N.Y., 1945.
100. *Conversion Table of Code and Title Changes between Second Edition and Third Edition, Dictionary of Occupational Titles*, Government Printing Office, Washington, 1965.
101. Cooley, W. W.: *The Classification of Career Plans*. Proceedings of the 73d Annual Convention, American Psychological Association, Washington, 1965.
102. *The Corpsman*, a periodical published by The Job Corps, Washington, for the men and women of The Job Corps.
103. Corre, M. P.: "Filing Occupational Information," *Occupations*, November, 1943, p. 122.
104. *Counselor's Guide to Occupational and Other Manpower Information*, Government Printing Office, Washington, 1964.
105. *Counselors' Information Service*, published periodically by B'nai B'rith Vocational Service, Washington.
106. A Counselor's Professional File, Chronicle Guidance Publications, Moravia, N.Y., 1964.
107. Cox, C. L.: Memorandum to R. Hoppock, October, 1952.
108. Cronin, A.: "Reclaimed Housewives," *Women's Education*, September, 1964, p. 5.

109. Crosby, M. J.: "Planning Vocationally and Finding a Job," in E. Lloyd-Jones and M. R. Smith, *Student Personnel Work as Deeper Teaching*, Harper & Row, Publishers, Incorporated, New York, 1954.
110. Crosby, O. A.: "Careers Unlimited," *Scholastic Teacher*, Feb. 16, 1956, p. 9-T.
111. Cuony, E. R.: "An Evaluation of Teaching Job Finding and Job Orientation," doctoral thesis, New York University School of Education, New York, 1953, summarized in E. R. Cuony and R. Hoppock, "Job Course Pays Off," *Personnel and Guidance Journal*, March, 1954, p. 389.
112. Cuony, E. R.: "The Follow-up Study in the Junior High School Orientation Program," *Personnel and Guidance Journal*, May, 1962, p. 812.
113. Cuony, E. R., and R. Hoppock: "Job Course Pays Off Again," *Personnel and Guidance Journal*, October, 1957, p. 116.
114. Dale, R. V. H.: "To Youth Who Choose Blindly," *Occupations*, April, 1948, p. 419.
115. Davenel, G.: "Retooling for the Space Age," *Journal of College Placement*, December, 1959, p. 21.
116. Davis, J. A.: *Great Aspirations: Volume I. Career Decisions and Educational Plans during College*, Report No. 90, National Opinion Research Center, University of Chicago, Chicago, 1963.
117. "A Day with a Social Worker," *Glamour*, November, 1953, p. 142.
118. Dempsey, F., and L. Z. Begnoche: "An Early Look at the Employment Market," *Vocational Guidance Quarterly*, Spring, 1960, p. 145.
119. *Developing Work-Study Programs for Potential Dropouts*, Bureau of Guidance, State Education Department, Albany, N.Y., 1965.
120. Diamond, E.: "Bring the Occupational File Out into the Open," *Vocational Guidance Quarterly*, Summer, 1959, p. 219.
121. Diamond, E.: "Publicizing Career Conferences," *Vocational Guidance Quarterly*, Winter, 1962, p. 113.
122. Dickinson, C.: "How College Seniors' Preferences Compare with Employment and Enrollment Data," *Personnel and Guidance Journal*, April, 1954, p. 485.
123. *Dictionary of Occupational Titles*, 3d ed., Vol. I, *Definitions of Titles;* Vol. II, *Occupational Classification and Industry Index*, Government Printing Office, Washington, 1965 (see new editions and supplements as issued).
124. Diener, T. F., and H. R. Kaczkowski: "Readability of Occupational Information," *Vocational Guidance Quarterly*, Winter, 1960, p. 87.
125. Dierkes, W. A.: *Evaluation of the Careers Unlimited Program for 1965*, Detroit Public Schools in Cooperation with the Institute for Economic Education, Inc., Detroit, Mich., 1965.
126. Dillon, H. J.: *Work Experience in Secondary Education*, National Child Labor Committee, New York, 1946.
127. Dingilian, D. H., R. D. Samson, W. T. Speers, and B. Stefflre: "Local Occupational Information," *Vocational Guidance Quarterly*, Summer, 1954, p. 109.

128. *Directory,* National Association of Trade and Technical Schools, Washington (see latest edition).
129. *Directory of Accredited Private Home Study Schools,* Accrediting Commission of the National Home Study Council, Washington (see latest edition).
130. *Directory of National and International Labor Unions in the United States,* Government Printing Office, Washington (see latest edition).
131. *Directory of National Trade and Professional Associations of the United States,* Columbia Books, Washington (see latest edition).
132. Dittersdorf, H.: "Subject Matter Centered Career Conferences," *Vocational Guidance Quarterly,* Summer, 1962, p. 248.
133. Dolan, M. C., and V. M. Yates: "We Collect Colleges," *Personnel and Guidance Journal,* February, 1954, p. 343.
134. Dresden, K. W.: "High School Seniors Survey Job Opportunities," *Occupations,* October, 1950, p. 32.
135. DuBato, G.: "Case Conference on Occupations," *Vocational Guidance Quarterly,* Summer, 1959, p. 257.
136. DuBato, G.: Memorandum to R. Hoppock, 1952.
137. DuBato, G.: "A Vocational Guidance Unit for the Non-College Bound," *Vocational Guidance Quarterly,* Autumn, 1961, p. 56.
138. DuBois, E.: Conversation with R. Hoppock, May 18, 1962.
139. Duffy, K. E.: "Vocational Guidance Begins in Grade One," *New York State Education,* June, 1950, p. 671.
140. Edmiston, R. W., and A. W. Scrivner: "Evaluation of Teaching Methods to Provide Occupational Information," *Industrial Arts and Vocational Education,* September, 1951, p. 262.
141. "Education for Jobs," *Changing Times,* June, 1966, p. 32.
142. *Education Is the Key to a Good Job,* Burroughs Corporation, Detroit, Mich., no date.
143. *Educational Media Index, Volume 7: Guidance, Psychology, and Teacher Education,* McGraw-Hill Book Company, New York, 1964.
144. Einbinder, W.: Memorandum to R. Hoppock, April 29, 1961.
145. *Encyclopedia of Associations,* vol. I, *National Organizations of the United States,* Gale Research Company, Detroit, Mich. (see latest edition and supplements in vol. III, *New Associations*).
146. *Encyclopedia of Job Descriptions in Manufacturing,* American Liberty Press, Milwaukee (see latest edition).
147. Engen, M.: "Wyoming High School Seniors Discover Their Community," *Occupations,* March, 1948, p. 361.
148. Englander, M. E.: "Influencing Vocational Choice: A Pilot Study," *Vocational Guidance Quarterly,* Winter, 1965–1966, p. 136.
149. *An Experiment: Job Clinics for the Graduating Senior,* Business Research Station, State College, Miss., 1949.
150. Faul, G. J.: "Vocational Planning and Adjustment Courses at Contra Costa College," in H. T. Morse and P. L. Dressel, *General Education for Personal Maturity,* William C. Brown & Co., Dubuque, Iowa, 1960, p. 161.

151. Feingold, S. N.: *A Career Conference for Your Community*, B'nai B'rith Vocational Service, Washington, 1964.
152. Feingold, S. N., and A. Jospe: *College Guide for Jewish Youth*, rev. ed., B'nai B'rith Vocational Service, Washington, 1963.
153. Felician, Brother, O.S.F.: Letter to R. Hoppock, no date.
154. Ferdian, J. J., Jr.: Letter to R. Hoppock, Jan. 5, 1966.
155. Fick, R. L.: "The Stockton Occupational Survey," *California Journal of Secondary Education*, December, 1948, p. 493.
156. Fink, A.: Letter to R. Hoppock, Dec. 2, 1952.
157. Flax, L.: Memorandum to R. Hoppock, Aug. 4, 1953.
158. Fletcher, F. M.: "Some Developments in Vocational Guidance and Counseling," in *Counseling Workshop, Summer, 1950: General Lectures*, Chico State College, Chico, Calif., 1950, p. 166.
159. Flowerman, S. H.: "Group-guidance through Ninth-grade English," doctoral thesis, New York University School of Education, New York, 1943.
160. Flynn, H. J., N. Saunders, and R. Hoppock: "Course for Dropouts," *Clearing House*, April, 1954, p. 486.
161. Forer, B. R.: "Personality Factors in Occupational Choice," *Educational and Psychological Measurement*, Autumn, 1953, p. 361.
162. Forkner, H. L., in R. K. Hall and J. A. Lauwerys, *Yearbook of Education, Guidance and Counseling*, Harcourt, Brace & World, Inc., New York, 1955, p. 403.
163. Forrester, G.: *Occupational Literature*, The H. W. Wilson Company, New York (see latest revision).
164. Forrester, G., and others: *A Syllabus for the Study of Occupations*, tentative revision, Board of Education, Newark, N.J., July, 1951.
165. Forte, J.: Memorandum to R. Hoppock, Aug. 6, 1957.
166. Fox, M. G.: "A Twelfth-grade Course in Occupations," *Bulletin of the National Association of Secondary School Principals*, January, 1950, p. 280.
167. Frank, R. L., and B. B. Patten: "A Three-Way Occupational File," *Vocational Guidance Quarterly*, Spring, 1960, p. 171.
168. Froehlich, C. P.: "Must Counseling Be Individual?" *Educational and Psychological Measurement*, Winter, 1958, p. 681.
169. Froehlich, C. P., and A. L. Benson: *Guidance Testing*, Science Research Associates, Inc., Chicago, 1948.
170. Frosch, A.: Memorandum to R. Hoppock, April 28, 1954.
171. Gachet, R. R.: "Filing Occupational Information for Women," *Occupations*, March, 1944, p. 354.
172. Ganley, A. L.: "Boston Follows through with Its Follow-up," *School Counselor*, no date, p. 1.
173. Gardiner, G. L.: *How You Can Get the Job You Want*, Harper & Row, Publishers, Incorporated, New York, 1962.
174. Gardner, J. W.: *From High School to Job*, reprinted from annual report of the president, Carnegie Corporation of New York, New York, 1960.
175. Gardner, L. C.: *Vistas for Women*, Report of a Special Project, Na-

tional Board, Young Women's Christian Association of the U.S.A., New York, 1963–1965.

176. Garrison, C. W.: "A Program for High School Dropouts in Bamberger's, New Jersey," in H. R. Northrup and R. L. Rowan, *The Negro and Employment Opportunity*, Bureau of Industrial Relations, University of Michigan, Ann Arbor, 1965, p. 343.

177. Gates, J. E., and H. Miller: *Personal Adjustment to Business*, Prentice-Hall, Inc., Englewood Cliffs, N.J., 1958.

178. Gaudet, F. J., and W. Kulick: "Who Comes to a Vocational Guidance Center?" *Personnel and Guidance Journal*, December, 1954, p. 211.

179. Gilles, L. L.: *Charting Your Job Future*, Science Research Associates, Inc., Chicago, 1957.

180. Ginzberg, E., S. W. Ginsburg, S. Axelrad, and J. L. Herma: *Occupational Choice: An Approach to a General Theory*, Columbia University Press, New York, 1951.

181. Ginzberg, E., and J. L. Herma: *Talent and Performance*, Columbia University Press, New York, 1964.

182. Glanz, E. C.: *Groups in Guidance*, Allyn and Bacon, Inc., Boston, 1962.

183. Gleazer, E. J., Jr., and A. M. Carroll (eds.): *American Junior Colleges*, 6th ed., American Council on Education, Washington, 1963.

184. Goedeke, M. T.: "Vocational Problems via Video," *Occupations*, January, 1951, p. 278.

185. Goldberg, H. R., and W. T. Brumber: *The Rochester Occupational Reading Series*, Science Research Associates, Inc., Chicago, 1958.

186. Goldman, L.: "Guidance Students Do Research in Occupations," *Personnel and Guidance Journal*, April, 1954, p. 475.

187. Goodwin, R. C.: *Annual Report of Services to High School Seniors and Dropouts, School Year 1964–65*, U.S. Bureau of Employment Security, Washington.

188. Grady, L. A., L. R. Malnig, and T. V. Tuleja: *Peacocks on Parade: A Survey of the Alumni of Saint Peter's College*, Alumni Association of Saint Peter's College, Jersey City, N.J., 1954.

189. Graham, J.: *A Guide to Graduate Study. Programs Leading to the Ph.D. Degree*, 3d ed., American Council on Education, Washington, 1965.

190. Graves, E. C.: *Ulrich's International Periodicals Directory*, R. R. Bowker Company, New York (see latest edition).

191. Greenberg, B.: Memorandum to R. Hoppock, April 20, 1966.

192. Greenberg, B.: Memorandum to R. Hoppock, May 4, 1966.

193. Grell, L. A.: "How Much Occupational Information in the Elementary School?" *Vocational Guidance Quarterly*, Autumn, 1960, p. 48.

194. Grube, G. E.: Memorandum to R. Hoppock, May 14, 1960.

195. Grunes, W. F.: "On Perception of Occupations," *Personnel and Guidance Journal*, January, 1956, p. 276.

196. Guerra, R. D.: *An Experimental Study to Determine the Effects of*

Presenting Occupational Information to a Ninth Grade Class, master's thesis, Northern Illinois University, De Kalb, Ill., 1963.

197. *Guidance Exchange,* a periodical, P.O. Box 1464, Grand Central Post Office, New York.

198. *Guide to College Majors,* Chronicle Guidance Publications, Moravia, N.Y. (see latest edition).

199. "Guidelines for Preparing and Evaluating Occupational Materials," *Vocational Guidance Quarterly,* Spring, 1964, p. 217.

200. Hahn, M. E., and A. H. Brayfield: *Occupational Laboratory Manual for Teachers and Counselors,* Science Research Associates, Inc., Chicago, 1945.

201. Hahn, M. E., and M. S. MacLean: *Counseling Psychology,* 2d ed., McGraw-Hill Book Company, New York, 1955.

202. Hamel, L. B.: "A Survey of the Teaching of Occupations in New York State Secondary Schools," doctoral thesis, St. John's University, Jamaica, N.Y., 1961.

203. *Handbook for Young Workers,* Government Printing Office, Washington, 1965.

204. Handville, R. M.: Letter to R. Hoppock, Sept. 22, 1953.

205. Hartley, D.: *Guidance Practices in the Schools of New York State: Tentative Report,* State Education Department, Albany, N.Y., 1949.

206. Havighurst, R. J., and others: *Growing Up in River City,* John Wiley & Sons, Inc., New York, 1962.

207. Hawes, F.: "Learning by Seeing," *Kiwanis Magazine,* February, 1952, p. 30.

208. Hawes, G. R.: *The New American Guide to Colleges,* rev. ed., New American Library of World Literature, Inc., New York, 1964.

209. Hayward, W. F.: "Alumni Day Program at Islip High School," *Vocational Guidance Quarterly,* Winter, 1953–1954, p. 49.

210. Heathcote, J., and R. Hayter, "The 'Carter Lodge' Experiment in Extended Visits to Industry," *Youth Employment,* 9 Carmelite St., London, England, Summer, 1964, p. 12.

211. Heayn, M. H.: Letter to R. Hoppock, Nov. 9, 1949.

212. Hedge, J. W., and P. W. Hutson: "A Technique for Evaluating Guidance Activities," *School Review,* September, 1931, p. 508.

213. Hefter, J.: "Employment and the Mature Woman," *Vocational Guidance Quarterly,* Summer, 1962, p. 251.

214. Hewer, V. H.: "Group Counseling, Individual Counseling, and a College Class in Vocations," *Personnel and Guidance Journal,* May, 1959, p. 660.

215. Hewer, V. H.: "Vocational Planning Courses at the University of Minnesota," in H. T. Morse and P. L. Dressel, *General Education for Personal Maturity,* William C. Brown & Co., Dubuque, Iowa, 1960.

216. Hill, G. E.: "The Evaluation of Occupational Literature," *Vocational Guidance Quarterly,* Summer, 1966, p. 271.

217. Hill, G. E.: *Management and Improvement of Guidance,* Appleton-Century-Crofts, Inc., New York, 1965.

218. Hill, W. P.: *Planning My Future: A Workbook in Educational and*

Vocational Planning, Science Research Associates, Inc., Chicago, 1958.
219. Holland, J. L.: *The Psychology of Vocational Choice*, Blaisdell Publishing Company, Waltham, Mass., 1966.
220. Hollingshead, A. B.: *Elmtown's Youth*, John Wiley & Sons, Inc., New York, 1949.
221. Hollis, J. W.: "Placement in the Secondary School," *School Counselor*, Winter, 1955, p. 29.
222. Hoppock, R.: "Courses in Careers," *Journal of Higher Education*, October, 1932, p. 365.
223. Hoppock, R.: "Employment Opportunities in Guidance and Personnel Work," unpublished excerpts from an address delivered at the annual meeting of the National Vocational Guidance Association, San Francisco, Calif., 1942.
224. Hoppock, R.: "Evaluations of Occupational Literature: IV, Physical Therapy," *Occupations*, October, 1945, p. 19.
225. Hoppock, R.: *Job Satisfaction*, Harper & Row, Publishers, Incorporated, New York, 1935. (Out of print; available in large libraries.)
226. Hoppock, R.: "More Pretests and Retests," *Occupations*, November, 1936, p. 157.
227. Hoppock, R.: "Pretests and Retests," *Occupations*, April, 1936, p. 684.
228. Hoppock, R.: "Teaching Occupations to Counselors," *Vocational Guidance Quarterly*, Spring, 1954, p. 74. How the laboratory study method was used.
229. Hoppock, R.: "Teaching Sources of Occupational Information," *Vocational Guidance Quarterly*, Winter, 1953, p. 50.
230. Hoppock, R.: "A Twenty-seven Year Follow-up on Job Satisfaction of Employed Adults," *Personnel and Guidance Journal*, February, 1960, p. 489.
231. Hoppock, R.: "Two Methods of Demonstrating Group Guidance to Counselors in Training," *Occupations*, December, 1951, p. 195.
232. Hoppock, R.: "Two Methods of Training Counselors for Group Guidance: An Experimental Evaluation," *Occupations*, May, 1949, p. 523.
233. Hoppock, R.: "What Is the 'Real' Problem?" *American Psychologist*, March, 1953, p. 124.
234. Hoppock, R., and E. R. Cuony: "Pretesting Equated Groups," *Educational and Psychological Measurement*, Summer, 1955, p. 163.
235. Hoppock, R., and M. D. Hardenbergh: "Courses in Careers," *Journal of Higher Education*, March, 1944, p. 157.
236. Hoppock, R., and M. E. Hoppock: "Renovating an Occupational Information File," *Vocational Guidance Quarterly*, Winter, 1960–1961, p. 84.
237. Hoppock, R., and N. Lowenstein: "The Teaching of Occupations in 1951," *Occupations*, January, 1952, p. 274.
238. Hoppock, R., and N. D. Stevens: "High School Courses in Occupations," *Personnel and Guidance Journal*, May, 1954, p. 540.

239. Hoppock, R., and V. Tuxill: "Growth of Courses in Careers," *Journal of Higher Education,* October, 1938, p. 357.
240. Houghton, H. W.: *Jobs for You,* Keystone Education Press, Inc., New York, 1960.
241. *How to Make Referrals,* Guidance Series, The Michigan State University Press, East Lansing, Mich., 1956.
242. *How to Visit Colleges,* National Vocational Guidance Association, Washington (see latest edition).
243. Hoy, W. C.: "A Survey of the Study of Occupations in Pennsylvania Secondary Schools," doctoral thesis, University of Pittsburgh, Pittsburgh, 1949.
244. Hoyt, D. P.: "An Evaluation of Group and Individual Programs in Vocational Guidance," *Journal of Applied Psychology,* February, 1955, p. 26.
245. Hoyt, K. B.: *S.O.S. Guidance Research Information Booklets,* Bureau of Educational Research and Service, University of Iowa, Iowa City, 1965. Sold only to counselors.
246. Hoyt, K. B.: *Wha' Happen'd,* Westminster High School, Westminster, Md., 1950.
247. Huey, M. L.: "Filing Occupational Information in the Atlanta Opportunity School," *Occupations,* February, 1944, p. 315.
248. Hughes, R. G., Jr.: "See for Yourself: A Doing Approach to Vocational Guidance," *Vocational Guidance Quarterly,* Summer, 1965, p. 283.
249. Hunt, D.: *Work Experience Education Programs in American Secondary Schools,* Government Printing Office, Washington, 1957.
250. Hutson, P. W.: *The Guidance Function in Education,* Appleton-Century-Crofts, Inc., New York, 1958.
251. Hyde, H.: "A Guide for Effective Preparation of New York State Public School Counselors and Utilization of Their Counseling Services," doctoral thesis, New York University School of Education, New York, 1950.
252. "Industry Visits Aid Realistic Counseling and Job Placement," *S.R.A. Guidance Newsletter,* November–December, 1965, p. 3.
253. Isaacson, L. E.: *Career Information in Counseling and Teaching,* Allyn and Bacon, Inc., Boston, 1966.
254. Jackson, R. M., and J. W. M. Rothney: "A Comparative Study of the Mailed Questionnaire and the Interview in Follow-up Studies," *Personnel and Guidance Journal,* March, 1961, p. 569.
255. Janney, A. C.: "Occupational Map," *The Beacon,* Lambertville, N.J., March 15, 1962, p. 8.
256. Jesmur, F. A.: Memoranda to R. Hoppock, Feb. 23 to Apr. 27, 1966.
257. Jessup, A. S.: "Measuring the Value of a Course in Occupations in the Ninth Grade," master's thesis, University of Colorado College of Education, Boulder, 1926.
258. *Job Guide for Young Workers,* U.S. Employment Service (see latest edition).

259. John Wanamaker advertisement in *The Philadelphia Inquirer,* April 26, 1953, p. A25.
260. Jolles, I.: "An Experiment in Group Guidance," *Journal of Social Psychology,* February, 1946, p. 55.
261. Jones, J.: *From Here to Eternity,* Charles Scribner's Sons, New York, 1951.
262. *Journal of College Placement,* published quarterly by the College Placement Council, Inc., Bethlehem, Pa.
263. Julius, Brother, F.S.C.: "Some Guidance Needs of High School Seniors," *Personnel and Guidance Journal,* April, 1954, p. 460.
264. Kaback, G. R.: "Occupational Information for Groups of Elementary School Children," *Vocational Guidance Quarterly,* Summer, 1966, p. 163.
265. Kaback, G. R.: "Occupational Information in Elementary Education," *Vocational Guidance Quarterly,* Autumn, 1960, p. 55.
266. Kagan, N.: "Three Dimensions of Counselor Encapsulation," *Journal of Counseling Psychology,* Winter, 1964, p. 361.
267. Katz, M. R.: *You: Today and Tomorrow,* Educational Testing Service, Princeton, N.J., 1959.
268. Kaye, J.: "Fourth Graders Meet Up with Occupations," *Vocational Guidance Quarterly,* Spring, 1960, p. 150.
269. Kearney, N. C.: *A Teacher's Professional Guide,* Prentice-Hall, Inc., Englewood Cliffs, N.J., 1958.
270. Keegan, V.: "Job Strategy: A College Credit Course in Job Hunting Techniques," *School and College Placement,* May, 1951, p. 40.
271. Kefauver, G. N., and H. C. Hand: *Appraising Guidance in Secondary Schools,* The Macmillan Company, New York, 1941.
272. Kemp, C. G.: *Perspectives on the Group Process. A Foundation for Counseling with Groups,* Houghton Mifflin Company, Boston, 1964.
273. Kenyon, L. B.: "A Course in Occupations," *Bulletin of the National Association of Secondary School Principals,* November, 1948, p. 131.
274. Kenyon, L. B.: "Dust Off That Tape Recorder," *Occupations,* February, 1952, p. 327.
275. Kilby, R. W.: "Some Vocational Counseling Methods," *Educational and Psychological Measurement,* Summer, 1949, p. 173.
276. King, H. R.: "Vocational Guidance for School Pupils: United Kingdom," in R. K. Hall and J. A. Lauwerys, *Yearbook of Education,* Harcourt, Brace & World, Inc., 1955.
277. Kirk, B. A., and M. E. Michels: *Occupational Information in Counseling,* Consulting Psychologists Press, 270 Town and Country Village, Palo Alto, Calif., 1964.
278. Kitch, D. E.: *Problems in Vocational Planning, California Guidance Bulletin No. 3,* rev. ed., State Department of Education, Sacramento, Calif., January, 1952.
279. Kline, M. V., and J. M. Schneck: "An Hypnotic Experimental Approach to the Genesis of Occupational Interests and Choice," *British Journal of Medical Hypnotism,* Winter, 1950, p. 1.

280. Kobliner, H.: "Literature Dealing with Vocational Guidance in the Elementary School," *Personnel and Guidance Journal*, January, 1955, p. 274.

281. Krieg, E. M.: Memorandum to R. Hoppock, April 22, 1961.

282. Krumboltz, J. D.: "Parable of the Good Counselor," *Personnel and Guidance Journal*, October, 1964, p. 118.

283. Kutner, J. E.: "An Evaluation of Occupational Field Trips Conducted by Paterson Technical and Vocational High School in Terms of Vocational Success," doctoral thesis, New York University School of Education, New York, 1957.

284. Lansner, L. A.: "Helping Seniors to Break the Job Barrier," *Journal of College Placement*, December, 1959, p. 27.

285. Lanson, E.: "The Elusive Dropout," *Vocational Guidance Quarterly*, Spring, 1961, p. 167.

286. Lapidos, M.: "Integration of Individual and Group Counseling with a J.V.S.," in *The Latest in Vocational Services: Proceedings of the Midwest Conference of Jewish Vocational Service Agencies, Jan. 12–14, 1951*, sponsored by the Jewish Occupational Council, Cincinnati, Ohio.

287. Larison, R. H.: *How to Get and Hold the Job You Want*, David McKay Company, Inc., New York, 1950. Includes directions for starting a job-finding forum.

288. Lee, J. M., and D. M. P. Lee: *The Child and His Curriculum*, Appleton-Century-Crofts, Inc., New York, 1950.

289. Leis, W. W.: *Occupational Survey of Pasadena*, City Schools, Pasadena, Calif., 1955.

290. LeMay, M.: "An Inexpensive Address File for Occupational Information," *Vocational Guidance Quarterly*, Autumn, 1965, p. 55.

291. Leonard, G. E.: "A Careers Class with a Special Mission," *Vocational Guidance Quarterly*, Spring, 1961, p. 193.

292. Leonard, G. E.: "Developmental Career Guidance Project in the Inner-City Elementary School: A Research Project," unpublished manuscript, Wayne State University, Detroit, Mich., 1966.

293. Lichliter, M.: *The Lindenwood Graduate, 1949–1958: A Profile*, Lindenwood College, St. Charles, Mo.

294. Lifton, W. M.: "The Elementary School's Responsibility for Today's Vocational Misfits," unpublished manuscript, 1959.

295. Lifton, W. M.: *Introducing the World of Work to Children: Teacher's Manual for "What Could I Be?"* Science Research Associates, Inc., Chicago, 1960.

296. Lifton, W. M. (ed.): *Keys to Vocational Decisions*, Science Research Associates, Inc., Chicago, 1964.

297. Lifton, W. M.: *What Could I Be?* Science Research Associates, Inc., Chicago, 1960.

298. Lifton, W. M.: *Working with Groups*, 2d ed., John Wiley & Sons, Inc., New York, 1966.

299. Lifton, W. M., and A. Williams (eds.): *Widening Occupational Roles Kit*, Science Research Associates, Inc., Chicago, 1962.

300. *Lincoln Directory of Career Information for Use Now and After Graduation*, Abraham Lincoln High School, Brooklyn, N.Y. (see latest edition).
301. Lincoln, M. E.: "Educational and Vocational Information as Part of a Guidance Program with Criteria for Measuring Results," doctoral thesis, Harvard University Graduate School of Education, Cambridge, Mass., 1934.
302. Lippman, E.: Memorandum to R. Hoppock, May 13, 1960.
303. Lipschitz, B.: Memorandum to R. Hoppock, 1965.
304. Little, W., and A. L. Chapman: *Developmental Guidance in Secondary Schools*, McGraw-Hill Book Company, New York, 1953.
305. Logie, I. R., and M. R. Ballin: "Group Guidance for Adults," *Occupations*, April, 1952, p. 530.
306. Logie, I. R., T. F. Humiston, and M. R. Ballin: "Adult Group Guidance: A Pilot Plan," *Occupations*, January, 1951, p. 287.
307. Long, C. D.: *School-leaving Youth and Employment*, Teachers College Press, Columbia University, New York, 1941.
308. *Looking at Private Trade and Correspondence Schools, A Guide for Students*, American Personnel and Guidance Association, Washington, 1963.
309. Losi, C. R.: *Dropouts—Guidance Practices for Improving School Holding Power*, Annual Report, Department of Guidance, Board of Education, Newark, N.J., 1963.
310. Lovejoy, C. E.: *Lovejoy's College Guide*, Simon and Schuster, Inc., New York (see latest edition).
311. Lowen, W.: *How and When to Change Your Job Successfully*, Simon and Schuster, Inc., New York, 1954.
312. Lowenstein, N.: "The Effect of an Occupations Course in High School on Adjustment to College during the Freshman Year," doctoral thesis, New York University School of Education, New York, 1955, summarized in N. Lowenstein and R. Hoppock, "High School Occupations Course Helps Students Adjust to College," *Personnel and Guidance Journal*, September, 1955, p. 21.
313. Lowenstein, N., and R. Hoppock: "The Teaching of Occupations in 1952," *Personnel and Guidance Journal*, April, 1953, p. 441.
314. MacCurdy, R. D.: "Characteristics of Superior Science Students," *Science Education*, February, 1956, p. 3.
315. Magoun, F. A.: *Successfully Finding Yourself and Your Job*, Harper & Row, Publishers, Incorporated, New York, 1959.
316. Mahler, C. A., and E. Caldwell: *Group Counseling in Secondary Schools*, Science Research Associates, Inc., Chicago, 1961.
317. Mahoney, H. J.: *Occupational Information for Counselors*, Harcourt, Brace & World, Inc., New York, 1952.
318. *Manpower Implications of Automation*, U.S. Department of Labor, Washington, 1965.
319. Martinson, W. D.: *Educational and Vocational Planning*, Scott, Foresman and Company, Chicago, 1959.

320. Maslow, A. H.: *Motivation and Personality*, Harper & Row, Publishers, Incorporated, New York, 1954.
321. Mason, L. G.: "Guidance Aids for Incoming Freshmen," *Clearing House*, March, 1950, p. 419.
322. Maye, G. A.: Letter to R. Hoppock, Dec. 2, 1952.
323. McCracken, T. C., and H. E. Lamb: *Occupational Information in the Elementary School*, Houghton Mifflin Company, Boston, 1923.
324. McKinney, W. D.: "Another Slant on Career Day," *Occupations*, April, 1952, p. 534.
325. McKown, H. C.: *Home Room Guidance*, 2d ed., McGraw-Hill Book Company, New York, 1946.
326. Menninger, K. A.: "Work as a Sublimation," *Bulletin of the Menninger Clinic*, November, 1942, p. 170.
327. "Mental Patients Guided into Jobs," *The New York Times*, reprint, Fountain House, 412 W. 47 St., New York, July 10, 1960.
328. Metcalf, W.: *Starting and Managing a Small Business of Your Own*, Government Printing Office, Washington, 1962.
329. Mich, D. D., and E. Eberman: *The Technique of the Picture Story*, McGraw-Hill Book Company, New York, 1945.
330. Miles, M. B.: *Learning to Work in Groups*, Teachers College Press, Columbia University, New York, 1959.
331. Miller, A. E., and B. I. Brown: *National Directory of Schools and Vocations*, 2d ed., State School Publications, North Springfield, Pa., 1963.
332. Miller, D. C., and W. H. Form: *Industrial Sociology*, 2d ed., Harper & Row, Publishers, Incorporated, New York, 1964.
333. Miller, H.: "Getting Local Occupational Information through a Volunteer," *Vocational Guidance Quarterly*, Autumn, 1952, p. 6.
334. Miller, J. N.: "Seven Steps toward Getting a Job," *Reader's Digest*, March, 1963, p. 72.
335. Miller, R. A.: "Courses in Vocational Adjustment at Fairleigh Dickinson University," in H. T. Morse and P. L. Dressel, *General Education for Personal Maturity*, William C. Brown & Co., Dubuque, Iowa, 1960, p. 189.
336. Miller, R. A.: "A Study of the Relative Effectiveness of Two Techniques for Imparting Occupational Information," doctoral thesis, New York University School of Education, New York, 1951.
337. Minkin, V. F.: Memorandum to R. Hoppock, March 26, 1952.
338. *Missouri Filing Plan for Unbound Materials on Occupations*, College of Education, University of Missouri, Columbia, Mo., 1950.
339. Mooren, R. L., and J. W. M. Rothney: "Personalizing the Follow-up Study," *Personnel and Guidance Journal*, March, 1956, p. 409.
340. Morelli, E. A.: "Group Counseling in an Employment Service Setting," *Employment Service Review*, December, 1964, p. 17.
341. Morse, H. T., and P. L. Dressel (eds.): *General Education for Personal Maturity*, William C. Brown & Co., Dubuque, Iowa, 1960.
342. Mosback, C. R.: Letter to R. Hoppock, July 22, 1949.

343. Moyer, D.: "Advice from the Apprentices," *Occupations,* March, 1940, p. 411.
344. Munson, H. L.: "At Your Fingertips: A File Full of Information," *Vocational Guidance Quarterly,* Spring, 1955, p. 90.
345. Munson, H. L.: *Guidance Activities for Secondary School Teachers.* Five pamphlets: *Guidance Activities for Teachers of English; Guidance Activities for Teachers of Foreign Languages; Guidance Activities for Teachers of Mathematics; Guidance Activities for Teachers of Science; Guidance Activities for Teachers of Social Studies;* Science Research Associates, Inc., Chicago, 1965.
346. Munson, H. L.: *How to Set Up a Guidance Unit,* Science Research Associates, Inc., Chicago, 1957.
347. Murphy, G. C.: "Counselor Dominance," doctoral thesis, New York University School of Education, New York, 1957.
348. Murphy, J. M.: *Directory of Vocational Training Sources,* Science Research Associates, Inc., Chicago, 1964.
349. Musselman, D. L., and L. A. Willig: "The Science Fair: A Vocational Guidance Opportunity," *Vocational Guidance Quarterly,* Spring, 1961, p. 153.
350. *NVGA Bibliography of Current Occupational Literature,* American Personnel and Guidance Association, Washington, 1966.
351. *National Study of Existing and Recommended Practices for Assisting Youth Adjustment in Selected Elementary Schools of the U.S.,* Ann Arbor Publishers, Ann Arbor, Mich., 1953.
352. Neal, E.: "Filing Occupational Information Alphabetically," *Occupations,* May, 1944, p. 503.
353. Nelson, A. G.: *Colleges Classified. A Guide for Counselors, Parents and Students,* 4th ed., Chronicle Guidance Publications, Moravia, N.Y., 1964.
354. *New York State Plan for Filing Unbound Occupational Information,* State Education Department, Bureau of Guidance, Albany N.Y., 1961.
355. *The New York Times Index,* published periodically by *The New York Times,* New York.
356. *News-Bulletin,* New York State Counselors Association, January, 1955, p. 8.
357. Nick, E. W.: "High School Boys Choose Vocations," *Occupations,* January, 1942, p. 264.
358. *1965–1966 Directory of Approved Counseling Agencies,* American Board on Counseling Services, Washington, 1965.
359. Nolfo, J. A.: "Follow Up Facts and Figures While They're Hot," *Vocational Guidance Quarterly,* Summer, 1958, p. 202.
360. Norris, W.: *Occupational Information in the Elementary School,* Science Research Associates, Inc., Chicago, 1963.
361. Norris, W., F. R. Zeran, and R. N. Hatch: *The Information Service in Guidance: Occupational, Educational, Social,* 2d ed., Rand McNally & Company, Chicago, 1966.
362. Nosow, S., and W. H. Form (eds.): *Man, Work, and Society: A*

Reader in the Sociology of Occupations, Basic Books, Inc., Publishers, New York, 1962.

363. *Occupational Abstracts,* published periodically by Personnel Services, Inc., Jaffrey, N.H.

364. *Occupational Index,* published periodically by Personnel Services, Inc., Jaffrey, N.H.

365. *Occupational Outlook Handbook,* Government Printing Office, Washington (see latest edition).

366. Odgers, J. G.: Memorandum to R. Hoppock, July 31, 1956.

367. Orrico, A. J.: "School Club Gives Preview of Nursing," *Occupations,* December, 1945, p. 156.

368. *Our Youth—Five Years after Graduation.* A Follow-up Study of the Class of 1959, High School, Jamestown, N.Y., no date.

369. "Outlook for Summer Jobs—a Reappraisal," *Occupational Outlook Quarterly,* February, 1964, p. 29.

370. Oxhandler, A.: "What Makes an Occupational Information Pamphlet Popular?" *Occupations,* October, 1950, p. 26.

371. Parker, H. S.: "Ever Hear of a Job-O-Rama?" *Vocational Guidance Quarterly,* Autumn, 1958, p. 11.

372. Parmenter, M. D.: *You and Your Career,* University of Toronto Guidance Centre, Toronto, Canada (see latest edition).

373. Patterson, C. H.: *Counseling and Guidance in Schools: A First Course,* Harper & Row, Publishers, Incorporated, New York, 1962.

374. Paul, D. S.: *Earning a Living in Philadelphia,* Board of Public Education Print Shop, Philadelphia, 1951.

375. Peagler, O. F.: Memorandum to R. Hoppock, April 30, 1960.

376. Perks, D.: "Abraham Lincoln High School Directory of Career Information," *Guidance News,* February, 1965, p. 5.

377. Peters, H. J., and W. Brown, Jr.: "Making a Movie of Local Vocations," *Clearing House,* February, 1951, p. 350.

378. Pitt, G. A., and R. W. Smith: *The Twenty-minute Lifetime: A Guide to Career Planning,* Prentice-Hall, Inc., Englewood Cliffs, N.J., 1959.

379. Plummer, R. H., and V. Ingram: "They Call It the Career Carnival," *Nation's Schools,* August, 1955, p. 48.

380. Poppel, N.: "Summer Activities for Students," *Vocational Guidance Quarterly,* Winter, 1963–1964, p. 99.

381. Preston, E. L.: "Students Conduct Job Survey," *California Guidance Newsletter,* May, 1954, p. 3.

382. *A Profile of Jobs for Women.* A series of leaflets. The Harvard-Radcliffe Program in Business Administration, Radcliffe College, Cambridge, Mass., no date.

383. *Psychological Abstracts,* published periodically by American Psychological Association, Inc., Washington.

384. Purcell, F. E.: "Helping Students Use Occupational Information Files," *Vocational Guidance Quarterly,* Autumn, 1961, p. 55.

385. Rauschkolb, J.: "A Key Club Group Conference," *Vocational Guidance Quarterly,* Spring, 1960, p. 147.

386. *Readers' Guide to Periodical Literature,* published periodically by The H. W. Wilson Company, New York.
387. Recktenwald, L. N.: "Attitudes toward Occupations before and after Vocational Information," *Occupations,* January, 1946, p. 220.
388. Redefer, F. L., and D. Reeves: *Careers in Education,* Harper & Row, Publishers, Incorporated, New York, 1960.
389. Reed, A. Y.: *Guidance and Personnel Services in Education,* Cornell University Press, Ithaca, N.Y., 1944.
390. Reed, C. L.: Letter to R. Hoppock, Dec. 29, 1965.
391. Reeves, D.: "A Survey to Ascertain How Widely Job Getting Techniques Are Presented by Colleges and Universities, the Manner of Presentation, and Reactions to Them," doctoral thesis, New York University School of Education, New York, 1957.
392. *Resource Units in the Teaching of Occupations,* Board of Education, New York, 1956.
393. Richardson, H., and H. Borow: "An Evaluation of the Efficacy of Group Preparation for Vocational Counseling," *American Psychologist,* July, 1950, p. 349.
394. Richmond, S. S.: *Career Plays for Young People,* Plays, Inc, Boston, 1949.
395. Ritzman, E. R.: "Subject Career Day," *Vocational Guidance Quarterly,* Spring, 1960, p. 155.
396. Robinson, H. A., R. P. Connors, and A. H. Robinson: "Job Satisfaction Researches of 1963," *Personnel and Guidance Journal,* December, 1964, p. 360.
397. Roe, A.: "The Implications of Vocational Interest Theory for Vocational Counseling," unpublished manuscript, 1958.
398. Rogers, C. R.: *Client-centered Therapy,* Houghton Mifflin Company, Boston, 1951.
399. Rogers, C. R.: *Counseling and Psychotherapy,* Houghton Mifflin Company, Boston, 1942.
400. Rogers, C. R.: "Facilitation of Personal Growth," *School Counselor,* January, 1955, p. 1.
401. Rohr, G. E., and D. Speer: "The Guidance Service Uses the School Newspaper," *Occupations,* March, 1948, p. 363.
402. Rosengarten, W., Jr.: "The Occupational Orientation of High School Seniors," doctoral thesis, New York University School of Education, New York, 1961, summarized in W. Rosengarten, Jr. and R. Hoppock, "Another Job Course Pays Off," *Personnel and Guidance Journal,* February, 1963, p. 531.
403. Ross, M. J.: "Significant Concepts of Occupational Information," *Occupations,* February, 1952, p. 323.
404. Ross, R. G.: *Occupational Information,* State Department of Education, Guidance Services, Des Moines, Iowa, 1954.
405. Ross, V.: *Handbook for Homeroom Guidance,* The Macmillan Company, New York, 1954.
406. Rothney, J. W. M.: "Interpreting Test Scores to Counselees," *Occupations,* February, 1952, p. 320.

407. Rubinfeld, W. A.: "Weekly Group Conferences on Careers," *Personnel and Guidance Journal*, December, 1954, p. 223.
408. Rubinfeld, W. A., and R. Hoppock: "Occupations Course Evaluated Eight Years Later," *Vocational Guidance Quarterly*, Autumn, 1961, p. 45.
409. Ruderman, V.: "A Report on an Occupational Survey of 'Alumni' of a Federal Correctional Institution," master's thesis, New York University School of Education, New York, 1947.
410. Rundquist, R. M.: "Tape Recorded Interviews Vitalize Occupational Information," *Vocational Guidance Quarterly*, Winter, 1955–1956, p. 62.
411. Ruth, R. A.: "Readability of Occupational Materials," *Vocational Guidance Quarterly*, Autumn, 1962, p. 7.
412. Sachs, G. M.: *Evaluation of Group Guidance Work in Secondary Schools*, University of Southern California Press, Los Angeles, 1945.
413. *Salary Survey*, prepared and published periodically by the College Placement Council. (Mailed without charge to subscribers to the *Journal of College Placement*.)
414. Santolo, R.: "Field Trips for Guidance?" *School Counselor*, May, 1963, p. 183.
415. Saterstrom, M. H., and J. A. Steph: *Educators Guide to Free Guidance Materials*, 4th ed., Educators Progress Service, Randolph, Wis., 1965.
416. Schaffer, R. H.: *Job Satisfaction as Related to Need Satisfaction in Work*, Psychological Monographs, no. 364, 1953, p. 1.
417. Scherini, R., and B. A. Kirk: "Keeping Current on Occupational Information," *Vocational Guidance Quarterly*, Winter, 1963, p. 96.
418. *School Boards in Action*, Twenty-fourth Yearbook of the American Association of School Administrators, Washington, 1946.
419. Schreader, B. M.: "The Detroit Job Upgrading Program," *Vocational Guidance Quarterly*, Autumn, 1961, p. 53.
420. Schubert, R. M.: "File Your Occupational Information by Student Interests," *Vocational Guidance Quarterly*, Spring, 1953, p. 17.
421. Schwartz, J.: *Part-time Employment-Employer Attitudes on Opportunities for the College-trained Woman*, Alumnae Advisory Center, 541 Madison Ave., New York, 1964.
422. "Seen in the Field," *Highlights*, State Education Department, Albany, N.Y., December, 1959, p. 15.
423. Senesh, L.: *Our Working World. Families at Work*, Science Research Associates, Inc., Chicago, 1963, 1964.
424. *Services to Older Workers by the Public Employment Service*, U.S. Bureau of Employment Security, Washington, May, 1957.
425. *Sewanhaka Offers Young Men Information on Job Opportunities on Long Island*, Sewanhaka Central High School District No. 2, Floral Park, N.Y., 1957.
426. Shartle, C. L.: *Occupational Information*, 2d ed., Prentice-Hall, Inc., Englewood Cliffs, N.J., 1952.

427. Sherrill, A. C.: *The 3rd Bridge*, Pittsburgh Plate Glass Company, Pittsburgh, Pa., no date.
428. Shoemaker, W. L.: "Tapping a New Source of Educational Information," *Vocational Guidance Quarterly*, Spring, 1960, p. 149.
429. *Simmons College Bulletin*, Simmons College, Boston, November, 1955.
430. Sinick, D.: Letter to R. Hoppock, Jan. 22, 1962.
431. Sinick, D.: *Your Personality and Your Job*, Science Research Associates, Inc., Chicago, 1960.
432. Sinick, D., W. E. Gorman, and R. Hoppock: "Research on the Teaching of Occupations 1963–1964," *Personnel and Guidance Journal*, February, 1966, p. 591.
433. Sinick, D., and R. Hoppock: "Research Across the Nation on the Teaching of Occupations," *Vocational Guidance Quarterly*, Autumn, 1965, p. 21.
434. Sinick, D., and R. Hoppock: "Research by States on the Teaching of Occupations," *Personnel and Guidance Journal*, November, 1960, p. 218.
435. Sinick, D., and R. Hoppock: "Research on the Teaching of Occupations 1945–1951," *Personnel and Guidance Journal*, November, 1953, p. 147.
436. Sinick, D., and R. Hoppock: "Research on the Teaching of Occupations 1952–1953," *Personnel and Guidance Journal*, October, 1954, p. 86.
437. Sinick, D., and R. Hoppock: "Research on the Teaching of Occupations 1954–1955," *Personnel and Guidance Journal*, November, 1956, p. 155.
438. Sinick, D., and R. Hoppock: "Research on the Teaching of Occupations 1956–1958," *Personnel and Guidance Journal*, October, 1959, p. 150.
439. Sinick, D., and R. Hoppock: "Research on the Teaching of Occupations 1959–1960," *Personnel and Guidance Journal*, October, 1961, p. 164.
440. Sinick, D., and R. Hoppock: "Research on the Teaching of Occupations 1961–1962," *Personnel and Guidance Journal*, January, 1964, p. 504.
441. Sinick, D., and R. Hoppock: "States Report Research on the Teaching of Occupations," *Personnel and Guidance Journal*, February, 1955, p. 328.
442. Skahill, F. J.: "The Group Approach to College Recruiting," *Personnel*, American Management Association, January–February, 1963, p. 53.
443. Slotkin, H.: "New Programs for Dropouts in New York City: A Coordinated Approach," *Vocational Guidance Quarterly*, Summer, 1962, p. 235.
444. Slotkin, H.: "A Technique for Self-measurement," *Personnel and Guidance Journal*, March, 1954, p. 415.

445. Slotkin, H.: "Three Experimental Programs for Dropouts," *Guidance News,* Board of Education, New York, November, 1961, p. 2.
446. Smith, L. J.: *Career Planning,* Harper & Row, Publishers, Incorporated, New York, 1959.
447. *Socio-Guidramas,* Methods and Materials Press, 6 S. Derby Rd., Springfield, N.J.
448. *Sociological Abstracts,* published periodically by Sociological Abstracts, Inc., New York.
449. *Sociological Studies of Occupations. A Bibliography,* Manpower Administration, U.S. Department of Labor, Washington, 1965.
450. Sondern, F., Jr.: "Judge Cooper's Remarkable Experiment," *Reader's Digest,* June, 1956, p. 53.
451. Southern, J. A., and R. M. Colver: "Looking a Gift Horse in the Mouth," *Vocational Guidance Quarterly,* Winter, 1955–1956, p. 46.
452. Spiegler, C., and M. Hamburger: *If You're Not Going to College,* Science Research Associates, Inc., Chicago, 1959.
453. Splaver, S.: "What High School Freshmen and Seniors Want in Occupational Books," doctoral thesis, New York University School of Education, New York, 1953.
454. Splaver, S.: "What High School Students Want in Occupational Books," *Personnel and Guidance Journal,* September, 1954, p. 15.
455. Splaver, S.: *Your Career If You're Not Going to College,* Julian Messner, Publishers, Inc., New York, 1963.
456. *Standard Industrial Classification Manual,* Government Printing Office, Washington, 1957.
457. Stevens, A.: *1956 Pilot Study: Final Report,* Diablo Valley College, Concord, Calif., June, 1961.
458. Stevens, N. D., and R. Hoppock: "College Courses in Careers," *Personnel and Guidance Journal,* April, 1956, p. 502.
459. Stevens, N. D., and R. Hoppock: "High School Courses in Occupations," *Personnel and Guidance Journal,* December, 1955, p. 213.
460. Stevens, N. D., and R. Hoppock: "Junior College Courses in Careers," *Vocational Guidance Quarterly,* Autumn, 1954, p. 21.
461. Stevenson, R. L.: *Virginibus Puerisque and Other Papers,* Charles Scribner's Sons, New York, 1902. See "An Apology for Idlers," pp. 107–127.
462. Stiles, H.: "Career Exploration," *California Guidance Newsletter,* March–May, 1961, p. 7.
463. Stone, C. H.: "Evaluation Program in Vocational Orientation, 1938–1940," unpublished manuscript, University of Minnesota Committee on Educational Research, Minneapolis.
464. Stone, C. H.: "Evaluation Program in Vocational Orientation, 1941," in *Studies in Higher Education,* biennial report of the University of Minnesota Committee on Educational Research, Minneapolis, 1938–1940. Out of print. Revised and reprinted under the title "Are Vocational Information Courses Worth Their Salt?" *Educational and Psychological Measurement,* Summer, 1948, p. 161.

465. *Summary Report of the Seven College Vocational Workshops 1962– 1966*, Placement Office, Barnard College, New York, 1966.
466. *Summer Vacation Jobs in Federal Agencies*, U.S. Civil Service Commission, Washington (see latest edition).
467. Super, D. E.: "Group Techniques in the Guidance Program," *Educational and Psychological Measurement*, Autumn, 1949, p. 496.
468. Super, D. E.: *The Psychology of Careers*, Harper & Row, Publishers, Incorporated, New York, 1957.
469. Super, D. E.: "A Theory of Vocational Development," *American Psychologist*, May, 1953, p. 185.
470. Super, D. E., and J. O. Crites: *Appraising Vocational Fitness by Means of Psychological Tests*, rev. ed., Harper & Row, Publishers, Incorporated, New York, 1962.
471. Super, D. E., and P. L. Overstreet: *The Vocational Maturity of Ninth Grade Boys*, Career Pattern Study Monograph 2, Teachers College Press, Columbia University, New York, 1960.
472. Super, D. E., R. Starishevsky, N. Matlin, and J. P. Jordaan: *Career Development: Self-Concept Theory*, College Entrance Examination Board, Princeton, N.J., 1963.
473. Sutherland, D. M.: "The 'College Opportunities' Course," *Simmons College Bulletin*, February, 1949, p. 4.
474. *Technician Education Yearbook*, Prakken Publications, Ann Arbor, Mich., 1963–1964.
475. Tennyson, W. W., T. A. Soldahl, and C. Mueller: *The Teacher's Role in Career Development*, rev. ed., National Vocational Guidance Association, Washington, 1965.
476. *Thomas Register of American Manufacturers*, Thomas Publishing Company, Inc., New York, published annually.
477. "Three Types of Plant Visitation Illustrate How Practical Knowledge of Industry May Be Obtained," *Trends in Education-Industry Cooperation*, February, 1947, p. 4.
478. Tiedeman, D. V.: *Career Pattern Studies: Current Findings with Possibilities*, Harvard Studies in Career Development, no. 40, Graduate School of Education, Harvard University, Cambridge, Mass., July 20, 1965.
479. Tiedeman, D. V., and R. P. O'Hara: *Career Development; Choice and Adjustment*, College Entrance Examination Board, Princeton, N.J., 1963.
480. Toporowski, T. T.: *A Critical Evaluation of an Experimental Occupational Information Unit Taught to High School Seniors by Social Studies Teachers*, doctoral thesis, School of Education, Boston University, Boston, 1961.
481. *Toward New Horizons*, Fountain House, 412 W. 47 St., New York, no date.
482. Travers, R. M. W.: "A Critical Review of Techniques for Evaluating Guidance," *Educational and Psychological Measurement*, Summer, 1949, p. 211.

483. Tsugawa, V. U.: "What Should I Be?" *Occupational Outlook*, Department of Education, Honolulu, Hawaii, February, 1962, p. 11.
484. Turner, R. H.: *The Jobs You Get*, New York University Press, New York, 1962.
485. Tyler, L. E.: "The Antecedents of Two Varieties of Vocational Interests," *Genetic Psychology Monographs*, 1964, p. 177.
486. Tyler, L. E.: "The Future of Vocational Guidance," in M. S. Viteles, A. H. Brayfield, and L. E. Tyler, *Vocational Counseling: A Reappraisal in Honor of Donald G. Paterson*, The University of Minnesota Press, Minneapolis, 1961.
487. Tyler, L. E.: Letter to R. Hoppock, Feb. 9, 1962.
488. Tyler, L. E.: *The Work of the Counselor*, 2d ed., Appleton-Century-Crofts, Inc., New York, 1961.
489. Ubell, E.: *New Horizons in Science. Yardstick Applied to Social Agency, New York Herald Tribune*, Reprint, Fountain House, 412 W. 47 St., New York, June 24, 1962.
490. *A University Education in Agricultural Science*, New York State College of Agriculture, Ithaca, N.Y., no date.
491. Valdez, A.: "20 Years of Youth Placement," *Employment Security Review*, March, 1963, p. 11.
492. Van Dusen, A. C.: "Group Discussion in an Adult Counseling Program," *Educational and Psychological Measurement*, Autumn, 1949, p. 521.
493. *Viewpoint. Entry Employment in San Diego*, County Department of Education, San Diego, Calif., Summer, 1965.
494. *Vocational Guidance Quarterly*, National Vocational Guidance Association, Washington. Includes lists of "Current Occupational Literature" recommended by the Career Information Review Service of the association.
495. *Vocational Opportunities in Metropolitan Denver*, Public Schools, Denver, Colo., 1961.
496. *Wage Scales and Employment Opportunities in Atlanta Area*, Smith-Hughes Vocational School Counseling Department, Atlanta, Ga., no date.
497. Walker, Sister Mary Catherine: "The Influence of Instruction in Occupations and Self-appraisal Activities upon the Vocational Preferences, Vocational Interests, and Vocational Attitudes of High School Girls," doctoral thesis, Northwestern University, Evanston, Ill., 1955.
498. Warner, W. L., and J. C. Abegglen: *Occupational Mobility in American Business and Industry, 1928–1952*, The University of Minnesota Press, Minneapolis, 1955.
499. Warren, S. L.: Letter to R. Hoppock, with enclosures, Aug. 25, 1947.
500. Warters, J.: *Group Guidance: Principles and Practices*, McGraw-Hill Book Company, New York, 1960.
501. Warters, J.: *High School Personnel Work Today*, McGraw-Hill Book Company, New York, 1946.

502. Washville, V. F.: "Job-for-a-Day," *News Letter of the New Jersey Personnel and Guidance Association*, October, 1954, p. 6.
503. Wasserman, P., and H. W. F. Mason: "A Proposed Method for Finding a Position: Information Sources for Occupational Guidance by Geographic Area," *Personnel and Guidance Journal*, February, 1958, p. 408.
504. Watson, D. E., R. M. Rundquist, and W. C. Cottle: "What's Wrong with Occupational Materials?" *Journal of Counseling Psychology*, Winter, 1959, p. 288.
505. Weaver, G. L.: *How, When, and Where to Provide Occupational Information*, Science Research Associates, Inc., Chicago, 1955.
506. Weiss, M. J.: *Guidance through Drama*, Whiteside, Inc., New York, 1954.
507. Weitz, J.: "Job Expectancy and Survival," *Journal of Applied Psychology*, August, 1956, p. 245.
508. Wellington, A. M.: *Occupational Information Reference File*, Counselor Education Press, State College, Pa., no date.
509. Wellman, F. E.: "Utilizing a Community Occupational Survey for In-service Education," *Personnel and Guidance Journal*, April, 1954, p. 477.
510. *What to Do This Summer*, U.S. Bureau of Employment Security, Washington (see latest edition).
511. White, V.: Letter to R. Hoppock, April 5, 1949.
512. White, V.: *Manufacturing Industries of Waukegan and North Chicago, Illinois*, Waukegan Township High School, Waukegan, Ill., 1948–1949.
513. White, V.: "Occupational Orientation Day," Waukegan Township High School, Waukegan, Ill., 1949. (Unpublished manuscript.)
514. *Why Young People Fail to Get and Hold Jobs*, New York State Employment Service, New York, no date.
515. Wiley, E. J.: "Organizing the Liberal Arts College for Vocational Guidance," *Middlebury College Bulletin*, February, 1923, p. 6.
516. Williams, F. E.: *Adolescence*, Holt, Rinehart and Winston, Inc., New York, 1930.
517. Williams, H. F.: "The Town Tells Teens about Jobs," *Personnel and Guidance Journal*, January, 1954, p. 266.
518. Williamson, E. G.: *Students and Occupations*, Holt, Rinehart and Winston, Inc., New York, 1937.
519. Wilson, D. J.: Unpublished report to the Board of Education, Galt, Ontario, Oct. 12, 1949.
520. Wilson, E. S., and C. A. Bucher: *College Ahead!* rev. ed., Harcourt, Brace & World, Inc., New York, 1961.
521. Wilson, J. W., and E. H. Lyons: *Work-Study College Programs*, Harper & Row, Publishers, Incorporated, New York, 1961.
522. Wilstach, I. M.: "Career Guidance Center Sponsored by Office of Los Angeles County Superintendent of Schools," *Vocational Guidance Quarterly*, Summer, 1962, p. 245.

523. Wintman, C.: "There's Much to Be Said for Career Week," *Vocational Guidance Quarterly,* Spring, 1961, p. 215.

524. Wolfbein, S. L.: "The Outlook for the Skilled Worker in the United States: Implications for Guidance and Counseling," *Personnel and Guidance Journal,* December, 1961, p. 334.

525. Wolfbein, S. L., and H. Goldstein: *Our World of Work,* Science Research Associates, Inc., Chicago, 1961.

526. Wolfman, E. F., Jr.: "A Medical Careers Day Conference," *Vocational Guidance Quarterly,* Summer, 1961, p. 217.

527. *World of Work,* Metropolitan School Study Council, ser. 8, New York, 1949.

528. Wright, B. H.: "A Method of Using the Group Conference as a Guidance Device," *Vocational Guidance Magazine,* October, 1928, p. 26.

529. Wright, M.: Letter to R. Hoppock, April 9, 1954, quoting B. H. Reeves, vice-president and general manager of Rockbestos Products Corp.

530. Wyatt, G.: "Who's on Top—You, or Company Literature?" *Journal of College Placement,* May, 1957, p. 33.

531. Young, F. M.: *Survey of 1960 Work Experience Program,* Marion Central School, Marion, N.Y., 1960.

532. Youngberg, C. F.: "An Experimental Study of 'Job Satisfaction' and Turnover in Relation to Job Expectations and Self Expectations," doctoral thesis, New York University Graduate School of Arts and Science, 1963, summarized in *"Realistic" Job Expectations and Survival,* Life Insurance Agency Management Association, Hartford, Conn., 1964.

533. Youngberg, C. F.: Letter to R. Hoppock, Nov. 30, 1965.

534. *Your Future Occupation,* published twenty times a year by Randall Publishing Company, Washington.

535. Zapoleon, M. W.: *Girls and Their Futures,* Science Research Associates, Inc., Chicago, 1962.

536. Zapoleon, M. W.: *An Outline of the Steps to Be Taken in a Community Occupational Survey,* Chronicle Guidance Publications, Moravia, N.Y., 1963.

537. Ziegler, R. A.: *The Oregon Pilot Project in Teaching Creative Job Search Techniques to the Unemployed and or Underemployed,* and *A Leader's Guide for Group Guidance in Creative Job Search Techniques,* Oregon Bureau of Labor, Portland, Ore., 1962.

Name Index

See also the Bibliography for names of authors, which appear there in alphabetical order.

Subject Index

Abstracts (*see* Information)

Abstracts of Sociological Literature, 151

Academic versus vocational high schools, 488

Academy of Teachers of Occupations, 479

Accredited school or college, minimum for, 370–372

Adjustment, emotional, 101, 102
  versus vocational, 100–103
  familial, 101
  social, 101

Administrators, 12
  school and college, suggestions for, 370–372

Advancement, 21, 24, 39, 156–157

Alumni (*see* Follow-up; Group conference)

Ambition, a symptom of maladjustment, 481–482

American Association of School Administrators, 199

American Board on Counseling Services, 107

American Child, 537, 546

American Institutes for Research, 488

American Junior Colleges, 543

American Universities and Colleges, 542

Apology for Idlers, An, 482

Appraisal of occupational literature, 44–56
  (*See also* Publications)

Apprenticeship, 39

Approved schools, 38

Aptitude, 35, 49, 116, 153

Aspiration, 86, 106

Assembly speakers, 343

Assignments, for observers of interviews, 502–506
  for use in counselor education, 541–558

Associations, 33, 36

Attitudes, 352

Audio-visual media, 313–322

Automation, 496–500

Averill Park, New York, 220

Banks, 10

Barnard College, 181

Beginners, suggestions for (*see* Suggestions)

Beginning jobs (*see* Survey, of employment market)

Biased information (*see* Information, sources of)

Big three, 12

Biography, 49

Blind, 509

Blood pressure, 35

Book budget, 54

Books (*see* Publications)

Boonsboro, Maryland, 216

Boston, Massachusetts, 478

Brown University, 479

Bulletin of the N.A.S.S.P. (National Association of Secondary School Principals), 537, 546

Bulletin boards, 316

Burroughs Corporation, 315

Buzz groups, 374

Capital, 39

Career clubs, 339

Career day, 339–342

Career development (*see* Vocational development)

Career Insights Program, 236

Careers (Largo, Fla.), 52

Careers Unlimited Program, 388

Case conference, 286–297
  comment on, 296
  demonstration of, 440–450
  leading discussion, 290
  live cases, 290–292
  purpose of, 286
  selecting cases, 286–290
  what students learn, 292

Chamber of commerce, 10, 498